A Geography of Economic Behavior

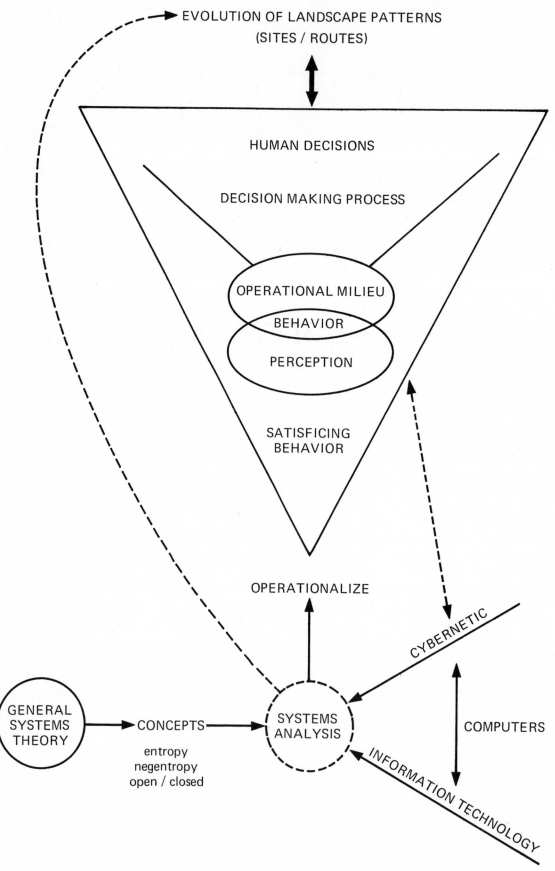

EVOLUTION OF LANDSCAPE PATTERNS
(SITES / ROUTES)

HUMAN DECISIONS

DECISION MAKING PROCESS

OPERATIONAL MILIEU

BEHAVIOR

PERCEPTION

SATISFICING
BEHAVIOR

OPERATIONALIZE

CYBERNETIC

GENERAL
SYSTEMS
THEORY

CONCEPTS

entropy
negentropy
open / closed

SYSTEMS
ANALYSIS

COMPUTERS

INFORMATION TECHNOLOGY

Frontispiece. *A conceptual framework for analyzing economic behavior. (From an idea by J. B. Sellers.)*

A Geography of Economic Behavior
An Introduction

Michael E. Eliot Hurst

Simon Frasier University

Duxbury Press
North Scituate, Massachusetts
A Division of Wadsworth Publishing Company, Inc.
Belmont, California

Acknowledgments

L.C. Cat. Card No.: 72-075109
ISBN 0-87872-002-2
Printed in the United States of America

2 3 4 5 6 7 8 9 10—76 75 74 73

American Psychological Association for the excerpt from C. E. Osgood and T. A. Seboek, "Psycholinguistics: A Survey of Theory and Research Problems," J. of Abnormal and Soc. Psych., *vol. 49, 1954.*

Ballantine Books for the excerpt from Power, Politics, and People *by C. Wright Mills.*

C. Campbell for the excerpt from "An Approach to Research in Recreational Geography," British Columbia Occ. Paper No. 7.

Institute for Social Research, The University of Michigan, for the excerpt from Bogue, 1949.

The Johns Hopkins Press for the excerpt from The Economics of Outdoor Recreation *by M. Clawson and J. Knetsch. Published by The Johns Hopkins Press.* © *1967 for Resources for the Future.*

Landscape *for the excerpt from J. T. Snow, "The New Road in the United States,"* Landscape, *vol. 17, no. 1 (Fall 1967).*

Methuen & Co. Ltd., London, for the excerpts from Economic Development in the Tropics *by B. W. Hodder and* Essays in Political Geography *edited by C. A. Fisher.*

Monthly Review for the excerpt from K. Gough, "Anthropology and Imperialism," Monthly Review, *vol. 19, no. 11. Copyright* © *1968 by Monthly Review, Inc. Reprinted by permission of Monthly Review, Inc.*

Princeton University Press for the excerpt from Long Range Economic Projection: Studies in Income and Wealth *by Isard and Freutel. Copyright 1954 by Princeton University Press.*

Random House, Inc., and Methuen & Co. Ltd. for the excerpt from The Caucasian Chalk Circle *by Bertolt Brecht.*

Scott, Foresman and Company for the excerpt from "A Theory of Buyer Behavior" by John A. Howard and Jagdish N. Sheth in Perspectives in Consumer Behavior *by Harold H. Kassarjian and Thomas S. Robertson. Copyright 1968 by Scott, Foresman and Company.*

The University of Chicago, Department of Geography, for the excerpt from E. A. Ackermann, Research Paper No. 53.

To Our Parents

The first rule for understanding the human condition is that men live in second hand worlds. They are aware of much more than they have personally experienced; and their own experience is always indirect. The quality of their lives is determined by meanings they have received from others. . . . Their images of the world, and of themselves, are given to them by crowds of witnesses they have never met and never shall meet. Yet for every man these images . . . are the very basis of his life as a human being.

C. Wright Mills, *Power, Politics and People*

Preface

The concern in this book is with the real world of the decision maker in economic situations rather than with the normative and optimal world of the economist's model, "economically rational man." The book's frame of reference is composed of a wide range of concepts from allied disciplines, not the least of which is the "systems approach." This approach is used to focus on the totality of relationships found in the economic landscape. The book thus differs from the two principle streams of economic geography—the descriptive stream and the quantitative and predictive stream.

Descriptive economic geography located and described, but did not generally attempt to explain why something was where it was. It had its roots in the desire to amass information about the newly revealed environments of Darwin's world. There was little concern with change, uncertainty, or human fallibility.

Quantitative and predictive economic geography has its roots in the more recent past. Its concern is with precision, measurement, and normative situations. This concern has led to the adoption of a wide range of statistical tools and models, which have proved extremely useful.

Most recently, a third stream has been growing in economic geography (and geography as a whole) which focuses attention on man himself. Geographers must no longer be content with merely outlining the "objective" dimensions of economic and social patterns in space. We need also to incorporate the subjective dimensions in order to increase our understanding of the human condition and man's behavior.

This book falls firmly within the newly emerging third stream. Much of what it presents is tentative in nature; no "definitive truth" is presented. Neither description nor quantification are mutually exclusive, nor are they the only approaches. The following chapters combine these two approaches with a humanistic view of man's behavior. The purpose is to present a tentative multidimensional framework, commensurate with a world of subjective human values.

To this end, the many behavioral and physical influences, cultures, institutions, and political systems that affect economic activities are contained within a three-component "environmental system": a *phenomenal* component (physical, biotic, and certain human processes); an *operational* component (culture, technology, institutional and political subsystems); and a *behavioral* component (the perceived and experiential environment).

There are difficulties in translating the multisensate environment of the real world into the linear coolness of the written word, but I hope that the ideas and relationships of this newly emerging third broad stream in economic geography do not suffer from this added constraint.

It would be impossible for me to list all those who have helped me with this book. Many do not know me and are not aware of how much their books, articles, and ideas have added to my understanding of human behavior and economic geography. Obviously, in utilizing such a wide-ranging approach I have also leaned heavily on the advice and criticism of many people at all levels within the academic community. I am particularly indebted to Bob McDaniel, Jim Simmons, and Phil Wagner, who read an early draft of the book; to Wendy Eliot Hurst, Ed Gibson, and Paul Koroscil, who gave helpful comments on the concept of the "operational milieu"; to Maxim Berg, Reg Golledge, and Ian Joyce, who let me borrow some of their ideas; to Jim Sellers, who provided teaching assistance and intellectual stimulation of the highest caliber; to Peter Mueller, for his help in the abridgment of the preliminary edition and who corrected some of my sloppy errors in the chapters on agriculture and industry; to Louis Skoda and Karl Renkel, who executed the diagrams; to Archie MacPherson, who fostered the growth of the department at Simon Fraser which provided the milieu within which the economic geography course was taught; to those anonymous reviewers of various drafts who helped so much in turning a crude monograph into a readable text; to Michael Edwards, for straightening out my English prose; and last, but not least, to Alex Kugushev of Wadsworth/Duxbury, who displayed so much skill and tact in steering a temperamental author through the various drafts and legal entanglements that this book has experienced.

Whatever usefulness this book may have is largely due to these friends, known and unknown; but, needless to say, the ultimate responsibility for any errors or distortions lies with the author.

Contents

A Geography of Economic Behavior

one

Toward a Geography of Economic Behavior

Introduction

What is economic geography? One way of answering this question is to point to the results of economic *behavior*, as they appear in the landscape around us. The concern is with present *and* past behavior; the landscape as we now see it has gone through many stages, and is always changing. Since behavior, as the term will be used here, denotes the actions of individuals or groups, it follows that economic phenomena in some way reflect individual and group values, policies, and decisions. In order to understand the individual and group decisions that have led to any particular landscape pattern, we must widen our attention to include the circumstances under which those decisions were made. We must know what physical, cultural, and political influences were present at that point in time, what information was to hand, and how competent the decision makers were to make use of it. Economic geography can be called the subdiscipline that, in seeking to explain landscape patterns, takes all these factors into account.

Although some basic ideas in economic geography are drawn from economics, it remains essentially geographical. It has inherited traditional geography's interest in the relations between space, time, and behavior, as well as between physical features, on the one hand, and cultural phenomena, on the other. From economics comes the emphasis on man's efforts to define, coordinate, and integrate economic activities. Thus economic geography has become the study of such efforts, and of all they mean to a creature whose decision making abilities are limited by his own perception of the alternatives available, and by certain physical and cultural phenomena of which he may or may not be aware.

Economic geography has itself undergone changes. Until recently it was concerned largely with the spatial distribution of economic phenomena. In the early 1960s, for instance, a popular textbook in the subject saw it as "an enquiry into the production, exchange, and consumption of goods by people in different areas of the world." Another textbook defined the scope and method of economic geography in terms of the following three basic questions:

1. *Where is the economic activity located?*
2. *What are the characteristics of the economic activity?*
3. *To what other phenomena is the economic activity related?*

To these questions later studies have added:

4. *Why is the economic activity located where it is?*
5. *Would it not be better located elsewhere, to better satisfy certain economic and social criteria?*

Obviously, the answers expected to questions 1–3 are descriptive ones. Questions 4–5, however, introduce a **normative** dimension.* This development, unfortunately, is not quite as promising as it sounds. It is true that the additional dimension is concerned with finding the best or most efficient solution to whatever the economic problem happens to be. But it also depends heavily upon the assumption of economic rationality, that is, of a decision maker who is an **economic man,** with perfect knowledge and a per-

Words shown in boldface are defined in the Glossary.

fect ability to use that knowledge. This is a concept long used in economics, and there can be no question about its applicability within the closed confines of that discipline. With it, economists are able to proceed a long way in their analyses without making any assumptions at all about behavior: all they need to do is to study the nature of the alternatives available, and then calculate the **opportunity costs** of the activity in question. Thus economists are concerned above all with the analysis of *consistent* activity.

What many economic geographers have done, however, is to take normative economics from its own domain and have then tried to apply it in the geographical domain. Because it quite deliberately ignores all but one narrow dimension of human behavior, normative economics largely fails to explain what occurs in the multidimensional domain with which the geographer is concerned. Of course, geographers should not completely abandon the concept of economic rationality; there are specially defined situations where it can be used. But neither should they adopt normative approaches without realizing their implications for the study of man. Concern with man makes us humanists, not scientists, and humanism is not served by doctrinaire insistence on scientific purity and rigor.

The New Economic Geography

In the last few years there has been a movement away from the exclusive focus on economic man, and toward considering man as one who is constrained on virtually all sides by a variety of environmental factors, both human and nonhuman. The whole range of these factors constitutes a **milieu** of which he is never free.

This movement comes at the end of a period of some significance to economic geography. The last thirty years have seen six major areas of reorientation: increasing use of quantitative methods, the impact of the mathematical concept of probability, reliance on **models,** a growing preference for the **nomothetic approach,** convergence of economic geography with neighboring disciplines and subdisciplines, and adoption from these disciplines of such techniques as **systems analysis.** Some grasp of these trends is essential to proper use of this textbook.

Quantitative Methods

Through the use of high-speed digital computers, massive amounts of information can now be processed both quickly and easily. Moreover, a computer can be programmed to handle virtually any kind of statistical technique. The computer revolution, as it is aptly called, has affected economic geography no less than other disciplines, and a number of texts now show geographers how to take advantage of it. However, the use of computers has as many pitfalls as advantages. Both quantification and computerization are means, not ends, and the scientist who goes overboard on computer techniques may find himself in the position of the amateur photographer who takes worse pictures with his brand new, fully automatic single-lens reflex than he used to take with his box camera.

Probability and Random Processes

For some time, social scientists have been questioning the total predictability of human action and behavior. The original impulse for this came from the pure sciences, especially physics, which has elevated unpredictability into a formal principle—the so-called uncertainty principle. According to Werner Heisenberg, who formulated the principle (or one version of it) in 1927, some natural phenomena can never be completely described. Before the work of Heisenberg and his colleagues physicists had taken a more *deterministic* approach; specific results were thought to be wholly predictable from specific conditions. In contrast, the principle of uncertainty, or indeterminacy, introduced a world in which physical laws no longer completely described or predicted anything, but instead yielded statistical approximations of very high probability. Thus the entire nature of science was changed.

There is no need, of course, for geographers to jump to the conclusion that the earth's surface is governed by the mechanics of a roulette wheel, or to see economic development as a "permanent floating crap game." More important is a proper appreciation of the different ways in which chance, or randomness, can enter into economic affairs. It can stem from the imperfection of human decisions, since the limits on man's perceptual abilities at any one time are considerable. It can arise from the many apparently equal choices that can confront us on occasion—for example, there are more potential routeways than routes, and more town sites than towns. It can arise because, after all, the goals of individuals and groups do vary over time. Finally, it can arise because of what has been called "background noise," that is, the infinite number of factors that, although present, could not be taken into account at the time of the actual decision or occurrence.

In geography, recognition that the traditional modes of explanation do not always apply stems to a great extent from the influence of other social sciences, which have brought dissatisfaction with available methods and concepts, and an increasing realization of the unpredictability and uncertainty of human choice. This recognition, as we have seen, has been accompanied by the growth of sophisticated statistical techniques. Frequently, however, use of probabilistic techniques reflects not philosophical belief in indeterminacy but simply admission that we may not know enough about the events under study. Whatever their philosophical foundation, some probabilistic approaches have been very successful in simulating the patterns of the real world. Thus one study of farmers in Ghana used a gaming procedure, which is a technique of analysis involving chance, or randomness. The farmers had a choice between five crops that produced yields of different sizes according to whether it was a wet or a dry year. Since they had to find a solution through trial and error, with error meaning starvation, they were literally gambling with their lives. Obviously, this type of study is more capable of describing the processes involved than it is of explaining them.

The Use of Models

A **model** is an idealized representation of reality that is intended to demonstrate certain properties of the real world. By model-building we abstract certain factors from reality, so that rather than having to consider simultaneously a whole host of them, we can deal with what we perceive as the essential few. By their very definition models cannot convey the whole truth, but only a comprehensible part of it.

Models have many uses. They can be a set of working hypotheses for the researcher; guides to the visualization of complex interactions; organizational frameworks for the classification and manipulation of data; or simple and effective teaching aids. Thus models can be concepts, notions, or just hunches. They are useful chiefly because they are economical. Not only do they transmit general information in a highly compressed form; they can in certain circumstances express a theory as precisely as any verbal formulation. They can also draw our attention to the difference between abstraction and reality, and provide a simple picture for the student. In short, models are designed to make understanding easier. Some of the simplest models are in almost everyday use. They include maps, aerial photographs, floor plans, and flow charts. Others are used on the pioneer fringes of research. We shall be meeting them throughout this book.

Types of Models

Various types of classifications of models have been suggested. Table 1 categorizes these and other models commonly used in geography.

Different types of models have different properties and represent reality in varying degrees. Thus *analogs* utilize one property of a thing to represent another, the way distances on a slide rule represent quantities, or contour lines represent changes in height and slope. On the other hand, *physical models* allow one to dissect the socioeconomic structure into any number of component parts. These parts can be unscaled, in which case they constitute "hardware models," or they can be full-fledged "mathematical models," expressed in quantitative or symbolic terms. Also in this group are "experimental models," which are subject to testing under some experimental design. The third group, *systems*, emphasizes the linkages between components. "Synthetic" systems are built to simulate reality in a structural way, while "partial" systems are concerned with approximating relationships that are not wholly understood. Finally, a "black box" is a model of a system the internal workings of which are not understood, so that many of the relationships between components are established through intuition. Of course, none of these categories are mutually exclusive. Indeed, many of the models put forward in this book transcend these boundaries altogether.

A final distinction should be made between *internal models*, which deal with small parts of reality, and **paradigms**, which are the "grand theories" from which most models are derived. Thus Ptolemaic astronomy rested on a geocentric conception of the cosmos. The crisis of Ptolemaic astonomy did not arise from any change in the functioning of the heavenly bodies. Rather, the geocentric paradigm became increasingly unsatisfactory as a basis for *explaining* observed phenomena. The questions we ask are therefore fundamentally limited and conditioned by the underlying paradigm we adopt. Evidently, selecting one paradigm to help explain phenomena can become more of a hindrance than a help. This is particularly true in the social sciences, because the social reality reflected by any one paradigm frequently undergoes fundamental changes, and the vested interests of individuals, groups, and classes may obstruct change.

The Nomothetic Approach

Another important new influence on all branches of geography has been the change from an **idiographic** to a **nomothetic approach.** This change, which is part of the general scientific revolution created by modern physics, has come more easily to the other social sciences. In geography, however, the strongly individual character of the world and its component regions has always influenced the methods used, and geographers in general have always been inclined to prefer a descriptive analysis of what they see in front of them. The idiographic approach (from the Greek *idios*, "unique") stresses the special qualities of particular places. Its characteristic expression is the descriptive and its characteristic way of drawing conclusions is by **induction.**

The main criticism now leveled at this approach is that piling fact upon fact may be self-defeating. Unique phenomena cannot be explained—or, to put it another way, to generalize about something is to say what it has in common with something else. To be nomothetic is to look for repeated patterns, and so to develop principles, generalizations, and concepts. Geographers are beginning to see this need because they want to summarize what they think they see in the real world around them, so that they can codify information and better understand and explain the relationships between phenomena. It is of course true that the individual members of all biological species are unique. No two human beings are identical in a physiological sense. The same is true of the economic behavior of different individuals or, for that matter, the economic characteristics of different regions. Yet, if we do not admit the possibility of similarity the concept of uniqueness has no real meaning. For unless, by argument based on analogies between situations, we look for common denominators, unless we seek norms or standards, no single case can ever be described as unique. Facts

Table 1. *A Typology of Models*

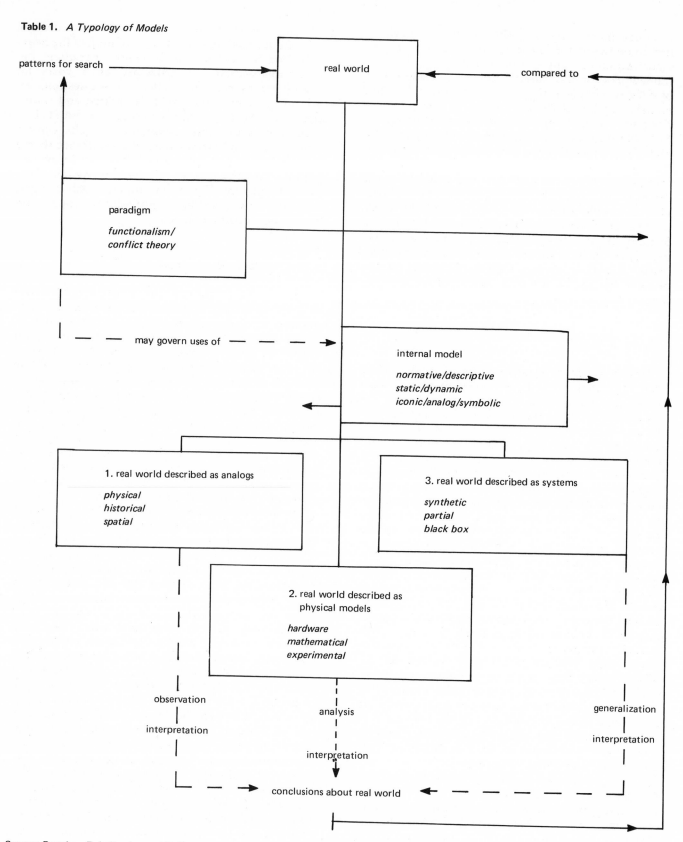

patterns for search ⟶ real world ⟵ compared to ⟵

paradigm

*functionalism/
conflict theory*

— — — may govern uses of — — — ⟶

internal model

*normative/descriptive
static/dynamic
iconic/analog/symbolic*

1. real world described as analogs

*physical
historical
spatial*

3. real world described as systems

*synthetic
partial
black box*

2. real world described as
physical models

*hardware
mathematical
experimental*

observation

interpretation

analysis

generalization

interpretation

interpretation

conclusions about real world

Source: Based on R.J. Chorley and P. Haggett, eds., *Models in Geography* (London: Methuen, 1967).

increase in significance only in proportion as we develop intellectual tools for dealing with them.

Convergence

The new methods and approaches discussed above are not the exclusive property of economic geographers, though perhaps the latter have made more use of them. They are used in nearly all branches of geography, and provide some common interplay between them. By itself, such interplay is insufficient; the boundaries of disciplines are artificial, and the most recent trend in economic geography has been to disregard them as much as possible. As often as not, very little of value is brought back from these excursions. Behavioral variables have long been neglected in economics and economic geography. In the rush to fill this void, good intentions have sometimes given way to hasty and illogical incorporation of behavioral notions into traditional location analysis. For example, one devastating indictment of traditional economic postulates, despite the intellectual excitement it generates, fails to improve on what it has destroyed.

The dangers of adapting superficial explanations and notions from poorly understood neighboring disciplines are indeed very real. We need a precise understanding of these concepts to make proper use of the interdisciplinary convergence that seems to be taking place regardless of the difficulties involved. It is a fact that geographers have been influenced by recent work in sociology, anthropology, and psychology. From psychology comes our present concern with behavior, and the forces that influence behavior, whether it be economic or social. Hence our concern with the perceived environment, that is, with the mental images held by man of the space around him. Obviously, these images influence how we decide about or locate our economic structures, patterns, and processes. Man thus decides to grow crops and animals for his sustenance, not arbitrarily, but because he sees the world around him in a certain way. For instance, we now know that traditional economic factors, like transport costs, have declined in importance, and that the decision to locate an industry or business may be increasingly related to the image an area has in the minds of a few key people. The scenic, recreational, cultural, and intellectual resources of an area may now play their role. None of this preempts the use in economic analysis of more traditional factors, but it does encourage us to look beyond the blinkers that traditional economics imposes. The role of behavioral factors is examined in more detail in chapter 4.

Systems Analysis

The concept of a system has been with us for some time. Indeed, we are all familiar with such terms as solar system, economic system, and social system. More recently, this rather loose usage has been defined and structured to represent highly complex systems and processes.

The basic concept is simple enough. A **system** is a set of identified elements so related that together they form a complex whole. Systems analysis means considerations of such a whole *as* a whole, rather than as something to be analyzed into separate parts. A system as opposed to a mere assemblage (one might almost say "heap") is not just a totality of parts, but rather a totality of relations among and including those parts. **Systems analysis** is an approach or methodology rather than a philosophy or a scientific paradigm. In other words, it is an analytical technique or tool that can aid in the understanding or elucidation of complex structures, not a generalized theory in itself—although some of its champions may see it as one.

It has been said in criticism of systems analysis that everything can be considered a system—the human body, a business organization, the national economy, the weather, and even the universe itself. And this is true: all phenomena are susceptible to systems analysis, since they are all made up of interconnected parts. Thus we can look on the world economic scene as an extremely complex network of flows of people, money, energy, goods, and information—in short as a system.

Economic geographers utilize the system concept in order to better understand the component elements of some part of reality, and the relations between them. To continue with our example, if we look at the world economic scene as an entity, we can break it down into component subsystems. Given this better understanding of the structure, we could then perhaps try to rearrange the elements spatially in order to maximize some human welfare function. And in fact the acceptance by some economic geographers of this notion of the world economy is regarded by some as one of the major conceptual advances of recent years. This insight will not be neglected here. As one proceeds through this book, one should gain a growing awareness of the interrelatedness of things, and thus be led, almost subconsciously, into a consideration of what is the nature of the interrelatedness among any set of phenomena. To cope with the whole earth will seem increasingly impossible, and eventually one will turn to extracting from a particular environment a system, and to subdividing this into subsystems.

Toward a Geography of Economic Behavior

The approach to economic activities taken in this book is based on two areas of recent development: systems analysis, as a conceptual tool, and convergence with other disciplines as a guiding principle. Other innovations, especially probability theory and such tools as models, are also utilized. The main topic thus becomes not so much the economic landscape as economic behavior. We are concerned with the behavior of the entrepreneur, the policy maker, and the consumer; with how such behavior leads to overt decisions that alter and affect the landscape around us; and with how such behavior can be related to surrounding systems of phenomena. Systems analysis remains the organizing framework, but it is not utilized as *the* overriding paradigm. The relationship of all these elements to analysis of the economic landscape is shown diagrammatically in the frontispiece.

Determinism ruled in geography until after 1945. In some ways, deterministic geography was like economics when it was still dominated by the concept of economic man: decisions affecting the economic landscape could only be explained along rationalistic lines.

Since 1945, probabilistic ideas have slowly seeped into the social sciences from such areas as physics. In geography, however, it was not until the late 1950's that their influence began to be felt, chiefly through the influence of the behavioral sciences. Incorporation of the behavioral science outlook into geography is known as **behavioralism.** Man's behavior is seen as the result of his perception of the environment, and that perception as molded by his individual and group values, his learning processes, and so on. Futhermore, this behavior is indeterminate, that is, it can be neither described nor predicted with certainty. This lack of certainty stems from the fallibility of human decision making, the multiplicity of choice, and the impossibility of screening out causal "background noise." A number of geographers have used these concepts in such fields of study as flood plain occupance, individual farmers' views of their agricultural environment, and the relation between traffic and individual movements.

Noneconomic Man

In rejecting deterministic viewpoints, we also reject economic man. What can we put in his place? Obviously, a new model of man, closer to the human reality. H. A. Simon expresses the difference between the old and new models as follows. Economic man is the **optimizer,** that is, his actions are always optimal, certain, and rational. But since no one can possibly be aware of all the alternatives when he comes to make an economic decision, and since none of us can know the final outcome of our actions, it makes more sense, according to Simon, to speak of a man who *satisfices*, that is, who seeks a course of action that is "good enough." In other words, what we opt for is not necessarily the best in economically rational terms, but merely what we find acceptable. Having found that line of action we adopt it, without necessarily being concerned about whether or not there may be a better one. In this view economic decisions are not *determined* by physical environment, economic rationalism, or anything else. Instead, they are the product of the individual's *acquired* abilities: he learns about possible courses of action, and goes on learning.

Simon has another concept that is applicable here: that of **bounded rationality.** In the real world, an individual does not have complete information—and if he did, he would not have learned how to assess it. Thus his rational powers are limited, or bounded. Within his perceptual bounds the **satisficer** chooses as it were along a preference scale, which varies from person to person and from group to group. This can be thought of as extending from the optimal solution to a choice that actually makes the chooser worse off, although the range of choices in any given instance would be more restricted. As individuals, when we come to make a decision we select a course of action that we think will satisfy our particular set of needs. Such a course of action is frequently the most practicable given the more limited framework of man the satisficer; as we will see in later sections, high incomes and high profits can still be the results of satisficing behavior!

By contrast, the optimizer, or rational economic man, lives in a more deterministic world than the one we inhabit, and has more information at his disposal. As a model—an abstraction from the real world—he has his uses. But we must not forget that in the real world the individual decision maker is also a learner who always seeks to better his choice, but is perpetually groping in uncertainty.

So we end up with an economic geography that is both probabilistic and behaviorally oriented. Instead of an economic man to whom all things are an open book, we have a figure who gropes his way toward what is *to him* a satisfactory solution or activity. This satisficer lacks complete knowledge, may sometimes lack the incentive to learn, and may often lack the money necessary to search for a better solution.

The Plan of This Book

Utilizing the components sketched in the frontispiece, chapters 1–5 introduce the means of analysis. Chapter 2 introduces various basic spatial and economic concepts, and explores certain notions of economic behavior. Chapter 3 further elaborates the idea of systems analysis. Chapter 4 introduces a conceptual model for all geography, with special reference to the effect of the behavioral environment and the operational milieu on economic activities. Chapter 5 illustrates some of the efforts that have been made to represent the relationships outlined in chapter 4.

The core of any approach to economic geography, descriptive or otherwise, must be some account of the traditional economic sectors or subsystems; agriculture, manufacturing, tertiary activities, and transportation. Chapters 6–13 present this core material from both the classic and the behavioral viewpoints.

Having dismembered the economic system in this way, in chapter 14 we shall go to the other extreme and study complex economic processes at the regional level. Chapter 15 examines some of the reasons why an optimal system does not occur in reality. Here we shall have occasion to discuss political differences in the world, a subject not often treated by economic geographers, and to analyze the various concepts of "development" and "underdevelopment."

Finally, chapter 16 synthesizes the behavioral, operational, functional, and dysfunctional parts of the system, to form a conceptual model of the economic landscape.

Summary

1. *Economic geographers study the overt results of economically oriented behavior as they appear in the landscape.*

2. *The subdiscipline draws on the basic concepts of two disciplines—geography and economics; but in addition to spatial and economic factors, physical, cultural, and political influences are also taken into account.*

3. *Put in simple terms, economic geographers in the past have posed five basic questions concerning the location, characteristics, relationships, decision making, and normative conditions of economic activities.*

4. *However, in the last thirty years a number of changes have occurred which modify and/or advance these basic questions.*

5. *Quantitative techniques have been developed, for example, which can aid the empirical investigations involved if they are used judiciously and carefully. Similarly, the use of a nondeterministic approach (probability) has also widened considerably the techniques available for describing the overt results of human decisions.*

6. *The use of models—notions or ideas set in a simple diagrammatic fashion—enables us to hand on generalized information in a compressed form, provides a simple working picture in the classroom, and heightens understanding by allowing a comparison between the basic abstract features of the model and real-world conditions.*

7. *To supplement the descriptive approach (idiographic) so long used in geography, nomothetic approaches have been utilized. This latter format stresses generalization, broad principles, and basic conceptualizations, rather than the uniqueness of phenomena.*

8. *Statistical representation, the search for law-like principles, description, and the use of models have been supplemented by increasing interest in the concepts and notions of neighboring disciplines. One result of this convergence has been a concern with behavioral factors and the process of perception.*

9. *Finally, the adoption of systems analysis has aided economic geography. A system is simply a set of identified elements so related that together they form a complex whole. The use of such a conception stresses the study of the whole as well as of the parts. Thus the world economy can be regarded as a set of interlocking parts and subsystems.*

10. *Two of these changes—the behavioral approach and systems analysis—are utilized in this book as frameworks for studying and analyzing economic activities.*

11. *Within those bounds of study, emphasis is placed on man the satisficer, rather than economic man. Hence, in analyzing the decision making processes generated by economic activities, we are dealing with man bounded by his own inabilities to perceive all of the environment, learning as he proceeds, but groping forward in an uncertain and "incomplete" environment.*

12. *These frameworks and notions will be developed in later chapters before they are applied to the "core" of economic geography, the subsystems of agriculture, manufacturing, tertiary activities, and transportation.*

Further Reading

A lengthy introduction to the two disciplines contributing to the subdiscipline of economic geography is provided by

Chisholm, M. *Geography and Economics* (London: Bell, 1966), especially chapter 2.

while general simple statements about the subdiscipline will be found in

Brown, R. C. and Eliot Hurst, M. E. "Recent Change in Economic Geography," *Journal of Geography*, vol. 71, no. 1, 1969, pp. 41–45.

Haggett, P. "Changing Concepts in Economic Geography," in R. J. Chorley and P. Haggett, eds. *Frontiers of Geographical Teaching* (London: Methuen, 1965), chapter 6.

Thoman, R. "Economic Geography" in D. L. Sills, ed. *International Encyclopedia of the Social Sciences* (New York: Macmillan Company, 1968), pp. 123–129.

More detailed statements about some of the recent areas of change will be found concerning

quantitative methods, in

Gould, P. "Methodological Developments since the Fifties," *Progress in Geography*, vol. 1, 1969, pp. 1–50.

probability, in

Curry, L. "Chance and Landscape," in P. W. English and R. C. Mayfield, eds. *Man, Space, and Environment* (New York: Oxford University Press, 1972), pp. 611–621.

models, in

Haggett, P. and Chorley, R. J. "Models, Paradigms, and New Geography" in *Integrated Models in Geography* (London: Methuen, 1967), pp. 19–41.

perception, in

Brookfield, H. C. "On the Environment as Perceived," *Progress in Geography*, vol. 1, 1969, pp. 51–80.

Sonnenfeld, J. "Geography, Perception, and the Behavioral Environment," in P. W. English and R. Mayfield. *Man, Space and Environment* (New York: Oxford University Press, 1972), pp. 244–250.

systems, in

McDaniel, R. and Eliot Hurst, M. E. *A Systems Analytic Approach to Economic Geography* (Washington, D.C.: Commission on College Geography, General Series, Publication no. 8, 1968).

To gain some general idea of the study of economic activities within the general field of geography, a glance through

Haggett, P. *Geography: A Modern Synthesis* (New York: Harper and Row, 1972).

might be helpful. This book provides a broad-ranging review of contemporary geography, and the interlocking nature of physical, economic and cultural geography is made clear.

In addition, it would also be helpful to look through recent numbers of some of the principal geographic journals to see what work economic geographers are currently undertaking. *Economic Geography* (quarterly), *Tijdschrift Voor Econonische en Sociale Geografie* (every two months), *Canadian Geographer* (quarterly), *Transactions of the Institute of British Geographers* (three times a year), *Geography* (quarterly) and the *Annals of the Association of American Geographers* (quarterly) are all useful journals from which to assess general work in economic geography. More specialized topics will be covered in other journals, which can be tracked down by consulting *Geographical Abstracts, C, Economic Geography* (every two months).

two

Some Basic Concepts

Some Economic Terms

Over the centuries, man has succeeded in establishing certain relationships between himself and his **milieu,** or the environment as he perceives it (figure 1). These relationships are related to the availability of **resources,** the distribution of population, the **value system,** the **political system,** and the current state of the **technological system.** Every relationship of this kind can be regarded as a form of economic organization, that is, a means of exploiting valuable resources for the benefit of a given population, and of compensating for the uneven distribution of such resources in space and time.

The Economy

Man has intervened in the natural environment to the point at which neither the changing seasons nor the uneven distribution of resources need seriously hurt him. Human values and human intervention together create what economists call **utility,** that is, what is added to resources when they are converted into something useful to man.

Through manufacture, man adds **form utility.**
Through transportation, man adds **place utility.**
Through storage, man adds **time utility.**

For example, iron ore is virtually useless in itself, but it acquires form utility after it has been extracted, smelted, and converted by manufacture into iron goods. If such goods can be transported to a place where they are both needed and absent, then they

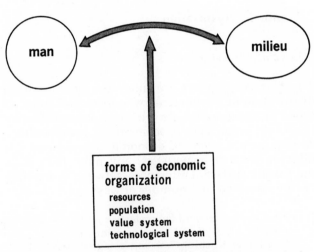

Fig. 1. *Man-milieu relationships. Between man and his perceived environment are certain economic forms or systems representing resource evaluation, tools, technology, etc. These forms of economic organization intercede between man and his general milieu.*

have place utility. Finally, storing them against the day of need will give them time utility.

Taken together, these attempts to make the natural environment more amenable to exploitation create an **economy.** The economy has two basic functions:

1. *To produce goods and services.*
2. *To distribute these goods and services among users.*

Here, the type of institution that takes charge of economic production and distribution will be called the **firm,** and its clients **consumers.**

The Firm

The part of the economy engaged in production can be divided into four distinct but interrelated systems, usually labeled primary, secondary, tertiary, and quarternary (table 2).

Primary activity includes agriculture, forestry, fishing, the extraction of minerals, and, in general, the exploitation of energy resources. All primary production is closely related to the natural environment.

Secondary activity is production that results in some transformation of primary products through the addition of form utility, or the change in form of some existing item. Most of it comes under the head of what we would ordinarily call manufacturing.

Tertiary activity consists mainly in rendering services that can give place and time utility to products that have already passed through the primary and secondary stages. Thus this group includes transportation and wholesaling, as well as the activities of the service-oriented professions and occupations. Because of this high service component, there is some overlap between tertiary activity and consumption.

Quarternary activity, a relatively new concept, applies to the growing class of service occupations for which advanced training and education are required. The reason for distinguishing these occupations from all others is their importance, far out of

Table 2. *Classification of Economic Activities*

A. Production. *The transformation of resources and producer goods, adding value and/or form (the addition of form/utility).*

    1. Primary. *Direct acquisition from the natural environment, or systematized production from land or sea. (Agriculture, grazing, forest products, fishing and hunting, mining and quarrying.)*

    2. Secondary. *Transformation of primary products and producer goods. (Manufacturing—handicraft to factory production.)*

    3. Tertiary. *Services, wholesaling and retailing consumer goods. (Retailing, banking, trading, entertainment, etc.)*

    4. Quarternary. *Service for which advanced training and education is required.*

B. Exchange. *The addition of time and place utility; the sale of goods in the market place and the change in location so entailed.*

    1. Trade. *Increasing the value of producer or consumer goods by selling or barter, thus changing their ownership. Time utility may be added in this process. (Wholesaling and retailing.)*

    2. Movement. *Increasing the value of producer or consumer goods by adding place utility. (Transportation—freight and passenger.)*

C. Consumption. *The using up of goods and services to satisfy human wants and needs.*

    1. Consumer goods. *Food, shelter, clothing, etc., used in direct satisfaction of human wants. Found at all levels of economic organization.*

    2. Producer goods. *Used for indirect satisfaction; consumed in the act of further production of goods. Restricted to higher levels of economic organization.*

proportion to their numbers, in the actual operation of an economic system, particularly in the realm of decision making.

The Consumer

The other major division of the economy is that involved in **exchange** and **consumption**. The process of exchange overlaps with some of the productive activities mentioned above. Transportation, a tertiary production activity, increases the value of a good by changing its location. But what of the movement, or flow, of people and ideas? It is hard to put an exact price on an idea. But there is no doubt that some ideas increase in value when transplanted from one country to another, especially when the country of origin, for whatever reason, is not a suitable place to try them out. Change of ownership is another mechanism through which exchange can be said to increase value. Thus the materials in a loaf of bread increase in value at each stage of their journey from field to meal table.

The **consumer** is the end of the line for the economic activity system. Investment, production, and all the other economic activities so far discussed, are merely means to consumption. Of course, there are many different kinds and degrees of consumption. It may be fast, as when a food or drug is consumed, or so slow that, as in the case of an appliance or a machine, we think of wearing the good out rather than consuming it (hence the term "consumer durable," applied to this class of goods). Consumption may also involve the use of some resource or good for a specific purpose—for instance, the use of the Rocky Mountains as a recreation area. Perhaps the strangest form of consumption, from the ordinary person's point of view, is the payment of vast sums for some object, such as an old postage stamp, simply because it is rare. But the same economic principles apply to the production and consumption of pearls, diamonds, and other so-called precious commodities. The stamp trade is peculiar not because stamps are peculiar but because collecting them is an activity valued by a very limited class of consumers.

Economic Organization

Organizational Categories

Just as geographers are interested in the varied distribution of phenomena over space and time, so economic geographers are interested in the distribution of different types of economies. Clearly, neither economies nor forms of economic organization exhibit uniform characteristics, any more than does the earth's surface. Differences between economies can be classified in a number of ways:

1. *They can be classified by production technique. The result of a host of such terms as* plant gathering, hunting and fishing, hoe and plough cultivation, pastoralism, *and* manufacturing. *An alternative set of terms, representing man's supposed economic evolution, is the* hunting and gathering, agricultural, industrial, *and* scientific stages. *All such types of classification are too simplistic; they fail to take account of societal as distinct from purely economic variations.*

2. *They can be classified into* **subsistence** *and* **profit economies.**

2(a). *As a modification of the above, they can be classified into subsistence and* **exchange economies.**

In a so-called subsistence economy, the family, whether **nuclear** or **extended,** usually performs all the functions of production, exchange, and consumption. Thus the small family unit is both firm and consumer, since it produces what it consumes, and consumes what it produces. Raymond Firth has even rejected the term "subsistence" in favor of "primitive." The reason for this is that virtually every real-life economy that has been tagged with the subsistence label does in fact produce more than *just* food, clothing, and shelter; for instance, it is likely to include some exchange while lacking a general medium of exchange, such as money.

In an exchange economy more than one family or social unit takes part, and goods and services are distributed by more sophisticated and formal methods. Production, exchange, and consumption take on the complex characteristics defined in table 2, above.

This third, and now widely accepted, categorization can of course be further broken down. For example an exchange economy can be **reciprocal** (exchange is regulated by tradition, ceremony, and status), **redistributive** (exchange is controlled by a strong central agency and the society is highly stratified), **peasant** (small-scale producers who enter marginally into the exchange system, although they rely mainly on subsistence practices), and **market** (no specialized agency of exchange except the market itself).

We can now recognize five broad types of economic organization:

1. *Subsistence.*
2. *Reciprocal exchange, with subsistence.*
3. *Peasant, with primary reliance on self-produced food, but containing some exchange elements.*
3(a). *Market peasant (for instance, a peasant economy existing on the edge of a market economy).*
3(b). *Redistributive peasant (such as might exist in a feudal economy).*
4. *Market-commercial.*
5. *Redistributive, or* **state socialist,** *with an urban elite (not a pure type, but sharing elements from some of the above).*

Many of the characteristics of these five types will be found summarized in table 3.

Some Organizational Characteristics

We, of course, are most familiar with the market-commercial system, in which all economic relations tend to be somewhat impersonal. And even if they are not, the individuals concerned are usually considered to be replaceable. As economic units, it is not their total social characteristics that matter, but the nature of their direct contribution to the economic process. In privitive economies, on the other hand, the individual is likely to hold his economic position by virtue of his social position—and not, as with us, the other way around.

Table 3. *Characteristics of Types of Economic Organization*

subsistence	reciprocal	peasant	redistributive	market-commercial
absence of machine technology			*complex technology*	
limited exchange marketless	*reciprocal exchange*	*peripheral market*	*"State" market*	*market*
	value of "gifts"	*money variable*	*all-purpose money*	
production unit: the family, kinship			*production state-managed*	*production by institutional unit*
distribution relatively complex			*distribution state organized*	*distribution by market*
production and distribution units: multipurpose social units			*production and distribution units economically oriented*	
primary activities dominant			*secondary and tertiary activities dominant*	
crafts specialized		*cottage industries*	*industrial units large*	

The main organizational differences between primitive and industrial economies can be summed up as follows. In industrial economies, technology has reached a high level of development but the distribution process, which depends mainly on the market principle, has remained relatively simple. The reverse situation is found in primitive economies; the technology is relatively simple, but the distribution system may be very complex, both in organization and in the principles involved. Of course, major structural changes do occur. In particular there has been a historical trend away from activities that are primary and rural, and toward those that are secondary and urban. Today, the trend seems to be in favor of tertiary activities (figures 2 and 3).

According to one theory, tertiary employment increases relative to total employment during the course of development. More specifically, the theory suggests that both secondary and tertiary activities have grown in importance somewhat as follows:

1. *Growth occurs through specialization in primary activities, accompanied by improvements in transport. Both industry and services remain small in scale, the former consisting mainly in handicrafts.*
2. *Secondary industries are introduced, and the economic* **infrastructure**—*transport, schools, and so on—develops in proportion. Population pressure increases, and returns from primary activities decrease.*

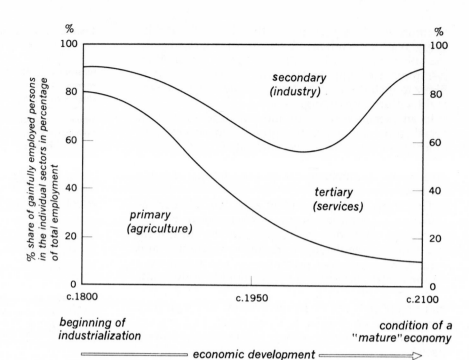

%
100

% share of gainfully employed persons
in the individual sectors in percentage
of total employment

80

60

secondary
(industry)

40

20

0

primary
(agriculture)

tertiary
(services)

c.1800

c.1950

c.2100

%
100

80

60

40

20

0

Fig. 2. *Development of primary,
secondary, and tertiary activities: France.
(After Jean Fourastié,* La Productivité,
Paris, 1964.)

beginning of
industrialization

condition of a
"mature" economy

economic development

3. *The secondary industries grow more diverse and the
economy more complex. Internal industrial linkages
develop. It is at this point that there are sustained
rises in real incomes per head of population.*

4. *Specialization occurs in certain tertiary activities.*

This model is known as the Clark-Fisher thesis,
after its inventors. Over the last twenty years it has
come in for a great deal of criticism, though some
recent research seems to bear it out. In any case, it
is a useful working hypothesis.

The world distribution of the various forms of
economic organization discussed above is shown in
figure 4. In areal terms, the bulk of the earth is devoted to something other than a market-commercial
economy. The bulk of its population still lies within
the peasant and subsistence economies. To use
another measure, something like 54 percent of the
world's labor force are still agricultural workers, and
most of these are peasant or subsistence cultivators.
Of the remaining 46 percent, most live in countries
dominated by peasant or subsistence economies, and
most are still associated with crafts and services at a
preindustrial level. The proportion of commercial
cultivators is very small indeed.

It should not be assumed that these types of economic organization represent stages through which
a society *has* to pass. They can be viewed either as a
series of end states or as more or less arbitrarily defined stages in a nation's history. The concept of
development, whether social or economic, is notori-
ously hard to define; most definitions, as we shall

see in chapter 15, concentrate on one factor exclusively, and neglect structural shifts in the economy.

Economic geography is concerned with the spatial
distribution of all these types of economic organization and activity, and with their variation over time.
By studying these factors, it hopes to explain the
variations in economic behavior. The key questions
seem to be, What is produced—and by what groups?
What is the purpose of production? How is the final
product distributed, and what structural or institutional mechanisms exist to this end? How is the
economy related to the social structure, and to what
degree are economic factors independent of social
ones? As we shall see in chapter 4, all these relationships are highly complex.

Economic Behavior

This book is concerned with behavior in economic
situations. This goes beyond the traditional concern
of economists and economic geographers with one
abstract dimension of human behavior, that is, so-
called rational behavior under a set of very rigid
constraints. These a priori constraints or assumptions, sometimes implicit sometimes explicit, can
be reduced to six:

1. *That production and exchange are predominantly motivated by the attempt to maximize profits, usually in the
short run.*

2. *That economic behavior is predominantly rational, and*

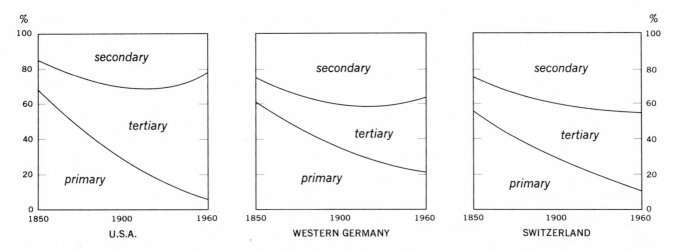

percent share of gainfully employed persons in the individual sectors
in percentage of total employment

Fig. 3. *Development of primary, secondary, and tertiary activities. As an economy "develops" in the Western sense, the proportion of the labor force in the three basic sectors changes, with particular emphasis on the tertiary, or service, sector. (After Francesco Kneschaurek, "Wachstumsbedingte Wandlungen der Beschaftigungsstruktur," in* Strukturwandlungen einer wachsenden Wirtschaft, Schriften des Vereins fur Socialpolitik, Neue Folge Band 30/II. *Berlin: Verlag Duncker & Humblot, 1964, pp. 720–39.)*

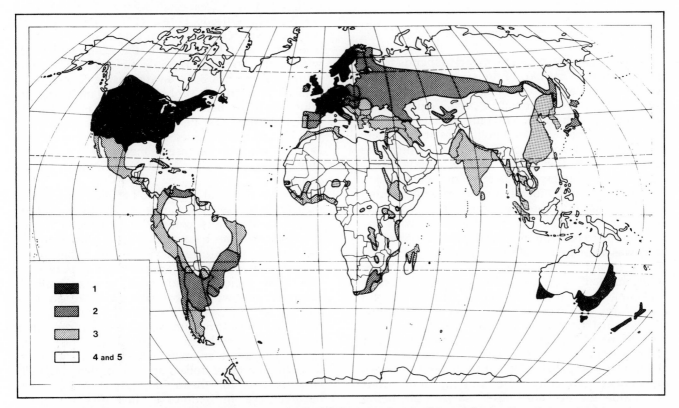

Fig. 4. *Kinds and levels of economic development. (1) high level of productivity, predominantly exchange economy; (2) intermediate level of productivity, generally of exchange economy but with large sectors of subsistence economy; (3) low level of productivity, generally of subsistence economy but with large sectors of exchange economy; (4) low level of productivity, almost completely of subsistence economy; (5) largely undeveloped for production, with no distinction as to kind or level of the economy that does exist. Sections (4) and (5) are not distinguished from each other on this map. (From N. Ginsburg, "Essays on Economic Development," Research Paper No. 62, 1960, p. 22, reprinted by permission of the University of Chicago, Department of Geography.)*

based on more or less complete knowledge of the market and more or less perfect anticipation of the results of alternative choice. (This assumption is necessary in order to make the first assumption meaningful.)

3. *That additional units of consumption and income bring progressively less satisfaction. (This is known as the principle of diminishing **marginal utility**.)*

4. *That total wants inevitably exceed the means of satisfying them. (This is known as the principle of scarcity.)*

5. *That satisfactions are to some extent substitutable for each other.*

6. *That any change is gradual and nondisruptive, and tends toward a general equilibrium.*

With the help of these assumptions, plus the assumption that all other things remain constant, various general postulates are derived. One such postulate is that price will move toward the point at which supply equals demand; another is that all economic systems tend toward a state of equilibrium. Many economists and economic geographers believe these postulates to be true, at least for most of the time.

Traditional Economic Assumptions

Much of classical economic theory depends for its validity on the first two of the six assumptions set out above, while the sixth assumption is the foundation for theories of general or partial equilibrium. But these assumptions are only social products, derived from the values and prejudices of the society in which the classical economists lived, which was the only society they knew. Their economic theory was partly an attempt to describe the social reality of their time—the "liberal" society of early capitalism—and partly a utopian conception of a fully developed market society that they foresaw as one day coming to realization. Classical economic theory, then, was a fairly adequate description of a particular economic and social reality, even though its "laws of the market" were arrived at by pure deductive reasoning rather than observation. This reality did not endure, however, and the social and economic changes that have since occurred are far from any classical utopia. Thus, small-scale businesses have given way to the corporate enterprise and the conglomerate; competition is quite imperfect, since monopolies frequently arise; and the motivations that guide the decision maker, so far from being reducible to a few principles, are exceedingly complex.

Economists and others who use economic propositions (including geographers) have been curiously blind to these changed circumstances. Instead of rejecting these now untenable classical assumptions

in order to provide a sounder cultural and psychological base for economic analysis, most economists have attempted to exclude all so-called noneconomic influences, including behavioral ones, as irrelevant to their purposes. Instead, a body of "pure" economic theory has arisen. This takes the approach that economic behavior is concerned mainly with the disposition of scarce means for given ends, and that this is an almost ubiquitous determinant of human behavior (the principle of scarcity, mentioned above). No attempt is made to deny the existence of noneconomic motives and relationships; they are simple categorized as irrelevant to economic behavior, which is defined as consistent behavior in the disposal of scarce resources for given ends. The reasons why these ends have been chosen are not considered important to the economist. In fact he can proceed quite a way without making any assumptions at all about behavior, as he studies the nature of alternatives and calculates the direct (and sometimes the indirect) cost of pursuing any particular end to the exclusion of others.

Over the last 150 years, this paradigm has been explored by such great economists as Alfred Marshall (1842–1924), Vilfredo Pareto (1848–1923), and John Maynard Keynes (1883–1946), and many interesting problems have been posed. But continued study within this framework has yielded diminishing returns. There has been an increasing concern with smaller and trivial problems, to compensate for which there has been increasing use of elaborate and refined techniques. Perhaps it is time to reaffirm that economic principles continue to be useful only as long as they represent meaningful postulates about human motives, behavior, and social organization.

In neglecting real economic behavior, the economist finds himself producing explanations that are independent of any cultural of behavioral reality. Such explanations, because they lack social reference, are devoid of empirical content. The propositions of pure economic theory are like those of pure logic: they state logical relationships, but say nothing about the real world. Economic postulates indicate what is to be expected *if* economic behavior is rational and seeks to maximize profits or returns. These postulates are felt by most economists to be empirical, since people in many situations are seen by them to seek more dollars and to calculate rationally what is best for them. Empirical studies reveal, however, that individuals in their varying roles as consumers, savers, investors, managers, workers, or landlords frequently act in nonrational and noneconomic ways. Empirical studies reveal not just the "what" of the classical economist, but also how much, where, when, why, and to what else the action is related. The truth of classical economic theory is the truth of tautology, that is, it is true by definition, and brings us no news about the real world.

In some areas, there has been a movement away from pure theory. For example, in some studies of the **business cycle,** the theory of money, and the economics of savings, it has been possible to dispense with the unrealistic assumption that human beings react mechanically to economic forces. Certain "classical" assumptions are still widely used, in particular the assumption that rational economic behavior is a model that can be used to describe economic patterns. Defendants of classical theory usually argue that economics should not be expected to explain all behavior in economic situations, but should limit itself to an analysis of the "purely economic aspect" of human behavior. But this is only a piece of special pleading to the effect that all factors likely to inconvenience the researcher should be held constant. In similar vein, so-called noneconomic factors are frequently dismissed as subjective, immeasurable, and ephemeral.

Much of economics, then, remains essentially normative. It takes the existing social system for granted, and assumes implicitly that the capitalist system is permanent. Instead of trying to understand how the socioeconomic system actually works, many economists are engaged in ideological apologetics coupled with what they take to be social engineering. At fault is the underlying paradigm, the six dimensions of which were described above. This paradigm no longer applies to a certain aspect of reality. Rather, it remains only a framework within which certain ways and means can be devised to manipulate certain variables.

Human Behavior

Obviously, economic behavior is not to be constrained by the six assumptions of classical economics. Habit, custom, institutions, technology, political systems—all have their economic aspects, as well as such psychological factors as satisfaction in doing a job well, achieving prestige or status, and conforming to the "spirit" of the current business system. In other words, economic behavior must be related to human behavior in general. It must also be related to the particular problems of the farmer, businessman, wholesaler, retailer, industrialist, and consumer. How else can geographers explain patterns of economic recession ("poverty areas"), or the immobility of labor in such areas, where workers may turn down better employment opportunities and better living conditions elsewhere, preferring to stay in the community and occupation with which they are most familiar? The explanation of such behavior needs a much more subtle approach

than the simplistic classical economic postulates make possible.

Man the Satisficer

An alternative to the traditional postulate of "economic man" is badly needed. Such an alternative would recognize that possible choices are not given, but must be sought and searched for, and that some economic decisions may have results that are satisfactory or "good enough" in a particular context, but are not necessarily the best from a purely economic point of view. The businessman's or consumer's information about his environment encompasses only a small fraction of the total reality. When we come to make a decision we usually draw on only a small section of the available information. The environment generates millions of pieces of information every second, but the bottleneck of our perceptual apparatus—eyes, ears, nose, and skin—cannot absorb more than 1,000 pieces per second, and probably much less. Another bottleneck occurs when that information reaches the brain, which never seems to draw as many inferences as it is theoretically capable of doing.

With such incomplete information it is obviously not possible to be certain about any economic outcome. Factors may influence the consequences of our decision that we simply had not perceived. Moreover, we know too little about economic processes to predict the future on the basis of present knowledge. In any case, given the principle of uncertainty mentioned in chapter 1, all predictions are of limited value. Not only do we fail to anticipate the consequences of our choices because of our own lack of information, but our brains cannot at a single moment grasp the consequences of a choice in their entirety. Instead, attention shifts from one piece of information to another, and from one value to another, with consequent shifts in preference.

The concept of man as satisficer rests, as we have seen, on an essentially practical and realistic view of the likely alternatives. Thus an economic decision maker is thought of as searching the environment or his own informational store for alternatives the outcomes of which are assessed not automatically as "the best," but as "good enough" in terms of his **aspiration level.** The conditions for satisfaction are thus not static, but are adjusted upwards or downwards on the basis of new experience and new aspiration levels. When the outcome of a decision falls short of the decision maker's level of aspiration, he either searches for new alternatives, or adjusts his level of aspiration downwards, or both. The goal is to reach levels that are practically attainable.

Table 4 sets out a typical range of choices. Number

Table 4. *A Choice Scale of Decisions*

possible range of choices

1. maximin *solution: optimal, maximum-minimum payoff*
2. fairly optimistic *solution: minimization of regret at not choosing the optimal solution*
3. satisfactory *solution: a choice that is just "good enough" within the known range of choices.*
4. fairly pessimistic *solution: up to a 75 percent chance of a less-than satisfactory payoff*
5. worse off *solution: much less than satisfactory; usual payoff unsatisfactory; chances of satisfactory solution minimal*

1 on this scale is the optimal solution, that is, the best solution from the point of view of classical and normative economics. This is the decision that economically rational man, the optimizer, invariably takes. In real life, however, it is likely to be the *least* frequent choice. Most people settle for other grades of satisfaction, from fairly optimistic to fairly pessimistic (numbers 2 and 4), that may be sufficiently satisfactory to be acceptable. Also included in table 4 is the "worse off" choice (number 5), presumably due to lack of information (though in some economic situations, such as gambling, the decision maker may secretly want to lose).

Thus we can replace the notion of economic rationality with that of **bounded rationality.** None of us has more than an incomplete notion of the real world. The satisficer, within his perceptual bounds, chooses as it were along a preference scale, like the one in table 4, which varies in width from person to person and from group to group. Through learning, the scale may be adjusted. To sum up:

Being an *optimizer* would require a more deterministic and predictable world than in fact exists; more information than man normally handles; and decision processes at levels higher than those at which man normally operates. Economic rationality is a useful model to compare with real economic behavior, but that is about the extent of its usefulness.

Being a *satisficer* is a form of decision making in which man is guided by his ambitions, goals, and drives—in short, by his aspiration level. If the outcome of his choice does not meet his aspirations, the next time he is faced with a similar situation he will presumably aim higher. Certainly, he will not settle for less than the previous solution.

Decision Making

So far we have dealt with economic decision making only in the most general terms. We must now turn to the processes by which the generalized pursuit of satisfaction results in overt, particular actions such as building a new factory at a new location, taking a particular route to work, planting a particular crop, or buying a particular brand of margarine. The decision making process is a convenient term to cover the whole complex of influences that bear on a single decision. In order to better understand this process, let us first examine the "closed" system of economic man's decision making, and then the more complex "open" process of the satisficer.

"Closed" Decision Making. Economic man makes a choice on the basis of:

1. *A known set of relevant alternatives with known outcomes.*
2. *An established rule or relation that produces an ordering of the alternatives.*
3. *Maximizing utility (which may be defined in terms of profit, income, or physical goods).*

This choice situation is considered "closed" because it minimizes the effects of the environment on the decision maker. Each course of action taken here is likely to lead to one of several possible consequences, but the outcomes are all known, and are chosen with a view to producing the optimal consequence.

"Open" Decision Making. If a decision maker is continually influenced by his total environment, then he is engaged in "open" decision making. There is no assumption here that all goals and feasible alternatives are recognized. On the contrary, as we shall see in chapter 4, the lesson of the behavioral sciences is that man's cognitive abilities are as limited as his environment is complex.

The satisficer faced with a single choice can be considered to go through three phases in coming to a decision:

1. *He settles on an aspiration level (or at least decides not to change the one he already has).*
2. *He engages in* **search activity,** *and defines a limited number of outcomes and alternatives, but not rigorously.*
3. *He weighs the alternatives with a view to finding a solution consistent with his aspiration level.*

Thus there are no predetermined goals, alternatives, or outcomes; the criterion is not the best outcome possible but one that satisfies the aspiration level.

Table 5 illustrates the basic elements of the open decision making procedure, for both single- and multiple-choice situations. The distinctive feature of the latter is the difference between the levels of aspiration and degree of satisfaction with the eventual outcome. Such a difference will nearly always arise, except when a habitual choice is being made, since the satisficer will not be able to equate aspira-

Table 5. *"Open" Decision Models*

a. single-choice model

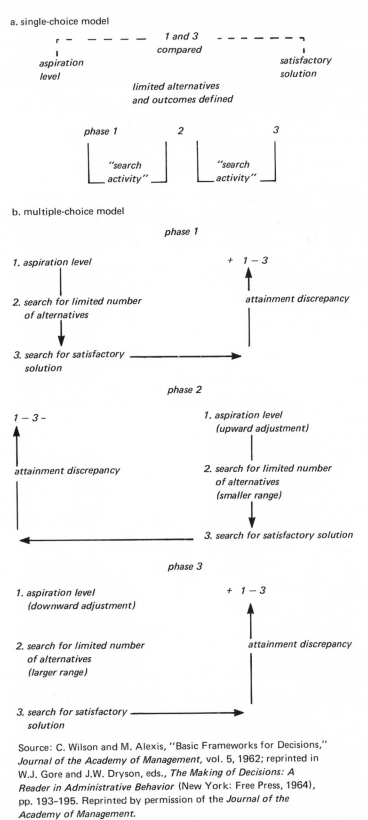

b. multiple-choice model

Source: C. Wilson and M. Alexis, "Basic Frameworks for Decisions," *Journal of the Academy of Management,* vol. 5, 1962; reprinted in W.J. Gore and J.W. Dryson, eds., *The Making of Decisions: A Reader in Administrative Behavior* (New York: Free Press, 1964), pp. 193–195. Reprinted by permission of the *Journal of the Academy of Management.*

tion and outcome with perfect accuracy. As can be seen from table 5, a *positive* discrepancy between aspiration and outcome – the decision maker gets more than he expected – increases the level of aspiration and narrows the range of search (5b, phase 1, leading to phase 2). A negative discrepancy — the decision maker gets less than he expected — has the opposite effect (5b, phase 2, leading to phase 3). Thus each new decision is the product of earlier ones.

The type of decision making that is the concern of economic geography can be classed as *problem solving behavior* – decision making with such results as new locations for shops, farms or factories. Decisions like these can cause the most abrupt changes in landscape patterns. However the other categories of decision making – *weakly motivated* behavior and *habitual* response – may well be more frequent. Obviously, they are also important in maintaining landscape patterns. Routine or habitual behavior usually follows the path of least effort, serves to reduce uncertainty (since the outcome has already been experienced), and minimizes the consideration of alternative courses of action.

Economic Behavior

Every economic decision, as we have seen, is made in a particular economic milieu, or situation. The claim that these decisions can be adequately described in terms of an autonomous model or so-called pure theory is illusory. The concrete behavior of the social individual includes elements of noneconomic meaning that can be understood only within the broad structure of his society. This milieu or situation is comprised of elements to be examined in some detail in chapter 4, but we can categorize them here as:

1. *All the factors of the* **operational milieu,** *including institutions, culture, political system, technology, and the particular economic system, which integrate the isolated economic act or the particular economic activity into the fabric of a society.*
2. *The* **behavioral environment** *of the decision maker, which includes his aspiration levels, his expectations, and his perception of the operational milieu.*
3. *A limited amount of information about the economic system – wage levels, prices, interest rates, competitors, competitive brands – that the decision maker has, and that he believes to be pertinent to his decisions.*

If we start from these three elements in the economic milieu, we find that, in order to understand economic behavior, we need to ask questions such as the following:

1. *Who are the policy and decision makers?*
2. *What kinds of* **interaction** *are involved in the decision making process?*
3. *What attitudes, beliefs, values, habits, and knowledge are important, and how influential are they are each decision making situation?*
4. *How are these values, etc., transmitted?*
5. *How receptive are decision makers to new ideas and innovations?*
6. *How do final decisions become translated into overt decisions?*
7. *How do overt decisions affect the distribution of economic activities over time and space?*

To this abbreviated list many other questions could be added. But it is long enough to show why economic geographers should occupy themselves with economic behavior, and why the classical notion of economic man has proven to be less than satisfactory.

Conclusion

Until recently, most geographers utilized the normative, optimizing construct of economic man. Thus in studying consumer behavior, production behavior, or journey and trip behavior, geographers have assumed that the decision maker has perfect knowledge of the kinds of trip he can make, or a stable array of ordered preferences for goods and services. As a reaction to these unrealistic assumptions some have turned to the probabilistic approach already noted in chapter 1. This approach, however, while it represents a suitable gesture of humility in the face of complex processes, does not necessarily help us to explain why and how particular landscape patterns have emerged. Other geographers have made use of various behavioral patterns, with apparently promising results. Many of these studies will be discussed in later chapters.

The Domain of Space and Time

All of man's activities occur in time and space. Conceptions of time and space therefore play a large part in explanations of human behavior.

Spatial Concepts and Principles

Space has frequently been cited as one of the principle dimensions with which the geographer is concerned. Traditionally, geographers have treated both man and space as simultaneously given – which is to say they have tended to take both for granted. More recently, however, their attention has been directed explicitly toward the evaluation of space. Spatial reference and orientation systems are no longer thought of as having just positional qualities or abstract geometrical dimensions. With this new concern, it has become obvious that geographers in fact conceive of space in many different ways, ranging from the Aristotelian conception of geography as the study of the earth's different *parts*, or regions, and their coordinates, to the Newtonian conception of it as concerned with absolute space, to which there is no end and no beginning. In our own century, as a result of Einstein's discoveries, we tend to think in terms of a space-time dimension. This too, has had its effect on geography, though probably more by way of reaction against the physicists' notion of an abstract space and time entirely divorced from human needs and interests. Thus it can be maintained that man can, in fact, only define his actions in spatial terms, and that space can only be defined in terms of man's behavior. "An individual is not distinct from his place; he is that place."

Spatial Reference Systems

Geographers commonly talk both of **location**—where something is on a grid reference system—and of **relative location**—where something is in relation to other points of activity. The latter concept is taken one step further by the related concept of links between such points—links in the form of flows of goods, people, or information. An economic activity thus has both an absolute and a relative location. The latter can change with a person's image of the area, or as technology changes (figure 5).

Absolute location is sometimes referred to as the **site** of an activity. By itself, however, a site is no more than a grid coordinate reference on a map, an actual point in space. The geographer is concerned with something more—with relative location and **situation.** For instance, an iron and steel plant has a grid coordinate. But the plant is not an activity unto itself. Rather, it is part of a larger manufacturing system, within which the plant has a particular situational relationship. So the plant is not a separate entity, but an activity that has contacts or relations with other sites, places, and activities. The differential association and location of activities over space and time imply a pattern of mutually oriented interaction systems.

A Spatial System of Geography

According to the system developed by E. N. Thomas in 1964, the basic units of geography are

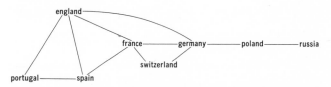

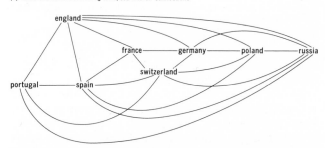

Fig. 5. *Relative locations and interaction. (Adapted from W. Bunge,* Theoretical Geography, *Lund, Gleerup, 1962, pp. 104–105. Reprinted courtesy of the author and the Department of Geography, Royal University of Lund, Sweden.)*

geographic facts. These are expanded into the concepts of **spatial distribution, spatial interaction,** and **areal association,** which in turn are combined to build up **regions.**

Geographic facts have been defined by Thomas as referring to "the character of a place, or of the quantity or quality of some phenomenon which occupies a place at a given time." A spatial distribution is a set or assemblage of geographic facts "representing the behavior of a particular phenomenon or characteristic in many places on the surface of the earth." Thus the spatial distribution of automobile assembly plants, iron and steel foundries, or department stores could be plotted for the whole earth or any region of it.

Very frequently we deal with the spatial distribution not of one activity, but of several. If we can detect some connection between these several distributions, then we say they are **areally associated.** However, this does not necessarily imply a causal relationship. Various statistical means can be used to test whether such associations are causal or not. Finally, the geographer will want to go further than similarity or postulated causal relationship, and

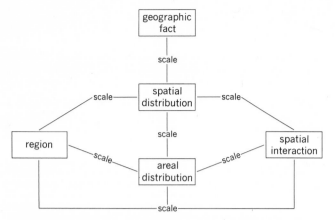

Fig. 6. *A structure and system of geography (see glossary for definition of terms). The basic concepts used in the geographical approach are related to each other in a systematic way. (From E. N. Thomas, "Some Comments About a Structure of Geography," 1964, reprinted courtesy of the Department of Geography, University of Iowa.)*

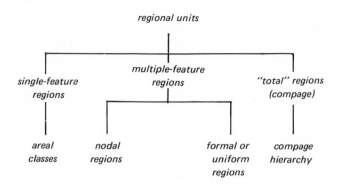

Table 6. *Categories of Regions*

There are three broad categories of regions, varying with the number of criteria used to delimit the region.

A. Single-feature regions: *based on one phenomenon only (category of slopes, an element of climate, language, etc.). Because of their simplicity, they cannot be further divided, but are sometimes called areal classes.*

B. Multiple-feature regions: *differentiated on the basis of combinations or associations of features. Formal regions are uniform in that several features vary equally. Nodal regions are organized with respect to a focus to which the region is linked by lines of circulation.*

C. The compage, or total region: *the most complex region. It is conceived in terms of the entire human occupance of an area — all the physical, social, and economic features combined in a complex totality. A hierarchy of compages of increasing size and complexity can be identified from the locality to the realm.*

Source: D. Whittlesley, "The Region, Theory and Practice," in P.E. James and D.F. Jones, eds., *American Geography: Inventory and Prospect* (Syracuse: Syracuse University Press, 1954), pp. 32–51; P. Haggett, *Locational Analysis in Human Geography* (London: E. Arnold, 1965), p. 242.

explore the underlying process that led to the relationship and continues to sustain it.

Spatial interaction is a concept that refers to the relationship between clusters of geographic facts. Particular locations, as well as territorial or areal specialization, demand connections between areas so that goods can be exchanged. One point might specialize in mining iron ore, another in fabricating iron products; each — in theory — would exchange its own product for the product it does not have. Thus a spatial interaction or movement would occur.

The spatial structuring of geographic facts helps to initiate movement. With increasing specialization, demand and supply become separated. Spatial interaction — movement — is the means of correcting any spatial imbalance. Such interaction consists of the movement of messages, ideas, people, goods, money and energy. This is a theme to which we will return below, when considering transportation (chapter 12).

From the concepts of spatial distribution, areal association, and spatial interaction, the concept of region can be synthesized. Through areal association and spatial interaction, certain geographic facts may show a particular likeness or patterning in one area that makes it convenient to call that area a region. Any area with some kind of internal homogeneity can be distinguished from surrounding areas as a "region." The regional concept is a convenient way of treating and organizing spatially distributed information, and several categories of regions have grown up with its usage (table 6).

There are obvious disadvantages to the regional concept. Theoretically, the earth's surface could be divided into an infinite number of regional patterns. People in general are probably conscious only

of the **compage,** the most complex type of region (table 6); other categories of regions do not interest them. The selection of regional boundaries is often both difficult and arbitrary. Rather than abrupt boundaries between regions, there are zones of gradation from the core of one to the core of the next. Finally, the regional concept is a static view of reality with validity for only one point in time, not part of a dynamic world system. Despite the conceptual and practical difficulties, regions have been widely used in all branches of geography since the early nineteenth century.

Implicit in this discussion of spatial concepts is yet another concept of the same type: **scale.** All such organizing concepts have been equally applicable to small and large areas — that is, at different scales. In a large-scale study of an area like Los Angeles, it would be possible to describe the spatial distributions, areal associations, and spatial interactions of Los Angeles as compared with (say) the rest of California. Manufacturing, shopping, and residential areas or regions, each localized in some particular part of the area, would all appear in such a study. In contrast, a small-scale study of Los Angeles would show it as one dot or point among the several hundred metropolitan areas in the United States.

The scale of an investigation makes a great difference to the generalizations drawn from it. Thus in a large-scale study of a small area, the location of particular iron and steel foundries might appear to be strongly conditioned by factors such as zoning regulations, local water supply, or the presence of a local labor pool. But these factors would be of little importance in a study of the location of iron and steel industries throughout the North American continent. The nature of the problem determines the scale of the inquiry, which in its turn influences the level of generalization.

Conceptions of Space

Traditionally geographers have assumed, usually without being aware of it, that the space within which we order our information is that of Euclidean geometry. Terms like "locational element," "spatial variable," and "spatial significance" assign causal and explanatory roles to space. In this way we impose our culturally influenced definitions onto a socially constructed reality that may have little congruence with them. The entrepreneur locating his new factory or warehouse may not conceive of space as we geographers are accustomed to do. We must therefore take care not to impose our own conception of reality on the behavior of others.

Conceptions of space do vary among cultural groups. Town plans and village layouts have been shown to be closely linked to the social structure of a group, as well as to economic factors. Most obvious, to the eye of the social scientist, is the shift in space evaluation among groups and individuals as certain types of space become a scarce resource. Thus in Thailand, a very simple system of measurement was found adequate until the first quarter of this century, when it was replaced by a more definite scale. This transformation coincided with increased pressure on available garden land and a concomitant rise in land values. Religious and ideological factors are also of importance. In Malaysia, for example, houses should not be built on promontories of any sort, since such places are frequented by spirits. A review of anthropological literature makes it clear that there are almost as many conceptions of space as there are cultures.

Time

Time is a continuous variable, yet as geographers we frequently slice through it in order to examine some timeless segment. Most of the data we utilize is based on discrete observations made at some point in time. Yet time, like space, can be measured in relative as well as absolute terms, and is no less subject to cultural variation. Time, in short, is a measure geared to the process of living, and conceptions of time are as varied as living itself. Time in a peasant or subsistence economy, tied to seasonal rhythms, is essentially different from time in a market-commercial economy.

Time Reference Systems

The time that most of us use as a point of reference is time as measured by a clock. But clock time is not the only reference system. The changing of the seasons, phases of the moon, progress of plant life, biological aging—all measure the passage of time.

Time has many uses. It can indicate succession, duration, or location. Locational time is used for

Table 7. *Time as a Reference System*

locational time ("when")
measured by
> *the sundial*
> *the hourglass*
> *clocks and watches*
> *time zones*
> *daylight savings time*
> *moon time*
> *the calendar*
> *atomic clocks*

durational time ("rate," "length")
measured by
> *the aging process*
> *the seasons and plant growth*
> *the calendar*
> *the growing season*
> *the harvesting season*

successional time ("past," "present," "future")
measured by
> *the cycle of religious rites, harvests, festivals, other agricultural work and household activities*
> *the preparation and scheduling of future events and projects*
> *the preservation of genealogies and other legends*
> *thoughts about "future" existence*

Source: G.M. Clemence, "Time Measurement for Scientific Use," in J.F. Fraser, ed., *The Voices of Time* (New York: George Braziller, 1966); E.W. Eliot Hurst, "Cross Cultural Conceptions of Time," unpublished manuscript, Simon Fraser University, Department of Political Science, Sociology, and Anthropology, 1969.

classifying and distinguishing discrete temporal units. Durational time is a measure of the rate at which time passes; it can be measured by many means, including our own aging process. Successional time, as its name indicates, applies to the order in which events occur. The measured round of agricultural work, religious rites, and household activities; the preservation of genealogies and legends; and thoughts about our future existence—all fall within this time reference system. Obviously, time is an all-pervasive concept.

Statics and Dynamics

Researchers, including geographers, can call upon a number of techniques when analyzing society. As far as time is concerned, the principal metholodogical distinction is that between static and dynamic analyses. A static analysis assumes a constancy of factors—for example an absence of invention, technological innovation, price change, and market variation. In what is commonly called "comparative statics," a static model can be placed in an environment of change. In other words, the model responds to change but does not generate changes out of itself. Thus a change in the environment would upset the system's old equilibrium, and its components would rearrange themselves in a new stationary equilibrium appropriate to the new conditions. For example, in a market system, where price is fixed by demand and supply, if consumer demand and, say, technology were constant, there would be a price equilibrium. However, if those variables changed, prices would also change, until they reached some new equilibrium level.

Dynamic models involve temporal processes even more directly. Between the initial disturbance in equilibrium and the final equilibrium state occurs a long sequence of related events. In terms of our example, the price at any intermediate time is the consequence of changes that occurred in the preceding period. Thus a dynamic model can represent the economy, or any complex system, as the consequence of its state a moment ago, and as an antecedent to the state it is about to enter. As we shall see in chapter 3, in order to go on changing the system would have to be open. In a closed system the change, or initial push would be built in. Eventually, the system would reach a state of equilibrium in which it would remain unless its boundaries were opened up. Most attempts to represent the time dimension in geography have relied essentially upon comparative statics; truly dynamic models, which would come close to the dynamics of the real world, are very difficult to build at present.

Conceptions of Time

In the everyday world, time is a social and personal concept—the time of sense-perception, feeling, thinking, imagining, and making decisions. This kind of time—evaluatory time, as it may be called—contrasts with mathematicians' time, which is a homogeneous dimension in which all points have the same validity. Evaluatory time, on the other hand, is always social and subjective, reflecting some succession of events experienced in the past or anticipated in the future that are of sufficient interest to an individual or group to be noted, evaluated, and conceived in a particular way. Both conception and evaluation are derived from the socioeconomic values and structure of the system or subsystem in which the individual or group is living. In other words, it reflects their experience. Thus to the American middle class, time is rational, impersonal, and harnessed to some plan or schedule. This is one reason why middle-class Americans tend to perceive groups with the opposite conception of time as "lazy." Thus conceptions of time play an important role in the behavior of groups and individuals, including their economic behavior.

In a highly bureaucratized society like ours, life tends to become a constantly repeated series of crescendos towards deadlines. The deadlines can be short-term, medium range, or long-term, even extending over several years, as in the case of large-scale resource development. Most, however, are set so close to the initiation point that they can be achieved only if a medium to high intensity of work is constantly maintained. In practice this evolves into a pattern of low and high intensity work periods. Concomitantly, there develops a work ethic in which time plays a large part. To be constantly "busy," to be "rushed off one's feet," to have "virtually no time for anything," becomes the desired and desirable state of things. Small tasks are magnified and prolonged so that this state can always be present.

The social result is a particular kind of alienation, different from the alienation of the worker on the assembly line, but just as destructive of human relationships. Indeed, it may be even more destructive. Recent studies have shown that most workers have a much higher tolerance for mechanical and repetitive activity than middle-class researchers had previously thought. At the same time, workers are cushioned from the "deadline syndrome" and the "busy-every-second" ethic. Nor are most of them likely to be worried—consciously, at least—by their lack of meaningful relationship with the system as a whole. But as one moves up the occupational scale, the role of time conceptions becomes increasingly prominent, if only because at these levels the individual has to schedule his work for himself. The idea of time may not be an independent factor, but it does appear to be a reinforcing one.

In a subsistence society, technologically simple groups may lack anything that we would recognize as clock time. However, they will have day time or seasonal time, and the passage of time will be important to them. Thus the Navaho people live in different residence units according to age group. Time also affects their attitude toward wealth: since wealth is seen essentially as something that can be accumulated, resource controllers wield considerable authority. Finally, age is allotted merit on the grounds of increased wisdom and competency. Thus, to a Navaho the future is a series of inevitable changes of residence, with the possibility of becoming a resource controller, and the ultimate gaining of status through age. Change is conceived as continuous, inevitable, and nonreversible. Such conceptions have to be taken into account in dealing with any group's economic behavior or milieu.

Space and Time

Although we have arbitrarily separated space and time, they are closely related in what one author has called a *space-time manifold*. Nothing is *just* "in space" or "in time"; it is always both. Rejection of the concept of absolute space is one of the chief achievements of modern physics. The relativistic view of space as four-dimensional, with time as the fourth dimension, has also affected geography. If there is no such thing as pure space, then geographers should divest themselves of the illusion that they are studying purely spatial relationships. Something in the landscape is always changing. What are the processes that cause it to change? Clearly, the model we need for studying any evolving spatial pattern is a dynamic one.

Space Through Time: Relations to Economic Activities

The space-time manifold in which economic activities take place is by definition not static. Moreover, the economic relevance of the key spatial and temporal factors has changed over the centuries. Let us attempt briefly to place some of these factors in their historical context.

Specialization of Labor and Area

Factors of location become noticeably important to a society only when it includes some occupational or institutional specialization. In prefarming cultures, nearly every kind of work known to the society can be found performed within the family or extended family group. Only in certain circumstances are there specialized occupational groups—for example, the blacksmiths of certain African societies. In this early stage of technological evolution, socioeconomic organization often consists of small nomadic groups, economically self-sufficient, whose wanderings are governed only by the availability and location of water for themselves and their flocks.

In later stages, as crops are cultivated, location becomes of increasing importance. This is the stage at which man begins his long struggle to transform the raw natural environment into a landscape that reflects his culture. But despite some specialization and diversification, the great majority of the population still lives directly from the land. The chief technical advances are the development of metal smelting and pottery. Agriculture improves to the extent that a small nonagricultural minority can be supported on the surplus. Communications also improve: both information and goods travel over space, and with the development of an alphabet information receives a temporal dimension. The nonagricultural minority—administrators, educators, military, politicians, priests—establish the first cities. Soon there is a regular exchange of goods and services between the city and the rural hinterland. In time, there are wider market relations with more distant areas. All these expanding developments and interactions result in **feedback** to the society itself, strengthening the sociopolitical powers of the urban elite, who in turn stimulate further developments.

From these **hearth areas** of intensive agricultural development, high population density, and strong economic and political organization, technological, cultural, and economic innovations spread to other locations. There seems to be only limited agreement among archeologists and social anthropologists as to the nature and extent of these diffusions. The main hearth areas stand out as highly creative centers rather than passively receptive ones; nevertheless, there were catalytic contacts between Mesopotamia and Egypt, and between Egypt and Greece. Less is known at present about the other hearth areas. In the Old World, Shang China, the Indus Valley centers of Harrappa and Mahenjo Dero, and, in the New World, pre-Spanish Mesoamerica and Peru, all seem to have undergone similar developments at different points in time. Each of these areas attained **civilization** by parallel trends and processes—agricultural development, followed by urbanization, militarization, bureaucratization, and so on. In the New World, of course, these processes were cut short by the Spanish Conquest.

The key to these changes was the production of a dependable surplus of food. This surplus provided a base for a marked increase in population, and, through the accumulation of wealth and the corresponding development of leisure, to the support of nonagricultural pursuits that led to major changes in social organization. Urban life stimulated increased complexity in the economic and political systems, because mechanisms had to be set up to insure that food reached the urban centers. The procurement of raw materials for manufacturing, the exchange of manufactured items for food, the transportation of goods and ideas, and all the other elements of a complex economic system, created interdependence among large groups of people. The technological achievements of these so-called civilizations, and the factors of location that went with them, set productivity levels for many centuries, in both the Old World and the New.

With the developments that led to the second **Agricultural Revolution** and then to the **Industrial Revolution,** the former interdependencies and location patterns were broken. As a result, patterns of organization—economic, social, and political—were transformed. The second Agricultural Revolution established an agricultural minority that could produce enough surplus food on its commercial farms to support a by now nonagricultural majority. Release of labor from the rural areas created a pool of labor for industry to exploit. The large surpluses of capital, productively invested, created new industries and enlarged the existing ones. Through labor-saving machinery, as well as the growing skills of the industrial labor force, productivity was increased. Household and handicraft skills gave way to the new factory system which, like all other nonagricultural activities, was increasingly concentrated in the urban centers. The apparatus of industrialism—communications, transportation, market relationships, investment, exploitation of resources—became worldwide. The new transportation technology, in particular, was vital not only to the internal movement of goods, ideas, and people, but to external relationships, as the newly industrializing countries, of which England was the first, sought to expand their resource bases beyond their own boundaries. This external relationship played a crucial role in helping to finance the capitalization of these new societies.

The development of industry, the rise of commercial farming, and the expansion of Europe overseas, dramatically affected the importance of factors of location. Through the growth of specialization, demand was physically separated from supply. A major feature of this growth stage was the increasing **division of labor.** With it came geographical separation of the occupations themselves, and a corresponding specialization of areas. This specialization could not have existed without the growing interaction and movement of goods, information, and people between areas.

More recently there have been further developments that may in the near future change patterns of location once more. This is the era of automata. Automatic machinery, computers, and cybernetic systems can control programs of production with fewer and fewer human overseers. The new role of the labor force promises to be devising, maintaining, and supervising these automatic machines. Society is changed as the balance between the old productive and locative forces changes. Thus changes in commercial farming may well increase both the specialization of areas and the importance of the locative factors in general.

Both preindustrial and industrial society are now part of history. Technocratic society may already be upon us. In all three forms of society, one trend stands out: increasing specialization of areas and of the links between them. Land use patterns result from decisions and choices about where to locate, what to produce, how to produce it, where to buy and sell goods, and how to overcome the distances between the various producing and consuming areas. The decisions reflect the perception of the decision maker as to what differences will arise from alternative locations. The nature of the alternatives depends on environmental differences such as the location of raw materials; the importance of relative location to production and consumption; the space requirements of the activities themselves; and the cost of overcoming spatial separation.

Comparative Advantage

The structural features of society, when combined with environmental differences, give rise to the hypothesis of **comparative advantage.** Decisions as to locative factors shape the geographical patterns of land use, which in turn reflect the society's economic activities. The whole process is illustrated in figure 7.

Comparative advantage has interested many economists and geographers. They used to stress how people or areas tend to specialize in the activities for which they are most suited. Nowadays, however, a more realistic and complex view is taken. For instance, a study of central Iowa and western Kansas has shown that wheat is not always grown in the

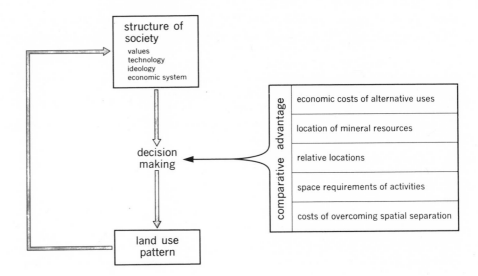

Fig. 7. *Geographic factors in location. Elements of comparative advantage.*

areas best suited to it. The reason suggested by the authors is that each area tends to produce those products for which its **ratio of advantage** is greatest, up to a point at which market demands are best satisfied by diversion to some less advantageous activity. Thus a given quantity of labor and capital can produce a wider range of products with a higher level of efficiency on the very fertile lands of central Iowa than on the less fertile lands of Kansas or most other farming areas in the United States. Yet it is not physically possible or economically sound to produce in Iowa all of the products that are well suited to that region. This is because the national market for agricultural products is best served by using the more highly valued central Iowa lands for products for which it is best suited *compared with other areas.* Hence agricultural practices in Iowa concentrate on maize, pigs, fodder crops, soy beans, and dairy products. Little or no wheat is grown even though the area is well suited to it. The reason for this is that crops such as wheat can be grown in the less fertile semi-arid regions, including western Kansas, which are not suited to many crops. To use Iowa land for wheat would merely deprive the national market of products that Kansas and other wheat regions either cannot grow or cannot grow well. In this instance, Iowa farmers concentrate on the products for which they have the greatest comparative advantage, while Kansas farmers concentrate on wheat, for which they have the least comparative disadvantage.

This is still a rather simplistic application of comparative advantage; the reality tends to be much more complex. It has been shown that comparative advantage varies in space, over time, according to the level of technological information, with external economics, and with the level of satisfying and per-

ception. In fact, major regional shifts of resources, as well as extra capital in the form of improved transport, crops, or livestock, have produced changed geographical patterns of comparative advantage.

Other Factors

In addition to the factors of location described above, there are others that, under the proper circumstances, are just as powerful. They include the benefits and economies of concentration, scale economies and the thresholds for production and consumption, other market influences, transfer costs, government intervention, and the size and complexity of the country. There is also government intervention in location, which can take several forms: normal fiscal controls, such as credit or taxation; direct legislative intervention; and quasi-military force, including the transfer of whole populations. This last point touches on the differences between economic ideologies. Capitalist decision making can produce land use patterns quite different from those produced by socialist decision making. Some systems combine both capitalist and socialist elements, and these again lead to characteristic location patterns. Military or religious roles may also have powerful economic effects.

Finally, the location of particular economic activities may not be explicable in present terms because it results from decisions made under conditions that no longer have relevance to the present economic system. Changes in power sources, certain changes in technology, or the exhaustion of a particular resource may all have removed the original locative forces. Yet a number of economic activities may remain despite this locational obsolescence. New, more flexible power sources, the existence of a skilled pool of labor, financial capital invested in the plant, social capital invested in an area or its people, plus lags within the economic system (which, it should always be remembered, can for a while maintain activities for which there is no real economic justification)—all these and other historical factors too may have to be used to account for the existence of apparently inexplicable locations.

Summary

1. Man's attempts to make the natural environment more amenable to exploitation creates an economy.

2. The economy can be divided into production and consumption sectors.

3. Production (the firm) involves the addition of form, place, and/or time utility to resources. This resource enhancement ranges from primary, to secondary, tertiary, and quarternary activities, encompassing productive activities from the farm to the research laboratory.

4. Consumption is the end point of the economic activity system. Consumption activities vary from day-to-day household expenditures to military expenditures and recreational activities.

5. There is not one economic system, but many. These systems can be categorized in a number of ways. Five basic economic types are used in this book, based primarily on the forms of exchange of goods used (or its absence), and on the degree of involvement with the exchange system.

6. These categories do not represent stages through which a "subsistence" economy, for example, has to proceed. "Development" is a complex factor and is analyzed in detail in chapter 15.

7. However, it is possible to recognize some difference in the complexity or the use of production activities from one economic category to another (e.g., table 3). In particular, the technological complexity, the presence or absence of the market institution, the relative complexity of the production and distribution systems, and the development of secondary manufacturing activities and tertiary service activities seem to accompany increasing economic and exchange complexity.

8. Economic geographers are concerned with describing and explaining the spatial-temporal distribution of these types of economic activity.

9. The approach of this book is to describe and explain such distributions by adopting behavioral notions other than those traditionally used in economics and economic geography.

10. The assumptions and postulates of traditional economic approaches have been conceived within a "closed," narrowly defined framework, largely divorced of any cultural or behavioral reality.

11. As an alternative, the conception of "man the satisficer" is again introduced, and a comparison made between two decision making models as to the outcome of using this more "open" behavioral notion in economic situations.

12. Such decision making is made, in fact, in a range of economic situations which are influenced by the whole fabric of a particular society (its operational milieu), the behavioral environment, and the limited set of information concerning the economic system.

13. In addition, decision making takes place in the domains of space and time.

14. Although both space and time are said to have "absolute" referents (location in a space or time grid system), they also have "relative" meanings which involve particular situational relationships.

15. Time and space relationships involve notions of site (when and where) and situation, areal association, spatial interaction, region, and scale. All of these are traditional concerns of the geographer.

16. Yet both space and time are also culturally influenced conceptions. The evaluatory meanings applied to these conceptions may be of vital importance since they vary from group to group (of geographers, as well as of decision makers).

17. To carry this further, although traditionally separated, space and time must also be seen as interacting elements of a four-dimensional world.

18. This space-time manifold becomes particularly important when points of production and consumption become separated. When demand and supply are virtually coterminus in time and space (e.g., when the "firm" and the "consumer" are the same, as in a subsistence economy), very little spatial interaction takes place. However, when groups of people are no longer sulf-sufficient, a spatial separation of demand and supply occurs, and the economic landscape becomes more highly differentiated. Historically, the change from self-sufficiency and interdependency can be traced and matched against landscape and other changes.

19. From such structural features, and through environmental differences, comes the idea of comparative advantage. There appears to be a tendency for areas or regions to specialize in the

production of crops where their ratio of advantage is greatest compared to other areas. More recent work has shown that rather than being a static concept, comparative advantages vary through time with cultural and technological change.

20. Thus we come full circle from defining an economy and its production-consumption components to behavioral notions of decision making, situational influences on that activity including the time-space manifold, and the space-time variations in the landscape patterns of production and consumption.

Further Reading

Basic traditional economic concepts can be tracked down in any standard economic text such as

Samuelson, P. *Economics: An Introductory Analysis*

Radical critiques and theories are presented along with traditional economic postulates in

Hunt, E. K. and Sherman, H. J. *Economics: An Introduction to Traditional and Radical Views* (New York: Harper and Row, 1972).

The geographic approach to economic activity systems is thoughtfully analyzed in

Wagner, P. L. *The Human Use of the Earth* (New York: Free Press, 1960).

These themes are carried forward in terms of human communication in

Wagner, P. L. *Environments and People* (Englewood Cliffs: Prentice-Hall, 1972).

The spatial diversity of man's impact on the natural environment in a time-space sense is treated in

Brock, J. O. M. and Webb, J. W. *A Geography of Mankind* (New York: McGraw-Hill, 1968).

Thomas, W. L., ed. *Man's Role in Changing the Face of the Earth* (Chicago: University of Chicago Press, 1956).

Other questions raised in this chapter can be answered in part by the following references—non-Western contemporary economies, in

Firth, R. *Primitive Polynesian Economy*, 2nd ed. (London: Routledge, Kegan, Paul, 1965).

Firth, R., ed. *Themes in Economic Anthropology* (London: Tavistock Publications, 1967).

Belshaw, C. S. *Traditional Exchange and Modern Markets* (Englewood Cliffs: Prentice-Hall, 1965).

Marx, K. *Pre-Capitalist Economic Formations*, edited and with an introduction by Eric J. Hobsbawm, translated by Jack Cohen (New York: International Publishers, 1964).

—man, the satisficer, in

Simon, H. A. *Models of Man* (New York: Wiley, 1957), chapters 14 and 15.

—space and time, in

Harvey, D. *Explanation in Geography* (London: Edward Arnold, 1969), chapters 14 and 21.

three

The Systems Approach

Introduction

There is nothing very new about the systems approach as such. Astronomers have long found it useful to speak of the solar system, and biologists of ecosystems. A leading contemporary sociologist has argued that society is best understood as a social system. In geography, "region" and "system" are two concepts with a lot in common. The thread connecting all these uses is the notion of a complex, interrelated whole. One would think such a notion would come in handy almost anywhere in science, but the fact is that, until recently, most disciplines treated it as a side interest. In the last ten years, however, it has firmly established itself in such fields as engineering, transportation, communications technology, and planning. This book is committed to showing, among other things, that it can be just as useful in geography.

But first, what is the systems approach? Perhaps the best way to begin answering that question is to ask why such an approach should be needed. There are two main reasons:

1. *Social scientists have begun to realize that society is not like a machine; it can not be taken apart and examined bit by bit.*

2. *Because of scientific specialization, human knowledge is being divided up into separate compartments, with little or no communication between them.*

The second point deserves expansion here because it raises the specter of a science with no future. One leading thinker—he happens to be an economist, but would probably reject any such label—

wonders if scientists may not end up as hermits, each one mumbling to himself in a language none of the others understands. His solution is that specialists should be trained to develop "generalized ears," so that they can catch what other specialists are saying. This is not just a matter of communication between different scientific disciplines; in geography, for instance, we are fast reaching a point at which the various kinds of experts no longer talk to each other. Hence the attractiveness of the systems approach, which can be applied to almost any field of knowledge.

Some critics of the systems approach have claimed that it is nothing more than a dressed-up version of common sense. But, to judge from the overspecialized condition of modern science, there is nothing very common about it, although its essentials are easy to grasp. They are:

1. *Although each part of a system may play an individual role in the system's operation, no part is entirely independent of the others.*
2. *A change in the operation of one part will have significant repercussions throughout the system.*

Although the systems approach has been gaining ground, there is some disagreement over how it should be applied. Granted, it can be argued that a human body, a business, and a national economy are all systems, inasmuch as they consist of interconnected parts. Where do we go from there? Three main directions can be identified.

General systems theory is essentially a general theory of organization that aims at the unification of all science. As such it often resembles the search of medieval alchemists for an elixir, the one secret ingredient that would turn base metal into gold. Like all such searches, it is not likely to prove successful.

Systems analysis, although it implies a common definition of "system" and various other technical terms, is an analytical tool rather than a grand theory. It was first used in engineering and communications technology.

Systems notions are models that, for convenience, portray reality in simplistic systems terms. They are used mainly in teaching.

Of course, these three categories overlap to some extent. But it is important to note that systems analysis and systems notions, unlike general systems theory, are tools in a search for generalization, not ends in themselves. Moreover, they represent only one class of tools among a whole series of techniques that can aid in the analysis of complex structures. These tools, unlike general systems theory, have been tested and shown to work. In teaching, they have also provided a framework for the identification of problems, rather than simply an aid to problem-solving. At this level, the systems approach is not hard to apply, but it does require mastery of the basic technical concepts. The following sections explain those concepts.

System

Systems analysis involves treating both phenomena and the concepts used to organize phenomena *as if* there existed organization, interaction, interdependency, and integration of parts and elements. In other words, it assumes the existence of some structure, recognizable within some more or less arbitrarily chosen time period, that constitutes an organized whole. It is the way in which the parts are connected and interact with each other that makes it a system. Thus systems analysis is not an attempt to describe reality—a task to which there is no end—but rather a convenient abstraction from it.

Open and Closed Systems

A system is said to exist in relation to an *environment*, which is simply what surrounds it (the environment may of course be seen as a larger system). In relation to that environment, the system may be either *open* or *closed*. An **open system** is not isolated from its environment, but exchanges materials or energies with it. A **closed system** operates without such exchange. A system may also contain *subsystems*, that is, smaller systems within it; these are said to be its *components*. This implies that some parts of a system may be more closely or actively connected than others.

The main differences between open and closed systems can be illustrated by the example of a domestic heating system of the hot-air variety. Such a system consists, in essentials, of a number of ducts, gratings, fans, and filters, all linked to a furnace by the flow of air. As separate unconnected elements, the ducts, furnace, and so on, have a different meaning than as a connected whole. Since energy enters the system from without, in the form of gas for the furnace, and leaves it as warmed air, *energy transference* occurs across the limits of the system. A closed system has no energy transference; it can change only as a result of innate elements. Given those elements, it is possible to predict how the system will develop. In geography, this latter kind of system is rare, if indeed it occurs at all. The open system has the advantage of being less deterministic, since it allows random effects to occur, and can be applied in a much greater variety of situations.

Other Types of Systems

It is also useful to distinguish between *simple action* (or *nonfeedback*) *systems* and **feedback systems** A simple action system is one in which the chain of cause and effect runs all in one direction; for example, rainfall affects the rate of soil erosion, but soil erosion has no effect on rainfall. A feedback system involves not only action but reaction, as when a TV program gets poor ratings, thus causing the sponsor to cancel it. Most economic systems are of the feedback type. The different kinds of feedback are discussed below.

Feedback systems can be divided into two main varieties: *uncontrolled* and *controlled* (or *cybernetic*). In a free market system, supply, demand, and price are nearly always interrelated. Thus prices tend to rise as demand increases or supply decreases. Of course, it is possible that either supply or demand may remain constant. But this kind of stability is not something built into the system, which is therefore said to be uncontrolled. A controlled system, in contrast, is one in which at least one component or variable is kept at a constant level. The classic example is a thermostat. Controlled systems are often called cybernetic systems, from a Greek word meaning to "guide" or "steer."

Any of the above kinds of systems can also be treated as either *real* or *conceptual,* that is, they can exist in the world of space and time, or they can be theoretical, in whole or part. Finally, systems can be classified according to the way in which they involve man. Thus *mechanistic* systems, which are typical of engineering, offer only limited options, but *adoptive* (or *variable utilization*) systems allow the user to make choices that modify the system being used. Most systems in human geography are of this latter type.

Equilibrium

Much controversy surrounds the question of whether all systems tend toward a state of internal stability. A number of terms are commonly used. **Equilibrium** refers to a system that maintains some kind of balance instead of being in a transient or everchanging state. *Homeostasis* implies that the balance is at a fixed point or level. A *steady state* is an equilibrium that does not depend on a fixed point or level. *Morphogenesis* is the process that leads to changes in a system's form, structure, or state, so that it comes to exist at a new and more complex level of equilibrium.

Normally, we can recognize two categories of equilibrium: *stable* and *dynamic.* Stable equilibrium includes both *homeostasis* and *steady state,* as defined above. In a homeostatic social system there is always activity, but it does not alter the balance between the system's components. A social system that was in a steady state would be equally stable, but it would also change—in an orderly way. Dynamic equilibrium refers to the process by which a slight disturbance engenders constant change throughout the system. If feedback is present this kind of change can go on indefinitely, at least in theory. Because societies consist of conscious, reasoning individuals, many social scientists have doubted whether any social system can truly attain equilibrium. In any case, because of the controversy over the notion of equilibrium, it should be used with great care, especially when dealing with socioeconomic systems.

Feedback

Feedback may be viewed as either *positive* or *negative*. One familiar example of negative feedback is the operation of a thermostat, since it opposes the working of the main driving force (the furnace). Increasing the flow of warm air—for instance, by setting the thermostat to 100° F. on a cold day—creates positive feedback.

A third way of looking at feedback depends on the concept of *amplification*. Imagine a large, uniformly fertile plain. Some hardworking farmer is lucky enough to open the first farm on it—the so-called *initial kick*. Others follow his example. The farmers open various kinds of store to supply each others' needs, and before long they have a regular village. As the farms prosper, the village becomes a city. The city has grown because of the way in which positive feedback has been amplified from one farmer to another. It was just an accident that some farmer originally chose to settle in that particular spot. If that had been all, there would never have been a city. But the other farmers, by settling nearby, created a socioeconomic system in which deviations from a steady state were *amplified* through positive feedback. As the settlement became a village, and the village a city, the structure of the system was completely changed. In other words, it was a morphogenetic system.

Because they change less, systems that are not morphogenetic usually end up resembling each other more than systems that are. Morphogenetic systems, on the other hand, become increasingly unlike. The result is paradoxical: nonmorphogenetic systems have dissimilar beginnings and similar end structures, while of morphogenetic systems the opposite is more likely to be true. Similarity of end structures is known as **equifinality**, and its opposite as **multifinality**. An example of equifinality would be the manufacturing region or agglomeration (chapter 8), which assumes a typical structure regardless of its origin. Multifinality can be seen in cities with different sites and patterns but founded by people with very similar initial cultures; very often, as in Classical Greece or Renaissance Italy, they end up with different socioeconomic systems. These different kinds of relationship between structure and process are summarized in table 8.

Entropy and Negentropy

Entropy is often referred to as a measure of disorder or disorganization. Basically, it is an expres-

Table 8. *Levels of Systems Analysis*

Buckley's progression of systems levels

a complex of interrelated entities and elements

| mechanical systems ◀- - - - - - - ▶ sociocultural systems |
| (nonmorphogenetic) | (morphogenetic) |

normally closed	*more and more open*
components:	*components:*
simple	*complex*
stable	*unstable*
relatively unaffected by	*alterable by workings*
workings of system	*of system*
tendency to entropy	*tendency to negentropy*
transmission of energy	*transmission of information*
relationship of parts:	*relationship of parts:*
organized simplicity	*organized and disorganized*
rigid structure	*complex*
restricted (few degrees of	*more fluid structure*
freedom in behavior)	*more flexible (increasing range*
functional links	*of alternate behavior)*
equifinality	*conflict, functional, and*
	competitive links
	equifinality and multifinality

◀- - - - - - - ▶

example:	*example:*	*example:*
the clock	*the missile*	*socioeconomic system*
the "pre-	*the "cybernated*	
cybernetic	*machine"*	
machine"		

Source: Adapted from an idea by J.B. Sellers.

sion for the degree to which energy has been unable to perform work. As such, it is closely linked to the second law of thermodynamics, which states that "systems can only proceed to a state of increased disorder." *Negative entropy* (or **negentropy**) is therefore a measure of order. For an organism, keeping alive is a matter of being able to extract negentropy from the environment. Maximum entropy, the state toward which all organisms move, is death.

These two concepts are perhaps best illustrated by an inanimate example. If you put sugar in your coffee there will be an increase in entropy, since the sugar crystals, which would otherwise have held their shapes indefinitely, will dissolve. If you heat the coffee, entropy will increase further, since the increase in heat motion will dissolve the sugar faster. Any closed system tends to increase its entropy in this way, and will finally approach the inert state of maximum entropy. An open system, on the other hand, can maintain a fairly low level of entropy by interacting with its environment. As a result, it will tend to develop a more complex structure.

It is useful to think of entropy and negentropy when studying socioeconomic systems because it makes us ask how organized they are. Norbert

Wiener, who invented cybernetics in the course of his pioneering work in communications engineering, has drawn a comparison between information and entropy that is very relevant here. Whereas entropy brings disorder, information is thought to bring order, or negentropy. In a social system, entropy means not knowing what to expect; if entropy is maximized, then, as we say, anything can happen. At the other extreme, in a perfectly negentropic system there would be maximum circulation of information, and we would be absolutely certain about the behavior of the system.

Cybernetics

The techniques of systems analysis and **cybernetics** are commonly linked. Cybernetics can be defined as the scientific analysis and control of animate and inanimate systems of organization, based on their methods of communication. Thus there is an emphasis on the unity of all systems, especially on functional parallels such as "natural networks" and "electrical circuits." In other words, although constructed differently, man, machines, and societies are very similar in structure, particularly insofar as all depend for their functioning on information flows. Cybernetics is often cited as the real-world application of general systems notions and concepts. Similarly, geocybernetics is the geographical study of man-machine relationships in the control of spatial organization. The messages of control between man and machine, machine and man, and machine and machine, are seen to play an increasing role in society. The spread of the automated and cybernated factory would of course have an effect on the economic landscape. The latest computation machines, with their ability to calculate, compute, retain in memory, react to environment, and select free alternatives on the basis of experience (i.e., to duplicate to some extent the human system), provide the background for current thinking and work in cybernetics. These developments, together with our ability to transmit information between spatially separate points at the rate of 224 million pulses per second (say, the equivalent of about 40,000 average books an hour) could revolutionize the landscape in the not too distant future. This is speculation, however, and implies considerably more control of our time-space economy than the following chapters reveal we have today, or can conceivably afford.

A Simple Economic System

So far, we have dealt with the systems approach mainly in the abstract. Let us now attempt two simple applications of it.

First, one might consider the iron and steel industry as a system. A number of components, or subsystems, can be identified:

1. *The extraction of raw materials, and the network of sites and routes associated with it.*
2. *The blast furnace operation, and the shipment patterns associated with it.*
3. *The manufacturing of steel, and the shipment patterns associated with it.*
4. *The fabrication of steel, and the input-output relationships associated with it.*

We can see how the various forces of supply and demand might be in a state of equilibrium at any given point. However, changes in the location of supply and the magnitude of demand will result in new locations for all these activities, and consequently in new shipment patterns. The iron and steel industry is therefore an open system.

At a different level of analysis, the basic variables of economic theory can themselves be depicted as systematically interrelated. Figure 8 shows a very simple model of an economic system. In this example, the input is the demand or need for goods or services in the particular area we want to study. The system is an open one because as many functions as we want—cultural factors, price constraints, technological development—can be added to it. In more technical terms, the input variables are independent of the model system itself, and the values and measures of those inputs are determined by the operator of the model. The output of the model system is the supply of services. It is entirely dependent upon what goes into the model system, so that the output will vary with the character of the input.

A third characteristic of this simple model system has to do with the structure of the model itself. This is the class of **status variables** so named because they specify the particular conditions under which the system operates. In the case of an economic system the status variables would specify the type of economic organization—for instance, whether it was a *subsistence* or an *exchange* economy. In figure 8, economic organization modifies the link between **demand** and **supply**. There is also a feedback effect, as demand (the input) is further modified by increasing satisfaction or dissatisfaction with supply (the output).

Criticisms of the Systems Approach

Systems analysis is extremely useful to economic geographers because it encompasses a number of key concepts, such as interaction and spatial rela-

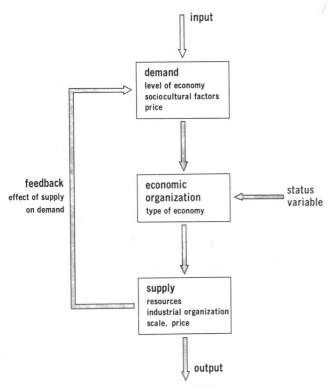

input

demand
level of economy
sociocultural factors
price

feedback
effect of supply
on demand

economic
organization
type of economy

status
variable

supply
resources
industrial organization
scale, price

output

Fig. 8. *A model of a simple economic system.*

tionships, in terms of processes within socioeconomic systems. Nor is this its only advantage; it can also encompass value-directed behavior such as decision making and goal-seeking, not to mention symbolic cognitive processes. Nevertheless, it is vulnerable to certain criticisms, which must therefore be discussed here. One of them is that the systems approach tends to crowd out all the others. This is a danger against which the present book tries to guard. Other criticism comes from those who believe systems analysts claim too much, both scientifically and ideologically.

On another level, the concepts of entropy and homeostasis have been called in question on the grounds that systems are not things but abstractions from people's observed behavior—abstractions that exist only in the minds of the people who are concerned with it. But even if the systems identified in this book have no further meaning than was in the author's mind when he identified them, they are at least consistent with one particular view of geography (see chapter 4). They may be arbitrary illustrations, but they are also convenient ones.

Another frequent objection is that the systems approach somehow carries with it the assumption that all social systems either are or should be in a state of equilibrium. Some analysts believe that this would be true only of closed systems, and that nearly all societies are open systems. The objection has

some force. Obviously, many societies are far from harmoniously integrated; social institutions are changing radically, traditional types of political organization, marriage, economic production and consumption are all breaking down. There is indeed a danger that the only harmonious integration may be in the mind of the observer. It is only too easy to assume that the components of a system must be functionally related, that is, related in such a way that each component somehow contributes to the stability of the system. In this book, such an approach has been called the **functional paradigm**; its exponents, of whom the most influential is the sociologist Talcott Parsons, are generally known as *functionalists*.

Fortunately, it is not necessary to be a functionalist in order to use the systems approach. Any description of a system necessarily catches it at one point in time, and what seems functional today may be a source of conflict tomorrow. Society is not static or stable in a functionalist sense; it is continually changing, and discloses few simple cause-and-effect relationships. It may well be structured in some way, but not necessarily in any particular way.

Conclusion

It has been said that philosophers create systems because it gives them a nice warm comfortable feeling inside. The same might be said of some systems analysts. Certainly, to force society into a systems framework creates at best an illusion of scientific progress, even when the framework is decorated with mathematical formulae. Nevertheless, if systems analysis is viewed as one of a bag of tools, models, and theories among many, it can be put to good use in economic geography as in other fields.

Summary

1. The systems approach emphasizes the study of phenomena as complex, interrelated wholes. As such it can be applied to almost any field of knowledge. It has been used for three main purposes: as a wide-ranging paradigm, or metaphysic; as an analytical tool for the sciences and social sciences, pure and applied; and as a general organizing concept for use in the classroom. In this book, the last two purposes are preferred.

2. Systems may be open or closed, according to whether or not they interact with their environment. Simple action systems contain only one-way chains of cause and effect, whereas feedback systems also contain reactive elements. Other useful ways of classifying systems are as uncontrolled or cybernetic; real or conceptual; and mechanistic or adoptive.

3. A system in a state of equilibrium is one in which there is a tendency toward balance among its components. This is not a quality that can be attributed to all systems by definition; many or even most of them may be in a constant state of internal conflict.

4. Feedback is the conversion, in whole or (more usually) in part, of output to input by means of linkages that are part of the system. Positive feedback enhances the main driving force of a system, and negative feedback opposes it. Amplification feedback is a cumulative stimulation of the driving force that may result in morphogenesis, or change in the system's structure.

5. Entropy is the tendency of systems to fall into disorder, and negentropy is its opposite. In sociocultural terms, we can say that the relations between an open system and its environment are mediated by an exchange of information that leads to increasing order (negentropy). Closed systems tend to be entropic, and altogether less complex.

6. In economic geography the systems approach can be applied either descriptively—for instance, in the analysis of one segment of manufacturing—or in model form, in order to show the interrelationships between input and output as specified by certain status variables.

7. In using the systems approach it is necessary to guard against the philosophical implications of concepts such as "equilibrium," "organic wholeness" or "functional unity"; the distortions that can arise when physical analogies are applied to human situations; and the danger of reading an implicit structure into a situation when perhaps a more relativistic viewpoint would be appropriate.

8. The systems approach is of great value to economic geographers if it is used as just one bag of tools among many.

Further Reading

There are a number of introductory statements about systems analysis. The best of these is still

Chorley, R. J. "Geomorphology and General Systems Theory," U.S. Geological Survey, Professional Paper no. 500B, 1962.

Other useful statements which apply to its use in human geography are

Borchert, J. R. "Geography and General Systems Theory," in S. B. Cohen, ed. *Problems and Trends in American Geography* (New York: Basic Books, 1967), pp. 264–272.

Foote, D. C. and Greer-Wootten, B. "An Approach to Systems Analysis in Human Geography," *Professional Geographer*, vol. 20, 1968, pp. 86–89.

Wilbanks, T. J. and Symanski, R. "What Is Systems Analysis?" *Professional Geographer*, vol. 20, 1968, pp. 81–85.

A particular application to economic geography will be found in

McDaniel, R. and Eliot Hurst, M. E. *A Systems Analytic Approach to Economic Geography*, Commission on College Geography, General Pub. no. 8, 1968.

A criticism of the use of the framework is set out by

Chisholm, M. "General Systems Theory and Geography," *Transactions of the Institute of British Geographers*, vol. 24, 1967, pp. 42–52.

Its use outside geography in the other social sciences is explained in

Buckley, W. *Sociology and Modern Systems Theory* (Englewood Cliffs: Prentice-Hall, 1967).

Buckley, W. *Modern Systems Research for the Behavioral Scientist* (Chicago: Aldine, 1968).

More complex presentations of the use of certain systems concepts in geography will be found, for example, in

Berry, B. J. L. "Approaches to Regional Analysis: A Synthesis," *Annals of the Association of American Geographers*, vol. 54, 1964, pp. 2–11.

Berry, B. J. L. "Cities as Systems within Systems of Cities," *Papers and Proceedings of the Regional Science Association*, vol. 13, 1964, pp. 147–163.

Berry, B. J. L. and Schwind, P. J. "Information and Entropy in Migrant Flows," *Geographical Analysis*, vol. 1, 1969, pp. 5–14.

Woldenberg, M. J. and Berry, B. J. L. "Rivers and Central Places: Analogous Systems?" *Journal of Regional Science*, vol. 7, 1967, pp. 129–139.

Finally, the only comprehensive use of the systems framework in the textbook field is

Chorley, R. J. and Kennedy, B. A. *Physical Geography: A Systems Approach* (Englewood Cliffs: Prentice-Hall, 1971).

four

Natural and Human Milieux: An Overview

Introduction

Paradigm Changes

Up until the 1920s, geographers tended to view the world as static, fixed, and determined. There were two forms of this outlook. At first, human behavior was seen as predictable in terms of a given set of environmental factors, which were always physical—climate, soils, landforms, and the like. This school of thought we now term **environmental determinism.** Such terms as "geographic factor," "geographic influence," and "physical influence," still current in popular scientific literature and journalism, are relics of it. Today they must be rejected, since the form of explanation they offer is too narrow.

Later, environmental determinism gave way to **environmental possibilism,** according to which environmental factors were necessary rather than sufficient conditions. The environment was conceived as a set of opportunities to be fashioned by man, sometimes with ease, sometimes with difficulty. But although the possibilists granted man freedom of choice, they still thought of him as essentially all-knowing. Thus their paradigm was a deterministic one, because the long-range outcome was wholly predictable.

Neither of these two earlier paradigms of man-environment relationships took man's psychological processes into account. Accordingly, neither was able to provide a working frame of reference for explaining human choices and decisions in the context of such relationships. One attempt to remedy this defect is the paradigm of the **behavioral environment.** This approach assumes that man responds only to the environment that he *perceives*, and that his decisions and behavior with respect to economic or indeed any other activities can have meaning only within this perceived environment. Man's behavior is thus determined neither by his physical environment, nor by any all-encompassing rationality. Because the behavioral environment can be interpreted only by reference to man's psychological processes, all explanations and assumptions regarding its nature must have a psychological basis. This is true whether one is viewing the world from the standpoint of sociology, political science, cultural anthropology, geography, or economic geography.*

The Relevance of "Environments" to Economic Geography

Economic activities cannot be divorced from certain environmental concepts, since, as we have seen, such concepts provide the **operational milieu** within which the activities are carried on. No individual can be fully described, in a behavioral sense, without some mention of the social group or groups to which he belongs, his various roles and statuses in them, and the culture of the group itself. To divorce economic geography from this set of operating conditions would be to set up a mechanical, simplistic model divorced from the real world.

*This newer viewpoint has appeared under the guise of a number of names such as "behavioral geography," "psychogeography," and "environmental perception." A number of publications have also appeared, some of which are reviewed below (see especially chapter 5).

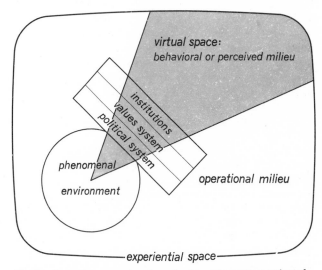

Fig. 9. *An environmental system. A schematic representation of the milieux spaces in which economic activities occur.*

An Environmental System

The relationship of a whole set of environments to each other is shown in figure 9. Here we see, first, a **phenomenal environment** that is both a storehouse of certain physical resources and a physical or biological setting for man's activities of production, consumption, and exchange. Between the phenomenal environment and the actor is an **operational milieu** that consists of various interrelated elements: a political system, a value system, and so on. These elements govern the machinery of production, consumption and exchange. Third, there is a **behavioral milieu.** This is the sociopsychological realm of the individual or group perceiver; it takes account of the difference between the significance of environmental objects to the perceiver and the properties of those objects as they exist in reality.

It should be noted here that the terminology used in figure 9 is not entirely standard. Thus H. and M. Sprout use "operational milieu" to denote what is here called objective reality, which is conceived as the total set of relations as they would appear to an observer who sees all and knows all. On the other hand, J. Sonnenfeld uses the same term to denote only those portions of the environment that impinge on man and influence his behavior in some way. Throughout this book it denotes a set of operating characteristics within whose constraints economic activities take place.

To the three milieux sketched in figure 9, two additional components should be added. The first is **experiential space.** As was made clear in chapter 2, all human interaction, including economic activity, takes place in a spatial context. Experiential space is the space "known by sight and touch, by free motion and restraint, far and near sounds. . . . " It is what is actually in the physical environment to be experienced. The second is **virtual space,** which is "the created domain of human relations and activities. . . . " It is therefore a particular way of perceiving experiential space, and can be called a function of both the behavioral and the operational milieux.

Finally, it should be remembered that figure 9 depicts all these relationships as occurring in one frozen instant of time, like one frame in a movie. Elements of the phenomenal, operational and behavioral environments as they coexist at this one instant are the result of previous developments and occurrences, as well as the forerunners of future patterns. So although for purposes of study we isolate one episode in a dynamic process, the patterns we identify are the result of the evolution of cultural forms over time. The same is true of the physical landscape: it may change slowly, but change it does.

The Phenomenal-Behavioral-Operational System

The first two paradigms described at the beginning of this chapter, environmental determinism and possibilism, considered man and environment as two quite separate entities. But it is obvious from figure 9 that there is a unified field or system that embraces both of them. Within this system, shown in figure 10, the division is not between two entities, man on one side and environment on the other, but between interlinked phenomenal, operational, and behavioral milieux. In this book, the whole system will be called the **geographic environment.**

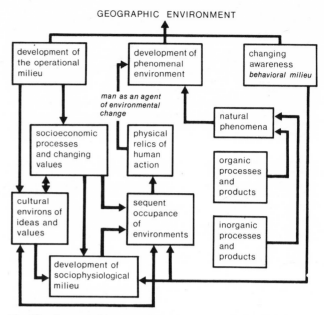

GEOGRAPHIC ENVIRONMENT

Fig. 10. *A geographic environmental system. Here the behavioral, operational, and phenomenal milieux are shown to interlink, producing the geographic environment that is the setting for man's behavior. (Adapted from W. Kirk, "Problems in Geography,"* Geography, *vol. 48, 1963, p. 364.)*

The Phenomenal Environment

The term "phenomenal environment" includes not just the natural environment but everything in it that has been altered or created by man. Thus it places the physical environment in a dynamic framework that includes the results of man's actions. The phenomenal environment is a physical realm undergoing ruthless exploitation as well as constructive transformation. Even what we call natural ecosystems have often been created or modified by man over the course of time.

Natural Phenomena

Figure 11 shows the relations between natural phenomena, both organic and inorganic, in the form of an **ecosystem.** The concept of ecosystem was put forward as long ago as 1935 by the plant ecologist A. G. Tansley. Although it is generally thought of as biological, it has considerable relevance for geography.

In terms of systems theory, the ecosystem is an open system tending toward a steady state, or equilibrium. However, everything in it is viewed from a dynamic viewpoint. Moreover, any change in any single element of the ecosystem sooner or later has repercussions throughout the entire system. Thus for millions of years slight changes have been occur-

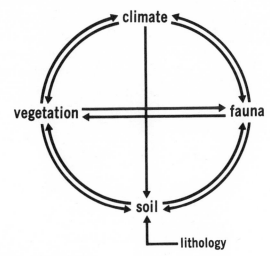

Fig. 11. *The ecosystem.*

ring in the degree of tilt of the earth's axis, and these in turn have caused climatic changes affecting plant and animal species.

Man as an Agent of Environmental Change

It was only recently that man intruded into the complex terrestrial ecosystem. As he increased in numbers, continually adding to his repertoire of technological skills as his socioeconomic system evolved, he inevitably began to disturb the ecosystem's balance. Natural vegetation was cleared, in some instances to be replaced by planted species, in others, by towns and cities. The removal of a forest changes an area's climate; the removal of natural vegetation gradually changes its soil texture, watershed capacity, and many other features. The results can be anything from total destruction and loss of the soil, as in the case of the Dust Bowl, to catastrophic erosion, as on many Caribbean islands.

Some of these changes have been documented over substantial periods of time. For instance, the Plains Indians used to set fires, probably every year, that modified the forest margins of the Middle West. Similar practices have been observed in Eastern Europe, where the forest borders the steppe. Apart from the regular grazing and burning practices of the peasantry, the military authorities of Moscow used to burn off the steppe in order to deny fodder to the horses of infiltrating Tartars. All this burning seems to have kept the forest back. Similar results have been achieved by similar methods in the pampas of South America. In the tussock grasslands of South Island, New Zealand, firings of vegetation by the aboriginal moa-hunting Polynesians have reversed the normal vegetational pattern of the area.

Grasslands now occur in areas with as much as 80 inches of rain per year, while areas with as little as 30 inches, but no man-set firings, are occupied by native beech.

Conclusion

The present phenomenal landscape can be thought of as the product of two sets of forces. On the one hand there are the organic and inorganic processes and, on the other, the activities of man. The present phenomenal landscape has been produced by the interaction of these two sets of forces. Of course, this is not a simple static relationship. In the past, the physical landscape was regarded as a static framework for man's activities. This was the outlook that we labeled environmental determinism. Freed of determinism, we can now regard the physical landscape as a complex and dynamic open system. Man's modifications of the ecosystem, from Los Angeles smog to the Punjab irrigation schemes, must have affected all the other elements in it. Soil, areal climates, vegetation, water availability—all have been modified by man's intervention.

The physical environment as such has therefore changed considerably. The elements of the present landscape, and the balance of the ecosystem, are not the same as existed before man's appearance, or the same as existed at earlier stages of man's occupancy of this planet; in fact, they may well have changed beyond recognition. This makes historical studies of settlement extremely difficult, since the past physical setting usually has in some way to be reconstructed.

In economic geography we are concerned first of all with the phenomenal environment, representing as it does the state of the ecosystem at this point in time, a state affected by the actions of man.

The Behavioral Environment

The idea of a behavioral environment is not an entirely new one in geography. Cultural geographers have made use of it for some time under the guise of "changing ideas and attitudes toward the earth" and similar phrases. More recently, however, they have begun to see the need for a more formal statement. Some of their attempts to construct such a theory are summarized in the following sections.

The Environment Perceived

An individual's or group's behavioral environment may differ substantially from its physical environment. In other words, the objective factors of

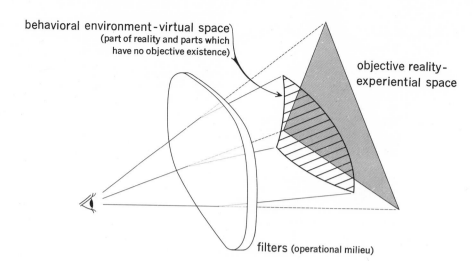

behavioral environment-virtual space
(part of reality and parts which
have no objective existence)

objective reality-
experiential space

filters (operational milieu)

Fig. 12. *Perception and reality. A simplistic breakdown. (Cf. fig. 18.) (From an idea by J. B. Sellers.)*

the physical environment may not be recognized by the group, so that its physical and behavioral environments may be in conflict. Evidence for such conflict comes from studies of settlement in the short grass prairies on the edge of the American Desert, of the perception of the drought hazard in the Great Plains, and of settlement in eastern Oregon. The evidence consists in such indicators as the frequency of out-migration, rate of decrease in business and community activities, and revelations of conflicts in letters and local newspaper accounts. The words used, attitudes shown, and hostilities revealed all indicate a stubborn and persistent clinging to a particular value system, including a particular way of viewing economic activities, as the individuals and groups in question attempted to transfer a behavioral milieu brought from elsewhere to a physical environment that could not support it. There could be no better demonstration of the fact that the behavioral environment does not consist of external phenomena but of images and ideas.

Much of human behavior, then, is governed by responses to images or symbols of the environmental and social milieux. To the extent that these images and symbols vary among individuals and groups, so does human behavior, including economic behavior. Variation in these images and symbols among groups results from **selective perception,** as well as from man's general tendency to make symbols out of observed objects. Members of the same cultural group will have some values and experiences in common, and hence some symbols in common. It is with these *social* symbols that we are concerned here.

The perceived environment can therefore be postulated as a milieu of social illusion and social symbols. As one geographer has aptly said, "man has the peculiar aptitude of being able to live by notions of reality which may be more real than reality itself." A person responds to his environment only as he perceives it. If landscape objects, for in-

stance, are not recognized or symbolized in terms of past experiences, then they are not part of that person's environment. Perceptual processes do not present the individual with a picture of the objective world: the past experience, conceptualizations, symbolizations, attitudes, needs, and purposes of the perceiver determine to a large extent what shall constitute a stimulus and what shall not. In short, perception involves learning. From this point of view no consideration of economic activities can take place apart from consideration of the environment as perceived. Economic decisions and economic behavior can have meaning only within the perceptual environment of the group making the decisions.

A number of explanatory models have been developed by geographers and others to represent the relation of man to his phenomenal and behavioral environments. The most important of them have drawn on gestalt psychology, so-called S-R theory, and Osgood's conception of cognitive processes.

Gestalt Psychology

It is not necessary here to go into the details of gestalt psychology. Suffice it to say that it is a theory of perception (the German word *Gestalt* means "shape" or "figure") with two basic principles:

1. *That the objects we view in the world have a different meaning when viewed as a whole rather than as individual parts.*
2. *That perceptual organization is not chaotic or haphazard but attempts to achieve an ideal state of order and simplicity. This tendency of perception is not a learned trait but a natively given property of the central nervous system.*

An illustration of the first proposition is given in figure 13.

Fig. 13. *A perceptual illusion. (Adapted from a sketch by Toulouse Lautrec.)*

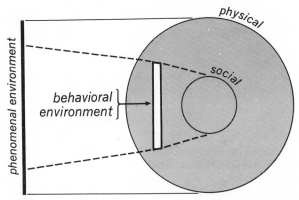

Fig. 14. *Kirk's model of the behavioral environment. (From Kirk 1963, p. 366, reprinted by permission of the editors of* Geography.*)*

This is part of a sketch by Toulouse Lautrec, in which lines and shading are used to depict a representation of a female figure. "The pattern which emerges is clearly more than the mere sum of the physical lines drawn by the artist—it has shape, cohesiveness, and meaning added to it by the act of human perception"—in other words, the whole is greater than the sum of the parts. But despite its appearance as a real object (a phenomenal pattern), if you look at the drawing a second time, instead of a young female the lines can be reconstituted to look like the head of a hook-nosed old crone. That is, the spatial pattern is a subjective feature, each picture mutually exclusive, which picture or gestalt that is accepted depends on the perceiver.

One application of these principles to geography is W. Kirk's model of the behavioral environment (figure 14). Kirk suggests that, at one level, physical man is in direct contact with phenomenal environment, and that physical action will lead to changes on both sides of the relationship. At a second, equally important level, however, the facts of the phenomenal environment will enter man's behavioral environment. But they will do so only insofar as they are perceived by human beings, with motives, preferences, modes of thinking, and traditions drawn

from their social and cultural context. The same empirical data may have quite different meanings for people of different cultures, or at different stages in the history of a given culture. Kirk sees man as a conscious, reasoning, purposive being, basing his decisions on a rational appraisal of the total situation.

This sounds suspiciously like our old friend, economic man—but with a difference. In Kirk's model the behavioral environment is portrayed as a product of interaction between the "real" environment and the group's cultural values. Human action is therefore guided not by the external environment but by a distorted psychological representation of it. However, Kirk's model does not specify by what processes this alleged distortion takes place, beyond placing it in a broad gestalt framework. Nor does it account for the learning element in perception. The fault lies, of course, in gestalt psychology itself. We now know, for example, that the perceptual distinction between figure and background is probably not innate but has to be learned. Indeed, the whole idea of a gestalt is being called into question as a result of various cross-cultural studies as well as experiments with people born blind.

S-R Theory

Another branch of psychology that can help to shape the concept of the behavioral environment is so-called **S-R theory** (stimulus-response theory, or learning theory). The basic notion here is that of a linkage between a stimulus and a response: gradually, this linkage is *reinforced* through repetition. As first put forward, S-R theory did not strictly include the process of perception. Now, however, S-R theory insists that learning influences perception rather than vice versa. Thus setting a group down in a completely different physical environment does not necessarily change that group's way of perceiving the world. Of course, a change in the physical environment can place obstacles in the way of the group members' normal behavior patterns. The group, then, has the choice of removing those obstacles by changing its collective reactions, or of maintaining them, but at great cost. It is the history of the group that determines the general pattern of individual responses.

Perception is thus a long drawn out process of learning by which we learn to respond to particular parts of a pattern before we recognize the whole of it as a stimulus. Man's actions depend not so much on the physical-cultural environment envisioned by Kirk as on a socioeconomic environment that he has to *learn*. Gestalt theory presents man as conscious and reasoning. S-R theory gives a less rationalistic view: man perceives what he has learned to perceive, and responds principally to the stimuli that he has learned to respond to. This latter view provides a more realistic view of economic behavior. But if geographers are going to use S-R theory, they will have to give up the idea that either the physical or the social environment can determine the behavior of man by itself. Changing a group's physical environment does not immediately change its way of perceiving the world.

Neither gestalt nor S-R theory takes note of the variables that are internal psychological events in the actor. Although S-R theory identifies a stimulus (a symbol) and a response (a decision), it does not identify what goes on between them, the mediating events that lie hidden in the mind while a decision is actually being made. Those mediating variables, however, are genuine enough to be considered. Both earlier models are too simplistic to be used to explain the behavioral environment. We must turn to explanatory devices which do attempt to take those intermediary events into account.

There are a number of explanatory devices we could choose from works in psychology. We will use the well known explanation of C. E. Osgood.*Osgood and others have shown with convincing, although indirect, evidence that behavior cannot be explained in terms of gestalt or S-R only. Rather, behavior requires for its explanation a third intervening variable, an internal mechanism that reorders, reworks, or in some sense transforms the stimuli in such a way that a whole range of behavior from habitual to innovative and creative decision making is possible. No device yet can say what these intervening variables actually are in terms of neurophysiological processes, although we have many clues. We can say, however, what they appear to do, and we can describe them, as we do certain of the unobservables of physics, as being a *black box*; something which is

*The only work in geography that directly utilizes Osgood's model is that of Joyce 1969.

an intrinsic part of a given system, but which is known only through its input/output relations with the remainder of the system. Behavior is a system as just described, and the mediators between the input of information and the response output are clearly a black box in the system. Osgood's black box is a process (not a product) whereby we can define a set of operations designed to code environmental information and subsequently to decode it as overt behavior.

The Osgood Model

Because it takes account of symbolism and the reaction to a perceived rather than an objective reality, the model devised by Osgood is of more relevance than either of the two psychological theories discussed above. Osgood has taken the basic S-R model and divided it into two stages: an *encoding* stage and a *decoding* stage (figure 15). Decoding is the association by an individual of a sign or cue with a disposition to respond to that sign in a particular way. Such internalized functions are called *representational mediators*. Thus an individual may associate a buzzer (the sign) with an electric shock. Internalization of the buzzer sounds represents and mediates the anticipated shock; in fact, the sound of the buzzer symbolizes the shock. Encoding involves the way the response is actualized. Thus the disposition to respond to the buzzer may manifest itself in shrinking away from the source of the noise, crying out, hair standing on end, and so on. In symbolic terms, the stimulus S will become associated with some portion of the total behavior elicited by the significate S. The significate could be anything from a value, like national pride, to an object, like a ball. The stimulus could be the national anthem, or just a word, like "ball." In either case, the appropriate response could be produced by the appropriate stimulus.

The same basic framework can be used to describe human communications (figure 16). Each human communication unit is able to send and receive messages, which he both **decodes** and **encodes**. In decoding, some form of physical energy, such as sound or light, is first recoded into nerve impulses via the receiving apparatus (ears, eyes, skin, and so on) and is then interpreted in the **black box** (for which see below). In encoding, some motive centered in the black box, after being transmitted to the motor areas, is recoded into the physical movements (speech, gesture, and so on) that are the output of the communications unit. Thus the input is the stimulus, the receiver is the perception, destination and source are the cognitive processes of the black

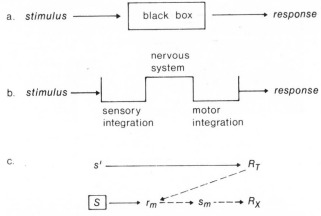

Fig. 15. *The Osgood Model. The earlier stimulus-response approach is adapted here to take account of the black box (a), sensory and motor integration (b), and decoding and encoding (c). See also figure 16.*

s' = the significate, any stimulus that in a given situation regularly and reliably produces a predictable pattern of behavior.

R_T = the behavior produced by a significate, such as the cry of pain from an electric shock.

$\boxed{S}$ = a perceptual sign of a significate, such as the buzzer associated in the mind with an electric shock.

r_m = the response or "disposition" within the individual that R_T represents.

s_m = the self-stimulation that results from r_m.

R_X = a variety of possible "instrumental acts" that take account of the significate.

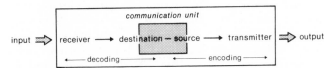

Fig. 16. *Osgood's communication unit. The extension of the decoding/encoding stage of fig. 15 into the communication situation.*

box, the transmitter is the motor skill and organization, and the output becomes the response.

The Black Box

The notions of stimulus, response, and mediating cognitive processes are illustrated in figure 17. Both stimulus and response are related to individual goals, on the one hand, and the goals of the group to which the individual belongs, on the other. But the information-processing system also involves learning, thinking, deciding, and the whole range of motor responses. The black box is a convenient name for the "place" where all this goes on. We should think of this box as set down in an environment from which it is continually receiving messages that it has to answer.

We have seen already that what man sees, reacts in, and reacts to is something less than reality, a perceived environment set by needs, desires, learned abilities, past experiences, and awareness. Within this perceived environment, he makes the decisions that lead to economic activity. Clearly, the information on which he bases these decisions is not complete, either. Various mechanisms of which the value system is perhaps the most important from an economic point of view, ensure that certain types of messages are "filtered out."

What else is in the black box? In recent years, there has been much speculation about certain biological drives and physiological factors. For instance, it has been suggested that man has a basic drive to organize and lay claim to territory. This drive, called territoriality, is supposed to be inherent in all animals, including man; it is defined as behavior by which an organism characteristically lays claim to an area and defends it against members of its own species. Territoriality also involves the capacity to determine "critical distance," that is, the distance at which the presence of another species is perceived as a threat, and social and personal distance for interaction with members of the same species.

Man's physiology is also a factor in cognition, though its exact contribution is difficult to assess. The main question is how the sensory organs are influenced by the socioeconomic complex. Cross-cultural experiments have shown that persons brought up in some cultures do in fact perceive certain objects differently from people brought up in some other cultures.

Finally, we cannot exclude what was earlier called "the hidden world" of our minds, a cognitive structure of the black box. This hidden inner world of the individual may influence behavior more than does the external environmental stimulus. Several contemporary geographers have already intimated this—J. K. Wright in a famous essay, *"Terrae incognitae—the place of imagination in geography,"* concludes, ". . . perhaps the most fascinating *terrae incognitae* of all are those that lie within the minds and hearts of men." Essentially Wright argues that it is not so much what we see, but how we feel about what we see that is crucial to understanding behavior. Lowenthal emphasizes this dimension when he says our personally apprehended milieu ". . . varies with mood, with purpose, and with attentiveness." What we think and feel about the environment thus also falls into the black box. J. W. Watson also hints at this notion of an inner world of meaning: "Not all geography derives from the earth itself; some of it springs from our *idea* of the earth. This geography within the mind can at times be the affective geography to which men adjust and thus be more important than the supposedly real geography of the earth. Man has the peculiar aptitude of being able to live by notions of reality which may be more real than reality itself." In an earlier essay Watson

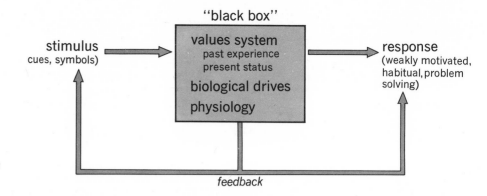

stimulus
cues, symbols)

"black box"

values system
past experience
present status

biological drives

physiology

response
(weakly motivated,
habitual, problem
solving)

feedback

Fig. 17. *The black box. The relationship between the ideas of S-R theory and the intervening black box.*

links this factor to the geographic landscape. In a description of the Canadian Maritimes he says:

Yet the sea is something more than a maritime economy. It is part of the thought and sentiment of the people. The sea as a felt reality, more than tides, capes, coastal meadows or little settlements primed to the shore, more than the call of the sea in fishing and whaling and carrying and trading; the sea as man's battle with storms and disasters and, indeed, with life itself—all these are in the heart and mind of a people who, because of these things, think of themselves as different from dwellers in the Canadian interior.

The black box thus contains this world of meaning, but it is mostly unexplored territory. Like the earth of a hundred years ago our minds still have unmapped Africas and South Americas. Nevertheless they exist, and as such cannot be ignored. In general, the lesson of the black box approach is that economic actions involve not just stimulus and response, but a complex process of interaction and feedback between the environment and a whole range of cognitive and physiological processes that are still poorly understood.

Toward a New Model of the Behavioral Environment

We have now moved to a point at which we must amend the simplistic ideas about the behavioral environment with which we began this section and which were illustrated in figure 12. Figure 18 shows virtual space as part of the cognitive structure that we have called the black box. The general frame of the diagram represents experiential space, which is everything that can be experienced through the senses. Experiential space is subject, first, to the constraints of the human time span and brain capacity, and second, to the biological limitations of the human sensory apparatus (b). Information is transmitted to the black box, which is where the operational milieu is partly **internalized.** Thus objective reality is transformed within the black box

into the subjective human reality of virtual space, composed now of select elements and symbols of reality mixed with elements and symbols of illusion. It is virtual space that supplies the container or frame of reference for behavior, including economic behavior.

If we turn back to figure 9, we can see that, in order to make allowance for the models so far discussed, it will have to be modified. Figure 19 represents such a modification. Here we take the essential elements of figure 9—experiential space (the container of all further elements), the phenomenal environment (the cultural and physical landscapes), and the operational milieu (cultural values and institutions)—and express their point of overlap as virtual space, that is, as part of the black box. Still using the basic frame of figure 9 it is possible to show that within the black box virtual space is broken down into a whole series of cognitive structures, depicted in figure 20 as cognitive *symbolic* spaces.

The notion of symbolic spaces deserves expansion; indeed, it is crucial to this entire approach. The ability to create and use symbols is peculiar to the human species. Without it, the higher thought processes could not exist. Symbols remove the organism from an environment of sounds, shapes, and smells to an environment of meaning. An act of symbolization can mediate between a stimulus and a response. Through many such acts, entire human groups can orient themselves to the phenomenal environment. Human society itself has been said to consist in shared symbolism.

One symbolization that concerns us very much in this book is *space,* of which there are at least five kinds. **Cultural space** is a set of landscape objects that are part of a group's cultural values, as expressed by designating such objects as "historic landmarks," "national monuments," and the like. **Social space** is the set of spatial arrangements that reflect the social structure, values, and aspirations of a community; it is an important element in any system of **social stratification,** as when the location of a person's house indicates his social status. **Ideological space**

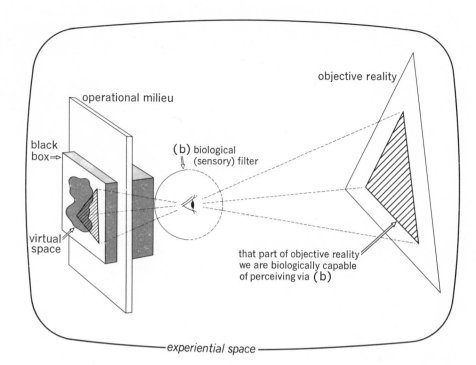

Fig. 18. *Perception and reality: now incorporating the idea of the black box. (From an idea by J. B. Sellers.)*

Labels in figure:
- objective reality
- operational milieu
- black box⇒
- (b) biological (sensory) filter
- virtual space
- that part of objective reality we are biologically capable of perceiving via (b)
- experiential space

symbolizes the way in which a nation or other community and its relation with other areas is conceptualized. As will be seen in chapters 6 and 8, different kinds of ideological space involve different locations for agriculture and industry. **Movement space,** the perceived part of the environment in which travel generally occurs, is that part of space within which direct stimuli and symbols are pre-

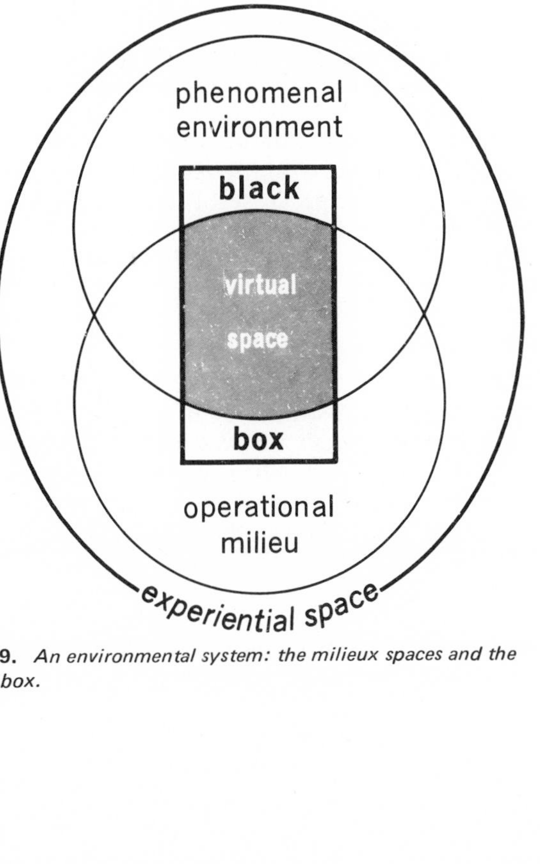

Fig. 19. *An environmental system: the milieux spaces and the black box.*

Labels in figure:
- phenomenal environment
- black
- virtual space
- box
- operational milieu
- experiential space

sented to the economic decision maker. Finally, **economic space** may be symbolized in a variety of ways, including the well-known "time-cost dimension," and the numerous measures of economic interaction between groups.

Conclusion

From the foregoing sections it is evident that the behavioral environment cannot be located anywhere in physical space, but only in the psychic space of groups and individuals. Consequently, these sections have dealt with human psychological processes. It is evident that man is capable of great adaptability. He selects and organizes his milieu in terms of his past heritage, present situation, and future expectations. This milieu is no less psychological than natural, and man's actions, economic or otherwise, can only be understood in relation to it. It has already been suggested that geographers have become increasingly aware of man as a creature set in a milieu of illusion and symbolic meaning more real than any so-called objective reality. Behavior, especially adult behavior, can be considered as learned from symbolic communication rather than from individual trial and error or conditioning. The learning process involves decoding and encoding sign and stimulus, not mechanical response to physical stimuli. Man lives in a symbolic environment into which the majority of physical stimuli are admitted only in symbolic form. In this way they acquire

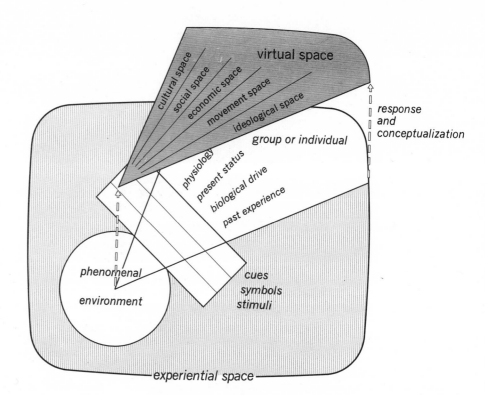

Fig. 20. *An environmental system: symbolization and space.*

social meaning, and circulate between individuals, groups, and generations.

J. G. Myers (1968) has identified the dimensions of such a symbolic milieu (table 9). At the cultural level X_{C_1}, for example, all Americans will have some common symbolism for specific foods, but it will vary among the subcultural groups within the culture (X_{S_1}), or among different social groups (X_{G_1}), or among individuals X_{I_1}, one individual strongly liking a good or identifying with a symbol and another not. This dimension of group aggregation could also be used as a spatial dimension, from a region (X_{C_1}) down to a located site (X_{I_1}). The time dimension can be incorporated in similar fashion. Thus the meaning and symbolism attached to buggy whips or hot cereal in the North American culture region are significantly different today (X_{C_1}) from what they were in 1850 (say X_{C_4}), though the change has been a con-

tinual process broken only by new innovations or chance occurrences. In much shorter cycles, the meaning of a symbol like a television set or an air conditioner to a group of middle-class families may change from one year (X_{G_1}) to the next (X_{G_2}).

The importance of all this to economic geography is fairly obvious. Not only is man nonrational in the sense that he spends his time groping about in uncertainty, but he also sees around him only a selection of the alternatives that are actually there. Thus the economic decision maker's course of action depends on the values he holds, on his past and present experiences, on the situational feedback, on certain biological and sensory aptitudes, and on an array of symbolic cognitive processes. Facts that do not enter his behavioral milieu will not influence his economic behavior.

The Operational Milieu

Culture, social institutions, the political and technological systems—all are powerful factors influencing the economy, and hence economic behavior. The interrelationships between these factors are complex. There is no doubt that feedback occurs between the economy and the other components (figure 21). Indeed, it is often argued, especially by Marxists, that the economy is the key institution, and that it determines the form taken by all other institutions. In this book, however, a more Hegelian viewpoint

Table 9. *The Dimensions of the Symbolic Environment*

level of aggregation	1	2	3	4	5	6
region/cultural	XC_1	XC_2	XC_3	XC_4	XC_5	XC_6
region/subcultural	XS_1					
region/group	XG_1					
site/individual	X_{I1}					

Source: Adapted from J.G. Myers, *Consumer Image and Attitude* (Berkeley: University of California I.B.E.R. Special Publication, 1968), p. 46.

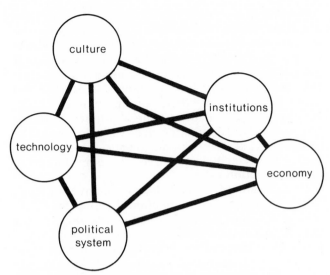

Fig. 21. *The interrelatedness of the operational milieu; the economy, seen at a simplistic level, as influenced by and influencing the other operational components.*

is taken, and the economy is seen as only one element in an interrelated system. The different components in that system are discussed below.

Culture

Certain aspects of the cultural system influence economic activities. In fact it has been argued that culture ascribes meaning to everything. However, it is much harder to define what culture is. Man is surrounded by culture all his life. It shapes his thinking, his behavior, his participation in ways of life; culture changes man from an organism into a human being. Culture is shared; it influences not only how one behaves but how one expects others to behave toward oneself. Culture contains within it a number of components, some conscious, others unconscious. The conscious elements are overt behavioral patterns; the unconscious elements are unstated values and norms. Thus one group may unconsciously and habitually assume that every chain of action has a goal, and that when this goal is reached tension will be reduced or disappear. To another group, life may consist not of a series of purposive sequences, but rather of disparate experiences that may be satisfying in and of themselves, rather than as means to an end.

These patterns of behavior are not only shared by groups. They are passed on from generation to generation by the learning experience, which extends throughout the society. Patterns of eating, sleeping, sexual behavior, even so-called physical reactions such as response to pain—are all carried on within the learned cultural system. It has been said that "Man has to eat to live, but whether he eats steak or snails will be determined by his culture." For this reason, perhaps the most satisfactory recent definition is that of Clifford Geertz, according to whom culture is "an historically transmitted pattern of meanings embodied in symbols, a system of inherited conceptions expressed in symbolic forms by means of which men communicate, perpetuate, and develop their knowledge about and attitudes toward life."

It should be emphasized here that cultural symbols are not abstract ideas or values but concrete embodiments of such ideas and values. Perhaps the best way to think of a cultural symbol is as a meaning attached to an object or act. In Redfield's well-known formulation "the meanings are conventional and therefore cultural insofar as they have become typical for members of that society by reason of intercommunication among the members." There is therefore a relationship to be observed between a cultural system's physical components—its artifacts, buildings, social institutions, and so on—and the values, symbols and beliefs held within it. Thus two cultures having similar or identical institutions and artifacts, but attaching different meanings to them, are different cultures. In other words, the differences between cultures center not on their physical components but on their culturally determined values, beliefs, and symbols.

Despite these differences, the cultural subsystem is composed of a number of elements that are fairly common in most cultures. Such elements are often termed **cultural universals,** and efforts have been made to compile lists of them. One famous list, which does not claim to be exhaustive, contains seventy-three items. Among them are age grading, calendars, systems of counting, cosmologies, division of labor, dream interpretation, food taboos, games, gift giving, incest taboos, language, law, magico-religious systems, penal sanctions, sexual restrictions, status differentiation, tool making, and trade. Obviously, not all of these things are of equal importance to a society; for instance, it could probably get along without dream interpretation, and might have little or no trade. But it could not get along without language, the basis of most communication. Since language is a set of symbols, and since culture itself is communicated mainly through language, it is possible to reduce cultural patterns and subpatterns to symbolic systems or complexes.

People are not born knowing the symbols of their culture; rather they are born into an operational milieu that consists of such symbols. This is what anthropologists mean when they say that cultural symbols are *extrinsic* to the individual; they lie outside him, are independent of him, and will go on existing after he is dead. Culture shapes individual behavior through institutions, which convert cultural symbols into processes of **socialization.** In order to take part in society, human beings have to learn the meaning of various sets of symbols so that responding to them becomes second nature. Geertz has called these sets of symbols "cultural patterns"; without them, he writes, "man's behavior would be virtually ungovernable, a mere chaos of pointless acts and exploding emotions, his experience virtually pointless." Thus the total of these cultural elements or patterns, "culture," is an essential condition for normal human behavior.

Many cultural patterns are in fact very widespread. Thus marriage, tool making, age grading, and games are found in virtually all known cultures. But they take on many different forms. Some of these patterns are set out in table 10.

Groups and Classes

Groups and classes represent the framework for the day to day operation of a culture: they carry out the social functions of a culture, see that its standards and values are adhered to and, if necessary, modify or abolish them. But not all values have equal significance for the whole society, or even for major regions of it. Many values have efficacy only within quite narrow sectors of such regions. Thus in the economic region, groups may differ in their values as much as the National Association of Manufacturers differs from the Consumers Union. Nevertheless, both are essentially the same *kind* of group. Political scientists have called it the **interest group,** because it is formed to protect its members' (mainly economic) interests.

Groups can be classified in many other ways, all of which have relevance for economics. Thus *primary groups* are small, intimate groups like the family or extended family unit. **Secondary groups** are larger and less interdependent, but are still characterized by face-to-face contact, fairly close acquaintanceship, and a complex of common goals. A good example of a secondary group is the neighborhood. Other kinds of group, both formal and informal, include peer groups; cults, sects, and denominations; ethnic and subcultural groups, cliques, clubs, and sets; large-scale, formalized bureaucratic organizations such as large corporations, large universities, or the Pentagon; and a host of **reference groups,** that is, groups that are taken into account in deciding what one's values should be.

A **group** can be called a system of interaction. Much of its importance stems from its influence on the attitudes and opinions of its members. Through this influence it creates much of the immediate cultural milieu within which individual decisions are made. Those belonging to a particular group use a "vocabulary" of motives, attitudes, and values peculiar to that group and its members. When people interact they take account of one another. Interaction is based on attitudes toward others and expectations about the actions of others. Group membership involves cooperation toward the attainment of some common goal. Cooperation may vary from slight to compulsory; it may be antagonistic, hateful, rivalrous, or extremely cooperative. The point to note is that cooperation exists.

Usually, an individual belongs to many formal and informal groups. But more often than not they have the same sets of values. In other words, most people do not exist as totally separate and unaffected beings. Cultural values and norms, opinions, attitudes, and actions, are transmitted for the most part through group influences. People adjust to cultural patterns in different ways, and these adjustments are reflected in and influenced by their particular group memberships.

If we turn to *class,* we find that, like culture, it has many definitions. Basically, it is a system of social stratification within a society or cultural group that assigns a person standing, or prestige. Members of the same social stratum, or "class," would be acceptable to one another for social interaction. Such interaction is equated within the cultural system as symbolic of equality. A person's standing in any ranking system is closely related to his behavior. The full effects of a class system can only be explained in terms of the individual's attitude toward social stratification, including his own efforts to maintain or improve his position in the system.

Each class tends to have its own **life style,** which distinguishes it from other classes in the same society. Life styles include such subcultural variations as speech patterns, personal grooming, posture, gesture, residence location, type of house, consumption patterns, occupation, "taste," and so on.

Not all the characteristics noted here as identifying social classes are used in the same way in all societies. Thus kinship connections are less important in the United States than in China or Great Britain; ethnic characteristics are more important in the United States than in France or Brazil; education is less of a barrier in the United States than in Germany, Holland, or Sweden. Nor are class boundaries always rigidly or formally set. Different people may define the class system of the same society in very different ways. But since any clearcut definition is more or less arbitrary, it may be impossible to say who is "right."

Class, like group or culture, acts as a kind of behavioral screen, limiting the range of the individual's values and actions. But since cultural values and, to

Table 10. *A Matrix of Cultural Elements*

primary message systems	interactional	organizational	economic	sexual	territorial	temporal	instructional	recreational	protective	exploitational
interaction	communication vocal qualifiers kinesics language	status and role	exchange	how the sexes interact	places of interaction	times of interaction	teaching and learning	participation in the arts and sports (active and passive)	protecting and being protected	use of telephones, signals, writing, etc.
association	community	society class caste government	economic roles	sexual roles	local group roles	age groups roles	teachers and learners	entertainers and athletes	protectors—doctors, clergy, soldiers, police, etc.	use of group property
subsistence	ecological community	occupational groupings	work formal work maintenance occupations	sexual division of labor	where the individual eats, cooks, etc.	when the individual eats, etc.	learning from working	pleasure from working	care of health, protection of livelihood	use of foods, resources, and equipment
bisexuality	sex community (clans, sibs)	marriage groupings	family	the sexes masc. vs. fem. sex (biological) sex technical	areas assigned to individuals by virtue of sex	periods assigned to individuals by virtue of sex	teaching and learning sex roles	participation in recreation by sex	protection of sex and fertility	use of sex differentiating decoration and adornment
territoriality	community territory	group territory	economic areas	men's and women's territories	space formal space informal space boundaries	scheduling of space	teaching and learning individual space assignments	fun, playing games, etc., in terms of space	privacy	use of fences and markers
temporality	community cycles	group cycles	economic cycles	men's and women's cyclical activities	territorially determined cycles	time sequence cycles calendar	when the individual learns	when the individual plays	rest, vacations holidays	use of time-telling devices, etc.
learning	community lore—what gets taught: and learned	learning groups—educational institutions	reward for teaching and learning	what the sexes are taught	places for learning	scheduling of learning (group)	enculturation rearing informed learning education	making learning fun	learning self-defense and to stay healthy	use of training aids
play	community play—the arts and sports	play groups—teams and troupes	professional sports and entertainment	men's and women's play, fun, and games	recreational areas	play seasons	institutional play	recreation fun playing games	exercise	use of recreational materials (playthings)
defense	community defenses—structured defense systems	defense groups—armies, police, public health, organized religion	economic patterns of defense	what the sexes defend (home, honor, etc.)	what places are defended	the When of defense	scientific, religious, and military training	mass exercises and military games	protection formal defenses informal defenses technical defenses	use of materials for protection
exploitation	communication networks	organizational networks—cities, building groups, etc.	food, resources, and industrial equipment	what men and women are concerned with and own	property—what is enclosed, counted, and measured	what periods are measured and recorded	school buildings, training aids, etc.	amusement and sporting goods and their industries	fortifications, armaments, medical equipment, and recorded safety devices	material systems contact with environment meter habits technology

Source: From *The Silent Language* by Edward T. Hall, pp. 174–5. Copyright © 1959 by Edward T. Hall. Reprinted by permission of Doubleday and Company Inc.

a lesser extent, primary and secondary group values, are so all-pervasive that one is not usually conscious of them, class values, since they are intended to differentiate one group from another, are encountered every day.

The class structure is only one of the social mechanisms linking the economic subsystem to the cultural subsystem, just as economic behavior is only part of an interrelated system of social action and symbols. Table 10 already illustrates this point. It is not possible, then, to consider any economic action in isolation. Rather all economic actions have to be seen as constituting an integrated system of values, actions, symbols, and behavior, with all the interrelationships implied by use of the term "feedback system." The mutual interdependence of the system's components arises from their subordination to its environment, which is a common set of values and symbols. Such a total system of action is set out in figure 22, where the environmental value system in question is that of the United States.

Economy and Society

It has been suggested that the economic subsystem is linked to the whole societal milieu in three ways: by **normative integration,** by **functional interdependence,** and by **causal interaction** Let us explore each of these dimensions in turn.

Normative Integration. Economic activities, as we have seen, derive their meaning from the general values held by a society or culture. Thus people engage in economic activities (production, consumption, and exchange) for benefits that frequently lie outside the economy itself. Economic motives are not the only ones; the economic decision maker may frequently be involved with other types of goals — independence, freedom, prestige, power, security, ritual, creativity, or craftsmanship. Even the profit motive is not clear-cut. Some researchers have identified a whole range of economic motives and business goals. In peasant and primitive societies the norms and values used to define a resource or a commodity, to control other goods and services, and to set standards of economic behavior, are the norms governing most social interaction. The economy is not so different from the rest of society that it has to have its own set of values.

Functional Interdependence. Functional interdependence arises from the joint roles people play in the workings of society's different subsystems. Thus the same person plays a role in the economic, kinship, magico-religious, and political arenas — for example, as farmer, father, believer, and voter. Because he plays these joint roles, they must obviously fit together in some way, that is, the decision maker

must be able to find the values called upon to some extent compatible. It is easier to use examples from anthropological studies of non-Western societies, where these relationships involved in functional interdependence are more clear-cut than in our own experience.

For instance, among a tribe called the Nayar, descent is through the female line. This is functionally compatible with the occupational role of the males, who are warriors and live apart from their wives. Such interdependency of the components of a societal system means that there are always limits to the development of economic and societal organization in certain directions. Theoretically, incompatible types of economy and values could exist side by side for a short while. In the long run, however, there must be functional interdependency between subsystems, or the society will fall apart.

Causal Interaction. Manning Nash has described causal interaction as follows:

> *For given forms of social structure a given variety and volume of goods and services are required, and if there are shifts in facilities available, there will be shifts in the rest of society. Conversely, shifts in the social structure will change the volume and variety of goods and services a society produces.*

In this causal way, the provision of facilities acts as a pivot for the interaction of economy and society. Much of the empirical evidence for this interrelationship comes from the study of societies undergoing cultural and economic change, particularly recent studies dealing with the spread of Western forms of economic activity and their associated values. These and other studies have shown only too clearly how the spread of Western cultural patterns and values disrupts existing economic and societal organization in non-Western societies.

Conclusion

Implicit in our earlier rejection of "economic man" was the notion that man is activated by motives other than the maximization of profit. "Keeping up with the neighbors" is important from Melanesia to the San Fernando Valley. Thus for the European or American suburbanite, an automobile is no less a prestige symbol than a means of transport. Profit and material advantage are replaced or supplemented as motives by what Raymond Firth has called the "status-increment motive." Whether culture is thought of as systems of belief, values, groups or classes, or patterns of symbols, it filters the stimuli received by the individual from the phenomenal environment and the objective world. To the extent that only selected stimuli or symbols are apparent

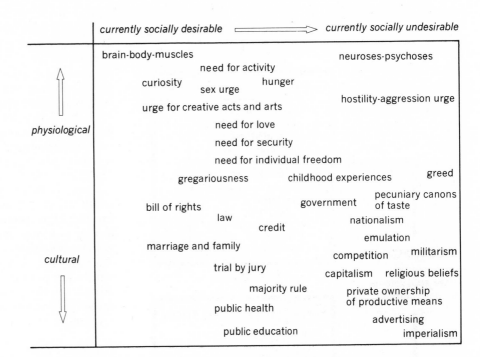

Fig. 22. *A matrix of North American "values." The relationship of certain widely held or widely despised values. (Reprinted courtesy of F. B. McFarland, "Toward an Interdisciplinary Conception of Economics," 1969, p. 7.)*

to the individual, economic decisions are reached with only a particular part of objective reality in mind. It is not possible, therefore, to understand economic behavior without understanding the makeup and structure of the behavioral-phenomenal system. The symbolic network of beliefs, expressions, and values within which economic activities are carried out provides the mechanisms needed for economic behavior to take place. Cognition, economic or otherwise, depends upon the existence of external symbolic models of reality within the operational milieu. Thus E. Isaac has related the symbolic use of the citron (a lemon-like fruit) in the Jewish faith to the present-day distribution of the fruit in the economic landscape.

The Political System

Cultural attitudes, groups, values, and classes are only a part of the operational milieu; further constraints or cognitive filters occur with the **political system.**

All peoples have developed customs that may be termed political. The essence of a political system is sharing territorial rights and providing for mutual services such as protection. From such activity comes recognition of group membership, usually expressed through shared symbols, although in some societies the symbols may be more diffuse than a flag or constitution. The extended organization of society results in governing bodies whose functions are *internal* (social control and welfare) and *external*

(relations with other groups and societies). Thus the political system is also concerned with the authoritative allocation of values within a society. And since it is responsible for this wide range of factors, including goal attainment and policy formation, the political system can have a considerable influence on the economic landscape.

Since the early 1950s, there have been a number of important attempts by social scientists to analyze political relationships in systems terms. Several such attempts have been combined to produce the model of the political system shown in figure 23. It will be seen that the model has the same general features as other open systems: inputs, outputs, various conversion functions, and feedback. But it also has certain special features, of which the most noteworthy are the two classes of input, **demands** and **supports.** These inputs are generated internally by political elites (legislators, royalty, nobility, and so on) and by the domestic society as a whole, as well as externally by demands and supports from other political systems.

Demand inputs include:

1. *Demands for goods, such as food and clothing, for services, such as education, and for welfare measures, such as regulation of working conditions.*
2. *Demands for social control, such as safety in the streets and highways, or honest weights and measures in the market.*
3. *Demands to participate in the system by voting, or holding political office.*
4. *Demands for various kinds of symbolic output, such as*

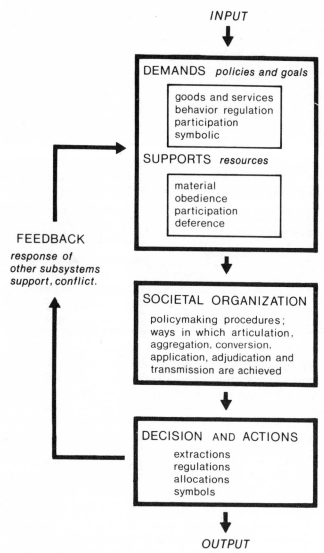

INPUT

DEMANDS *policies and goals*

goods and services
behavior regulation
participation
symbolic

SUPPORTS *resources*

material
obedience
participation
deference

FEEDBACK
*response of
other subsystems
support, conflict.*

SOCIETAL ORGANIZATION

policymaking procedures;
ways in which articulation,
aggregation, conversion,
application, adjudication and
transmission are achieved

DECISION AND ACTIONS

extractions
regulations
allocations
symbols

OUTPUT

Fig. 23. *The political system. Based on ideas expressed by Easton, Almond, and other political scientists, this is essentially the same type of "systems model" as fig. 8.*

the display of power during periods of crisis or external threat.

Support inputs include:

1. *Material factors, such as taxes, levies, or military service.*
2. *Obedience to sanctions, laws, and regulations.*
3. *Participation, by voting, joining organizations, etc.*
4. *Deference to public authority in all its aspects, including the purely symbolic ones.*

The way in which inputs are dealt with depends on the mechanism or *status variable* of the system—in this case, varying societal organization. Obvi-

ously, the intermittent political structure of a migratory hunting group will differ from the complex structures of a contemporary redistributive and commercial-market society. Likewise, a localized group dealing with the environment in terms of magico-religious beliefs, and aiming at bare survival, may have a relatively simple structure, while a government bureaucracy dealing with everything from international crises to domestic party and interest group politics will have status variables that are infinitely more differentiated and complex.

Laws, policies, and enactments, all of which directly affect the economic system, are formulated through the interest group mechanism, through formal policy proposals, through the conversion of policy proposals into authoritative rules, and through the transmission of information, both within the political system and from it to the societal milieu. In this way the inputs of the system are converted into its outputs.

Outputs can be roughly categorized as:

1. *Extractions such as taxation.*
2. *Social control, including control of economic behavior.*
3. *Methods of allocating goods and services (market structures, systems of collection and distribution, etc.).*
4. *Symbolic outputs, including the affirmation of societal values through ritual and ceremonial.*

Having elicited outputs, which for most purposes are identical with specific acts of policy making, members of the societal group respond through supporting the existing policies or advocating new ones by the same means. This kind of feedback may well produce conflict between the society and its policy makers. But, if the system works, changes in policy will result. It is this continuing two-way flow between the political subsystem and the society that constitutes the policy making process, or one aspect of it.

Polity and Society

For our purposes, political factors can be said to exert influence at three levels:

1. *At the first level, the concern is the "state" or "nation-state."*
2. *At the second level, politics can be viewed as coercive authority within a territorial framework.*
3. *At the third level, politics is relations among groups (business, stockholders, labor, consumer organizations, etc.).*

The State. Viewed simply as political space, the world presents a highly diversified appearance. It is fragmented into strange partitioned areas called nation-states. Nationalism is the group feeling about the particular area of partitioned space. The idea of sovereign territory is common to all cultures. The tie to territory is largely ecological for man as for other species. But for man this tie is supplemented by sentiment, myth, religion, and other forms of collective symbolism.

Each nation-state, however rich, is limited in the range of choices it can make. Thus both Russians and Americans display considerable pride in having dominated the vast areas that make up their national territories. Yet for all of man's ingenuity, the limitations presented by a nation's financial resources are still important. As one geographer has pointed out, man can move mountains—but not without floating a bond issue. Problems in the political or technological spheres often turn out to be problems of cost. As the United States now knows so well, money spent on the military complex and space programs cannot also be spent on foreign vacations, education, or the war on poverty. Nor is this kind of choice confined to the United States. The Soviet Union chooses to invest in heavy industry rather than consumer goods; China chooses a "cultural" revolution instead of an industrial one. The tolerance, then, for choosing between various kinds of alternatives varies among nation-states and from ideology to ideology.

Any attempt to classify ideologies is inevitably value-laden. However, the terms "capitalist," "state-capitalist," "socialist," and "state socialist," can be used to tell us much about the relations of the nation-state to its economic activities. An alternative classification is considered below. Meanwhile, we should note that the nation-state may not only be dominant over its own territory. Dominance of a nation-state beyond its borders is usually known as colonialism. It may be economic (as with United States relations with most of the West), or military (as with British colonialism in the past, and Soviet colonialism in the present). Of course, these two types of colonial dominance may overlap. But they do not necessarily reinforce each other.

Territorial Authority. Many national economic decisions are as much political as economic. According to one economist there are three possible relationships between political authority, at this level, and economic activity:

1. *Is the government engaged in expansionist activity, or does it rely on the intrinsic productive resources of the existing territory? Expansionism includes the active extension of territorial limits, as in the case of the nineteenth-century United States. Contemporary Spain, Denmark, Finland, and certain other countries could be said to be intrinsic since they rely, as far as any nation does, on their present productive capacity.*

2. *Is the political unit dominant over its own territory, or is it a satellite of some outside political or economic force? Most nineteenth-century Western European nation-states were "dominant," as are the United States and the Soviet Union today. It could be argued that virtually all other states are "satellitic" and that no one can be neutral. A few states, like China, are neither totally dominant nor are they satellites. In their case, we shall have to wait and see.*

3. *Does the political unit allow economic activity to proceed in an autonomous way, or does it attempt to induce such activity? Many governments today find they have to take an active part in guiding and stimulating economic growth, some by direct control of all sectors, others, like the United Kingdom, by policy control, monetary and fiscal policies, and part government ownership. Most states, however, permitted autonomous economic activity until the Soviet Union, in the 1920s, showed that this was not the natural order of things.*

Governments can also control economic activity by other means than economic planning. For instance, the racist policies of the Republic of South Africa, known as *apartheid*, or the separate development of so-called racial groups, have definite economic effects. Through apartheid an economic system is being shaped with two quite separate parts:

1. *A European subsystem of the market-exchange type—based, however, on African labor.*

2. *An African subsystem, peasant oriented, but receiving some money flows from the European sector. The two subsystems interact, but such interactions are kept to a minimum.*

No other national economic system, with the possible exception of Rhodesia's, is shaped in quite this way. In South Africa, the operational milieu provides the medium for two economies and two landscape subsystems. On the one hand, there is the urbanized, industrialized landscape, with all or most of the attributes that we in the West associate with twentieth-century living. On the other hand, there are the African reservations, or Bantustans, from which most of the male labor has been siphoned off to feed the European subsystem and which are backward, neglected, and based on an economic system that depends on unscientific and unprofitable pastoralism and agriculture.

Political Relations Among Groups. Political relations at the group level involve relations among firms, as well as relations between firms and other groups organized to protect their economic interests.

One form that may be taken by relations among firms is concentration of economic power. The increasing size of companies, with their greater economic pull and manipulative powers, can increase the rate at which smaller firms are edged out of the market. The effect on the economic landscape may be profound, as the economist Neil Smelser has pointed out:

> As the size of the firm increases, its immediate capital problem recedes more into the background; if the firm controls a portion of the market, even demand ceases to be as active as a determinant in their behavior. At such a point their production and pricing policy comes to be more oriented to the behavior of other firms in the industry. Thus economic behavior comes to reflect more and more the political relations among firms.

This one-sided picture may provoke agitation from consumer organizations for the regulation of prices and standards. As a result, they may actually establish cooperatives to distribute goods and services. So far, however, it is labor that has been able to mount the most substantial response. If labor relations in a given area are bad, new industries may settle elsewhere, and present industries may reach a point where they would rather move. Further analysis of such situations is beyond the scope of this book, but they are our concern to the extent that they can and do influence economic behavior and landscape patterns.

Conclusion

As with cultural influences, it is evident that the political system and its interrelationships, including those at the legislative, executive, and judicial levels, do constitute a part of the operational milieu and affect economic activities.

The Technological System

Although technology is closely bound up with economic activity, the technological system is distinct from the economic system. It is impossible even to think about the economic process without taking account of certain kinds of relationships between human beings. However abstract economic thinking may become, it always returns to those basic relationships—buyer and seller, debtor and creditor, giver and recipient. Technology is concerned primarily with things; the fact that these things are for human use is taken for granted. Pottery, tools, weapons, buildings—all these are evidence of a technological order. But, like other cultural artifacts, they may symbolize much more than their basic functions. A house may be much more than shelter; for instance, it may be the home of a god. In other words, technology, like economic activity, has to be viewed in relation to the rest of society.

Technology and Society

Technology is a system of ideas, principles, techniques, and tools with which man attempts to control or modify his natural or phenomenal environment. **Technique** refers to a specific way of operating tools. Thus operating each major group of tools—the potter's wheel, agricultural implements, the loom, and so on—involves a sequence of coordinated movements or operations through which some task is accomplished.

Tools can be defined as material objects especially designed for the application of energy in precise and controlled ways. Two categories of tools can be distinguished: tools proper, which transmit bodily action directly or indirectly; and facilities, which include containers, barriers, and so on. **Material culture** is a term used by anthropologists that includes both tools and facilities.

The technological system, then, is the consistent and extensive use of tools and techniques. And, like certain other cultural traits, it is a learned pattern. Some anthropologists, notably Leslie A. White, see learned technological patterns as the very basis of society, around which economy, culture, and other societal components are arranged. In fact, White has outlined a mechanistic development or evolution of economic systems based on the transmission of increasingly complex technological patterns. Most social scientists, however, view the relationship between technology and the societal subsystems as a mutual one: they shape technology as much as it shapes them. Certainly, the systems approach postulated in this book would lead one to expect that change in any part of the societal system must have repercussions elsewhere. Thus a technical change like electric light has effects far beyond those on the gas mantle and match industries; for instance, people are less likely to imagine that they see ghosts.

Stages of Technology. Every major technological advance—cultivation by means of a digging stick or hoe, plowing, irrigation, domestication of large herds of animals, machines driven by steam, electricity, computers—has widened the spectrum of economic activities. The relationship is as simple as that. In fact, of course, the relationships in the real world are not just between technical feats and economic activities. But technical knowledge is indispensable. Without it, man could not make economic use of the raw materials provided by his environment. He could not even use his own labor effectively. In other words, between a people and their habitat stands their technology.

Table 11 sets out one comprehensive taxonomy of mechanical and technical properties. It includes certain symbolic techniques—writing, painting, mak-

Table 11. *A Taxonomy of Technology*

1. symbolic (writing, art)
2. material
    a. tools
        implements (knife, hammer)
        missiles (javelin, boomerang)
    b. facilities
        containers (pot, house, boat)
        bases (floor, road)
        barriers (fence, dam)
        lines (cord, knot)
    a-b. simple machines *(firedrill, bow, cart)*
    c. energy convertors
        prime movers:
            engines (steam engine, internal combustion engine)
            motors (electric motor)
        batteries (storage battery)
        dynamos
        heater (electric furnace)
        reactors
        friction devices (matches, etc.)
    a-b-c. power machines *(lathe, gun)*
    d. instruments
        natural objects (foot, stick)
        tools (= a) (calipers)
        facilities (= b) (basket)
        machines (= a-b) (scale, violin)
        power machines (= a-b-c) (electron, microscope)
    a-b-c-d. automata
        manufacturing automata (pipeline, chemical plant)
        automatic signals (radar, weather signals)
        calculators (computer)
    b-c. nonmechanical power devices *(sailboat, plow)*

Source: P.L. Wagner, *Human Use of the Earth* (New York: Free Press, 1960), p. 99.

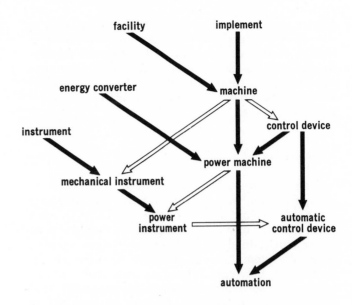

arrows indicate the incorporation of simpler into more complex types of artifacts

Fig. 24. *The family tree of tools. The growth in complexity of tools from the "simple" firedrill to the automatic and computerized tools of the present day. (Reprinted by permission of the Free Press, from P. L. Wagner,* The Human Use of the Earth, *1960, p. 103.)*

ing masks and insignia—that may not always be thought of as technologies. But the bulk of this scheme consists of physical techniques and tools that transmit or restrain motion in some way, transform energy, and incorporate certain symbolic functions.

Figure 24 illustrates the developmental process, from simple tools to more complex ones. At the least complex stage, there are *implements* and missiles; the main distinction here is between the direct and indirect transmission of bodily motion. Implements include knives and hammers, which essentially are extensions of the hand and arm; missiles, like blowpipes and javelins, are propelled. At this simple level also we find *facilities,* such as baskets, pottery, or fences, which direct or control liquids, gases, or animate objects. They represent an important class of technical device since they are used for storage, transportation, and certain processes like brewing or dyeing.

A *machine* is a more complex tool consisting of one or more moving parts. In its simplest form a machine can be a bow and arrow or mortar and pestle. Relatively complex machines, such as cranes and pumps, have been known for more than two thousand years. *Energy converters* are machines that convert one kind of energy into another, as a dynamo converts mechanical energy into electricity. Most machines with which we are familiar today are a combination of mechanical machines and energy convertors. For this reason, they are properly called *power machines.* In their early stages they still require applications of human energy for continuous operation. Later, they need only fuel and occasional maintenance. The technological advance represented by power machines can hardly be overestimated.

Also an important development were *instruments,* which transmit energy impulses and thus register the variations in some other object or activity. In so doing, they make possible a great degree of control over power machines and other technical and economic activities. In time these instruments have acquired powered controls and ultimately automatic controls, removing bodily motion ever further from the operation. The computers, cybernetic techniques, and **information technology** are important recent developments. Through them, man can be supplied with enormous amounts of information, increased control, and complex analytical tools. Already the new machines seem capable of performing most of the mental operations we associate with human beings. Moreover, it is now technologically feasible to place all spatial aspects of the economy under continuous electronic surveillance. Clearly, the interaction of technology and economic activity is entering a new stage.

Conclusion

Each set of tools and techniques available to groups of men presents those men with particular means to exploit the environment. However, each such strategy of adaptation must be thought of as being constrained by still further factors: culture, political systems, and institutions. So although the connection between techniques and economic activities may seem direct, it has to be viewed as part of the entire societal system. However, by considering technology by itself for a while, we have been able to see what an important place it occupies in the operational milieu.

Institutions

The concept of **institution** is closely connected not only with the economy but with the other three sectors of the operational milieu. It is an inescapable fact that economic activity takes place within an institutional framework. Accordingly, we need to have a clear idea of what an institution is.

To call a set of social arrangements an institution is to imply two kinds of things about it. First, it involves certain normative patterns of human behavior: something is not only happening on a regular basis, it is also what is "supposed" to be happening. Second, certain arrangements—certain rules, regulations, and other social machinery—have been created to insure that what is supposed to be happening will go on happening. Thus a particular set of kinship relationships will determine who may or may not marry whom.

Kinship, like marriage, family, church, or property is an easily recognized institution with a definite name and function. Other institutions may be more elusive. Thus the medical code of ethics, although the essence of it can be found in the Hippocratic Oath, is really a complex set of informal understandings that have never been written down, and probably could not be. Nevertheless, they exist, in the sense that they have meaning for people and influence their behavior.

Standardized norms and modes of behavior become *institutionalized* in a group of people under the following general conditions:

1. *A large number of the members accept the norms in question.*
2. *Those who accept the norms take them very seriously.*
3. *The norms are sanctioned; that is, certain members of the group are expected to adhere to the norms under appropriate circumstances. If they do not, they expect in turn to undergo* **sanctions,** *which may vary from social disapproval to physical deprivation.*

Institutions can also be safeguarded and sustained by positive inducements, instruction, and in some cases by what one anthropologist has termed "dramatizations." Adherence to the standardized modes of behavior may be approved of with inducements like rewards and prizes that express the group's appreciation and also draw attention to the norms themselves. Institutions are sustained by educational activities, both formal and informal, which inculcate not just the norms, but the sanctions and inducements attached to them. Dramatizations include the demonstration or commemoration of desired modes of action through ceremonials, festivals, and holidays such as Thanksgiving or Veterans Day.

Operation

The normative patterns that institutions purvey may be of two types. First, there are patterns supported by common moral sentiments, which are widely conformed to. Second, there are utopian patterns, which may be widely approved, but are lived up to by only a few. Insofar as these patterns (particularly the first group) are mandatory, they "direct" or "determine" actions, or at the very least, set limits beyond which deviance is sanctioned negatively. Thus the institution of marriage is a complex normative pattern that applies to all marriages in a particular societal group or, as noted below, in a particular social status group in a segment of that societal system. Particular marriages in the group or subgroup will conform to the pattern in varying degrees, but all members of the group *know* the pattern itself, and if it is a strong pattern they will regard it as morally valid and binding.

The actual strength with which a norm is seriously accepted may vary a good deal. Some norms, such as that of mutual sexual fidelity, are supported with some vehemence among many groups in North America; others, like the desirability of a husband mowing the lawn at weekends, are not. Institutionalized patterns may also apply differentially to different members of a group—for instance, according to their social status. It is not necessary to understand a norm in order to disapprove of its being violated. For instance, the detailed workings of the United States stock market are understood only by

Table 12. *A System of Institutions*

OPERATIVE   REGULATIVE

somatic—*individual physical existence (sex, age, treatment of disease, etc.)*
economic—*contract, property, occupational role*
recreational—*leisure time, clubs, groups*
    scientific—*technology, techniques, research innovations*
       magico-religious—*ceremony, ritual, church, supernatural and mystical beliefs*
          educational—*school, apprenticeship*
            political—*authority, leadership, power*

                                   legal—*control and maintenance through sanctions of the operation of*
                                         all other institutions and groupings
                                  kinship—*control and maintenance through descent (family, marriage,*
                                       inheritance, etc.)

Source: Adapted from S.F. Nadel, *The Foundations of Social Anthropology* (London: Cohen and West, 1951), p. 135

experts. But most people approve of punishing those who violate the regulations of the Securities and Exchange Commission. Finally, it is also possible to institutionalize beliefs by making them dogmas or doctrines.

The operation of an institution, therefore, unifies the various elements of a society or group. The institutional controls within which the economic system operates govern factors like the division of labor, the disposition of property, and the methods of distribution or exchange. These controls provide answers to questions like, Who does what? Who controls what (and whom)? and, Who gets what? Institutions integrate the isolated economic activity or economic mechanism into the society's value system. Thus an economic subsystem consisting of businessmen and firms operates in a society that includes the social myth of free enterprise, the laws of contract and property, formal business codes, and profit and loss. All these different elements combine to form the institution known as "American business."

Classification

Table 12 illustrates the gradations and interrelationships between the various institutions. The **operative institutions** fulfill a purpose immediately by rendering a particular service; the **regulative institutions** achieve their purpose by allowing the others to operate, that is, by safeguarding them. The distinction is not absolute; there is a continuum, and the same institutions may appear in different contexts to be either operative or regulative. Here, economic institutions have been placed in the "operative" category. However, it is also possible to consider them as institutional complexes centered around the notions of "contract" and "property," and therefore as primarily regulative. The real question here is what it is that one considers distinctively

economic—the activities of production, exchange, and consumption, or the norms that regulate those activities.

Particular services tend to be institutionalized in terms of particular occupational roles, such as "banker," "craftsman," or "farmer." Since certain of these roles involve **authority,** as of an employer over his employees, there are links to political institutions at this point. All occupational roles are of course regulated by other institutionalized activities such as taxation and labor legislation.

Some institutions, such as the magico-religious complex, provide both operative and regulative frameworks. Religion shapes social order by serving as a source of general conceptions about the world. In this way it provides the operating conditions for relations between individuals and groups, and for their sociopsychological dispositions. But religious institutions may also directly regulate such activities as the time of year for particular behavior, or the food that may be eaten on certain days of the week, and it may regulate other institutions, such as kinship and marriage.

The central component of political institutions is authority, which has been aptly defined as "the generalized right to invoke binding obligations in the interest of collective goals." Such institutions include all those intended to control and maintain whole corporate groups of society, if necessary by the ultimate use of force. These, therefore, are the institutions that enforce such policies as **apartheid.** The medium through which authority is exercised is **power.** Thus political institutions are by nature regulatory. Within the legal framework that they provide, economic resources and interests are exploited.

Finally, kinship institutions include all norms intended to control and maintain groups based on descent. Marriage, family, inheritance—all are kinship institutions. The relationships between them are complex, but they can be studied. Thus it has been shown that certain changes in kinship groups between them lead to certain changes in descent, which finally leads to a change in the kinship terms that people use for each other. A good example of the regulative nature of these institutions, and their interrelatedness with the economic subsystem, comes from a study of the Algonkian-speaking hunters of the Easter Subarctic, in North America. Among these groups, marriage is permitted between cross cousins (the children of a father's sister or mother's brother), even though it is forbidden for other kinds of cousins. This helps the bands of hunters to remain small and isolated, so that they can effectively exploit their hunting areas, and at the same time retain some unity and strength.

Institutions and the Economy

In itself the economic process (production, consumption, and, in some societies, exchange) is just the mechanical and biological interaction of certain elements necessary for human survival. In the absence of the appropriate societal conditions — culture, political system, and particularly institutions — the interaction that we call economic activity has no social meaning. On the other hand, relations between institutions and the economy can be very complex, and can have a profound effect on economic activity. Rules of inheritance may, for example, divide land equally among all male heirs, which may lead in time to small fragmented parcels of land and small scattered plots, as in southern France until recent years. The effect of such fragmentation is to reduce agricultural efficiency.

Institutions provide the applications of labor and capital, no less than the distribution of roles and authority. Thus the choice between "capitalism" and "socialism" is not just an ideological one, but refers to two different ways of instituting technological systems. The economy is so embedded in institutional relationships that religion and government may be as important to the functioning and operation of the economic process as financial institutions or the availability of tools and machines.

Thus institutions are regulatory devices that limit and define economic action by determining the ends that the economy should serve, and providing the means to make economic activities conform with values. Institutions put the economic aspects of human behavior within the context of the structure and operation of the behavioral environment and the operational milieu. In short, economic activities are molded, constrained, directed, and limited by the institutional framework.

Conclusion

The paramount reality in human experience is the everyday world of common sense objects and practical acts. This is the world with which we have the most direct contact, and from whose pressures and requirements we have the least escape. The operational milieu, summarized in table 13, surrounds this "reality," or behavioral environment, cuts us off from the world of "objective facts," and colors the individual's conception of the established world, including his conception of economic activity and processes. Culture, religion, and education both legitimate and motivate the economy, especially through the legitimation of economic roles. Family and kinship supply labor and land. Political systems supply the legal order in which economic decisions are made, and the legal institutions that make credit and investment possible. But, of course, it is not a one-way affair. Figure 25 suggests that there are feedbacks from the economy to the rest of society — the economy returns wages and income, goods, and services. Sometimes, as in a subsistence society, the feedback is almost direct. In other kinds of society, the feedback is indirect and institutionalized through special social codes or mechanisms that may or may not involve money. The economy supplies resources for culture, religion, and government.

One fact that stands out from this necessarily brief overview is that the small-scale, highly personal subsistence economic systems, with few or no market facilities and no money medium, stand in marked contrast to the characteristic Western institutional framework of business enterprise, with its machine technology, automata, impersonal labor market, profit orientation, banking and credit, and trading links over wide spatial areas. The differences lie in the structure of the operational milieu governing behavior.

Another important fact is that the interchange between the objective world of phenomenal facts, behavioral environment, and operational milieu is multidirectional. Government actions affect culture, religion, and family, as well as the economy — and vice versa. Figure 26 attempts to specify a few of these interactions.

The operational milieu — the political, cultural, technical, and institutional systems — are of course interdependent, so much so that it is difficult to study one without studying at least the elements of the others. A study of the economic system by a geographer would obviously be incomplete without reference to this milieu. No economic landscape can be understood without reference to values, ideologies, techniques and norms.

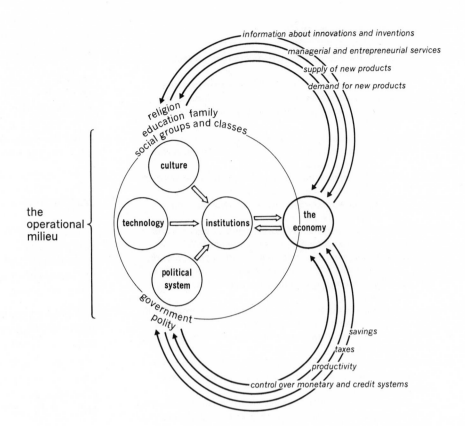

Fig. 25. *The operational milieu and the economy. (Adapted from a diagram by K. Deutsch in "Integration and the Social System," 1964, p. 191, by permission of J. B. Lippincott Co.)*

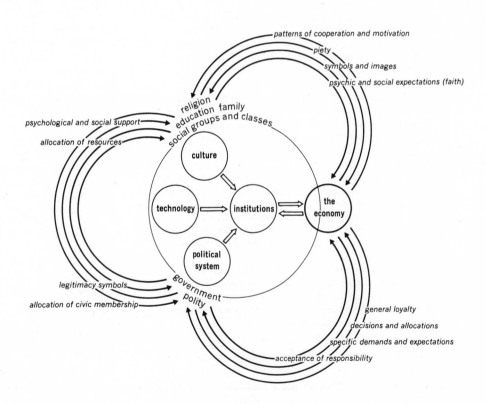

Fig. 26. *The operational milieu: some other relationships. (Adapted from a diagram by K. Deutsch in "Integration and the Social System," 1964, p. 191, by permission of J. B. Lippincott Co.)*

Table 13. *The Operational Milieu*

A. Culture: *"An historically transmitted pattern of meanings embodied in symbols."*
1. elements *(extrinsic): age grading, calendars, systems of counting, cosmologies, division of labor, food taboos, gift-giving, laws, magico-religious systems, toolmaking, etc.*
2. operates by *groups, classes, culture regions.*
3. via *(a) normative integration (economic values, part of general values of a society).*
    (b) functional interdependence (joint roles played in society, some economic, some social).
    (c) causal interaction (facilities shared by economic and social systems).

B. Political System: *"A system of sharing rights of territory and mutual service, like protection, via shared symbols."*
1. elements: *the nation state in international relations; the state within a territorial framework; political relations among groups (firm, consumer, stockholders, labor unions).*
2. operates by *dominance, coercion, use of power and authority, induction, laissez faire, etc.*
3. via *government, legislation, political authority, judiciary, etc.*

C. Technology: *"A system of techniques and tools by which man attempts to control, ameliorate, or modify the phenomenal environment."*
1. elements: *symbolic techniques (writing, painting, printing, sculpture, etc.); physical techniques (tools and weapons).*
2. operates by *conceptions and applications concerning direct and indirect energy transmissions, bodily motions, etc.*
3. via *appreciation of phenomenal environment, search for natural law and causation.*

D. Institutions: *"Structure or normative patterns which represent and sanction standardized modes of behavior."*
1. elements: *a large number of people who accept the norm and take it seriously; sanctions.*
2. operates by *acceptance of norms and sanctions: dispersed or centralized codes of diffusion of rules and information.*
3. via *unification of the various elements of a society or group; institutionalizing roles in society; division of labor; application of labor and capital; distribution of rules and authority.*

E. Economic system: *"A system of allocation and disposal of scarce goods, the goods having alternative uses and varying satisfaction."*
1. elements: *the firm; consumer; contract; property; division of labor; means of production (primary, secondary, tertiary, quaternary); consumption (food, shelter, clothing, producer goods); and exchange market, quasi-market, trade, etc.)*
2. operates by *addition of form-, place-, and time-utility; value; exploitation of resources and compensation for their uneven distribution in space and time.*
3. via *systems of organization (subsistent, peasant, redistribution, market-exchange, etc.).*

The implications of this phenomenal-behavioral-operational framework for economic geography are fairly obvious. Not only is man nonrational in the strict sense, but he perceives around him only a selection of the alternatives open to him. Man, the decision maker, has his scale of preferences and choices set by his values, which in turn are the product of past and current experiences. He perceives only what is filtered through the highly selective screen of the operational milieu. Thus facts that exist in the phenomenal environment but do not enter the behavioral milieu of an individual or group have no relevance to behavior.

Summary

1. A new concept of the geographic environment is introduced as an interlinked system of phenomenal, operational, and behavioral milieux—a substitute for the earlier paradigms, environmental determinism and possiblism.

2. The phenomenal milieu is the natural or physical environment, plus man's actions as a landscape-seascape-climate-forming agent.

3. The concept of an ecosystem is introduced to represent the natural environment and man. The ecosystem is a functioning, interacting system of fauna, flora, soils, and climate.

4. Into the complex state of dynamic equilibrium that seems to be assumed by ecologists to represent an "ideal" man-environment ecosystem, man has recently intruded on a rather massive scale. Intrusion and disequilibrium have increased as socioeconomic and technologic developments have grown more complex. The grazing of animals, the setting of fires, the development of advanced agricultural systems, manufacturing systems, and the whole complex of settlement have changed the balance, and, in many cases, completely altered vegetation, soil structure, or the microclimate.

5. The phenomenal milieu is both the storehouse of certain physical resources and the biological setting of man's economic activities or production, consumption, and exchange.

6. The concept of the behavioral environment, although not new, has only recently received widespread attention in geography. A basic notion is that an individual's behavioral environment may differ substantially from the phenomenal environment. Such selective perception as occurs, therefore, is of importance to us since economic behavior will obviously be influenced by the particular perceived environment of the decision maker.

7. A number of models have been developed to represent this behavioral process. One of the earliest by a geographer was put forward by William Kirk in 1952. Kirk's model was based on gestalt *psychology*, and the behavioral environment was conceived as a "psycho-physical" arrangement of patterns and structures (gestalter). Kirk does not, however, specify how the perceived environment becomes a distorted representation of the objective environment, other than placing it in a broad gestalt framework.

8. Many of the gestalt notions are now openly challenged, so that another branch of psychological theory is turned to, the so-called stimulus-response theory (S-R). This approach to behavior is based on the notion of a linkage between a stimulus and a response, reinforced by repetition.

9. Although the theory was extended to include notions of learning and perception, it remained incomplete since it still did not account for the mediating process between receipt of a stimulus (e.g., a symbol) and a response (e.g., a decision to do something). This mediating process, the human brain and mind, is sometimes called "the black box."

10. A third model, that of C. E. Osgood, does provide some details about this mediating process, although it has not been widely used in geography. By using concepts of encoding, decoding, and representational mediators, Osgood's model helps us understand some of the cognitive processes at work. In particular, we can see how such a model fits into the general framework of "human communication."

11. Although by using the idea of a black box lying between symbolic stimulus and overt decision, we have moved some way toward an understanding of the behavioral process, we still lack full knowledge of its workings. We can add biological and physiological drives to the fairly mechanical conception of mediation, but we are still left with a largely "hidden world" of the mind. There is no doubt that those hidden areas of the mind largely control what we think and feel about actions and environments. The black box thus contains the whole world of meaning, although it is still a largely unexplored area.

12. At this point, we can modify our simplistic ideas about the behavioral environment to include the black box and notions representing select perceptions of the objective environment. One way to show this is to identify common cognitive symbolic spaces.

13. The behavioral environment thus rests in the psychic space of groups and individuals, rather than in physical space. Factors that do not enter the behavioral milieu of the economic decision maker do not directly influence his economic behavior.

14. Turning to the third element of the geographic environment, the operational milieu, it can be seen that cultural, institutional, political, and technological systems limit the capacity of an "economy" to transform habitats.

15. Culture, variously defined, shapes man's way of thinking, his behavior, and his actions via a set of transmitted symbols. These symbolic components contain sets of information which govern, for example, the avoidance of certain foods, restrictions on the use of land, restrictions on particular occupations, and other organizational impediments or enhancements. Without these components behavior would be chaotic and formless.

16. Particular functions or symbolic components of culture are transmitted to the individual via groups and classes, which provide the day-to-day framework for its operation. "Economic value" becomes a function of culture by way of these groups and classes, and thus economic behavior always has a social content that constantly alters economic realities.

17. Links can be identified between culture and economy by way of "normative integration," the holding of a common values system for economic and noneconomic behavior; "functional interdependence," the holding of joint roles for economic and non-economic actions; and "causal interaction," the provision of joint facilities for social and economic services.

18. The political system, the second subcomponent of the "operational milieu," influences economic actions at the state level in international relations, just as at the local level it governs relations between groups, and, between the two extremes, governs the distribution of activities within a territorial framework. The effect of the "apartheid" policy in the last instance has had a powerful influence on shaping the economic landscape in South Africa.

19. Technology, the third subcomponent, is a system of techniques and tools, rather than a set of relationships like the economic system. There is, however, a strong relationship between the two, since knowing how to deal with a particular set of environmental opportunities (tools and techniques) and knowing how to deal with human organizations are clearly related.

20. The final subcomponent of the "operational milieu," the concept of institutions, is interrelated with the other three subcomponents. An institution involves certain normative patterns of human behavior and rules or regulations to ensure that the normative patterns are adhered to. All economic activities in fact occur within an institutional framework.

21. This framework governs factors like the division of labor, land tenure, inheritance laws, and methods of distribution and exchange, that are apparent in the

use of words like "capitalism" or "socialism," each of which denotes differing institutional frameworks.

22. The operational milieu surrounds the everyday world of perceived objects (the behavioral environment), and is interposed between the individual and objective reality. This filtering process colors the individual's conception of his place, temporally and spatially, his normative and motivational orientation, and thus shapes his economic and noneconomic behavior.

23. The three elements of the geographic environment and their subcomponents have obvious implications for any study of the economic landscape.

Further Reading

In addition to the comprehensive reviews already noted by Wagner (1960, 1971) and Thomas (1956), and the explication of the physical environment by Chorley and Kennedy (1971), the following readings may be useful concerning the phenomenal environment:

Chorley, R. J., ed. *Water, Earth, and Man* (London: Methuen, 1969).

Kates, R. W. "Links between Physical and Human Geography: A Systems Approach," Commission College Geography, Pub. no. 5, *Introducing Geography: Viewpoints and Themes*, 1967, pp. 23–30.

Stoddart, D. R. "Organisms and Ecosystems as Geographical Models," in R. J. Chorley and P. Haggett, eds. *Models in Geography* (London: Methuen, 1967), chapter 13, pp. 511–548.

Tuan, Yi Fu. *Man and Nature*, Commission of College Geography Resource Paper no. 10, 1971.

Watt, K. E. F. *Ecology and Resource Management* (New York: McGraw-Hill, 1968).

the behavioral environment:

Downs, R. M. "Geographic Space Perception: Past Approaches and Future Prospects," *Progress in Geography*, vol. 2, 1970, pp. 65–108.

Kirk, W. E. "Historical Geography and the Concept of the Behavioral Environment," *Indian Geographical Society Journal*, 1951, pp. 152–160.

Kirk, W. E. "Problems of Geography," *Geography*, vol. 48, part 4, November 1963, pp. 357–371.

Osgood, C. E. "A Behavioristic Analysis of Perception and Language as Cognitive Phenomena," in W. Buckley, ed. *Modern Systems Research for the Behavioral Scientist* (Chicago: Aldine, 1968), pp. 186–203.

Sprout, H. & M. *The Ecological Perspective on Human Affairs* (Princeton: Princeton University Press, 1965).

Tolman, E. C. "Cognitive Maps in Rats and Man," *Psychological Review*, vol. 55, 1948, pp. 189–208.

More general information on environmental perception will be found in

Lowenthal, D. ed. *Environmental Perception and Behavior* (Chicago: University of Chicago, 1967), Department of Geography, Research Paper no. 109.

Lowenthal, D. "Geography, Experience, and Imagination: Towards a Geographical Epistemology," *Annals of the Association of American Geographers*, vol. 51, no. 3, 1961, pp. 241–260.

Prince, H. C. "Real, Imagined and Abstract Worlds of the Past," *Progress in Geography*, vol. 3, 1971, pp. 1–86.

Russell, D. C. "Psychology and Environment," *Planning Outlook*, vol. 6, no. 2, 1964, pp. 23–37.

Saarinen, T. F. *Perception of Environment*, Commission on College Geography, Resource Paper no. 5, 1969.

Watson, J. W. "The Role of Illusion in North American Geography: A Note on the Geography of North American Settlements," *The Canadian Geographer*, vol. 13, no. 1, 1968, pp. 10–27.

Wright, J. K. "*Terrae Incognitae:* The Place of Imagination in Geography," *Annals of the Association of American Geographers*, vol. 37, 1947, pp. 1–15.

Aspects of the operational milieu as they relate to economic activities are treated in

Nash, M. "The Organization of Economic Life," in Sol Tax, ed. *Horizons of Anthropology* (Chicago: Aldine Publishing Company, 1964) pp. 171–180.

Smelser, M. J. *The Sociology of Economic Life* (Englewood Cliffs, New Jersey: Prentice-Hall Inc., 1963).

Tucker, W. T. *The Social Context of Economic Behavior* (New York: Holt, Rinehart and Winston Inc., 1964).

Readings covering selected aspects of the operational milieu will be found in

Cohen, Y. A. *Man in Adaptation: The Cultural Present* (Chicago: Aldine Publishing Company, 1968).

Deutsch, K. W. "Integration and Social System: Implications of Functional Analysis," in P. E. Jacob and J. V. Toscana, eds. *The Integration of political communities* (Philadelphia: J. B. Lippincott Co., 1964).

Hall, E. T. *The Silent Language* (New York: Doubleday and Company Inc., 1959).

Hall, E. T. *The Hidden Dimension* (New York: Doubleday and Company Inc., 1966).

Isaac, E. "The Act and the Covenant: The Impact of Religion on the Landscape," *Landscape*, Winter 1961–2, pp. 12–17.

Johnson, H. M. *Sociology: A Systematic Introduction* (New York: Harcourt, Brace, and World, Inc., 1960).

Kroeber, A. L. and Kluckholm, C. *Culture: A Critical Review of Concepts and Definitions* (New York: Vintage Books, 1952).

Sahlins, M. D. "Culture and Environment," in *Horizons of Anthropology*, op. cit., pp. 132–147.

Salter, C. L. *The Cultural Landscape* (North Scituate, Mass.: Duxbury Press, 1971).

five

Some Models of Natural and Human Milieux

Geography in recent years has been enriched by a number of theories and models that, although they do not deal explicitly with the phenomenal-operational-behavioral system discussed in chapter 4, are of great help in understanding it. In particular, they demonstrate that, no matter how specialized the topic, human geography, including human economic behavior, both can and must be studied as one field, not a conglomeration of separate fields.

Zimmermann's Functional View of the Resource Process

A number of investigators have analyzed the **resource process,** that is, the means by which the landscape's resources are recognized and utilized by a society, and have come up with various interpretations. Some have taken a cultural view, others an economic one; most, however, stress the human side of the process, since in the final analysis everything depends upon the characteristics of the people themselves. Among these characteristics an important part will be played by population size and age structure, by the society's level of technical knowledge, and by the ordinary working man's desire for material betterment and willingness to make the sacrifices necessary to attain it.

The model of Erich W. Zimmermann is an attempt to conceptualize a functional interaction between man and his physical environment. By calling resources functional, Zimmermann means that they are "inseparable from human wants and capabilities." Thus natural conditions are essentially neutral material into which man as it were drives a wedge of culture. In so doing man converts some aspects of this neutral material into resources, but at the same time he meets with what Zimmermann terms "resistances."

Figure 27 is an attempt by Zimmermann to illustrate a simple relationship between man and the physical environment at a relatively low level of socioeconomic development. Aspects of this environment that are used in the satisfaction of man's wants and needs can be called "resources," and aspects that harm or hinder him can be called "resistances." The extent of basic want satisfaction is a function of resources and resistances, not just of resources. Man at this level is swamped by his environmental surroundings and impinges on them very little. Since he is unaware of so much, he is capable of only limited evaluation and appraisal. In fact, he sees only that small portion of the environment with which he comes in direct contact in order to satisfy his simple needs. In the same way, the resistances of which he is aware are the ones that impinge on him directly. Because of his low level of development, they are often difficult to overcome. For the same reason, population growth is static or nearly so.

Thus in figure 27 man is linked with environment in a simple feedback system. Man is shown to have certain basic wants or needs that he can satisfy only to the extent that his native physical and brain power allows him to see and utilize certain objects in the natural environment—berries, fruits, game, perhaps timber for shelter. Thus there is a link from $a+$ to $b+$, and also from $b+$ to $a-$, since these resources satisfy his basic wants. At this level the physical environment impinges on man more directly, creating resistances, $b-$, that have to be overcome in order to

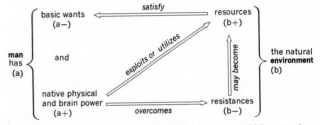

Fig. 27. *Dynamic interrelationship between man and his natural environment at relatively simple socioeconomic levels. (Reprinted by permission of Harper and Row, from Erich W. Zimmermann's* Introduction to World Resources, *edited by Henry L. Hunker, 1964, p. 16.)*

realize certain resource potentials. Of course there are other resistances, such as disease, that man at this societal level is barely equipped to tackle. In general, this type of relationship between man and his natural environment can be described in fairly simple terms: satisfaction of basic needs or wants is a "function" of resource evaluation and resistances.

By increasing use of his intelligence, however, man ceased to play a passive role. He learned to light fires, build shelters, use tools, domesticate animals, and many other things. Each of these innovations represented a major gain in adaptability. It is important to note that many of man's so-called natural resources are not natural in the strict sense. Very few usable elements of the natural environment are offered directly to man; most of them are accessible only after various obstacles have been surmounted. Most resources are the result of slow, patient research. Thus coal or iron ore are found in the natural environment; some coal seams do outcrop directly, and there are minerals called native ores that can be beaten or flexed while cold. But the amount and variety of such easily accessible materials are very small indeed. Man must first be capable of devising methods to extract ores, and then of producing very high temperatures to smelt them. He must also create an institutional and political system capable of organizing the exploitation and distribution of such products.

Figure 28 illustrates a more advanced socioeconomic level, and therefore a much more complex relationship between man and the environment. Man has here freed himself from direct contact with natural forces; they no longer control him in the way shown in figure 27. Man now affects and changes his environment; he is capable of quite complicated evaluatory abilities. This more complex relationship cannot be divorced from the value system, technical system, and level of socioeconomic organization because it is through economic, cultural, and technological developments that resources become available. The concept of resources is functional, that is, inseparable from human wants and capabilities. Zimmermann pictures this very complex relationship as a spearhead driving ever deeper into the physical environment and converting ever more of it into resources. As a result of feedback, more complex resistances are also created. Man's wants and abilities, his demands and capabilities, now interact to produce the socioeconomic complex shown in figure 28. This complex is not static, but is constantly developing with man's values and technical systems.

Resources, then, are dynamic in the sense that they increase as knowledge increases. They are also responsive to changes in individual wants and social objectives. They change in response to peace or war, capitalism or communism, conservation or expansion. They change as groups become more complex— for example, as labor force composition changes from predominantly unskilled to predominantly skilled. Many aboriginal inhabitants of North America lived in a harsh environment. For them there was no iron ore, oil, or coal. Water power went unused; agriculture was minimal and crude. Both social structure and food production methods combined to keep the various tribal groups small and mutually hostile. Yet this is essentially the same environment as North Americans now live in. Most geophysical processes of change are too slow to have much visible effect over that period of time. Yet as we look backward at human development since the first European colonists landed, the resources appear to have changed. For example, the Rocky Mountains were once barriers to several levels of economic organization. Now, on the contrary, they appear as a tourism resource.

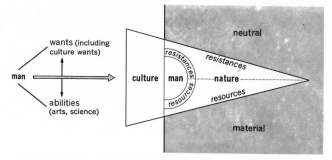

Fig. 28. *Dynamic interrelationship between man and his natural environment at more advanced socioeconomic levels. (From Zimmermann 1964, ibid., p. 17; see fig. 27.)*

In short, as Zimmermann says, "resources *are* not, they *become.*" The progression from the simple functional relationship shown in figure 27 to the far more complex one in figure 28 is one way of illustrating this fact. The resources of any one society at a given time represent an evaluation, through the behavioral environment, of the physical environment at that point in time. Thus the entire resource picture is liable to rapid change.

Kirk's Decision Model

Human communities, and individuals within those communities, are constantly confronted by problems concerning their particular environments. As a result, they are continually making decisions that have geographic consequences. To illustrate this, W. Kirk set up a device based on his earlier gestalt framework, where the social and physical facts of the phenomenal environment are shown to reach the decision maker only after they have penetrated a highly selective filter of values, as shown in figure 29. Clearly, facts which do not enter the perceived milieu of a group have no direct relevance to their decision making behavior, although they may ultimately affect the long-term impact on the landscape.

To further illustrate this point Kirk constructed a simple decision making model (figure 30). He assumed that there were three groups of communities — *A, B,* and *C*. Since this is a model, certain initial assumptions have to be made: that the groups enjoy some measure of equilibrium, and that there are no stresses or conflicts within their behavioral environment. Then the equilibrium fails, whether from an increase in total population without an expansion of the food base (the Malthusian situation), or from social or technical innovations that lead to a reappraisal of the environment (the introduction of the plough in agriculture, or the formation of a powerful elite and a subservient peasantry). It could also fail

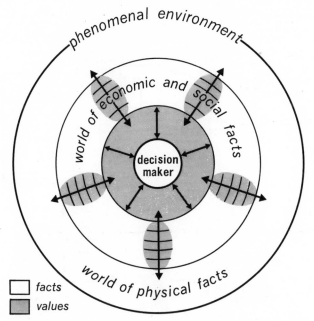

Fig. 29. *The behavioral environment of a decision maker. (Adapted from Kirk 1963, p. 367, reprinted by permission of the editors of* Geography.*)*

facts

values

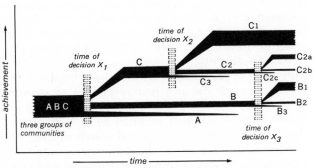

Fig. 30. *Decision making through time and at various levels of achievement. (From Kirk 1963, p. 369, reprinted by permission of the editors of* Geography.*)*

because of the exhaustion of a traditional resource. Whatever the cause, some change occurs that introduces the need for a major decision. (X_1).

Group *A* is not aware of the change. In other words, the change has occurred in the phenomenal environment, but it has not impinged upon the group's behavioral milieu. Accordingly, no conscious decisions have been taken. In a way this has the same result as the least satisfactory decision on our preference scale. Eventually, the conflict within the behavioral environment acts against the group, and it does not survive.

Group *B*, however, recognizes the problem and decides to do something about it. The group chooses, within the constraints of its value system and its incomplete knowledge, a solution that it finds "good enough." But the decision turns out to be wrong: the group does not raise its level of achievement, finding instead that the new situation is working against it. Nevertheless, unlike group *A*, it somehow survives, and so is confronted with a second major decision (X_3). At this point a number of things can occur: having learned from its earlier mistakes the group can make a satisfactory choice leading to improvement and extension of its economic activities (B_1); it can make a less than satisfactory choice and go on as before or die out (B_2); or, like group *A*, it may not be aware of this latest change, and either continue in ignorance, surviving by chance, or die out (B_3).

Group *C*, however, not only perceives the change at X_1, but finds a more than merely satisfactory solution, through which it is able to enter a phase of rapid progress and economic expansion leading to a higher overall level of achievement. Having moved through one learning situation successfully, the group is able to perceive environmental problems that previously escaped it. New stimuli, unperceived by groups A and B, can permeate the value filter of group C. Again, there is a time of choice (X_2). Through experience and learning—or perhaps just by chance—the group may choose the near-optimal solution, and achieve an even higher level of socioeconomic progress (C_1). Or it may reach a less than satisfactory decision that allows it to survive, but at the same level of economic activity (C_2). Finally, the decision may be not only unsatisfactory but disadvantageous, so that the group does not survive at all.

Group *C*—or C_2, as it is now called—may itself react at another time of decision making, X_3, as reached by group *B*. Again, there are three possibilities: an advantageous decision (C_{2a}); a less than satisfactory decision that nevertheless results in survival (C_{2b}); and a disadvantageous decision that results in nonsurvival (C_{2c}).

This is, of course, a *model*, that is, an abstraction from reality. The model holds constant such processes as **diffusion,** not to mention the chances of one group overwhelming another one by force. But despite these oversimplifications it reveals some of the results of actual geographical processes. In particular, it shows how variations in perceptual and decision making ability, combined with chance, can lead initially similar groups in similar phenomenal environments to eight or nine different types of socioeconomic outcomes. Above all, it reminds us that behind almost any sign of economic activity, especially fixed features such as roads, crops, or communities, lies a whole series of decisions as to where that activity should take place.

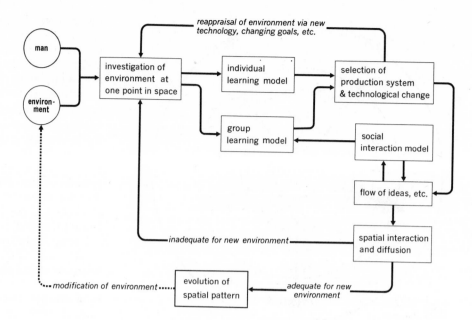

Fig. 31. *A synoptic model system: the evolution of spatial patterns. (From D. W. Harvey, "Models of Spatial Patterns in Human Geography," 1967, p. 596, reprinted by permission of Methuen and Co.)*

Harvey's Synoptic Model

Economic decisions are constrained by cultural experience. Thus Carl Sauer has stated that culture *is* a group's learned traits, formalized as conventional activities and symbols. These traits originate at a particular point in time, and gain acceptance over time. Acceptance is limited, both spatially and temporally, only by the presence of adverse conditions or alternative traits.

Harvey has attempted to conceptualize this evolution of spatial patterns by means of the model shown in figure 31. In this no one part is more important than another; a change in one part reverberates throughout the system. Thus a change in technology or aspiration level will cause a reappraisal of the environment, and so change the spatial landscape patterns.

Harvey begins by examining the position of a decision maker operating under conditions of uncertainty and ignorance, and trying to work out a production system that will insure his survival. Such an individual may devise a system that is satisfactory and yields a living above subsistence level, but he will not usually search further than this. In fact, any environment can be used for a number of production systems. But they will not all satisfy the producer in the same way; the solutions will range all the way from less than satisfactory to optimal, as illustrated in figure 32.

Harvey goes on to envisage a process in which the individual producer will search the environmental production systems until by chance or otherwise he hits on what is to him a satisfactory solution (figure

33). This search will, through time and experience, yield a great deal of knowledge about the environment and its productive systems. The choice made at any particular point in time thus becomes a function of previously accumulated experience and knowledge. The entire process can be described in terms of a **stochastic** learning model that leads to the selection of a satisfactory production system in the face of uncertainty.

By itself of course, this is a simplistic notion; learning and search are not just responses to environmental stimulation. The group's organizational and technical skills are just as vital; so is technological change. Nor is the learning and search process confined to isolated individuals. Rather, it is undertaken by group members with particular spatial and visual information fields, both public and private, and with varying abilities to use that information. A group of individuals searching for a satisfactory production system, within the same environment, with the same values and goals, and with perfect ability to receive and transmit information, would, if one producer found a satisfactory solution, adopt it unanimously—provided there were no effect upon the condition of the environment. However, if the environment were affected—through a price change for example—then adoption of that one solution would necessarily prevent the others from following suit. Adaptive behavior is exhibited over time, and the order in which the various alternatives are discussed will largely determine the decisions made.

To the components enumerated above must be added that of space. Individuals or groups do not exist in isolation at one point in space, but as part

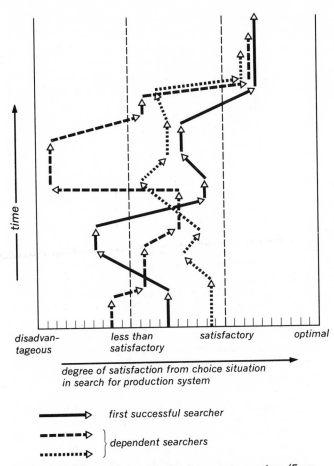

first successful searcher

-----▷ }
.......▷ } dependent searchers

Fig. 32. *Random search for a production system over time. (From Harvey 1967, ibid., p. 594; see fig. 31.)*

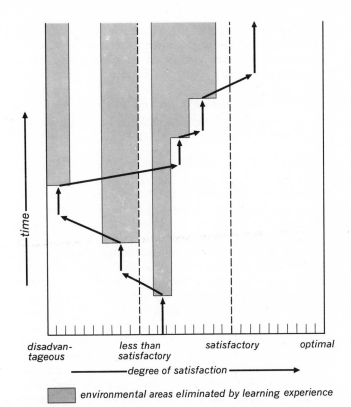

environmental areas eliminated by learning experience

Fig. 33. *Search for a production system over time, with recognition of unsatisfactory production systems. (From Harvey 1967, ibid., p. 594; see fig. 31.)*

of a spatial pattern. Individual points are linked by flows of ideas, goods, people, and so on (compare figure 31).

Thus man's behavior is determined neither by his physical environment, nor by his rationality. Rather, all his actions contain an irreducible element of uncertainty. Man seeks a course of action that is "good enough," but not necessarily the best in terms of economic rationality. Behavior is constrained by the learned abilities of the individual, on the one hand, and by the components of the operational milieu, on the other. In the real world we never have complete information at one time; our decisions are a probabilistic amalgam of choice, calculation, perception, and chance.

Pred's Behavioral Matrix

Another contemporary economic geographer who rejects the concept of economic man is A. Pred. Instead, he has tried to devise a model that repre-

sents man as a creature with imperfect knowledge and fallible rationality.

Adoption and Adaption

Pred began by examining the ideas of A. A. Alchian and C. M. Tiebout. Alchian has suggested that instead of using a world of perfect information as our basic assumption, we should begin with a world in which there is no information whatsoever, and then work out the implications. What happens is that certain ways of organizing resources are adopted purely by chance, while others are rejected in the same way. As we have seen, the technical term for a way of organizing resources is a **firm.** What happens if Alchian's assumption of "perfect" non-information is slightly relaxed? If the first information a firm receives is about the success or failure of other firms, then the system will be characterized by a great deal of imitative behavior. But since not even the little available information will be perfect, innovation and change will take place unintentionally. Clearly, we have to assume that firms would have more information than just the bare facts of each other's success and failure. But, according to Alchian, it need not be much more before this hypothetical system begins to approximate reality. The characteristics of the system are:

1. *Economic activities are adopted by chance.*
2. *Such activities rationally adapt themselves to the system or environment.*

Thus there are two processes at work: *adoption* and *adaption.* Particular practices, activities, or locations are said to be adopted by chance because the decision makers in question are acting with imperfect information, or with no information, or without perceiving the information available. Adaption, on the other hand, is as rare as economic rationality itself. Normally, the most that can be hoped for is that environmental or societal conditions may be such that these decisions do not clash with the environmental system in a negative way. Also relevant here are the concepts of success and unsuccess. Thus a successful adoption would be a chance positive relationship with the environmental system; unsuccessful adoption the chance selection of an unsuitable act or location; successful adaption the satisfactory positive outcome of rational choice (the same, in fact, as successful adoption), and unsuccessful adaption a less than satisfactory choice.

To sum up: Alchian's original formulation, although it is a great improvement on the models it is intended to replace, is of limited use as an explanatory tool, since it does not tell us a great deal about the "information condition" of each choice or act, nor about the individual's or group's receptivity to such information.

The Behavioral Matrix

Pred has overcome some of the deficiencies of Alchian's model by suggesting that each decision—by which he means a decision that produces clear, abrupt, and substantial change in some nonroutine problem-solving situation—should be interpreted in terms of information level. In Pred's **behavioral matrix** a decision making situation is depicted as a function of the quantity and quality of *perceived* information available in an environmental situation, and of the individual's or group's ability to use such information (figure 34). Each matrix is in turn a function of the environmental system, since this governs both the availability of information and the perception of its usability.

It should be emphasized that Pred's matrix is intended only as a heuristic device, that is as something that leads to the discoveries that will replace it. In fact, our state of knowledge about communi-

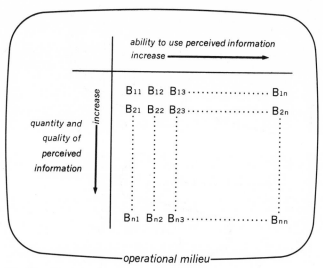

Fig. 34. *The behavioral matrix. (Adapted from Allen Pred,* Behavior and Location, *1967, p. 25, by courtesy of the Department of Geography, Royal University of Lund, Sweden.)*

cations and decision making are not advanced enough to measure so complex a process in any environmental situation. The following observations may be made about this device:

1. *The position of a person on this matrix represents his perceived information, and his ability to use it. This distinction must be made because, while motivation is one of the factors affecting the decision maker's ability to use information, empirical studies have shown that the decision maker's own perception of his decision-influencing motivations either may or may not accord with his actual motivations.*
2. *The matrix represents one point in time and space.*
3. *The decision makers are boundedly rational satisficers—or, in other words, no person could fall into cell B_{nn} (perfect knowledge, perfect ability to determine an optimal solution).*
4. *Each matrix is unique in its degree of information availability and perception, by virtue of a particular operational milieu.*
5. *Roughly the lower half of the matrix (especially the lower right-hand corner) corresponds to "adaptive acts," and the upper half to "adoptive acts."*

Variations in Quantity and Quality of Information

Both the quantity and quality of information available at any one time depend on certain attributes of the operational and behavioral milieu of groups. The existing technological system dictates what communications systems are to hand to disseminate information. The institutionalization of relationships controls the ease or difficulty of paths and flows of information. Theoretically, each group or individual should be surrounded by a circular array of information that decreases as distance from the center increases (figure 35). But such determinants of social contact as group relationships, kinship ties, or religious affiliation can introduce irregularities into an information flow. Thus the ratio of potential information to actual information will vary from group to group. Well-established public information systems encourage the dissemination of information through urban areas. But how an individual simplifies and modifies even these sources of information (if they exist at all) will depend on his learning situation and perceptual abilities, which in turn are bounded by his operational situation. These contexts govern whether the information is recognized at all, whether its content is deemed relevant, and whether any binding action is undertaken. Learning or past experience plays a role in determining whether the information accords with past situations, or whether it is part of a trial-and-error situation.

Variations in the Ability to Use Information

Whether or not a piece of information produces a positive action depends on a number of conditions. The aspirations, goals, and values set by a particular culture may reduce or enhance the likelihood that people will respond to a particular stimulus or piece of information. The cultural milieu of a particular group may set very high or very low threshold levels of utility or achievement. It may discriminate against failure, or favor the continuance of habitual and traditional practices. As a result, new information, although perceived, may not be acted upon. Group norms provide guidelines and scales of reference for such situations. They are usually backed up by sanctions, prizes, or rewards, which vary from group to group.

If uncertainty is reduced, the ability to use information is affected. Almost any decision making behavior is likely to take place with incomplete information. The reliability of communication channels may also vary over time and space. But if previously learned behavior is successfully repeated, or some prestigious other successfully imitated, then the decision maker is likely to gain emotional reassurance, at the very least. Uncertainty can also be reduced by gaining reassurance from the values, norms, and goals held by the group and institutionalized into various patterns of action and behavior. Other cultural criteria may also be important here: the values that form part of an individual's personality structure, constraints (whether real or imagined) stemming from the political system, and in general

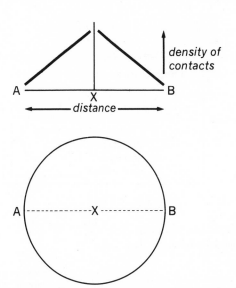

Fig. 35. *An information field. The circular decay of information with increasing distance from the individual.*

any cultural mechanism that appears to mediate between the individual and reality.

Brookfield's System Model

An approach similar to Pred's is that of H. C. Brookfield, who developed a simple system model. Like Pred's behavioral matrix, this model is intended as a heuristic device. Indeed, there are many difficulties in applying any such device directly to individual or group behavior, largely because of problems of measurement. At the general level, however, the model is highly suggestive.

The simplest version of Brookfield's model consists in a man-environment system at the local level. This is an open system, which means that it is influenced by other local systems, and by energy exchanges within the phenomenal environment. Within this system there are a number of subsystems. They represent the technological and cultural aspects of the society; the action sybsystem; the phenomenal environment; the behavioral or perceived environment; and the operational sybsystem, which affects the other three subsystems mainly through the decision making process (table 14). It will be noticed that there are separate boxes for the perceived environment and the objective environment. This is because, however much they may come to resemble each other, they remain separate and distinct. The difference is an important one, since even though the objective environment may in time become a largely human creation—in which case we call it the phenomenal environment—it is only the perceived environment that is always and

Table 14. *Brookfield's Man-Environment System*

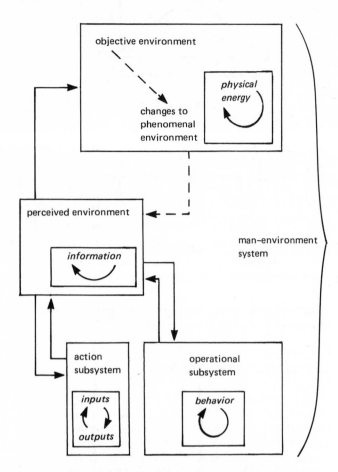

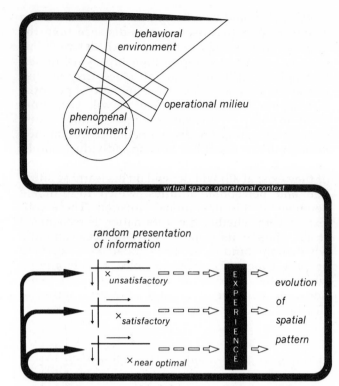

Fig. 36. *Frame of reference for economic behavior and its impact on the landscape.*

wholly a cultural artifact. Hence changes in the perceived environment may take place without any corresponding changes in the objective environment, and vice versa. Having described the elements of Brookfield's model, we can now proceed to apply it—though only in a tentative way, of course. Let us imagine a group moving into a new environment (table 15). It has a given stock of technological, institutional, cultural, and political means and a given set of imparted information (1A). Thus it can assess the objective environment to produce an initial perceived environment (1B). Such an assessment adds to the group's stock of information, and so provides a basis for decision making. The decisions in turn produce results that, if perceived, will be evaluated to modify future decision making (1C–2A). If there were no changes in its objective environment, means, information, or (we must add) population, the societal system represented in table 15 would achieve a steady state. If there were no further modification of the perceived environment, a virtually closed system would result. As Brookfield points out, this would be rare historically, though

palaeolithic society may have come close to this model, and a number of so-called primitive groups, especially in Africa and South America, still exhibit features of it. Usually, however, the various system components are subject to change. The objective or phenomenal environment changes as a result of the removal, destruction, disturbance, or addition of elements—all through the agency of man. The means that man has to hand vary through technological innovation, whether native or imported, and may be lost through disease, natural disaster, or warfare. The society's needs may vary with its population size and composition, living standards, social requirements, wealth, external demands, and physical resources. Both the quality and the quantity of information may vary, as new information is generated within the system through discovery or innovation, and new means, such as compulsory education, arise to distribute it. Changes in the rate of population growth will affect all these needs and demands. Finally, the system itself may grow larger or smaller, or change its relationship with other systems.

Brookfield, like Pred, has made it clear that the distinction between objective and perceived reality is a very useful one. It is not enough to relate human decisions to the objective environment alone, just as it is unrealistic to ignore the objective environment altogether. The perceived environment, the

Table 15. *Sequence of Events in Changing Societal System*

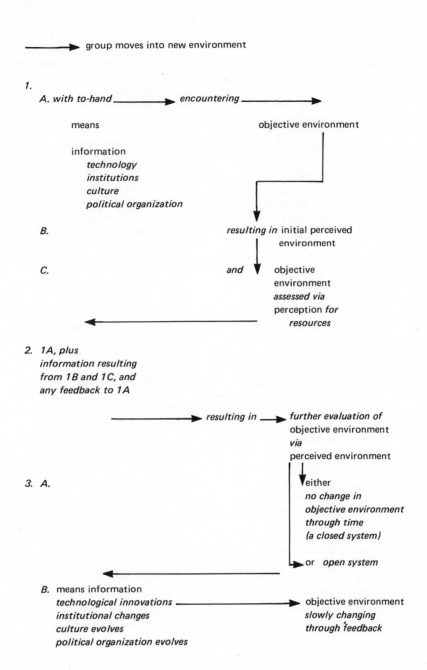

operational subsystem, and the phenomenal environment all contribute to the total man-environment system.

Conclusion

The concepts and principles introduced in this chapter can be linked with the phenomenal-operational-behavioral system (for which see chapter 4) in order to form an overall frame of reference for the chapters to come. Figure 36 tentatively depicts that frame of reference. With its help, and with the other conceptual tools developed in these first five chapters, we can now proceed to look at the behavioral-economic contexts of the resource, agricultural, manufacturing, tertiary, and transportation subsystems of the economic system.

Summary

1. A number of models exist in geography, which, though not explicitly dealing with the geographic environment and its three components as set out in chapter 4, may be used as aids to making these new conceptions more tangible.

2. The simplest of these is Zimmermann's functional view of the resource process. Landscape appraisal (the phenomenal environment) is seen from this viewpoint as a function of a particular cultural, political, technical, and economic relationship (the operational milieu), and as a function of human wants and capabilities. This conceptualization involves a dynamic element, in that the appraisal of resources varies with the changing cultural and economic beliefs and conceptions (behavioral milieu) of a people in a particular area.

3. In his decision model, Kirk postulates the existence of three groups or communities which encounter a moment of problem solving. While some groups are aware of the information presented by the environment and can perhaps make a "satisfactory" choice, others may not even perceive the problem presented. Those who perceive the choices available learn by experience from the outcomes of particular decisions.

4. Harvey's synoptic model begins with the decision maker operating under conditions of uncertainty. By a combination of chance, search behavior, and learning processes, a "satisfactory" outcome is reached. To this basic frame Harvey adds cultural attributes, group values, technical abilities, and spatial factors, so that the final patterns seen in the landscape are a comination of probabilities, perceived opportunities, and cultural constraints.

5. Pred details some of the factors influencing decision making behavior by reference to Alchian's concepts of adoptive and adaptive acts and to his own "behavioral matrix." Adoption and adaption distinguish between chance survival and deliberate, intendedly rational choices which fit into the environmental system. The matrix goes further and details the actual "information conditions" available at the time of decision, and the ability of the individual or group to utilize that perceived information. Availability of information is controlled by such factors as perception and by elements of the operational milieu like technology and institutions. Ability to use information again rests on perception and various factors of the cultural subsystem such as group values, norms, and aspiration levels.

6. Finally, Brookfield's simplistic local-level system model is examined. The man-environment system is divided into distinct subsystems like the objective environment (phenomenal), the perceived environment (behavioral), and the needs, demands, and techniques which are available to a group (operational milieu). Viewing this as predominantly an open system, the changing relations among its components can be examined.

7. It is possible to link these concepts together, as in figure 36. This frame of reference for economic behavior is in part our guide to the various components of the economic system examined in the rest of the book.

Further Reading

These five models can be examined in their original contexts in

Zimmermann, E. W. *Introduction to World Resources*, edited by H. L. Hunker (New York: Harper and Row, 1964).

Kirk, W. "Problems of Geography," *Geography*, vol. 48, 1963, pp. 357–371.

Harvey, D. "Models of Spatial Patterns in Human Geography," in R. J. Chorley and P. Haggett, eds. *Models in Geography* (London: Methuen, 1967), chapter 14.

Pred, A. *Behavior and Location*, part 1 (Lund: C. W. K. Gleerup Ltd., 1967).

Brookfield, H. C. "On the Environment as Perceived," *Progress in Geography*, vol. 1, 1969, pp. 51–80, especially pp. 62–67.

six

*Agricultural Systems:
An Overview*

Introduction

Primary economic activity was defined in chapter 2 as including "agriculture, forestry, fishing, the extraction of minerals, and, in general, the exploitation of energy resources." In short, primary activity is concerned with natural resources. Since, as we have seen, a resource becomes one only when it is recognized as such by some human group, natural resources—the basic elements of the physical or phenomenal environment—can be regarded as a slowly changing "stock" that includes both known and unknown factors. This stock is separate from but linked to human and cultural resources. Human resources are people, viewed both quantitatively, as manpower, and qualitatively, as possessing certain skills and other desirable attributes. People become resources when they are forced to sell their labor on the market in order to survive. Cultural resources are the means by which an attribute is expressed or made known; they can be divided into **hardware,** such as tools and artifacts, and **software,** such as beliefs and attitudes. Figure 37 suggests that all these kinds of resources are linked in a complex feedback system. In other words, both resources and primary economic activity lie in a sociocultural frame of reference, since both exist for the satisfaction of certain human needs.

It is no part of this book's purpose to catalogue the world distribution of natural resources or sites of primary economic activity; such catalogues can be found in any good economic atlas. Rather, its purpose is to develop useful generalizations concerning production, consumption, and technological trends by examining part of each subsystem in some

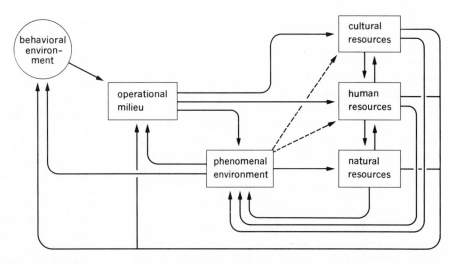

Fig. 37. *Elements of a resource system which interact to produce the three most commonly used meanings of "resource."*

detail. In the case of primary activity, this approach is definitely remedial. Thus although the literature on mining, fishing, and forestry is extensive, there are very few articles or books that deal with other than specific commodities, such as oil, or specific producing areas, such as the Middle East. Attempts at an integrated body of theory dealing with the location of these primary activities have not yet appeared. This is not to dismiss lumbering or fishing as unimportant in themselves. But compared with agriculture they are intellectually underdeveloped areas. Accordingly, this chapter and the next examine agricultural activity sites as part of the primary activity subsystem.

Agriculture is the science or art of cultivation; here, "cultivation" includes both the planting of crops and the tending of animals. An agricultural system is a set of interrelated elements, including the elements through which cultivation takes place, that is functionally related to natural resources and to the total economic and cultural systems in such a way as to satisfy the society's elementary biological needs (figure 38).

Agriculture is one of man's oldest activities. Although enormous technological advances have been made since the first crops were harvested, the basic agricultural processes have remained the same. Moreover, man still depends on agriculture as heavily as he did in neolithic times. Despite the rising significance of secondary, tertiary, and quaternary economic activities, agriculture still employs most of the world's labor force. About 60 percent of the world's gainfully employed workers are in agriculture, while 15 percent are in manufacturing, 15–17 percent in trade and services, and the remainder in forestry, fishing, and mining. These are

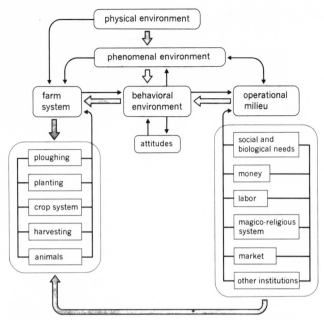

Fig. 38. *The agricultural subsystem. The factors involved in the development of the agricultural landscape, including the needs of society, values and attitudes, and the constraints of the physical-phenomenal environment.*

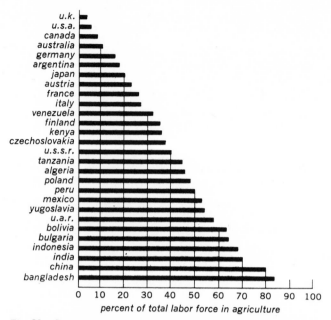

Fig. 39. *Proportion of the labor force employed in the agricultural sector. (Based on data in the* United Nations, Yearbook, *1964.)*

averages for the whole world, of course; the proportion engaged in agriculture does vary a great deal from country to country (see figure 39).

Just as the percentage of the labor force employed in agriculture varies over the earth's surface, so do a number of related factors: the contribution of agriculture in the society, and level of agricultural technology. Moreover, very primitive and very advanced technology can exist side by side, even in the same society.

Primitive agricultural technology is characteristic of subsistence economies. Many of the world's so-called farmers are subsistence farmers; only when their family needs have been met, and an allowance made for seed, does any surplus reach the distribution or marketing channels. Thus, a large proportion of the world's agricultural output does not enter any distribution system, let alone world markets. Moreover there are very few farmers who do not have to pay at least some taxes. Under subsistence conditions, it is only too easy to fall into debt; at best, when taxes or rent are owed the farmer may take an alternative job, often leaving the rest of the family to tend to the land.

At other levels of organization, agriculture is part of an exchange economy. In some cases this is fully commercial; the output is for sale, and final consumption may take place hundreds of miles from where it was grown. The income from the sale of these goods is expected not only to support the farmer and his family, but to bring in a reasonable

return on the capital invested in the farm, and a profit that will encourage the farmer to remain in business. If these expectations are not realized, it is common practice for the government to intervene with price supports, soil bank plans, and other forms of subsidy.

Whether agriculture is subsistence or exchange, on the whole it is an economic activity that tends to offer only meagre returns to those engaged in it. In all types of economic systems the income per capita from agriculture is much lower than in other types of economic activity. Usually, the reasons are a low capital investment per worker, small units of production, biological and climatic vagaries, plurality of products from one unit, lack of flexibility, or a long tradition of subsistence farming. Occasionally, great fortunes are made in certain lines of agricultural production, but these are exceptions.

The distinction between subsistence and exchange agriculture is also important when we consider locational factors. The locational decisions involved are very different, and lead to differences in the landscape pattern. In subsistence agriculture the operating unit as producer and consumer is the household or extended household unit, and choices and decisions are made within that context, which differs entirely from that of commercial farming.

Environmental Constraints

Viewed as an independent system, agriculture contains at least three subsystems: subsistence farming, commercial farming, and redistributive farming. Some of these subsystems can themselves be further broken down into such forms as plantation, dairying, or mixed farming, all of which are components of the commercial system. Through competition, farms in a commercial or exchange economy are interlinked. Because of their economic interdependence, the operation of each farm is a function not only of its own climate or environment but also of the climate and environment of other farms in other areas. Moreover, each farmer is competing with others not only for markets but for labor, transportation, and storage facilities. Indeed, the farmer in a market economy is in competition with far more than nature!

Nature, however, is still the main competitor—and here man seems to be winning. While he may still be limited in his agriculture practices by his relationship to the phenomenal environment, improvements in these practices are creating a new kind of relationship. To control climate, or rather to offset climatic extremes, the technological systems at certain socioeconomic levels have given rise to such varied means as irrigation, greenhouses, smudge pots, afforestation, and cloud seeding. Methods have been developed to increase productivity by using fertilizers and better techniques of working the soil. Through **hydroponics** dependence on soil is entirely eliminated. Control of the life processes of plants and animals has been achieved through improved breeding, development of hybrids, research into such basic processes as photosynthesis, and finally, control of pests and weeds through the development and manufacture of pesticides and herbicides.

Use of these methods of surmounting environmental hazards ultimately depends, however, on the attitudes of the individual farmer. Two basic attitudes can be delimited:

1. *The farmer takes a long-term view, such as an owner mindful of his family might, and is therefore more likely to practice genetic agriculture, whereby he seeks to maintain the fertility of his land.*

2. *He takes a short-term view, as might be expected of a tenant farmer who is anxious to maximize his annual return, and is therefore more likely to "mine" the soil by omitting to replace the elements removed through cropping.*

These are by no means universal attitudes or the only attitudes; for instance, the value of genetic agriculture may not be known at all. Then again, even the most conscientious genetic agriculturalist must operate within the limits or constraints set by his own knowledge. So-called scientific agriculture is often confounded by unforeseen side effects when

new elements are introduced into a farming system. Thus it is still not fully known to what extent the application of fertilizer can replace the elements removed, nor to what extent the use of various kinds of machinery upset the texture, structure, and moisture regime of the soil.

In subsistence agriculture, what the farmer receives in return for his labor depends to a large extent on the phenomenal or natural environment. Of all economic activities, agriculture is probably the one on which the phenomenal environment impinges most. Although it is no longer believed that the phenomenal environment actually determines types of human activity, it does set limits that, if they are perceived, have to be taken into account. The scientific farmer also has to deal with the phenomenal environment, but technological and genetic progress have given him at least some tools to overcome climatic extremes, increase soil productivity, and adapt crops and livestock to particular climatic (and market) conditions. Again, some limits are set within which a farmer might have to work; for example, there will probably be specific climatic conditions under which the desired crop can best grow. These limits are found only in certain areas of the world, so that there are physical limits both on the optimal area for the crop, and on whether it will grow at all. Neither type of limit is absolute or unchanging. There may be further limits on where the crop can best be grown commercially; these will nearly always be somewhere where it can be grown easily, but the cost of transporting it to the nearest market may be prohibitive.

However, as we have seen, man has had a good deal of success in pushing back environmental constraints. Thus the physical, optimal, and commercial limits change with the changing technology, as well as with man's changing motivations and perceptions. But some crops, particularly such tropical products as bananas, are very much more restricting in their demands than others. Very often a high latitude country will invest in a low latitude area to produce one of these more environmentally restricted plants for its own consumption. This is one of the ways in which plantation systems of agriculture grew up, to supply high latitude countries with such crops as bananas, rubber, palm oil, cocoa, and coconuts.

It follows that the actual distribution of crops and livestock as shown, for instance, on a map of world crop patterns, cannot be understood solely in terms of climate and other natural conditions. If that were the case, potential growth would nearly always coincide with natural growth, or at any rate could be explained solely in terms of it. It is obvious, however, that farmers in an exchange economy do not just devise strategies against nature, but are equally concerned with market conditions.

Finally, agriculture is subject to various hazards peculiar to itself. First and foremost is the weather. The size of the crop is never certain until it is about to be harvested. Figure 40 shows some of the fluctuations in yields of prairie wheat experienced over the last few decades (of course, these fluctuations were sometimes due to economic factors rather than climatic ones). Another factor to be borne in mind is the inflexibility of biological characteristics. Living things cannot be suddenly programmed to grow differently. Hence agriculture is relatively inelastic in response to changes in demand, that is, agricultural practices cannot avoid being slow in adapting to changes in the market, which itself may change very rapidly indeed. Tree crops, for example, require several years from their initial planting before they bear fruit. But in the time that the trees are maturing, the demand that initially stimulated the planting of the trees could have fallen. When this extra fruit reaches the market, the combination of falling demand and plentiful supply will mean a low price for it. But obviously the farmer cannot just stop the tree producing fruit, and it may take several years to phase this particular crop out of his production system. By that time demand may have risen again! This is in great contrast to the manufacturing subsystem, which is much more flexible and under greater direct control. Even with annual crops it is not easy to effect a sudden increase in output; unless the land is properly prepared at the right time and climatic conditions are favorable, a whole season can be lost. Thus both upward and downward adjustments of production are difficult, particularly since in agriculture fixed costs—of machines, land, labor, etc.—are usually a high proportion of total costs. These fixed costs are incurred whatever the size of the crop produced. Only in types of farming where fixed costs are relatively low, as in smallholder rubber production, does output show a rapid response to price stimuli.

Attitudinal Variations

If a farmer is to be successful, he has to do more than just react to climatic or market conditions. He has to have the motivation, perception, and knowledge to make use of some of the tools or strategies available in the economic system of which he is part. He may react strongly and develop the ability to use these tools wisely. But even the best farmer cannot see all the implications of his practices. In any case, his inability to foresee climatic or market conditions places him in a position of risk.

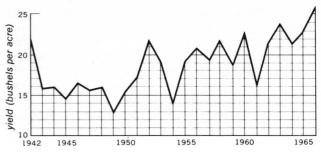

Fig. 40. *North American wheat yields. (Based on data supplied by the U.S. Department of Agriculture.)*

In what does this risk consist? The following list of factors is from J. Wolpert:

1. *Personal factors such as the farmer's health and ability to work.*
2. *Institutional arrangements such as government policy and landlord-tenant relationships.*
3. *Technological changes.*
4. *Market structure.*
5. *Physical factors such as weather, blight, and other environmental variables.*

The extent to which farmers actually take risks will vary with age, income, accumulated capital, farm size, level of education, and the society's value system. Both noneconomic and economic goals may enter into the decision, and the degree to which farmers aspire to these goals will vary with their awareness of social pressures, on the one hand, and economic pressures, on the other. For example, farmers may vary considerably in their perception of what is their lowest acceptable level of income.

Such variations of attitude among farmers have a major impact on the landscape because decision making is much more spatially dispersed in agriculture than in manufacturing. Thus even such agricultural innovations as the spread of a new harvester or strain of wheat will, because of the dispersed decision making pattern, exhibit greater variability in their diffusion patterns than will similar innovations in manufacturing. The individual farmer must make decisions with respect to crop or livestock alternatives, investment in machinery, and so on. His goals may vary along the whole range of decisions, from optimal to less than satisfactory. The information available to the farmer at the time he makes these decisions cannot include all the facts about market conditions, demands, prices, costs, or technical changes, and, as has already been pointed out, no man has access to all information. Biological and climatic processes contribute further uncertainties. Within this context of uncertainty the farmer has to make his decisions. To minimize risk, he tends to favor traditional and familiar practices that have worked before. All farmers are faced with these decisions and choices, but of course their approach to them will vary according to their motivations, both personal and economic, level of knowledge, and circumstances.

In a study of farming on the Great Plains, an attempt was made to ascertain the farmers' range of choice as they themselves perceived it. In this case, the salient environmental fact was the hazard of drought. The study dealt not with the optimal or theoretical range of choice, but rather with what to the Great Plains farmers were the practical alternatives. Some 45 percent of those interviewed felt that their present practice was the best available. Table 16 presents some of the data pertaining to those who felt they had a choice. Among the findings were that the greater the experience with drought, the lower the proportion who saw other choices possible; the greater the experience with varied crop and livestock types, the less the range of choice perceived (the data for this category do not appear in the table). Thus experience of drought, type of operation, and aridity influenced the Great Plains farmers' perception of alternative land uses. Almost half the farmers saw no choice at all.

Table 16. *Effect of Experience on Perception of Other Land Use Possibilities*

a. drought experience

months of drought experience	% who see other choices
0 - 72	63
88 - 143	45
174 - and over	57

b. type of operation

grain	63
diversified, grain emphasis	48
diversified, grain 50%	46
diversified, livestock emphasis	71

c. practical range of choice

in order of average preference:
  more grass
  other crops
  irrigation
  more grain
  more livestock
  more feed

Source: T.F. Saarinen, "Perception of the Drought Hazard on the Great Plains," Chicago, University of Chicago, Department of Geography, Research Paper No. 106, 1966, pp. 78–80.

At other socioeconomic levels, differences in technology, values, and economic methods give rise to other attitudinal variations. Unfortunately, this is a difficult area to survey because most anthropological surveys deal with economic problems only tangentially. Subsistence farmers and others till the land that is traditionally theirs to cultivate, and grow the crops they need for their customary diet and crafts. Farmers at this level can seldom choose the land they farm, the crops they grow, or the tools and facilities they use. Their motivations and attitudes stand in direct contrast to farmers at other socioeconomic levels. Subsistence farmers are uninformed about alternative methods and kinds of production; they neither perceive nor conceive of such alternatives, as they persist in their traditional and familiar patterns of behavior, even though in a given situation other techniques might be more productive. This is not to say that in all cases this would be so; under the constant threat of starvation many groups have probably evolved methods of production that approach some kind of optimum for the conditions involved.

Table 17 shows the yearly calendar of agricultural events for the Nuer, a Sudanese tribe who, though they are basically pastoral, include the growth of millet and maize in their agricultural practices. The attitude of the Nuer toward their neighboring tribes is influenced by their love of cattle and their contempt for tribes that do not have any. The calendar shows not just crop or livestock practices, but illustrates the complex interrelationships to be found in such an economic system. Taste preferences, societal and magico-religious beliefs and practices, traditions, customs, and location of settlements are all interwoven with the Nuer agricultural attitudes and practices, and with their perception, or conception, of time.

Figure 41 shows how the systems relationships also include conceptions of space. Because of these complex interrelationships, agriculture in these societies has been referred to as "a complex of farming and nonfarming activities," including fishing, gathering forest products, making simple tools, providing shelter, and other activities such as simple metalworking, ornaments, and services. Per capita incomes in these societies are low, and a large proportion of their income is spent on agricultural products. The pattern of demand is modest; it rarely goes beyond staple cereals or other subsistence foods, as shown in table 17. Under these conditions, there can be only limited savings, if any, so that the capital for further development is rarely available. But availability of resources should not be confused with motivation to use them. Adherence to traditional patterns is of course a factor, and may appear

Table 17. *The Nuer Calendar of Events*

May	June	July	August	September	October	November	December	January	February	March	April
			RAINS					DROUGHT			
		RIVERS RISE					RIVERS FALL				
				HORTICULTURE							
preparation of gardens for first millet			preparation of gardens for second millet				BURNING OF BUSH				
								FISHING			
	sow first millet	harvest maize		harvest first millet						preparation of gardens for maize	
							BUILDING AND REPAIRING				
	sow beans	sow Jack millet			harvest beans		harvest Jack millet				
											sow maize
		sow tobacco		sow second millet	harvest tobacco		harvest second millet				
	FOOD SCARCITY				FOOD ABUNDANCE				HUNTING AND COLLECTING		
	FISH AND MILK				GRAIN AND MEAT					FISH AND MILK	
				VILLAGES				CAMPS			
OLDER PEOPLE RETURN TO VILLAGES	YOUNGER PEOPLE RETURN TO VILLAGES					younger people in early camps		everyone in main dry season camps			
				weddings, initiations, mortuary, and other ceremonies							

Source: Adopted from E.E. Evans-Pritchard, *The Nuer* (Oxford: Clarendon Press, 1947, pp. 78, 83, 97, by permission of the Clarendon Press.

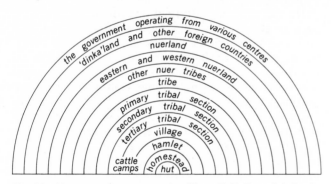

Fig. 41. *Nuer sociospatial categories. (From E. E. Evans-Pritchard,* The Nuer, *1940, p. 114, reprinted by permission of the Clarendon Press, Oxford.)*

to act as a barrier to change. But this tendency among so-called primitive peoples should not be overrated. For instance, there is evidence in Malaysia of willingness to change radically in response to income incentives very similar to those occurring at high socioeconomic levels.

Obviously, more study is needed of which cultural patterns appear to stimulate or retard agricultural production. There are indications that, over centuries of trial and error, even farmers in non-market economics have been moved by something like a profit motive. These economies look as if they are static only because they return very little in proportion to the amount of labor invested in them. Morevoer, the operational milieu itself varies from group to group. Not every group can derive the same kind of motivational return from productive effort as some Western capitalist farmers do; some may turn to what has been called **productive leisure.** This term is not very satisfactory, and so the term **status increment** is substituted in table 18.

In short, it is beginning to look as if no society's technology is so static that innovations cannot occur. It has also been pointed out that capital investment does occur in so-called underdeveloped societies, though not in forms recognized by the Western value system. It has even been suggested that these "static" societies may in the past have reached a point in their socioeconomic development that is optimal as far as they are concerned. Thus in a study of small farming in Jamaica, it was noted that the farms were technically poor, but that they did appear to represent a reasonable response to the conditions under which farming had to be practised there.

Table 18. *Summary of Systems of Agriculture in Four Basic Types of Economic Organization*

attribute	1. subsistence	2. peasant	3. commercial	4. redistributive
values	*magico-religious status increment*		*receptive, economic, and social optimizers*	*economic optimizer*
goals	*family consumption and survival*	*family consumption*	*income and net profit*	*planned production*
decision making	*arational, traditional*	*traditional satisficer*	*"rational" and choice-making*	*intentionally rational, managerial, planned*
agricultural regulator	*labor supply*	*labor supply/market*	*market*	*state*
farm input	*family labor*	*family labor*	*family – hired*	*combine*
technology	*static, traditional, nonmechanical, little innovation*	*static, traditional, some mechanization*	*dynamic and rapid innovations. mechanized*	
factor proportions and rates of return	*high labor/capital ratio low labor return*	*high labor/capital ratio medium labor return*	*low labor/capital ratio high labor return*	*medium labor/capital ratio medium-high labor return*
distribution	*deficient and imperfect*	*deficient and imperfect barter-market*	*efficient and well-developed market*	*market (planned and pre-scribed) deficient*
proportion agricultural sector in total economy	*very large*	*large*	*small*	*medium-small*

Source: S.H. Franklin, "Systems of Production: Systems of Appropriation," *Pacific Viewpoint,* vol. 6, 1965, pp. 145–166; C.R. Wharton, "Research on Agricultural Development in Southeast Asia," *Journal of Farm Economics,* vol. 45, 1963, pp. 1161–1174.

Economics of Agriculture

Land on its own is not economically productive. For it to become productive, at least one other factor has to be present, no matter what the socioeconomic level. That factor is labor. Like capital, it is an investment, or input, frequently associated with land in huge quantities—and, like capital, it is needed in different amounts according to the goal being pursued.

Labor Inputs

Labor requirements for different varieties of crops and livestock vary considerably. Table 19 illustrates this variation for one particular societal and agricultural system. It will be seen that annual labor input varies by output from 0.10 man-days per head for certain stages of poultry farming to 15 man-days per head for dairy cows, and from 0.25 man-days for grazing grass to 1,320 man-days per acre for greenhouse horticulture. Activities requiring a lot of labor are called **labor intensive** and those requiring a little **labor extensive.** Labor intensive crops tend to yield more per acre. Thus the highest yields per acre come from truck farming and from small plots such as

gardens, which are labor intensives. The best-known crop of this kind is rice grown in a wet field, or paddy, which can utilize over 4,000 man-hours per hectare per year. A family farming some 2½ acres of wet rice would have to work for about 6½ hours per day all year round in order for the crop to feed a dozen people. In contrast, in the farms of the U.S. and Canadian prairies, labor inputs are small compared to the total areas, mechanization is high, and production units large. Actual inputs per hectare are under 8 man-hours per hectare, but the ratio of actual yields to labor input is high.

The distinction between labor intensive and labor extensive practices can be made the basis for a comparison between Eastern and Western agriculture. In the East, production units—usually, the peasant and his family—have been small, and labor plentiful. Accordingly, maximum production per unit has been attained by labor intensive practices. Irrigation systems have been perfected, and whole communities organized to manage them. By such methods, two or more crops a year have been grown in the same field. In the West, on the other hand, there has been more land available for farming, but labor has become progressively more expensive. The situation has therefore encouraged the development of labor extensive practices, such as grazing beef cattle, that are prodigal of land. This in turn has meant ever larger production units and, finally, substitution of machines for human and animal power, until huge areas are farmed with very little labor input. In the East, by contrast, instead of more crops per man-hour, intensive farming aims at more crops per acre.

No crop, however, can absorb more and more labor input indefinitely. If labor inputs are increased beyond the optimal level, the return from the extra labor is zero. This statement, of course, is true by definition, but there are real-world examples of its coming true. Thus the wet-rice cultivation described above is frequently overmanned in comparison with the yields obtained.

Mechanization

A major trend at high socioeconomic levels has been that labor and land of themselves have had an ever smaller impact on the efficiency of agricultural output. In part this has arisen as technological developments and increased awareness of them have removed many of the environmental constraints. In particular, four factors have been listed as having had some effects on increases in output per unit of land and per man at these levels:

1. *Mechanization, including the shift from manual labor to horsepower, and from horsepower to mechanized power. Mechanization has speeded production, improved outputs or yields per man input, and increased the general ability of farmers to cope with agricultural processes.*
2. *A steady rise in crop yields per acre. This has been made possible by new and improved crops and pastures, increased use of fertilizers, and disease and pest controls.*
3. *Steady rises in yields per unit of livestock. New and improved stock, better management, and a shift from economically less efficient to more efficient stock have all contributed to this result.*
4. *Improvement in the general societal system. Under this head can be grouped improvements in education, health, welfare, and transportation.*

Economic growth at the higher socioeconomic levels has meant increases in agricultural output. In the United States this increase has reached a yearly rate of from 0.8 to 1.35 percent, which would double the output of each agricultural worker every thirty-two years. These changes have come about not only through technical improvements, but through the accumulation and investment of capital, and its substitution for labor and land. In this way capital can be used to better the skills and ideas of labor. It can substitute for labor through mechanization, and for land through fertilizers, irrigation, and land

drainage. Capital can also be used in association with these other production factors to widen and intensify the scope of agricultural practices.

Specialization

In chapter 2, the changing importance of various location forces was traced, and attention was drawn to the specialization of labor and areas. The changes outlined above have been accompanied by specialization within the agricultural system, and have given rise to various farming subsystems. The major factors encouraging specialization in agriculture are what are known as **economies of scale.** By specializing in only a few products, farmers can gain the advantages of larger scale production combined with increased efficiency. In other words, they enjoy better levels of output per unit of input (whether that input is land, labor, or capital) until some stage of diminishing returns is reached. Such increases in efficiency, what we have termed *economies of scale,* involve changes in the size or *scale* of the farm units involved. The changeover to mass production of a few items within one farm unit, such as "industrial" farming of chickens, is an *internal* economy of scale, because it takes place inside one production unit. It is distinguished from external economies of scale, which involve the relations between production units—for instance, when many farms of the same type concentrate in the same area in order to enjoy the same advantages of marketing, transfer, and transportation. Such external economies arise from the scale of the region's production and not necessarily or even usually from the scale of production of the individual farm unit. For example, let us suppose that there are two areas of dairy farms, X and Y (figure 42). Area X is small and isolated from other similar areas; area Y is very large. On the whole, the farmers in area Y will be better off than the farmers in area X, because they benefit by being members of a large system supplying certain processing factories. For those factories to operate economically, they need a concentration of farms, above some threshold level; they could not subsist on a level below that supplied from scattered areas like X.

Specialization can also occur with a combination of enterprises. Thus supplementary, complementary, and even competitive relationships may exist between crops and livestock. While a farmer may stress the enterprise for which he has the greatest **comparative advantage,** he may gain by adding one or more supplementary practices. Several practices may be combined because they help to maintain and boost soil fertility; for example, clovers, which are rich in nitrogen, may be rotated with cereal crops. The

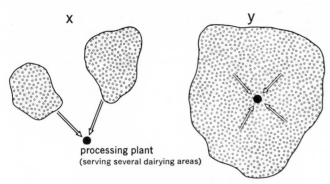

x   y

processing plant
(serving several dairying areas)

Fig. 42. *Location of farms and processing plants. A processing plant may serve several small agricultural regions or one large region.*

presence of clover may lead to the raising of livestock. These mixtures of interest must, however, be properly controlled, otherwise they are likely to increase costs. Diversification may also be used to offset the uncertainties of weather and climate, or of market conditions.

Table 19. *Agricultural Labor Inputs: England and Wales, 1964*

	man-days/acre
greenhouse horticulture	*1320*
hops	*100*
orchards with small fruits	*55*
flowers, nursery stock	*50*
small fruits	*45*
vegetables	*40*
orchards	*25*
vegetables (roots)	*21*
fodder beets and roots	*21*
vegetables (cabbage, etc.)	*20*
potatoes	*20*
sugar beet	*17*
dairy cows	*15*
vegetables (peas, beans, etc.)	*12.5*
turnips, swedes	*12*
dairy heifers	*9*
bulls	*7*
beef cows	*4.5*
oats, mixed corn	*4.5*
pulses for stock	*4*
hogs	*4*
wheat, barley, rye	*3.5*
other cattle	*3*
hay	*2*
lowland sheep, one-year-old and over	*1*
upland sheep, one-year-old and over	*0.50*
bare fallow	*0.50*
poultry, 6-months-old and over	*0.30*
other sheep	*0.25*
grass for grazing	*0.25*
poultry, under 6-months-old	*0.10*

Source: L. Symons, *Agricultural Geography* (New York: F.A. Praeger, 1967), pp. 222–223

Comparative Advantage

An agricultural area or region tends to produce those products for which it is perceived to have a special ability or physical advantage, or the least disadvantage compared with other areas. This observation is known as the principle of comparative advantage. It rests on the following simplifying assumptions:

1. *A state of pure or perfect competition exists in which there is complete flexibility of wages and prices.*
2. *Farmers are economically rational beings whose prime aim is to maximize gain and minimize loss.*
3. *Farmers have complete knowledge of all alternatives and developments.*
4. *The decisions taken on one farm do not affect the economic conditions on any of the others.*
5. *The advantages of external economies or of increases in cost do not exist.*

These assumptions are of course unrealistic, but they do allow us to detect some of the principles underlying farm location and production. It must be remembered, however, that the case examples noted below are both simplified and imaginary. In order to make them realistic, the five assumptions would have to be relaxed. As a result, however, the examples would become so complex as to disguise in large part the workings of comparative advantage. The case examples are derived from a 1966 work of R. McDaniel.

Two regions are considered: A and B. Each produces crops of wheat and garden produce. In the following table, production is shown in arbitrary units intended to reflect both labor and capital inputs. The fractions on the right denote the domestic ratio between yields, that is, the proportion of each crop produced by A and B respectively.

Case 1

	A	B	B_1	
Wheat	40	40	50	
Garden Produce	60	60	75	$\frac{2}{3} = \frac{2}{3}$

Here, the domestic ratio is the same for both producers. Even if B's yields were to rise to 50 and 75, as shown in B_1, the ratio would remain the same. Under these conditions, there can be no advantage from either trade or specialization.

Let us explore this last point in more detail. Suppose B_1 specialized in garden produce. The application of 2 composite units of labor and capital would result in the production of 150 (2×75) garden produce units. Then if *A* specialized in wheat the application of 2 composite units of labor and capital would produce 80 (2 × 40) units of wheat. If each area thus specialized, it would have to trade in order to gain the product it no longer grew. Thus in order to replace the lost production of garden produce, *A* would import 60 units from B_1 leaving B_1 with a surplus of 15 units (150 − [60 + 75]) after its own demand for 75 units had been met.

On the other hand, B_1 would take 50 units of *A*'s wheat. But after *A* had met its own demand for 40 units, there would be only 40 units left (80 − 40) to export to B_1, so that the latter would be left with a deficit of 10 units of wheat. Note that in *A*, 10 units of wheat is the equivalent of (in terms of composite units of labor and capital) 15 units of garden produce. But this is true also of B_1. Therefore, *either* *A* could produce another 10 units of wheat and trade them to B_1 for 15 units of garden produce, *or* B_1 could transfer the appropriate amounts of labor and capital into wheat, and produce its own wheat *instead of* the 15 units of garden produce. But after all this, neither *A* nor *B* would be any better off than before. Therefore, there is no advantage here in specialization of trade.

Case 2

	A	B	
Wheat	40	50	
Garden Produce	60	40	$\frac{2}{3} < \frac{5}{4}$

In this case, the domestic ratios are different. It can therefore be concluded that there would be an advantage in the two regions specializing and trading. *A* has an absolute advantage in garden produce, and *B* an absolute advantage in wheat. Therefore, they specialize in those commodities.

For 12 garden produce units, *A* will trade 8 units of wheat, these being the equivalent to the garden produce in terms of labor and capital; similarly, for 12 garden produce units, *B* will trade 15 units of wheat. There is, then, a basis for trading 12 garden produce units for from 8 to 15 units of wheat. The determination of the actual trading ratio will depend upon the **terms of trade,** that is, the conditions of demand within each region and the powers of bargaining that each enjoys.

Suppose, however, that trading equilibrium is established at the rate of 12 garden produce units for 10 of wheat. Thus *A*, which is producing garden produce, will *gain* 2 units of wheat over and above what it could produce itself for an equivalent amount of labor and capital. *B*, on the other hand, will *save* 5 units of wheat in that it produces 15 units but trades 10 for its desired amount of garden produce.

Both *A* and *B*, therefore, profit through specialization and trade, when each has an absolute advantage in different commodities desired by both. In the real world, however, these advantages are not always perceived.

Case 3

	A	B	
Wheat	40	70	
Garden Produce	60	65	$\frac{2}{3} < \frac{14}{13}$

Here again, the domestic ratios differ. However, in this instance *B* has an absolute advantage in both wheat and garden produce. But *A* has a least comparative disadvantage in the production of garden produce. Nevertheless, it can be shown that there is a mutual advantage in *A*'s specialization in garden produce and *B*'s specialization in wheat.

Case 4

	A	B	
Wheat	40	45	
Garden Produce	60	90	$\frac{2}{3} > \frac{1}{2}$

Once more, the domestic ratios differ. As in case 3, *B* has an absolute advantage in both commodities. This time, however, *A* has a least comparative disadvantage in wheat (that is, only 5 units less than *B*). But unlike the earlier cases, wheat (40 units) is not the most productive here in terms of yield units when compared with garden produce (60 units). Nevertheless, as in case 3, it can be shown that both *A* and *B* will profit if *A* specializes in wheat production and *B* specializes in garden produce.

Economic Relationships

Two sets of economic relationships interact to determine ratios of advantage of disadvantage for farming systems. The first of these can be referred to as the physical production possibilities. These are the physical inputs such as land, labor, and capital, together with their interrelationships and ultimate output. The physical possibilities themselves are influenced by the interaction of two further subsets of factors. These are land types and production functions. Land types are important because, other factors being equal, the better the physical conditions (soils, climate, drainage, etc.), the better the physical production facilities. Ultimately, this shows up as lower cost per unit of output. The other subset, production functions, consists in the physical relations between inputs and outputs—for example, how much land, labor, or capital is required to gain a unit of output of a selected good. Increasingly, these production functions are being affected more by abilities, knowledge, risk taking, and technological developments within the operational milieu, and less by land type.

The second set of relationships is that between prices and costs. Obviously, the agricultural system and its comparative advantages are affected by the physical conditions described above. But while these may greatly affect prices and costs at the farm level, marketing conditions, which are beyond the individual farmer's control, are also very important. Price-cost relations can affect the rate of technological change, as well as the farmer's final choice of what to grow and how to grow it. Few systems of production are ruled out in the Western capitalist operational milieu simply for technical reasons. Indeed, if paid to do so, a Western farmer can simulate almost any physical condition.

A number of other structural and locational conditions are important to the exchange agricultural system. The inelasticity of supply to meet changing demands has already been mentioned. But not only is supply inelastic; **inelasticity of demand** may also affect agricultural practices. A fall in the price of food does not necessarily stimulate demand to any great extent, as it does in industry. Once a person or household has attained an adequate level of diet, the reaction to a fall in the price of foodstuffs is not to consume very much more. One influential formulation of this truth is **Engel's Law,** so named after the German statistician Ernst Engel (1821–1896); it holds that as economic development proceeds and people grow richer, they spend proportionately less of their income on food, and more on consumer goods and services. The changes that do occur are mainly qualitative ones, as when the proportion of the diet composed of starch declines and consumption of proteins increases. For example, in the eighteenth and nineteenth century in Ireland, a family of six could be supported on a quarter acre of land—but it meant that each member had to consume 2.3 pounds of potatoes each day. Naturally, as the economy developed the proportion of potatoes in the diet declined. Such changes in diet particularly reflect the change in protein, usually associated with the intake of animal rather than plant proteins. Animal products are expensive, since they take more time to produce, and the process by which vegetation is converted into steak is very wasteful of calories. Animal farming can yield a high profit or return to the individual farmer, but it generally demands a favorable overall ratio of land to farmers. When land is short, the animal must either be a work animal, or one that can graze on areas useless for

crop production (a sight more common in underdeveloped nations).

To exploit the rising world demand for more protein and other dietary improvements, agricultural production has expanded both through increased production and through the opening of new areas in the New World and Oceania. These changes have also stimulated the amount of interaction between regions, which in turn has led to new means of transporting produce. One effect of improved contact has been the development of bulk carriers, cool storage, and refrigeration, which have allowed farmers to resort to ever larger and more distant sources of demand. Thus farmers in exchange economies have become increasingly influenced by urban markets, often quite distant from their farms. In addition, improved transportation, while giving the farmer access to the market economy and to new sources of technological information, has also tended to free him from the locational pull of particular urban markets, thus allowing him to select the physically best land inputs.

Such economic relationships are of course culturally determined. Thus the greatest obstacle to the transfer of American and Western European experience in agriculture to peasant or other non-Western economies is the confusion of socioeconomic attributes with technological means. Technology is at least theoretically transferable between dissimilar societies; the relative values of land, labor, and capital, are not. Thus the family farm in the United States is an example of smallholder agriculture: such farms usually have no more than a two-man labor force, supported by heavy capital investment. The underlying operational situation is of course the ability to substitute capital for labor. But this is not all. The farming operation in the United States is part of an integrated system of activities dominated either by the suppliers of inputs, or by the processing and distributing interests. The result may well be a highly efficient system from a technical point of view. But it is also one that is so completely embedded in its own operational milieu that it cannot properly be described as just another farming system. In fact, it will probably be more accurate to describe it as a part of American culture as a whole—a part that is rapidly shrinking.

Location

All agriculture necessarily takes place within an economic-spatial framework. Such **economic space** centers in exchange economies on urban-industrial nodes, which are the core areas of each economic subsystem. One of the effects of the systematic interplay between urban center and farm is the development of "industrial" or "factory" farms that produce beef and veal, or eggs and poultry, under intensive conditions. Such industrial farms normally locate in the rural-urban fringes of the major urban centers.

The conception of economic space includes that of **relative location. Centrally placed** farmers are those who can participate in the economic system in an efficient way because they are intimately tied to the system's mainstream. A kind of multiplier-accelerator effect enables them to participate increasingly in economic growth. By contrast, **peripherally placed** farmers have, for various reasons, come to participate in an increasingly inefficient manner in the mechanism of growth. This very mechanism tends to widen the gap between the extremes. A multiplier-accelerator mechanism applies to the peripherally placed groups with depressing effects. Of course, the term "peripheral" here cannot be defined in terms of any actual distance from urban centers. Rather, it refers to relative distances that vary with socioeconomic level, stage of technological development, information level, and accessibility.

Farmers can also be peripherally placed in another sense. We have already noted that, for any particular crop or livestock, there is an optimal physical location. Away from this location, production costs might rise and returns fall until eventually this particular practice would become uneconomic, although still physically possible. Such a declining **margin of profitability** may coincide with the margin that denotes increased returns from some other crop or livestock enterprise. Of course, any margin will change as the gap between prices and costs changes. If prices increase, an area that was unprofitable will become profitable. In some marginal areas, prices and costs are continually changing.

Government Intervention

In considering economic factors, government intervention also has to be taken into account. Few societies can allow their agricultural systems to function unaided by the central authorities since, despite its relative decline in importance, agricultural production is obviously a staple factor in virtually all economic systems. Government intervention or assistance may take several forms: **guaranteed prices, deficiency payments,** direct **subsidies** or **bounties,** and **protective duties** or **direct embargoes.** The government may also enter the area of land development itself. In the Western capitalist economies, agriculture is carefully nurtured and heavily pampered. In none of these areas do governments allow agriculture to stand or fall entirely on the basis of its efficiency in a free market. Even so, agricultural

incomes per capita remain lower than those in other economic activities, largely because of the farmers' inability to discharge labor quickly enough as mechanization proceeds and technical efficiency increases. The results, particularly in North America, are recurring surpluses, since products cannot be sold at prices sufficient to cover costs. The schemes of government assistance are in fact various means of transferring income from the nonfarming to the farming community. Very often these aids help the large efficient farmer most and the smaller farmer, who probably needs more help, least of all. Quite often, a high subsidy on, say, cereal production, hinders transfer of interest toward greater livestock production. Moreover, by delaying the removal of workers to nonagricultural activities, such a subsidy can in fact slow down the rate of overall economic growth within the system.

Obviously, government intervention is not confined to Western capitalist systems; it also occurs, if only by implication, in the centrally planned economies. In the latter case, however, there is a shortage, not an overabundance of supply. Russia's enormous wheat purchases in recent years make it clear that agriculture both there and in Eastern Europe is barely adequate. Among the commonly cited reasons for this are unwillingness to make large investments in the agricultural compared to the industrial sector, and wages insufficient to provide incentive for farm workers. Markups of several 1000 percent are reported on the produce obtained from the collective farm before its sale by the state. An exception to these statements would be the case of China, where a much greater emphasis has been placed on agrarian development than on industrial development, particularly since the early sixties. China is now virtually self-sufficient in foodstuffs, and in fact it has been exporting a range of products. The commune system, by its ability to mobilize large numbers of people, helped avert famine during a series of climatic hazards in 1959 and 1960; these communes operate now as integral entities determining their own production, savings, and future plans in collaboration with the state, rather than as units of a centralized state planning mechanism such as has characterized Russian agriculture.

Difficulties also occur at the lower socioeconomic levels. Frequently, as in the socialist economies, the problem is shortages. The United Nations Food and Agricultural Organization (F.A.O.) has estimated that in many countries the daily per capita calorie intake is often below the minimum acceptable level, so that although the population may not be starving, it experiences considerable hunger. In such countries a substantial increase in domestic food production is imperative. Realization of this goal is, however, extremely difficult, partly because there are difficulties in utilizing all the capital and land at the disposal of the farmer, and partly because governments often discourage peasant initiative by paying low prices for farm products, which they then dispose of at considerably higher prices. This occurs at present in many parts of South America, West Africa, and Southeast Asia.

Agricultural Structure

In the complex of social and economic relationships that are part of the agricultural system, particular structural attributes can be identified. Among the most important are farm size and layout, land tenure, and marketing. Variations in these can change the entire character of a particular subsystem or component.

Farm Size

Farm size can vary from $7\frac{1}{4}$ million acres for one unit in the Northern Territory of Australia, through 100,000 acres for many **Sovkhoz** (Russian collective farm), all the way down to units of 1 or $1\frac{1}{2}$ acres in the peasant economy of Java. Farms at this lowest extreme are frequently too small to be genuinely economic, and provide the farmer with a barely acceptable income. In North America and Western Europe, there is little doubt that many farmers on the smallest farms could earn a higher income in a nonagricultural activity. Some of these farms are so small that they cannot provide continuous employment for the farmer; for example, in Malaysia some rice farmers are underemployed for nine months of the year.

The type of farming practiced is often closely aligned to the size of holding. Most farms under five acres, for example, have little place for livestock other than poultry. In advanced economies, a farm under 100 acres will tend to specialize in dairying or truck farming, and yet may often have a margin of economic insecurity. It should also be pointed out that there are exceptions. Thus Belgium has an average farm unit size of four acres, much of it devoted to very intensive truck farming, which is profitable. In grain production, however, the existence of substantial economies of scale is one of the best established facts of modern agriculture. Despite very high grain prices, agriculture in Western Europe, where farm sizes average well above 10 acres, is faced with a persistent structural problem of scale. In Britain, commercial grain growing is heavily concentrated on farms exceeding 100 acres, and in Canada there is a strong trend toward holdings of 1,000 acres or more. Some observers maintain

that the huge size of some state farms in the Soviet Union (50,000 acres or more) is a weakness of the Soviet agricultural system. But the movement toward larger farm sizes is almost universal in the agriculture of developed countries, and the Soviet Union is no exception.

Land Tenure

Land tenure is another structural attribute of considerable significance for the agricultural system. Tenure is the institutional framework within which decisions are taken about the distribution and use of land resources. In social terms, land tenure denotes the varied relationships of man to the land. The actual structure of the framework varies from nation to nation, from subsistence to market-exchange economy. Nevertheless there are common features and relationships that make it possible to classify and compare the land tenure systems of the world. Broadly speaking, there are four basic types of land tenure: **communal tenure, latifundia, freehold,** and **tenancy.**

Under *communal tenure,* there is no individual right to land ownership; land is held on a village, group, or tribal basis, and individuals enjoy **usufruct** (the right to use and profit) simply by virtue of their group membership. It is a tenure system of some antiquity, and was once widespread in many subsistence and peasant economies. Accordingly, it has resisted absorption into a money economy. But it usually gives way to private ownership of some kind unless the government intervenes. Contemporary examples of government-sponsored communal tenure are the Russian **kolkhoz,** the Israeli **kibbutz,** the Mexican **ejido,** and the Chinese **commune.**

Also of some antiquity are *latifundia* or large estates such as are still found in Portugal, Spain, Italy, and parts of South America. In the past the latifundium used slaves and serfs. Now it generally uses wage laborers of some sort, although in the *inquilino* (tenant) system of Chile a peasant is allowed to cultivate a plot of his own, in return for working on the estate for a given number of days per week. Frequently the owner of the estate does not cultivate the area himself, but rents out small plots to the local population. Two variants of this system are the *agribusiness,* or corporate farm, of North America and the *plantation;* in contrast to the traditional latifundium, both are heavily capitalized and generally use only wage labor, under strict contract. In addition, the plantation is usually under foreign ownership.

The term *freehold* denotes virtual outright ownership by the farmer. Many freeholders own only small units; for example, in Western Europe the average is less than 50 acres, and in Asia 10 acres would be a considerable holding. In both North America and Western Europe, the freehold system is regarded as ideal from a moral and cultural point of view. But the small size of freehold units, their frequent undercapitalization, and lack of government aid often lead to inefficient or below optimum operation. Elsewhere, in Southern Europe and Asia, the system suffers from inheritance laws that require an equal division of land between all the male offspring, which obviously both reduces and eventually fragments units that are often too small already.

A system of *tenancies* occurs when farmers pay owners for the use of the land. There are many examples of this system, especially in peasant and subsistence economies; the major types are *labor*, *slave*, and *cash* tenancies. Under labor tenancy, the tenant helps the landlord several days a week in return for the use of his own plot or holding. The system is now quite rare. Share tenancy, or share cropping, is still found in the southeastern United States and in Southern Europe. In a share tenancy, the tenant pays the landlord part of the crop, usually between 30 and 50 percent, in lieu of cash. In market exchange economies, however, share tenancy is far less common than cash tenancy under which the farmer pays a cash rent for the use of the farm. In most countries the cash tenant has considerable legal protection; for instance, he usually receives compensation for improvements (which does not occur under slave tenancy), and is protected against landlord exploitation in general.

Land tenure in its broadest sense comprises *rights* over land. It therefore sets relationships with other members of the group. Because land tenure systems differ, their capacity to affect the use and distribution of resources and relationships also differs. To the extent that such systems affect the agricultural landscape different patterns will result from the different systems. Tenure rights also look at once backwards into the past and forward into the future. Some are limited to the life of the holder; others devolve upon a long line of successors. Redistribution of tenure rights upon death of the tenure holder can in some societies exert a most powerful effect upon what can and will be done with the land in the future.

A farmer's financial and economic well-being, his social habits, and his very outlook on life can be influenced by the land he holds and how he holds it. In particular, the type of tenure system may affect the operation of the farm in six distinct areas:

1. *Through its effect on management and planning over the long term.*
2. *Through the extent to which investments in the farm can be realized if necessary.*

3. *Through the extent to which the occupier is dependent solely on his own resources in exploiting the farm.*
4. *By determining how much income (money or crop) must be set aside to meet obligations in respect of rent and mortgage.*
5. *By determining preference for investment in the land as compared with investment in livestock or other movable capital, investments off the farm, or consumption.*
6. *By determining the possibility of extending or contracting operations through purchase or sale of land, or adjustment through letting.*

Marketing

Marketing arrangements can also affect the structure of an agricultural system. At least some marketing structure is nearly always necessary because sales directly from farm to consumer tend to be rare. Very often, farmers are dealing with markets too distant or too impersonal for any direct contact. Unless they can combine in some way, they are in a weak, divided, and isolated relationship with the market. The smaller farmer usually has only a limited output for sale. For this reason, he frequently has no choice but to deal through an intermediary, or middleman, who by dealing with many farmers can collect enough goods to make the use of formalized marketing channels worthwhile. The middleman's overheads are frequently high, so the charge for his services are quite high too. Moreover, since the middleman is dealing with many farmers, he can easily dictate the terms on which he will buy.

For these and other reasons, farmers have often found themselves forced to organize their own cooperative marketing systems. But these have not always been successful. Some farm products lend themselves to such schemes more readily than others. Dairying is the prime example, but eggs, tomatoes, small fruits, potatoes, cucumbers, and other kinds of produce have also been marketed cooperatively in various parts of the world. In Western Europe, cooperative dairying in particular has achieved great success; liquid milk is collected from numerous small farms and either marketed rapidly as fresh milk or processed, refrigerated, and later packaged as butter or cheese. In this latter process, both the consumer demand for a more standardized product and the high levels of government health inspection are met. In return, the cooperative can often buy farm supplies for its members in bulk at a great saving.

Cooperatives exist not only in centrally planned and Western capitalist societies, but in the developing economies too. Here, colonial governments or native administrations have often made use of cooperatives to dispose of their products on world markets. Such concerted action may serve to protect

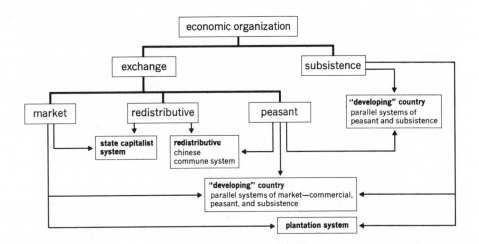

Fig. 43. *The world agricultural systems. The interrelationships of the various forms of agricultural economic organization.*

them against the wild swings in world prices that sometimes occur. Both the British and French ex-colonial territories in Africa have such organizations, which often make advances of seeds or seedlings to farmers, and help them with transport, storage facilities and even credit. They also buy the crops from the farmer, sell them on the world market at the current rate, and, if necessary, retain a surplus against the time when world prices will be higher. Such organizations exist to market coffee and palm kernels in the ex-French territories, cocoa in Ghana, Sierra Leone, and Nigeria, and cotton in Nigeria.

The existence of cooperative marketing agencies is of considerable importance to the continuance of many agricultural systems. Without them, a crop's production may be seriously curtailed. High costs from middlemen, uncertainty of markets, and fluctuating prices, can all force a farmer to abandon a particular crop or crops; through cooperatives, these hazards are avoided. In the less developed economies, such hazards could force the farmer to return to subsistence or near-subsistence practice.

The effect, then, of farm size, land tenure, and marketing on farming organization cannot be overstressed. It is obvious that these structural attributes have effects thoughout the system, and that a change in one of them can affect not only agriculture but the entire geographic and economic landscape.

Agricultural Organization

Having examined some of the structural attributes of agriculture, we can now attempt some classification of agricultural practices. The problem of classifying agricultural systems is one that has occupied the attention of a number of geographers, including E. Hahn (1882), D. Whittlesey (1936), E. Ottremba (1950–60), N. Helburn (1957), and D. Grigg (1969). It is not easy to encompass so many diverse and complicated elements within a single framework and any such classification necessarily contains an element

of compromise. For our purposes we can take the basic fourfold division of economic organization that we used in chapter 2 and apply it to the agricultural subsystem (figure 43). Within each major division of agriculture—*subsistence, peasant, market-exchange,* and *redistributive*—a number of distinctive attributes can be identified (table 18). But these distinctions are by no means clear-cut, and within each major division a number of subtypes are also identifiable.

Subsistence Agriculture

Subsistence producers consume their own output, and have a very limited division of labor. There is a relatively low differentiation of economic roles, that is, each member of the household tends to do most kinds of jobs. Moreover, there is virtually no specialization by area; each area tends to form a small, functional region of quite diverse activities focused on a single point, whether that point is fixed, like a village, or moving, like a camp. There may be some exchange, especially if a limited amount of specialization has occurred, but specialized regions or areas arising out of such exchange tend to be simple and territorially limited.

Most of these groups' resources are spent on obtaining subsistence products from the land. They have a limited stock of capital and a very limited capacity to substitute capital for land and labor; in fact, labor is the chief regulator of the subsistence agricultural subsystem. Motives, values and goals center around the household group, or around the society and its magico-religious beliefs. This is not, however, to deny the existence of quite complex economic traditions in some of these groups. But their technology is basically nonmechanical, with little or no innovation, and the agricultural complex is directed toward maintaining rather than increasing capital assets.

Within this broad grouping, a number of sub-types can be identified: shifting cultivation, pastoral nomadism, and rudimentary sedentary tillage.

The practice of periodic cultivation of an area until the yields from it fall to some minimal level is known as *shifting cultivation*. An area is cleared for cultivation, cropped until yields fall, which usually takes one to three years, and then abandoned in favor of another area. Thus a cyclical pattern is established: clear a patch of ground; let it dry; burn it over; till (usually with a digging stick); sow the first crop; sow subsequent crops the same year; repeat in the following years until yields become poor; abandon, and clear next patch. Originally, return to the original patch may take over thirty years. But as the population grows, the area for shifting becomes more restricted, and a serious imbalance occurs between population and resources. Moreover, erosion occurs as land is overworked. Technology is simple: the primary or secondary forest is cut with an axe or blade, and then fired. The return from the land in the form of maize or millet and various vegetables is only just sufficient for the household's or group's needs, and continual shifting makes overworking inevitable. The existence of the tsetse fly, which carries sleeping sickness and other diseases, together with the low returns from animals, restricts the keeping of livestock. Shifting cultivation, or slash-and-burn agriculture as it is often known, occurs in Malaya and Indonesia (*ladang*), Central America (*milpa*), Vietnam (*ray*), the Philippines (*caingin*), South America (*conuco* and *roca*) and parts of Africa (*masole*, etc.). It should be noted that, given the physical conditions of these areas, this particular system may well be the best available.

As an agricultural system, *pastoral nomadism* is primarily a subsistence appraisal of steppe and semi-steppe areas too dry for crops. It is based on a variety of animals (cattle, sheep, goats, camels, reindeer) since it occurs from the dry margins of intertropical Africa and Asia to the subarctic tundra. Limitations of water and pasture limit the stay of the herds in any one place, so that the pastoral group is always moving on. Because of this constant movement, material belongings are at a minimum, and technology is fairly simple. In recent years the movements of pastoral peoples have become restricted by the intrusion of market-commercial or redistributive livestock ranching, and by the collectivization of agriculture.

Subsistence crop combinations occur at varying degrees of intensity of cultivation. The least intensive is *rudimentary sedentary tillage*, which utilizes plots of land in rotation; as a system, it is hardly more advanced than the shifting cultivation described above. Many groups using this system have now become peasant farmers, as their contact with com-merce has led to the cultivation of such marketable crops as cacao, oil palm, and rubber. At a higher level of intensity is *dryfield* subsistence farming; it is used where lack of water restricts the growth of very high yielding cereals, such as rice. Even if the land is irrigated, the emphasis is on dry grains—maize, wheat, millet, and sorghums—rotated with soybeans, garbanzos, and so on. There is also a type of intensive subsistence rice tillage known as *sarvah*. Both types occur in South and Southeast Asia, as well as in North Africa and Mexico. Sarvah is the dominant form in the deltas, floodplains, coastal plains, and till terraces of South and Southeast Asia. Where the area is very wet, and rice is therefore most successful, it supports very high rural population densities. Rice, in fact, yields more grain per acre than any other cereal, and very high yields are regularly obtained from holdings of two or three acres through multiple cropping, intense labor input, and fertilizers.

With economic growth and the expansion of information systems, many of these subsistence groups have come into contact with other systems, and an increasing proportion of their agricultural output enters local commercial channels.

Peasant Farming

Peasant groups have been variously defined. The terminological boundaries are vague between "peasant," "subsistence," and certain smaller market-commercial farmers. In popular usage, the term "peasant" has connotations of rusticity, coarseness, and dullness. But it also implies a permanent link with the soil. Both types of connotation include an element of truth. The peasant agricultural subsystem consists of small-scale producers with relatively simple technology and equipment who tend to rely for their subsistence on what they themselves produce. In other words, the peasant is a farmer who uses his resources primarily for purposes other than exchange, though in certain situations peasants have been known to exchange up to about 60 percent of their crops. Thus the values of the peasant may differ only in degree from those of the subsistence farmer. Those values can be summed up as family consumption governed by tradition, and aiming at productive leisure. Family labor is used, but if the family is small or under certain other disadvantages, other help may be needed. Land holdings are small, both absolutely and relatively: 10 acres may be the limit in some areas, while in others it may go up to 40 acres. When found in the same environment as market-exchange holdings, peasant holdings are always much the smaller, as for example in Indonesia, Turkey, and India. They are often effectively diminished in size by fragmentation, especially outside North America and the U.S.S.R. Technology is not usually well developed among peasants, though in some instances mechanization may be present. Generally a large range of produce is grown, including cereals, vegetables, and tree crops. The ratio of labor input to capital input is still high, but because of some mechanization and the use of more complex tools and techniques, there may be a higher return than in subsistence economies. Such small-scale production has its own concomitant systems of capital accumulation and indebtedness, marketing and distribution.

The peasant economy is closely linked with a certain way of life. In peasant society, economic relationships are personal relationships; there is no such thing as a purely economic service or even a purely economic goal. Everything economic is seen in terms of the entire social situation. Thus the peasant economy is characterized by its type of socioeconomic relationships rather than a particular group of tools or economic structures.

Sol Tax has suggested that three factors differentiate peasant from subsistence economies:

1. *Land ownership and inheritance are more important to the peasant than to the subsistence farmer. Accordingly, the peasant places more emphasis on inheritance laws and is more likely to have his land fragmented as a result of division between heirs. Property, savings, and investment enter into all his calculations; he need not necessarily own the land to be concerned with it.*

2. *Domestic animals, where they are a part of the system, make man a slave to time as well as to property.*

3. *Individual motivation and competition begin. In subsistence societies, on the other hand, individual competition is secondary.*

As an example of a group of peasant farmers we may examine the Fur-speaking hoe agriculturalists of the southern Sudan. Thanks to its location on the slopes of Jabel Marra (10,073 feet), this area has perennial streams and a partly forested landscape. There is a dry season from October to May when winter crops are grown on irrigated land; during the rest of the year rainland crops are grown. The staple crop is millet grown on dry terraces but receiving summer rains; it is sown at the onset of the rainy season in May and harvested in September. Low terraces by streams are irrigated and used to grow onions, garlic and wheat. In the summer, tomatoes are also grown (they were introduced by Egyptian troops about a century ago). The impingement of nearby market-exchange economies has led increasingly to the growth of citrus, mangoes, papayas, and other fruits on these terraces. Animals are limited to the donkey as a pack animal, a few

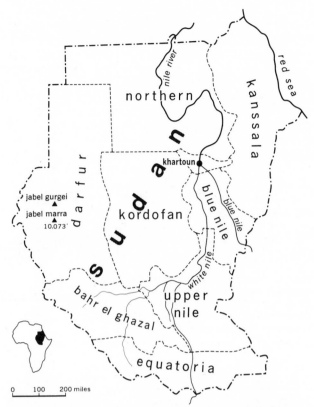

Fig. 44. *Geographic location of the Mountain Fur group (the Darfur area).*

goats, and some cattle. The latter are kept for resale; they are neither bred locally nor milked.

Four factors in the operational milieu of the Fur people affect their agricultural system:

1. *The size and composition of the households are important because economic activities are a matter of individual concern. Husband and wife cultivate separate fields, and store their produce separately. Obligations in marriage mainly concern services: the wife must provide labor, especially for cooking and brewing beer; the husband in return supplies cloth to the wife and her children. Cloth is spun and woven by men. Children are fed by their mother from her stores.*

2. *The institution of land ownership is a very loose one. Nominally, land is owned by a representative of a kin group. But all others in the kin group have usufruct rights, and land is made available to all without any significant rent.*

3. *Exchange of labor tends to be on an individual basis, for the direct satisfaction of one's own needs. However, there is a matrix of obligations and institutionalized opportunities, of which the most significant is the beer party. Any person who needs help in the fields or in building a house throws a beer party in order to get it.*

4. *The medium of exchange is the market. The marketplaces are active for one day a week each, and are so spaced around the perimeter of the mountain that no community*

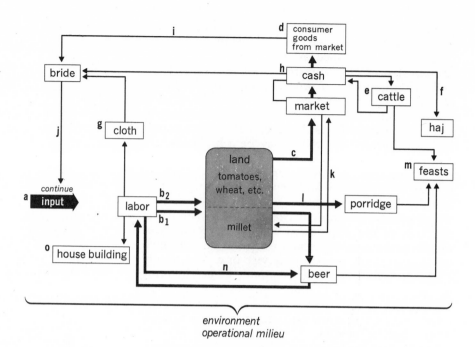

Fig. 45. *The* Fur *economic system. The pattern of standard alternative choices for an economic unit among the* Fur. *(After Frederik Barth, "Economic spheres in Darfur," 1967, pp. 149–174.)*

is farther than one day's return journey away. Millet is rarely marketed, but tomatoes, wheat, garlic, and onions, are sold for cash, as are, in some cases, cattle. The money so obtained is used to purchase goods from traveling pedlars and some local craftsmen. Among these goods are pottery, implements, imported industrial consumer goods, and sugar.

The Fur economic system is set out in figure 45. The input to the system (a) is the individual's own time, used as labor. To start production the individual needs access to land, which is obtained from a parent or close relative who is a title holder. Two alternative production systems are open (b_1 and b_2): millet and some onions for basic subsistence, which enter the exchange system only as beer (b_1), and tomatoes, or other produce, grown for cash needs (b_2). The balance between these two systems depends on individual skills and preferences, usufruct rights to irrigated land, and obligations to wives, children or husbands. Women tend to concentrate more on millet, while men, especially if they have several wives, will need more cash to meet clothing needs, bridewealth, and so on.

Tomatoes and wheat (c) are sold in the local market, and the cash is used to buy a variety of consumer goods (d)—tools, donkeys, and young cattle. Cattle rearing forms a small loop in the system: the cattle are tended by the children of the owner for several years, and are fattened for eventual resale. Only cash and manure reenter the main system, since the cattle are neither bred or milked. Some of the cash leaves the system via a once-in-a-lifetime pilgrimage to Mecca (haj-f).

The men may weave cloth for their families (g); in any case, the cotton is usually grown and spun by them. A major cash expense is bridewealth (h), including payments to the wife and her family. It consists mostly of purchasable items such as cattle, swords, and donkeys, or their equivalent in cash. For the rest of his life, the husband is obligated to provide his wife and small children with basic necessities from the market (i). In return the wife provides sex, cooking, and the brewing of beer (j).

Some individuals find they have chosen the wrong balance between cash crops and subsistence crops, but their error can be corrected in the marketplace (k). Visits to the market would also occur if in any one year an excess of millet was produced. Millet is used for both porridge and beer (l), about one-fifth of the crop going to the latter. Most of the porridge is consumed directly, but it is also used in feasts (m), along with beer and, occasionally, cattle. Feasts are given on special occasions, such as funerals and weddings. Most of the beer is consumed in the course of feasts or work parties, since it does not keep long, and has to be specially produced (n). Reciprocal exchanges of labor for house building (o) or work in the fields (b_1 and b_2) are repaid by these beer parties.

This description of a particular peasant system clearly illustrates the mutual interrelatedness of agriculture and the operational milieu. Agriculture to the peasant is both a livelihood and a way of life. He uses a relatively simple technology to raise some crops for profit in addition to his subsistence crops. In summary, we could say that peasant cultivation is still *nonscientific husbandry*, dominated by tradition. Most of the labor is provided by the peasant and his family, and most production is for home consumption.

Commercial Farming

Commercial (market-exchange) farming involves specialization of both labor and areas, as patterns of links emerge between urban centers and rural areas, on the one hand, and between the various areas of specialization, on the other. Such links occur not only between farms, towns, and cities, but also between regions, some of them separated by great distances.

As part of an exchange economy, farmers tend to maximize profits. However, they are also constrained by their particular operational milieu, which means that they have imperfect knowledge and limited perception and experience. The main difference between commercial farmers and subsistence or peasant farmers in this respect is that they respond to market demands from a world system as well as to the circumstances of their local area and environment. Technology and investment have also introduced major differences. Here, a principal factor is the investment in *people*—investment to change people's awareness of, and willingness to adopt, new techniques, and to enhance the return from labor.

One result has been a widespread decline in the relative economic importance of primary activities. Thus it has been noted that the rural work force in peasant societies often exceeds 70 percent of the total work force, whereas in market-exchange economies it is frequently below 15 percent. Modern agriculture has become part of a highly urbanized industrial system in which it is allotted the lesser role in national budgeting and planning—though, as we have seen, all governments intervene to keep the agricultural sector viable. There has been a qualitative shift away from basic foods such as cereals and toward so-called industrial crops, especially for textiles. To meet the expanding demand for such crops, and to help exploit new resources released by an ever-growing technology, there has been massive use of capital, particularly through the substitution of capital for labor and land. Thus there is a low ratio of labor to capital, with a correspondingly high return on the labor input.

Extensive commercial crop systems are found in both market-commercial and redistributive agricultural systems. The rise of the commercial crop system coincided with the development of the steel plough, harvesting machinery, and numerous improvements in transportation. It is found in the mid-

latitude continental interiors, and is particularly highly capitalized, especially in North America and Australia. Grain production is virtually the only source of income, and originates in large units of 1,000 acres or more. This extensive size is needed for the economic deployment of a wide variety of mechanical equipment with a low labor input. Although productivity per worker is high, yields are very low. The principal grain crop is wheat, rotated with other easily harvested grains such as rye, oats, and maize. Where grain crops compete with livestock farming there is some hazard from drought.

Extensive commercial livestock farming represents an exchange-economy application of practices similar to those of pastoral nomadists. It was instituted by sedentary populations from Europe (including European Russia), who had migrated and settled in the dry interiors of North America, the U.S.S.R., South America, South Africa, and Australia. The areas used are largely unimproved with low stock carrying capacities—as low as 1 sheep for every 15 acres in some areas. But as in the extensive crop areas, there is a high capital investment per worker. This represents the optimum use of large areas too dry for crops, where poor transportation links and limited markets are often additional handicaps for the grain family.

Intensive commercial livestock farming includes dairying and industrial beef farming. What these activities have in common is the intensive production of livestock for closely linked urban industrial markets, whether commercial or communal. It is usually capital intensive, though a peasant-commercial variety, producing butter and cheese, that occurs in Scandinavian countries has much lower capitalization rates and poorer transportation links. In market-commercial examples, the farm is small— 50 to 100 acres. It is also labor intensive, since dairy livestock needs much care though there is some substitution of capital for labor through mechanized production systems. In redistributive systems, collectivization has formed larger holdings, though nearly all the eggs in the U.S.S.R. and about half the meat and milk are produced on the much smaller personal plots.

Besides these subtypes two very distinctive commercial subsystems are to be found: mixed farming and truck farming.

In *mixed farming*, as the name implies, diversity and flexibility are maximized. There is a high degree of interdependence between crops and livestock, each contributing a large part of the farm's output. In commercial economies, the development of mixed farming is governed closely by marketing possibilities and tariffs. For example, in Western Europe wheat is a large earner. But in spite of rather than because of the system, it is also heavily subsidized.

Moreover, production costs are often high because of too much mechanization. In North America and the U.S.S.R., on the other hand, the emphasis in mixed farming is on feedstuffs as a low cost production item; livestock (cattle, pigs, and sometimes sheep) are kept largely for meat.

Specialized intensive crop production is also found in *truck farming*, which occupies only a very small area in any total economy. Truck farming is closely associated with urban markets, as a local source of soft fruits and vegetables that may not travel well. Land values are high in these situations, and there is intense competition with alternative real estate usages. Thus the farms are worked with special intensity; labor input is high, and there is much use of fertilizers and cultivation under glass. The alternative for truck farmers is to be highly specialized but more distant from the market, in order to be able to supply crops out of season to the local truck farmers. Such crops may be labor or capital intensive. If capital investment is high, as in California, it is more likely to be devoted to a single crop than where levels of investment are lower.

Redistributive Farming

In contrast to the three types of agricultural organization discussed above, redistributive agriculture is subject to direct control through a socialized planned economy. The state through various agencies owns and operates the secondary, tertiary, and quaternary sectors of the economy, directs resource exploitation, and itself engages in farming through the institution of state farms. It also largely controls other farming through collectives. All these aspects of the agricultural economy, with other sectors of the economy such as banking or trade, are subject to systematic planning by the state. A small sector of market exchange often occurs, but overall the state is dominant. The market-exchange systems and peasant systems of other nations are of course subject to government influence, insofar as there is state manipulation of prices and other measures that limit the farmer's initiative. But in a redistributive economy the dominant planner, owner, and operator of economic activities is the state, and national, rather than individual, planning is the tool for economic change.

Most of the nations that now have redistributive economies (the U.S.S.R., Poland, etc.) previously had peasant economies with low productivity, rural overpopulation, and limited industrial development. Although in each case the state achieved control over the urban-industrial subsystem at an early stage of the redistributive planning process, the agricultural subsystem has remained peculiarly resistant to such overall control.

The basic approach of the state planners has been made through so-called collectivization. In all essentials, this is equivalent to rationalization of agricultural production on the factory model. It is undertaken as a means of serving the urban-industrial demand and, in the case of the U.S.S.R., as a logistic system to funnel agricultural products from what were originally about 25 million peasant holdings. Here, collectivization consisted of agglomerating these small peasant farms into larger farming units.

In the U.S.S.R., two main types of farm units have been utilized to rationalize agricultural production: the **sovkhoz** and the **kolkhoz.** The sovkhoz, a factory type state farm, employs on the average about 800 workers or wage-laborers, on an average unit of some 28,000 hectares (average sown area, 10,100), with an average of 2,400 cattle, 2,000 pigs, and 5,000 sheep and goats. Of course extremes do occur, and some state farms are units in excess of 70,000 hectares with 50 to 70 settlement nodes, some of which are 100 miles apart. Today there are about 12,000 state farms; they account for about 43 percent of the Soviet sown area. In contrast, the kolkhoz, or collective, averages about 6,000 hectares with about one-third the livestock. Originally the 500 workers of the average collective shared in the net income of the farm. More recently, however, there has been a move toward a guaranteed income. In both cases workers also have small plots for their personal use. This preponderance of large units with large labor forces stands in distinct contrast to the normal farming practice of market-exchange economies. In this respect Soviet agriculture is more comparable to the latifundia of South America: the subsidiary private economy of the Soviet farm population, with its small garden plots and livestock holdings, is comparable to the small plots of many agricultural laborers on the latifundia. On the other hand, the purely peasant cultivator is rare in the U.S.S.R. This is not the case in many other redistributive economies, particularly those of Eastern Europe.

Despite the formation of collective farming institutions, some traits of peasant organization remain. In the 1930s the original collectives were basically peasant oriented, though the basic processes of grain cultivation (and a few other crops) were mechanized. Similarly, the larger amalgamations up to the present day still exhibit some of the basic peasant attitudes and methods in new guises. Hence contemporary Soviet agriculture has been subject to severe handicaps; production levels are relatively low and costs generally high. The revolution in agricultural yields and techniques that took place in the market-exchange economies has largely bypassed the redistributive economies. The latter are especially handicapped by their primitive marketing mechanism; little attention has been given to distribution and its effect on product specialization.

Hence there tends to be a lack of specialization in high yield crops adapted to local areas of comparative advantage, as well as a lack of area specialization in livestock production. Of course specialization does occur. Grain, cotton, mixed farming, and truck farming are all to be seen in the Soviet Union in forms not very unlike those they assume in market economies. On the other hand, the lack of improved systems of marketing and distribution means that although a subsystem of some fifty suburban agricultural zones was organized around Soviet cities between 1937 and 1953, 80 percent of purchases of fruit and vegetables, 50 percent of meat, and 30 percent of dairy products were still made on the open or collective farm market in 1955.

Outside the Soviet Union, redistributive economies have also had mixed success in dealing with the agricultural subsystem. Cuba, before 1959, was basically a colonial "sugar mine" for the United States, with a plantation economy. The revolution of 1959 led to the expropriation of the sugar plantations and their conversion to state farms and cooperatives without their ever having passed through a peasant smallholding stage. Today there are about 700 state owned farms and 1,000 not yet collectivized, but both sectors are directed by a National Institute for Agrarian Reform. The Institute's efforts to diversify Cuban agriculture (for instance, by cattle breeding) while increasing the output of traditional crops, such as sugar, have met with very mixed success, despite the fact that they enjoy popular support.

In Eastern Europe, attempts at the reform of the basically overpopulated rural peasant systems had taken place before the changeover to a redistributive economy. But most of these attempts were doomed to failure because the economic system was dominated by the military, urban capitalists, and the landed aristocracy. Since the changeover, the peasant agricultural system has been subjected to periods of both collectivization and decollectivization. Today, most Eastern European nations have a large sector of small peasant farms subject to state direction, and a small sector of kolkhoz. In Poland, the kolkhoz occupy only 1 percent of the whole agricultural area.

The governments of most redistributive economies have mainly emphasized heavy industry and mining. In contrast, the government of the People's Republic of China (although it has placed considerable emphasis on industrial cities, as mentioned above) has made considerable efforts to improve the agricultural system, and to incorporate the relatively isolated rural economy into the planned economic system. About 85 percent of the Chinese population is rural, and more than 80 percent of the consumer goods and almost all the food and clothing consumed originates directly or indirectly in the agricultural

sector. The major planning techniques in China have been to:

1. *Intensify production through the increased use of chemical fertilizers, irrigation, pest control, and new crop varieties (mechanization has been introduced more slowly).*

2. *Increase the total area cultivated.*

3. *Conserve water.*

4. *Collectivize—this policy began rather poorly, but the introduction of* communes *seems to have overcome peasant opposition. In contrast to a purely agricultural cooperative, a commune is a device to link town and country by introducing light manufacturing into the agricultural base.*

Although particular phases of planning have emphasized the industrial sector strongly, on the whole agriculture has received a heavier emphasis than in the other redistributive economies.

In summary, agriculture, with the distinctive exception of China, has been a somewhat neglected sector in the state planned redistributive economies, most of which have placed emphasis on the urban industrial base. This is not just a matter of investment policy; the land sector has also been comparatively neglected for ideological reasons, because the urban working class is seen as the spearhead of the economy and the backbone of the revolution. The result has been a lower ratio of labor to capital than in most market-exchange systems, with yields frequently lower than in the latter (see table 19, above). But the potentials, via technological development remain just as great.

Transitional Categories

As figure 43 makes clear, many agricultural activities are in process of change, or have recently changed. The farming types mentioned earlier under the "subsistence" heading may soon become peasant activities. They may even merge into a commercial system, as in Japan, the Irrawaddy delta, or the Sudan (particularly with cotton). As long as less than a quarter of a system's crops enter distribution channels we can continue to think of it as basically a subsistence system with the earnings used to pay taxes. However, as the proportion of crops and livestock entering distribution channels rises, the system begins to approximate the peasant type. This process has been called **agriculturalization;** as it proceeds, it overwhelms the peasant society and gradually incorporates it in the market economy. Such agriculturalization, with its weakening of traditional values, occurred in Europe just prior to and during the Industrial Revolution. Whereas in much of Europe this process has given rise to a fully commercial system, the peasant element is still strong in developing countries undergoing the same process.

Another kind of transitional phase takes place when some novel agricultural practice is superimposed on a previously subsistence-peasant economy. One example of this is collectivization; another is the plantation. We have already defined the plantation as an intensely commercial form of agriculture. One reason for this is that all its products enter world exchanges. Historically, it was one means by which Western values were introduced into an alien environment. It was a device to procure desired quantities of produce that were ceasing to belong to the luxury class but could not be produced in the middle latitudes. Usually considered attributes of the plantation system are its tropical or semitropical location, crop specialization, advanced cultivation and harvesting techniques that ensure the product is of uniform quality, large operating units, management centralization, labor specialization, massive production, and heavy capital investment. As will be recognized, these are largely attributes of the market-commercial system, but placed in another latitude and in another system.

Operated virtually always in the past by an alien labor force, usually because the indigenous population was unable or unwilling to engage in a system operated from without, the labor problem was solved by using slaves. This happened first in the sugar plantations and later in the tobacco and cotton plantations. At the present time, the indigenous population are more familiar with the commercial-exchange system and are therefore more willing to enter the plantation labor force. Plantations have also changed with changing markets. Thus, for example, much of the production of the Brazilian sugar plantations now enters the domestic market, while ownership lies in the hands of local entrepreneurs, distributors, cooperatives, and the state. Some crops, however, remain plantation-dominated, like tea, while others, like coconuts, lie almost entirely with smallholders. The same crop may now be plantation-grown in some areas but not in others.

Conclusion

Attempts to abstract or isolate the important processes that influence agricultural landscape patterns are complicated by the wide range of factors involved: chance and uncertainty, climatic and topographic exigencies, market conditions, factors of the operational milieu, and behavioral influences all play their part. A farmer is not only subject to all these risks to an unusual degree; in most countries, he also has incomplete control over the results of his labors.

All agricultural activities take place within the framework of the operational milieu. Thus the decisions that are made within that framework are a function of the farmer's behavioral environment. The operational milieu establishes the economic organization, the units of production, the units of consumption, the units of investment, and structural attributes such as farm size, land tenure, and distribution systems. It is to the behavioral environment that we must look to explain why subsistence farmers often retain their small properties even though their marginal returns are lower than if they worked as wage laborers in a nearby city. Thus each farmer seems to make his own productive decisions according to his own particular preferences and a particular set of variables that affect his situation. These decisions and these situational variables are of course not random or individual. They are the result of a long set of previously realized social and economic relations, shaped by the perceptions and conceptions of the behavioral environment, and organized by the institutions and interrelationships of the operational milieu. Each farmer or farming group acts within a given socioeconomic situation and a given phenomenal context.

Summary

1. Only one primary production activity has been chosen for study, and that is agriculture. Although agriculture is one of man's oldest activities, and although certain sectors of the system have undergone enormous technical change, man is still heavily dependent on agriculture. Agricultural occupations still account for over half of the world's labor force, particularly in certain regions of South America, Africa, and Asia.

2. In those nations where over half of the labor force is employed in agriculture, usually part or all of the produce never reaches a national marketing system. There is also a tendency for such nations to utilize unsophisticated equipment and to be labor intensive. In contrast many Western nations have a sharply declining agricultural work force as capital is substituted for land and labor.

3. Along this continuum from labor intensive to capital intensive agricultural practices, many different locational and landscape patterns occur.

4. Although the phenomenal environment does not "determine" human activity, it appears to set certain limits to agricultural production—each crop has an optimal and a marginal area of production imposed by the plant's temperature, rainfall, and frost-free requirements. Only somewhere between 7 and 10

percent of the earth's total land surface is cultivated (about 1 acre per person).

5. Within the wide areas of possible growth, production actually occurs in limited areas, often as low as one-fifth of the total possible. This spatial restriction can be accounted for in terms of human choice and attitudes. Man selects his points of production—some selections are made by fairly careful consideration of economic costs and return (economic optimality and marginality), but in other areas, random change, historical inheritance and tradition, and emotional ties are very important.

6. Farmer-to-farmer variations in attitude are important because decision making in farming is dispersed spatially, and so can reflect from farm to farm and from field to field the availability of information to the farmer, his ability to use that information, as well as market and societal pressures.

7. Where innovations and information are more restricted, and where societal organization constrains the perception and use of such information, then farmers persist in their traditional and familiar patterns of behavior, as with the Nuer. Such societies have a complex interrelationship of farming and nonfarming activities. But conservative habits can also be seen in many farmers, as the study of the Great Plains showed.

8. Land is not productive as such, without the input of labor. The labor input can be intensive, as with gardens and small plots, or extensive, as with the U.S. and Canadian Prairie wheat farms.

9. Increasingly, capital has become another important land input. Capital application is associated with mechanization, fertilizers, pest and disease control, improved crop and stock, and an upgrading of the links to and from agriculture and the socioeconomic system in general. Capital is thus substituted for labor and land.

10. Specialization has also occurred with increasing capital inputs. Economies of scale, both internal and external to the farm, regional specialization, and factors of comparative advantage have become increasingly important to commercial and redistributive farming systems.

11. Agricultural goods are consumer rather than producer goods. They tend to be in short supply in subsistence and peasant economies, and in surplus in some Western economies. In the latter areas agriculture tends to focus on large metropolitan nodes, and to be increasingly operated along business lines (agrobusiness) by large corporations.

12. Despite its relative decline in labor force terms in Western economies, agriculture remains a staple factor, and as such has frequently drawn the attention of political and government action through subsidies, bounties, and protective tariffs.

13. Particular structural attributes within the operational milieu are important in determining farmer decisions and consequent land use patterns. In particular, farm size, tenure, and marketing systems are of importance. Farming practices are often closely aligned to the size of holding; to the stability of tenure, determining extractive and genetic attitudes; and to the ability to distribute the crops to regional or national marketing channels when the farmer is part of more than a subsistence system.

14. Having examined some of the basic components of an agricultural system, a broad categorization of agricultural practices can be set up—subsistence, peasant, market-commercial, and redistributive. Within each of these categories further subtypes can be identified according to the intensity of production and the particular crops or livestock emphasized.

15. Subsistence farmers consume their own output, are concerned largely with a local immediate area, and have little or nothing to contribute to an exchange system. Labor is the chief regulator of this category of farming, technology is simple, and the effect of the phenomenal environment is most direct.

16. Peasant farming systems are also basically small scale with relatively simple technology, and although production is not basically for exchange purposes, a substantial proportion of the output may reach the market. It is a nonscientific husbandry with emphasis on social as much as economic relationships.

17. Market-exchange farming involves specialization, mechanization, intensive application of capital, and links with a well-developed urban based distribution system. The work force in agriculture frequently falls below 15 percent of the total work force.

18. Redistributive farming is distinguished by the role of the state in systematically planning, and in some cases directly operating, the agricultural sector of the economy. There are variations on some of the subtypes already identified—large scale collective and state farms, smaller scale plots, and even sales on a "free" market.

19. In addition to those four broad categories and their subtypes, a fifth "transitional" sector can be identified. The impact of collectivization, agriculturalization, and the imposition of a plantation system on a subsistence and peasant economy, can result in the occurrence of several different landscape-forming systems side by side.

20. *All agricultural activities take place within the framework of the geographic environment previously identified.*

Further Reading

The distribution of crops and livestock on a world scale (and for that matter energy resources, fishing, manufacturing, etc.), can be gauged by reference to an economic atlas, such as

Oxford Economic Atlas of the World (London: Oxford University Press, 1970).

In addition, many regional atlases contain larger scale geographical and economic maps.

Several sources exist which give a general introduction to the agriculture system:

Buchanan, R. O. "Some Reflections on Agricultural Geography," *Geography*, vol. 44, 1959, pp. 1–13.

Coppock, J. T. "The Geography of Agriculture," *Journal of Agricultural Economics*, vol. 19, 1968, pp. 153–169.

Gregor, H. F. *Geography of Agriculture* (Englewood Cliffs: Prentice-Hall, 1970).

Henshall, J. D. "Models of Agricultural Activity" in R. J. Chorley and P. Haggett, eds. *Models in Geography* (London: Methuen, 1967), pp. 425–460.

Morgan, W. B. and Munton, R. J. C. *Agricultural Geography* (London: Methuen, 1971).

Reeds, L. G. "Agricultural Geography: Progress and Prospects," *Canadian Geographer*, vol. 8, 1964, pp. 51–64.

Symons, L. *Agricultural Geography* (London: G. Bell, 1967).

A standard text by an agricultural economist is

Heady, E. O. *Economics of Agricultural Production and Resource Use* (Englewood Cliffs: Prentice-Hall, 1952).

Types of farming systems are analyzed in

Blaut, J. M. "The Ecology of Tropical Farming Systems," *Revista Geografica*, vol. 28, 1961, pp. 47–67.

Clark, C. and Haswell, M. R. *The Economics of Subsistence Agriculture* (London: Macmillan, 1964).

Courtenay, P. P. *Plantation Agriculture* (London: G. Bell, 1965).

Duckham, A. N. and Masefield, G. B. *Farming Systems of the World* (London: Chatto and Windus, 1970).

Dumont, R. *Types of Rural Economy: Studies in World Agriculture* (London: Methuen, 1957).

Dumont, R. *Lands Alive* (New York: Monthly Review Press, 1965).

Franklin, S. H. *The European Peasantry: The Final Phase* (London: Methuen, 1969).

Franklin, S. H. "Reflections on the Peasantry," *Pacific Viewpoint*, vol. 3, no. 1, 1962, pp. 1–26.

Fryer, D. W. Section 2, "Agriculture . . ." in *World Economic Development* (New York: McGraw-Hill, 1965), pp. 47–216.

Grigg, D. "Agricultural Regions of the World," *Economic Geography*, vol. 45, 1969, pp. 95–132.

Gregor, H. F. "The Changing Plantation Systems," *Annals of the Association of American Geographers*, vol. 55, 1965, pp. 221–238.

Karez, J. F. *Soviet and Eastern European Agriculture* (Berkeley: University of California Press, 1967).

Lentnek, B. "Economic Transition to Commercial Agriculture: El Llamo, Mexico," *Annals of the Association of American Geographers*, vol. 59, 1969, pp. 65–84.

Strauss, E. *Soviet Agriculture in Perspective* (New York: Praeger, 1969).

Walker, K. R. *Planning in Chinese Agriculture, 1956–1962* (Chicago: Aldine, 1965).

Farms have been analyzed in the following papers:

Blaut, J. M. "The Economic Geography of a One-Acre Farm in Singapore: A Study in Applied Micro-Geography," *Malayan Journal of Tropical Geography*, vol. 1, 1953, pp. 37–48.

Heller, C. F. "The Use of Model Farms in Agricultural Geography," *Professional Geographer*, vol. 16, 1964, pp. 20–23.

Henshall, J. D. and King, L. J. "Some Structural Characteristics of Peasant Agriculture in Barbadoes," *Economic Geography*, vol. 42, 1966, pp. 72–84.

For those interested in other types of primary production the following skeletal readings are suggested:

Burton, I. and Kates, R. W., eds. *Readings in Resource Management and Conservation* (Chicago: University of Chicago Press, 1965).

Coull, J. R. *The Fisheries of Europe* (London: 1972).

Gordon, R. L. *The Evolution of Energy Policy in Western Europe* (New York: Praeger, 1970).

Haden-Guest, S. et al. *World Geography of Forest Resources* (New York: Ronald Press/American Geographical Society, 1956).

Kromm, D. E. "Sequences of Forest Utilization in Northern Michigan," *The Canadian Geographer*, vol. 12, no. 3, 1968, pp. 144–157.

McDivitt, J. F. *Minerals and Men* (Baltimore: Johns Hopkins Press, 1965).

Manners, G. *The Geography of Energy* (London: Hutchinson, 1964).

Odell, P. R. *An Economic Geography of Oil* (London: G. Bell, 1963).

Utton, A. E., ed. *National Petroleum Policy: A Critical Review* (Albuquerque: University of New Mexico Press, 1970).

Voskuil, W. H. *A Geography of Minerals* (Dubuque, Iowa: Wm. C. Brown, 1969).

seven

Some Models of
Agricultural Behavior

Introduction

Agricultural patterns, as we have seen, are difficult to analyze in reality. We now turn to some theoretical conceptualizations of these patterns. Such conceptualizations make use of simplifying assumptions in order to help disentangle the complex reality. This is why they are often called **models.** By devising and applying appropriate models we can hope to reach a better understanding of the factors that underlie the location of agricultural activities in the real world.

In this chapter and those that follow reference will be made to *location theory*, and to a general category of *location models.* The latter are models that attempt to identify principles and constructs helpful in explaining such phenomena as: the location of farm sites; patterns of agricultural land use; location of manufacturing sites, settlements, and sites of tertiary economic activity; and the general spatial makeup of regions and nations. General theories of location have been largely grounded in the equilibrium theory of economics, and in fact in their early development dealt with site locations as point locations, neglecting or underplaying the spatial dimension. Explicit consideration of the spatial dimension of the economy and its subsystems began with Johann Heinrich von Thünen (1783–1850), Carl Friedrich Launhardt (1832–1918), Alfred Weber (1868–1958), and August Lösch (1906–1945), and culminated in the present work of Walter Isard (1960) and the discipline of *regional science*.

There are two basic approaches to location theory within the equilibrium framework. One is a *partial* equilibrium approach, with primary emphasis on minimizing cost factors; it was largely developed by

Alfred Weber. The other follows a *general* equilibrium approach, and can be seen, for instance, in Isard's works. In this chapter, as well as in chapters 9 and 10, the theories examined fall largely into the partial equilibrium category. Here, most extraneous locational forces are held constant. This means that locations are discussed, for the most part, in terms of a homogeneous plain, so that influences like political boundaries or uneven distribution of population and resources are not initially taken into consideration. Instead, the location and cost of all resources are considered fixed, so that the effects of one variant—say transportation costs—can be better examined. Unfortunately, for all its theoretical attractiveness, this partial equilibrium approach is too simplistic and naive to represent the complexities of the real socioeconomic system, and has therefore come to be replaced by general equilibrium theory, of which there are many forms. Some aspects of it are presented in chapter 14; here, we are concerned mainly with general equilibrium concepts that, under ideal conditions, would enable us to explore every aspect of the behavioral and operational milieux. Thus Isard's attempts have focused on the spatial regional economy in its virtual entirety, emphasizing the links and interdependencies between all sectors and location sites of the economy. Not surprisingly, most attempts at applying general equilibrium theory involve research tasks too difficult and complex for much hope of success at the present stage of the social sciences.

One word of caution must be inserted about any equilibrium approach. The socioeconomic system is in fact constantly subject to disturbances, conflicts, and uncertainties. Under their impact, the system changes both internally and externally. Thus processes of change and adjustment are constantly in operation, and socioeconomic systems are never in a state of equilibrium. However, there is some heuristic value in viewing location problems as produced by a socioeconomic system tending toward some optimal steady state. Indeed, if this were not true we would no longer spend much time discussing such partial equilibrium theorists as Weber and von Thünen.

Von Thünen's Model

The analysis of land use patterns has long been one of geography's basic concerns. At first, it might appear as if agricultural land use is little affected by relative location, once the factor of a suitable market has been acknowledged. Indeed, the farmer does adapt his land use to site conditions, climate, landforms, and soils. However, the effects of the market situation cannot be disposed of as easily as all that. Johann Heinrich von Thünen, German economist and estate owner of the early nineteenth century, developed a theory of farm management that is still worth considering. This model, as we would now call it, is based on an econometric analysis of his estates in Mecklenburg. As a model it is inherently descriptive, but in the twentieth century it has been adapted to normative use.

Von Thünen's approach falls within the partial equilibrium category of location theory. He sought to find laws that could determine what form of agricultural production would best be carried on at a given place. He began with a set of simplifying assumptions; the area to be dealt with was physically homogeneous, completely isolated from the rest of the world, with only one market at its very center which set the price for all agricultural commodities. Moreover, transportation costs were assumed to increase at the same rate with distance, in all directions. Thus with the market price, for say, wheat, being the same for every producer, the return to the farmer would depend on how much he had to pay for transportation. To a farmer living nearby, the return might be high enough to allow intensive farming, with wheat as one of the rotation crops. A farmer living farther away would get less for his wheat, allowing him to grow only this crop, and to invest very little capital or labor in it. Still farther away, at the very margin of the estate, transportation costs to the market would be too high to grow any crops at all. Only goods of high value per unit collected without great input of labor, such as furs, could stand the cost of transportation.

Since transportation cost is the only variable in von Thünen's model, and since it is proportionate to distance in all directions from the central city, the resultant types of land use form concentric rings. If only one product is cultivated, the intensity of production of that product will, other things being equal, depend on the price the farmer gets for his crop. If that price is in turn dependent solely on transportation costs, intensity of production will vary with distance from the market. This is the first of two distinct aspects of von Thünen's model and is known as his *intensity theory*; it is based on the realization that a given crop can be cultivated under different systems, some more intensive than others. Local prices will be higher near the central market than away from it.

Von Thünen applied his intensity theory to two different farming systems; an improved system, and a three-field system. He decided that since the former system incurred higher costs, it would cease to yield a profit nearer to the center market than the latter system. He also decided that when several products were introduced, different commodities would have different profits of monetary yields according to their distance from the market, since the impact of transportation costs would vary according to the bulk and perishability of the commodity. This second aspect of von Thünen's model is known as his *crop theory*. It is important to remember that the model does have these two distinct aspects, since the crop theory, as can be seen from figure 49, does not follow a simple rule of intensity. The following pages deal mostly with this latter aspect of the von Thünen model.

Can the model be applied to reality? One simple demonstration of it is to suppose that a given amount of dairy production from a given acre of land can be sent to the market in one of three forms:

as 25 lbs. of milk, 10 lbs. of cream, or 1 lb. of butter. It can easily be shown that, with a fixed unit transportation cost per pound, the produce will be sent as milk close to the market and as butter furthest from the market, with cream sent from the zone between the two (see figure 50). Using this type of analysis, the agricultural location theorists have demonstrated how a regional differentiation in land use will occur over space according to distance from the central market. Deviations from this simple pattern can then be considered. Von Thünen showed the importance of such factors as crop combinations, differentials in transport facilities, the existence of multiple markets, and variations in the cost of production. He also considered external factors, such as tariffs, that might interfere with the spatial structure of prices.

The assumptions of von Thünen's model can be placed in seven main categories:

1. *There is an "isolated state" (as von Thünen called his model economy), consisting of one market city and its agricultural hinterland.*
2. *This city is the market for surplus products from the hinterland and receives products from no other areas.*
3. *The hinterland ships its surpluses to no other market except the city.*
4. *There is a homogeneous physical environment, including a uniform plain around the city.*
5. *The hinterland is inhabited by farmers who wish to maximize their profits, and who adjust automatically to the market's demands.*
6. *There is only one mode of transport—the horse and wagon (this is 1826!).*
7. *Transportation costs are directly proportional to distance, and are borne entirely by the farmers, who ship all produce in a fresh state.*

Within this framework, von Thünen considered the relationship of three factors:

1. *The distance of the farms from the market.*
2. *The prices received by farmers for their goods.*
3. **Economic rent.**

The relationship between the first two is simple: the price received by the farmer is the market price set by the central city, minus the cost of transportation which increases directly with distance from the city plus the costs of production. Thus any given product is of greatest value closest to the market.

The third factor, sometimes also referred to as "land rent," is a concept drawn from classical economics. Put simply, this "rent" represents the difference between the revenues obtained from the land and the costs of working that unit of land.

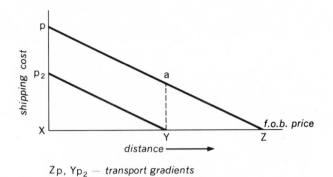

Zp, Yp$_2$ — transport gradients

Fig. 46. Von Thünen: (1) economic rent considering one crop.

Thus it is a surplus left after all costs, strictly including such costs as interest on invested capital, have been deducted. It was assumed by von Thünen that the farmers in his model economy wished to maximize that surplus.

Economic rent can be defined by the equation

$$R = E(p - a)Efk,$$

where R is the rent per unit of land, k is the variable quantity, distance, and E, p, f, a are constants of fixed values for particular commodities. Thus E represents yield per unit of land, p the market price per unit of commodity, f the transportation rate per unit of distance for each commodity, and a the production cost per unit of commodity. For any single given commodity, the relationship between R and k can be shown graphically, as in figure 46.

The market is at X. Assume that the demand at X is such that all farmers along the line XZ, including the farmers at Z, must produce the commodity if the demand at the market is to be satisfied. Thus the people at X must be willing to pay a price, p, for the commodity that will enable the farmer at Z, the most distant from X, to grow the commodity, ship it to X, and yet be able at least to break even. In this sense the farmer at Z sets the price for the commodity at the market. There are three reasons for this: the market demands just so much; to supply that quantity we must include all farmers up to Z; and it is not possible to distinguish among the various producers.

However, if costs of production, a, are held constant, then all the farmers along the line along the base line will have the same costs, and that base line can be designated **F.O.B. price.** The line Zp is the **transport gradient,** and Xp measured in, say, dollars and cents is the cost of shipping a unit of the commodity from Z to X. Thus the delivered price, p, is made up of the cost of production of the unit of the commodity (the F.O.B. price) *plus* the transport cost from Z to X. The farmer at Z is the **marginal producer,** the last farmer brought into production

in order to just satisfy the market demand, and it is he who sets the price.

Let us now consider an intermediate location, Y, where a farmer is also producing the commodity to ship to X. His costs of production and transport (a and f in the original equation) are the same as for the farmer at Z, as is the yield, E, and market price, P. Thus the transport gradient Yp_2 is parallel to Zp, but the cost of shipping a unit of the commodity from Y to X is only Xp_2. Since the market price, p, is the same, as just stated, the farmer at Y receives a profit represented by $p2p$ (equivalent to Ya), which is the economic rent.

In order to show how if we apply the crop theory aspect of the model, economic rent can result in varying patterns of agricultural production, figure 47 depicts an example involving three commodities.

In figure 46 any line perpendicular to XZ represented economic rent. Similarly, in figure 47 economic rents for horticulture, forest products, and intensive arable products may be determined from lines drawn respectively from pL, qM, and rZ, perpendicular to XZ. Note, however, what happens at point a where the transport gradients for horticulture and forest products cross. Exactly at a, or more correctly at the point A where aA is perpendicular to XZ, the economic rents for horticulture and forest products, Aa, are equal. But if we move slightly to the left of A, then the economic rent for horticulture, ce, is greater than the corresponding economic rent for forest products, ed. It follows that the farmer at e will gain more if he specializes in horticulture. On the other hand, if we move to the right of A, we find that the opposite condition holds, and the economic rent for forest products, fh, is greater than that for horticulture, gh.

A similar argument can be developed at point B. To the left of B, the economic rent for forest products is greater than that for intensive arable products. It follows that a farmer left of B will specialize in forest products. To the right of B the opposite condition holds: the farmer will specialize in intensive arable products. The locational relationship between these commodities is the relative slope of the transport gradient ($-Ef$). Thus the competitive strength of a product is related both to yields per unit farmed and to the transportation rate. Where commodities have low yields and/or low transportation rates, they will have gradients at a lower angle, and will tend to be produced at greater distances from the market—hence rZ.

If the model (figure 47) is now rotated about its axis, Xp, a nested set of rings is generated with radii XA, XB, and XZ, within which horticulture (to XA, the **margin of transference**), forest products (to AB), and intensive arable products (to BZ) are produced, as figure 48 illustrates. This is in fact a

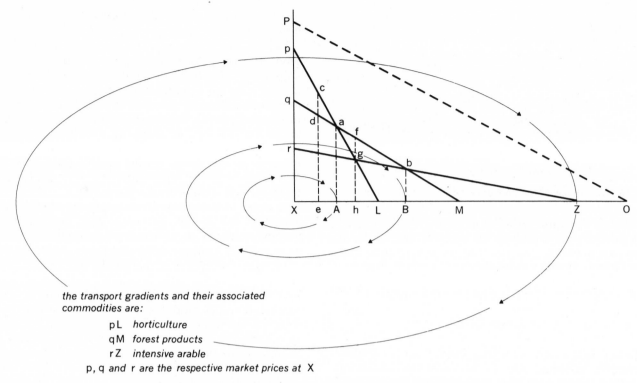

the transport gradients and their associated
commodities are:

    pL   horticulture
    qM forest products
    rZ   intensive arable
p, q and r are the respective market prices at X

Fig. 47. *Von Thünen: (2) economic rent considering three crops.*

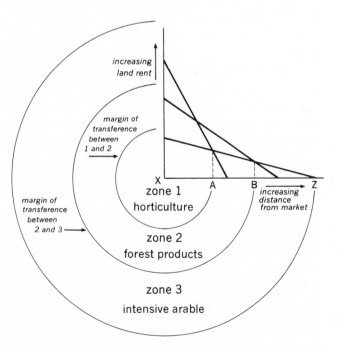

Fig. 48. *Von Thünen: (3) a simplified model.*

simpler version of von Thünen's scheme, which used six commodities and developed six concentric rings around the central city (figure 49, upper half). We do not have to confine ourselves to those particular crop sequences; for instance we could use our milk production example, or some combination of wheat and sheep (figure 50). In all these figures illustrating a von Thünen type analysis the particular position of a crop or farming system depends on its economic rent (which in our case is shown as a function of the slope of the transportation gradient). There are alternative methods of illustrating economic rent; they tend to stress the relative profits per land area and other distance effects, as well as take into account transportation costs. It suffices for our purpose, however, to view transportation costs and economic rent as the basic factors underlying this process of agricultural differentiation.

Modifications of the Model

As a further illustration, let us suppose that an industrial plant to process sugar beets is located at *X*,

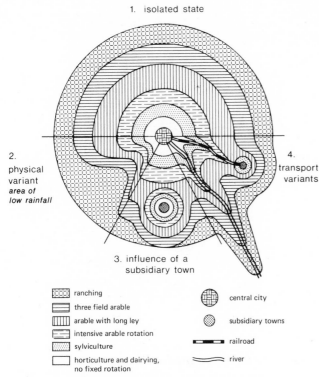

1. isolated state

2. physical variant *area of low rainfall*

4. transport variants

3. influence of a subsidiary town

Legend:
- ranching
- three field arable
- arable with long ley
- intensive arable rotation
- sylviculture
- horticulture and dairying, no fixed rotation
- central city
- subsidiary towns
- railroad
- river

Fig. 49. *Von Thünen: (4) the spatial expression of the basic model (the "isolated state") and three variants.*

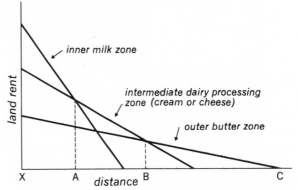

inner milk zone

intermediate dairy processing zone (cream or cheese)

outer butter zone

land rent

X   A   *distance*   B   C

a simplified model applied to a threefold zonation of dairying around a market

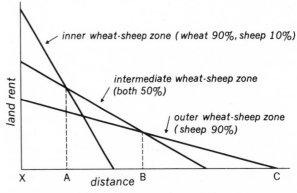

inner wheat-sheep zone (wheat 90%, sheep 10%)

intermediate wheat-sheep zone (both 50%)

outer wheat-sheep zone (sheep 90%)

land rent

X   A   *distance*   B   C

a further model suggesting zonations within a wheat-sheep region

Fig. 50. *Von Thünen: (5) alternative crop/livestock combinations. (From J. Rutherford, M. I. Logan, and G. J. Missen,* New Viewpoints in Economic Geography, *1966, p. 44, reprinted by permission of Martindale Press.)*

and offers the price *P* per unit of beets (figure 47). The transportation gradient is shown as *PO*; it overlaps all the other gradients, thus implying that a higher land rent is possible if the whole area is changed to sugar beets. How would this changeover take place?

Figure 51 suggests that the new pattern might develop in a rather uneven manner. The introduction of the new crop might well be more a function of human attitudes than of the natural environment. The high price might bring more land into production—land that previously had not been worked because it could be utilized only at a loss. The gradual spread of sugar beet cultivation over the landscape would reflect the diffusion of information about sugar beets—that is, the rate at which farmers became aware of, made a decision on, and acted to take advantage of the possibility of increased profit in sugar beet cultivation. But the introduction of this new crop would disturb the balance of the market system. The forces of supply and demand, conditioned by human tastes, would operate to bring about a new equilibrium, which might imply higher prices for horticultural, forest, and intensive arable products. On the other hand, the market at *X* might find it to its advantage to import these commodities from much further afield, thus extending its spatial system of food production and consump-

tion. This situation could, in turn, encourage formerly subsistence or peasant farmers to join or enter more fully into the exchange economy, or it could encourage foreign entrepreneurs to move into the area and establish plantations. This development might then upset the political balance of power—and so on, in a chain of events typical of a world economic system that is both complex and interrelated.

Von Thünen himself relaxed certain assumptions of his model. First he introduced a canal along which transportation costs were lower than by horse and wagon. The effect was to create a series of wedge-shaped land use zones along the canal (figure 49, sector 4). Second, he introduced a second and smaller market, around which he postulated that a series of separate zones would be created (sector 3). Similarly, we could relax the assumptions by introducing yet another means of transport, such as a railroad (sector 4), or allow variation in the physical environment (sector 2). The extent to which these

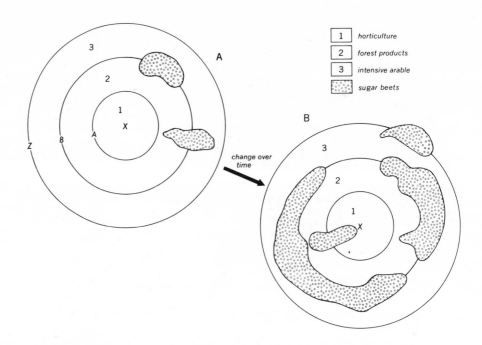

Fig. 51. *Von Thünen: the possible effect of the introduction of a fault commodity. (From an idea by R. McDaniel.)*

relaxations affect the simple von Thünen model (sector 1) will depend on how they affect the simple conceptual framework put forward earlier.

Some researchers have used von Thünen's model as a general framework for interpreting the spatial framework of the economy. Others have worked on a more direct basis. Thus von Thünen's model has been applied to the distribution of European agriculture in 1925 (figure 52), and to conditions on the Edwards Plateau in Texas (figure 53). Neither of these studies found a direct and absolute relationship between distance from the market and the gradation of land uses.

More recently, in the 1960s the von Thünen agricultural system has been applied on both a continental scale by Schlebecker and Peet and a local one by Dickinson, Chisholm, and Horvath. Two recent empirical studies have also used aspects of the model. A study of the Wisconsin cheese industry concluded that the factors of relative market location and freight rate differences governed the location of cheese production only in a general way and did not determine location at any particular point. A similar study of the Kentish hop industry noted the tendency for hop growing to be related to distance from the center of production.

Obviously, the patterns noted by von Thünen in 1826 have been radically modified by changes in transportation, in the evaluation of resources, and in technology. One result is that the radius of land use is much greater; in order to recognize the pattern of concentric circles it is now necessary to study whole continents.

Limitations of the Model

Von Thünen's model contains several built-in assumptions that limit its applicability to real-life situations. It assumes the complete availability of information or, at best, assumes that lack of information is only a short-term problem with no long-term effects. It also assumes completely rational economic behavior on the part of individuals who must be prepared to change the land use system in order to reap even a very small gain in land rent. These assumptions are not defects in the model as such. But they do indicate where we might look to understand differences between the model and reality.

The von Thünen model is also static and deterministic. Today we know that economic growth and changes in demand will alter the spatial patterns of agricultural systems and land use, which in their turn influence the rate of change. It might be possible to postulate a dynamic von Thünen model that could be applied to the expansion of settlement from a coastal origin to the interior of, say, the United States, Australia, or parts of South America. But the model, despite these possible manipulations, is really static, since it represents a land use system at one point in time. Von Thünen was not concerned with transitional changes, since he and most of the direct extenders of his model assumed that any change in technology, demand, or transport cost would automatically be accompanied by an adjustment in the land use system. As has already been suggested (figure 51), changes of this kind are complex; a new innovation might be adopted only spo-

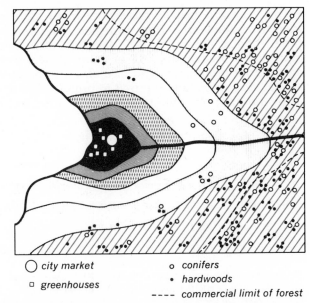

○ city market   o conifers

□ greenhouses   • hardwoods

                   - - - - commercial limit of forest

Fig. 52. *Model of the zones of production around a theoretical isolated city in Europe. (From O. Jonasson, "The Agricultural Regions of Europe,"* Economic Geography, *vol. 1, 1925, reprinted by permission of the editor.)*

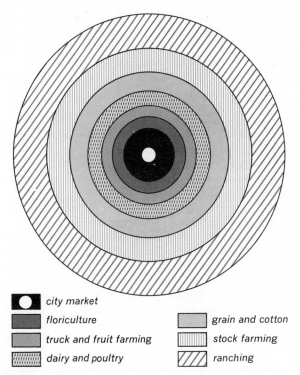

■○ city market

■ floriculture   grain and cotton

truck and fruit farming   stock farming

dairy and poultry   ranching

Fig. 53. *Zoning on the Edwards Plateau of Texas. (From O. Jonasson 1925, ibid.)*

radically, so that a pattern of discontinuity results. It has also been suggested that when von Thünen's model is used as a technique of **marginal analysis** it fails to make the point that production systems may have their costs altered according to the scale or extent of their development. Thus it is assumed that the productive system developed around a metropolitan market like Seattle has no scale advantages over a production system developed around a much smaller community like Olympia. This is unrealistic; economies of scale achieved around a large market may substantially lower production costs relative to the smaller market. If this **cost advantage** to the larger city more than offsets the transportation costs in supplying the smaller market, then the land use pattern around the latter can be modified to a high degree.

It would be possible to go on making modifications and revisions of the von Thünen model; some geographers have. However, none of these attempts has altered the basic concepts behind the model, which are largely independent of the real world.

Economic Models

Von Thünen was concerned above all with the spatial dimension; he identified zones of land use that, at **margins of transference,** changed from one function to another. Instead of using this spatial technique, however, some economic models conceptualize such areas as points. Producers or farmers,

production factors, products, and consumers are all treated as if they were located at a series of discrete points with transportation costs held constant. Provided trade takes place, analysis of comparative advantage indicates differences in the type of production at different points. Such models are of two basic types: *input-output models,* and *spatial equilibrium models.* Recent improvements have extended the basic interregional equilibrium framework to include transportation costs. The general problem has been stated in 1951 by Enke in this way:

There are three regions trading on homogeneous good. Each region constitutes a single *and* distinct market. *The regions of each possible pair of regions are separated—but not isolated—by a transportation cost. . . . For each region the functions which relate local production and local use to local price are known, and consequently, the magnitude of the difference which will be exported or imported at each local price is also known. Given these trade functions and transportation costs, we wish to ascertain:*

1. *the net price in each region;*
2. *the quantity of exports or imports for each region;*
3. *which regions export, import, or do neither;*
4. *the aggregate trade in the commodity;*
5. *the volume and direction of trade between each possible pair of regions.*

This is more complex than the problem of comparative advantage. But it is still an essentially static conceptualization, taking no account of capital, labor, skills, or entrepreneurs, all of which are mobile in response to changes in resources.

Input-Output Models

Regional agriculture is sometimes analyzed in terms of input-output models. These were originally devised with entire national economic structures in mind; the regional application refers to product subsectors within the U.S. Department of Agriculture's type-of-farming areas. For purposes of demonstration, a very simple example is set out below. It is divided into two basic sectors: primary agriculture and secondary agriculture. The former sector includes crop production, the latter livestock. Only two regions are considered here, although the original study dealt with six groups of regions.

The numbers in the row for sector 1 (primary agriculture) in table 20 show that this sector, for region 1, in the course of delivering 55 units of output as end products to "final demand," and 20 units as feedstuffs to sector 2 (secondary agriculture), delivers 25 units of its output to itself (let us say as seed). "Final demand" includes the goods consigned to investment and export as well as to current consumption in the households of the region. The total output of 100 units from the primary agricultural sector of region 1 satisfies both the "direct" final demand for its end products, and the "indirect" demand for its intermediate products. On the input side, taking the primary agriculture of region 1 again, in order to produce 100 units of total output this sector absorbs not only 25 units of its own produce as seed, but also 14 units of input (fertilizers, etc.) from the secondary agricultural sector of that region together with 80 units of labor and capital.

Table 20. *Input/Output Analysis: Two Agricultural Regions* *

input

	sector prim. 1 agric.		sector sec. 2 agric.		final demand		total output	
	region 1	region 2	region 1	region 2	region 1	region 2	region 1	region 2
sector 1	25	15	20	10	55	15	100 units	45 units
sector 2	14	5	6	5	30	100	50	110
labor, etc.	80	30	180	300	40	30	300	360

*This table displays outputs from each sector in two regions in a corresponding horizontal row, and the inputs to each sector in a vertical column.

This matrix is usually recast into input ratios or coefficients (table 21). Thus, in region 1, where crop production is dominant, 0.25 of a unit of primary agricultural production, 0.14 of a unit of secondary agricultural production, and 0.80 of a unit of labor, capital, and so on, are required to produce 1.00 unit of total output from the primary agricultural sector.

Table 21. *Input/Output Coefficients* *

	sector 1		sector 2		final demand	
	region 1	region 2	region 1	region 2	region 1	region 2
sector 1	0.25	0.33	0.40	0.09	0.183	0.042
sector 2	0.14	0.11	0.12	0.05	0.100	0.278
labor, etc.	0.80	0.68	3.60	2.73	0.133	0.083

*In this matrix, the input-output table (table 20) has been recast into input ratios or coefficients. The columns display the ratio between each input to a sector and the total output of the sector for each of the two regions.

These models describe existing relationships, but they can be manipulated so as to encompass sectoral changes, and hence changes in regional specialization. They are also difficult to operate because of the large numbers of regions that would normally be included, and the numerous commodities that could be specified—for which, incidentally, statistics are not always available.

Spatial Equilibrium Models

The purpose of **spatial equilibrium** models is not just to analyze the agricultural economy at one point in time, but to determine if possible where agricultural production ought to be located if certain goals are to be achieved. One of the goals to be achieved could be the highest average profit among all producers. Or it might be something less ambitious. The whole approach is very difficult to summarize because each model used varies according to the problem to be solved and the data available. Here, a simple example will serve to show how the spatial equilibrium model could operate.

Imagine two regions, X and Y, with maize traded between them. X is a surplus region, and Y is a deficit region. If no movement of maize took place between the two regions, the price per unit produced would be low in X and high in Y, following the equation

$$P = 300 - 2D$$

where D is the amount consumed, and P is the

regional price. The condition in each region, then, before any movement or trade takes place is

X	Y
100 units	*25 units*
$2.00 per unit	*$3.50 per unit*

Trade will occur if the costs of moving maize from X to Y are low enough for producers in X to sell to Y at a higher price than they can get locally. Trade to Y will continue until the supply is large enough for the spread in price between the two to be equal to the transportation costs between them. If the latter is 50 cents per unit then, after trade, supplies and prices are

X	Y
75 units	*50 units*
$2.50 per unit	*$3.00 per unit*

Spatial equilibrium is reached after 25 units of maize have been moved from X to Y.

If the commodity values before and after are compared, a net payoff can be noticed:

I. Before trade:

X: *100 units at $2.00 = $200.00*
Y: *25 units at $3.50 = $ 87.00*

II. Transportation costs:

25 units at $0.50 = $ 12.50

III. After trade:

X: *75 units at $2.50 = $187.50*
Y: *50 units at $3.00 = $150.00*

The net payoff amounts to the after-trade value of the maize, less the before-trade values, less transportation costs. In this case, ΣI = $287.50 + II $12.50 = $300; ΣIII $337.50; $337.50 less $300 = $37.50 net payoff.

Another example of the spatial equilibrium approach is a study of grain production in the United States. Its objective was to determine how grain production could be distributed regionally while either maximizing farmers' incomes or minimizing costs to the consumers. The United States was divided into 140 grain-producing areas, for each of which data were collected on production costs and yields. Three models were then constructed. Two of them assumed that differences in regional prices accurately reflect differences in transport costs (the influence of von Thünen is obvious). Efforts were then made to estimate how farmers should allocate their profits with respect to regional prices, follow-

ing methods roughly parallel to those illustrated above. The third model also attempted to allocate marketing areas for the grain using certain calculated freight rate costs. That is, it attempted to explain agricultural patterns by taking into account the interaction between regional production costs, distributing costs between regions, and regional demands.

These models have the advantage over the von Thünen type in that they use exact empirical measures for prices, transport, and regional demand. Empirically measured inputs of labor, machinery, fertilizers, seeds, and so on, are also used, so that they have a strong empirical foundation, though this does not necessarily make them nearer to reality. The von Thünen model, on the other hand, consists of rather loosely connected qualitative statements.

Linear Programming

The agricultural economic system of a group such as the Fur can be represented in matrix form (table 22). If this matrix were quantified, the effect of changes in the values of particular cells could be measured, and changes in the total pattern would be revealed. This kind of matrix analysis, often called **linear programming,** has been used in the study of relatively self-contained farming systems in India and East Africa. The results of changes in such variables as resource availability, technology, markets customs, and values have been studied. No claims are made to represent actual behavior in these studies; rather, they analyze the alternatives implicit in the ecological, technological, and economic components of the operational milieu.

Table 22 shows a range of possible cultivating activities (P_{1-10}) for the Fur economy. The direct input requirements for those activities—land, labor, manure, and so on—are represented by the first six rows ($P_{101-104}$). Labor resources can be increased by "hiring" labor (P_{17}) at the cost of beer (P_{105}). Beer in turn requires millet (P_{106}) and brewing services (P_{107}). Millet can be obtained by cultivation (P_1) or by purchase (P_{25}). This matrix form can also be used to represent custom, as with the role of women in brewing (P_{107}), dowry commitments (P_{112}) or hut building (P_{16}). The nonzero values shown in the matrix illustrate the interdependence of millet production on land and male labor. They also demonstrate the possibilities of using other male labor for cultivating by hiring through beer payments, which in turn depends on the availability of millet and brewing labor. It does not, however, show that there are alternative uses for land and labor, nor that millet may be bought as well as cultivated.

Table 22. *Matrix Representing the Mountain* Fur *Economy**

constraints			resources available	summer raingrown crops			irrigated - winter		irrigated - summer			irrigated - orchard		livestocks			collecting and gathering	hut building	series reciprocal given (by periods)
				millet	wheat	tomatoes	wheat	onions	garlic	chillies	herbs	potatoes	orchard bearing	orchard establishment	cattle	goats			
			P_0	P_1	P_2	P_3	P_4	P_5	P_6	P_7	P_8	P_9	P_{10}	P_{11}	P_{12}	P_{13}	P_{14}	P_{15}	P_{16}
land-unirrigated	P_{101}		1	1	0	0													1 2 …
land-irrigated (summer)	P_{102}	1	0	0	0	0													
(winter)		2	0	0	0	0													
manure	P_{103}		0	0	0	0													
series labor—non-brewing (by periods)	P_{104}	1	1	1	0	0													
		2	1	1	0	0													
		!																	
series beer—at different times	P_{105}	1	1	0	0	0													
		2	1	0	0	0													
		!																	
millet	P_{106}		1	1	0	0													
series brewing beer	P_{107}	1	0	0	0	0													
		2	0	0	0	0													
		!																	
series reciprocal labor commitments	P_{108}	1	0																
		2	0																
		!																	
series livestock feed	P_{109}	1																	
		2																	
		!																	
series subsistence & feast requirements millet for porridge, and own beer (possibly in storage form)	P_{110}	1																	
		2																	
		!																	
cash requirements - tools, consumer goods, etc.	P_{111}																		
cattle requirements, feasts, dowry	P_{112}																		
tomatoes	P_{113}																		
wheat	P_{114}																		
onions	P_{115}																		
garlic	P_{116}																		
chillies	P_{117}																		
herbs	P_{118}																		
potatoes	P_{119}																		
fruit	P_{120}																		
cattle	P_{121}																		
goats	P_{122}																		

*The labor - millet - beer relationship is illustrated; the numeral one indicates some value above zero.

Linear programming is looked at in rather more detail in chapter 13.

All the models discussed so far have been essentially static, or at best only partly dynamic. Thus they are not easily adapted to changes in technology, information, ideology, motivation, or demand. It is very difficult to build a dynamic model for, as pointed out earlier, changes in time dimensions are associated with changes in spatial dimensions, and there is a causal or functional relationship between the two that affects the patterns of agricultural systems. The difficulty with the time dimension in the von Thünen model has already been noted. In one attempt to overcome this difficulty, the land use system in one year was treated as the function of land use systems (as measured in costs) in the previous year, plus some component of change determined by linear programming. However, no explicit account was taken of the entrepreneur's or farmer's decision making, which obviously affects the evolution of a land use system. Most research of this type uses a deterministic framework, whereas there is much to be gained by a more probabilistic approach.

Decision Making Models

The drawback of all the economic models is their inability to take into account the multiplicity of factors, past and present, that actually determine land use patterns and farming behavior. Any pattern that is studied is the result of a large number of individual decisions made for less than rational reasons, with only incomplete knowledge to hand.

Game Theory

One set of decision making models makes use of **game theory,** a mathematical discipline that originated in the 1920s and reached definitive form in the 1940s. Game theory concerns the rational choice of strategies in the face of competition from an

series reciprocal labor received (by periods) p$_{17}$	series brew beer (by periods) p$_{18}$	series sell labor (by periods) p$_{19}$	cloth making p$_{20}$	buy cattle p$_{21}$	buy goats p$_{22}$	buy wives p$_{23}$	buy tools p$_{24}$	buy millet p$_{25}$	sell millet p$_{26}$	sell tomatoes p$_{27}$	sell wheat p$_{28}$	sell onions p$_{29}$	sell garlic p$_{30}$	sell chillies p$_{31}$	sell herbs p$_{32}$	sell potatoes p$_{33}$	sell fruit p$_{34}$	sell cattle p$_{35}$	sell goats p$_{36}$
1 2 ...	1 2 ...	1 2 ...																	
0 0		0 0																	0
0 0		0 0																	0
0 0		0 0																	0
1 1		0 0																	0
1 1		0 0																	0
1 1		0 0																	0
1 1		1 1																	0
1 1		1 1																	0
0 0		1 1																	0
0 0		1 1																	0
0 0		1 1																	0
0 0		0 0																	0
0 0		0 0																	0

opponent. Competition can also concern locations where the values depend on the locational choices of others, or competition in terms of man choosing certain strategies to overcome or outwit his environment. Thus a study of an area of variable rainfall, in which several crops have their yields differentially affected by differing amounts of rain, sought to discover what proportions of land should be planted with what crops to ensure the largest possible minimum yield of food in any year.

As an illustration of the game theory approach the following example should prove quite simple, although the mathematical techniques involved are complex. Suppose that a farmer is confronted with four different crops or cropping systems, of which he can choose only one. The income from these crops depends upon weather conditions, and only six different types of such conditions can occur. From this information, it is possible to construct a **payoff matrix,** showing the potential returns (table 23). The "game" is to determine the best solution. The ranking system of choices outlined in chapter 2 is relevant here: the farmer might take the economically rational choice that would maximize his minimum income no matter what the weather conditions. In table 23 this would mean choosing crop A, which gives the highest minimum income of $1,300 under the worst weather conditions. This is the short-term solution. However, if the farmer takes a longer view and decides to maximize his average income, then he would choose crop C. This would give him an average return of $2,666 even though on 50 percent of the occasions his crop failed altogether. If he chose

Table 23. *Payoff Matrix: Crop Type, Weather Conditions and Potential Revenue (in dollars)*

crop	weather conditions					
	1	2	3	4	5	6
A	1300	1600	1800	1500	1450	1380
B	2100	900	2700	1000	1260	2400
C	0	3000	0	9000	4000	0
D	1800	0	1100	700	0	800

A, his average would be $1,505; if B, $1,726 — and so on. The point to note is that different decisions would produce very different land use patterns.

The limits of game theory in this type of situation have brought criticism that it is psychologically and behaviorally unreal, and that it tends to simulate or represent patterns without explaining why they occur. A farmer will not usually have the knowledge and foresight to rationalize this problem in the form of a game theory matrix. Even if he were able to, his actual choice-making behavior would be influenced by a whole range of other factors, such as experience, age, income, and so on. Obviously, he could assess a game theory presentation only after much experience. Until he has acquired this experience he has to grope around in uncertainty, gradually and imperfectly learning his way on the basis of trial and error.

Diffusion Models

A second approach to decision making concerns the diffusion of information and the resulting patterns of land use. A key distinction here is that between the physical and social distribution of the same geographic phenomenon. This distinction is made to emphasize the tie between the landscape patterns and the elements of culture. According to the model of spatial innovation diffusion, acceptance of an idea (say, a new crop) is related not only to the receipt of information about it but also to various behavioral, psychological, and economic factors.

A study of the diffusion of innovation in rural southern Sweden dealt with a government subsidy to improve pasture, and with control of bovine tuberculosis. The vehicle for the diffusion process was the network of social contacts, including newspapers, radio and television broadcasts, books, talk, and observation. Most important, however, was oral communication. Various differences in the nature of the communications network occur with differing socioeconomic groups: some individuals are bound to the local plane, others operate on the local and regional planes, and still others operate on all three planes of social communication (figure 54). Interpersonal communications, however, seem to be of most importance for the transmission of information at the local level.

The diffusion of an innovation has been simulated in a number of models that use a probabilistic statistical method. The rules governing the system are:

1. *Only one person carries the item at the beginning.*
2. *The item is adopted at once when heard of.*

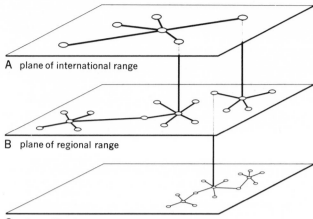

A plane of international range

B plane of regional range

C plane of local range

Fig. 54. *Planes of communication. A hypothetical matrix of social communications: A = international range; B = regional range; and C = local range. (From T. Hagerstrand, "On Monte Carlo Simulation of Diffusion," in W. W. Garrison and D. F. Marble, eds.,* Studies in Geography, *no. 17, 1967; Northwestern University Press, reprinted by permission.)*

3. *Information is spread only by face-to-face communication.*
4. *Such communication takes place only at certain times and at constant intervals.*
5. *The chances of being paired with a carrier of the item depend on the actual distance between teller and receiver.*

Later models were changed to obtain a more realistic representation. In particular, a group of "resistances" was added to represent various categories of resistance to acceptance. This later model is shown in figure 55.

Figure 56 illustrates the diffusion of an innovation over space and time. The importance of these processes to agricultural patterns should be obvious. If information is spread through the resistances — channels of communication that are constricted — then there are bound to be lags between the invention of a new agricultural practice and its adoption, with unmistakable effects on agricultural land use. There may also be a lag in the diffusion of information about market conditions and technological changes. Studies of diffusion have shown a difference between the availability of a certain piece of information and its acceptance, although for more complex reasons than these diffusion models can embody. Thus a particular new technique may be available to all U.S. farmers at approximately the same time, but acceptance of it may nevertheless vary over space.

Behavioral Models

One thing that most of the models so far examined have in common is that they make unrealistic as-

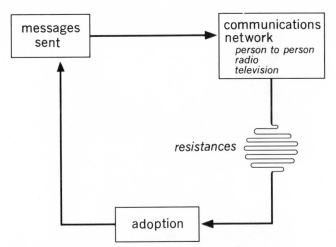

Fig. 55. *Diffusion of innovations: a simple schema.*

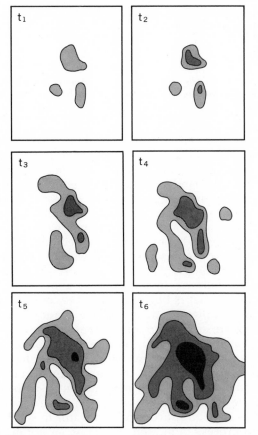

Fig. 56. *Areal diffusion of a hypothetical innovation over successive time periods* (t_1, t_2 ... t_6). *(From T. Hagerstrand,* Innovationsforloppet ur korologisk synpunkt, *1953, by courtesy of the Department of Geography, the Royal University of Lund, Sweden.)*

sumptions about human behavior. Thus most geographic studies assume that all the land use patterns and practices now part of the landscape are optimal systems, because only the best have survived. This

cannot be accepted. Many areas are subject to suboptimal land use simply because, for whatever reason, the optimal solution is simply not perceived. But although any agricultural model ought to incorporate some of the elements of learning and communication theory, not to mention decision making, almost none of them do. Let us review some of the few exceptions.

One study examined the behavior of livestock farmers in New Zealand. Attempts were made to treat some of the elements affecting a farmer's decisions. For this purpose, an "uncertainty framework" was used, where uncertainty represents either the indeterminacy inherent in the situation or simple ignorance of what is likely to happen. For example, these farmers must schedule the timing of operations from period to period, while weighing up in their own minds the probabilities of gain and loss.

Also worth mentioning here is a 1962 study of flood plain use that was one of the first full-length studies to be concerned with the decision making behavior that underlies any type of land management. Simon's concept of bounded rationality turned out to be relevant here, since the resource managers were in fact operating in a boundedly rational way, the bounds being set by the limits of their experience. It also turned out that there were few signs of the conscious optimizing or maximizing that virtually all the other models assume as standard. Indeed, it was hard to discern consistent use of any economic criteria. In short, the managers' behavior was that of *satisficers*.

This notion of satisficing — behavior that goes only some way toward economic rationality — is obviously a useful one for future studies. Lack of interest in the optimal solution means paying attention to the perceived environment rather than the objectively described environment. Thus actions may be intendedly, though boundedly, rational in terms of an individual's perception of crop failures or success, while in statistical and absolute terms the only term for them is suboptimal.

Another study combining both normative and behavioral analysis, raised questions concerning farmers' perception of goals and risk situations. It examined the hypothesis that the farmers in the study area (Middle Sweden) did not achieve profit maximization, and that productivity was not limited just by the amount and combination of available resources. Actual labor productivity was at substantially less than its theoretical optimum (figures 57 and 58). Less than half the area studied had a labor productivity of more than 70 percent of the optimal level, and in some places was as low as 40 percent of this. In other words, the average farmer achieved less than two-thirds of the productivity that his resources would have allowed. The con-

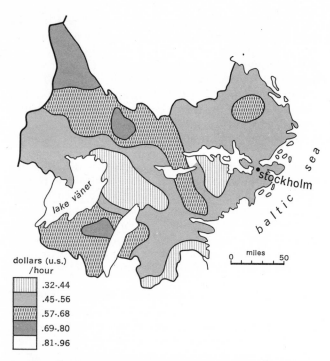

dollars (u.s.)
/hour

	.32-.44
	.45-.56
	.57-.68
	.69-.80
	.81-.96

miles
0   50

Fig. 57. *The Swedish Mellansverige: the actual surface (the satisficer) of farm labor productivity. (From Julian Wolpert, "The Decision Process in Spatial Context,"* Annals of the A.A.G., *vol. 54, 1964, p. 540, reprinted by permission of the Association of American Geographers.)*

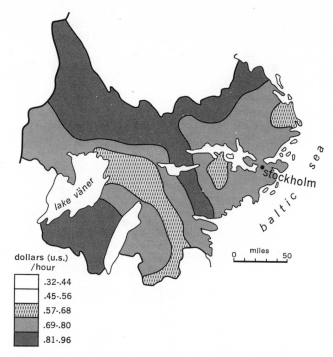

dollars (u.s.)
/hour

	.32-.44
	.45-.56
	.57-.68
	.69-.80
	.81-.96

miles
0   50

Fig. 58. *The Swedish Mellansverige: the potential surface (the optimizer) of farm labor productivity. (From Wolpert 1965, ibid., p. 541.)*

clusion drawn was that the prerequisites for optimum production (perfect knowledge and optimization behavior) simply were not present. And in fact production levels were later found to be guided by:

1. *The fact that farmers chose what was to them a satisfactory solution, but which in an absolute sense was suboptimal.*

2. *The fact that there were regional lags in the diffusion of information from centers like Stockholm and Uppsala, so that the level of information available to farmers was uneven (this unevenness was correlated with variations in awareness of alternatives and their consequences).*

3. *The fact that further uncertainties existed as to the profitability of particular crop and livestock combinations, not to mention uncertainties about weather and market prices, and such personal uncertainties as health.*

In the study just described, all the assumptions of economic rationality had to be relaxed before certain spatial variations in agricultural practice could be interpreted. Yet these assumptions are the very ones utilized in most models of agriculture and, as will be seen later, of manufacturing and tertiary activities. The assumption of perfect knowledge was disproved by the existence of unpredictable changes and lags in the communication and percep-

tion of information. If the distribution of satisficing farmers is considered in the light of these changes and lags, then the spatial variations in farming practice and land use may be more clearly understood. A study of agriculture along these lines would be more realistic. But it would still contain assumptions that set it apart from the real world. The fact that a model is behaviorally oriented does not mean it explains or represents all real-world processes.

A more comprehensive framework might be applied as follows. Imagine an area of subsistence agriculture that is beginning to have contacts with a general market economy. If we assume that the farmers are anxious to learn about this new system, and that the social, technical, and economic conditions of the existing system are unsatisfactory to them, then the farmers, or some of them, may succeed in learning that a new and more satisfactory land use system is available. Given these conditions, it takes only one successful innovator to set the diffusion process in motion. Thus one farmer may discover a satisfactory cropping system. When this discovery is communicated to the less successful farmers close by, many of them will adopt it. In time, the whole area may adopt the new cropping system. In an adjacent area, however, farmers for various satisficing reasons may choose another solution that also gives rise to distinctive patterns of land use. These two agricultural patterns may

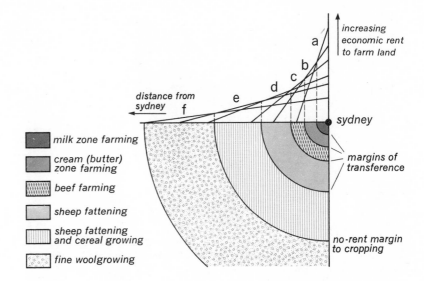

milk zone farming

cream (butter) zone farming

beef farming

sheep fattening

sheep fattening and cereal growing

fine woolgrowing

Fig. 59. *Types of farming regions in New South Wales. Hypothetical to real. Stage I, Thünian type model. (From J. Rutherford, M. I. Logan, and G. J. Missen,* New Viewpoints in Economic Geography, *1966, p. 46, reprinted with permission of Martindale Press.)*

diffuse until they reach other areas that are already satisfied.

This latter framework utilizes decision theory, study of behavioral attitudes and diffusion processes, learning theory, and communication theory. Even so, it by no means exhausts the range of concepts that could be cited.

Actual and Theoretical Agricultural Locations

Attention has already been drawn to the fact that models represent only part of reality. How far they diverge from it should already be obvious. Two divergent views have been presented in this chapter and the previous one. In chapter 6 we dealt with such concrete aspects of agricultural reality as farm structure, tenure, and market and economic conditions and attitudes. In this chapter, we reviewed attempts by geographers and others to represent parts of reality by means of models. How far do these two approaches really diverge?

Reference to the von Thünen model may help here. Figures 59–62 show the progressive relaxation of certain of the model's simplifying assumptions, as applied to the farming patterns of New South Wales, Australia.

Figures 59 and 60 stress the tendency toward concentric zonation, a function of distance from Sydney, which is the primate city and largest market. Both of these diagrams assume, as in the original von Thünen model, that the state of New South Wales is a homogeneous plain, and that the transportation costs are uniform in all directions from Sydney, except that (as can be seen from figure 60) the pattern is truncated by Sydney's coastal position.

The zones of land use shown here are based on real levels of profit around Sydney, less transportation costs, which are taken to increase at a uniform rate. The margin between zones *e* and *f* is the environmental limit for cropping.

In fact, however, physical conditions are not uniform over the whole state. Figure 61 shows that, rather than concentric zones of land use, a sectoral pattern might appear. The north-south alignment of actual land types causes a north-south alignment of land uses, especially in the interior. Thus by allowing these physical factors, especially rainfall, soils, and topography, to enter the model, the concentric pattern is distorted.

Figure 62 goes one step further. Sydney is not the only market, though it is the principal one. Accordingly, there is a tendency toward a pattern in which

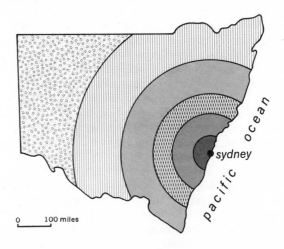

Fig. 60. *Types of farming regions in New South Wales. Stage II, introduction of state boundary and coast. (From Rutherford, Logan, Missen 1966, ibid.)*

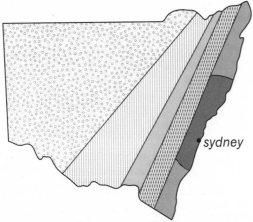

Fig. 61. *Types of farming regions in New South Wales.* Stage III, *distortion with introduction of physical variables. (From Rutherford, Logan, Missen 1966, ibid.)*

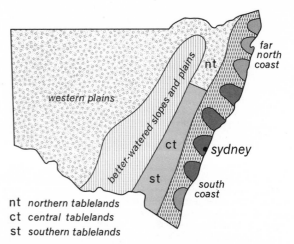

nt *northern tablelands*
ct *central tablelands*
st *southern tablelands*

Fig. 62. *Types of farming regions in New South Wales.* Stage IV, *introduction of multiple nuclei. (From Rutherford, Logan, Missen 1966, ibid.)*

a number of towns act as nodes of land use along the coast, rather than toward simple concentric zones or sectors. Allowance is also made in this diagram for further physical factors such as the existence of the Northern Tablelands, which receive less rain than the slopes of the central table lands. Once again, we can start with the simple assumptions of the von Thünen model, and then, by relaxing some of its constraints, can better understand the patterns in the landscape around us. The diagrams show some of the reasons why, in a market-exchange economy, patterns of land use are distorted by various phenomena. However, figure 62 still assumes that farmers are at heart economically rational. The complicating effects of transportation routes are ignored, as is the use of irrigation. Figure 63 illustrates actual land uses in New South Wales.

Two other recent studies by Pred have examined conditions at the so-called margin of transference (the point of change from one land use to another). They showed that, with varying farmer aspiration levels, income, farm size, and education characteristics, no such sharp boundary occurs. Land use patterns in fact overlap in an almost disorderly way due to the presence of a wide range of boundedly rational satisficing behavior instead of the rational profit maximization postulated by von Thünen and others. The farmer may actually choose the poorer alternative—for instance, forest products instead of horticulture. Thus in the real world, as opposed to von Thünen's model, cultivation of forest products can occur on either side of the alleged margin of transference. Other factors besides these strictly behavioral matters might also cause land use to overlap—the intermingling of different farm sizes, land tenure systems, small scale variations of soil, slope, and climate, and so on. If the transport gradient changes as the price changes at the market with

demand differentials, this may open up new land use opportunities not perceived by all farmers.

Some of these factors are shown in figure 64. A line joins each farmer's location in the landscape to the cell in the matrix that best summarizes his information and general receptivity. Farmers utilizing land use schema *a* beyond even *b* are shown to have limited information and limited abilities to use such information. Their ultimate survival therefore depends on how long they can survive sustained losses. Farmers utilizing *a* within ring *b*, where net returns per unit of land are higher on land use *b*, do so because of poor ability to use information or because of low information levels. Not all farmers adopting land use *a* within the "von Thünen limits" for *a* do so because of good information and ability levels; obviously, some of them select the optimal decision by chance.

Conclusion

This consideration of agriculture has swung from the real world to models, and then firmly back to the real world again. But our understanding has surely been improved by the use of these theoretical concepts. There are certain economic concepts that can be understood more clearly just because the systematic relationships that they involve have been simplified. Behavioral factors have been stressed because the models have pointed to the inadequacies of those same economic concepts, which at first seemed so important.

Each farmer is not only competing in the market place, or devising a strategy against nature; he is also competing for, among other things, labor, transport, and storage facilities. Each of these com-

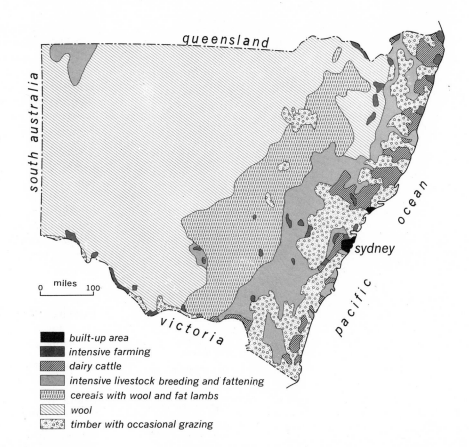

Fig. 63. *Types of farming regions in New South Wales.* Stage V, *the actual pattern.*

Legend:
- built-up area
- intensive farming
- dairy cattle
- intensive livestock breeding and fattening
- cereals with wool and fat lambs
- wool
- timber with occasional grazing

petitive situations is linked to the farmer's perceptual abilities, and these in turn are linked to his learning, education, and value system, all of which are affected by the milieu in which they occur. Because of the interdependence of anyone (apart from subsistence farmers) acting within a particular economic system the operation of each farmer is a function not only of his own abilities but, indirectly, of the abilities of others. Thus, once again, a return is made to the systems approach, which rightly stresses the interdependence of phenomena.

Summary

1. Because of the complexity of real-world patterns of agriculture, a number of models (abstractions, or simplifications) will be looked at, principally that of von Thünen.

2. Von Thünen's model, which falls into a category we call a partial equilibrium *approach, was devised in the early nineteenth century. The model is constrained by a series of simplifying assumptions which remove the effects of competing regions, many markets, variable physical factors, intended rationality, and varying transportation rates.*

3. Transportation cost is the only variable, and it is assumed to increase directly with distance. One application of the model, the intensity *aspect, occurs where only one crop is cultivated, and since the return to the farmer varies solely with transportation costs, intensity of production varies with distance from the market. The nearer the farm is to the market, the more intensive the method of farming.*

4. The crop *aspect of the model occurs when several crops are raised, each with different monetary yields. The underlying factors causing specialization of crop production in such a situation are transportation costs and economic rent. Since the simple model assumes only one market and an homogenous plain with equal lines of access, concentric rings of crop use result.*

5. Modifications of this basic model can be made to allow for a lag in adoption of a newly introduced crop, alternate means of transportation, secondary market centers, variations in physiography, etc.

6. However, no matter what modifications are made, a number of built-in assumptions limit the model's ability to replicate the agricultural landscape. The model is static, deterministic, unable to account for scale changes, and, most importantly, assumes that the farmer is "economic man."

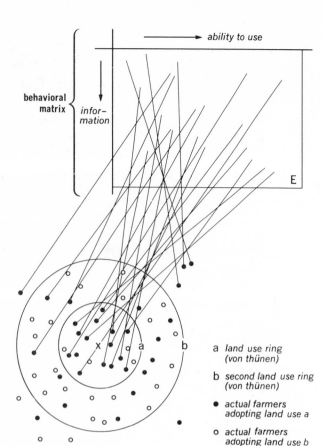

a land use ring
   (von thünen)

b second land use ring
   (von thünen)

● actual farmers
   adopting land use a

○ actual farmers
   adopting land use b

Fig. 64. *Pred's behavioral matrix and the agricultural model. (Adapted from Allen Pred,* Behavior and Location, *1967, p. 76, by courtesy of the Department of Geography, Royal University of Lund, Sweden.)*

7. A second type of model has been developed where transportation costs are held constant. These economic models utilize techniques such as input-output analysis, spatial-equilibrium approaches, and linear programming to take account of comparative advantages within and between regions. Again they assume economic rationality and, although they utilize real-world data, are still too simplistic to offer real understanding of agricultural practices.

8. Decision making models can be utilized in an attempt to overcome some of these drawbacks. Game theory and diffusion simulations, which can incorporate the multiplicity of factors determining land use decisions, have been successfully used to replicate land use patterns fairly realistically. Unfortunately, successful replication does not produce successful or realistic explanations of farmers' behavior and crop patterns.

9. Because of the inadequacies of these three earlier types, a fourth group, behavioral models, are examined. These vary from probabilistic analyses of

livestock farming to comparisons of optimal and satisficing land use patterns. In particular, one investigator was able to operationalize the behavioral approach and to recognize that farmers took a satisficing approach to agricultural decisions, had less than perfect information, and were subject to considerable uncertainty as to weather and market conditions.

10. Finally, a real-world pattern of agricultural land use in New South Wales and a von Thünen formulation are compared. Again, as the optimal conditions of the model are relaxed one by one, real-world forces become more apparent. Agricultural use patterns are found to overlap in disorderly patterns (although basically within the constraints of the phenomenal environment) which can only be accounted for in terms of the behavioral and operational milieux.

Further Reading

Theoretical approaches are dealt with by

Chisholm, M. *Rural Settlement and Land Use,* 2nd ed. (London: Hutchinson, 1968).

Found, W. C. *A Theoretical Approach to Rural Land Use Patterns* (Toronto: Macmillan of Canada, 1971).

Harvey, D. W. "Theoretical Concepts and Analysis of Agricultural Land Use Patterns in Geography," *Annals of the Association of American Geographers,* vol. 56, 1966, pp. 361–374.

Munton, R. J. C. "The Economic Geography of Agriculture" in R. U. Cooke and J. H. Johnson, eds. *Trends in Geography* (Oxford: Pergamon Press, 1969), pp. 143–152.

The von Thünen formulation and the concept of economic rent are set out in

Chisholm, M. "Agricultural Production, Location, and Rent," *Oxford Economic Papers,* vol. 13, 1961, pp. 342–59.

Dunn, E. S. *The Location of Agricultural Production* (Gainesville: University of Florida Press, 1954).

Garrison, W. L. and Marble, D. "The Spatial Structure of Agricultural Activities," *Annals of the Association of American Geography,* vol. 47, 1957, pp. 137–144.

Grotewald, A. "Von Thünen in Retrospect," *Economic Geography,* vol. 35, 1959, pp. 346–355.

Hall, P., ed. *Von Thunen's Isolated State* (Oxford: Pergamon Press, 1966).

Two recent attempts at modification and application of the basic von Thünen scheme are

Horvath, R. J. "Von Thünen's Isolated State and the Area around Addis Ababa, Ethiopia," *Annals of the Association of American Geographers,* vol. 59, 1969, pp. 308–23.

Peet, J. R. "The Spatial Expansion of Commercial Agriculture in the Nineteenth Century: A Von Thünen Interpretation," *Economic Geography*, vol. 45, 1969, pp. 283–301.

A few references to the heavier-going of economic models are

Day, R. H. and Kennedy, P. E. "On a Dynamic Location Model of Production," *Journal of Regional Science*, vol. 10, 1970, pp. 191–198.

Heady, E. O. and Egbert, A. C. "Programming Models of Interdependence among Agricultural Sectors and Spatial allocation of Crop Production," *Journal of Regional Science*, vol. 4, 1962, pp. 1–20.

Howes, R. "A Test of a Linear Programming Model of Agriculture," *Papers of the Regional Science Association*, vol. 19, 1967, pp. 123–140.

Judge, G. T. and Wallace, T. D. "Estimation of Spatial Price Equilibrium Models," *Journal of Farm Economics*, vol. 50, 1968, pp. 801–20.

Mighell, R. L. and Black, J. D. *Interregional Competition in Agriculture* (Cambridge, Mass: Harvard University Press, 1951).

Some approaches to decision making models in agriculture are covered in

Berkman, H. G. "The Game Theory of Land Use Determination," *Land Economics*, vol. 41, 1965, pp. 11–19.

Bowden, L. W. *The Diffusion of the Decision to Irrigate*, Department of Geography, University of Chicago, Research Paper no. 97, 1965.

Dillon, J. L. and Heady, E. O. *Theories of Choice in Relation to Farmer Decisions*, Iowa State, A.E.S. Bulletin no. 485, 1960.

Gould, P. R. "Man against His Environment: A Game-Theoretic Framework," *Annals of the Association of American Geographers*, vol. 53, 1963, pp. 290–297.

Gould, P. R. "Wheat on Kilimanjaro: The Perception of Choice within Game and Learning Model Frameworks," *General Systems Yearbook*, vol. 10, 1965, pp. 157–166.

Lipton, N. "The Theory of the Optimizing Peasant," *Journal of Development Studies*, vol. 4, 1968.

Behavioral models are treated by

Pred, A. *Behavior and Location*, parts 1 and 2 (Lund: C. W. K. Gleerup, 1967 and 1969).

Saarinen, T. F. *Perception of Drought Hazard on the Great Plains*, Department of Geography, University of Chicago, Research Paper no. 106, 1966.

Wolpert, J. "The Decision Process in Spatial Context," *Annals of the Association of American Geographers*, vol. 54, 1964, pp. 537–558.

eight

Manufacturing Systems: An Overview

Introduction

Scarcely any of the primary products are usable in the form they come in from the farm, forest, or mine. Wheat is milled, logs can be converted into wood pulp, ores are smelted. This transformation of commodities from one form into another form, which we have called *form utility*, is the essence of manufacturing, or the secondary group of economic activities.

Manufacturing covers a wide range of activities, from handicraft and cottage industries producing hand crafted items, to the smelting and refining of ores and the assembly of complex electronic equipment. Each type of secondary activity varies in its particular inputs of *materials*, *labor*, and *capital*, in the particular sources from which it draws these, and in particular outputs that it provides for purchase. The locational pattern, and so the impact on the landscape, varies from industrial group to industrial group with these variations in inputs, sources, and outputs. Each branch of a manufacturing group is also liable to be affected as scales of production and scales of management change from the cottage industry, to the multiplant industry, to the multiindustry firm, and to the state managed and planned industry. Other variables that can affect the landscape patterns of manufacturing are entrepreneurial attributes, temporal change, technological change, change in resource evaluation, quantitative and qualitative economic growth, growth in scale of regions, nations, and international groupings, and market changes. Figure 65 conceptualizes some of the factors that influence the decision to begin an industry at a particular location or "explain" its existence as part of a particular geographic pattern.

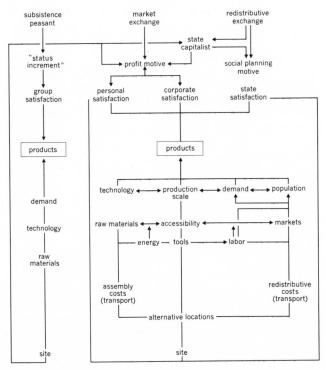

subsistence peasant

market exchange

redistributive exchange

state capitalist

profit motive

social planning motive

"status increment"

group satisfaction

personal satisfaction

corporate satisfaction

state satisfaction

products

products

technology ← → production scale ← → demand ← → population

demand

raw materials ← → accessibility ← markets

technology

energy — tools — labor

raw materials

assembly costs (transport)

redistributive costs (transport)

alternative locations

site

site

Fig. 65. *The industrial subsystem. The range of factors influencing the establishment and location of industry. (Adapted from F. E. I. Hamilton, "Models of Industrial Location," 1967, p. 365, by permission of Methuen and Co.)*

For centuries industrial transformation was conducted at the home of the consumer, with specialization and supply without the household growing very slowly. The specialization of large numbers of people in exchange economies carrying out these transformational or manufacturing activities is a phenomenon of the last 200 years. The step from the first steam engine to the first satellite and space probe has been encompassed in that time span. Today about 95 million people are employed in exchange manufacturing systems, about 10 percent of the world's labor force. As figure 66 shows, the proportions vary tremendously (compare with figure 39); some nations have a very small industrial labor force, while a few technically advanced areas like Western Europe, the U.S.A., and U.S.S.R. have large numbers employed in manufacturing.

The simplest type of transformation, the **household** or **cottage industry,** is sited at the source of raw materials and mostly at the site of consumption; it produces clothing, furniture, utensils, tools, and ornaments. These cottage industries are not just confined to the historical past, but are found widely in the so-called developing countries today. In some areas, besides supplying a household or village market they now supply on an exchange basis national and international markets (Indian handwoven cotton cloths are a good example). Neither have these cottage industries always been confined completely to the home, as the bread baking, fulling, brick making, and pottery workshops of the Roman Empire testify. However, capital is limited in these circumstances and equipment crude and simple, so that the industrial sites are small and frequently scattered. This spatially dispersive character results from a number of factors. In the **eotechnic** phase, so termed by Mumford in 1934, energy and raw materials were found nearly everywhere in the form of wood, wind, water, clays, sands, skins, and wool; the labor available was plentiful, and labor inputs could therefore be high; population and therefore markets were dispersed and scattered; transport was slow, difficult, and very costly. Regional dif-

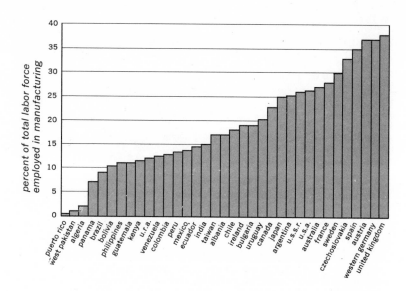

Fig. 66. *Proportion of the labor force employed in the industrial sector. (Based on data in the* United Nations, *Yearbook, 1969.)*

ferences arose through the lack or growth of industries that processed materials like wood or metals and produced valuable products like cloth that could be transported by water.

The Industrial Revolution, with some roots in late eighteenth-century England, began to change the emphasis within the industrial structure (figure 67). It allowed or made possible the specialization of labor, so that no longer was it necessary to have 80 percent of the labor force concerned with agriculture. Mechanization and new energy sources are two prime attributes of the Industrial Revolution, which allowed a concentrative force to come into action. This is Mumford's **paleotechnic** phase. Transport was still a controlling factor, and the availability of a cheap mode (water) a great asset. The increased use of coal, a bulky material, as an energy source, localized the rapid growth of existing and newly founded industries to coal fields or their immediate proximity. A further localizing factor was the association of other raw materials with coal—fireclays, iron ore, and so on. As these base areas grew, certain feedback effects occurred, so that the areas grew in strength as markets expanded and more and more capital and skill were tied to the coal field localities. However as technology and transportation improved, in particular via railroads, the hold of the raw material sites began to loosen in favor of growing urban markets. Space and distance, resistance factors of a high order until this period in the nineteenth century, were decreasing as obstacles to mobility.

The last 100 years have seen further shifts still—Mumford's **neotechnic** phase. Increased efficiency in transport is of particular importance, and instead of low efficiency and high costs, transportation costs now form only a small proportion of final costs. Transportation costs are still vital in some cases, as industries operate on smaller and smaller cost margins. However, this general decrease in transportation costs has been accompanied by a smaller change in production costs, even with the growth of mass production techniques. Mass production, with all its interrelational systems implications, is another important structural attribute of the neotechnic phase. As these changes have occurred, emphasis has shifted towards strong market orientations, a shift that is aided by technical changes within energy (mobility), growing skills, and the search for noneconomic factors (amenities, recreation). Thus nowadays there is considerable flexibility of location choice.

A. Pred's 1965 study of this process in a few North American centers between 1860 and 1910 shows how the progressive concentration of manufacturing arose there. From the initial setting up of industries, through random or intendedly rational processes, their growth caused a multiplying effect and feedback as the growing productive system stimulated technical changes, attracted labor, and developed skills. Once these centers were established, three factors ensured future growth, and discouraged growth and development at comparatively inefficient or nonproductive centers. These were changes in transportation, the relative lowering of production costs, and the growth of an industrial establishment, the latter blocking growth to unwanted competitors.

Elements of the System

This brief historical sketch introduces some of the factors important in a study of manufacturing. As figure 65 emphasizes, evolutionary schemes can illuminate the present as much as the past. The neotechnic phase coexists in the contemporary world with the paleotechnic and eotechnic phases.

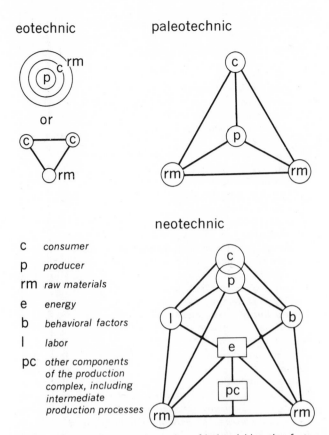

eotechnic   paleotechnic

neotechnic

c   consumer
p   producer
rm *raw materials*
e   energy
b   *behavioral factors*
l   labor
pc *other components
    of the production
    complex, including
    intermediate
    production processes*

Fig. 67.   *The historical transformation of industrial location factors.*

The manufacturing subsystem encompasses all activities where man assembles raw materials at an establishment (household, workshop, or factory), where their usefulness is enhanced (the addition of form utility), and where those products are shipped to the consumer. The focal point of this manufacturing activity is the place of transformation, the **factory,** which serves as a link with both the source of raw materials and the area of consumption. The interaction of this system, as figures 65 and 67 show, focuses on the site or location of the factory. So the elements of the subsystem that are important are the elements that influence the choice of factory site—source of raw materials, transportation costs, energy, labor supply, capital, entrepreneurial attitudes, and certain other elements of the operational milieu.

The ideal manufacturing area would provide the factories with four essential requirements—raw materials, one or more sources of energy, labor, and a market. But since ideal requirements rarely exist, most factories must choose between locations that have some but not all of those elements. The orientation of an industry determines which single requirement seems to the entrepreneur to be the most important in establishing the location of a factory. For example, a factory that was oriented toward raw materials might tend to be located nearer to raw ma-

terial sources than to either labor or markets. A market-oriented factory, on the other hand, might place a premium on being located nearer to customers.

It is hard to analyze the locational procedures followed by entrepreneurs, as we have seen already in the case of agriculture. The economic needs of factories differ from industry to industry, and vary with the size of the individual firm. Managerial attitudes to location also differ widely. In some cases managers have tried to take a rational view and have estimated carefully within the limits of their abilities; in others, very little thought has been given to the problem. Existing locations are also not necessarily the most favorable in terms of present-day Western strategy; in older industrial areas the original reasons for location may be lost in the past, and managers may be unwilling to move, despite new ties, because of **geographic inertia.** Irrespective of the reason why these locations were chosen and the decision made, over time it has led to a similarity of result, a concentration of manufacturing in areas, belts, or agglomerations in many "advanced" nations.

Figure 65, a diagram of an industrial system, tries to categorize and structure some of the locational factors involved. As with the agricultural subsystem, this subsystem is placed in a particular socioeconomic context, as we can see from its recognition of subsistent-peasant, market-exchange, and redistributive economic organization. Since many market-exchange economies are subject to some state planning, and some redistributive economies have a so-called private sector, another category is introduced. For convenience, it is called **state capitalism.** These differences in economic organization are reflected in the locational decisions eventually made, though with the exception of subsistent-peasant, they are essentially dealing with the same set of locational factors, which are therefore shown in the diagram as common to the systems. Even subsistent-peasant economies are rarely without some contact with an exchange economy—that is, with the main system.

The approaches made to the location problem do differ however, and these vary with time and place. During the Industrial Revolution, locations were determined mainly by *private capitalists;* the same is true of the early stages of industrialization, when capital requirements are small. As the need for capital investments outstrip the capital resources of one-man businesses, this role is taken over, at least in capitalist countries, by *corporations, conglomerates,* and powerful *stock companies.* This change is typical of twentieth-century Western Europe and North America. The state, on the other hand, plays a powerful role in redistributive economies and in a growing number of market-exchange economies as the planning abilities of the competitive corporations fail to meet the responsibilities of long-term growth and planning.

In most theoretical discussions it is assumed, as in von Thünen's agricultural model, that entrepreneurs strive to maximize their profits by making thoroughly rational locational decisions. This assumption of course is openly questioned, and applied and empirical research has shown that the noneconomic or personal motives of entrepreneurs have exerted a considerable influence on location decision making. Some of these motives, as with agricultural motives and attitudes, are difficult to systematize. The earlier notion of status increment is used for the subsistent-peasant group; this term refers to motivation in a noneconomic way. Profit is the motive of most decisions in the market-exchange and of some in state capitalist economies; consideration of social benefits and costs motivates the decisions under a centralized government agency. The divergences between individual entrepreneur (individual, corporate, or state) are accounted for by different levels of satisfaction. Thus given the same business or plant to locate, no two entrepreneurs would judge alternative locations by the same maximizing criteria of profit or social benefit. The rest of the diagram deals with demand, which itself is influenced by such factors as: population size and occupation structure; scales of production; technology; assembly and distributive costs; raw materials; and the labor force and its technological attributes.

Some order appears to exist, despite the lack of rational decision making. The long-term pressures of the economic systems have exerted powerful influences on the seemingly noneconomic motives of individuals. Accordingly, the factors depicted in figure 65 do seem to play some role in the location pattern of industry. In fact, as will be seen later, irrespective of the reasons why location decisions are made, over time they have led to a similarity of result in market-exchange, redistributive, and state capitalist economic systems: a concentration of manufacturing in areas, belts, or agglomerations.

Economic Structure

The major economic factors that influence the location decisions of an entrepreneur, consciously or unconsciously, are summarized in this subsection and in table 24.

Material and Resource Availability

As we have seen, the location of certain industries is strongly oriented to raw materials, though with technological development there has been a strong

Table 24. *Summary: Descriptive Elements of the Industrial System*

1. influence of materials:
    weight losing?
    perishable?
    value per unit of weight?
    substitutability?
    how many materials used?
    freight rate structure?
2. market influences:
    high transportation costs on finished product?
    perishable?
    personal contact?
    relatively cheap product?
    size of market area?
    market capacity?
3. transfer costs:
    distinguish between transport *and* transfer *costs.*
    form of transport?
    return cargo?
    nature of commodity?
    volume of traffic?
    structure of freight rates?
    break-of-bulk point?
    fabrication-in-transit?
    restrictive practices?
4. energy
5. factors of production:
    a. *labor: geographic variation in cost?*
        geographic variation in supply?
        geographic distribution of specific skills?
        attitudes?
        unionization?
        availability of food?
    b. *capital: effects of political boundaries?*
        existence of financial institutions?
        inertia of fixed capital?
    c. *enterprise: mobility?*
        in underdeveloped regions?
6. geographical concentration: *the development of the concept of "linked" industries.*
    a. *economics of scale (internal).*
    b. *external economics: localization economics — resulting from being near to suppliers, subcontractors, and similar firms.*
        urbanization economics — agglomeration of unlike industries gives rise to savings in costs of police protection, insurance, and municipal services generally.
7. government activity:
    legal restraints?
    taxation?
    government expenditure?
    direct government influence?
8. other:
    site requirement?
    building?
    services?
    local attitude?
    promotional activities?
    water supply?
    local taxation?
    climate?

tendency for this factor to decline in significance. Obviously, however, the availability of materials to be transformed in the industrial process is crucial, and all industries are to some degree concerned with the costs of procuring those materials. Raw materials are distributed in an uneven manner, and they are not everywhere economically accessible. Other matters being equal, an industry utilizing resources will be located with regard to the costs of procuring them. Of course other matters are rarely equal, and technical change has increasingly made it possible for resources to be used more efficiently and to be transported over greater distances. Thus the degree of attraction exercised by resources will vary with the resource, the processes which they undergo, and the techniques of distribution. There are still some industries, however, that continue to be oriented toward raw materials, and they are influenced by a number of factors.

Weight Loss

If the material or resource loses much of its original weight when it goes through the manufacturing process (i.e., if it is **gross**), then the industry will tend to be attracted to the resource site itself, so that transportation costs can be kept to a minimum. Thus in processing sugar beets, seven-eighths of their weight is lost in refining to sugar; pulp and paper lose three-fifths; milk to form butter and cheese about five-sixths; and iron ore to form pig iron from two-thirds to three-quarters. Loss of bulk or weight can be overcome through the use of mineral concentrators. However, industries with these great weight losses are attracted to the source of raw materials. Thus sugar beet refineries tend to be in the midst of beet growing areas, and blast furnaces tend to be on orefields or coalfields (although in recent years this tendency has decreased). This simple proposition can be modified because of freight charges, economies gained through integration, and other factors.

Perishability

If a material is highly perishable like fresh fruits, vegetables, or milk, it is common for processing to occur near the points of raw material production. This particularly applies when the market areas are distant. The notion of partial processing enters here too. Just as there are ore concentrators, which remove bulk or in this case some degree of perishability, some processes occur in two stages. Thus sugar cane, for instance, is first milled, and then reduced in bulk and perishability so that it can be moved more cheaply (and frequently more slowly) to its final processing near or at the market.

Value Per Unit of Weight

Transport costs add less proportionately to the cost of a material of higher value than to one of lower value, even though there may be a freight differential against more valuable cargo. Thus the more highly priced the material in relation to the value added in manufacturing, the more likely it is to be carried over long distances. Thus a material of high value like wool can more readily bear the costs of transportation, than a material of low value per unit of weight like copper ores.

Substitute Materials

The ability to substitute one material for another is growing as technology advances. In the choice of location for a steel making plant, the choice could be either one near to pig iron, or one near to scrap metal. When materials can be substituted like this, the pull of either (or any, if there are more than two) is reduced. Capital can also be substituted for raw materials, when more efficient techniques allow the use of smaller quantities of raw materials; an example again is the iron and steel industry.

Number of Materials Involved

The number and relative importance of the resources used is important. Industries rarely use just one raw material, and the more materials they do use the lesser the influence again of any one, unless it loses a great deal of weight in processing. For example the iron and steel industry uses not just iron ore, but coking coal, limestone, and scrap. For each material the conditions of supply may vary. In the case of the electronics industry many components in small quantities and of more or less equal importance are used, so that none of them exerts much influence on the location decision.

Freight Rate Structure

The influence exerted by a raw material can be reduced or enhanced by the freight rate structure. If raw material production sites have access to sea transport, for example, distant users may take advantage of the relatively low freight rates that operate over great distances. North American iron and steel industries are heavily dependent on water transportation of ores. Railroads usually offer tapering freight rates — that is, lower rates per ton as the distance increases (these are considered in more detail below, in chapter 13). Changing rate differentials between livestock and meat products were an important factor in the struggle between rival centers of the meat packing industry in the United States. So not only distance, but the actual rating procedures are important.

Finally, a note should be added that many industries do not of course draw directly on primary products, but rather on the products of other intermediate industrial processes. In their case, everything said above about raw materials sites applies to intermediate process materials sites.

Material procurement costs still remain of importance, despite technical changes and capital substitutability, especially to industrial activities that directly process bulky primary products — lumber mills, copper smelting, sugar refining and so on. Even here, however, the directness of this relationship is modified by remoteness from markets, lack of transportation facilities, and the use of partial processing, all of which may alter the basic pattern. Obviously, transportation is a basic factor. With this in mind it is obvious that the less developed the transportation facilities, the greater the role played by the materials.

Market Factors

The attractions of a market location have become increasingly important as the influence of raw materials has declined. The attraction of a materials location is often weighed against the attraction of the market, the latter being a concentration of other industries or consumers. Again a number of sub-elements can be identified.

Transportation Costs

While there may be a reduction in volume, weight, or perishability through processing, there may equally well be an increase. In this case the cost of moving the finished product is such a high percentage of the total costs that processing must be very close to the market. Bulk in manufacture occurs in processes that add water, for example brewing and soda water manufacture.

Perishability

Perishability may be added by manufacture, as in the baking industry with bread and cakes, and these tend to be manufactured close to the consumer. Perishability of another kind is added by the glass industry, for its finished product is more difficult and thus more costly to transport than its raw materials. A third category of perishability is news, so that local newspapers tend to be of little value outside their own localities. Thus newspaper production is strongly attached to its market.

Personal Contact

Personal contact between producer and consumer can be important, as with the fashion clothing industry, where close personal contact between manufacturers, designers, and department stores is essential. This provides one of the reasons for the concentration of high class clothing industries near the downtown cores of Paris, New York, and London.

Low Value Products

Low value products, with low initial costs, but some bulk, can have a substantial cost addition if they are far from the market. Cement is probably the best example, since it is a low value product with high distribution costs that is located in market areas because of this factor.

Market Size

Local, regional, national, and international markets offer different locational problems. If the market is very concentrated and specialized, it usually pays to be close to it. Thus textile machinery manufacturers will tend to be near textile centers. This "pull" of the market reflects in part lower transportation costs on the finished product, personal contacts, and so on. If the markets, on the other hand, are scattered or diffused over a large area, a number of choices are open to the entrepreneur. The problem is often made more difficult by the entrepreneur's desire for plants to serve large markets in order to gain the maximum economies of large-scale production. If, through this, transportation costs become greater than the savings arising from large-scale production, the plants may be made smaller in size and more diffused, in order to be near each local center (once more, brewing is a good example). If, however, the output of a few enterprises serves a national market and transportation costs are not prohibitive, the location chosen will be a good distribution point, that is, a nodal point on a transportation network.

Market Capacity

Some industries, such as iron and steel, gain maximum economies in production when they can operate on an enormous scale. If productive capacity goes beyond the market capacity of the immediate market area, then this will be balanced against the extra transportation costs incurred. Smaller productive capacity may in this case raise the cost substantially to the consumer. This is an important argument against establishing iron and steel, chemical, or automobile industries in newly industrializing or developing countries.

These are only some of the important market factors; others are a concentration of labor, and spending power. The pull of the market is thus a very powerful one indeed, and there is a tendency to regard the market location as the norm, and to explain nonmarket locations in terms of cost advantages.

Transfer Costs

The importance of transportation costs has been underlined in the previous two subsections. However, a distinction should be made between **transportation costs** and **transfer costs.** Transportation costs are the direct freight costs; transfer costs are the transportation charges plus other indirect expenses such as interest or insurance. Thus freight charges alone do not express all movement costs. Speed, regularity and dependability can also be included as part of these indirect costs. The requirements vary of course with the nature of the product. For bulky and low value goods speed is rarely essential; of more importance is the ability of the mode of transport to carry large quantities at low cost. By contrast a highly perishable or valuable product requires above all speedy movement, and this urgency may outweigh the higher transportation costs of road or even air transport.

Transport, despite its declining significance, must be considered an integral part of the productive process, for a commodity has to be moved from the point of production to the point of consumption. The cost of assembling materials and distributing products varies in relative terms from industry to industry, but in some industries it still forms a large proportion of total costs. Even movements over short distances can significantly affect costs in this latter group; for example, the Lorraine iron and steel industry is strongly affected by the freight rates of the nationalized French rail system, which can add up to 30 percent onto total costs. Some firms are therefore acutely interested in variation in transportation costs from area to area. Other things being equal they tend to locate where aggregate transfer costs are at a minimum. Even where transport costs are not so important there is still a heavy dependence on an efficient system of transference.

Mode of Transport

The mode of transport has a special significance (see chapter 13). Different modes of transport may also be in competition. This in turn may give rise to special rates, as for example when a railroad is in competition with an inland waterway or pipeline.

Back Haulage

The possibility of a return cargo is significant if wagons, barges, or trucks have to return unladen. Otherwise, freight charges will have to be high enough to pay the costs of the empty return journey.

Commodity Type

The nature of the commodity may incur extra transfer charges if special containers are needed for liquid or refrigerated goods, or those kept under pressure, such as liquefied gases, or if special care is needed for highly perishable or fragile goods, or finally because of special loading or unloading facilities.

Volume of Traffic

A large volume of traffic may create special rates. This can have an adverse effect on smaller firms in competition with larger plants, or on new enterprises whose growth may be restricted by having to absorb higher transfer costs than their larger competitors, who qualify for freight rate reductions.

Freight Rates

The structure of freight rates is a complex but important topic. Charges vary according to the commodity to be carried. One mode of transport can fix rates so that locations that perhaps are no longer strictly viable because of technical change are perpetuated because of the unfavorable rate charges to new or existing plants that in fact are in more favorable locations. On the other hand, low commodity rates or special privileges can be extended in order to foster new industrial developments. Bulky goods are normally carried at low ton-mile rates, and finished and semifinished products can usually bear a higher transportation charge because of their higher value. In terms of weight, fixed charges would favor raw materials. But these latter are in fact less costly to move than the fabricated products, which reduces the pull of the raw material site in favor of the market location. These cheaper rates for heavy raw materials enable them to be transported further than would be economic if the same rate applied equally.

Distance is also important; freight rates fall with increasing distance, but not in a uniform way. A high proportion of the total cost of movement is incurred at terminals; the costs of handling, loading, discharge, and storage are especially high. These remain the same, however, no matter what the length of the haul, and the hauler can therefore quote lower charges per ton mile as distance increases. So sheer distance can be less of a handicap than might appear at first sight. Break of bulk between modes or across political boundaries may disrupt the economies of long distance haulage. This was particularly important in the Western European steel industry, where products crossed many political boundaries until the rationalizing effect of the European Common Market made itself felt.

Fabrication in Transit

Obviously, the rates for two short distances are going to be more than the rate on one journey of the same overall length. But special charges may be granted by a railroad company, for instance, in order to allow a stop for manufacturing. The now transformed good continues to the wholesaler or to another fabrication point, at the original freight rate. Such fabrication-in-transit privileges exist in the United States for the products mentioned in table 25. These privileges allow the producer to locate between the material source and the market, and to save transfer costs by still using a long haul rate, even though two shorter hauls have now been substituted.

Table 25. *Commodities with Fabrication-In-Transit Privileges in the United States*

commodity	privileges
grain	milling, inspection, mixing, grading, sacking, and storage
lumber	manufacturing and further improvements
marble and granite	finishing
lead and zinc ore	refining
livestock	grazing and fattening
iron and steel products	fabrication
cotton and hay	compression
butter, eggs, dairy products, and dressed poultry	concentration
miscellaneous products	storage

Source: M. Fulton and L.C. Hoch, "Transportation Factors Affecting Locational Decisions," *Economic Geography*, vol. 35, 1959, pp. 51–59.

The milling-in-transit privilege means that both grain and grain products such as flour and breakfast foods are hauled at the same freight rates. This has tended to equalize freight burdens, thus permitting mills in the Eastern United States to compete with those in the Middle West.

Restrictive Schemes

Of more general importance than in-transit privileges is the operation of restrictive schemes, either by governments or by groups of producers. These basing-point systems can place certain areas of a country in a favorable position for industrial growth. Probably the classic example of this was the "Pittsburgh Plus" basing-point scheme, which from 1900 to 1924 required all U.S. steel to be sold at the Pittsburgh price plus the cost of moving it from Pittsburgh, although the steel might be produced elsewhere. This scheme naturally reinforced the dominance of Pittsburgh in the U.S. steel industry at the expense of other areas. It was replaced, from 1924 until 1948, by a multibased system, but one that still favored Pittsburgh. After 1948 the industry introduced a rating structure that gave local mills a competitive advantage in their local areas.

Thus the best location for the transport oriented industry is one that minimizes the costs of assembly and distribution. Holding other matters constant, wherever the product is much lighter or less bulky than the materials used the process tends to be attracted toward the material source. If the product is more expensive to transport than the materials, production is likely to be attracted toward the market. In a less clear-cut case (like the majority of instances) a location may be chosen because of its accessibility to and from a wide area. It may be that a location where total transfer costs are lowest is not the most favorable site for an industry, because of lower processing costs (considered below), and other factors that may offset a nonminimum transfer cost location.

Factors of Production

There are many processes for which the costs of assemblage of raw materials, including energy and the costs of distribution, are a small percentage of total costs, given the existence of a satisfactory transportation service. For example the shift of cotton textile production from New England to the South is not explainable in terms of savings on the transfer of raw materials. While the southern mills do save 20 to 30 percent on freight costs for cotton as compared to New England, this saving, it is estimated, represents only 0.3 to 0.7 percent of total manufacturing costs.

The optimal location in these cases may be where there is an optimum combination of processing and other production costs. Processing costs mainly involve costs of labor, capital, services, and levels of taxation. If any one of these factors is unevenly distributed in space, then industries may seek out locations that minimize one of these production factors. Such spatial variations can often be offset by the mobility of the production factors; thus the mobility of capital makes it unlikely that the price of capital (i.e., interest rates) will vary much over the surface of the same country. On the other hand, labor can be relatively immobile, and regional variations in wage rates can be the decisive factor that induces an industry to locate at point A rather than point B. So all of the production factors are available to the manufacturer—at a price. These prices can then vary geographically because of the imperfect mobility of the factors of production. However, the entrepreneur can offset some of the geographic variation in these factors by restricting the use of a high-priced input (labor) and substituting another input such as capital. Thus automating a plant would offset high labor costs. This could also be done by using one piece of capital equipment for longer hours, that is, substituting labor for capital by working a shift system. This ability to substitute one input for another gives the manufacturer considerable flexibility in his location choice.

Labor

This is one of the most important cost items in the structure of industry, although it varies from industry to industry; it is particularly important where labor costs are a large proportion of total costs. In such industries the geographic differences in labor costs may be of great significance in a location choice. These industries include those where techniques are not highly mechanized, and the final product thus has a high labor component. Some idea of the range of labor costs as a proportion of total value added by processing in the United States can be gained from table 26.

Geographic Differences in Labor Costs. Labor intensive industries such as clothing, textiles, and leather, where labor costs exceed 50 percent of the value added by manufacturing, are attracted to sites where a plentiful supply of labor and relatively low wages can be found together. Tables 27 and 28 indicate some of the regional differences that can occur in two particular countries. Table 27 indicates that there are considerable variations in average hourly earnings by area and occupation, and shows one of the reasons why there has been a substantial net migration into Southeast England for several dec-

Table 26. *Labor Costs as Proportion of Total Value Added by Manufacture (United States, 1956)*

clothing industries	62%
leather industries	60%
textile industries	51%
fabricated metal products	43%
	average 37%
machinery (except electrical)	34%
electrical machinery	30%
chemicals	29%

Source: R.C. Estall and R.O. Buchanan, *Industrial Activity and Economic Geography* (London: Hutchinson, 1961), p. 83. Reprinted by permission of the publisher.

Table 27. *Average Hourly Earnings* in Engineering and Other Metal-Using Industries, U.K.*

	hourly workers			piece workers		
	skilled	semi	unskilled	skilled	semi	unskilled
Midlands	105	98	100	110	110	107
East and South England	103	111	111	96	112	109
London and S.E.	102	111	105	104	95	107
South Western	101	89	97	93	99	92
Wales	101	94	103	96	97	98
North Western	94	88	93	91	88	94
Northern	92	86	95	96	88	95
Scotland	90	89	97	94	90	101
Yorks. and Linc.	90	90	95	92	91	94
national average	100 [92.6]	100 [81.7]	100 [65.2]	100 [99.6]	100 [91.4]	100 [69.4]

*including overtime

Source: M. Chisholm, *Geography and Economics* (London: G. Bell, 1966), p. 126

Table 28. *Regional Variation in Wage Rates; U.S. Manufacturing Industries 1907–1946*

(100 = Northeast wage rates)

	Northeast	South	Midwest	Far West
1907	100	86	100	130
1919	100	87	97	115
1931-2	100	74	97	113
1945-6	100	85	101	115

Source: M. Chisholm, *Geography and Economics* (London: G. Bell), p. 126.

Table 29. *The Institutional Framework of Entrepreneurial Behavior*

	political institutions	economic institutions	business institutions	other institutions
values and behavior	authority, power *relation of national or regional government to the firm and the individual*	systems *of exchange, factors of production, value, and distribution* economic *costs*	the business ethic *"free" enterprise* profit motive *individual satisfaction business welfare*	tradition *social codes religious practices societal attitudes and motivations*
structure	*the military-industrial complex* constitution legislation	*the firm the multiplant firm the corporate enterprise*	*stock exchange marketing and management schools chambers of commerce other clubs*	*trade unions professional organizations churches nonbusiness clubs and societies*
means	*antimonopoly commissions* antitrust laws tariffs, quotas pressure groups state planning and management	*board of directors entrepreneur marketing and distribution advertising*	*lobbies manipulative practices patents*	*labor organizations (strikers, bargaining, restrictive practices) pressure groups consumer unions*

ades. In the United States, by contrast, the geographic variation in wage rates and earnings appears to be getting less. In 1907 wage rates in the Far West were the highest, topping those in the Northeast by some 30 percent. By 1945–46, however, the difference was down to 15 percent, as shown in table 28.

Geographic Variations in Supply. An industry will normally wish to find an adequate pool of the kinds of labor required at a prospective location. By locating in an area already provided with a pool of labor the employer also finds the essential **social capital,** such as housing, water supply, sanitation, and schools. On some occasions plant construction may precede the labor supply, but this considerably raises the initial capital requirements. This kind of situation occurs when industry moves into such previously undeveloped and sparsely populated areas as northern British Columbia. For example, the Aluminum Company of Canada founded a new town, Kitimat, to draw labor to its new aluminum smelting plant on the central coast of British Columbia.

Normally, large labor concentrations are very attractive to industry, since an employer may find the bulk of the labor to suit his needs. In addition, there is normally some organization through which he can quickly obtain more workers.

Geographic mobility of labor occurs in response to differences in opportunities and earnings. As we have seen, regional differences in earning power can be considerable. Local mobility rests on the costs (in both time and money) of personal transport, and in advanced economies industries can draw on a wide catchment area. Regional mobility rests on more complex bases; social, economic and often political upheaval may have to occur to induce people to leave

their home areas. A great deal of work has been carried on to try to measure why people migrate; the image of the areas to which people move is important, as are their expectations; absolute differences in wage levels, and so on, may be of smaller importance.

Skills of Labor Supply. Labor supply concerns not only the physical supply of labor but the age, sex, and skills of the supply. Because of the high costs involved in training workers in some industries, rapid turnover of labor can greatly increase production costs. In general, manufacturing industries need a higher level of skill, as modern plant and equipment are introduced. Thus a major problem of developing countries quite frequently is not so much the physical numbers of workers, but rather their general lack of skills to operate technically advanced machinery. While this general level of skill has been increasingly in demand, the demand for specialized skills has declined. Mechanization and standardization in production have replaced the craftsman. Some industries, however, do still call for a high degree of manual skill. These tend to be concentrated in the area where the industry first arose. Naturally, the area attracts new plants in that industry to it—specialized steel products such as cutlery, custom-made furniture, tailoring, and pottery, for instance. Skill continues to be demanded, but more at the semi-skilled level.

Skills in this latter sense can be transferred from industry to industry. Thus in the United Kingdom skills have been transferred, in an area like the Midlands, from sewing machines to bicycles to automobiles. But they have not been transferred so easily in Northeast England or South Wales, where the specialized skills of coal mining and shipbuilding were not as universal. Factors like these can be crucial for the prosperity of entire nations, since to develop is to adapt. Thus the Swiss watch industry was originally an attempt—and a highly successful one—at overcoming the handicaps of a remote location and poor national resources by developing skills already possessed by the Swiss people.

Attitudes of Workers and Influence of Trade Unions. In older industrial areas militant trade unions may be well entrenched, which—rightly or wrongly—can cause strained worker-management relations. This image of an area might dissuade many employers seeking new locations, and in fact could also stimulate existing firms to open branch plants in areas with more favorable attitudes. Industries moving to new areas will study very carefully the history of labor-management relations. It has been suggested that attitudes, trade unions, and labor-management relations have led to the decline of a number of British industries, including shipbuilding and the Lancashire cotton industry.

Workers' attitudes are also reflected in productivity. In a long established area a tradition may grow up concerning the work load, with opposition to innovation. Automation, too, actively involves trade unions and labor attitudes. Interindustry mobility, which is of importance to modern industries in replacing older skills, may be restricted by union activities.

Food Supply. Food supply is taken for granted in most market-exchange and redistributive economies. But on a world scale, it must be remembered that industrial development is not possible without adequate food supplies to sustain industrial workers. Industries either need an efficient agricultural base, or at least connections with an area of food surplus. However, in much of the world these prerequisites do not exist, and there is little or no food surplus above and beyond the needs of the agricultural workers. This situation is made more complex by the inability of the agricultural worker to afford to purchase the products of the industrial sector. Thus in developing countries the adequacy of food supplies is of major significance to industrial location and labor supply, as of course it was also in the initiation of the Industrial Revolution.

Capital

A trend was noted above for capital to be increasingly substituted for labor. At the national level, **money capital** is quite mobile, and there are few areal variations in the supply. Capital in this sense is probably the most mobile of all production factors,

moving quickly to areas of growth that offer good investment possibilities. Despite this mobility there are still areas that develop the reputation of being sources of capital—Toronto, Montreal, New York, Chicago, Los Angeles—while other areas may have difficulty, real or imagined, in attracting capital. However, within some countries, such as Denmark and Norway, governments may take special steps to increase capital liquidity and holdings in some regions that still fail to attract capital.

At the international level, movement of capital is much more difficult. National boundaries can hinder the flow of capital and lead to an uneven variation on a world scale. The potential to attract money capital is a function of two main factors: rate of return on the investment, and stability (low risk). Thus the political environment of a nation may play a great role, and the threat of nationalization of plantations, banks, industries, or oil installations will frighten off all but small capital sums. Hence political instability in West Africa, Central Africa, parts of Southeast Asia, the Middle East, and parts of the Caribbean tend to deter capital investment. Investment in industries in these areas is also held back by the lack of the overhead facilities and institutions—banking, insurance, savings and cooperative credit associations, communications, stock markets, and so on. The lack of banking and credit facilities not only hinders existing industrial growth but deters further capital investment.

The international mobility of capital is also limited by balance-of-payments problems. Heavy outflows of capital for a lengthy period might seriously affect an investor-countries balance of payments. Attempts to reverse the process might raise the costs of capital internally and externally.

Besides money capital there is also **fixed capital.** Fixed, or physical, capital is relatively immobile; it includes machinery, buildings, capital equipment, and social capital such as houses. Heavy investment in fixed capital tends to lead to inertia and immobility, since this kind of equipment is not easily written off until its useful term of life has been served. As long as some kind of depreciation costs can be applied against the fixed value, an industry is better off staying where it is than moving elsewhere. However, if either the raw materials or market change locations this may no longer hold. A plant is not worth much as scrap.

Enterprise

The efficient application of labor and capital varies with the general level of business organization and management, both of which can vary regionally. If men with skills in technology, administration, systems analysis, and marketing are not present, then the establishment of industries is difficult, if not impossible. Industrial management must be capable of formulating policies, planning production, setting standards, forecasting future growth potential, and planning the marketing of the good or goods. For these reasons the cost of management is often separated from the general production cost of labor.

From the locational standpoint, established manufacturing areas will be seen as having supplies of this kind of labor, while other areas will have to be assessed according to their ability to attract people of this training and caliber. This means usually that the area must have some physical or social desirability. As industry is released by technical developments from being tied to transportation costs, a firm may well look to an area's scenic and recreational facilities, its cultural assets, and so on. Snow and mountains are not essential to the assembly of electronic components, yet New Hampshire and Colorado contain industries of this type that have been attracted partly by the physical environment.

Geographic Concentration

Of equal importance with the factors discussed above are the economies a firm may gain by locating in a major center of industrial production, and sometimes by close geographic association with other productive units in the same industry. Manufacturing activities of most types, in fact, tend to cluster or agglomerate at nodes. It has already been noted that market influences can attract industries to large cities or nodal locations, but this does not always explain particular concentrations of industry, especially within a city or nodal region. The reasons for such concentrations can be expressed in terms of the economies gained by such locations, sometimes called **agglomeration economies**. Three categories of such economies can be identified:

1. *Large-scale internal economies, achieved by the increase in each single firm's scale of production.*
2. *Localization economies, for all firms within a particular industrial category in one area, due to the increase in total output.*
3. *Urbanization economies, for all firms in all industries in one area, due to the better market conditions and economies of management that are achieved by an increase in total economic size.*

As an aid in the understanding of these economies, the concept of **linkage** can be used. Linkage in this context means a group of geographically associated establishments that pursue the same kind of process or take part in the same sequence of operations. Four common types of linkage can be recognized: vertical, horizontal, diagonal, and multiple.

Vertical Linkage

The interrelationship of separate firms, each normally forming one stage in a series of operations, is known as vertical linkage (figure 68). This chain of production sequence can be seen in the nonferrous metal trades: the first stage is refining by one set of firms or plants; the second is the shaping of the metal by another set; the third is the further processing of rough shapes; and the fourth is the finishing of a particular product. Each member of the chain draws economies simply by being near the other members, a phenomenon known as external **economies of scale**. In other cases, the individual firm might expand its share of the production chain, finally undertaking the whole process previously carried out by a number of small firms, or scattered plants of one firm. One example of this process would be the integrated steel mill; this would be an internal economy of scale.

Horizontal Linkage

The kind of linkage referred to here is when separate firms produce many individual parts and accessories that are not a chain of processes, but that are brought together at some later stage to be assembled into a finished product. An example would be automobile component manufacturers and their convergence on Detroit from a radius of 150–200 miles.

Diagonal Linkages

When a firm produces a good or provides a service that is required at various stages in the vertical or lateral process it is said to be related to other firms in the area by diagonal linkage. An example would be a machine-tool firm that supplied a number of industries in any one area.

Multiple Linkages

The total linkage of industries using the common services and skills of one particular area is known as multiple linkage. It can be measured by various techniques including input-output analysis. Thus, a study of interindustry relations in the Philadelphia region identified the role of agglomeration economies

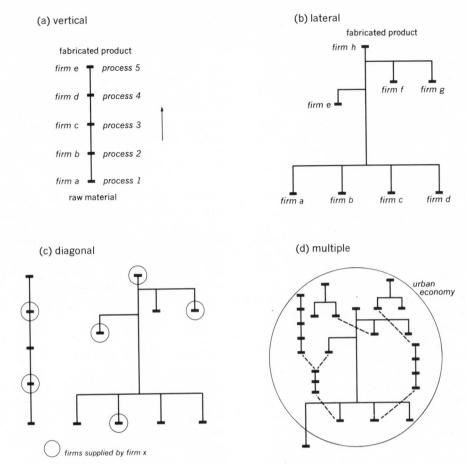

(a) vertical

fabricated product

firm e — process 5

firm d — process 4

firm c — process 3

firm b — process 2

firm a — process 1

raw material

(b) lateral

fabricated product

firm h

firm e   firm f   firm g

firm a   firm b   firm c   firm d

(c) diagonal

○ firms supplied by firm x

(d) multiple

urban economy

Fig. 68. *Industrial linkages.*

in influencing location in large metropolitan complexes. Information from this study could be used to analyze the way in which many industries locate close to one another so as to be assured of an inexpensive, efficient, and flexible supply of goods and services.

Figure 69 shows the kinds of economies that can be achieved in a situation of high urbanization: lowered transportation costs, labor costs, and energy costs, as well as lowered ancillary costs, such as those of education. Other parts of the social infrastructure, such as the availability of recreation facilities, also occur at cost savings to the firm.

The Agglomerative Forces

The economies gained by concentration are of various types. The raw material of one factory is another factory's output; both will obviously gain by being close together. Also firms that use the waste products of other firms would reduce costs of trans-

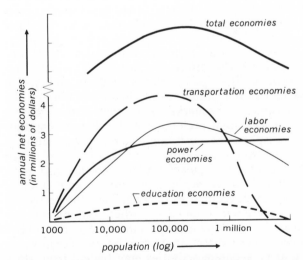

Fig. 69. *Hypothetical economies of scale occuring with increasing urban size (as measured by population). (Reprinted from Walter Isard,* Location and Space Economy, *by permission of the M.I.T. Press, Cambridge, Mass. Copyright ©1956 by the Massachusetts Institute of Technology.)*

port by agglomerating. Areas of manufacturing may develop into large complexes where a wide range of firms can locate, linked in the ways suggested above. Here, a good example is the automobile industry. Agglomeration economies tend to coincide with those market factors noted early—concentrations of consumers, and labor. The cumulative gathering of such advantages gives certain manufacturing areas very great attractive powers. Each location decision is made with reference to the existing pattern of distribution of population and economic activities. As a result, that pattern tends to perpetuate itself and multiply. Because fixed capital is invested as a result of these location decisions, the decisions tend to have a high degree of permanence. Firms try to depreciate their investment profitably over a long period of time, which assures the continued use of the investment even though the reasons for the original location no longer hold.

Thus this cumulative process is of great importance to location analysis. Whatever the reasons for the initial establishment of industries in an area, later industries have joined them. Some may want to use the products of already established firms; others may want to use the by-product or waste of another industry. As the nucleus grows it becomes a center of concentrated earnings and purchasing power, and so a bigger and better market for the consumer goods industries. Thus as the center of industrial activity expands from its initial nucleus it provides these opportunities for achieving certain economies.

This tendency has grown with technical change. Technical advances in processing industries have reduced the importance of raw material locations, as these advances serve to lower raw material costs as a proportion of total production costs. Changes in demand have had their effect too, as economic growth in market-exchange economies has stimulated demand for more complex goods, such as automobiles. The spatial effects of these changes in the fabricating industries has been to underline the importance of the market orientation. Firms with less strong locational preference as far as raw materials or transportation costs are concerned are naturally attracted to the concentrated market power of urban agglomerations. Transport improvements also make it possible for large units or firms to gain internal and external economies of scale. Thus the breweries and bakeries mentioned in earlier sections are now released from dependency on the local market. Other forces are less direct; there may be indirect linkages —that is, separate activities may benefit from close location, for instance by drawing on "moonlighters" or personnel with different but allied skills. Thus a cosmetic manufacturer may be able to "borrow" color-matching specialists from an adjacent printing-

ink establishment. Spatial concentration of manufacturing plants (despite the drawbacks suggested in figure 69, above) can be an efficient system. In any case, it is a trend found throughout the advanced market-exchange and redistributive economies.

On the negative side it should be stressed that, for instance, it is rare that plants can be relocated to achieve localization economies without imposing further costs. Existing points are more likely than any hypothetical point to act as centers of agglomeration. And finally, as suggested in figure 69, even the savings from locating in a major urban center do not rise in direct proportion to the size of the center, but after some point the costs of congestion and decreasing economies (for instance, in power production) lead to decreasing returns. In other words, beyond a certain point the added costs of rising land values and congestion may well outweigh the gain of the convenient urban location.

Other Locative Factors

If these are the five major categories of economic attributes, there are still a number of other factors that for particular industries or areas may have some importance, or may be completely dominant. Factors such as direct government planning, indirect government activities, the role of the general economy, geographic inertia and historical processes, energy sources, and local site factors may all play their role as locative influences.

Government Activity

External to the productive process, but prevalent in all economies, is the activity of the central government. Governments in both market-exchange and redistributive economies are becoming increasingly involved in the function and location of industry. The influence can be direct, indirect, accidental, or planned. Governments are obviously involved as central planning agencies in redistributive economies. But they also have an interest in market-exchange economies, because of the ability of manufacturing to multiply economic activities and job opportunities, and to stimulate the general process of economic growth. The location of an industry can have important effects on the overall growth of a particular area within a nation, and these areas or regions are often in competition in their efforts to attract industry.

Indirectly government activity can affect locations through such routine economic measures as budgetary contracts, credit restrictions, legal restraints (e.g., minimum wage laws), and taxes. Among the most important of these measures have been the differential tax policies that tend to operate in some federal systems, particularly the U.S.A., Canada, and Australia. There may be wide and marked differences from state to state in the rates of taxation. Wisconsin, for example, has a high rate of taxation, while neighboring Illinois has no state tax on industry. Other state legislation may be important too; some states even forbid the manufacture of certain commodities. Thus Wisconsin, a leading producer of dairy products, does not allow the manufacture or sale of margarine. Differential tax policies may also occur to decelerate or accelerate the continued growth of particular areas. For example, the Japanese government imposes higher than average taxes on industries wishing to locate in Tokyo, while the British government may refuse industrial development certificates in the London area. A government also has an effect on industry and location simply by being the largest spender in an economy. General government expenditure can stimulate new growth or bolster up old units and areas, whether through specialized agencies, such as the U.S. Atomic Energy Commission (A.E.C.), or through military spending.

Direct government action can also occur through tariffs erected to protect particular industries. Governments may even direct firms to particular areas. Successive British governments have created so-called industrial estates, to ease unemployment in certain areas. In Australia, state governments have given freight concessions, cheap land, and housing to attract industries to locate outside state capitals. The government of the U.S.S.R., which actively plans all industrial location, anticipated the German invasion of 1941, and began to decentralize industries to both the Urals and Kuzbas (Kuznetsk basin) as early as the mid-1930s. Finally, the U.S. government has acted both directly, as it did when establishing an inland iron and steel plant (the Geneva Steel Plant at Utah, Colorado) during the Second World War, and indirectly, through the impact of defense contract awards, particularly as it affected the aerospace industry. Further mention of the redistributive economies is made below.

Energy

In the early phases of the Industrial Revolution energy was virtually immobile. Industrial plants were therefore build alongside rivers, or where coal or charcoal were available. Today the influence of energy is much less important. Technical advances toward the end of the nineteenth century and in the twentieth century have made energy more mobile and transmittable. However, because of the fixed capital involved in these earlier locations, many in-

dustries have remained in their original situations. New power sources—oil for instance—have been substituted for coal or wood, since oil has the great advantage of being easily moved over great distances by pipeline. Electricity is now also mobile, although in its early stages electrical generation was as immobile as coal. The introduction of grid transmission systems has allowed electricity to be distributed in a flexible and economically rational way. There are some industries, however, that need cheap, very high-voltage power that cannot easily be transmitted over long distances. They are attracted to areas where such power, generated by hydroelectric installations, is readily available.

Geographic Inertia

Almost any industry tends to stay where it is because the advantages of its present location, the original reasons for which have changed, usually far outweigh the advantages of relocation. This is known as **geographic inertia;** the factors contributing to it include fixed capital in plant, the existence of a large skilled labor force, the local development of social capital, and the existence of linkages with other industries in the same area. Such factors make relocation of even **footloose industries** a major operational risk. The power of a region to hold an industry may well exceed its power to attract new industries, since the attractions of the new locality must exceed those of the current one by a margin sufficient to offset the factors enumerated above. Equally, the very existence of an area with established manufacturers may provide the regions with a head start over new regions in competitive terms. Such established regions with these factors making for inertia may well be found to be initiating changes and innovations in order to maintain their lead over newly emerging regions. In this way, inertia may well provide a temporal advantage that balances any disadvantages of older machinery or plant.

Technical Change

General technological progress has progressively freed industry from the exact locational requirements of raw material or energy sites. Transportation improvements have lessened the frictions of distance. The effects of change have thus been to disperse industrial locations, yet through economies of scale and integration to encourage concentration. Various studies of branch plant locations have isolated some of the variables that control the dispersive tendency, especially variations between parent and branch plant in the costs of transport and administration.

Thus in Britain, branches that manufacture components for footloose industries are usually within a sixty-mile radius of the parent plant, in order to tap available labor supplies, while others may be located 150 miles or further away. Many of the latter are self-contained plants, set up to supply growing regional markets more efficiently. Technological progress makes such dispersion possible.

The rate at which technological change is taking place varies from industry to industry. This variation can have a feedback effect on the differences between regions and relate to their relative ability to attract further industries. The output of industries where technological change has been most rapid increases at above-average rates, and areas that contain these industries can also attract more industries. Thus Southeast England, which contains growth and change industries such as electronics, contrasts favorably with areas of Northern England, where the dominant industries of textiles, steel, and shipbuilding are undergoing slow change or even decline.

Behavioral and Random Factors

Other locative factors have a quality of chance about them. Henry Ford just happened to be working as a machinist in Detroit; had he been born in Illinois, not Michigan, the automobile capital of the world today would probably be Chicago. The purely personal motives of entrepreneurs must also be considered. One may seek a large level of profit, another a much lower level. In redistributive economies, bureaucrats replace entrepreneurs—and no bureaucrat or bureaucratic agency judges social cost benefits in the same way. This divergence of opinion and attitude of course makes explaining site choices all the more complex. Other circumstances peculiar to each entrepreneur also influence motives and thus final location choice. Personal considerations of either an economic nature or social character can also be important. Chance conditions can mean that small beginnings like those of Henry Ford may, in response to a combination of favorable local conditions, combined with a willingness to operate in a known local environment, lead to an industrial combine the size of the present Ford Motor Company and its subsidiaries. However, when a firm grows to this size, personal factors are subordinated to the interests of the shareholders and to the efficiency of the various plants in their highly competitive markets. Location decisions are now made at a corporate level, and tend to include such factors as the spatial, technical, and economic relationships of new plants to existing plants, division of the market to ensure adequate supplies, and other intendedly rational rea-

sons. Of course, noneconomic factors are still present. But the whole subject of entrepreneurial behavior deserves a section to itself.

Entrepreneurial Behavior

The attitude of the entrepreneur toward the industrial milieu in which his business is conducted is as vital a consideration as the attitude of the farmer toward the various components of his milieu. The term "entrepreneur," or businessman, is used very widely here to denote not just a proprietor who risks his own or his friends' capital, but a manager who has little capital and whose income derives mainly from his salary. However, as we shall see later, this is a broad framework and the attitudes at either end of the spectrum may be very different. The industrialist's view of the business world around him is in reality much more complex than traditional location theory holds it to be. Traditionally, the businessman is thought to maximize profits and operate in conditions of perfect knowledge. But in fact we now know that businesses have objectives other than profit, that entrepreneurs have personal motives, and that merely satisfactory returns may be good enough. Similarly, information is not given to the firm, but must be searched out. In light of these factors, and with help of modern organizational theory, it is possible to look at industrial decisions of location within a behavioral framework.

The Institutional Framework

The industrial subsystem is firmly entrenched in the institutional framework that forms part of any societal group's operational milieu. Decisions that lead to the creation of industrial regions take place in terms of the human institutions of a particular group. Flows of ideas, technical know-how, and management decisions—all are subject to this institutional framework. Thus industrial decision making in redistributive economies differs from that in market-exchange economies; decision making in the United States varies, though not quite so sharply, from that found in the United Kingdom or Sweden. Decision making in the cottage industries of India or Indonesia differs from all of these. Some of the differences can be accounted for by differences of scale. But the gross difference between, for instance, the United States and the U.S.S.R. can be accounted for by differences in the institutional setup.

Table 29 attempts to disaggregate some of the institutional influences that influence the entrepreneur, the manager, or the state planner when he comes to make a decision about locating a new industry, or perhaps expanding an old one. This should be compared with the systems framework of figure 66.

A particular societal group may institutionalize its value system through government and legislative activities. Thus the value system of a particular group may be translated into legislation that hinders monopolies, emphasizes individual welfare, fosters common social benefits, or sets up a code of business ethics. This legislative and sanctioning activity is a feedback from the society's traditions, social codes, religious practices, attitudes, and motivations. As a process, it may fall into the hands of a vast military-industrial complex, which funnels all industrial decisions through a manufacturing institution that has no end purpose but national or individual aggrandizement. Such was the case in Germany immediately prior to the Second World War; it seems to be replicated to some extent in both the United States and the Soviet Union today. The process also reflects the systems of production, distribution, and exchange utilized by a particular group—whether a capitalist money system, a redistributive state planned system, or some other variation. Within this socioeconomic framework certain formal and informal business structures arise. On the one hand, these may include the small businessman and investor, together with the firm (both single- and multiplant), the corporate enterprise, and the conglomerate; on the other, it may include investment brokers, stock exchanges, schools that specialize in training people to work within a particular business framework, and business clubs and organizations such as chambers of commerce. Thus an important article by the industrial geographer, R. B. McNee, on the Western capitalist corporation or firm concludes that it may be considered one of man's most effective tools in the attempt to organize space for human purposes.

While some societal groups have an institutional framework that fosters the expansion of the large private firm others, like the United Kingdom or Italy, replace the private capitalist in some industrial sectors with a state-planned firm such as British Railways. Yet others, like the Soviet Union, replace both the private and the state capitalist with state planners and economists who work with the "economic region" and the "complex" as their institutional tools. All three institutional frameworks can ultimately lead to very different landscape patterns.

A group's social values, like the American concept of prosperity, can have ramifications throughout its industrial subsystem. Entrepreneurs and consumers in the United States accept and maintain a framework that allows high cost, high waste, and high output. New appliances, new cars, and new plant equipment are purchased every few years. This value system makes the whole structure economically feasible, since the mass demand for new goods brings the costs of production down so low that it is cheaper to replace equipment or applicances than to repair them. One result of this is to create an artificial sense of abundance and "the good life." But whether this accelerated cycle of production and consumption really benefits society is quite another matter.

Entrepreneurial Decision Making

Industry in most areas outside the redistributive economies has two main categories of decision makers; the owner-manager, and the manager. Several subdivisions of these two categories have been attempted. The entrepreneur can be the self-made founder of the business, the head of a family business that he inherited, or an influential large shareholder in a company. The manager can have origins as a promoted employee, a technocrat, or a trained administrator. Each type tends to have a different motivation and outlook. Thus a whole complex of decisions underlies business activities. Table 30 suggests that five sets of motives can be distinguished: two distinct types of economic motive, one group each of psychological and sociological motives, and one of "alogical" behavior revealing no apparent motives.

The motive labeled *Economic A* (the "cash nexus")

Table 30. *Business Decisions and Motivations*

motives	entrepreneur	salaried manager
economic A	maximum profits	choice of greater salary
economic B	satisfaction—balance of profit and other utilities	satisfaction—balance of pleasing the shareholder and other utilities
psychological hobby, boss, and free man	power seeking empire building love of work	power seeking fear of others' power
sociological	prestige status-seeking in industry	identification with firm prestige from successful firm
alogical	"his own money to do as he wishes" tradition	no initiative or ideas from outside tradition

Source: Adapted from P.S. Florence, *Economics and Sociology and Industry: A Realistic Analysis of Development* (London: C.A. Watts and Co., 1964), p. 97.

is the traditional one of profit maximization. Such a motive probably still lurks in the heart of the owner-manager, but for the salaried manager it is probably quite rare.

The motive labeled *Economic B* ("real-cost nexus") takes other costs into account. Thus the owner-manager may balance his profits against satisfaction attained from some other source, like leisure. In other words, he is content if his total satisfactions outweigh his total problems. The manager has no profits to weigh against his problems, but he does value his own security and peace of mind. Accordingly, he may well choose a way out that pleases the shareholders and at the same time allows him some respite.

Among the *psychological motives* can be distinguished the "hobby nexus" (love of the work for itself), the "boss nexus" (love of power), and the "free man nexus" (love of being one's own boss). Evidence for the existence of these motives can be found in the reluctance of entrepreneurs and managers to accept mergers at the price of autonomy, despite the economic rewards.

Among the *sociological motives* are the nonowning manager's ability to identify himself with the interests of the firm he serves. Thus one study reports that the top executives in a sample of large corporations remembered their own and their competitors' volume of business and share of the markets, though not always their profits.

Patterns of *alogical* behavior that are relevant here include decision making from habit, and the sort of wilfulness that may result if the entrepreneur wishes to use his own money as he sees fit, and ignore managerial advice. Firms dominated by such behavior may survive—but by accident.

The individual decision maker is constrained by the institutional framework described above, and by a value system, outlined for a capitalist group in table 31. The kinds of managerial decisions that result in such a societal group are outlined in table 32, which shows a *managerial matrix*. The matrix represents on its two axes two dominantly identified values in a commercial economy; the desire for *profits*, and the desire for some other kind of *satisfaction*. The "task management" approach represents those decision makers whose central responsibility is to achieve production objectives and to maximize profits. The other extreme, the "country club" approach, also probably rarely exists in reality. In organizations dominated by this approach production and profits are entirely incidental to satisfaction. This probably occurs only in certain monopolies or near-monopolies and in official bureaucracies. "Impoverished management" de-emphasizes profit and other utilities. This results in what has already been called alogical behavior. In "team manage-

Table 31. *The Values System for an Entrepreneurial Decision Maker in a Commercial Economy*

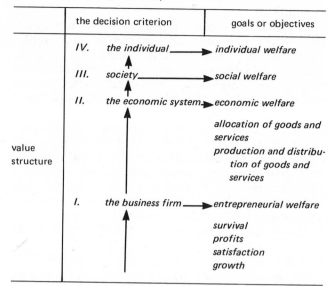

Source: Adapted from W.F. Bernthal, "Value Perspectives in Management Decisions," *Journal of the Academy of Management,* December, 1962, p. 195.

Table 32. *The Managerial Matrix*

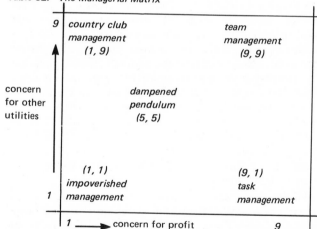

Source: Adapted from R.B. Blake, J.S. Mouton, and A.C. Bidwell, "The Managerial Grid," *Advanced Managements Office Executive,* vol. 1, no. 9, 1962, p. 13.

ment" decisions, the building block is the team, which attempts to maximize both its own satisfactions and the monetary success of the firm. Again, such an **ideal type** is probably rare in reality. Finally, in the center of the matrix (although many other combinations could exist) is a pattern of decision making aptly labeled the "dampened pendulum," where decisions are made partly to achieve personal satisfaction and partly to ensure the economic survival of the firm. The uncertainty of the future makes it impossible to plan entirely from economic motives. No firm can realistically plan ahead for more than a short period, and the younger the firm the harder it is for it to plan at all. Lacking relevant experience, management is likely to be guided by almost anything but long-term considerations.

Entrepreneurial decision making, constrained by the behavioral environment and operational milieu, is subject to other than purely economic pressures. Risk, uncertainty, imperfect information, varying values, institutional constraints, personal and group noneconomic goals—all influence the decision maker. His final choice is thus very different from the postulates of normative economic theory.

Corporate Decision Making

The industrial subsystem in both market-exchange and redistributive economies contrasts with the peasant economies. In the latter, and in the other economies of the nineteenth century, the basic decision making unit is the individual entrepreneur and the small business. But small decision making units are rapidly giving way to large ones. For governments and large corporations, the decision making process is simply on a different order from that of the individual entrepreneur and the small firm. In the United States, large corporate enterprises produce more than half of the total industrial output. They play a significant role in many urban and metropolitan regions, and their multiplier effects are often crucial to the decision making processes of the many smaller firms that produce components for the larger ones, as in the automobile industry.

Large corporate size is most usually associated with mass production industries such as automobiles, iron and steel, chemicals, aluminum, or petroleum. However, they occur in other industrial sectors such as the food industry. General Foods Corporation, for example, has sixty major installations in the United States and seventeen subsidiary organizations in other countries. Marketing two hundred products under thirty major brand names (Jell-O, Maxwell House, Post, Bird's Eye, Kool Aid, etc.), General Foods is a major landscape influencing organization (figure 70). The relative importance of the behavior of these units of operation increases as the proportion of the total output of a country from smaller firms decreases.

The corporate organization, unlike the firm with a single owner, is a coalition of individuals divisible into subgroups or subcoalitions, each with different formal tasks, responsibilities, and authority. In a business organization the coalition members include managers, workers, stockholders, suppliers, lawyers, and so on. Their opposite numbers in the redistributive economies' equivalent, the state corporation, would be administrators, planners, economists, workers, suppliers, and interest group leaders. Individual members have goals, whereas collectivities of people do not. Thus the objectives of the corporate body are reached by bargaining between members of a coalition or subcoalition, and are then stabilized and elaborated by such internal organizational processes within the enterprise as the budget. Through experience and search activity these objectives may be altered, though there are variations in the ability to handle, assemble, store, recall and perceive information.

Corporations also differ in the way they reach their collective decisions; some are relatively democratic, in the sense that they do at least try for a consensus, while others are ruled by small cliques. Despite these differences, however, corporations tend to resemble each other in producing collective decisions rather than individualistic ones. In part, this is due to the rise of the professional manager, itself made possible by the separation of ownership from control that is the essence of corporate structure. According to McNee, "the separation of ownership from control destroys much of . . . the classical assumption of profit maximization as the universal goal of business. Presumably, the personal goals of the manager, such as personal prestige or advancement may diverge sharply from the general, collective, company goal of profitmaking." This *managerial subculture,* as Kenneth Boulding has called it, whether in the United States or the Soviet Union, necessarily leads to more complex patterns of decision making than the decisions of individuals or small firms. The managerial elite acts as yet a further intermediary between perception of an environmental stimulus and its final translation into some corporate decision. It is the administrative decisions made within such a managerial subculture that create areal patterns, based as they are on compromise, competition, incomplete information, and uncertainty. The perceptions and feelings of each managerial group in each firm are accompanied by a particular degree of corporate autonomy, a particular tradition of planning, and a particular relationship with other corporations and trade unions, as well as the central government. Occasionally the milieu makes an impact largely through chance, as when a firm happens to have products, capabilities, and capacities that fit in with the changes occurring at that time. On other occasions, as a result of unawareness of changes in the business milieu, the result may be declining sales, and perhaps ultimate bankruptcy and liquidation. Of course, the individual entrepreneur and small firm can be placed in a similar situation. But with the corporation the effects of a less than satisfactory decision can be

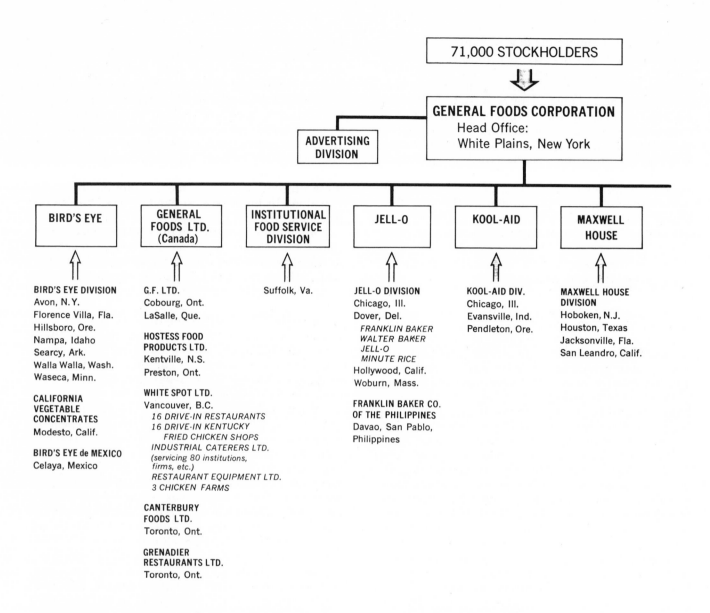

| 71,000 STOCKHOLDERS |

GENERAL FOODS CORPORATION
Head Office:
White Plains, New York

| ADVERTISING DIVISION |

| BIRD'S EYE | GENERAL FOODS LTD. (Canada) | INSTITUTIONAL FOOD SERVICE DIVISION | JELL-O | KOOL-AID | MAXWELL HOUSE |

BIRD'S EYE DIVISION
Avon, N.Y.
Florence Villa, Fla.
Hillsboro, Ore.
Nampa, Idaho
Searcy, Ark.
Walla Walla, Wash.
Waseca, Minn.

CALIFORNIA VEGETABLE CONCENTRATES
Modesto, Calif.

BIRD'S EYE de MEXICO
Celaya, Mexico

G.F. LTD.
Cobourg, Ont.
LaSalle, Que.

HOSTESS FOOD PRODUCTS LTD.
Kentville, N.S.
Preston, Ont.

WHITE SPOT LTD.
Vancouver, B.C.
16 DRIVE-IN RESTAURANTS
16 DRIVE-IN KENTUCKY
*   FRIED CHICKEN SHOPS*
INDUSTRIAL CATERERS LTD.
(servicing 80 institutions,
firms, etc.)
RESTAURANT EQUIPMENT LTD.
3 CHICKEN FARMS

CANTERBURY FOODS LTD.
Toronto, Ont.

GRENADIER RESTAURANTS LTD.
Toronto, Ont.

Suffolk, Va.

JELL-O DIVISION
Chicago, Ill.
Dover, Del.
FRANKLIN BAKER
WALTER BAKER
JELL-O
MINUTE RICE
Hollywood, Calif.
Woburn, Mass.

FRANKLIN BAKER CO. OF THE PHILIPPINES
Davao, San Pablo, Philippines

KOOL-AID DIV.
Chicago, Ill.
Evansville, Ind.
Pendleton, Ore.

MAXWELL HOUSE DIVISION
Hoboken, N.J.
Houston, Texas
Jacksonville, Fla.
San Leandro, Calif.

much more far-reaching, affecting a complex web of relationships in an entire industrial region. For instance, underestimation of the impact of the small compact car on the United States automobile market has produced a different landscape pattern than would have occurred had the American car manufacturers been able to perceive the market change at an earlier stage. The effect of corporate decision making on the landscape can be even greater when the multinational character of many of the enterprises is taken into account. Until recently only the Rothschilds and the Roman Catholic Church maintained vast international business enterprises. But now the central decision making of any number of corporations may affect the spatial diffusion of technology, product flows, and establishments in many countries.

Motivation and Behavior

Increasingly, empirical research in industrial geography and related disciplines is presenting evidence of the behavioral influences on a firm's decision making processes, and is openly questioning the economically rational postulates of classical location theory (see chapter 9). These studies can be subdivided into investigations of investment decisions, location decisions, and what is known as a firm's "range of tolerance."

Investment Decisions

The effect of cost factors, technological considerations, and other investment decisions influence the location and mobility of a firm, and hence of course

Fig. 70. *A corporate enterprise:* General Foods Corporation. *A breakdown of the corporate structure emphasizing the size and range of subcompanies, many operating under different names and in different parts of the world.*

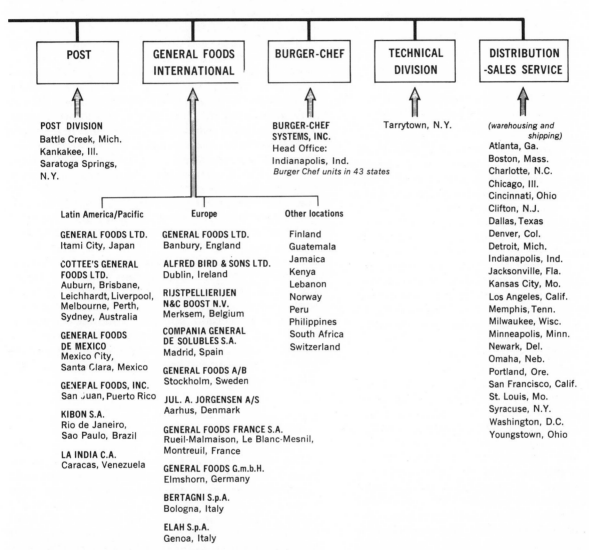

POST	GENERAL FOODS INTERNATIONAL	BURGER-CHEF	TECHNICAL DIVISION	DISTRIBUTION -SALES SERVICE

POST DIVISION
Battle Creek, Mich.
Kankakee, Ill.
Saratoga Springs, N.Y.

BURGER-CHEF
SYSTEMS, INC.
Head Office:
Indianapolis, Ind.
Burger Chef units in 43 states

Tarrytown, N.Y.

(warehousing and shipping)
Atlanta, Ga.
Boston, Mass.
Charlotte, N.C.
Chicago, Ill.
Cincinnati, Ohio
Clifton, N.J.
Dallas, Texas
Denver, Col.
Detroit, Mich.
Indianapolis, Ind.
Jacksonville, Fla.
Kansas City, Mo.
Los Angeles, Calif.
Memphis, Tenn.
Milwaukee, Wisc.
Minneapolis, Minn.
Newark, Del.
Omaha, Neb.
Portland, Ore.
San Francisco, Calif.
St. Louis, Mo.
Syracuse, N.Y.
Washington, D.C.
Youngstown, Ohio

Latin America/Pacific

GENERAL FOODS LTD.
Itami City, Japan

COTTEE'S GENERAL
FOODS LTD.
Auburn, Brisbane,
Leichhardt, Liverpool,
Melbourne, Perth,
Sydney, Australia

GENERAL FOODS
DE MEXICO
Mexico City,
Santa Clara, Mexico

GENERAL FOODS, INC.
San Juan, Puerto Rico

KIBON S.A.
Rio de Janeiro,
Sao Paulo, Brazil

LA INDIA C.A.
Caracas, Venezuela

Europe

GENERAL FOODS LTD.
Banbury, England

ALFRED BIRD & SONS LTD.
Dublin, Ireland

RIJSTPELLIERIJEN
N&C BOOST N.V.
Merksem, Belgium

COMPANIA GENERAL
DE SOLUBLES S.A.
Madrid, Spain

GENERAL FOODS A/B
Stockholm, Sweden

JUL. A. JORGENSEN A/S
Aarhus, Denmark

GENERAL FOODS FRANCE S.A.
Rueil-Malmaison, Le Blanc-Mesnil,
Montreuil, France

GENERAL FOODS G.m.b.H.
Elmshorn, Germany

BERTAGNI S.p.A.
Bologna, Italy

ELAH S.p.A.
Genoa, Italy

Other locations

Finland
Guatemala
Jamaica
Kenya
Lebanon
Norway
Peru
Philippines
South Africa
Switzerland

also its location decision. In one study of the investment decisions of 188 firms in Michigan it was found that businessmen make decisions on the basis of many considerations, not all of them rational. The authors interviewed firms that had expanded their plant or equipment in the recent past or planned to do so in the near future. Particular emphasis was placed on the varying *attitudes* of the businessmen toward these decisions in relation to the volume, type, and timing of the investment. In answer to the question, "Could you tell me what the considerations were which led you to decide to expand this plant?," the most frequent answers were "The demand for our product is growing," "To take care of increased business," or "To keep up with orders." Increase in business was interpreted to mean that an increase took place first, and that this stimulated firms to expand their facilities. In table 33 this category to response is shown as "current demand and current orders." Other firms did, however, report an

Table 33. *Reasons Given for Expansion of Firm*

motivating factors	% of firms recently expanded	% of firms contemplating expansion
current demand and current orders	61	45
policy of expansion	4	14
cost or efficiency considerations	17	20
future demand	8	13
change of product	10	8
	100	100
number of firms	103	89

Source: G. Katona and J.N. Morgan, "The Quantitative Study of Factors Determining Business Decisions," *Quarterly Journal of Economics* (Harvard University Press, 1952), vol. 66, p. 84.

expansion policy, the limits being available funds. It was deduced from these two categories of response that investment decisions are governed not ". . . by definite and carefully scrutinized expectations but a quasi-automatic response to certain circumstances, or a habitual action." There were more rational instances of investment in expansion: to reduce the costs of operations or to gain greater efficiency in operations; in response to a perceived future potential; and due to a diversification of production, when a new product was introduced. Thus certain investment decisions are seen to be routine or habitual, determined by previous actions and by standardized policies. In other instances, however, businessmen did base their decisions on definite expectations and on a definite weighing of alternatives.

A number of investigators have utilized these findings, particularly in West Germany. Here, questions have been posed about the predominant purpose of a firm's investment activity during a particular year with regard to expansion, modernization, automation, and replacement. Another line of questioning has pursued the dominant occasion and cause of investment with regard to periods of labor shortage and production changes. Thus two basic motives are seen to underlie investment decisions: response to change in the milieu, and expansion for its own sake.

Location Decisions

A number of empirical studies have been undertaken to analyze the decisions behind new locations, relocations, and expansion of existing facilities (which is only the confirmation of a previous location decision). Table 34 summarizes some of the survey results. There are, of course, certain drawbacks to this particular technique, including its subjectivity, the lack of information as to the firms'

particular economic milieu, and the complexity of particular decision making processes. However, the technique does make it possible to see the strong influence of personal factors on locational decision making.

Besides the kinds of study noted in table 34 there are two other empirical reports that deserve mention here: a study by Luttrell in 1962 of locational decision making and cost situations in a wide selection of British industries; and one by Whitman and Schmidt of plant integration in the General Foods Corporation. The first study is a detailed analysis of location choices in industries ranging from textiles, clothing, and hosiery to metal woodworking. Among the factors considered are physical site requirements, marketing and labor needs, and the personal motivations of entrepreneurs and managers. In almost every case, these motivations seem to outweigh the traditional location theory postulates. The second study concerns the awareness by General Foods in early 1960 that four of its existing plants in the Jell-O division (see figure 70) were not suitable for site expansion and that a new consolidated facility would have to be constructed on a new site. The study then details the elaborate decision making processes that are undertaken in such a corporate enterprise before the actual site choice is made. Location decisions proved to be an amalgam of the values of the managerial elite, certain optimal economic considerations, and certain efficiency solutions. The final choice of site rested on labor and wage differentials, low cost land and transportation facilities, and general living conditions.

Range of Tolerance

The extent to which an entrepreneur and a corporate management can survive noneconomically motivated decisions depends on what has been termed the *range of tolerance*. Usually, a firm could locate in or relocate to any one of several different locations, and still be economically successful. This tolerance can be accounted for by a variety of factors, such as near monopolistic situations, great efficiency, and so on (see chapter 9). According to one definition, the optimum location for an industry is the point that provides optimum access to its ingredients or component elements. It is possible to measure a firm's locational or **geonomic efficiency** in terms of how closely it is located to this hypothetical optimum point.

In short, firms appear to get away with their economically irrational behavior. It appears that some entrepreneurs and firms are perfectly adjusted to the economic milieu in which they operate, and

Table 34. *Location Decision Making: Empirical Results*

source and study	objective or question posed	most significant factors and reasons mentioned
Ellis (1949) *a study of why 106 new manufacturing firms located in New England*	1. *why did new establishments locate in New England?*	*personal reasons* *market advantages* *production relationships*
	2. *why did new establishments select specific communities in New England?*	*suitable building* *labor supply* *personal reasons*
Katona and Morgan (1952) *a study of why 188 manufacturing plants located in Michigan*	1. *how did your firm happen to locate this plant in Michigan rather than in some other state?*	*personal reasons* *to be near markets* *availability of plants or sites*
	2. *opinions on disadvantages of Michigan location*	*wages, rates, and labor* *pressure of organized labor* *distance from materials*
Mueller and Morgan (1962) *a later study of 239 further plant locations in Michigan*	1. *are there any minimum requirements which must be met for locating plants in this line of industry?*	*labor costs* *proximity to markets* *availability of labor* *industrial climate*
	2. *what were the main reasons for locating the plant in Michigan?*	*personal reasons* *chance opportunity—site, etc.* *proximity to customers*
Law (1964) *investigation of 28 firms which established plants in Northern Ireland*	1. *reasons for moving of 19 British firms*	*difficulty of obtaining labor* *difficulty of expanding parent plant* *board of trade dispersal policy*
	2. *reasons for location in N. Ireland of 27 firms*	*availability of labor* *factory available quickly* *financial assistance*
	3. *locational disadvantages experienced by 28 firms*	*transportation costs* *higher stocks* *unreliable transportation*
McMillan (1965) *a study of 200 new plant locations*	1. *what considerations are important in selecting a specific area or site?*	*trucking* *reasonable cost of property* *reasonable or low taxes* *ample area for expansion*
Logan (1966) *a study of 72 urban based manufacturers in the Sydney area (Australia)*	1. *main reasons for relocation of firms*	*lack of space for immediate expansion* *high land values* *move from rented premises* *nonconforming with zoning* *change in nature of operations*
Wabe (1966) *a study of 91 offices in London (England)*	1. *reasons for considering decentralization*	*expansion* *integration of several offices* *cost reduction* *lease expiring*
	2. *reasons given for not decentralizing*	*difficulty of retaining key staff* *loss of business connections* *disruptive effect of move* *remain in central London for meetings*

Source: G. Krumme, "Toward a Geography of Enterprise," *Economic Geography,* 1969, p. 34.

can make decisions that place them well within the limits of the tolerance range. Others, however, seem unaware of the spatial implications of their location decisions and economic behavior, and their location within the range of tolerance is by pure chance. But over the long term only those firms remain in business that are either correctly located (whether by choice or by chance) or have adjusted over time to their economic situation. Of course, the economic situation may be adjusted for them by some powerful outside agency. The government may not wish to see a firm liquidated in a depressed economic area, and may save it with subsidies. Or a financially strong concern or large corporate enterprise may be able to see benefits in taking over an ailing firm. The only certain conclusion is that firms either may or may not foresee the consequences of their decisions.

The Individual Firm

In studying the behavior of the firm, it is necessary to distinguish between *external* factors—those that actually exist in the firm's environment and affect its workings—and *internal* factors—those that, whether they exist or not, are imagined by the firm's leadership to be important. Thus a study of the shipbuilding industry in Northern Ireland showed that, although it responded initially to favorable economic conditions, it was unable to adapt successfully when those conditions changed. During the Second World War the shipbuilding facilities of many countries were destroyed and Japan and Germany were forbidden at first to construct ships. The urgent demand for new ships in the late 1940s and early 1950s found British shipyards some of the few able suppliers. Thus Northern Ireland was for various reasons external to the industry itself one of a few areas able to supply a booming market. As changes in technology put a premium on the building of very large vessels up to the "supertanker" range, Northern Ireland was again one of the few areas able to fulfill the demand. In time, however, changes in the world market led to the rise of Japanese shipyards, which became strongly competitive. Union restrictions, inefficient labor organization, and unenterprising management combined to hold Northern Ireland back. Certain features of the national milieu also militated against Northern Ireland and helped Japan. Thus the British government gave very little aid or subsidy and there was little national interest in shipbuilding, while the Japanese benefited not only from government support but from favorable credit facilities and vigorous research activity. However, the Belfast firm that was the special object of this study was able in time to recognize these problems and reorganize itself accordingly. The result was that "the firm of 1964 was quite different from that of 1950."

Conclusion

Figure 71 summarizes many of the points put forward in this section. The decision making behavior of the entrepreneur or managerial elite takes place in an institutional as well as a spatial framework. Decisions are influenced by a wide range of cultural and personal factors, are constrained by such institutional factors as legislation, business values, and economic organization, and become overt landscape patterns through the spatially adoptive and adaptive mechanisms of the firm itself and the economic system. Entrepreneurial and managerial behavior, and the spatial patterns that arise from it, are as important to an understanding of the North American manufacturing belt as of the Ukraine industrial region. The complex web of relationships is interpretable not only in terms of the mechanics of industrial structures or industrial economics, but in terms of the human values and institutions that exist in these regions.

Systems and Organization

Some of the factors that categorize different types of industries and economies are recapitulated in table 35. It is difficult to characterize one factor as being more important than another. A region of manufacturing could occur that consisted of one or two industrial types under a market-exchange economy that was technically advanced, mature, and economically healthy, and whose major locational attributes were raw materials and a pool of skilled labor. But such a systematization would not get us as far as it did with agriculture because of the complex systematic relationships involved. Some of these relationships are explored below.

Organization

Mention has already been made of the role that governments and economic institutions play in the structure of manufacturing. Government or the state can bring social and planning policies to bear upon decisions in the so-called private sector of a market-exchange economy. On the other hand much of that private sector is motivated by profit or some utility satisfaction and is governed in part by the market structure itself. This is true whether the private sector consists of private or corporate capitalists. The private capitalist determines decisions within industrial situations for which the capital

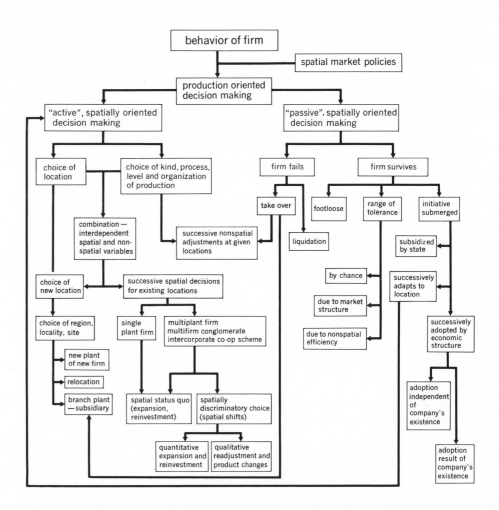

Fig. 71. *The behavioral interrelationships of firms. Two basic categories are designated: those firms that take an "active" role in decision making and those that take a more "passive" role. (From Gunter Krumme, "Toward a Geography of Enterprise,"* Economic Geography, *reprinted by permission of the editor.)*

requirements tend to be small, especially in the initial stages of industrialization. The corporate capitalist or stockholding companies wield much greater capital investments. The state not only determines location choices in redistributive economies, but also plays a role in most market-exchange economies. In theory, the state does not yield to personal influence in its location policies. Frequently, however, powerful groups may steer a project to a particular location even when planning is centralized. As against the profit or personal satisfaction motive, which is to maximize a satisfactory personal or corporate gain, the state system is motivated to maximize national socioeconomic benefits and interests. This may lead to very different spatial manufacturing patterns quite apart from the differences already ascribed to entrepreneural behavior. The government may wish to develop manufacturing to reduce a colonial-type policy of exporting raw materials for processing elsewhere, to reduce the dependence on imported capital goods, to allocate industry from a military-strategic

point of view, or to aid areas of distress or underdevelopment. These activities are increasingly common also in the state capitalist phase of market-exchange economies.

Planned Economies

Since the bulk of our knowledge and experience concerns market-exchange economies and the subsistence-peasant economies that come under their influence, a few notes should be added here about redistributive economies. Whether these latter apply Marxist or Leninist ideologies is of less importance than the fact that in them central agencies do control and direct industrial location. In particular, an economically deterministic viewpoint is taken. Thus close association between industry and sources of fuel and raw materials, on the one hand, and centers of consumption, on the other, is frequently invoked in the U.S.S.R. in order to justify, for example, the

Table 35. *Manufacturing Systems*

1. organization	2. health	3. age	4. technical system	5. attribute	6. type	7. example regions
subsistence	economic distress	infancy	backward	resource-oriented, transport intensive	coal iron ore smelting food lumber	U.S. manufacturing area
peasant		adolescence		market-oriented, transport intensive	bakeries newspapers	Japan
market-exchange		maturity		resource- and market-oriented transport intensive	iron and steel oil and gas	U.S.S.R.
state capitalist	economic health	old age	advanced	resource-oriented, power intensive	aluminum	Common Market
redistributive				market-oriented	clothing research publishing	
				general market, transport minor	machinery appliances automobiles aircraft	

N.B. Read by columns only. Only columns 5 and 6 should be read across.

massive investment and development plans in the eastern areas, from the Urals to Central Siberia. Much of this massive investment, however, has been dubbed by capitalist economists as "apparently non-rational."

The doctrinal requirements of "balanced" economic development, which call for the diversification and expansion of industrial activity in formerly backward and colonial areas, are still implicit in the so-called law of complex development. A complex can be broadly defined as a regional grouping of integrated economic activities. In practice it is usually a functionally organized area within which economic activities are sufficiently interrelated to form a single integrated unit; the unity of such complexes is based not so much on economic homogeneity as on interrelationships and linkages between a set of variable manufacturing sectors. This conception is used in locating new economic activities and new economic regions. The existing structure of complexes obviously also influences decisions on the location of expanded and additional production facilities.

Although the idea of the complex has roots in early Soviet planning, it owes much of its definition to one worker, N. N. Kolosovsky, who has emphasized the linkages that integrate particular industries into the complex. These include transport, energy, raw materials, partly fabricated goods, labor, and the infrastructure in general. Kolosovsky has identified a number of these linkages, which he has grouped into **production cycles:**

The *iron-steel cycle* includes all activities from the mining of coking coal and iron ore to smelting, rolling, metal working, and heavy machinery fabrication. It also includes such indirect linkages as those from coking coal to the chemical industry.

The *nonferrous cycle* includes the mining of such nonferrous metals as copper and zinc and of the fuels required to smelt them. It also includes industries, such as cable production and much of the chemical sector, that are based on nonferrous metals.

The *petroleum and petrochemical cycle* ranges from the extraction and refining of oil, gases, and salts to the great variety of chemical products obtained from these raw materials—plastics, fertilizers, and artificial fibers.

The *hydroelectricity cycle* includes all those industries that need plentiful cheap electric power—electrochemicals, electrometals, and **electrothemics.**

The *labor and market cycles* represent a large group of industries that are attracted to large population centers—precision machinery, building materials, food, textiles, and the footloose industries.

The *lumber cycle*, as its name implies, is made up

of lumbering, sawmilling, wood pulp, wood chemicals, and building materials.

The *agricultural-industrial cycle* refers to all non-irrigation agricultural products, including the agricultural practices themselves and the processing of crops and animals. In this group are leather, flour milling, tobacco, and so on.

The *irrigation-agricultural-industrial cycle* is the same as the previous cycle, but based on irrigation.

Kolosovsky suggests that knowing these cycles and their linkage patterns one could plan and locate all industrial facilities. But not all Soviet economic geographers and economists agree with him in all details. Critics do not attack the basic idea of the complex, but rather its detailed application, and in particular the production cycles themselves. They recognize linkages but, because of their intricate interrelationships, do not distinguish separate cycles. However, the basic idea of the complex has received wide recognition, and undoubtedly sheds light on Soviet reasoning and planning.

The redistributive approach to location differs from the market exchange approach in several ways. First and foremost, the individual profit motive is replaced by state guides to production and income levels. These involve careful planning to attain the maximum social and economic benefit. Because of the total planning it is also possible to have more certain locative factors, since the randomness and chance of the market-exchange milieu are removed. Final locations chosen reflect the outcome of careful planning between representatives of the various industrial sectors and the regional planners. The Yugoslav example suggests that exhaustive comparisons of locations are made.

Four basic principles of location can be noted besides the idea of the complex. Industries should be located:

1. *Near sources of raw materials and fuel.*
2. *Near consumers (to minimize transportation costs).*
3. *So as to achieve an even spread of industries, that is, to ensure that the development of production in one area does not hinder that in others.*
4. *So as to disperse plants in the interests of security and defense.*

The first two factors were mentioned earlier. Their foundation is similar to the division between the raw material and market-oriented industries of table 35. The two are of course linked, since as the market grows with industrialization and economic expansion, the high levels of production attainable may overcome the disadvantages of transporting the raw materials. This is a similar process to economic agglomeration, but there are forces that offset such concentrations: the certainty of planning and the lack of a need to be close to the market in order to take account of fashion and other consumer preferences.

Thus the social frictions inherent in urban crowding and urban sprawl are discounted for a more dispersed industrial pattern—the third of the four principles. This dispersion is not a standard ratio of employment to area or population, but it does aim at equalization of per capita income in the long term. Since in fact incomes are at present unequal, those areas with the lowest incomes receive planning priority, especially through industries that can employ local materials and energy, and are labor intensive. Industrial growth is of course planned for all areas, either as complexes or by economic regions. Prior to 1951 the economic region was intended to be as self-sufficient as possible, with the use of local fuels, peat, oil shale, wood, and coal without immediate regard to cost. Similarly, uneconomic steelworks were built locally (Rustavi in Georgia, Begovat in Uzbekistai, and Komsomo'Isk in the Far East), and token agricultural development was undertaken in adverse conditions to supply part of the needs of mining settlements in the Arctic North and Siberia. Special efforts were made to minimize freight hauls of firewood, potatoes, and other bulky low priority goods. Since that time there has been some consideration of the total costs of production as well as of absolute volume. Economic regions tend now to have specialties according to the size and scale of development. These are usually major items such as energy, steel, or metal fabrication, but may include food processing as allied specialties. Despite these specialties there is an overall tendency to dispersion without favoring any particular region, and within each region without regard to size of town. The fourth location factor is also of importance here.

The redistributive economies are varied of course; the U.S.S.R. is organized on a much vaster scale than the Eastern European countries because of its own vast size. The lateness of arrival of redistributive organization to Eastern Europe also means that the redistributive patterns are superimposed on an older capitalist industrial structure. China and other redistributive economies show yet other differences, but the general principles outlined here are operative, and in distinct opposition to many market-exchange structures.

Economic Health

In most economies there are regional industrial differences that reflect prosperity or economic health,

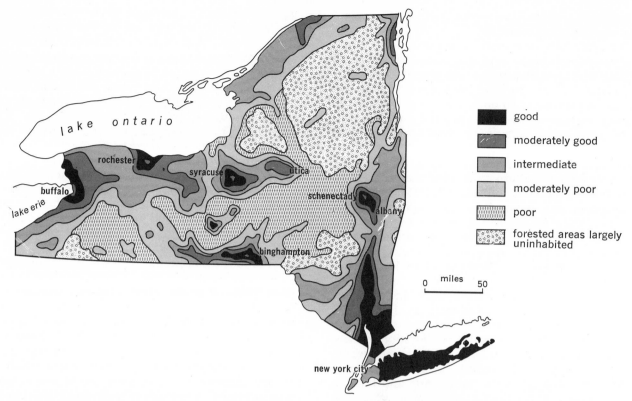

Fig. 72. *New York State: areas of economic health and stress, 1965. (From Thompson 1966, reprinted by permission of the American Industrial Development Council.)*

while others reflect lack of development or decline. The aim of much redistributive economic planning is to overcome such regional differences and to aid backward areas. There are various terms in use to describe these differences: "health" as against "distress," "stagnation," "underdevelopment," "depressed areas," or "areas of economic stress." Definitions of all these terms involve employment, income, and so on, as measures of an area's industrial success, or lack of it. Thus economic stress has been defined as per capita income below the national average or some other norm. Two types of stress have been identified:

1. *The area has experienced growth at an earlier time, but the growth has slowed because of changing technology, product demand, and reevaluation of resources. An example is a nearly exhausted coal mining area.*
2. *The area has never undergone rapid economic growth.*

The second type is of less interest for the study of existing patterns of manufacturing, since it is found mainly in rural areas.

An empirical study of economic health, with New York State as the subject, shows a ranking from good to poor (figure 72). The large urban areas had better

economic health than either the smaller centers or rural areas, though some urban areas were subject to stress, especially the central portions. Certain areas such as state-owned parks and rough terrain naturally registered as in "poor" economic health. A similar analysis has been made of Northwest England.

Age

Linked with an area's economic health to some extent is its *age*. Economic growth occurs as agricultural and primary industry decline in importance relative to secondary and tertiary industry. A cycle theory exists according to which an industry, once established, goes through a predictable sequence of changes, each with appropriate structural attributes. Individual manufacturing establishments are said to be young and vigorous, mature and stable, or old and declining. Although each changes at a particular rate of increase or decline, it is held that most exhibit a common course of development involving periods of experimentation, rapid growth, slow growth, and finally stability, with decline in many cases. Among the factors responsible are technical change, changing demand, competition, changing cost advantages, and management ability.

Manufacturing areas are also said to exhibit a similar growth curve, for similar reasons. At first industry is said to be largely extractive and oriented toward raw materials. But with the growth of other manufacturing, especially textiles, to supply a consumer market, the cycle enters **youth**. In terms of the Northeast United States this stage of the cycle corresponds to the time of the 1812 war and the Civil War, when no other part of the United States could compete with it. **Adolescence** was achieved when basic industries developed to serve the producer and consumer markets; industries were localized near energy sources, raw materials, and transportation nodes.

Once large-scale manufacturing has developed, with a complex system of transport, industry, and services, the area can be said to have reached **maturity**. This was the period of the First World War in the Northeast, with its tradition of industrial know-how, managerial and labor skills, good access to national markets, and active competition with the rest of the United States. The area could adapt reasonably well to technical and economic changes, as its skills and inventiveness stimulated progressive adaptation to new industries. This mature stage can be recognized in other areas such as New England and the English Midlands.

By the 1920s and 1930s population and market shifts had occurred, transportation improvements were nationwide, and new resources and processed materials were available. Thus many of the area's earlier locational advantages had disappeared, and symptoms of **old age** had set in, turning it into an area of economic stress. Labor costs had risen, trade unions were well developed and continually pressuring employers, urban development surrounded the industrial plants, taxes rose, products were now more difficult to sell in competition with newer areas elsewhere, and finally many of the smaller plants had not kept pace in terms of management quality and ability with the newer areas.

Some areas of course never pass through this cycle. Some industrial sites, especially those of mining exploitation, are hardly established before they are abandoned. Others are cut off from their base by political changes, while still others are rejuvenated by government intervention, since they cannot afford to waste so much human and social investment.

Technical Systems

The concept of technical systems is linked with several of those already mentioned, such as economic organization and the age of development.

Handicraft Industry

The simplest system is the handicraft or nonfactory manufacturing establishment, which is located both at the point of raw material sources and at the point of consumption. Raw materials are local in nature and usually simple—wood, straw, bamboo and native metals. Some household craftsmen do cater to a market outside the household unit itself, but still distribute their products locally. This is true of carpenters, blacksmiths, potters, and weavers. In addition, there may be small-scale hand industries that cater to national or international markets, as for example the hand production of cotton cloths in India.

These handicraft industries were widespread before the Industrial Revolution. They still occur in Southeast Asia, though the impact of the Western market-exchange economy has brought the handicrafts into competition with cheap machine-made products. However, the Indian government in particular has seen these handicrafts as an essential cultural attribute to be fostered and supported, and as an additional source of income for agricultural workers. But competition from mechanized industry is very strong, and the craftsman working by himself may give way to workshops that operate on a smaller scale than factories but that can employ up to fifty people, producing such items as leather goods, footwear and pottery. Workshops of this kind are found particularly in Indonesia, where the government has acted to support them. Small-scale workshops and factories are becoming increasingly common in these technically less advanced areas, particularly with the spread of power-driven equipment that enables them to complement rather than compete with large-scale industry.

Technically Advanced Industry

In technically advanced areas, processing continues to be important. But it is now based on the factory rather than the farm. This applies to the processing of dairy products, vegetables, fruits, sugar beet, and sugar cane. Advanced areas are further distinguished from developing ones by their capital intensiveness and labor extensiveness, as capital is substituted for labor. Although industries such as the ones just mentioned tend to be raw material oriented, there is a trend for them to increase in size and become market oriented. Improvements in transportation and refrigeration make it possible to carry so-called perishable materials longer distances for quite cheap rates. Any increase in transportation costs is usually offset by economies of scale.

As economic growth proceeds and technical changes occur, the pull of the market is strengthened. This is shown for instance by industries formerly reliant on coal as an energy source; the use of coal freed industry from water sites, but limitations of transport and the bulk/weight loss of coal merely tied industry to coalfield locations. Today, however, these raw materials are used more efficiently, and alternative power sources such as electricity are now available. This latter development has freed many industries from a raw materials or energy location. There is no less geographic inertia than before, but the new industries tend to locate at major urban nodes.

There are also processes at work in technically advanced economies that tend to lessen the locative influences of raw materials. The value added by the manufacturing processes is growing, so that raw materials now make up a smaller share of the product's final value. The lessening of transportation costs has also had a greater effect on assembly costs than on distributive costs. As noted before, increasing numbers of manufacturing processes are becoming reliant on the output of other factories. Technical progress and economic growth change the demand for goods from the processing industries to complex fabrication industries, where the fabrication of an item entails several production stages. This process, and the increase of the market pull, cause an increasing concentration in the urban nodes, so that economies of scale can be reaped.

A Model of the Evolution of Technical Systems

The two extreme types of technical systems— advanced and developing—also differ in the spatial patterns they impose on the landscape. The important difference is the concentrative pattern of advanced economies as compared with the dispersed pattern of the developing economies. In the latter, household crafts and workshops are distributed in accordance with population and resources. Technological change now makes it cheaper to transport raw materials, which promotes a concentrative nodal pattern. The nodes are large cities, which act not just as transportation nodes, but as markets, large concentrations of purchasing power, sources of credit, pools of labor, and so on, and can in turn act as the access points to even larger markets.

The evolution from one economic extreme to the other can be presented in terms of a model sequence (figure 73). Evenly distributed crafts and workshops are found in the *first phase*, with two small market centers, t_1 and t_2, for the limited exchange of pottery and woven items. In time these centers may themselves attract a number of workshops specializing in,

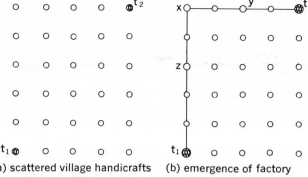

(a) scattered village handicrafts and two market towns t_1, t_2

(b) emergence of factory industry based on resources at x, y, z

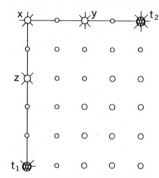 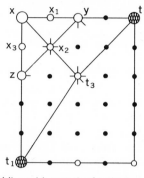

(c) transport feeders develop

(d) rapid growth of industry in transport nodes

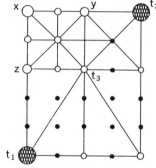 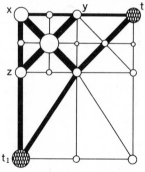

(e) completion of transport interconnection

(f) new pattern of localized manufacturing

Fig. 73. *A model of the evolution of a technically advanced industrial landscape. (From F. E. I. Hamilton, "Models of Industrial Location," 1967, p. 399, by permission of Methuen and Co.)*

say, carpentry or weaving. In the *second phase* a resource reevaluation, either internal or injected from without by alien entrepreneurs, leads to the discovery and exploitation of fuel and material resources at points x, y, z, t_1 and t_2, bringing the craft industries into a competitive relationship with mechanized industry, against which they do not survive. The *fourth phase* sees a further intensification of the transportation network, increasing the market areas of all five centers. Industry expands at all the centers,

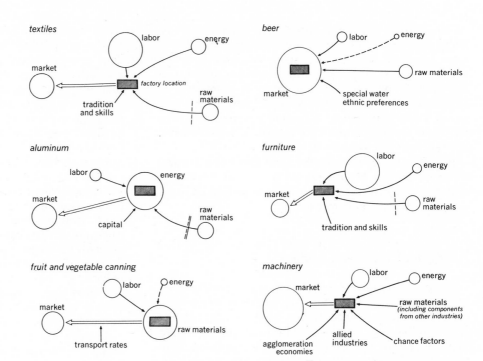

textiles

beer

aluminum

furniture

fruit and vegetable canning

machinery

Fig. 74. *Diagrammatic representation of some common relationships in a few industrial categories. (Adapted with the permission of the Association of American Geographers from the A.A.G. High School Project, unit 2, 1968, pp. 33–34.)*

as the agricultural base improves and a larger industrial population can be supported. By this time the household and workshop crafts are virtually extinct. Some, however, become the locations of larger workshop industries as new nodes arise on the transportation network and increase the effects of industrial growth around such centers as x_1, x_2, and x_3. With the virtual completion of the transportation network, which is the *fifth phase*, existing centers like t_1 and t_2 increase in importance due to their initial advantages and cumulative growth. The *sixth phase*, which is the last, sees the establishment of the polarized technically advanced pattern mentioned earlier, in contrast to the dispersed pattern of phase one. The pattern is based on an intensive linkage of industries, as well as on connections between assembly and distributive points, scale economies, inertia, and skilled labor forces. These cumulative advantages reinforce the pattern at the expense of some other node that, with equally good connective locations, by chance did not form part of the buildup stages.

Attributes

Demand, techniques, and plant economies condition the range of production, the number of plants of given size needed to supply a market, and the number of separate industrial units among which the production process can be divided. All these factors are in turn influenced by population and occupational structure. The scale of operation is also im-

portant since it can condition the degree of access that particular locations offer to materials, labor, and markets. The range of production, partly conditioning scale and cost structure, is now of importance. Within these frameworks of attributes an entrepreneur might compare the total costs of production, assembly, labor, and distribution. Thus for particular industries resource assemblage might be of special importance because of perishability, or weight loss in production. There is also, as we have seen, a difference between industries concerned with raw materials, and industries that use the parts, components, or tools produced by others.

It was suggested in table 29 that a systematic connection exists between these attributes of market, transport, and use of raw or secondary materials, and the various industrial types. Some further examples are illustrated in figure 74. Thus, even with a greater proportion of value being added in manufacture, the food, lumber, and coal industries are still oriented toward a raw material source because of transportation costs and frequent bulk losses in processing. Transportation costs can still be prohibitive for newspapers and bakeries; accordingly, they tend to be oriented toward a local market. Oil and gas, iron and steel, show a compromise locative position between assemblage and distributive costs, but transportation costs can be an important proportion of total costs. Intensity of labor use is characteristic of such industries as textiles, furniture, and electronics, and they tend to be oriented toward their source of materials, whether raw or secondary. But, as noted earlier, transportation costs are a small part of total costs, and this, with other attributes, may sway the final choice of location. Apart from aluminum smelting, which must have available a cheap high voltage energy source, the remaining examples are market oriented. Transportation costs are of slightly greater importance to some than others, but in all cases are minor. Thus entrepreneurs in the footloose industries are able to take a more flexible approach to the location decision.

In all cases, of course, the final decisions are influenced by the perceived and operational milieux, and the attributes listed above must be looked at as guides, not hard-and-fast rules.

Industrial Types and Regions

Geographers have traditionally studied industries in two ways; by industrial type, which is an analytical approach; and synthetically, by industrial region. It should be clear by now that both approaches have to some extent been replaced by the approach that takes the industrial type, or enterprise, as unit of analysis.

A number of industrial types are catalogued in table 36 and in earlier tables and figures; some of the relationships within an industrial type are illustrated in figure 74. Several, like iron and steel and chemicals, are of long standing and of fundamental importance to the operation of all technically advanced economies; others, like the electronics, aircraft, and space industries are of recent origin; still others, like automobiles, appliances, and clothing, pander to the shifting tastes of consumer fashion.

One industrial type, the iron and steel industry, is briefly analyzed below, but it is only one of the many examples that could have been chosen to illustrate this type of analysis.

The Iron and Steel Industry

The fabrication of iron and steel is one of the basic manufacturing activities. It has a **multiplier effect** in an economy, that is, it has very wide links and relationships with the occurrence and growth of other industries. Most national economies have within their structure one or another example of such an industrial activity, in a variety of locations. The existence of an iron and steel industry is usually thought to be basic to any long-term period of industrial and economic growth.

In its location pattern the iron and steel industry well illustrates Alfred Weber's analysis of location. It has one of the most concentrated patterns of all secondary activities, partly because of the relatively

small number of firms involved, and partly because of the orientation toward a few raw material sites. This trend is accentuated by the advantages of internal economies of scale, which are particularly marked. A throughput capacity of 1 million tons of steel per year is an approximately minimum size for a steel plant. Plants with a capacity of up to 8 million tons have been built, as for example the Bethlehem Steel Company's plant at Sparrow Point, Maryland. New growth tends to occur through the amalgamation and expansion of existing plants, and the trend toward rationalization is continually reducing the number of actual corporations.

The fundamental ingredient is iron ore, with varying quantities of coking coal. Iron ore in particular is needed in large quantities, and transfer costs are therefore high. Because of the size of the firms involved, at least in market-exchange economies, a modified vertical linkage occurs, with the ownership of raw materials resting in the hands of the firms themselves.

Because large quantities of coke were needed when the iron and steel industries were expanding in the early nineteenth century, firms were pulled toward coalfields (figure 74). At this time about 6 tons of coke were required to produce 1 ton of pig iron, compared at present to 1 ton of coke. The best locations, of course, were those in which coking coal and iron ores were found together, as in the case of the British Midlands, South Wales, and Central Scotland. Iron ores varied in quality. The presence of such impurities as phosphorus or sulphur prevented the use of certain ores until the technical means could be devised to deal with them. This took some time. Ores were usually moved to the coalfields if they were not present there. Frequently, however, seaboard locations were chosen for iron and steel plants so that they could gain access to otherwise inaccessible domestic ores or to foreign ores. Recent changes have reduced the quantities of coal and ore inputs, and new smelting techniques have allowed the use of soap in addition to pig iron in steel making. The locational significance of these changes is shown in figure 75. There have been other significant technical changes.

An extremely important innovation was the introduction in 1856 of the Bessemer converter, which by injecting blasts of hot air into molten pig iron burned off carbon, phosphorus and other impurities. But it could not deal with a high phosphorus content. The introduction of the open hearth process, which allows the use of scrap in steel making, reduced the pull of both coal and ore locations. In 1955 the open hearth or Siemens-Martin process accounted for 78 percent of world steel production. About 13 percent was accounted for by converter steel (a variation on the Bessemer process that uses a limestone lining to

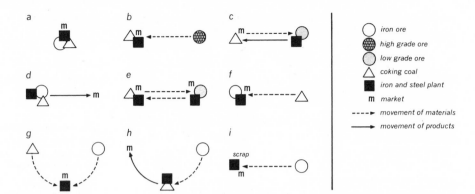

Fig. 75. *Diagrammatic representation of alternative locations of iron and steel plants. (From F. E. I. Hamilton, "Models of Industrial Location," 1967, p. 415, by permission of Methuen and Co.)*

remove high phosphorus impurities) and 9 percent by electric steel furnaces, a recent innovation. In the United States, open hearth steel accounted for 89 percent, but only 52 percent in Western Europe, with 37 percent from the converter process. Since this time, however, further technical modifications have occurred. In particular, the development of a high oxygen process by the Brassert Institute in Switzerland—the so called L-D process—has altered the 1955 figures. Other processes—the Swedish Kaldo and the German Rotor process—are also available; these tend to use lower proportions of scrap to pig iron, and may reverse the trend away from raw material locations.

Given the wide range in the quality of ores and coals that can be used to produce iron and steel, as well as the use of scrap, and the choice of basic Bessemer, Siemens-Martin, Kaldo, Rotor, L-D, electric hearth, and other processes, there is no longer a single optimum location where transport and other costs are at a minimum. Thus a study of Western European coastal steelworks found that they had greater freedom of choice between alternative reactions to change in the economic milieu than steelworks at traditional locations, whose integrated complex and ancillary industries suffered from **geographic inertia.** Indeed the higher flexibility of the coastal locations was one of the primary reasons for the original location decision.

In the United Kingdom six main points have been stressed as location factors by the state-owned industry:

1. *Nearly 10 percent of the total costs of iron and steel are transportation costs.*

2. *Market and raw material locations are important, with the latter sometimes gaining ground, but this is obscured by a general tendency in favor of seaboard locations, as iron ore is imported and fabricated products are exported.*

3. *The availability of labor.*

4. *The availability of scrap, since the United Kingdom uses about 50 percent scrap and 50 percent pig iron in steel production.*

5. *The location of domestic consumers of iron and steel.*

6. *Finally—a strategic decision after the Second World War—to emphasize domestic ores where possible.*

Since so many variables are involved, no clear pattern can emerge. The technical changes have altered the original locative factors almost beyond recognition, and the pull of changing markets is strong. Most supplies of scrap metal are to be obtained from large urban-industrial centers, which also happen to be the principal markets for the output. Automation may again affect these conditions by increasing the capital intensity of the industry, which is already high, and which explains the tendency for plants to be state owned or controlled by only a few corporate enterprises. These aspects of the operational milieu, as well as geographic inertia, are important in any account of the present-day location pattern of the iron and steel industry.

Industrial Regions

The distribution of industries on a world scale is obviously not even, although there is some correlation between the distribution of population and the distribution of resources. However, the major polarizing forces, described earlier for regions of high economic development, disturb that correlation. Some patterns do result from domestic national policies that protect their own industries and markets by tariffs. Other patterns result from the varying scales of states and the presence or absence of planning controls; for example, the government of the U.S.S.R. tends to distribute industry regionally and in complexes. In contrast to this, political fragmentation, as in Western Europe, can impose a dispersive character on industrial patterns. Rising levels of economic development, with enlarged markets and complex interaction patterns, give rise to large-scale activities. If unplanned, these tend to cause greater regional differences by locating in those nodes most accessible to the markets and most amenable to linkage patterns. Thus it has been suggested that integration in the European Common Market is consolidating employment in already existing centers.

Regions of manufacturing activity arise for the reasons already noted: the sharing of common links or facilities, the sharing of common resources, and the pull of associated markets. The national level of development—called here the technical system—will condition the size, extent, and intensity of regional development through the degree of vertical, lateral, and diagonal integration between industries, as well as through the transportation network. Such regions, or concentrations of manufacturing activity, are therefore complex spatial industrial interdependencies.

Given capital and market demand, differences in regional industrial patterns would thus be a function of the character, size, and variety of raw materials, the particular operational milieu, and the behavioral environment. Thus a regional structure associated with a coalfield, with its power source and associated raw materials, might be a complex of coal mining, coke-chemicals, gas-chemicals, electric power, heavy metals, glass, and cement. The bulkiness of the materials and of the output also ties heavy engineering to the region. Less localized industries, using lighter by-products or power from the coalfield, might also be associated with the region, employing much female labor to produce plastics, artificial fibers, and textiles. Large regions associated with large coalfields would give rise to major urban concentrations and complex transport networks, thus attracting consumer oriented and transport oriented industries to nodes around the coalfield. The Ruhr, the English Midlands, the Pittsburgh area, the Donetz Basin—all are examples of such industrial complexes. Somewhat similar complexes can grow around an orefield, and to a lesser extent around smaller coalfields, especially those with brown coal (lignite), which tend to attract only electric power, gas, and chemicals. Other regional structures include urban metropolitan regions; local concentrations of mining, concentrating, refining and energy sources; lumber mills and pulp plants; leather tanning, meat packing, and woolen textile complexes in response to commercial livestock rearing; food processing and canning, box-making, and machinery, fertilizer, and implement manufacturing regions. In fact, a multitude of regional complexes exist, giving rise to distinctive landscape patterns.

Conclusion

Three basic factors in the manufacturing subsystem have changed the traditional view of industrial activities taken by economists and geographers:

1. *The relative importance of transportation costs has declined. This has occurred not only because of a decline in actual costs, but because the industries that use transport intensively, such as iron and steel, are losing importance vis-à-vis the footloose industries. In commercial-exchange economies, increasing economic integration, by reducing institutional barriers, is also reducing the cost of moving goods from one place to another.*

2. *There is a trend toward greater interdependence in organization, greater organizational variety, and greater subjection to change. Firms grow and decline, change their characteristics through time because of technological, institutional, and economic system changes, maximize utilities other than profit, and are subject to governmental and other institutional controls that try to tie together spatial structure and societal goals.*

3. *The growth of the large multiplant firm and the multiregional corporation leads to a very different type of decision making to that studied in the one-plant firm. This is particularly true for spatially relevant decisions, and gives rise to very different types of landscape patterns.*

As will be seen in the following chapter, there seems to be a widening gap between theory and reality in the study of industrial activities. Traditional and conventional studies emphasize the linkage patterns in the industrial sector in terms of commodity flows. These are still important, but other linkages have arisen that also play a role in shaping industrial landscapes. The availability of technological change, and the tendencies toward both national and international economic integration, make available to the contemporary entrepreneur and professional manager a wide range of possibilities. These range from cooperative research and development, to exchange of technical information, to the greater mobility of capital. The decision maker is therefore confronted with very different criteria and different information from those that confronted his nineteenth-century forerunner. Initial causes of change are channeled through the operational milieu, a set of institutions that in turn affect and alter these causes, while themselves being subject to change and adjustment. In sum, a varying elasticity of entrepreneurial and managerial behavior is now possible. Despite the diversity in initiating factors, the final result is that certain regularities do occur. Despite many and various decisions, the range of "satisfactory" entrepreneurial behavior has limits.

Most locations of industrial activities seem to represent a compromise between the dictates of traditional industrial location analysis, and the variation of entrepreneurial behavior. The result of the compromise in each instance is some characteristic form of industrial organization, whether at a plant, industry, or regional level.

Summary

1. *The manufacturing subsystem encompasses all activities where man assembles raw materials at an establishment (household, workshop, or factory), where form utility is added, and from where products are shipped to the first stage of the marketing system. This subsystem includes small-scale cottage industries producing largely handcrafted items at one level, and large industrial corporations producing a wide range of mass-produced items at another level. The last 200 years have seen an increasing proportion of manufactured goods produced in that neotechnic set up, although eotechnic and paleotechnic establishments still exist.*

2. *The focal point of the subsystem is the site or location of the factory, with its feedback links to both raw material and consumer. This is the ". . . what comes in the back door and what goes out the front door of a plant . . ." approach. Such an approach is rather too deterministic and tends to exclude consideration of that all-important dimension—human behavior.*

3. *The "ideal" factory site should, however, provide easy access to raw materials, energy, labor, and a market. However, not all functions and production stages can be fully adjusted to a particular location. Each firm represents a combination of such functions and stages, not all of which are bound to the particular location with the same intensity. The initial reasons for the choice of a particular site may also have long since disappeared, but factors of "geographic inertia" may prolong the viability of a particular site.*

4. *Location decisions and the institutions regulating them vary from peasant, to commercial, and to redistributive economies. They also vary according to whether the decision maker is an owner-manager of a small firm, a professional manager in a joint stock corporation, or a state planner.*

5. *A number of major economic structures which underlie the entrepreneur or planner decisions can be identified; traditionally these factors alone were used to analyze industrial activities. Factors of material and resource availability, market structure, transportation and transfer costs, production factors (labor, capital, enterprise), and system structures like the advantages of geographic concentration, industrial linkages, institutional activities, geographic inertia, and technological change are partially isolated from the manufacturing subsystem. However, even here the role of behavioral and random processes has to be interposed.*

6. *In examining entrepreneurial and managerial behavior, it becomes obvious that information about the economy and the industrial subsystem is not simply presented to the decision maker(s), but is channelled to them and in many cases must be searched out. The degree to which search activity takes place, the use that is made of the information that is perceived, and the degree and type of institutional channelling profoundly influence the economic landscape.*

7. *The industrial decision making process is constrained by the operational milieu of each societal group. Some groups institutionalize their value system through government action, which may set up legislation to hinder or encourage monopolies, the common welfare, military support, or the wealth of the individual. In some cases a vast military-industrial institutional complex results through which most industrial decisions are funnelled, values here being defined in terms of national or individual aggression or aggrandizement.*

8. *The decision making process of the individual entrepreneur and manager in small firms is seen as taking into account factors of profit, real costs, leisure, satisfaction, power, and factors of habit. The landscape impact of such a process may be limited and local in scale, though the accumulative effect of many such decisions in nineteenth-century Britain profoundly changed and moulded both town and countryside.*

9. *In the contemporary world the multiplant corporation has been singled out as the most important institution affecting urban-industrial landscapes in both the West and in so called "developing" countries. The corporate decision maker is in fact a coalition of individuals, and frequently subcoalitions, each with different tasks and responsibilities. Objectives and decisions are reached by bargaining between individuals and subcoalitions (who individually may*

not be trying to maximize corporate profit), but are put into effect by the institutionalized process within the enterprise whose ultimate goal is maximization of dividends by virtually whatever means possible.

10. The differences between small firm and corporation can lead to very different landscape patterns, though frequently their effects lie side by side, with the increasing domination of the corporate enterprise.

11. The interweaving of the forces pulling towards an optimal or quasioptimal location, and the forces pulling towards the tolerable or satisfactory location decisions of the entrepreneur or manager are finally expressed in the landscape as systems and types of industrial regions and industrial complexes. There is a great variation from the unique character of, for instance, the iron and steel industry, the electronics industry, or the brewing industry, to the attributes and interrelationships of the metropolitan region, the port-industrial regions, or the economic complex of redistributive economies. This genetic approach, which has received considerable attention in economic geography, combines the dictates of industrial location theory with the real-world probabilities of the contemporary industrial subsystem.

Further Reading

General textbook coverage of industrial geography will be found in

Alexandersson, G. *Geography of Manufacturing* (Englewood Cliffs: Prentice-Hall, 1967).

Chisholm, M. *Geography and Economics* (London: G. Bell, 1966).

Estall, R. C. and Buchanan, R. O. *Industrial Activity and Economic Geography*, 2nd ed. (London: Hutchinson, 1966).

Hamilton, F. E. I. "Models of Industrial Location" in R. J. Chorley and P. Haggett, eds. *Models in Geography* (London: Methuen, 1967), chapter 10.

McNee, R. B. *A Primer on Economic Geography* (New York: Random House, 1971).

Miller, E. W. *A Geography of Industrial Location* (Dubuque, Iowa: Wm. Brown, 1970).

Individual structural aspects are covered in

Alderfer, E. B. and Michl, H. E. *Economics of American Industry*, 3rd ed. (New York: McGraw-Hill, 1957).

Harris, C. D. "The Market as a Factor in the Location of Industry in the U.S.," *Annals of the Association of American Geographers*, vol. 44, 1954, pp. 315–348.

Fulton, M. and Hoch, L. C. "Transportation Factors Af-

fecting Location Decisions," *Economic Geography*, vol. 35, 1959, pp. 51–59.

Lomas, G. and Wood, P. A. *Employment Location in Regional Economic Planning* (London: Cass, 1969).

Lutteral, W. F. *Factory Location and Industrial Movement* (London: N.I.E.S.R., 1962), two volumes.

Pred, A. "Industrialization, Initial Advantage, and American Metropolitan Growth," *Geographical Review*, vol. 40, 1965, pp. 158–185.

Rawstron, E. M. "Three Principles of Industrial Location," *Transactions*, Institute of British Geographers, vol. 25, 1958, pp. 135–42.

Segal, M. *Wages in the Metropolis: Their Influence on the Location of Industries in the New York Region* (Cambridge, Mass: Harvard University Press, 1960).

Smith, W. "The Location of Industry," *Transactions, Institute of British Geographers*, vol. 21, 1955, pp. 1–18.

The importance of behavior in industrial decision making are covered in

Florence, P. S. *Economics and Sociology of Industry: A Realistic Analysis of Development* (London: C. A. Watts and Co., 1964).

Krumme, G. "Toward a Geography of Enterprise," *Economic Geography*, vol. 45, 1969, pp. 30–40.

McNee, R. B. "Towards a More Humanistic Economic Geography: The Geography of Enterprise," *Tijdschrift Voor Economische en Sociale Geografie*, vol. 51, 1960, pp. 201–206.

March, J. G. and Simon, H. A. *Organizations* (New York: Wiley, 1958).

Pred, A., *Behavior and Location*, parts 1 and 2 (Lund: C. W. K. Gleerup, 1967 and 1969).

Steed, G. P. F. "Changing Milieu of the Firm: A Study in Manufacturing Geography," *Annals of the Association of American Geographers*, vol. 58, 1968, pp. 506–525.

Case studies of industrial regions and nations include

Estall, R. C. *New England: A Study in Industrial Adjustment* (London: G. Bell, 1966).

Fuchs, V. R. *Changes in the Location of Manufacturing in the U.S. Since 1929* (New Haven: Yale University Press, 1962).

Hall, P. *The Industries of London Since 1861* (London: Hutchinson, 1962).

Hamilton, F. E. I. *Yugoslavia, Patterns of Economic Activity* (London: G. Bell, 1968), chapters 6–8, 12, 13.

(Other studies by various authors on the industrial geography of Rumania, Poland, South Africa, etc., are under preparation.)

Karaska, G. "Manufacturing Linkages in the Philadelphia

Economy," *Geographical Analysis*, vol. 1, 1969, pp. 354–369.

Manners, G., ed. *South Wales in the Sixties* (Oxford: Pergamon Press, 1964).

Martin, J. *Greater London: An Industrial Geography* (London: G. Bell, 1966).

Rodgers, A. "Some Aspects of Industrial Diversification in the United States," *Economic Geography*, vol. 33, 1957, pp. 16–30.

Wise, M. J. "On the Evolution of the Jewellery and Gun Quarters in Birmingham," *Transactions*, Institute of British Geographers, vol. 15, 1949, pp. 57–72.

Individual industries are dealt with by such studies as

Airou, J. *The Location of the Synthetic Fiber Industry* (New York: Wiley, 1959).

Diones, L. *Locational Factors and Locational Development in the Soviet Chemical Industry*, Department of Geography, University of Chicago, Research Paper no. 119, 1969.

Estall, R. C. "The Electronics Products Industry of New England," *Economic Geography*, vol. 39, 1963, pp. 189–216.

Goodwin, W. "The Structure and Position of the British Motor Vehicle Industry," *Tijdschrift Voor Economische en Sociale Geografie*, vol. 56, 1965, pp. 145–56.

Hurley, N. P. "The Automotive Industry: A Study in Industrial Location," *Land Economics*, vol. 35, 1959, pp. 1–14.

Pounds, N. J. G. *The Geography of Iron and Steel*, 5th ed. (London: Hutchinson, 1971).

Rodgers, H. B. "The Changing Geography of the Lancashire Cotton Industry," *Economic Geography*, vol. 38, 1962, pp. 299–314.

An example of industrial relocation, the General Foods move, is covered by

Whitman, E. S. and Schmidt, W. J. *Plant Relocation: A Case History of a Move* (New York: American Management Association, 1966).

nine

*Some Approaches
to Industrial Location*

The fact that industrial regions continue to exist has prompted a number of highly abstract theoretical investigations into the phenomenon of industrial location. It was noted in the preceding chapter that three factors have separated traditional theory by a wide gulf from contemporary reality: decrease in importance of transport costs; increased organizational dynamism, interdependence, and variety; and the rise of the corporate enterprise. The traditional theoretical approaches have largely been of the normative type, concerned with partial equilibrium, static patterns, and economically deterministic explanations. Contemporary industrial activities, however, are the result of processes of change, adoption, adaption, and a wide variety of economic and non-economic factors. Most location theorists continue to deal with the location decisions of nineteenth-century entrepreneurs, who were strongly influenced by transport costs, and seem to ignore or hold constant the factors of the present mobile and dynamic industrial subsystem. Today only some 10 percent of the value added in manufacture in the United States is produced by the individual entrepreneur and the small firm. In other words, some 50 percent of value added is accounted for in the United States by just 100 corporations. To put this in perspective it is first necessary to outline traditional location theory.

Traditional Approaches to Industrial Location

The basic question posed by traditional theories of industrial location has been, "Where ought industries to locate?" The traditional answer has been,

"Where they derive maximum profits." Two separate systems of ideas have developed in justification for this answer. Both hold that an optimal location is determinable for every manufacturing production unit whether it be run by a single entrepreneur or a coalition of individuals.

The Least Cost—Cost Minimization Approach

The least cost approach is based on the following postulates:

1. *Firms seek to maximize profits with respect to costs.*
2. *There is perfectly competitive pricing.*
3. *Transport rates are homogeneous, while transportation costs are a function of weight and distance.*
4. *There is a given buying center and a given demand.*
5. *Raw material sources are fixed points.*

To Alfred Weber the optimal location, depending on the inputs and cost structure, was essentially one where:

1. *Total transportation costs per unit of output are at a minimum.*
2. *Failing this, transportation diseconomies are offset through economies of agglomeration and low labor costs.*

Thus within this Weberian least cost model, entrepreneurs will site their industries at the points of minimum costs achieved in response to three basic locational factors: relative transportation costs; labor costs; and agglomeration or deglomeration costs.

Holding two of these factors constant, Weber deduced how an industrial plant would locate with respect to the third factor. The logical conclusion of his approach was that an industrial establishment would locate at a point where the combined weight movements involved in the assembly and distribution of the firm's products are at a minimum.

The role of transportation costs can be explained by two simple examples.

First, if there is one market and one raw material, then there are three possibilities for location:

1. *If the raw material is evenly distributed over the landscape, then the factory will locate at the market, since it is at the latter that the lowest transportation costs occur for both raw material and finished product (figure 76).*
2. *If the raw material is located at one particular point, but weight is lost in the manufacturing process, then the industry will locate at the raw material source (it will be remembered that, according to the model's third postulate, transportation costs are directly proportional to weight).*

Second, if there is one market but two raw materials, then location can occur in four ways:

1. *If both raw materials, R_1 and R_2 are evenly distributed, then manufacturing will be carried out at the market, since again it is at this point that the lowest transportation costs prevail for both raw material and product.*
2. *If R_1 is ubiquitous, and R_2 is fixed at a point other than the market, and if neither suffers weight loss in manufacture, then the industry will locate at the market, and transportation costs will be high only on R_2. The reason for this is that if the factory were*

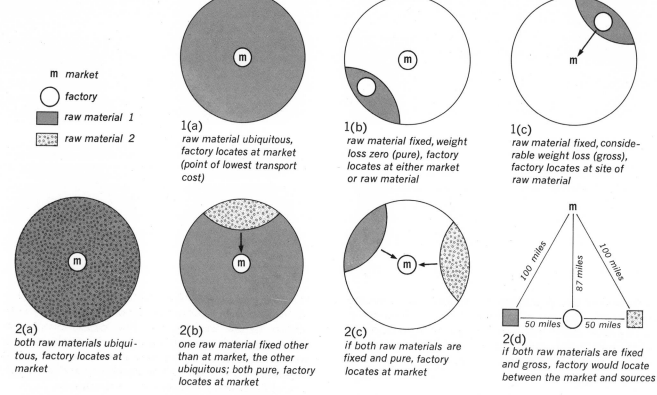

m market

○ factory

▨ raw material 1

▨ raw material 2

1(a)
raw material ubiquitous,
factory locates at market
(point of lowest transport
cost)

1(b)
raw material fixed, weight
loss zero (pure), factory
locates at either market
or raw material

1(c)
raw material fixed, considerable weight loss (gross),
factory locates at site of
raw material

2(a)
both raw materials ubiquitous, factory locates at
market

2(b)
one raw material fixed other
than at market, the other
ubiquitous; both pure, factory
locates at market

2(c)
if both raw materials are
fixed and pure, factory
locates at market

2(d)
if both raw materials are fixed
and gross, factory would locate
between the market and sources

Fig. 76. *Weber's theory of industrial location: (1) the role of transport costs.*

located at R_2 high costs would be paid on R_1 and on moving the finished product to the market, since the latter suffers no weight loss in manufacture.

3. *If both R_1 and R_2 are fixed, and if neither suffers weight loss in manufacture, then the factory will be located at the market. Both component materials will be sent directly to the consumption areas for processing, since this will give the lowest aggregate transportation costs. If the factory were located at either R_1 or R_2, additional transportation charges would have to be paid on that leg of the journey on which the product moved to the market. Thus any industrial process using* **pure** *materials from two sources will always locate at the place where finished products are consumed. The only exception would be if one of the raw materials, in being shipped to the market area, passed through the point where the other raw material was produced.*

4. *If both R_1 and R_2 are fixed, and if both suffer weight loss in manufacture, then the solution is a little more complex, involving as it does the use of Laundardt's locational triangle (figure 76). Thus if both R_1 and R_2 lose 50 percent of their weight in the manufacturing process, and 5,000 tons of each are required a year, then the total transportation cost each year, if the factory is located at X (the market), will be 5,000 tons × 100 miles × 2 (R_1 to X and R_2 to X), which equals 1,000,000 ton miles annually (ton miles are weight in tons multiplied by distance in miles).*

If, however, the factory were located at R_1, transportation would amount to 500,000 ton miles from R_2 to R_1 (5,000 tons × 100 miles), and 500,000 ton miles on the finished product from R_1 to X (5,000 tons + 5,000 tons raw materials, less 50 percent loss in manufacture = 5,000 tons × 100 miles). But if the factory were located at 0, midway between R_1 and R_2, the ton mileage would total:

5,000 tons × 50 miles (R_1 to 0) = 250,000 ton miles
5,000 tons × 50 miles (R_2 to 0) = 250,000 ton miles
5,000 tons (finished product) × 87 miles (0 to X)
   = 435,000 ton miles

which totals 935,000 ton miles. This is less than the burden facing an enterprise located at X, R_1, or R_2.

If the two raw materials do *not* have the same weight-loss ratio, and if differing amounts of the materials are required, the factory would tend to locate nearer one of the raw material sources so as to lower the burden of transportation costs. There are other situations that could be analyzed in this manner—for example 2 markets and 2 material sources, or 3 markets and 2 material sources.

There are two major drawbacks to Weber's analysis of transportation costs. First, freight rates are in fact

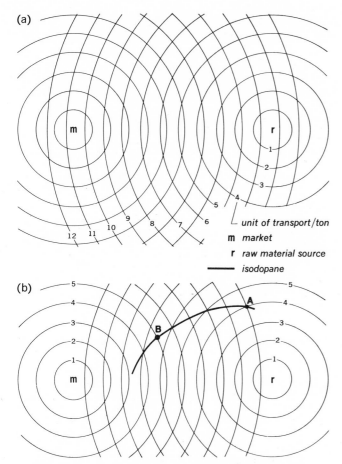

(a)

(b)

unit of transport/ton
m   market
r   raw material source
—— isodapane

Fig. 77. *Weber's theory of industrial location: (2) the role of labor costs.*

rarely directly proportionate to distance, as the model assumes. Second, freight rates are not usually, ton for ton, the same on finished products as on raw materials. This matter will be referred to again later.

Second, Weber considered the role of labor costs. He recognized that these could vary spatially and therefore wield an influence on the location of a factory. Thus a savings in labor costs could offset extra transportation costs.

To illustrate this, Weber used two devices that he called **isotims** ("equal in price") and **isodapanes** ("equal in expense"). Isotims are isolines of equal transportation cost for each item (raw material or finished product); they are shown in figure 77 as continuous lines. Isodapanes are isolines joining points of equal transportation cost; they are shown in figure 77 as broken lines. Here, m represents the market and r the raw material site. Again, transportation costs are assumed to be the same per ton mile for both raw material and finished product. The isotims around m represent transport costs from all points to m, and those around r represent costs to all points from r. Both sets of circles (isotims) rep-

resent a spacing of one unit of transport cost per ton. It is assumed that the raw material is **gross**, and that it loses 50 percent of its weight in the manufacturing process.

If the factory were located at r_1 every ton of the final product shipped from r to m would cost 10 units of transportation costs (10 intervals from r to m on the diagram). If the factory, on the other hand, were located at m_1 the cost would be 20 units of transportation charges, since double the quantity of raw material to final product has to be carried.

Alternative locations also exist. At A, the total transportation cost would be 18 transport units — 8 units on raw materials (2×4) and 10 units on moving the finished product. An isodapane can now be constructed representing all points that have a total transportation cost of 18 units. Thus point B carries 13 units on raw materials and 5 cost units on the finished product. All points on this isodapane in fact carry 8 units of transportation cost above that obtaining at R. The isodapanes reveal how great the labor cost advantage would have to be in order to offset higher transportation costs. If any cheap labor site with, say, at least 8 units advantage in cost terms, lies on the isodapane A–B in figure 77, then it could represent an industrial site. If its advantage is greater than 8 units, then in economically rational terms it would be an industrial site. If no sites exist with these advantages, then there will be no move to a cheap labor location. If more than one site does, then the firm will move to a cheap labor site — in fact, to the site of least labor cost.

Again, there are inadequacies in this approach, since the assumptions concerning labor costs are unreal. Thus there would be a tendency for substitution at the cheap labor site of cheap labor for those inputs of transport, through reduction in bulk, weight, or perishability of the product, provided production and other technical relations were not fixed. This kind of simplification can be expected with any model situation.

These first two differentials, labor costs and transport costs, were thought by Weber to interact, and thus to determine the regional distribution of industries. The third general location factor, *agglomeration-deglomeration economies*, was thought to act to concentrate or disperse industries within a particular region. Thus a firm or firms may seek locations that have a high overall transport or labor outlay. But an increase in production size is substituted for those higher costs if the costs per unit of production are thereby reduced.

Several individual units of production will agglomerate when together they can attain some threshold quantity of production, and when their critical isodapanes intersect (figure 78). The *critical isodapane* for any firm is the locus of points at which actual transportation costs exceed the transportation costs associated with the optimal transport point by a constant amount. Thus if an entrepreneur wished to locate four new units of production, he could locate each plant at its optimal transport point (least cost point), or he could locate them adjacent to one another at a center of agglomeration, thus achieving localization economies that would offset any transportation diseconomies. Similarly, Weber recognized that deglomeration might be advantageous when the costs of agglomeration rose above a certain threshold and began to impose further costs.

Weber's Theoretical Industrial System

To combine the interplay of the factors examined above, Weber used a **material index,** which is the weight of the localized material inputs divided by the weight of the product. This shows whether the point of "movement minimization" (i.e., the optimal site in least cost terms) would be near the source of raw materials or near the market. In the former case, the index is less than one, in the latter, greater than one. If a firm or industry has a high **labor coefficient** (ratio of labor cost to the combined weights of the material input and the product output), then the firm will be attracted to a point other than that with least costs in transport terms alone. Of course, this assumes that the savings in labor costs equal or exceed the transport diseconomies thus incurred. Agglomeration economies could also outweigh transport economies, thus giving rise to a third location type. By combining these factors, Weber was able to distinguish at least fourteen theoretical types of industries that combine transportation costs, labor costs, and agglomeration economies (table 36). Thus industries A, B, and D, processing ubiquitous materials, locate at the market to cut the transportation costs of hauling the finished product; industry F, using pure and fixed raw materials, locates at the market for the same reasons; industries E and H, with gross raw materials but different weight losses, locate nearest to the raw material source that loses most weight; industry G, with gross raw materials but equal weight loss, locates at an intermediate point (the locational triangle problem); industry C uses a pure but sporadically distributed raw material, incurring equal transport costs wherever it is located; industries I and J use fixed gross and ubiquitous materials, the location depending on the ratio of gross materials used to ubiquitous raw materials; industry K with a high labor coefficient (i.e., a savings in labor costs) locates where those savings exceed the transport diseconomies; industries L and M achieve agglomeration economies that exceed the transport diseconomies of such a location; and

(a) nonintersecting critical isodopanes: no agglomeration

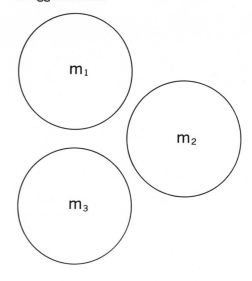

(b) intersecting critical isodopanes: agglomeration

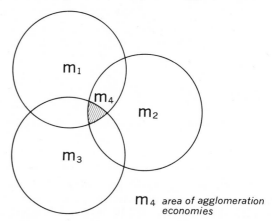

m_4 area of agglomeration economies

Fig. 78. *Weber's theory of industrial location: (3) agglomeration economies.*

finally, industry N, attracted to an urban center in the same way as L and M, finds the costs too high, and locates outside the agglomeration.

Conclusion

Weber's assumptions and framework, like any model situation, are unreal. But he can be criticized for the kinds of unreality he chose. Some of these have already been mentioned: transportation costs are not directly proportional to distance; freight rates are not equal on raw materials and finished products; both supply and demand change over space; raw materials and markets are not fixed points; and trans-

Table 36. *Weber's Theoretical Industrial System*

industry	raw materials ubiquitous	fixed pure	gross	labor costs	agglomeration	deglomeration	location
A	1						M
B	2 or more						M
C		1					any
D	1 or more	1					M
E			1				R
F		2					M
G			2 (equal weight loss)				O
H			2 or more (unequal weight loss)				R
I	1 or more		1				any
J	2 or more						any
K	not specified			high labor coefficient			L
L	not specified				agglom. econs.		A
M	not specified				agglom. econs.		A
N	not specified					deglom. econs.	D

locations: M = market location   O = intermediate location
       any = equally viable locations at market, materials, etc.   L = labor-cost-saving location
        R = raw material(s) source location   D = deglomeration
        A = agglomeration center

Source: A. Weber, *Theory of the Location of Industries* (Chicago: Chicago University Press, 1929), pp. 61–66. Translated by C.J. Friedrich.

portation costs are rarely even the basic cost criterion. Weber also underestimates the role of pure materials and overestimates the role of gross materials, ignores the fact that no industry uses just one material input, ignores both labor mobility and actual differences in wage levels, and underestimates the effects of agglomeration. And so the criticisms could continue, including not the least Weber's neglect of behavioral and attitudinal variations.

Similar least cost postulates have been developed by other investigators. In general, it can be said that the Weberian system of ideas, developed in a number of least cost models, seeks to explain the location of manufacturing by assuming a given demand and considering only the costs of location. Within its perfectly competitive framework it concludes that the optimum profit-maximizing location is the location where costs are minimized.

The Market Area or Profit Maximization Approach

Another school of thought has developed a system of ideas around the monopolistic potentialities of plant location. This approach, often referred to as the market area or locational interdependence model, can be represented by the following postulates:

1. *For each firm there exists a behavioral pattern such that it seeks to locate at the most profitable of the production points at which it can locate.*
2. *For each location there exist constant costs for the procurement and consumption of raw materials.*
3. *Buyers are evenly dispersed over an area, and have identical demands.*

One of the most significant advocates of this approach was August Lösch, in 1954. He disregarded spatial variations in production costs by holding them constant, and instead depicted optimal locations as occurring where the largest possible market area is monopolized—that is, where sales potential and total revenue potential are maximized.

The Löschian Schema

Again the real world environment is simplified considerably, although the framework established is broad enough to encompass not just the location problems of industry, but of cities, populations, and centers of concentration of economic activity in general. Overall, Lösch presents an elementary static model of a space economy.

If buyers are scattered over an area, sellers will locate accordingly, in order to gain maximum control over different groups of buyers. It must be stressed that, although the term "market area" refers to dollar volume of sales rather than square miles, the third postulate given above implies that the dollar volume of sales can be made synonymous with the number of miles of market area controlled by the firm.

Lösch established the hexagon as the ideal market shape, and viewed the trading area of the various products as the nets of such hexagons. Figure 79 helps to explain his choice of the hexagonal form. First, a net of hexagonal market forms will completely cover any area under consideration, whereas circular areas will either leave utilized areas or will overlap. Second, of all the regular polygons (hexagon, square, triangle, etc.) that will cover an area, the hexagon deviates least from the circular form and in consequence minimizes transportation expenditure in supplying a given demand.

Lösch then attempts to find the maximum profit

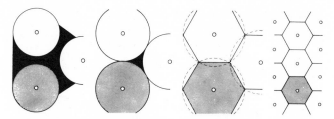

Fig. 79. *Development of market areas from circular to final hexagonal form. (From August Lösch,* Economics of Location, *1954, p. 110, reprinted by permission of Yale University Press.)*

location by comparing, for different locations, both the costs of production and the market area that can be controlled. Within the framework of this competitive situation, the location chosen may not be the least cost location, as the Weberian school would have it. Instead, it will be the maximum profit location built on sales revenues rather than production and distribution costs. Thus for each commodity or production type, the economic landscape is dissected into a series of hexagonal nets of market areas. These nets are grouped according to the size of their respective market units. After allowance has been made for the minimization of transport effort, the resulting nets are ordered around a common center. By turning the nets around this center the pattern shown in figure 80 results, with six sectors where production centers are most frequent. Thus, according to the model, at the center of the economic landscape a large metropolis would arise with all the advantages of a large local demand. With population and settlement localized into "rich" sectors, industries become agglomerated in the same zones to gain economies through linkage. As a result, the greatest number of locations coincide, the maximum number of purchases can be made locally, and the sum of the minimum distances between industrial locations is least. Moreover, not only shipments but also transport lines are reduced to a minimum.

Lösch identified a number of real situations that he believed compared with his model situation (figure 81). In these cases a barren area occurs immediately around the metropolis, as only a few local goods can be produced with profit in the neighborhood of such a center.

If the simple uniformity assumptions that are basic to the model were relaxed, that is, if there were inequality of raw materials, labor, and capital, as well as uneven population distribution, an extremely complex situation would result. Nevertheless, two basic factors seem to arise: the agglomerating cost factor promotes interindustry concentration, but the demand factor leads to a honeycomb type of dispersion of firms within an industry. In other words, each entrepreneur is seen to occupy a particular spatial position that maximizes his profit, so that as a result

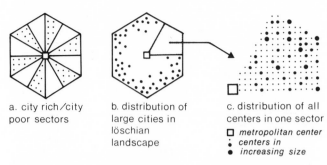

a. city rich/city poor sectors

b. distribution of large cities in löschian landscape

c. distribution of all centers in one sector

□ metropolitan center
· centers in
● increasing size

Fig. 80. *Lösch's theoretical landscape, achieved by the rotation of the many k system. This produces a strong pattern of variation between sectors with distance from the central metropolis. (From Lösch 1954, ibid., p. 127; see fig. 79.)*

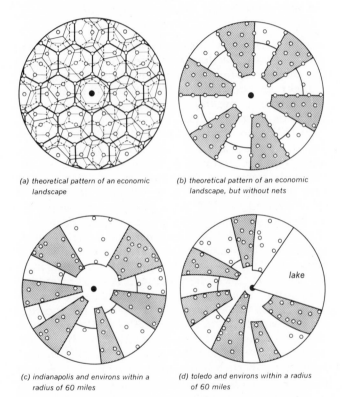

(a) theoretical pattern of an economic landscape

(b) theoretical pattern of an economic landscape, but without nets

(c) indianapolis and environs within a radius of 60 miles

(d) toledo and environs within a radius of 60 miles

Fig. 81. *Examples of Löschian landscapes. (From Lösch 1954, ibid., p. 125.)*

he will have no desire under economically rational conditions to move position. Consumers select a location with the same idea in mind. Thus an individual as a producer selects the maximum profit location, and the consumers select the cheapest market.

A number of criticisms have arisen concerning this Löschian industrial landscape. For instance, the model is based on the assumption that the price of a commodity is a simple function of the demand for it, and this is frequently unrealistic.

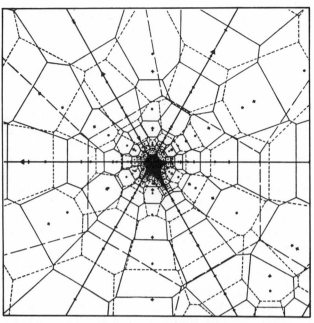

Fig. 82. *A simplified Löschian landscape. (Reprinted from W. Isard,* Location and Space Economy, *p. 270, by permission of the M.I.T. Press, Cambridge, Mass. Copyright ©1956 by the Massachusetts Institute of Technology.)*

Other Market Area Approaches

Isard has modified the Löschian schema, in an attempt to make it more realistic. In his version, the system has ever larger hexagons (market areas) as distance from the metropolis increases or population density declines. This creates a concentric zonal rather than a sectoral pattern (figure 82). An attempt by M. L. Greenhut to change the model admits the factor of uncertainty. Thus an entrepreneur seeking location with minimum cost and maximum profit increases the number of factors by which he can be influenced, and as his market increases it becomes doubtful and uncertain. Such a situation arises from the existence of differing costs at alternative locations, and from uncertainty about the profits and policies of competitors. In this case each entrepreneur chooses a line of action that could be analyzed in terms of game theory. Uncertainty and rivalry can lead to industrial location where firms think that rivals can achieve optimum sales at lowest cost. This would be particularly true of footloose industries.

A difference in emphasis, but one that still utilizes the same system of ideas, led to the locational-interdependence approach of Harold Hotelling in 1929. Where Lösch is concerned primarily with the size and shape of the firm's market area, Hotelling stresses the impact of the demand on location, confining his interest to the factors that cause firms to be attracted or repulsed by each other. For methodological simplicity he modified the third postulate, assuming a linear, evenly dispersed market. He reasoned that firms would concentrate at the midpoint of the entire market area, so that each could supply buyers located at the extremities while not surrendering locational advantage to rivals. Hotelling explained this locational strategy in the terms of an analogy, the so-called ice cream vendor problem. In terms of figure 83, X-Y represents a mile of beach, with two ice cream vendors, each selling the same brand of ice cream at the same price. The bathers on the beach all purchase equal amounts of ice cream, and select a vendor on the basis of which one is nearer to them. Locations at a and b would provide each ice cream vendor with a half mile of beach from which to draw his customers. However, each ice cream vendor can improve his position by moving toward the central position, M, as in figure 83 (b). The final solution to the problem, (c), is for both vendors to establish their stalls side by side at the midpoint of the beach. In this way, each retains one-half of the market and the situation remains stable, since there are no advantages to be gained by moving. It has been pointed out, however, that many firms would still in fact locate at the quartile points, a and b. This would occur particularly if customers beyond the quartile points, when both vendors are located at M, decided this was too long a trip to make for ice cream, and decided either to give up ice cream or to substitute another product.

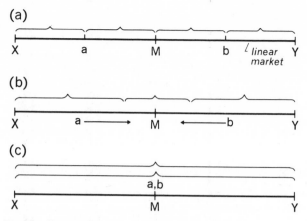

Fig. 83. *Hotelling's* linear market *solution (see text).*

The Traditional Approaches

The concern of these normative location models has basically been to identify where industries should or ought to locate. This has been couched in terms of profit maximization. What does it mean to maximize profits? Total profit is usually defined as the difference between total revenue and total cost. We have now reviewed two systems of ideas that attempt to justify this answer. Yet one of them, the least cost school, is totally concerned with costs, leaving demand constant; while the other is wholly concerned with demand, this time leaving costs constant. Any choice between these two possible ways of explaining manufacturing locations would be purely arbitrary. Further, neither model by itself gives a satisfactory explanation of profit maximizing behavior; a maximum profit location would have to satisfy both systems. Within the context of both models this is not possible, since the fourth postulate of the least cost system (there is a given buying center and a given demand) is incompatible with the third postulate of the market area approach (buyers are evenly dispersed over an area, and have identical demands). Both approaches seem to fail to pro-

vide a satisfactory answer to the location question; they fail because they are *closed* models, unable at our present state of knowledge to interact with one another. In addition, the two approaches are *static* and so fail to provide sufficient explanation of the variables they consider.

In failing to consider demand, the least cost approach uses an arbitrary concept of agglomeration, an unrealistic account of factor costs, and an inadequate framework for transport costs. The market area approach, by failing to consider costs, places its dispersed market assumption on a completely ad hoc basis. This approach disregards factors of concentration, that is, it assumes that firms are never attracted to the same location as their rivals. Thus it fails to explain cases where firms have the same market areas, or cases where demand is concentrated at one point. The locational-interdependence framework is less misleading when it places the location decisions of firms in the context of rival firms' location decisions of firms in the context of rival firms' location patterns. But this analysis, by utilizing assumptions in such a way that costs are not considered, fails again to provide any useful explanation of the profit maximizing location. The closed static framework of these models places a severe constraint on finding any operationally meaningful reasons for industrial location decisions. As Lösch himself admitted, "... there is no scientific and unequivocal solution for the location of the individual firm . . . hence Weber's and all other attempts at a systematic and valid location theory for the individual firm were doomed to failure."

Alternative Approaches

Chapter 8 listed and elaborated on a large number of factors influencing industrial locations. The relative importance of each of these factors varies among industries and firms. Essentially, these factors together make up a system, although the importance of a particular component will vary from example to example. However, this variation, and the fact that we are dealing with a dynamic not a static situation, makes the building of some grand overall explanatory framework very difficult. Just as the classical approaches simplified real-world conditions, so do most of the alternative approaches described below. Some, however, choose their constraints more wisely.

A "Spatial Limits" Model

D. M. Smith, in attempting to provide a theoretical framework for industrial location, has attempted to utilize the perfect competition-least cost approach of Weber, with some reference to the monopolistic competition-market area approach of Lösch. Basically, he relies on the least cost approach, since it allows for the effects of spatially variable supplies of material and labor. Under Lösch's assumptions of uniform plain and scattered population, this cannot be done. However, Smith attempts to relax such assumptions as that of constant demand, or of spatial variations in the size of the potential market, within the basic spatial limits set by external economic forces—that is, within the margins of tolerance.

When a businessman or entrepreneur makes a location choice, if the assumption is economic rationality, then he will make that choice on the *maximin* basis (maximize profits, minimize costs). No choice is ever made in isolation. This applies particularly to choice of industrial location, which has to take account of such considerations as scale, market conditions, competition, and certain behavioral factors. The maximin location may vary with factory size or different combinations of factors, and demand may vary with the location chosen. The interrelation of these different factors makes location analysis, as has been seen from the earlier examples, a difficult problem.

Figure 84 illustrates the effects of spatial variations in cost and price. Looking for the maximin location, it can be assumed that:

1. *Costs cannot be manipulated by entrepreneurial skills.*
2. *Output is constant over space.*
3. *Variations in demand are shown by price variations from point to point.*

In figure 84a costs are variable, and demand (price obtainable from the goods) is constant. In this case, with revenue everywhere the same and only costs varying, *O* represents the point of maximum profits,

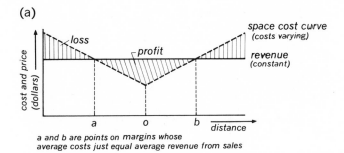

(a)

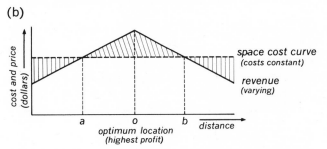

a and b are points on margins whose average costs just equal average revenue from sales

(b)

optimum location (highest profit)

(c)

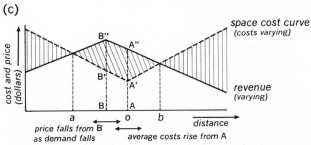

price falls from B as demand falls

average costs rise from A

Fig. 84. *The Smith model: (1) optimal locations and spatial profitability margins. (Figs. 84–91 are from D. Smith, "A Theoretical Framework for Geographical Studies of Industrial Location,"* Economic Geography, *vol. 42, 1966, p. 96; reprinted by permission of the editor.)*

the optimal location. The limits of profitable operation, or **margins of profitability,** *a* and *b*, can also be seen. Beyond this margin costs exceed revenue, and a firm could only operate at a loss. This is essentially the Weberian solution. The reverse situation is shown in figure 84b. Here, costs are the same everywhere, but with spatial variations in price or revenue. In figure 84c the situation becomes more realistic with both cost and price varying from place to place. Maximum profits obtain at *A*, where costs are lowest (profit = $A' - A''$), and where profits are also highest, higher in fact than at the point of highest price ($B' - B''$). The entrepreneur seeking maximum profits will therefore choose the least cost location, despite the lower total revenue obtainable here. The reverse situation, with maximum profits at the high price location, can be obtained by simply altering the slopes of the cost and revenue gradients. A number of propositions can be derived from these diagrams:

(a)

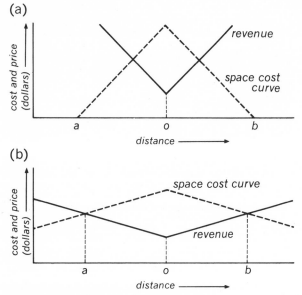

(b)

Fig. 85. *The Smith model: (2) optimal locations and spatial profitability margins — slope gradients. (Ibid.)*

1. *In a cost-price situation of this type, spatial variations in total costs and revenues impose limits to the area in which any industry can operate at a profit.*

2. *Within those limits the entrepreneur can locate anywhere, unless he seeks maximum profits.*

3. *The steeper the cost or price gradients, the greater is the spatial variation and the more localized the location choice; conversely, the shallower the gradients, the wider the location choice—unless again maximum profits are sought (figure 85).*

These factors become more meaningful if we subdivide per unit costs on all labor, material, and other factors, into **basic costs** and **locational costs** (figure 86). Basic costs are those incurred no matter what the location, such as the cost of a raw material at source, or the cost of labor irrespective of transportation cost. Locational cost, then, is the cost involved in getting those basic materials to the location point. The importance of the variations of these costs varies from industry to industry. The spatial variation of the particular cost factor that contributes most toward total costs will be of the greatest importance to the location of a particular industry. A cost factor that has little spatial variation normally has little influence.

Bearing in mind these factors, Smith postulates a simple location model based on the following assumptions:

1. *All producers are in business to make a profit (but not necessarily the maximum profit).*

2. *All producers are fully aware of spatial variations in costs and profits.*

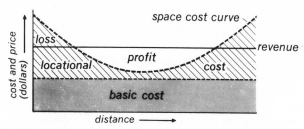

Fig. 86. *The Smith model: (3) locational and basic costs. (Ibid.)*

3. *Sources of production factors (land, labor, capital) are fixed, and supplies are unlimited, but no substitution can take place between them.*

4. *Demand (revenue) is constant over space.*

5. *No firm tries to take advantage of scale economies.*

6. *No firm influences the location of another firm.*

7. *All entrepreneurs are equally skillful.*

8. *No location is subsidized.*

The model is therefore static, analyzing just one point in time. If there is an industry with certain requirements for land and labor, selling a single raw material to a dispersed market, it can be assumed that the material is found at *A*, the labor is concentrated at *B*, and the market at *C*, while land costs are the same everywhere. In order to manufacture the end product the firm needs, let us say, $100 worth of materials; $75 worth of labor; and $25 of land. Let us further assume that sales costs are $50 at a location in the center of the market. In sum, basic costs are as follows:

A (*materials*)	$100
B (*labor*)	75
C (*market*)	50
Land	25
	$250

To calculate locational costs, for every $100 of material let it cost $2.50 a mile to transport it, and for every mile let labor costs increase by $2.50, and average cost of marketing by the same amount. Land costs are ubiquitous, so there is no variation. Treating *A*, *B*, and *C* as having spatial locations 30 miles apart, space-cost curves can be constructed, as in figure 87. This diagram shows concentric circles at 5-mile intervals (at a set increment in material, labor, and market costs of $15). Superimposed on these circles are isocost lines (points of equal cost per unit of production). These show that costs rise away from a point *O*, in this case in the center of a triangle formed by *A*, *B*, and *C*. This solution is essentially similar to that of Weber. If each article is produced for $504 then, given the assumptions noted earlier, the $300 isocost line becomes the margin to possible

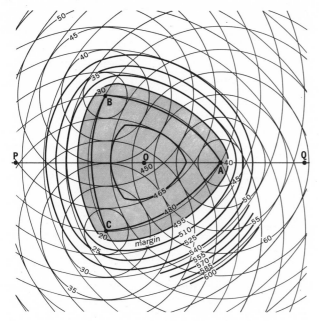

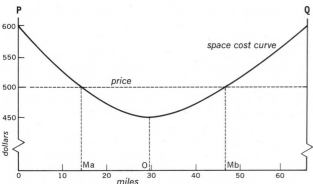

Fig. 87. *The Smith model: (4) isocost lines and space cost curves. (Ibid., p. 103.)*

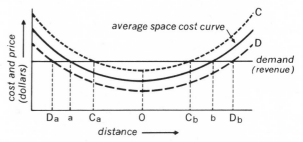

Fig. 88. *The Smith model: (5) the effect of entrepreneurial skill. (Ibid., p. 105.)*

locations. Within this line the entrepreneur makes a profit; without it he does not. He could locate at *A*, *B*, and *C*, where the least costs for labor, materials and marketing occur. But he can make more profit by locating nearer to *O*.

Underlying the isocost map in figure 87 is a graphic section across the area. Profitable areas occur between *A* and *B*. At the optimum location, *O*, costs are minimized at $453 per unit of production, giving a maximum profit of $51. At this point and all other points the basic cost is the same, but at this point alone locational costs are minimized. It should be added that *O* will not always be at the center of the triangle *ABC*. The stronger the pull of any one of these factors (lower movement costs in this case), the nearer the optimum location will be to it.

Three complications of the real world will now be allowed to enter the model: entrepreneurial skill, various behavioral or personal factors, and a dy-

namic aspect that will be explained below. Smith also deals with other factors such as the existence of subsidies and external economies.

The degree of **entrepreneurial skill** that a businessman has obviously varies, and this variation may influence choice. In economic cost terms, there will be wider margins of location for the highly efficient entrepreneur than for the less efficient one. Figure 88 sets out the space cost curve for such an occurrence. It is assumed that a particular firm, through high entrepreneurial skill, can lower production costs 10 percent below the average. The space cost curve, *CC*, for this firm shows that it could operate within the margins *Ca*, *Cb*, as opposed to margins *a*, *b*, for the average firm. Similarly, if a firm has a less efficient management and operates at, say, 5 percent or 10 percent above the average costs, its space cost curve, *DD*, will construct the profitable area of operation to *Da-Db*.

The *behavioral factors* included here are factors of chance and personal attitudes. The operation of noneconomic factors has been stressed throughout. But as long as they do not place the firm outside the margins of profitability, it can survive. Attempts have been made to develop a maximum profit theory that allows for conditions of uncertainty and subjective probability. The most usable result of these attempts is the concept of **psychic income**. This is a measure of social, psychological, or other noneconomic satisfaction that a particular location choice might offer to an individual businessman. Smith attempts to deal with these personal factors as a relaxation of his assumption of economic rationality. This can be done by remembering that there are outer margins of profitability within which freedom of choice exists to some extent. Within those outer margins, the exact location of any firm may be determined by noneconomic factors.

Figure 89 utilizes the psychic income concept. The isocost lines show the average profit as noted above, while the dotted lines indicate average losses. Point *x*, a location within the margin of profitability, has a certain attraction for a particular entrepreneur because a golf club or a health spa is located at that

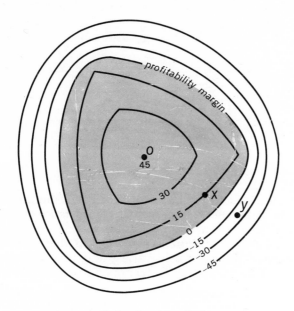

O *maximum profit (least cost location)*

Fig. 89. *The Smith model: (6) psychic income and isosatisfact lines. (Ibid., p. 108.)*

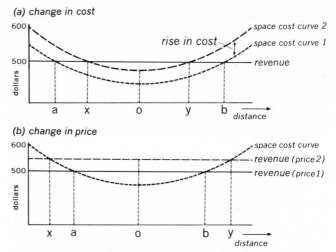

Fig. 90. *The Smith model: (7) dynamic changes (i). (Ibid., p. 110.)*

point. Instead of isocost lines these can be thought of now as lines of satisfaction, or *isosatisfact lines,* as we might call them. The golf club oriented businessman will site his factory at *x* if the psychic income he can get there exceeds the loss of profit resulting from obtaining only $15 per unit item instead of the $45 per unit item obtainable at *o*. If and when he does this, his factory is diverted from the maximum profit location by personal factors. To pursue this line of thought still further, the businessman may choose to ignore economic constraints altogether, and find a level of satisfaction at *y* that more than overcomes the fact that he loses over $15 on each item he produces. Such a situation is probably rare, but the other situation—less profit for the sake of more psychic income—is not.

The main drawback of Smith's model is that it is a static one, confined to a particular point in time, with definite locations for optimal points and margins of profitability. In fact, conditions in the real world are dynamic; for instance, the optimal location and the margins of profitability are changing through time as the spatial cost-price situation changes. Manufacturers in fact may never even try to find the most profitable location, because they realize its spatial location will change. The businessman might therefore choose a location within the broad constraints of the profitability margin, relying on his efficiency and enterprise to build up profits over the long term.

Figures 90 and 91 illustrate some dynamic elements that can be encompassed in the simple model. If there is a change in cost it can be shown as a new

space cost curve, above or below the existing curve depending on whether a rise or fall in costs is involved (figure 90a). The optimal location remains the same under these conditions, but the margins contract with a rise in costs, and expand with a fall. Change in price extends the profitable area upwards; a decrease in price has the reverse effect (figure 90b).

Changes in factor costs are a little more complex. If an industry operates with two factors of production, the basic cost of each being $30 per unit of output, and their sources *a* and *b* (figure 91), then their factor cost curves can be shown as *ca* and *cb*. Amalgamation of these two gives the earlier space cost curve, or total cost curve, *ct*, with margins of profitability *a* and *b*. Change in costs may occur to increase the costs of *B* by, say, 50 percent, resulting in a $15 increase in the cost of each unit of output. The new cost curve becomes *cb'*, and the new total cost curve *ct'*, while the margin of profitability contracts.

The effect of a change in location costs can also be illustrated by figure 91. Let us suppose the cost of moving factor *b* from its source is twice as much as before because of an increase in freight charges. In this case, the effect is not only to contract the area of profitability but to shift the optimal location from *o* toward *o'*, nearer the source of *b*.

Figure 91 also shows the effect of a simultaneous change in basic and location costs. If the quantity of *b* required in production is halved, as it might be by some technological improvement, then this results in the basic and location costs being halved, giving rise to a new cost curve for *b*, *cb^x*. There is also a new total cost curve *ct^x*, the result of which is to widen the profitability margins and to shift the optimal location toward *a*, the locational pull of which is thus strengthened.

These are, of course, only crude attempts to encompass dynamic elements. But increasing realism

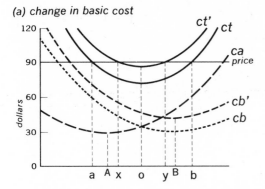

(a) change in basic cost

ct' ct
ca
price
cb'
cb

dollars

a A x o y B b

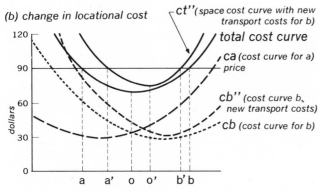

(b) change in locational cost

ct'' (space cost curve with new transport costs for b)
total cost curve
ca (cost curve for a)
price
cb'' (cost curve b, new transport costs)
cb (cost curve for b)

dollars

a a' o o' b' b

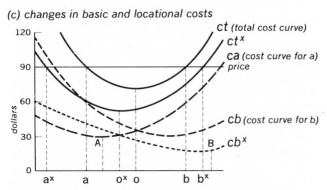

(c) changes in basic and locational costs

ct (total cost curve)
ct x
ca (cost curve for a)
price
cb (cost curve for b)
A
B cb x

dollars

ax a ox o b bx

Fig. 91. *The Smith model: (8) dynamic changes (ii). (Ibid., pp. 110–111.)*

means increasing complexity, and if we want to encompass uneven changes in space, eventually we will have to use three-dimensional space cost curves. Some of the complexities of change with economic growth processes have already been outlined in chapter 8. Technological change in the advanced economies is in itself a major industry, through research and development work. Of greatest importance here are the changes that affect operating costs and thus locational advantages. So far we have dealt only with hypothetical changes of 50 percent in basic or locational costs, or both. But change may mean the cessation of growth for all or some industries, while other industries may discover new advantages in addition to those they had before the innovation

reached them. Because of inertia through fixed capital, such changes rarely result in mass plant relocation; rather, it is plants about to be located for the first time that are affected.

Technological change within a single industry may be as far-reaching as the introduction of nonwoven artificial cloths, which bypass traditional weaving and spinning processes. At least 25 percent of all the products we use now were unknown twenty years ago, so that industries that continue under an old name, like machine tools, may be completely transformed and have new locational needs. The addition of new production steps, such as the packaging and freezing of baked goods, may alter the maximum location. Finally, changes in factors of production have occurred. These include diversification and increase in the number of units per input, substitution of one raw material for another, substitution of one fabricated material for another, new products and materials, and changes in market characteristics that free plants from direct dependence on fixed production inputs. Smith's approach is basically to assume that the gross locational patterns are determined by the forces of the economic system, but within those limits locations at the microscale are subject to personal and other motives. The drawback of such an approach of course is that the gross limits are only superficially dealt with, and we have little further understanding of industrial location processes at the macroscale.

The Principle of Substitution

A number of elements of the industrial system have been listed, and we have seen how a change in any one of them reacts upon the others. It is possible to look at these elements as if they contained some force of attraction or repulsion that acts upon an industry or firm. Thus we could conceive of an industry as being pushed or pulled over space until an equilibrium point is reached. Just such a **principle of substitution** over space was first put forward by the German economist A. Predohl in 1928. The concept as further developed by Isard and Moses in the late 1950s leads to the conclusion that if one allows for factor substitution and assumes a nonlinear production function, then the optimality of a location will depend on the characteristics of the input, the level of output, and the nature of the demand schedule. Thus, if the process of production is viewed as a combination of inputs to produce a specific output, the principle of substitution will have two components:

1. A change in the size of operation (level of output) may change the proportion of inputs.

2. For certain production processes, the entrepreneur has, within technical limits, a freedom to choose among alternative proportions of inputs to produce a distinct output or combination of outputs.

Basically, the principle of substitution implies that the entrepreneur has some freedom to change, though within certain limits. Every time a firm is moved over space to effect a savings in some factor, some other factor must also change. Thus when a firm moves from New York City to Rochester to take advantage of lower labor costs at the latter point, it may in effect be substituting increased transport costs to the market which may still be in New York. Accordingly, the savings in labor costs will have to more than offset any increases in other costs.

In the mid-1960s R. McDaniel developed a simple locational model based on three types of substitutions:

1. Substitutions between transport inputs (ton miles) and outlays (costs), and revenues associated with the various commodities used in the production process.

2. Substitution among sources of materials.

3. Substitution among markets.

Thus the whole location process may be conceived as a complex substitution problem in space.

Figure 92 shows two sites, c (market) and r_1 (raw material), with a transport link between them. The problem is where should p, the production point, be located. Borrowing a concept from production theory in economics, a **transformation line** can be constructed, assuming the same ton-mile cost for the raw material and the finished product. In this case there are two distance variables: distance from c; and distance from r_1. When these two variables are plotted, a straight transformation line with a slope of -1 is obtained. Since the transformation line is a straight line, it turns out in this instance that p can locate at any point along CR_1.

Let us take a more complicated case. Suppose production requires a second raw material available at one source, r_2. Suppose that the distance pc is a constant, or in other words that p can locate anywhere along ts. Again a transformation line can be constructed, though this time it turns out to be a curve (figure 93).

As before we assume that the cost of shipping a unit of r_1 is the same as for r_2, and that one ton of each is required in the production process. A further assumption is that transportation rates are proportional to distance. A series of isocost lines can be inserted (figure 93). The least cost transport location is where the isocost line just touches (is tangential to) the transformation line. Since the value of the

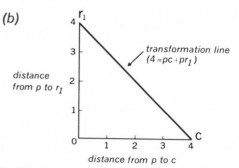

Fig. 92. *The substitution principle — (i) the use of the transformation line. (From R. McDaniel, "Elements of Economic Geography," 1966, used by courtesy of the author and the Department of Extension and Summer School, University of Western Ontario.)*

isocost lines increases as one moves away from the origin, it follows that the minimum transportation cost point along ts must be given by the tangential isocost line.

It might be possible to find a still lower transport cost point by taking a new distance, cp, as the constant, thus giving a new locus t_1s_1. One could continue in this manner, holding one distance constant and letting the other two vary, but attempts to find the least cost point might well be futile. This is so because every time one distance is changed, of necessity the others are changed too. The actual solution to this requires solving a set of simultaneous differential equations.

Besides the actual production process, substitution principles can be extended to the organizational level. There may be many alternative ways in which a firm or a branch location can be managed and operated, but for a particular location or a number of potential locations only a few organizational forms may be possible. The form that is finally chosen will depend on how well it combines with all other factors and functions; changes in these other components may change the organizational form itself.

Game Theory

It is possible to regard each industrial entrepreneur as devising a business strategy, and to analyze his behavior in terms of game theory. Let us take a simple example.

Imagine two entrepreneurs competing for industrial sites along a linear market, perhaps a highway

(a)

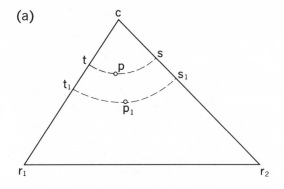

(b)

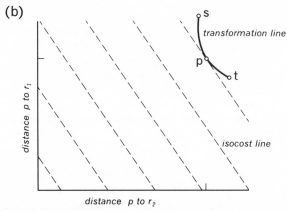

Fig. 93. *The substitution principle — (ii) the introduction of isocost lines with two raw materials. (Ibid.)*

or railroad, in such a way as to maximize their profits (figure 94). The first assumption is that buyers would always purchase from the entrepreneur with the lowest delivered price (f.o.b. price plus transportation costs). Figure 94 shows the simple linear market as 40 units long, with possible industrial sites *a, b, c, d,* and *e* equally spaced along that line. Further assumptions hold that the f.o.b. price for both entrepreneurs is $1 per unit; that both operate without cost; that there is a uniform transport rate of 2.5 cents per unit of commodity per unit of distance; and finally, that one buyer per unit of length will buy one unit no matter what the cost. If both entrepreneurs occupied the same location they would split the available market equally. Table 37 sets out the payoff matrix. Under these simple conditions if producer I located at *a* and the other at *c*, they would split the market between *a* and *c*. The producer at *a* would sell to the ten consumers between *a* and *b* and have sales of $10, while the producer at *c* would capture the whole

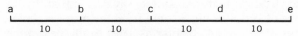

Fig. 94. *A simple linear market (see text).*

market from *b* to *e*, with sales of $30. The payoff to the seller at *c* would be $30 − $10 = $20.

The strategies of producer I are in the left-hand column of table 37, with positive payoffs, and the strategies of producer II are listed across the top of the table in negative values. If producer I entered the market first and located at *a*, when producer II entered the market he would locate at *b* and gain an advantage of $30. Producer I would then move to *c* within an advantage of $10. Finally, producer II would also move to *c* and all advantages would be eliminated, so that neither could gain by moving from this point. However, if the strategy were to minimize costs to the consumers and transportation costs, producer I would be at *b* and producer II at *d*. In fact much more complex situations than this can be dealt with. Much more research would be needed, however, to establish the vagaries of private and board room strategies with greater precision.

Table 37. *Payoff Matrix for Location Strategy (in dollars)*

		producer II					
	locations	a	b	c	d	e	min.
	a	0	-30	-20	-10	0	-30
	b	30	0	-10	0	10	-10
producer I	c	20	10	0	10	20	0
	d	10	0	-10	0	30	-10
	e	0	-10	-20	-30	0	-30
	max.	30	10	0	10	30	

Source: B.H. Stevens, "An Application of Game Theory to a Problem in Location Strategy," *Papers and Proceedings of the Regional Science Association*, vol. 7, 1961, pp. 143–157.

A Model for Redistributive Economies

In addition to these models of the so-called capitalist market-exchange system, there are models to represent the rather different conditions of a redistributive economy. The Polish economist T. Mrzyglod has recently put forward such a model. He returns to the earlier idea of complexes, as a means of avoiding too concentrated or too dispersed an industrial pattern. As we have seen, the complex is a close spatial association of industries based on local raw materials, local labor, and based on interrelated industries. Thus specialization and concentration arise, but without neglect or abuse of local resources or dependence on long distance hauls. The actual number of plants that comprise a complex varies with the economic possibilities, but they are always planned with the available labor supply in mind. In practical terms, this means labor supply areas.

All this fits in with the ideological requirement of balanced economic development; the picture of the

U.S.S.R. presented by all current Soviet regional geographies is one of balanced and sustained expansion and development. According to the official ideology, the purpose of industrial growth and expansion is to absorb labor surpluses in formerly "backward" and "colonial" areas. Mrzyglod suggests three variations on these ideas (figure 95). In case (a), resources can be utilized by a spatially separated but linked industrial process, where there is a high value output, low transportation costs, and a labor surplus evenly divided between three subregions, a, b, and c. The linked processes can then be rationally divided: subregion a produces and refines the raw material, while subregions b and c manufacture the semifinished and finished product of the vertically linked process. In case (b), the same conditions exist, but the labor force is heavily concentrated in subregion b, which is therefore allocated all the final processing stages. In case (c), subregion a has a very large labor surplus (or a gross raw material), and all processes are carried on within its borders. Thus these models discuss industrial location from a socialist planning point, which includes total direction as part of an overall national plan.

Regional Models

The theoretical approach outlined so far, with the exception perhaps of Mrzyglod's models, has emphasized individual plant locations. A category of models exists, however, that assigns number of plants to a range of locations. Frequently they use a process of analysis called **linear programming.** In industrial location problems this technique is used to find optimum production points for a number of plants by assigning optimum capacities among them. Other techniques assign optimal locations by computer simulation; the solutions use location shifts, shifts in patterns of materials and product flows, and efficiency changes.

Linear Programming Models

M. J. Beckmann and T. Marschak set out a model (figure 96) that makes allowances for several raw materials, plants, and markets. They were concerned with the flow of raw materials from source to plant, and with the flow of finished products from plant to market. The question they pose is, What flow pattern will meet market demands at minimum cost, without violating certain capacity limitations on plants and raw materials? Given were raw materials and their source, the plants, and a number of final markets. The capacity constraints placed on the plants and sources obviously restrict the amount of the

(a)
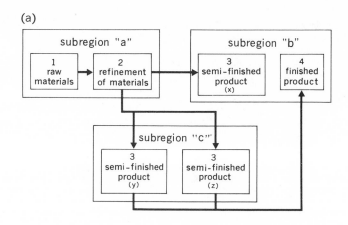

(b)
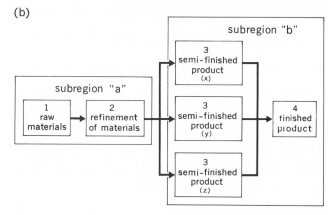

(c)
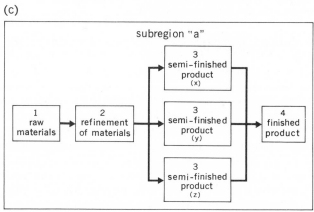

Fig. 95. *The redistributive economy: three industrial planning strategies. (From F.E.I. Hamilton, "Models of Industrial Location," 1967, p. 385, reprinted by permission of the author.)*

final product that can be sold at the market. The objective is then to select raw material and product flows that maximize net revenues. This is done by a linear programming formulation. It deals with situations where plant b's demands exceed the output of the cheapest material source, say ar_3, so that the balance of supplies must come from the more expensive sites at ar_1, or ar_2, insofar as sales to the best priced markets realize maximum profits (figure 96).

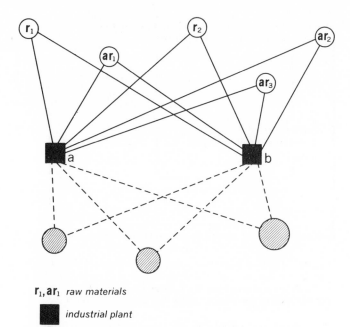

r₁, ar₁   *raw materials*

■   *industrial plant*

◯   *market*

Fig. 96. *The Beckmann and Marschak linear programming solution. There are several raw materials, factories, and markets. What flow pattern will meet market demands at minimum cost, without violating capacity limitations on factories and raw materials? (Adapted from W. Garrison, "Spatial Structure of the Economy,"* Annals of the Association of American Geographers, *vol. 49, no. 4, 1959, by permission.)*

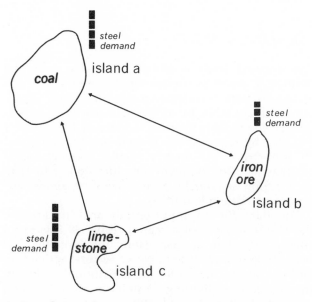

Fig. 97. *Goldman's linear programming problem. Where should iron and steel capacity be located in order to meet demands for iron and steel at least cost? The availability of "backhaul" cargo space affects the minimum cost solution. (From W. Garrison, "Spatial Structure of the Economy," part 2,* Annals of the A.A.G., *vol. 49, 1959, p. 479, reprinted by permission of the Association of American Geographers.)*

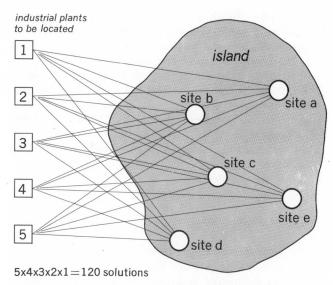

5x4x3x2x1 = 120 solutions

Fig. 98. *Koopman and Beckmann's linear programming problem. Five plants are to be assigned to five locations, and there are 120 ways this can be done. In the linear assignment problem the profitability of one plant at a location is not affected by the location of the other plants, but the profitability of a given plant varies from location to location. The problem is to select from the 120 different location patterns that pattern which maximizes the combined profitabilities of the plants. (From Garrison, 1959, ibid., p. 481.)*

Figure 97 presents a model complementary to that just considered, put forward by T. A. Goldman in 1958. He uses the problem of hauling several goods when one good may be handled as a back haul from another good. Consider three model islands, each with one raw material—iron ore, coal, and limestone—and each using steel products. The problem, then, is where to locate the iron and steel plant and set up the flows so as to minimize empty back haulage that would otherwise raise costs. The solution through linear programming shows that the optimum locations are a function of total demand, not cost, and that the plants may best be located when higher transport costs are in fact incurred.

T. C. Koopmans and M. Beckmann have dealt with the more complicated case of assigning n manufacturing plants to n locations in such a way as to achieve maximum combined profits from the plants (figure 98). The diagram shows the objective—just 5 plants to 5 locations—which can be achieved in $5 \times 4 \times 3 \times 2 \times 1 = 120$ ways. In the linear assignment problem (assigning plants to sites so as to maximize profits or satisfaction) the profitability of one plant at a site is not affected by the location of other plants, but the profitability of a plant does vary from location to location. The procedure is to find which of 120 different location patterns maximizes the combined profitabilities of the plants.

There are two phases to this analysis. The first uses the linear assignment approach, which treats the plants individually. This phase allocates plant *a* to the most profitable location, plant *b* to the next most profitable, plant *c* to the next and, finally, plant *n* to the least profitable. The second phase involves a so-called quadratic assignment problem that deals not only with the plants and the transport between them, but also with how the profitability of one plant becomes dependent upon the locations of the other plants. Naturally, the problems of computation involved here are formidable. Attempts are actively under way to apply linear programming and to overcome these problems.

The Multiplier Model

An approach to the regional location of industries can also be made through the *multiplier* model (figure 99). This technique is useful because it emphasizes the systems links, so that it is possible to trace the effects of any change in plant location or expansion on the rest of the region. It can also take account of general economic and social changes, and can demonstrate the direct and indirect economic effects of the construction of new industries or the closing of old ones. It can be used to demonstrate the overall selective effects on industry of specific technological changes, or of more general economic and social change. New manufacturing functions, whether or not they serve local markets, will have an initial multiplier effect through the stimulation of new local demands created by the factories and the new labor force. The multiplier effect will be greatest where systems linkages are most highly developed.

W. Isard and R. E. Kuenne have analyzed the total and regional effects of the location of a steel combine in the New York-Philadelphia area. Figure 100 represents the long-term local impact of this project in a systems framework. The actual changes, if the components of the system were quantified, would have various impacts according to the area under consideration. The main variables would be capital availability and degree of entrepreneurship, but socioeconomic changes in the system would also affect regional industrial growth and location. W. Z. Hirsch, in a 1959 analysis of the St. Louis metropolitan area, shows that an increase in market demand affected (for example) printing, textiles, and transportation equipment in the way of employment changes (and perhaps new plant locations) more than it did such other industrial sectors as furniture, lumber, paper, and even petroleum. Thus the growth of the local market was found to be crucial.

In a later study (1960) the same authors continued this analysis and noted the effects of eight past and present changes in state consumer and industrial markets upon twenty manufacturing industries.

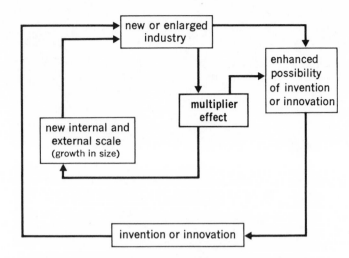

Fig. 99. *The basic multiplier model. (Reprinted from Allen Pred, The Spatial Dynamics of U.S. Urban-Industrial Growth 1800–1914, p. 25, by permission of the M.I.T. Press, Cambridge, Mass. Copyright © 1966 by the Massachusetts Institute of Technology.)*

The twelve industrial groups strongly influenced by these changes are noted in figure 101. Durable goods industries were found to be equally and strongly oriented to the market, as noted within the systems framework of the diagram. Each of the industries is affected by the eight measures of demand, except for leather working, which seemed to locate in areas of excess labor. Once again computational difficulties had to be overcome, but in this case the state of the raw data was found to be at fault.

Input-Output Analysis

A type of analysis closely associated with the multiplier model is input-output analysis. The objective of an interregional interindustry input-output analysis is to construct a matrix of input-output coefficients identified not just by industry but also by region. Thus if there are 5 regions and 50 industries, the matrix would contain 62,500 coefficients. One frequent simplification is to treat each region separately, as if it were an almost autonomous economic unit.

The data for an input-output analysis are the flows and services of a region. Table 38 sets out a simple hypothetical case. Here, the economy has been broken down into only two sectors, agriculture and manufacturing. From the agricultural sector, in the course of delivering 55 units of output as end products to *final demand*, and 20 units as raw materials to the manufacturing sector, it delivers 25 units of its own output to itself. "Final demand" can be taken to include the goods and services consigned to investment and export, as well as to current consumption in the households of the economy. The

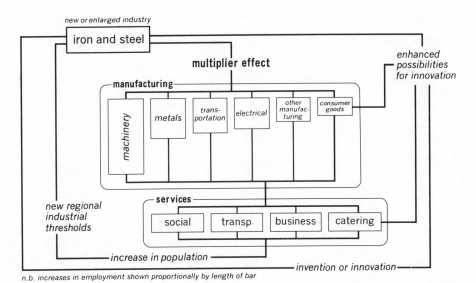

Fig. 100. *The multiplier effects caused by the introduction of a new integrated steel plant into the New York-Philadelphia regional system. (From F.E.I. Hamilton, "Models of Industrial Location," 1967, p. 413, by permission of Methuen and Co.)*

n.b. increases in employment shown proportionally by length of bar

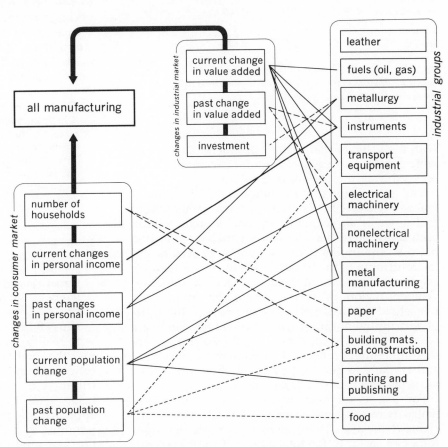

Fig. 101. *Systematic relationships: interregional demand. (From Hamilton 1967, ibid., p. 414; see fig. 100.)*

total output of 100 units from the agricultural sector thus satisfies both the "direct" final demand for its end products and the "indirect" demand for its intermediate products. On the input side, the numbers in the column labeled "agriculture" show that in order to produce those 100 units of total output, this sector absorbs not only 25 units of its own products, but also 14 units of input from "manufacture" (e.g., implements and tools), and 80 units of labor, capital and other prime factors from the sector called by convention "household services." Thus the spaces in each horizontal row of the matrix are filled in

Table 38. *The Leontieff Input-Output Technique*

(a) input-output matrix

| | INPUT | | | |
	sector 1 agriculture	sector 2 manufactures	final demand	total output
Sector 1 agriculture	25	20	55	100 units
sector 2 manufactures	14	6	30	50 units
household services	80	180	40	300 units

(b) input-output coefficients

| | INPUT | | |
	sector 1 agriculture	sector 2 manufactures	final demand
Sector 1 agriculture	0.25	0.40	0.183
Sector 2 manufactures	0.14	0.12	0.100
household services	0.80	3.60	0.133

Source: From "The Structure of Development," by W. Leontieff, *Scientific American*, 1963, p. 107. Copyright © 1963 by Scientific American, Inc. Reprinted by permission.

with the value of that sector's production, or *output*, which is sold to each of the other sectors as their *inputs* during the period under study.

The great virtue of input-output analysis is that it makes visible the indirect internal transactions and flows of an economic regional system. Within each sector there is a relatively invariable connection between the inputs it draws from other sectors and its contribution to the total output of the region's economy. This would hold also for an underdeveloped region or nation where the input from household services necessary to produce 100 units of agricultural output might represent 80 man-years of labor, as well as for a more developed area, where this input might reflect a large component of capital, and is likely to be offset by inputs from the manufacturing sector of fertilizers, and so on.

For use as an analytical tool, the input-output matrix is recast in the form of input ratios or coefficients (table 38*b*). These coefficients relate the input from one sector to the total output of another sector, and can be used to analyze the effects that growth in one sector, manufacturing, will have on the other sector (in our simple example, agriculture). In other words, an input-output model shows that changes in production or output in one sector affect production in the other sectors. Thus in table 38, 0.25 units of agricultural output, 0.14 units of manufactures, and 0.80 units of prime factors from household serv-

ices are necessary to produce one unit of total output from the agricultural sector. Calculation of the full effects on the other sectors is carried out by the "iterative" method which computes input requirements "round by round."

Conclusion

These highly abstract approaches to the simulation and explanation of industrial patterns, from the substitution principle to the multiplier model, still utilize concepts drawn from the real world. But they ignore many of the complexities of the real world. Of course, as has been emphasized a number of times, it is only by simplification that the location problem can be reduced to fundamentals. As each of the simplifying assumptions is relaxed the situation begins to resemble reality much more closely. But it also becomes more complex.

In addition to the two classical approaches and the alternatives noted above, still other approaches exist. The study of industrial location has in fact been made on two broad fronts:

1. *The approach taken at times by P. Sargant Florence (1962), W. Smith (1955), G. T. Renner (1947), and in part by E. M. Hoover (1947), which is essentially a search for indices to help explain existing spatial patterns. Sargant Florence has also tried to show whether major existing patterns are economically feasible. The more recent* **shift-share technique** *can be added here. These approaches are not strictly theoretical; rather, they are empirical tests and techniques undertaken to help understand existing patterns.*

2. *The second line of approach is seen in the work of Weber, Lösch, Predöhl, Isard, and others. The chief aim of this approach is to formulate a location theory within the partial equilibrium approach, and so to modify economic theory by taking space as well as time into account.*

Thus whereas the first approach is concerned with reality, and by implication with margins forming the boundaries to profitability, the latter is concerned with ideal locations, the equilibrium distribution of plants, and the attainment of that illusory goal, the optimum location. Thus the latter approach suggests that industrial locations are determined by a rigid set of locational forces, whereas the first approach, and the factors reported in the previous chapter, suggest that the location theorists' approach is oversimplified and misleading. Location theory explains neither the behavior of industrialists in a spatial context nor the spatial patterns that result. We need to know far more about how decisions are made, particularly in the corporate context, in order to understand a suboptimal type of organization like the firm.

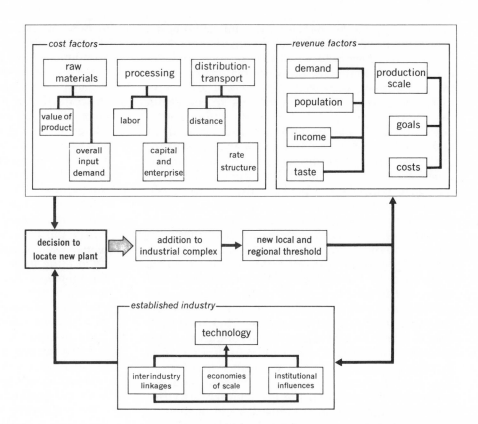

Fig. 102. *A model of new industrial locations and an established industrial area.*

Locational Factors

Bearing in mind the classical and modern approaches to industrial location, and the inadequacies of both of these to solve the problem, we can undertake two further sorties into the real industrial system. First we will examine why, irrespective of the way location decisions are made, they lead over time to a similar result: a concentration of manufacturing in areas, belts, or agglomerations in many Western countries. Second, we will attempt to compare some real-world patterns of industrial behavior with the theoretical postulates already examined.

The Effect of Established Locations

Given the existence and influence of established industries, it can be postulated that these locations are those where most new industries will locate. The basic assumption of such an approach still has to be profit maximization. However, account is taken of the interaction between four factors: total costs, total revenues, personal considerations, and the location of established industries. Considerations of cost are considered interrelated with revenue, the extent of one being determined by the extent of the other. The location of established industry then becomes one of the most significant factors in the loca-

tion decisions of entrepreneurs, for whether or not it is directly involved in their locational reasoning, it cannot possibly be ignored when they come to consider costs and revenues. The forces set into action by the established industries reinforce the strength of their position. Though the first manufacturing plant set up in the United States may have located where it did for any number of reasons, the fact of its location at a particular site had a dynamic attractive power for other industries. And as industries and economic landscapes evolve, and the original conditions for the locational decision cease to exist, the established industrial pattern can go on generating a locational pull, thereby causing new industries to reinforce an existing locational pattern.

Components of the Model

A schematic diagram of the approach just outlined sets out some of its basic components (figure 102).

Despite the assumptions of the market area approach most *raw materials* are not available to industries at constant costs; they are unevenly distributed and the costs of procuring them vary widely. The raw material pull can be determined by weight loss in manufacture, perishability, value per unit of weight, and substitution. These factors have been influenced by the demand side of the manufacturing system. The price mechanism of the finished product is also the price mechanism of the inputs. Increased demand for the product will call for increased demand for raw materials. But since raw materials are in fixed supply, increased demand will lead to an increase in price—that is, an increase in costs from the manufacturer's point of view. But the increased demand, which may result in an increased value of raw materials per unit of weight, may also enhance the possibility of the development of close substitutes, as well as technological improvements affecting weight loss and perishability. For the profit maximizing entrepreneur any increase in costs would provide great inducement for innovation. Generally, the influence of these cost factors has been greatly modified by this demand factor working through the location of established industry. This is because the interindustry linkages, economies of scale, and institutional forces (patents, quotas, etc.) provide the incentive and atmosphere for everchanging technological innovation. This serves not only to affect the raw material basis of industry, but increases the linkages and economies of scale, thus increasing the possibilities of further innovation. The resulting specialization of technique and development of horizontal linkage between activities lead to the aggregation of industries and people.

The *market influence* on the location decision may be the factor that offsets the pull of raw material sites. The main factors considered would be perishability, desirability of personal contact, the type and value of the product, the extent of the market, and market capacity. Again it must be stressed that the fact of one industry or a group of industries locating near a market center reinforces the pull of that market center, not through its original demand *per se*, but through the derived demand instituted by the location of industry at that point. Location in regard to demand involves seeking a certain type of demand for the product of the seller, as well as the power to pursue and establish a certain price and price system by virtue of occupying a particular location. The revenue the firm is able to derive is determined not only by the demand factor but by the scale of production, which again is interdependent with costs and established industry. The location of established industry will influence population and income distribution within the market area, and also, through cost considerations, the production scale. Likewise, transportation costs in the distribution of the finished product play a determining role in the pull of the market.

Both the influence of materials and the influence of markets seem to a large extent to be conditioned by *transfer costs*. The structure of existing transfer costs and facilities are dependent, of course, on the pattern of previously located plants. Warehouse facilities will be located in accordance with the de-

mands of existing industry; freight flows, cost structures, and so on, may well reflect the antecedent economic landscape. Transportation costs are a function of factors other than weight and distance; for instance, established firms may so influence the rate structure that the result is price discrimination in favor of established enterprises. Localities offering a large volume of traffic may induce transport agencies to offer reduced rates. This can feed back to new areas whose growth may be restricted by having to absorb higher transfer costs than their established competitors, who qualify for freight rate reductions.

The same kind of reasoning can be applied to *production factors*—labor, capital, and enterprise. Again the location of labor with sufficient or particular skills is determined by an existing structure. By locating in an area provided with a pool of labor, the employer finds the essential social capital; the manufacturer may find a ready market for his products. Joint supplies of labor may also play a role, as when an industry employing mainly female labor finds it expedient to locate in the proximity of an industry employing mainly male labor. Labor supply and costs will also depend on the revenue considerations of the firm, reflected in the production scale and demand for the final product—for marginal labor costs will rise as more is demanded. However, these labor considerations must also involve the possibility of the substitution of capital for labor. This possibility again will depend on the revenue factors working through the forces set in motion by established industry. The other components could be analyzed in similar fashion.

This model of industrial location establishes the close interrelationship between the cost-revenue consideration and the influence of established industry. Why, however, do industries locating with a view to cost considerations locate in the same place as industries locating principally for revenue considerations? This involves consideration of the changes wrought in the structure and influence of various cost and revenue factors by technological change.

Technological Change and the Model

Just as the single industry can achieve internal economies as it expands output, so too can a group of industries achieve external economies of scale as the industrial capacity of an area grows. The economies to be gained by interindustry specialization, joint use of labor supplies, and cooperation in bringing about decreased transport costs have served to decrease the locational influence of raw materials. This increasing vertical *dis*integration of the production process has led to an even greater specialization of manufacturing functions. One result is that the successive stages of production tend to be located near each other. This is possible because increasingly many industries are assemblers of semi-manufactured goods and finished parts. The finished products have a high commercial value in relation to their weight. Economies of scale may set into action interindustry linkages. It is important to stress that linkage is a derived rather than an initial advantage. When, however, the initial advantages have declined in importance, these interindustry linkages will form a strong basis for geographic inertia and even exert a strong locational pull.

The initial effect of technological innovations is determined by the interrelationships between various industries in certain localities. Such innovations are no longer isolated phenomena. Though meant to have a direct effect on the cost and revenue situation of one particular industry, they affect, through linkages, vast number of industries. From this develops the concept of linked innovations. This may be illustrated by the Leland Falconer and Norton Company of Detroit, which successfully made the transition from the production of machine tools to that of automobile engines. In most location theories, however, relatively little attention is paid to technical changes and the flow of information in the economic landscape, or to the way in which these can affect the location of activities.

Technological change reflected in changes in labor requirements may exert strong effects on industrial location patterns. But, generally, any effect felt is in mature industries in which the processes have been standardized: the larger and better established industrial centers often stimulate the growth and development of new industries Even mature industries, though a standardization of process has lessened the pull of labor, will have to take into consideration the most decisive element—capital.

The mere fact of a standardization of process must mean an increase in fixed capital, adding to the linkage aspects of geographic inertia. Thus the industry, having substituted capital for labor, becomes more not less dependent on its location. Technological change will also engender a change in the role of raw material requirements. Changes reflected in yield of output relative to the input materials, changes as regards the introduction of substitutes, and changes in orientation from extensively produced to intensively produced materials—all have resulted from the needs of established industrial centers. But again, the processes involved in adapting to these new materials, and often those involved in obtaining them, presuppose a certain minimum of concentration. A growth in production consequent upon the use of new materials may act as a force pushing to greater concentration through new interindustry economies in procurement.

The nature of energy sources in the past may provide a partial explanation of the location patterns in the present. For though energy requirements have changed, as have the types of energy consumed, industries may continue to concentrate at the location of the original energy requirement. As long as energy used was nontransportable, plants using this energy had to concentrate at the site itself. The change from water power to steam engines served to concentrate industry in the coal regions.

Since the first effects of steam were felt in Britain before the coming of the railroad, concentration near navigable water also resulted. Steam, however, served as an agent for further concentration. Since it offered an infinite energy source, it could permit manufacturing agglomerations much larger than could have been sustained by direct use of water power. Later energy innovations tended to diminish the pull of coal on location. But the change to electric energy sources did not have the same effects as the change to steam. In fact, the inadequacy of electric energy to meet other than the power requirements of industry has diminished its locational pull. Indeed, its ease of transfer may well have reinforced existing locational patterns.

The innovations thus far discussed have resulted in a reduction of costs coupled with an extension of the market area. These technical innovations have provided a great impetus toward shifts in the scale of manufacturing and toward an urban concentration of production. Greater market areas have meant the division of fixed costs over a greater volume of production. This has led to higher optimal scales of production. But in the twentieth century the reduction in transportation costs has been greater than the reduction in production costs. Each innovation cheapens transfer, altering the entire structure of transportation costs, and with it the significance of distance and volume.

Study of the effects of transportation systems and innovations on the location and future development of an area provides insight into the explanation of certain existing industrial concentrations. Thus the pull of a certain industrial center may have resulted originally from its power to institute far-reaching *institutional* restrictions. One of the best known examples of this is the "Pittsburgh Plus" system. The system was imposed between 1900 and 1924 by the major steel producers. It required that all steel be sold at the Pittsburgh price plus freight costs from Pittsburgh no matter where it was produced or where it was sold. This institutionalized favoritism not only reinforced the concentration in Pittsburgh but handicapped the growth, at this crucial stage in American economic development, of industry in new areas.

Transfer costs on a partially finished product are a fraction of the costs on the totally completed product. This may be one of the factors accounting for the concentration of the U.S. automobile industry. The manufacture of finished automobiles is strongly concentrated in an area centered on Detroit, which has good access to the large market of the northeastern industrial belt. The final assembly of motor vehicles is being increasingly performed at market oriented locations. But the powerful concentration in Detroit is not in the final assembly of the automobile so much as in the production of component parts. Thus empirical evidence shows that, for many firms, transportation costs are no longer of essential importance to the locational decision. The advantages of large-scale economies, even in traditional transport oriented or regional restricted industries, now ranks higher than these other costs.

Conclusion

Whatever the motives for industrial location have been and are, they tend to have the same effect on the economic landscape: a pattern of concentration. Cost and revenue factors of location seem to be closely related to the locational pull of established industry. Figure 102 illustrates a scheme to show the influence of established industry on the cost and revenue factors of the whole industrial structure. Historical examples of industrial development show that, although the conditions giving rise to a location might change, development of the location may engender other powerful conditions that can more than offset the initial change; thus the entrepreneur may well locate the industry in the same place if he has to make the decision again. It should be noted, however, that concentration cannot by itself guarantee the continuance of an area; for instance, prolonged and severe economic depression may well curtail the locational pull of existing sites.

It might also be inferred that the diseconomies of scale resulting from excessive concentration would set in motion a reverse multiplier process. Diseconomies such as high labor costs (via unionization or labor shortage), high land rents, insufficient space for expansion, or transport congestion might persuade new industries to locate elsewhere, and existing industries to eventually shift the bulk of production to branch plants in other areas.

The increasing flow of goods and ideas that occurs when human activities are concentrated at particular nodes may lead to overextension of communications links, deterioration of services, and congestion. Increased costs may therefore be imposed. However, it is just as likely that this positive feedback stimulation will result in communications innovations and improvement. This accords with the notion of the multiplier effect, and with the generally positive nature of agglomeration. An important motivating factor in agglomeration is the need for contacts and exchange of information between the increasingly specialized parts and linkages of the industrial structure. It seems that many important contacts cannot be efficiently carried out by letter or telephone, but need face-to-face contacts between managers and administrators. These contacts are probably confined mainly to the administrative part of manufacturing (the decision units), which receive, process, and transmit the bulk of the information flow. Contacts will be maintained with other firms and institutions, including government, banks, and research sources. A regional agglomeration of information units could bring about considerable savings for industry.

The entrepreneur or corporate management group that chooses to locate away from an established center because of diseconomies of scale within that center is still locating under the influence of the established industrial location. The established center, instead of exerting a positive pull, is exerting a negative force, and if the location decision is dependent in any way upon the conditions in those established centers, much of what is said above is still applicable. One might also argue, however, that a threshold concept forms a valid reason for industrial dispersal. In other words, industries might locate in other parts of the economic landscape because population levels or other necessary technical preconditions have reached a point of potential profit. But the growth of these new regions, as we shall see, is also conditioned by existing industrial locations.

It seems then, that the forces of positive feedback generated by an established industrial area will tend to reinforce that area's structure rather than destroy it. The original conditions leading to the location of the initial firms may have changed; the pattern and form of the interrelationships may have changed; but the basic structure remains. The evolution of manufacturing, from the Industrial Revolution to the present, has altered the influence of various cost and revenue factors; has seen the general pattern in North America shift from an eastern seaboard orientation to a continental pattern; and has (more recently) seen a suburbanization of certain industrial types. But throughout this evolution there has been little change from the basic tendency for firms to agglomerate. Increasingly, we can ascribe this to the growth of information flows, and the contacts that exist between firms, organizations, and administrators.

Behavioral Patterns

Although the agglomerative force may be the logic behind many industrial locations, and although we may be able to say that the adaptive and tenacious structure that it produces is an example of the systems concept of equifinality, actual conscious decisions may be very variable. We must therefore attempt to determine what these decisions are, and how they are made.

Actual and Theoretical Industrial Behavior Patterns

A number of attempts have been made to test the location models through empirical research. The Weberian model, for example, has been tested extensively. Thus a study of the Mexican iron and steel industry in the mid-1950s found that the Weberian model helped in the analysis of location patterns. As figure 103 shows, the iron and steel industry is located in northeastern Mexico primarily because of the presence there of iron ore and coking coal. The two main plants at Monterrey and Monclova are at locations approximately intermediate between iron ore and coal supplies; additional considerations are accessibility to scrap metal supplies and to supplies of oil and natural gas from Texas. Material supplies do not vary regionally in price, though costs of transport do vary with length of haul. The industry thus acts as a classic example of the Weberian situation. This analysis showed that the optimum location was in fact approximately 100 miles to the west of Monterrey, thus making the latter, in terms of weights and distances, virtually an ideal site.

Even in this case, however, the effect of market areas cannot be neglected. The delivered price of steel to the consumer varies with distance from the steel mill. In this respect the Monterrey manufacturers, being in an important market, as well as closer to Mexico City, have a distinct advantage over the Monclova plants. The spatial separation of the industry from its main markets is a serious problem, which is having important effects on the functioning of the industry. There is a continuing trend for pig iron to be made in the northeast, and for steel making to develop in Mexico City, close to supplies of scrap and close to the market as well. So, through time, markets seem to be having more of an effect on the Mexican industry than any Weberian factors.

By contrast, a study of the Swedish paper industry has uncovered a strong Weberian link. Since lumber in Sweden is virtually a ubiquitous material, the localizing effect is small. Nevertheless, market factors were found to be important. This pull away from a raw material source was seen as arising from the areal spread of the resource, which increases the difference between higher freight rates for products and lower freight rates for raw materials of the same weight and bulk (a factor that Weber never

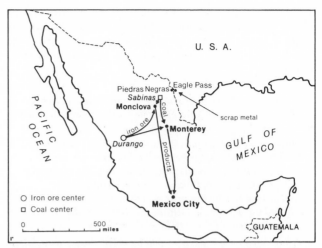

Fig. 103. *Location of the iron and steel industry of Mexico. (From J. Rutherford, M.I. Logan, and G.J. Missen,* New Viewpoints in Economic Geography, *1966, p. 318, reprinted by permission of the Martindale Press, Sydney.)*

recognized in the first place). It was also noted that the size of the demand in the market area was of importance in determining distribution costs. Thus there was a tendency for entrepreneurs to choose market locations, which offered them larger perceived benefits than least cost locations.

Other empirical research has tended to take one of three approaches: comparative cost analyses; normative models; and spatial association. A number of studies of specific industries have been undertaken in order to explain existing patterns by the comparative cost advantages that different location sites or regions could offer. One such study is that by R. Lindsey, who examined the U.S. oil refining industry. He pointed out that a raw materials location for oil refineries could serve the New York-Philadelphia area, and a market location for refineries could serve the Great Lakes. For consuming areas west of the Mississippi an even stronger market cost advantage was evident. This pattern appeared stable, though he was unable to take account of any future physical or technological changes that might reveal new oil deposits or reduce refining and distribution costs. Shifts in demand were foreseen, however, because of regionally differentiated population growth. In cost terms the major advantages would seem to be shifting in favor of the New York, East North Central and West South Central areas.

Normative studies have utilized linear programming techniques. These were not as successful as in the analysis of agricultural location problems, probably because of the more complex situation. A third approach has been the analysis of spatial associations in manufacturing location patterns. A number of techniques exist, including shift-share analysis and regression analysis. The difficulties associated with the latter analysis are mentioned in H. H. McCarty's major testing of this technique in 1956. Taking the group of machinery industries in the United States and Japan, he tested three hypotheses:

1. *That the occurrence of machinery industries will vary directly with the degree of specialization in manufacturing.*

2. *That the occurrence of machinery industries will vary directly with other industries in the linkage sequence, either horizontally or vertically. For example, in the metal products industries machinery occurs relatively high in the vertical linkage sequence (table 39). According to this hypothesis, machinery industries should vary directly with the location of industries manufacturing fabricated metal products.*

3. *That machinery industries will be more closely associated, in spatial terms, with metal-using than non-metal-using industries.*

Statistically significant correlations were found to exist between the proportion of workers in manufacturing and the proportion in machinery industries. A close spatial association was found between electrical machinery groups and the transportation category and — in the case of the United States only — with the fabricated metals industry. The third hypothesis was also substantiated. A high degree of areal association was found, then, between manufacturing industries and closeness to market and materials.

Table 39. *Production Sequence in Metal Products Industries*

1. *ore*
2. *blast furnaces; primary nonferrous metals*
3. *secondary refining*
    (a) secondary nonferrous metals
    (b) electrometallurgical products
4. *shapes and forms*
    (a) steel and rolling mills
    (b) nonferrous metal rolling and drawing
    (c) iron and steel foundries
    (d) nonferrous foundries
    (e) miscellaneous primary metal products
5. *fabrication*
    (a) cutlery, handtools, and hardware
    (b) heating and plumbing equipment
    (c) structural metal products
    (d) metal stamping and coating
    (e) fabricated wire products
    (f) machinery (except electrical) ◄ – – – – – *sector studied*
    (g) electrical machinery
    (h) motor vehicles and equipment

Source: H.H. McCarty, J.C. Hook, D.S. Knos, and G.R. Davies, *The Measurement of Association in Industrial Geography* (Iowa City: Department of Geography, State University of Iowa, 1956), p. 66.

Behavioral Elements

The concept of economic man is a normative one. As such, it is free from the multiplicity of goals and the imperfect knowledge that introduce complexities into decision making behavior. Thus economic man has a single profit goal, together with perfect ability to perceive, reason, compute, and predict. For these simple reasons his behavior can be studied in a controlled environment.

The assumptions implicit in the economic rationality framework — perfect knowledge of alternatives and their consequences, the optimization of production or utility — must be relaxed in a behavioral analysis. The concept of psychic income is an example of such relaxation: the intended maximization of personal satisfactions may be the goal of many entrepreneurs. Allowance has also to be made for man's finite ability to gather, store, and analyze information. These limitations would remain even if profit were the only goal. However, it is more likely that profit and personal satisfaction are only two goals among many, and that satisfactory rather than optimal levels are the relevant criteria. The framework examined in chapter 7 can just as well be applied to decision making in the manufacturing firm, or indeed to any situation in which it is suspected that decision behavior is affected by factors that vary spatially.

A basic principle of modern organizational theory is that organizations are not naturally endowed with the information they need; they have to go out and get it. To this may be added the principle that the order in which possible solutions are discovered will have a substantial effect on the decisions made. In most real-life situations the process of searching for solutions has a strong component of chance, and some suggest that it may be regarded as searching at random in a given population of alternatives. For example, the establishment of the French rubber industry at Clermont-Ferrand in central France, away from the main flows of goods and information, is ascribed to the chance occurrence of a marriage involving a British entrepreneur and a local French family. Not only did this in a generation or two mean that Clermont became the center for Michelin, the largest French rubber producer, but also that when Dunlop entered the French market to fight Michelin they located their plant at Montluçon, 40 miles away. Montluçon had nothing else to distinguish it from hundreds of other potential sites except its nearness to Clermont.

Increasingly, the evidence coming to hand supports the picture of a real world full of satisficers and suboptimality. Investigation of factory location decisions have often emphasized that psychological ties to place, desire for social approval, and other personal and noneconomic factors are important in industrial decision making. Variation in the entrepreneur's skill, as previously noted, is a major factor; rarely are location decisions made on a long-term basis, and the decision maker's review of the environment is usually brief. Thus in one study it was noted that businessmen do not have definite expectations about all relevant trends, and that frequently, when faced with dynamic situations or new economic conditions, they decide to locate branch plants almost as if it were a habitual action. Lösch himself acknowledged the relevance of such behavioral influences. But he made no allowance for them in his location model.

An alternative framework, examined in more detail in chapter 10, is one in which the entrepreneur is seen as examining a number of different marketing strategies. The experience he gains from the operation and outcome of such strategies will indicate to him whether his choice in each instance was "satisfactory" or "unsatisfactory." Such learning through search activity would continue until the satisfactory choice was found. The sequence of successful and unsuccessful outcomes during search can be represented by 1 for success and 0 for its opposite, thus:

01110101101011000110   Search Activity
11111111   Learned Activity

During search activity information about the system is accumulated, and becomes the basis of learned or habitual decision.

What happens when a new decision is called for? The producer finds himself in a rather different position. He knows what to do in a given market situation. But the situation may well have changed. Given this element of risk, he can do one of three things:

1. *Exactly the same as before.*
2. *Something entirely different.*
3. *Something different that nevertheless includes part of what was done before.*

It can be seen from this schema how likely it is that present decisions will be conditioned largely by previous ones.

The kinds of attitudes built up over time, in response to perceived stable conditions, can be summed up in the following quotation, based on the kinds of remarks businessmen had made to the author, Eversley, over a period of years:

I am all right where I am. I am making a living. The home trade suits me. I don't like to move to a new location, it might be worse there. More income means higher taxes. Moving is a bother. Here I know where I am—suppliers, customers, workpeople, council officials, transport agents.

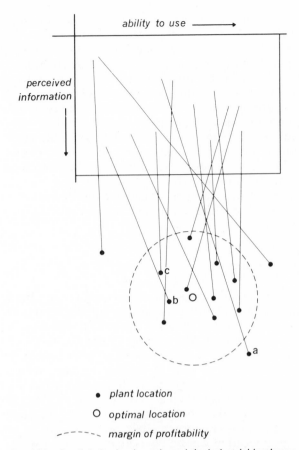

- plant location
○ optimal location
------ margin of profitability

Fig. 104. *Pred's behavioral matrix and the industrial landscape. (Adapted from Allen Pred,* Behavior and Location, *1967, by courtesy of the Department of Geography, Royal University of Lund, Sweden.)*

If I move I might be richer, but I might be poorer. I know of a chap who went bankrupt after he moved. I am too old to think of expanding very much. We've got all we need.

Finally, reference can once again be made again to Pred's behavioral matrix. Figure 104 relates the matrix to a hypothetical pattern in an economic landscape. The dotted line represents the margins of profitability, or tolerance. Within those margins a firm can make a profit; without them no profit can be made at this time. The fact that there are firms outside these margins could mean that these firms have just been founded, or that the margins themselves have recently changed. All three unprofitable locations are characterized by limited perceived information and ability to use it. It could be that two of the three copied the action of the other firm, which might have chosen its location at some earlier time when it was within the margins. All three firms' locations can be explained in terms of geographic inertia. The continued existence of such plants depends on capital reserves, willingness to absorb losses, and hope of change in the profitability margins.

In figure 104, plants *a* and *b* have the same level of perceived information, yet plant *b*, by chance, has chosen a profitable location. Plant *c*, whose ability to use information is low, has also made a profitable decision by chance. The remaining plants, whose entrepreneurs or managers have both high perception rates and high ability to use information, all lie within the profitability margins. Even though of 13 plants 10 have chosen profitable locations, variations in perceived information and varying entrepreneurial and managerial skills have led to choices other than the optimal or theoretically best location, *O*.

Conclusion

Increasingly, noneconomic criteria are being utilized in explaining manufacturing decision making and location choices. Behavioral elements of the simplest kind, like gaming strategies, have been incorporated into location models. Other behavioral concepts, such as that of psychic income, are obviously a closer approximation to the real world than the more abstract models. But many more steps remain to be taken before more realistic and therefore truly explanatory models and theories of industrial location can be devised.

Institutions, chance, and the vagaries of human behavior all play their role in shaping the manufacturing subsystem. And the role is multidimensional; it cannot be safely cordoned off in one particular area as Weber, Lösch, and others seem to have thought. This is not to decry their achievements. But they knew more about economic behavior than they were able to include in their conceptual schemes. Only subjective factors, combined with chance, can explain the decision making behavior of a Henry Ford or John D. Rockefeller. The problem is to determine how these personal factors interact with other, more impersonal ones to form a viable economic system.

Summary

1. Most industrial location theories treat patterns of contemporary manufacturing in a nineteenth-century framework—transport costs are strongly emphasized, the actions of individual entrepreneurs rather than corporate bodies are analyzed, and a somewhat static point of view is adopted.

2. These traditional approaches seek to find the optimal location for an industry or firm. Two principal systems of ideas are involved—the least cost and the market area approaches.

3. The least cost approach (associated with Weber) assumes entrepreneurs choose a factory site at that point where costs are minimized. Relative transportation costs, labor costs, and agglomeration/deglomeration costs are assessed; an increase in one cost due to increased transportation rates, for example, could be offset by choosing a point where labor costs are reduced and the cost advantages of an urban location are maximized.

4. The market area approach (associated with Lösch) depicts the optimal location of a factory as occurring where the largest possible market is monopolized; that is, where sales potential and total revenue potential are maximized.

5. Both of these approaches can be criticized for their unrealistic assumptions and closed, static viewpoints. The least cost school is totally concerned with costs, leaving demand constant; while the other is entirely concerned with demand, leaving costs constant. However, the two approaches are not complementary, and at least part of their approach is incompatible, denying any fusion between the two.

6. A number of alternatives to these two approaches have been devised. Smith in his "spatial limits" approach, grounded in the least cost school, attempts to utilize certain concepts of the market area school, and views industrial plants as being located within certain margins of tolerance (limits, set by external economic forces). Within those limits, the actual site chosen by an entrepreneur is seen as influenced by personal and other motives.

7. The principle of substitution, game theory, linear programming, input-output analysis, and a model applicable to redistributive economies, are also examined as alternatives. All seek to attain the optimum location, which seems an increasingly illusory goal. None satisfactorily explains the behavior of decision makers when they come to choose a factory site, nor do they help us to understand the economic landscape that results from those decisions.

8. Despite the difficulties in attaining a satisfactory explanation of industrial locative forces, some common forces must be at work since there seem to be common themes to industrial patterns. Many varying economic and noneconomic criteria and origins lead to a similar end result, manufacturing areas or regions (an example of the systems concept, equifinality). A number of these criteria are examined—the sheer locative pull of established industries and their associated infrastructure, the strength of fixed capital investment, geographic inertia, habitual behavior, low risk or uncertainty reduction—all seem to play their part in concentrating industrial locations or in some cases exerting a negative force towards dispersion.

9. Although the final patterns may be similar and although some basic economic threshold of profitability exists, we must turn once again to certain behavioral factors discussed in the previous chapter. A start can be made by comparing real-world patterns with the abstract landscapes of the location theorists, or by examining case examples of individual industries and the location decision making behind their site choice. It is apparent that under very similar external conditions two entrepreneurs may choose entirely different locations—and one may achieve personal success, the other, bankruptcy!

10. Investigation of decision making procedure lays stress to the entrepreneur's and manager's finite abilities, personal perceptual constraints, subjection to chance unforeseen occurrences, and their boundedly rational "satisficing" choice behavior. In such circumstances, with the decrease in importance of traditional economic factors like transport costs, the real-world industrial landscape becomes exceedingly complex to interpret.

Further Reading

In addition to the reading suggested for chapter 8, the following may be found useful:

Carrier, R. E. and Schriver, W. R. "Location Theory: Empirical Models and Selected Findings," *Land Economics*, vol. 44, 1968, pp. 450–460.

Cooper, L. "Generalized Weber Problem," *Journal of Regional Science*, vol. 8, 1968, pp. 181–97.

Garrison, W. "Spatial Structure of the Economy," part 2, *Annals of the Association of American Geographers*, vol. 49, 1959, pp. 471–52.

Golledge, R. "Conceptualizing the Market Decision Process," *Journal of Regional Science*, vol. 7, 1967, pp. 239–258.

Greenhut, M. L. *Plant Location in Theory and Practice* Chapel Hill: University of North Carolina Press, 1956).

Greenhut, M. O. *Microeconomics and the Space Economy* (Chicago: Scott Foresman, 1963).

Hoover, E. M. *The Location of Economic Activity* (New York: McGraw-Hill, 1948).

Isard, W. *Location and Space Economy* (Cambridge, Mass.: M.I.T. Press, 1956).

Karaska, G. J. and Bramhall, D. F., eds. *Locational Analysis for Manufacturing* (Cambridge, Mass.: M.I.T. Press, 1969), especially chapters 1 and 24–29.

Pred, A. *The Spatial Dynamics of U.S. Urban-Industrial Growth, 1800–1914* (Cambridge, Mass.: M.I.T. Press, 1966).

Richter, C. E. "Impact of Industrial Linkages on Geographic Association," *Journal of Regional Science*, vol. 9, 1969, pp. 19–28.

Roepke, H. G. "The Impact of Technological Change on Industrial Geography," *A.I.D.C. Journal*, vol. 1, no. 3, 1966, pp. 15–22.

Smith, D. M. "A Theoretical Framework for Geographical Studies of Industrial Location," *Economic Geography*, vol. 42, 1966, pp. 95–113.

Smith, D. M. *Industrial Location: An Economic Geographical Analysis* (New York: Wiley, 1971).

Stafford, H. A. "An Industrial Location Decision Model," *Proceedings of the Association of American Geographers*, vol. 1, 1969, pp. 141–45.

Streit, M. E. "Spatial Association and Economic Linkages between Industries," *Journal of Regional Science*, vol. 9, 1969, pp. 177–188.

The two classic references to the least cost and market area approaches are

Lösch, A. *The Economies of Location*, translated by W. H. Waglom and W. F. Stolper (New Haven: Yale University Press, 1954).

Weber, A. *Theory of the Location of Industries*, translated by C. J. Freidrich (Chicago: Chicago University Press, 1929).

Other references can be tracked down through

Stevens, B. H. and Brackett, C. A. *Industrial Location: A Review and Annotated Bibliography of Theoretical, Empirical and Case Studies* (Philadelphia: Regional Science Research Institute, 1967), Bibliography Series no. 3.

ten

The Tertiary Subsystem:
An Overview

Introduction

Workers engaged in tertiary economic activities probably make up only 5–10 percent of the world's labor force. They include retailers, clerks, government employees, teachers, lawyers, bankers, insurance salesmen, hotel maids, athletes, concert pianists, hairdressers, strip-tease artistes, and many others. Tertiary activity is a term that embraces all such pursuits. The characteristics they share in common are negative ones: they are not concerned with the harvesting of naturally produced phenomena, as are primary activities, nor do they involve any change in the form or location of commodities, as do secondary activities.

The number of people employed in this category is small on a world scale, but varies from nation to nation. In chapter 2 it was pointed out that the proportion employed in the tertiary sector seems to increase with economic development, a process somewhat unfortunately termed *tertiarization*. In the technically most advanced nations these tertiary activities actually form the largest single part of the total work force — over 40 percent in North America, and over 30 percent in much of Western Europe. These proportions compare to about 15 percent in the same areas in 1800, and 23 percent today in Mexico, or 13 percent in India, as shown in figure 105.

Just as manufacturing and agricultural activities vary spatially, so do tertiary activities. The general tendency seems to be for these latter activities to agglomerate in towns, cities, and other **central places**. This agglomerative tendency means, among other things, that retail stores are likely to be found in the

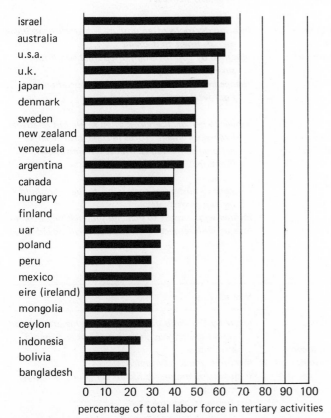

israel
australia
u.s.a.
u.k.
japan
denmark
sweden
new zealand
venezuela
argentina
canada
hungary
finland
uar
poland
peru
mexico
eire (ireland)
mongolia
ceylon
indonesia
bolivia
bangladesh

0 10 20 30 40 50 60 70 80 90 100

percentage of total labor force in tertiary activities

Fig. 105. *Percentage of the labor force employed in the tertiary sector. (Based on data in the* United Nations, *Yearbook, 1964.)*

same places as garages, law offices, or dentists. As a result, a large-scale pattern of specialization does not occur, so that there are no retail trade regions as there are regions of nomadic herding or commercial ranching. Because of this close areal association of tertiary activities, they are best studied in central places. This is not to say that central places consist only of tertiary activities; there are towns in market-exchange and redistributive economies where employment in the secondary occupations exceed those in the tertiary ones. And of course there are settlements where most of the labor force is employed in a primary activity — mining, fishing, lumber, or agriculture. However, the dominant trend in technically advanced areas is for service activities to outweigh, though rarely to exclude, the other activities.

Thus a study of tertiary activities is principally a study of urban based activities. The central places involved will vary in size from a small market village or roadside halt with just a gas station and general store, to a metropolitan center with thousands of such service establishments.

As a nodal region, the city performs a variety of economic functions, both for the population within its boundary, and for the population within its **hinterland.** The latter is variously defined, but can be thought of as an area of dependence, or trade area. The city-region relationship can vary from local to worldwide, according to function (consider, for instance, the dependence of the world diamond market on Amsterdam); the main thing is that it produces interaction in the form of movement of people, goods, information, money, and credit.

Cities, then, have both internal and external relationships with their tertiary services. The *internal* relationships are the actual spatial distributions of residences, shops, offices, wholesalers, and so on, and the circulation patterns associated with them. The *external* relationships are those that link the urban center to areas that look for urban tertiary

Table 40. *The Tertiary System: Characteristics and Location of Service, Trade, and Financial Establishments*

SERVICES	establishments	characteristics	location
recreation	theatre movie theatre dance hall cabaret bowling alley sports arena restaurants	subject to economic impact of tourism traffic located near customers major centers can support major-league football or hockey, art gallery, symphony orchestra, zoo, etc.	demand patterns: (a) frequent, near home; spacing dependent on threshold and range; (b) infrequent use; range considerable constrained by cultural attributes
vacation	hotels motels camps ski lodge (restaurants) souvenirs (gas stations)	natural and man-made seasonal spatial relationship of city to recreational area and movement pattern involved amount of money spent/visitor relationship between activity and journey in the recreational experience	dependent on resources and barriers; the barriers include cost and inconvenience of travel
medical	offices medical centers clinics hospitals	economic benefits by agglomeration. some gain by locating in shopping centers to benefit from multipurpose trips.	threshold of demand for support of a single physician thresholds increase as degree of specializaton of unit of supply increases
personal services	schools churches universities	highly correlated with demand for their services, but ratio of institute to population can be low (e.g., universities).	location decisions often obscure — historical, political, etc., nearness to demand modified by consideration of optimal size (often small) change in scale associated with transportation improvements
public administration	public safety	similar to personal services some special services dispersed for security of land space usage (e.g., missile sites)	similar to personal services, often small; but relatively large government offices in state, provincial, or national centers to centralize administrative functions
business and repair services	advertising accounting auditing bookkeeping auto repairs radio and T.V. repairs industrial repairs	special customer services	adjacent to businesses they serve, though threshold varies a great deal located with respect to demand (population, income) located with respect to demand (specialized industry)

TRADE	establishments	characteristics	location
retail	gas stations grocery stores drug stores liquor stores used-car dealers department stores specialty stores laundries dry cleaners farm equipment, etc.	subject to varying consumer perception, frequency of use needs to be accessible to population, income hold inventories at lowest level consistent with consumer demand	locate by threshold, range, clustering, hierarchies, and conditions of generative, suscipient and shared attraction low order goods (convenience) frequent and dispersed; high order goods (shopping, specialty) less frequent, agglomerated
wholesale	grocery wholesale bulk gas storage dry goods wholesale	most numerous, customer needs large and frequent less numerous, supply dry goods, furniture, jewelry, etc.	near to customers, consistent with threshold and range to maintain a positive net income often confined to medium sized centers and above

Table 40. (*continued*)

FINANCIAL	establishments	characteristics	location
banks	*clearing houses* *federal reserve banks* *local banks* *savings and trust organizations* *security and commodity exchanges*	*manufacturers of credit* *deal in services, usually of face-to-face nature, choice near customers* *major item of income: interest on credit*	*regional banks in major cities (threshold and range)* *local banks decentralized (hence subject to threshold entry)*
insurance	*offices* *agents*	*income via premiums* *much income from agents in the field*	*customer-oriented and associated with demand and income of an area; or central and branch offices, more highly centralized since fewer needed*
real estate	*offices*	*solicit customers and transport them to sales site* *appear wherever demand occurs*	*locate in sales territory* *locate in areas of speculative demand* *independent location, no need for regional or national organization* *decentralized, small, correlated to general business activity*

Source: H.H. McCarty and J.B. Lindberg, *A Preface to Economic Geography* (Englewood Cliffs, N.J.: Prentice-Hall, 1966); C.K. Campbell, "An Approach to Research in Recreational Geography," B.C. Occasional Papers, no. 7, 1966; W.L. Garrison et al., *Studies of Highway Development and Geographic Change* (Seattle: University of Washington Press, 1959).

activities; such relationships take the form of links in transport and communication.

Table 40 lists some of the elements of the tertiary subsystem. Some of its basic characteristics and location factors are also noted; the chief distinction recognized is that between *services, trades,* and a *financial* component. Thus in this and the next chapter we shall be concerned with the economic behavior related to recreational activities, vacations, medical services, education, public administration, retailing, wholesaling, banks, insurance, and finance. Varied though they are, they tend to share one dominant characteristic, that of being interrelated, directly or indirectly, through the behavior of their customers, in contrast to primary and secondary activities, which are interrelated through their inputs and outputs.

One way to describe *services* is to say that they satisfy certain human wants or needs, and at the same time bring monetary compensation to those who provide them. They involve such occupational roles as medical practitioners and aides, professional sportsmen, educators, and government administrators. Formerly perishability, nonstorability, and close personal contact were also important attributes of services. But the coming of the printing press, phonograph record, and other communications media have progressively altered some of these relationships. Second, *trading* includes both retail and wholesale activities. One indicator of their

importance in the United States is that they are second only to manufacturing as originators of **national income.** Their importance in the tertiary category is also fairly obvious. Third, the finance group, which includes insurance and real estate, also comes under tertiary activities.

The locational characteristics of these three groups are somewhat similar. Since they are all oriented toward the consumer, they tend to locate where most consumers are, that is, in central places. Thus tertiary activities are spatially distributed, but with a distinct tendency to agglomerate.

The tertiary subsystem will be examined from three points of reference:

1. *In the opening sections of this chapter, the mechanics of the subsystem will be examined, particularly as portrayed in central place theory and its extensions.*
2. *In the remainder of this chapter, certain elements of consumer behavior will be examined.*
3. *In chapter 11 some of the individual components of the tertiary subsystem (retailing, wholesaling, recreational activities, medical services) will be examined in more detail.*

Central Place Theory

The central place model was originally formulated by Walter Christaller in the 1930s. It was first applied to the *external* relationships between city and hinterland, the city being the focus of services, trades, and financial institutions. Later extensions of the model have attempted to apply it to the *internal* relations of the tertiary activities, that is, the actual distribution of shops and banks within the city. Together, these ideas of Christaller and later workers form a subdivision of partial equilibrium location theory that is called **central place theory.**

The Central Place Model

Much of the current work in settlements and their associated tertiary activities has its roots in the work of Christaller. Looking at the spatial distributions of settlements he was able to pick out a particular locational pattern. He attempted in fact to find the laws that determine the number, size, and distribution of towns. He was convinced, he wrote, that "just as there are economic laws which determine the life of the economy, so are there special economic-geographic laws determining the arrangement of towns." He asserts that the basic function of any city, other than towns like mining settlements or health resorts, is to be a central place providing retail goods and miscellaneous services for a surrounding tributary area. Because Christaller excludes manufacturing towns and other noncentral places from his framework it is a model of the location of tertiary activities and *not* a general model of urban systems. Even thus restricted it has a number of crucial inadequacies, such as unrealistic views of consumer behavior, and a failure to study feedback from tertiary functions to other sectors of the urban system.

Assumptions

If, for the moment, we accept Christaller's assertion that cities do result from the impact of so-called lawlike processes, then it follows that we would expect to find a relationship between the size of cities and the way they are distributed over an area.

As with all models, a number of limiting constraints or assumptions can be identified:

1. *The landscape is an unbounded plain with soil of uniform fertility and more or less evenly distributed resources. The term "unbounded," or limitless is used to remove the effect of any boundary problems.*

2. *There is an even distribution of population and purchasing power; thus demand is spread evenly, and no anomalies can arise through spatial variations in wealth. Such an initial settlement pattern is shown in figure 106. Each dot represents small groups of farmers, regularly distributed in an equilateral triangular grid, which permits the packing of as many settlements as possible in an area.*

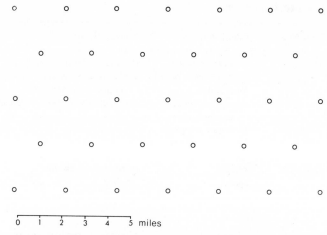

0 1 2 3 4 5 miles

Fig. 106. *Christaller's central place model: (1) first order settlements spaced 2¼ miles apart on an equilateral triangular grid*

3. *There is a uniform transportation network in all directions, so that all central places of the same type are equally accessible.*

Besides these physical constraints, there are a number of behavioral assumptions:

4. *A maximum number of demands for the goods and services should be satisfied.*

5. *The incomes of the people offering the goods and services should be maximized.*

6. *Distances moved by consumers to purchase those goods and services should be minimized—or, in other words, goods are purchased from the closest point or source.*

7. *The number of central places should be the minimum possible.*

8. *There is no intraproduct differentiation.*

Thus the model supplies not a general theory, but rather a descriptive account of the points or nodes in the settlement pattern that are primarily central places, and offer services of a tertiary nature.

The Basic Model

Within these assumptions and constraints, Christaller postulated a number of events in this landscape.

1. *A series of evenly spaced service centers would be established. The distance in questions was set at 2 hours of nonmechanized travel, since in the areas examined most central places had arisen before the advent of the automobile. Translated into physical terms, this 2 hours is the equivalent of about 4½ miles, since a man could walk or drive a team of horses about 2¼ miles in 1 hour. Thus if these first service centers were so situated that no person would be more than 1 hour from the nearest*

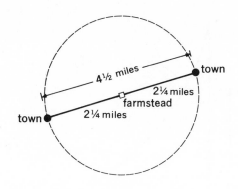

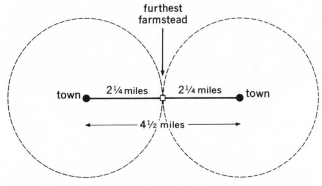

Fig. 107. *Christaller's central place model: (2) spacing of lowest order service centers.*

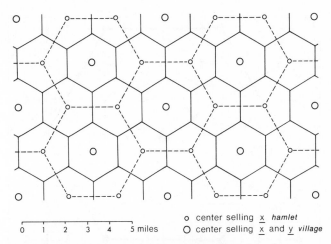

○ center selling $\underline{x}$ *hamlet*
○ center selling $\underline{x}$ and $\underline{y}$ *village*

Fig. 108. *Christaller's central place model: (3) pattern of two orders of service center generated by a k-3 hierarchy.*

center, the centers would be about 4½ miles from one another (figure 107). Theoretically, the trading area around each service center or town would be a circle of 2¼ miles in radius.

2. *Given the uniform population distribution, a hexagonal market area would in fact require the least average distance of movement to the centers for consumers, minimize the number of centers, and avoid areas of market area overlap or neglect. It would therefore be the most efficient form in a mathematical sense.*

3. *The basic settlement, service center, or central place reachable by a farmer in an hour or so would be small, and would provide only rather restricted services. Obviously, central places of this kind would be very numerous. The denser the rural population, the larger the service function of these first-order settlements would be. But the centers would not be closer together; they would remain 4½ miles apart.*

In addition to the frequent needs that the first-order centers can satisfy there are goods that are required less frequently—fertilizers and farm machinery, for instance. A first-order center could not afford to sell such items, since there would not be a large enough demand from one small area 2¼ miles in radius. However, if several trading areas were added together the total number of consumers they contain could support, say, a center dealing in fertilizers and simple farm machinery. Thus a *second-*

order center would arise (figure 108). All the earlier constraints would still operate except that now, for less frequently purchased goods, a consumer would be willing to travel further. Accordingly, there would be fewer second-order centers than first-order ones, and they would be farther apart. The trade area of one of these centers would be bounded by six of the first-order centers.

This process could continue on to a third and even a fourth level of centers, each higher order selling less and less frequently required goods, and therefore needing to draw on larger and larger numbers of consumers willing to travel further and further (figure 109). Each higher-order center would also supply a trading area of the order beneath it with lower-order goods. Thus a fourth-order trading center would combine all fourth-order functions for varying trading areas.

In his field area, southern Germany, Christaller identified seven orders of settlement, each with a precise quantitative relationship to the others (table 41).

Threshold and Range

Two concepts are fundamental to Christaller's grouping of service centers: **threshold** and **range**.

One approach to explaining these two concepts is to assume that, on the homogeneous plain, a shop is established to sell one product, X. Two factors will determine simultaneously whether this shop can be profitably established: the minimum level of demand needed for the shop to operate (the threshold); and the distance people will travel to buy X at a particular price. If people will not travel to the shop to buy X, whatever the price, then there is no way the shop can profitably exist. If the price, however, is such that people are willing to travel to the shop, and the

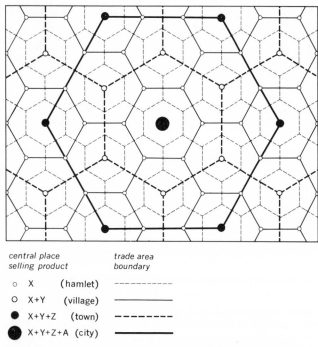

central place selling product		trade area boundary
○	X (hamlet)	– – – – – –
◯	X+Y (village)	————
●	X+Y+Z (town)	– – – – –
⬤	X+Y+Z+A (city)	————

Fig. 109. *Christaller's central place model: (4) four hierarchical orders.*

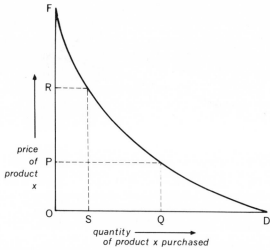

Fig. 110. *Demand curve for product x. (From August Lösch,* Economics of Location, *1954, p. 106, adapted by permission of Yale University Press.)*

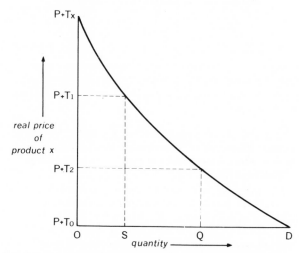

Fig. 111. *Demand curve for product x, allowing for real price (P + T). (From Lösch 1954, ibid., see fig. 110.)*

demand is such that it meets the minimum level of demand that it takes for the shop to operate at all, then the shop will remain in business.

Since the shop cannot exist unless a certain minimum level of demand is present, the threshold can be expressed in terms of the number of people required to support one particular function, in this case the sale of X. We can express it in population terms because one assumption of the model was that everyone had equal income and an equal propensity to consume. In terms of table 41, 3,500 people may be needed to support 40 different goods or services, or 350,000 people to support an array of 600 goods or services. Below the former population level the threshold would be so low as to support only a very restricted array of goods.

The range—the distance a consumer is willing to travel to purchase a good or service at a particular price—can be expressed even more precisely as the dimension of the trade area, or hinterland. Thus the range of an array of goods sold in a *Provinzstadt* (table 41) is 67.5 miles. In figure 110, the curve represents a hypothetical demand for product x. At price P, quantity Q of product x will be purchased by an individual. But should the price of x rise to R the individual will purchase less of x, or in other words quantity S. At price F we assume none of x is purchased at all. Such a simple statement ignores, of course, the spatial distribution of the purchasers. Each purchaser has to travel to the shop to buy x because of the spatial imbalance. So each purchase of

x involves the price of S *and* the costs of overcoming the spatial separation of the consumer's residence and the store. The real price of x to an individual is the price, $O - F$, plus the transportation cost, T.

Let us assume a fixed price along the range $O - F$ of prices of product x. In figure 111, price P has been chosen as an example. An individual who has to pay T_1 transportation costs to get to the shop would pay a real price of $P + T_1$, and would purchase Q amount of x. A person living farther away, and incurring a higher transportation cost (T_2), would pay $P + T_2$ for x and therefore purchase only S amount. On the other hand, somebody living next to the shop would incur practically no transportation costs, (T_0), and would therefore pay only the cost of the product, $P + T_0$. There is also a limit to the amount of transportation costs that an individual will tolerate when

Table 41. *Southern Germany: Christaller's Towns and Trade Areas*

order of town	no. of places	distance apart (miles)	service area (miles)	no. of types of goods offered	typical pop. of town	typical pop. of service area
1. Marktort (M)	486	4.5	18	40	1,000	3,500
2. Amstort (A)	162	7.5	54	90	2,000	11,000
3. Kreisstadt (K)	54	13.0	160	180	4,000	35,000
4. Bezirkstadt (B)	18	22.5	480	330	10,000	100,000
5. Gaustadt (G)	6	39.0	1,500	600	30,000	350,000
6. Provinzstadt (P)	2	67.5	4,500	1,000	100,000	1,000,000
7. Landstadt (L)	1	113.0	13,500	2,000	500,000	3,500,000

Source: Walter Christaller, *Central Places in Southern Germany,* © 1966, p. 67. Reprinted by permission of Prentice-Hall, Inc., Englewood Cliffs, New Jersey.

buying a particular item. This situation is represented as $P + T_x$, when no purchase is made.

Figure 112 illustrates the effect of transportation costs. The limit of the trading area of the store is set by the point $P + T_x$; this is called the maximum range of the store. The radius T_x demarcating the maximum trading area for product x is called the ideal limit; beyond this limit no purchaser will use this particular store. Since one of the assumptions of the model was a homogeneous plain with equal accessibility in all directions, the maximum range is circular.

So far the assumption has been one store, or shop selling one product over the homogeneous plain. Beyond radius T_x, however, transportation costs are such that other shops will be patronized. Each of

these, of course, has its own range and threshold values. In figure 113, plotting these ranges across the plain leads to the situation already described below: there will either be people not served at all (area *a*), or served by two overlapping service areas (*b*) that would cut into the threshold value of a shop. The most efficient shape, as we have seen, is where the service areas take a hexagonal form, and where the threshold limits lie within the perimeter of the hexagons. Since the hexagons are all of the same shape and size they interlock (figure 108, where ideal

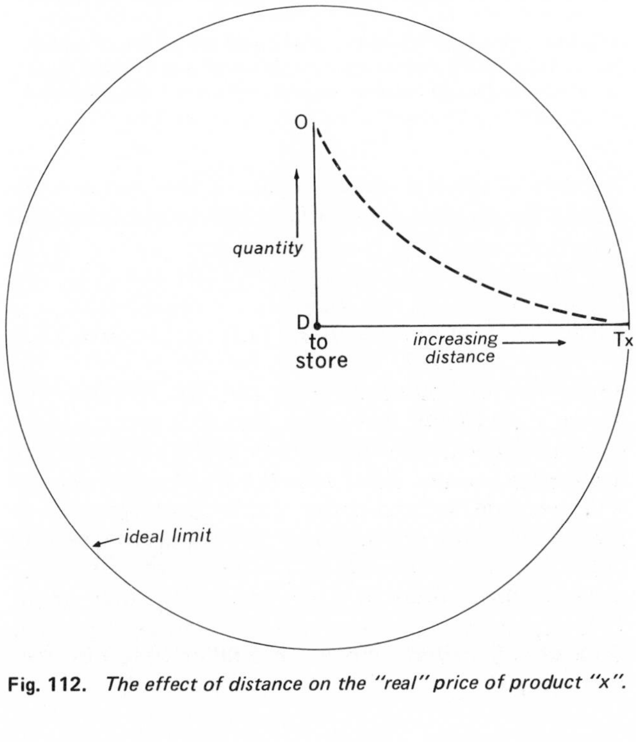

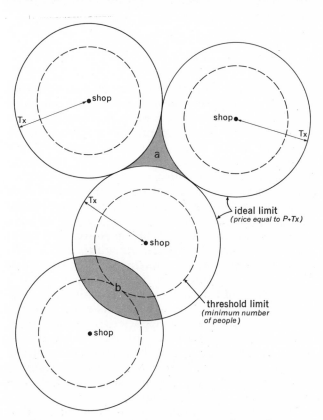

Fig. 113. *The ideal trading areas of a number of shops selling product "x."*

Fig. 112. *The effect of distance on the "real" price of product "x".*

and threshold limits are coterminous). Thus we have reached a stage at which product x is sold by many shops.

We can now take another step and add a shop or set of shops, separate from the set selling x, that sell product y. Let us suppose that y is an item of hardware and x an item of food. Hardware is sold less frequently than food, hence its threshold population must be larger and, since population is evenly distributed, its range of greater radius. If we assume that three times the population is needed to support the sale of saucepans than butter or bread, shops selling y will draw on an area at least three times that of x. Thus if a shop selling y locates at A, its service area or hinterland will not be just the service area of shop x but the closest one-third of the service areas of the six surrounding shops, giving a hinterland area three times the size.

The notion of threshold can now be extended. Products with a high threshold value, that is, ones that are expensive and bought less frequently, like clothing and appliances, need large service areas and large populations to support them. They are therefore found less frequently on the landscape. On the other hand, products with low threshold values, that are inexpensive and are needed frequently, like food and drugs, are retailed with greater frequency in the landscape.

The Hierarchy

The addition to a central place of a shop selling product y extends the service area in up to one-third of the six complementary regions that contain shops selling the low threshold product x. Thus if there were 300 central places containing shops selling x distributed over the homogeneous plain, 100 would *also* contain a shop selling product y. Those higher order places with y would be located so that each would be equidistant from six surrounding central places. In this particular example (figure 108) we have a twofold hierarchy of central places—one low order set with x, and a high order set with x and y. Obviously, the number of hierarchies could be extended (figure 109). An important factor to note is that a central place of a particular order in a hierarchy contains not just the function or functions characteristic of its order but also the characteristics of all orders below it. Instead of thinking in terms of one to four products, we can translate the complex of functions as being carried out from hamlet to city, or *Marktort* to *Landstadt* (table 41). Thus we have come full circle in describing Christaller's model.

The basic model outlined above is based on what Christaller called a **marketing principle.** A maximum

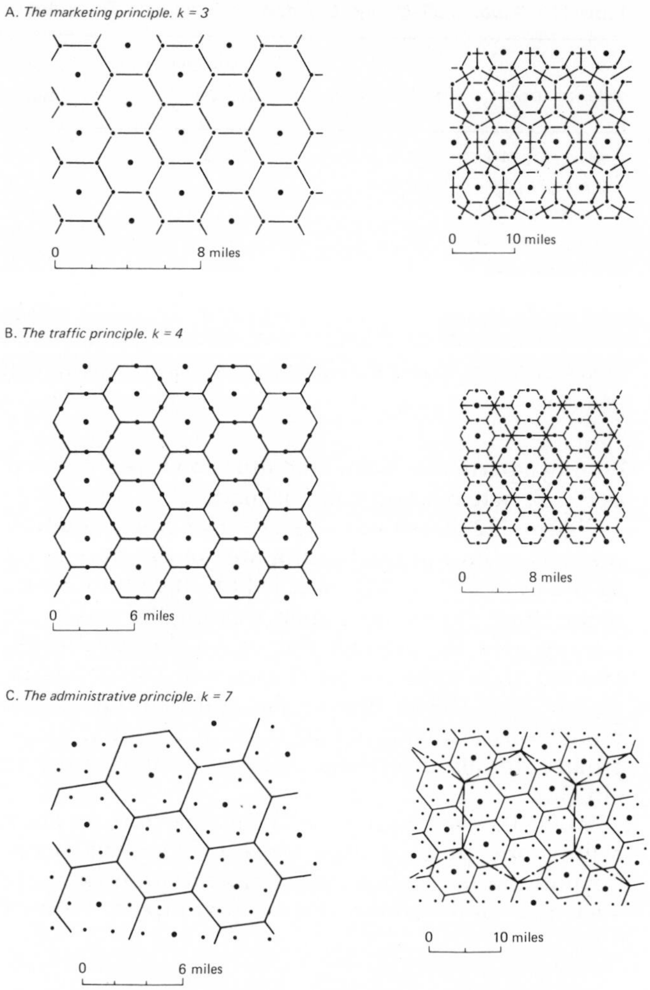

Fig. 114. *Christaller's central place model: the system of central places based on the marketing, transportation, and administrative principles. In the left column two orders of centers are developed; in the right, it is developed to a third order of settlement.*

number of central places result, if the above mentioned constraints (particularly the minimization of travel) are met. This particular system, known as the $k = 3$ network, is shown in figures 109 and 114a. The k value refers to the number of settlements at a particular level or rank in the ordering system. Thus in figure 109 each second-order center serves the equivalent of three first-order centers. This number is made up of the first-order part of a second-order function, plus a one-third share of the six bordering first-order centers. Similarly, the third-order centers will provide second-order goods and services to themselves and one-third of six bordering second order centers—in all, the equivalent of three second-order trading areas or nine first-order trade areas. This regular progression of $k = 3$ can be extended through all orders, since Christaller assumes that once the *k* value is adopted in any landscape it remains fixed, and thus can be applied to the ordering of all ranks of centers and trade areas. This is Christaller's fixed *k* hierarchy principle. In this network the progression of settlements (or trading areas), starting from the highest order center in the landscape, would be 3, 9, 27, 81, 243, 729, as in table 41.

Besides *k* = 3, the marketing or supply principle, Christaller put forward *k* = 4 and *k* = 7 networks (figure 114) to take account of some of the deviations from the *k* = 3 system. If the hexagonal net of that system is turned through ninety degrees, the border settlements are shared by only two central places, and the *k* value rises to four (figure 114b). Figure 114c shows the process of net enlargement moving one step further to produce a *k* = 7 system, where no settlements are shared between service areas.

Christaller suggested that a fixed *k* value of 3 (figure 114a) would develop where the supply of goods from the central places is to be as near the dependent places as possible. This marketing principle, as we have seen, maximizes the number of central places in the model landscape. The *k* = 4 network, Christaller's **traffic principle,** would develop where the cost of constructing transport networks is important. "The distribution of central places is most favorable where as many important places as possible lie on one traffic route between two towns." This leads to more higher order centers than with the marketing principle; the sequence is 4, 16, 64, 256, 1,024, 4,496.

Where, for protective or administrative reasons, it is necessary to group centers even more strongly, the rule of *k* = 7 arises. "Districts of practically equal area and population are created, in the center of which lies an administrative capital." This is known as the **administrative principle.** It leads to even more concentration on the higher order centers than either of the previous principles; the sequence is 7, 49, 343, 2,401, 16,807, 117,649. According to Christaller, "the three principles determine, each according to their own laws, the system of central places . . . any of these three principles can decisively influence the distribution of central places."

Empirical investigations of the ordering or ranking of settlements and the value of *k* have been carried out. Thus a *k* = 3 system has been identified in Ceylon, and both *k* = 3 and *k* = 4 networks in rural China. One of the difficulties associated with the fixed *k* assumption of Christaller when dealing with *k* = 3 and *k* = 4 networks is that dependent places are divided in their allegiance to the central places that are one higher in the order of settlement. Christaller overcame this through the concept of *nesting,* illustrated in figure 115.

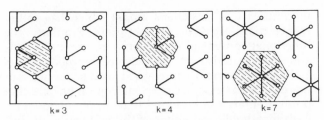

Fig. 115. *Alternative nesting principles in the Christaller fixed* k *landscape. (From Peter Haggett,* Locational Analysis in Human Geography, *1965, p. 122, reprinted courtesy of Edward Arnold, London.)*

Extensions of Central Place Theory

Central place theory has not been left in its original form; it has been subjected to a number of modifications and adaptations, including adaptation to non-Western situations.

The Lösch Model

Probably one of the major extensions of the theory has been that of Lösch, who put forward a scheme in the mid-1950s that extended and elaborated on the Christaller model. Lösch used the same hexagonal latices for his theoretical landscape, but he did not consider that a fixed *k* system approached reality. He therefore developed a more sophisticated format by superimposing the various hexagonal systems used by Christaller (*k* = 3, *k* = 4, and *k* = 7) and many more.

The market area for the supplier of any one good can be visualized in the Lösch model as a fish net, the size of the mesh being determined by the threshold of the good in question. Since different services have different thresholds, the complete landscape consists of many such fish nets, each with its own distinctive mesh size. In his model Lösch restricted himself to *k* = 1 through *k* = 25. He postulated that one point on the theoretical plain would by definition be a supply center for all goods, and this would be a central metropolis. Lösch then superimposed the 25 market area fish nets, and rotated them about the metropolis, so that the suppliers of the 25 different goods occupied various locations, but no two suppliers of the same good coincided. In this way he created six sectors with many relatively high order centers and six sectors where low order centers predominated.

By using a flexible *k* value Lösch built up a very different landscape from Christaller, and by allowing a variable *k* hierarchy the pattern of settlements he produced is much closer to reality. Thus it produces an almost continuous sequence of settlement size, in contrast to Christaller's model which has settlements distributed in distinct tiers. Similarly the functional content of settlements in terms of goods and services is also variable. Each center has function 1, the most frequently purchased good or service, but there is a greater degree of specialization beyond that point. Centers can be found that supply goods with high thresholds and goods with low thresholds, but not with anything in between. Thus identical arrays of services do not occur in settlements of the same size. The greater complexity of the Löschian model has made it less popular than Christaller's, despite the empirical evidence in its favor.

The Berry-Garrison Modification

Probably the best known modification of central place theory and the most widely used is that of Berry and Garrison. They emphasize the concepts of threshold and range. By concentrating on these two concepts they are able to bypass the assumption of uniform population distribution (Christaller) and that of hexagonal market areas (Lösch and Christaller). They note that *"whatever* the distribution of purchasing power (and whether in open countryside or within a large metropolis) a hierarchical spatial structure of central places supplying central goods will emerge."* Thus they remove Christaller's assumption that income is distributed homogeneously; instead of defining the market area as a 2¼ mile radius at the lowest level, the market area becomes equivalent to the threshold sales level. While centers are no longer thought of as equidistant, they are at a particular level equally accessible to an identical amount of consumer purchasing power. Figure 116 illustrates the concept of hierarchy within an urban area.

A hierarchy occurs because, to the seller or operator of tertiary activities, different functions have different threshold values and thus demand minimum trade areas of different sizes for their support. As we have seen, goods and services are purchased with varying degrees of frequency. Thus low threshold, high frequency functions are found in low order clusters, and high threshold, low frequency functions are found in high order clusters serving large trade areas, though these latter also contain the functions of the lower orders too. At the bottom of the hierarchy will be found low order convenience goods; the outlets supplying these goods and services will be spread throughout a city and their market areas will be small. Competition between these clusters will reduce the threshold and ranges to a minimum, so that they will form a dispersed geographic pattern. At the top of the hierarchy are found high order "shopping-specialty" goods clusters,

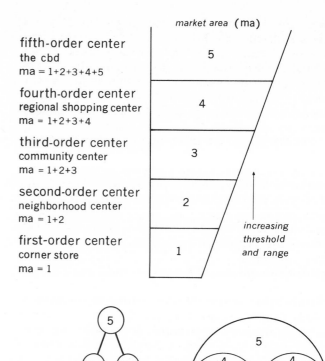

fifth-order center
the cbd
ma = 1+2+3+4+5

5

fourth-order center
regional shopping center
ma = 1+2+3+4

4

third-order center
community center
ma = 1+2+3

3

second-order center
neighborhood center
ma = 1+2

2

first-order center
corner store
ma = 1

1

increasing threshold and range

market area (ma)

Fig. 116. *Hierarchical nesting of tertiary centers within a city.*

with extremely large market areas. Berry and others noted that: "Higher order centers . . . also perform lower order functions . . . and for their low order goods have somewhat larger trade areas than centers which are exclusively of that lower level. The reason is the greater number of shopping opportunities in the higher order center, so that consumers can find additional reasons to travel somewhat further to purchase their convenience goods."

Thus just as Christaller identified orders or hierarchies of central places, Berry and Garrison have identified orders or hierarchies of shopping centers, from the frequent corner store to the usually single downtown area. Moreover, just as with Christaller's central places, each particular order in a hierarchy of shopping centers contains not just the functions characteristic of its class or order (supermarket, variety store, department store, etc.) but also the characteristics of all orders below it.

Most shops seek out other shops or groups of shops, and there does appear to be a regularity in the resulting grouping of business types. In other words, the commercial facilities within a city form a system, a set of interrelated elements that interact to create a recognizable structure. Knowledge of this structure and its elements has built up over several years of observation, classification, and deductive theorizing. As will be noted later, this apparently simple structure is disturbed by income differences, ethnic differences, discount trading, corridors of greater accessibility, and the existence of commerical ribbons and specialized functional areas.

Implicit in these ideas of hierarchy and structure are the concepts of threshold and range. In the real world application of these concepts is relaxed and widened somewhat. For instance, instead of measuring the threshold value of a shop by the number of people (which assumes that they all earn the same) it can be measured by the minimum amount of purchasing power needed to support such a shop. Other factors would be important too—population density and actual distribution, or cultural group and class (since they affect spending patterns). Range could still be measured in distance terms, but instead of using an actual cost distance or direct transport cost, a **utility measure** such as time-distance, or even some subjective measure can be used.

Although Berry and Garrison did not modify Christaller's concepts to this degree, they did initiate the use of central place concepts in internal city patterns. Berry, especially, translated these concepts into the system of centers noted above.

Moving-Point Solutions

Virtually all this chapter and chapter 11 are concerned with tertiary activities in Western multibased capitalist societies. But there are other patterns. For lack of literature it would be difficult to deal with pattern in redistributive economies. There is evidence, however, of distinctive patterns found in peasant and market peasant societies.

As one example of a non-Western system, we can look at a nonstatic solution to the retail distribution problem, the "moving-point" solution of Korea. The bulk of this book has dealt with static fixed locations, although some alternatives, such as nomadic herding, were noted in chapter 6. A moving-point solution in tertiary activities involves the use of *periodic markets* or (in our culture) fairs. In most peasant systems, markets are in fact periodic rather than permanent or continuous, although the trend toward specialization in all economies leads to a polarized and more static pattern. As we have seen, this interaction of complementary market area and city tends to lead to the appearance of fixed and permanent central places. In other areas of the world, however,

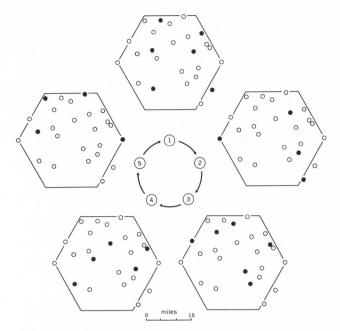

temporal characteristics of korean periodic markets

code	korean name	calendar of opening days *(adjusted to western calendar)*						
1	1–6	1	6	11	16	21	26	31(or 1)
2	2–7	2	7	12	17	22	27	2
3	3–8	3	8	13	18	23	28	3
4	4–9	4	9	14	19	24	29	4
5	5–10	5	10	15	20	25	30	5

Fig. 117. *Korea: space-time patterns of periodic markets. (From J.H. Stine, "Temporal Aspects of Tertiary Production Elements in Korea," 1962, pp. 70–71, reprinted by permission of the Bureau of Business and Economic Research, University of Oregon.)*

these same central functions are performed by mobile agents and their physical facilities, moving from place to place during a short period of time. In fact, if two or more merchants meet at the same location at the same time they can usually sell more than if their visits did not coincide. In Korea, a regular schedule of market visits is developed as an aid to both consumers and producers. Both in Korea and in many other countries, such as Great Britain, mobile and fixed markets exist side by side. However, in the case of Korea the periodic market has been the prime facility for most commercial transactions, and fixed exchanges are much more recent. The Korean markets meet once every five days (the specific times and dates vary from place to place). Figure 117 shows the opening days for all periodic markets in an area of central South Korea. Closed circles indicate markets meeting on the data shown by the ring of circled numbers. All other markets are shown by open circles.

In the same study of Korea, the concepts of threshold and range are used to explain the moving-point solution. The maximum range of a good is the distance at which the marginal consumer is located from the central facility. If we assume a homogeneous plain and the market is without competitors, this maximum range will describe a circle (figure 118). The minimum range, threshold, can also be looked on as circular, and contains the minimum total demand just large enough to ensure the success of the dealer at the market. Under certain circumstances (maximum range equal to or greater than the minimum range) the dealer can survive at a fixed location (118a). But when the maximum range is less than the minimum range the dealer will either lose money and go out of business, or keep moving from place to place (118b-d). This latter case would occur where the transport network was poorly developed, or transport technology was primitive, so that the distance consumers can travel to the market would be severely limited. The market would therefore change its location in space by "jumping" to meet the consumer within the limits of the latter's travel abilities. The length of each jump is a function of the maximum range, while the number of jumps necessary to reach the survival threshold is a function of the minimum range. The firms or markets will continue to make additional jumps until marginal costs equal marginal revenues.

In Korea, the conditions needed to stimulate market mobility are found: transport costs are high; travel is largely on foot, so that it is slow and costly, costs usually being measured as time lost on the farm; income levels are low, and thus are accompanied by high demand elasticity; income density is also low, though population density is high. Other studies of periodic markets and fairs point to similar conclusions.

Mechanistic Analyses

Besides central place theory, a number of other formulations have been used to help examine the mechanics of the tertiary subsystem. These include W. J. Reilly's so-called law of retail gravitation and D. L. Huff's model of retail behavior.

Reilly's "Law"

One group of work rests on the notions of **social physics,** which is the application of Newtonian gravity concepts to the movement of human populations. Here, it is applied to movement between centers of retailing activities and the consumer's residence. Such *gravity models* include one celebrated variation put forward by Reilly in an early 1930s study, where he stated that consumers moved to shop in certain

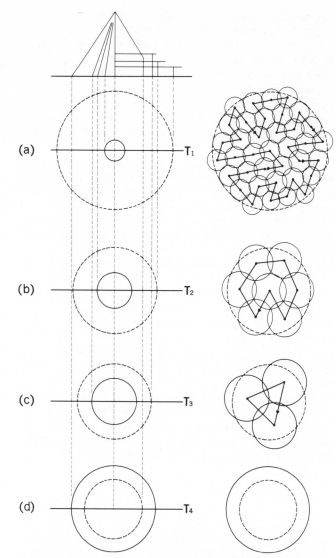

Fig. 118. *Stability and mobility of markets. Illustrating stabilization of a mobile firm under conditions of decreasing transfer costs. Dotted circles represent minimum range. Solid circles represent maximum range. Straight lines on the righthand side of the figure indicate path of mobile firm. The I's represent time instants. (From Stine 1962, ibid., p. 76; see fig. 117.)*

communities in accordance with a definite "law." He limited the application of his law to very high threshold goods ("style" or "specialty" shopping goods). The law states that "two centers attract trade from intermediate places approximately in direct proportion to the sizes of the centers and in inverse proportion to the square of the distances from these two centers to the intermediate place." This is the simple **gravity model,** usually restated as:

$$D_{jk} = \frac{D_{ij}}{1 + \sqrt{\dfrac{P_i}{P_j}}}$$

where D = distance

P = population

i and j are two settlements

and k is the "breaking point" between the two settlements, or the point at which a consumer would be equally disposed to shop at centers i and j.

Reilly and others have carried out a number of tests of this formula or "law"; the usual method has been to determine the limits of a trading center along all principal highway routes to competing centers, and then to compare the results with those obtained from a survey of consumer shopping habits in the trading area in question. The method has had a rather chequered career, and has been called" . . . marketing's first, most publicized, and possibly last 'law.'" The criticism is deserved: Reilly's law tells us nothing about why certain observed regularities occur. The weakness of Reilly's or any similar formulation, is that the concepts of physics are being used to approximate behavior, as if human movement could in some way be represented by the movement of electrons in a field of positive charges. Thus these models are static and descriptive; they miss out on the dynamics of the real world and the nonmechanistic bases of human behavior are missing. In Reilly's model in particular, there is no admission that places are simultaneously influenced by more than one other point in an interacting system. Finally, attention must be drawn to the long standing assumption, in both central place theory and gravity models, that consumers patronize the nearest center offering the desired tertiary service. From all the comments made about economic behavior in this book so far, it should be obvious that such a statement must be seriously challenged.

Huff's Formulation

The deterministic aspect of Reilly's formulation states that P_i/P_j represents the proportion of trade that moves in a particular direction. As an alternative notion, Huff in 1962 erected a model that allows for probabilistic situations. He allows some degree of choice between competing centers, within the overall constraint of a maximum distance that a consumer is willing to travel.

His model can be stated in this way: The *probability* that a consumer will be attracted from his residence, A, to a shopping center, 1, is directly related to the differing shopping opportunities of sizes S_1 to S_r which are located at travel times T_{A1} to T_{Ar} from A.

$$C_{A1} = \frac{\dfrac{S_1}{T_{A1}^x}}{\sum_{i=1}^{r} \left(\dfrac{S_i^a}{T_i^q} \right)}$$

where C is usually measured as retail expenditure by consumers at A as the shopping center 1, and the shopping center itself is usually measured in terms of floor space or retail sales volume, and distance often is driving time.

Unfortunately, in his calculation of relative utilities, Huff does not really go beyond Reilly. His numerator is a mass term, often measured as floor space devoted to the display of convenience goods or shopping goods, and his denominator a function of distance (travel time). A series of distance exponents can be used (the x of T_{A1}^x), varying with the threshold and range values of the goods and supported by evidence of varying consumer search efforts.

Berry waxes eloquent about this model: "It provides a very good replication of actual behavior . . . since his formulation stems, not from Reilly's empirical rules, but from a reasonable theory of individual choice behavior, it has sound foundations. . . ."

However, Thompson points out that Huff is still using only two variables, although there are in fact many more that affect consumer behavior. The real contribution of this formulation is the use of the probabilistic rather than deterministic aspect of consumer shopping patterns. Even here, Thompson queries the assumption of problem-solving decisions, attributing much consumer behavior to habit. Similarly, Huff assumes an economically rational framework to consumer decision making, whereas the perception of shopping alternatives by the "satisficing" consumer, with his imperfect ability to perceive his suburban milieu in all its objective complexity, may be very different. If Huff's model were really to represent consumer behavior, the **virtual space** of each consumer or class of consumer would have to be separated from objective reality. Only then could a model be designed to represent real-world consumer choices.

Toward Reality

Many of the analytic techniques discussed here, including the central place model, implicitly assume that the consumer purchases a good or service from the nearest source. Even the most critical revisors of the central place model have retained this particular supposition, and it is commonly used by marketing analysts. Christaller allowed only two exceptions to it:

1. *If by venturing to a more distant center of the same hierarchical order the savings incurred through purchasing "sale" items exceeds the additional transport cost.*

2. *If the consumer purchases both low order and high order goods at the same high order center, when that high order center is more distant than the closest low order center.*

However, it is assumed that the high order center *is* the nearest of its type to the consumer. Both of these "exceptions" of course still fall in the framework of economic rationality. Thus the consumer, in making a tertiary activity consumption decision, must under these ground rules:

1. *Be invariably motivated to minimize transportation costs and maximize purchases, under a great variety of individual circumstances.*

2. *Have perfect information about all distances to centers.*

3. *Have perfect information about all price variations among the standard tertiary items, and react rationally to even narrow price differences on each item.*

Deviations from the Assumptions

In the real world multipurpose journeys are frequent. This very expansion of trips (journeys to work, school, friends, entertainment, etc.) opens up a new and expanding information field. There are a growing number of feasible alternatives open to consumers in market-exchange economies as per capita income increases, education widens awareness of alternatives and decreases rural isolation, tertiary facilities expand with the "affluent" society, and general consumer mobility increases with increased automobile ownership. Thus Pred concluded that the array of tertiary choices confronting the increasingly motorized consumer is ". . . multiplied by the vastness of his visual information field, or more precisely . . . [by] . . . the exposure to alternatives that occurs is association with the journey to work and other trips whose primary objective is *not* that of purchasing goods and services. . . ."

A number of other real-world factors are of importance. It has already been noted that few people in market-exchange economies calculate detailed transport costs. Many potential savings are too small, irrelevant, or simply not perceived. Life style or class variations may be powerful influences in determining consumer preference. Such subcultural and socioeconomic variations also lead to blurring of the distinction between low order and high order goods. What is a convenience good to one group, subjected to only limited search, may be a shopping good and

subjected to much search activity by another group. Even within a group and among individuals or one individual, a convenience good at one particular time may be perceived as a shopping good at some other time.

Some empirical work has been done on the degree to which consumers do minimize their shopping trips in distance terms. Although some consumers consider distance reduction some of the time, they do not always do so. Clark was able to show that travel to the nearest center varies by order in the hierarchy and the degree of search involved. Trips for low order goods bought at neighborhood centers were usually limited to the nearest center, while trips for higher order goods or to higher order centers were rarely to the nearest center.

Model and Reality

Pred has attempted to compare the shopping patterns of the central place construct with what might happen in reality. Figures 119 and 120 show the residences of a number of consumers and two shopping centers (*m* and *n*) to which journeys can be made to purchase a single good.

In figure 119 each journey-to-consume is represented by a line from the residence to the center of purchase. These trips are shown to terminate at the nearest center, under central place model assumptions: all the journeyers to *m* live closer to *m* than *n*, and vice versa. In figure 120 the constraints are loosened, and four of the fourteen consumers are shown as traveling to nonproximate centers. Four of the six consumers traveling to *m* are behaving as expected from the central place model, but one is traveling in from *n*'s proximate trade area, and another from a market area to the south. A similar situation is found around *n*.

Figure 121 attempts to link the hypothetical pattern of figure 120 with the behavioral matrix in an attempt to interpret the consumer's imagined information and ability to use it. In this hypothetical situation, three out of the four consumers travel longer distances despite the fact that they are probably aware of the nearer centers. The reasons include low aspiration levels toward time and distance costs, combination with some other journey purpose, and miscellaneous personal factors.

The notable features of Pred's use of this heuristic device in the consumer situation is that it points to the fact that consumers are boundedly rational satisficers, not identically thinking economic men who seek to optimize by minimizing travel efforts. If the world were inhabited by such people all fourteen lines would terminate in the lower right-hand corner of the matrix.

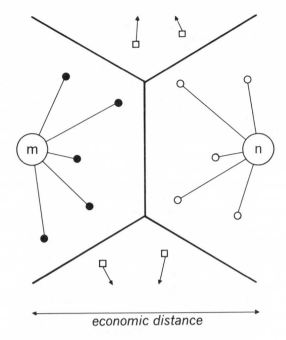

Fig. 119. *Journey to shop: trip destinations according to the central place model. (From Allen Pred,* Behavior and Location, *1967, p. 115, by courtesy of the Department of Geography, Royal University of Lund, Sweden.)*

economic distance

m,n   *shopping centers of the same rank*

———→   *movement*

● ○ □   *shoppers' residences*

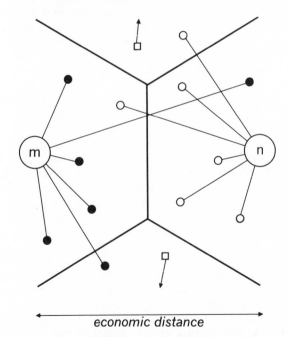

economic distance

m,n   *shopping centers of the same rank*

———→   *movement*

● ○ □   *shoppers' residences*

Fig. 120. *Journey to shop: trip destinations relaxing the assumptions of the central place model. (From Pred 1967, ibid.)*

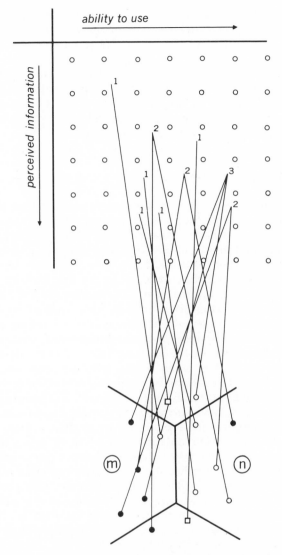

ability to use

perceived information

Fig. 121. *Journey to shop: linkage to Pred's behavioral matrix. (From Pred 1967, ibid., p. 118; see fig. 119.)*

The use of such a device in this consumer situation is supported by a wide range of literature. Pred goes still further by taking account of information fields, space preferences, and a variety of economic, psychological, and sociological factors. Thus he provides us with a first step toward a more complete understanding of consumer behavior, considered in the next section.

Consumer Behavior

Marketing geographers and others concerned with tertiary activities have recently begun to show more interest in the viewpoint of the consumer. The infinite number of factors that may influence the consumer at the time of his (or, more often, her) decision to journey in search of shop or service, or at the actual point of purchase, can no longer be ignored. Contemporary retail research draws on many fields. There is no simple way of explaining or understanding consumer behavior. But the fact that there is no neat solution to the problem is no reason for ignoring it—which is what happens when behavioral factors are held constant. The following pages are concerned with some of these factors.

Consumer Research

It has been pointed out in recent years that the consumer is neither wholly rational, as most economists would have us believe, nor wholly subject to whim and emotion, as many psychologists and advertisers seem to think. Nevertheless research work on consumer behavior tends to fall into two basic groups, one dominated by the rationalist and the other by the cognitive-symbolic view. In the former, economic motives, the allocation of scarce resources, and direct responses to economic stimuli, such as price changes, are the basis for decision. In the latter, some account is taken of cognitive and perceptual processes. The rationalist view suggests that motivations and attitudes are relatively unimportant, particularly with so-called convenience goods, and that shopping for food is no more than a weekly routine governed only by the desire to select the most convenient, best valued products at the nearest center. Motives, other than the purely economic, are seen as playing little or no role in the decision process. However, a growing sector of the research work is concerned with the consumer as heavily influenced by selective perception of advertising and packaging, as well as by group and class life styles and other cultural factors. The individual consumer has even been called a "dynamic symbol," fulfilling a particular life style that he shares with other members of his group. This continuum of views, from economic rationality to consumer perception, underlies the interdisciplinary perspective of the analysis of consumer behavior.

The Consumer

No consumer behavior is simply economic. It always is something more than a product that is sold, and something more than money that is the object of the sale. Indeed, the purely economic ingredient of a transaction may be almost nil.

The economic behavior of the consumer is much influenced by the specificity, communality, strength, and persistence of his *wants* or *needs*. All of these are related to his sociocultural situation.

The concept of *specificity of economic needs* covers a wide range. Specific wants and needs may be for anything from a particular brand of a product to "something to eat." At the opposite extreme are such vague desires as wanting to lead the "good" life, without bothering to think whether this means a particular job, a particular wife, or a particular reward. These vague needs are channeled into particular activities by cultural values or norms, which act as guides or referents for behavior. Thus in our culture, if one needs to maximize prestige he will do well to become a millionaire, write a best selling novel, or be a movie star. If, on the other hand, the need is for prestige with some small but elite group, he should set about acquiring the characteristics of that group.

The *communality of wants* is similarly bound up with cultural influence. This is illustrated by the *fashion cycle*. In capitalist societal systems this means that business subsystems of clothing and accessories develop styles with as wide a popular appeal as possible, given the nature of the group aimed at. The interactions between entrepreneurs, designers, fashion leaders, and customers are very complex, since they operate through such intermediaries as retail store buyers, advertising and fashion editors, and so on. The outcome is complex too, an interplay between industry trying to make women change their style of dress frequently, and consumers who from time to time want to change designs, materials and colors. Thus there is a communality of economic needs, but general needs are more widespread than specific ones. Every family wants a refrigerator, but only a limited number want four-foot high refrigerators in purple enamel!

The *strength of needs* or wants is closely related to cultural influences, especially through contacts with immediate face-to-face groups. Thus a group member may want an object because every other group member owns that object, or the member may want an object just because no one else in the group has it. How many present owners of Cadillacs would want to keep them if suddenly everybody could afford one? There is also a hierarchy of wants that for most of us is conditioned in part by group norms and in part by economic circumstances.

Finally, *persistence of wants and needs* is highly variable. A consumer may want a new car every year or every six years; he may want an ice cream every day or every month. Among the most persistent wants are the essentially cultural ones, which bolster the desire to belong to a group, or satisfy the desire for recognition.

The consumer, then, is culture bound. Most of the consumer's preferences are culture-bound preferences, decisions reached along the scale of choices postulated earlier (table 4). But they are constrained in the actual choice making situation by a cultural value-system. It may not be continually apparent to us in our roles as consumers that the choices we are making are both boundedly rational and culturally determined. But it is the culture that provides us with specific goals and norms.

Probably there will not be enough dried octopus, codpieces, and hookahs sold in Omaha in 1970 to support a single person's activities for a week, yet at one time or another and in one place and another, these have been standard items of use. All of them satisfy normal human wants that are in our culture directed in part toward the purchase of shrimp, hairdressing, neckties, and cigarettes . . . for the natural wants for excitement, one can attend a wrestling match, become a sports car enthusiast, take up skiing, purchase a scuba diving outfit, turn on television, or purchase a paperback mystery. One may not engage in a duel, shoot Indians, bait bears, or attend a cockfight.

Thus Tucker describes the culture boundedness of consumer decisions. He goes further, and identifies subcultural traits within the United States that persists despite the trend toward uniformity brought by the mass media, and which are reflected in the production and marketing of economic items.

The West Coast drinks more gin and vodka, the East more Scotch, and the South more bourbon . . . Artichokes are . . . important food items in the Italian section of Manhattan . . . in central Illinois or South Carolina they are rarities that most shoppers stare at in perplexity. Maxwell House coffee has a special blend for its western customers, a darker, stronger roast than is popular in the East. Beef supplied to northern and eastern markets is heavier and hung longer than that available in the South and West, where "baby beef" is popular. College dormitories in the Mid-West generally avoid serving lamb, because many of their occupants regard it as inedible.

Models of Consumer Behavior

Researchers in the area of consumer behavior have produced a number of alternative models, theories, and explanations to help explain consumer motivation and purchase patterns. Some have attempted to take account of the social milieu and the "state" of the individual at the time of decision making. Others have stressed the economic constraints within which consumer purchases are made, while at the same time recognizing the psychological component of the decision process. At least one comprehensive attempt has been made to represent consumer behavior in terms of a decision making process that leads from distributor or manufacturer to consumer and back again, via various feedback effects.

A more recent model by Howard and Sheth in-

cludes habitual responses and problem solving behavior in a framework of learning theory. Figure 122 shows a central box delineating the various internal variables and processes that represent the "state" of the buyer (compare the "black box" of chapter 4). The inputs to these internal states are internal stimuli and influences from the retail or tertiary environment and the socioeconomic milieu. The outputs include a range of responses based on the interaction between the internal states and external stimuli.

The left-hand side of diagram represents a set of three variables or inputs concerning brand choice, service choice, and center choice. Significate stimuli communicate information about price, quality, service, distinctiveness, or availability through the brand objects themselves; symbolic communication is linguistic or pictorial symbolization via advertising, mail-order catalogues, or some other selling technique. The third input to the internal state is the information that the decision maker's social environment (family, **reference group,** or friends) provides for him.

The internal variables fall into two categories in this model: those concerned with *perception*, and those concerned with *learning*. Among the components of the learning process are motives, evoked sets, decision mediators, predisposition, inhibitors, and satisfaction. Specific motives include such factors as the nutritional value or flavor of a food product; nonspecific motives would include, for instance, anxiety about overweight or ill health. To every set of brands, centers, or services, some label, symbol, or brand name is attached. This symbolism conveys certain meanings to the consumer, including an estimate of the object's potential to satisfy his needs or wants. Gradually the consumer works out a set of rules for matching objects with motives and ranking them in terms of their ability to satisfy him.

For any specific object, reinforcement of motivation (usually through satisfaction of a need or want by means of that object) creates a *predisposition* toward that object. But even when the consumer is thus predisposed, certain disruptive factors, or *inhibitors*, may distort the final choice. Examples of inhibitors are high price, lack of availability, pressure of time, and financial constraints. Continual occurrence of any of these inhibiting factors will sooner or later cause the consumer to place limitations on his own search behavior; for instance, he may stop going to any but the cheapest stores.

The last-named component of the learning process, satisfaction, indicates the degree to which the expectations in which the choice was made are met in the outcome. The resulting level of satisfaction or dissatisfaction, as compared to the original aspirations, can obviously influence the next choice.

The operation of all six learning variables depends

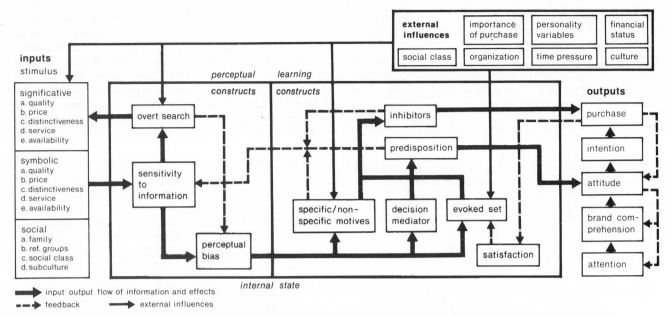

inputs
stimulus

| | perceptual | learning |
| significative | constructs | constructs |

significative
a. quality
b. price
c. distinctiveness
d. service
e. availability

symbolic
a. quality
b. price
c. distinctiveness
d. service
e. availability

social
a. family
b. ref. groups
c. social class
d. subculture

external influences — importance of purchase · personality variables · financial status · social class · organization · time pressure · culture

overt search

sensitivity to information

perceptual bias

inhibitors

predisposition

specific/non-specific motives · decision mediator · evoked set

satisfaction

outputs
purchase
intention
attitude
brand comprehension
attention

internal state

→ input output flow of information and effects
---► feedback
→ external influences

Fig. 122. *A model of buyer behavior. (From John A. Howard and Jagdish N. Sheth, "A Theory of Buyer Behavior,"* in Perspectives in Consumer Behavior *by Harold H. Kassarjian and Thomas S. Robertson. Copyright © 1968 by Scott, Foresman and Company.)*

to some extent on the length of the decision process. Thus *extensive* search behavior involves active information seeking, and deliberate reasoning, in the course of which extensive sets of objects are evoked. A major purchase such as a house or college education usually involves such behavior. By contrast, *limited problem solving* usually involves moderate predispositions, and information is sought on a relative rather than an absolute basis. Such behavior tends to accompany the purchase of goods or services that are frequently needed, but still far from routine—a new suit, say, rather than a pair of socks. Finally, routine or *habitual* responses are based on accumulated experience and information, with a high level of predisposition toward a known product or service center. The consumer is unlikely to actively seek information, and the information he does use will tend to support his habitual choice.

The function of *perceptual* factors in consumer behavior is to procure and process information relevant to the particular decision. Perceptual processes filter and select the objective information provided by the experiental environment (see chapter 4). In this way the decision maker's behavioral milieu is created.

The set of external variables that influence the consumer are internalized in his perceptual and cognitive processes. Both class and cultural factors are of major significance in these processes. Class differences seem to affect every aspect of learning except predisposition and satisfaction. The importance of financial constraints has already been noted. Per-

sonality constraints include self-confidence, anxiety, and risk reduction, all of which may widen or reduce the range of choices from which the final response is selected.

The outputs in figure 122 form a hierarchy of response variables similar to those used in research on other types of decision. "Attention" simply indicates the degree of awareness of the inputs, whether or not an environmental stimulus is received by the consumer. "Comprehension" indicates the degree of understanding, recall, and recognition that exists in the store of information, that is, it is to some extent a measure of the thought and remembrance attached to particular objects. "Attitudes" are the evaluations of the object or objects with respect to the aspirations of the consumer; they are directly related to the predispositions that allocate some degree of confidence to the outcome or eventual overt act. "Intention" has been described as "the buyer's forecast of which brand he will buy." "Purchase behavior" is the final overt act, the final decision to buy product X, utilize service Y, or patronize center Z.

A number of feedback effects are incorporated into this model. Thus learning indirectly governs perception; decision mediators are learned from past experiences and current information; information can arise from the tertiary environment or the whole socioeconomic environment; and the final choice feeds back to the distributor and the manufacturer.

Although models of this type are basically concerned with brand choice, more general implications of these relationships are obvious, and consumer behavior is clearly of relevance to geographers. But perhaps they are less concerned with the final brand choice between, say, Kellogg's or Post cornflakes, than with the actual site at which cornflakes (a convenience good) and/or a refrigerator (a shopping good) are purchased and supplied. However, it is difficult to separate these two factors. Brand choice may be uppermost in a consumer's mind at the time of deciding which shopping center to patronize, and the lack of availability of the desired brand may decide the final decision. Under certain pressures, such as time or money, both brand choice and site choice may be much more limited.

Conclusion

Traditionally, the reasons leading to brand, product, or site choice have been explained in purely economic terms derived largely from microeconomics (that is, the theory of the firm and pricing) and based on the principles of utility and satisfaction. According to these principles, the consumer will buy, and travel to buy, those quantities of products where the **marginal utility** (additional satisfaction from consuming one more unit) per dollar's worth of any one product equals the marginal utility per dollar's worth of any other product for a given time period. The assumption is that the consumer derives satisfaction from consumption, and that he seeks to maximize his overall satisfaction within the limitations of his income in relation to a given set of prices. Thus rational economic behavior is assumed in regard to the goods bought. We can add that in minimizing the costs of acquiring those goods he would minimize transportation costs and move to the nearest shopping center.

This microeconomic model falls short of satisfactorily explaining consumer behavior because of the assumptions about maximizing rather than satisficing behavior, because it omits other factors influencing behavior, and because of the difficulties of measuring "utility." Research has shown that most consumers in fact cannot tell one gasoline from another, cannot distinguish among brands of colas, cigarettes, or beers, and yet they display great brand loyalty. Apparently they are responding to more than a physical product, in fact to some symbol. Other kinds of consumer decision may well be made in this symbolic way.

Geographic Applications

Most geographic research in the tertiary sector has been concerned with describing retailing pat-

terns rather than with explaining how they arise. Thus any explanation has usually been of some limited nature, like the central place model. A few of the attempts at going beyond this simplistic level are described below.

Bucklin's Analysis

In a 1967 study of the Oakland retailing scene, L. P. Bucklin detected two basic types of consumer behavior, *full-search shopping* and *limited-search shopping*. He further divided the latter into *directed* and *casual*.

The activity known as *full-search shopping* involves, as its name implies, much time spent on the search process.

In part this is because the merchandise she (the consumer) wishes to buy possesses a high "social visibility," is highly differentiated, and is usually subject to rapid shifts in style. These products are not only seen by persons important to the consumer, but they provide a major basis for these persons to judge her taste—indeed, her very social position. Through careful selection of products of high social visibility, consequently, the consumer may reveal to others the type of person she is, and may publicize her achievements and social attainments.

In the case of *limited search (directed) shopping* the goods involved are both less expensive and less prestigious, but expensive enough to make their purchase a serious matter. Quality and product feature are still important, but price is now the chief criterion. However, because such goods form a smaller part of the social milieu, the actual search activity is more limited. Indeed, where standard items are concerned the search may be limited to known stores of a certain perceived image.

Finally, *limited-search (casual) shopping* is concerned with inexpensive items of everyday use that must be replaced quite frequently. For these the consumer turns to the nearest center.

Figure 123 shows these ideas within a **benefit-cost** framework. In figure 123a the relationship between the attraction and size of a center is plotted; each of the curves represents a different consumer attitude toward solving the good/service problem. With *full-search* shopping there is an increasing advantage with increasing center size, although the curve becomes less steep as very large centers have to be distinguished or chosen between. However, *casual* shopping has value in even small centers. On the other hand, *directed* shopping perceives the stores located in smaller centers as offering the best value. Very small centers have little worth, but

a. center size and level of attraction

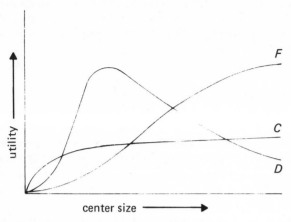

F-full search, C-causal, D-directed

b. user cost and distance

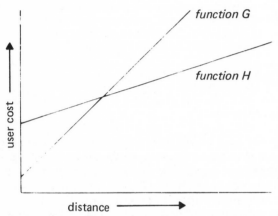

Fig. 123. *Patterns of shopping behavior as they relate to the attraction of a retail center and the cost of using that center. (Reprinted from L.P. Bucklin,* Shopping Patterns in Urban Areas, *1967, p. 124, by permission of the editor, Institute of Business and Economic Research Special Publications, University of California, Berkeley. Copyright © 1967 by the Regents of the University of California.)*

benefits climb steeply, falling only with large centers as they can add little or no benefit.

Figure 123b illustrates the shopper's perception of the costs of shopping relative to distance. The central place model, of course, portrays costs as comparable among all consumers. But here two alternative situations are postulated. Function G, as compared to function H, shows a much higher cost associated with distance. Such distances occur with varying time costs and the character of the shopping to be carried out. Both functions show positive costs at the origin, reflecting the degree of congestion about a local center or the lack of public transit. Thus the costs of using such a center may be high, regardless of distance.

The actual techniques utilized are, however, derived from the gravity model. Thus the size of the shopping center is seen as a proxy for the benefit the consumer receives from shopping at it; distance is used as a proxy for facilities. Although Bucklin attempts to take note of consumer decision making in his hierarchy of search activity, and to overcome the assumption of collectively perceived values assumed in gravity model, he still cannot overcome the inherent weakness of any such model, which is that it can account for spatial consumer movements only in terms of "mass" attraction.

A Shopping Center Utility Survey

R. G. Golledge has summarized the relevance of some forms of learning theory to geography, among which is the concept identification or **discrimination learning** model. This learning model has often been put into the framework of **S-R Theory.** Thus decision makers are seen as discriminating among responses according to the type, force, and frequency of reinforcement—in other words, in a *habitual* manner. A variant of this approach states that in fact responses are elicited by a set of stimuli after trial-and-error behavior has occurred. The discrimination-learning model is based on the task of finding which *cue* or *symbol* is relevant in a given problem situation. Once an action becomes learned, and the cue or symbol is recognized, future responses are based on that cue. In other words the consumer learns a response pattern and may develop a habitual response to it. It is in this context that market researchers have shown the use and value of brand names, particular distinctive packaging, and advertising. Geographers have examined similar situations, as in shopping journey patterns, where it is assumed that shoppers select alternative routes from a total array of routes and then test them. If a choice leads to an error or an unsatisfactory trip sequence, then that route may be discarded and a new choice made.

Despite the large number of criteria that may influence the choice of a response path, there are some cues or symbols that are more obvious than others. Thus for a shopping item that is the object of extensive search, the most relevant cues for achieving a satisfactory consumer response might be:

1. *The presence of a department store.*
2. *Some minimum range of functions.*
3. *The distance to be traveled.*

On the other hand, for a particular consumer irrelevant cues might be:

1. *The recommendation of a friend.*
2. *The presence of a restaurant.*
3. *The presence of a movie theatre.*

To some other consumer, these cues might be extremely relevant. In any case, perceived relevance determines which cues are acted upon.

Golledge conducted a small study of relevant cues in Columbus, Ohio; those he identified are ranked in table 42. These results should be compared with those given below for the two supermarkets. The conclusion he draws from his study is that there are relevant cues, particularly for limited search shopping, and that consumers do in part respond in their most frequent shopping trips to such symbolic factors. Thus as trip purpose changes the relevant cues change, from (say) a work trip to a shopping trip.

Table 42. *Cues for Selection of Shopping Centers*

attribute	frequency of rank 1	proportion of times attribute was ranked "1"
closeness	112	35.7
variety of stores	90	28.7
quality of products	32	10.2
parking	28	8.9
prices	15	4.8
service quality	6	2.0
freeway access	4	1.7

Source: Shopping Center Utility Survey, Dept. of Geography, The Ohio State University, 1967. Quoted in Golledge, 1969, p. 118.

Shopping Alternatives

A secondary analysis (i.e., later analysis of data collected earlier by someone else) of household shopping movements in Cedar Rapids, Iowa, focused on two main areas:

1. *The relationship between the location of stores actually visited by a consumer and their* **opportunity set.**
2. *The degree of repetition with which particular stores are patronized.*

The Opportunity Set. The term "opportunity set" is used in order to suggest that a consumer may view shopping opportunities as a "spatially arrayed set of alternatives from which one or more individual establishments are to be chosen." Figure 124 indicates the kind of opportunity surface that would exist around the "rational" consumer, since it contains complete information about the density and distribution of all grocery stores in Cedar Rapids.

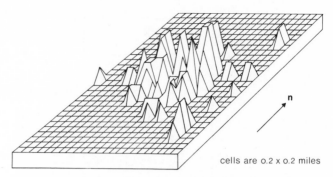

cells are 0.2 x 0.2 miles

Fig. 124. *Opportunity surface for grocery stores, Cedar Rapids, Iowa, 1949. The cells are 0.2 x 0.2 miles. The surface represents the spatial distribution of the alternate choices among, and the density of, grocery stores. (Reprinted from D.F. Marble and S. Bowlby, "Shopping Alternatives and Recurrent Travel Patterns," Studies in Geography, no. 16, 1968, p. 47, by courtesy of the Department of Geography, Northwestern University.)*

Distance is shown here as airline distance. It could also be represented as travel time, although this would cause short-run cyclical distortions in accordance with daily, weekly, and seasonal changes in traffic density and flow.

But spatial factors are only one side of the story. In any case, the consumer is most unlikely to have complete information about all stores in the area. Accordingly, an opportunity surface of a higher dimensionality is introduced. Partial or incorrect information, particular perceptions of price, quality, and brand images distort the objective location of shopping opportunities. Figure 125 illustrates this three-dimensional choice space. In this example, we could postulate that shop *Y* is chosen over shop *X*, even though the latter is closer to the consumer in physical distance terms, because *OX* is not perceived as nearer than *OY*. Thus the consumer may be selecting stores by price instead of distance. Hence stores selling goods at a lower rate than the consumer's threshold of price would occur in the choice space and others would not. This choice space would fluctuate with fluctuations in the stores' pricing policy if the consumer was aware of such changes. In reality the consumer has only very incomplete information, and each consumer's choice space may be very distorted. The consumer may be aware to some degree of this distortion (i.e., uncertain as to choice), and he may try to improve his chance of making a satisfactory decision by searching for additional information. To be motivated to undertake such search activity, the consumer would have to:

1. *Believe that a better choice does exist.*
2. *Be able to estimate the improvement in return he can expect for searching.*
3. *Be able to incur less than satisfactory returns if an incorrect choice is made.*

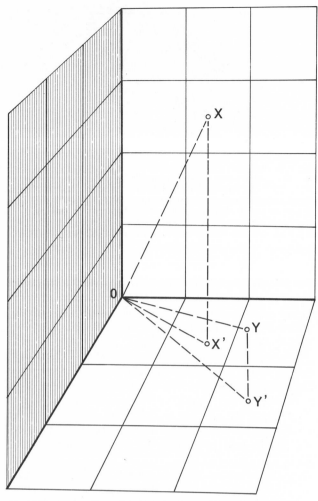

Fig. 125. *Three-dimensional choice space. Given the opportunity surface of fig. 124, the problem becomes one of choosing which grocery store you want to visit. In the terms of this three-dimensional choice space, this would be the point nearest to the origin of the coordinate system; this may lead to selecting a grocery store which is not the nearest in physical dimensions. Hence destination Y' would be closer, even though OX'<OY' since OY<OX, where the dimension XX' and YY' represents relative prices, qualities, etc. (From Marble and Bowlby 1968, ibid., p. 48; see fig. 124.)*

This search for additional information may lead to much switching of stores and brands. Such behavior can be explained in terms of **probabilistic clues** and incomplete **validation.** Where a low level of validation occurs, it is assumed that consumers quickly abandon attempts to search for better solutions, preferring to repeat some previously learned and moderately successful shopping trip. But if the search procedure is successful and the validation is high, the opportunity surface may include non-repetitive shopping trips.

Repetitive Behavior. Because of the complexity of the real-world choice situation, and the incompleteness of information about it, repetitive trips tend

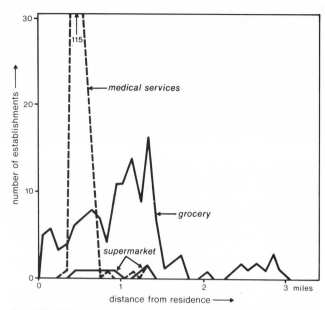

Fig. 126. *Number of establishments by distance from a sample household for selected functions, Cedar Rapids, Iowa, 1949. (From Marble and Bowlby 1968, ibid., p. 59; see fig. 124.)*

to be made when validation is slow and search activity minimal. If many stores sell the same convenience good, and this is the type of good required, then it is probable that little difference is perceived between stores. Thus the consumer's choice space will be relatively limited, and repetitive movements to the same store will occur. However, even where validation is high, search activity may be restricted if the good is of small unit value or of relatively low **social visibility.** Again in these cases trips would tend to be of a habitual and repetitive nature.

Empirical Tests. For each household for which data were available for the 30-day period under study an opportunity surface was set up utilizing a two-dimensional choice space (figure 126). Since Cedar Rapids was then only a medium-sized city of some 70,000 population (it now has over 100,000) it was assumed that most households were aware of the total set of opportunities.

Figure 127 shows the cumulative frequency distribution of distances to the nearest stores and services for the sample households. For the majority of consumers grocery stores were the most accessible, followed by supermarkets and medical services. For each store or service category it was possible to define a frequency distribution of household-to-store distances, as well as to calculate a minimum household-to-store distance. Obviously the distribution of minimum distances defines the limit of travel, below which no stores occur. Where shops are visited for other than distance or convenience reasons there will be a deviation from this minimum travel distance. Table 43 shows that there was con-

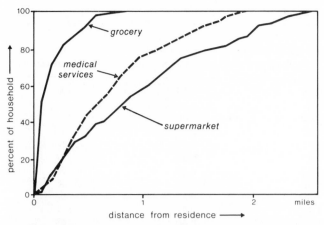

Fig. 127. *Distance from residence to nearest establishment for selected functions, Cedar Rapids, Iowa, 1949. (From Marble and Bowlby 1968, ibid., p. 60.)*

siderable variation in distance traveled. Supermarket trips were closest to distance minimization, while restaurant trips showed a much larger deviation, the mean distance for a restaurant trip actually exceeding the mean household-tertiary activity distance for all restaurants.

Table 43. *Comparative Distances for Four Selected Tertiary Activities, Cedar Rapids, Iowa, 1949*

	distance to tertiary establishment (in miles)			
function	mean minimum	mean	mean travel distance	percent single purpose trips
grocery	0.19	1.61	0.60	60
supermarket	0.70	1.37	0.78	34
clothing	1.23	1.33	1.30	4
restaurant	0.32	1.48	1.65	11

Source: D.F. Marble and S.R. Bowlby, "Shopping Alternatives and Recurrent Travel Patterns," in F. Horton, ed., *Geographic Studies of Urban Transportation and Network Analysis,* Northwestern University, Studies in Geography No. 16, 1968, p. 62.

In total trip terms (i.e., for all journey purposes), it was found that about 75 percent of the stops of an average household are to repetitiously visited locations, and that between 25 and 50 percent of these are repeated stops for retail purposes. There was considerable stability in the choice spaces of the consumers, and a large proportion of the 30-day total trips involved repetitious stops at 10 to 20 different locations. To measure this level of repetition, the ratio was calculated of the average number of repetitious trips to the total trips for each retail category. Thus in table 44 a value of 1.0 would indicate completely repetitive behavior, and zero no repetition. Stops for purposes with repetitious ratios over 0.8

are all made within 1 mile of the home, and stops for purposes with low repetition ratios were all 1 mile or more away from the consumer's residence.

One reason put forward for repetitious behavior was that it reduces uncertainty and search effort. Table 44 does not show any close relationship between habitual trips and the frequency with which trips are made. But when these are recategorized as in table 45, a new pattern emerges. The categories here are based on the degree of search activity and on the different types of goods and services. It will be seen that convenience and institutional trips appear as highly repetitious, followed by trips to entertainments and, finally, trips to purchase shopping goods. Only medical services seem to occupy an anomalous position, but this category includes a wide range of specialized and general services. As the repetition ratio declines, an increase in the distance traveled is noted, although this does not hold for all groups. Note that in every case consumers traveled further than the minimum average distance for even repetitious, low search convenience goods. Thus each consumer had a wide range of stores to choose from so that even the habitually visited location choice cannot be explained simply as an attempt to minimize physical distance. However, it does appear that the more repetitious and more frequent the convenience shopping, the shorter the average distance consumers normally travel.

The frequency of stops seems to be positively related to the repetition ratio for both convenience goods and entertainment (table 45). For other groups, however, there is no clear relationship. This seems to indicate that the higher value of shopping goods provides sufficient search motivation for different shops to be tried even on fairly frequent types of trips.

This simple analysis, although restricted to single-purpose trips, is an excellent first step toward a more realistic concern with consumer behavior. The same approach is now being extended to changes through time in opportunity sets.

Other Studies

Although very little other work has dealt directly with consumer behavior in geography, a few studies have dealt with the problem tangentially. Thus L. Curry, in the course of his attempts in the past ten years to modify the central place model, makes certain inferences about consumer behavior. Since he sees the behavioral milieu and the economic system as interdependent, he depicts consumer behavior as related to certain economic constraints. But the food stocks or appliances and clothes that a consumer

Table 44. *Repetition and Trip Purpose, Cedar Rapids, Iowa, 1949*

purpose	repetition ratio	average number of stops	average distance to repetitious stops (miles)	average minimum distance to establishment (miles)	total number of establishments
grocery	0.92	6.49	0.46	0.18	153
bank, loan, other financial	0.86	1.78	0.89	1.00	59
gasoline	0.85	1.17	0.93	0.26	97
supermarket	0.84	3.37	0.72	0.70	10
public office	0.83	2.84	0.83	0.38	107
tavern	0.80	1.05	0.63	0.45	63
general store	0.77	4.18	0.92	0.36	34
restaurant	0.73	3.53	1.68	0.34	98
theater	0.71	2.49	1.29	0.87	7
candies	0.70	1.12	0.99	0.50	25
bottle club	0.69	1.43	1.03	0.91	54
department store	0.67	2.64	1.61	1.15	5
variety	0.66	1.97	1.36	0.62	8
medical	0.64	1.49	1.66	0.76	168
clothing	0.61	2.09	1.42	1.24	17

Source: D.F. Marble and S.R. Bowlby, "Shopping Alternatives and Recurrent Travel Patterns," in F. Horton, ed., *Geographic Studies of Urban Transportation and Network Analysis,* Northwestern University, Studies in Geography No. 16, 1968, p. 69.

Table 45. *Repetitive Activities by Purpose Group, Cedar Rapids, Iowa, 1949*

repetition rank	convenience goods type	no. of stops	av. dist. to rep. stop	entertainment type	no. of stops	av. dist. to rep. stop.	shopping goods type	no. of stops	av. dist. to rep. stop	institutional type	no. of stops	av. dist. to rep. stop
1	grocery	6.49	0.46									
2										bank	1.78	0.89
3	super-market	3.37	0.72									
4										public office	2.84	0.83
5	general store	4.18	0.92									
6				restau-rant	3.53	1.68						
7				theater	2.49	1.29						
8							candies	1.12	0.99			
9				bottle club	1.43	1.03						
10							dept. store	2.64	1.61			
11							variety	1.97	1.36			
12										medical	1.49	1.66
13							clothing	2.09	1.42			

Source: Marble and Bowbly, *Ibid.*, p. 70.

stores at home, the standard of living the entrepreneur or shopkeeper expects to enjoy, are as much cultural and social as they are economic. Curry also notes that the types of goods offered are sanctioned by the system. Thus the decline in the number of bakeries, fresh fish shops, and butchers is a function of the less frequent shopping trips induced by the wide range of goods offered by the supermarket. This tendency is aided by the domestic refrigerator and freezer, both of which stimulate the sales of

(a) "discount" supermarket

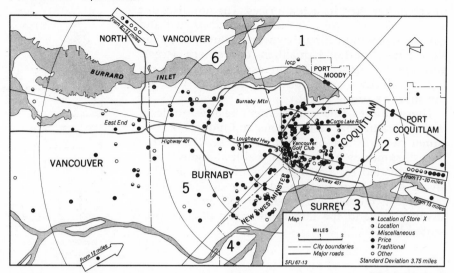

(b) "neighborhood" supermarket

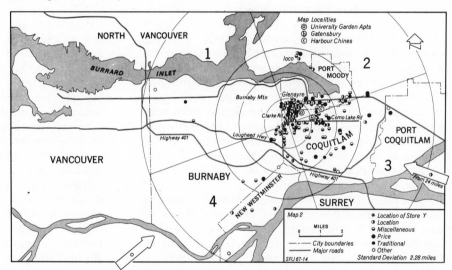

Fig. 128. *Trading areas of a "discount" and a "neighborhood" supermarket. From M.E. Eliot Hurst and J.B. Sellers, "An Analysis of the Spatial Distribution of Customers Around Two Grocery Retailing Operations,"* The Professional Geographer, *vol. 21, 1969, p. 185, reprinted by permission of the Association of American Geographers.)*

frozen and prepackaged baked goods, fish, and meats.

The system or structure that Curry generates through largely probabilistic and random processes does not have the symmetrical patterns of the central place model, his higher order centers do not include all lower order goods, nor does he assume discrete, nonoverlapping market areas. He sees that prices may be no more than "the posterior stamp of approval that society puts on a fairly efficient system."

Many of the empirical studies of shopping patterns also produce as a by-product certain observations about consumer behavior, though these are rarely systematized. For instance, a recent study of two supermarkets, one operating with a normal pricing

policy and the other with a discount operation revealed markedly different attitudes to the stores by consumers. The two stores showed a marked variation in their trading areas, although according to the central place model they both might be regarded as occurring at similar functional levels. Customers were questioned in an effort to detect the differences in consumer attitude apparently revealed by the distances they had willingly traveled to the discount supermarket. It was found that over half of this store's customers who were interviewed believed that the low prices attracted them. Their residences were scattered throughout the Vancouver metropolitan region; in some cases the distances traveled on single-purpose trips were considerable. But their behavior was related to their image of the store's prices rather than its actual prices. The nondiscount store's customers were spatially more restricted and gave answers indicating they were influenced by the store's neighborhood qualities, convenient access, and family "image." These results are of course highly selective, since consumer behavior was not the survey's prime target.

These studies, and many others besides, indicate that the traditional assumptions and models of consumer behavior are of only limited use. They show the consumer as a creature of habit at some levels, but motivated by a whole range of factors at other levels. Much more work needs to be done by geographers if models of consumer behavior are to advance beyond the largely heuristic devices presented here.

Conclusion

Berry has claimed that "central place theory constitutes a deductive base from which to understand" the apparent regularities of the tertiary activity system. But this seems open to question. It is obvious from our study of economic behavior up to this point that no adequate consideration of consumer behavior can be based on a mere cataloguing of business centers and other regularities over space and time. Any superstructure developed from such shaky foundations is bound to ignore the real world of price cutting, advertising, brand loyalties, brand switching, store images, entrepreneurial skill, consumer perception (itself based on a whole host of other factors), and past experience.

It has been claimed that tertiary economic activity can be understood exclusively in terms of central place theory. For this claim to hold, every tertiary supplier, whether retailer, physician or banker, would have to make an optimal location decision, and every consumer who used these tertiary services would have to be totally rational in so doing. Moreover, the supplier's decision to choose the site or situation for his shop, office, or bank, would have to be prescribed by the threshold notion. No central place activity could appear in an urban center unless the local population was of such size or wealth that the activity made a profit, or at least broke even. According to the central place model, a below-threshold activity would have to relocate at such a point in the hierarchy that it had greater access to consumers. Similarly, the entrepreneur or businessman would have to locate where profit was greatest.

In order to find the optimum location, however, the entrepreneur would need to know the location and consumption patterns of all his customers; the cost of getting goods for each consumer, from every

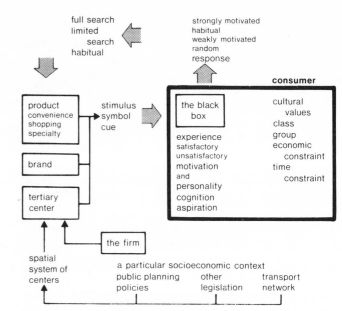

Fig. 129. *Summary: the tertiary system. This is an attempt to integrate some of the behavioral and other factors introduced in this chapter.*

competitive sales site; and the location and price-setting behavior of all his competitors, both present and potential. In addition, he would have to have an intimate working knowledge of urban land values. In other words, the model demands of the entrepreneur knowledge and capabilities that no human being (or computer) possesses or has access to. No satisficer could ever make the optimal decisions of the retailers described by Berry.

The central place model, as the concept of range implies, also requires the consumer to make a totally rational consumption decision. This concept assumes that movement will take place to the nearest source of goods and services. But for a variety of reasons, this does not always occur in the real world. The total rationality required of the consumer is apparently simple, and gives rise to the neat hexagonal service areas that have been illustrated above (figure 108). Consumer behavior, however, is neither totally rational, nor simple, nor neat.

Attempts to date have constituted a largely superficial examination of consumer actions. The attempts have been practical in the sense that they have been concerned with measures to help estimate the need for and location of new tertiary facilities, especially shopping centers, and most are still widely used. But, as several authors have pointed out, consideration of only one or two variables, with shallow empirical findings and no thorough theoretical underpinning, though giving reasonable results in the very short term, can in the long term only be disastrous. A thorough knowledge of consumer behavior would take into account such factors as attitudes, motivation, perception, decision making processes, and the whole complex of factors generated by the tertiary entrepreneurs. Our choice as economic geographers is between using "clean" but very "noisy" *gravity models*, or the less clean but much "quieter" *behavioral models*. As figure 129 indicates, the consumer must be viewed as a member of a particular dynamic socioeconomic environment, influenced by certain personality and psychological factors. The stimuli are denoted as "symbols" or "cues" that may have meaning for the individual or group. Thus consumers are shown as buying products not only for their intrinsic usefulness, but for what they mean and for the feelings they inspire. Only the behavioral model can encompass such variables.

Summary

1. In total, tertiary economic activities probably employ less than 10 percent of the world's labor force. But since these activities tend to increase with industrialization and urbanization, they may, on a smaller scale, employ over 40 percent of a nation's workforce. In addition, since they are dominantly urban activities, patterns of tertiary activities are concentrated in "central places."

2. The tertiary subsystem is made up of a service component, where the behavior of the customer is important—retailing, medical, education services; a trading component, such as various wholesaling activities; and a financial component including insurance and real estate. Since they are all oriented toward the consumer, all three groups have somewhat similar locational characteristics.

3. A central place model has been erected by Walter Christaller, and modified and extended by others, which purports to identify certain economic-geographic "laws" explaining the arrangement and location of retail and other activities. A relationship between city size, as measured by a greater range of tertiary activities, and the spacing of cities is postulated.

4. The model utilizes the now familiar partial equilibrium constraints (ubiquitous resources, population, purchasing power, etc., and economically rational consumer behavior). By developing the concepts of threshold and range, a system of orders or hierarchies of centers supplying tertiary services is built up. Low order centers with small threshold and range are spatially frequent, and the high order centers with large threshold and range are spatially infrequent.

5. The basic model has been extended and modified by a number of researchers including Lösch, but to date the most widely used has been the Berry-Garrison application to internal city patterns. Like the external pattern, the internal structure of cities includes nucleations of tertiary activities in a ranked order from grocery/corner store or neighborhood center up to regional centers and central business districts. This rank ordering again reflects increasing threshold and range, and decreasing frequency of occurrence.

6. In certain non-Western societies where transportation costs are high, movement slow and difficult, and income level low, a moving point or periodic market distribution system can arise. It can be partially explained in modified central place terms.

7. In addition to the central place model and its extensions, Reilly's "law" of retail gravitation, and Huff's probability model are examined. All share the same drawbacks—reliance on non-behavioral variables, assumption of economic rationality, and the use of unreal distance constraints which, among other things, assumes movement always occurs to the nearest city or shopping area.

8. A wide range of literature indicates, in fact, that the tertiary activity system is much more complex, and that the behavior of the consumer as satisficer, affected by store images, brand loyalties, and advertising, must be better understood if that complexity is to be satisfactorily explained.

9. Consumer research indicates that a wide range of factors, from economic motives to cultural and perceptual influences, provides the framework for consumer behavior. A number of models of behavior exist, but only one, set up by Howard and Sheth, utilizing a learning-perceptual framework, is examined here. Their approach encompasses a range of decision making from limited search and habitual routines to the more extensive full search procedures.

10. One application in geographical work of a similar conceptualization of consumer behavior is that of L. P. Bucklin, who examined patronage in Oakland retail outlets in terms of full and limited search shopping behavior. R. G. Golledge in another survey concentrated on habitual responses, and identified certain cues or symbols which once learned, were responded to in specific and repetitive ways. D. F. Marble and S. Bowlby identified a choice space or opportunity set which a consumer perceives and reacts to. They correlate habitual responses with repetitive visits to a small number of conveniently located stores, and full search problem solving behavior with non-repetitive trip making to a more limited in number, but dispersed, set of establishments.

11. These and other studies in geography and market research indicate that the traditional assumptions and models used to understand tertiary

economic activities are at best, superficial, and that further understanding can only come through more thorough behavioral analysis.

Further Reading

The "central place" approach to tertiary activity systems is best illustrated by

Berry, B. J. L. *Geography of Market Centers and Retail Distribution* (Englewood Cliffs: Prentice-Hall, 1967).

The original source for such an approach is

Christaller, W. *Central Places in Southern Germany*, translated by C. W. Baskin (Englewood Cliffs: Prentice-Hall, 1966). Originally published in German in 1933.

An annotated guide to the literature of central place studies is

Berry, B. J. L. and Pred, A. *Central Place Studies*, Regional Science Research Institute, Bibliography Series no. 1, 1961, with supplements.

The main modification to the basic central place model is stated in

Berry, B. J. L. and Garrison, W. "Recent Development of Central Place Theory," *Papers and Proceedings*, Regional Science Association, vol. 4, 1958, pp. 107–120.

The moving point solution is best introduced in

Stine, J. H. "Temporal Aspects of Tertiary Production Elements in Korea," in F. R. Pitts, ed. *Urban Systems and Economic Development* (Eugene: University of Oregon, 1962), pp. 65–68.

The general range of tertiary economic activities is set out in

McCarty, H. H. and Lindberg, J. B. *A Preface to Economic Geography* (Englewood Cliffs: Prentice-Hall, 1966), chapters 6, 7, and 8.

Some basic material on consumer behavior is covered in

Britt, S. H., ed. *Consumer Behavior and the Behavioral Sciences* (New York: Wiley, 1968).

Douglas, J., Field, G. A. and Tarpey, L. X. *Human Behavior in Marketing* (Columbus: Charles E. Merrill, 1967).

Howard, J. A. and Sheth, J. N. *The Theory of Buyer Behavior* (New York: Wiley, 1969).

Kassarjian, H. H. and Robertson, T. S. *Perspectives in Consumer Behavior* (Glenview, Illinois: Scott, Foresman and Co., 1968).

Nicosia, F. M. *Consumer Decision Processes* (Englewood Cliffs: Prentice-Hall, 1966).

The geographic behavioral case is put forward in

Bucklin, L. P. *Shopping Patterns in an Urban Area*, I.B.E.R. Special Publications (Berkeley: University of California, 1967).

Downs, R. "The Cognitive Structure of an Urban Shopping Center," *Environment and Behavior*, vol. 2, 1970, pp. 13–39.

Golledge, R. G. "The Geographical Relevance of some Learning Theories," in K. R. Cox and R. G. Golledge, eds. *Behavioral Problems in Geography: A Symposium*, Northwestern University Studies in Geography, no. 17, 1969.

Marble, D. F. and Bowlby, S. R. "Shopping Alternatives and Recurrent Travel Patterns," *Studies in Geography*, no. 16, Northwestern University, 1968, pp. 42–75.

Pred, A. *Behavior and Location*, parts 1 and 2 (Lund: C. W. K. Gleerup, 1967 and 1969).

Thompson, D. L. "Future Directions in Retail Area Research," *Economic Geography*, vol. 42, 1966, pp. 1–18.

eleven

Some Components of
the Tertiary Subsystem

In the previous chapter, we dealt with the tertiary subsystem as a whole. Here, we shall examine some of its individual components, as already listed in table 40. This will involve a fairly detailed review of retailing, and a somewhat briefer one of wholesaling, recreational activities, and medical services.

Retailing

The retail facilities of a city form a subsystem, a set of interrelated elements that interact to create a recognizable structure. H. F. Andrews has stressed the links between the behavior of the consumer and the entrepreneur—the subject of chapter 10—and the structure of the subsystem, dealt with here.

Retailing Processes

Figure 130 sets out the links that Andrews identifies, in terms of both a process-structure and a time-space framework. Taking up the theme where we left it in chapter 10, we can see how, in the retailing process, both consumer and entrepreneur exist in a particular spatial milieu. This milieu is determined by the perceptual-learning framework of the individual, on the one hand, and by the environment of social and nonsocial objects, on the other. This *experienced* and *felt* milieu has both time and space components. Thus the consumer may be concerned with, for example, some spatial allocation of expenditures at a particular point in time. The basic variables are depicted in the central box of the Howard-Sheth model (figure 122, above). But the situation also consists of social objects like family relationships and the extended social network in which the consumer has a role, including his social class and ethnic group. To these we must add nonsocial factors like the complete range of commodities and brands available in the society, or the type of shopping

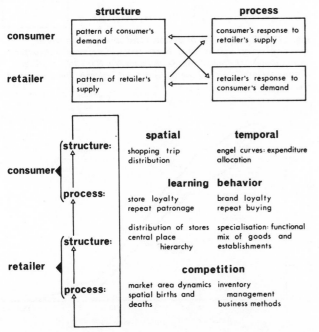

structure | process

consumer
- pattern of consumer's demand
- consumer's response to retailer's supply

retailer
- pattern of retailer's supply
- retailer's response to consumer's demand

consumer

structure:

spatial	temporal
shopping trip distribution	engel curves: expenditure allocation

learning behavior

store loyalty repeat patronage	brand loyalty repeat buying

process:

retailer

structure:

distribution of stores central place hierarchy	specialisation: functional mix of goods and establishments

competition

process:

market area dynamics spatial births and deaths	inventory management business methods

Fig. 130. *The tertiary system: the functional relationships between consumer and retailer and their spatial/temporal expression. (Reprinted from H.F. Andrews, "Consumer behavior and the tertiary activity system," London Essays in Regional Science, vol. 2, © 1971, Pion, London, figure 2, p. 8, by permission of Prior Press.)*

center from which the consumer is going to select his own purchases. However, these two categories, social and nonsocial, are interlinked, because nonsocial objects frequently invoke social feelings. In any case, faced with so much information and so many influences, including inputs from such other subsystems as recreation and the journey to work, the consumer has to filter this input in order to define a set of actions within which the final purchase may be made. But even when the point of final purchase is reached, he—or she—cannot be certain that the required good or service will be available at the point in time and space selected for the shopping trip. Similarly, the retail entrepreneur is faced with almost identical factors when he comes to choose his store location. Where should he locate? How much should he stock in the face of uncertainty of demand at any particular point in time and space?

As figure 130 indicates, the consumer's demands and responses and the entrepreneur's supplies and responses are linked through a feedback system. Thus the consumer learns about what particular shops stock—or learns how to assess his expectations of what they will stock—and hence over time develops a capacity to evaluate his perceptions of the retailer's supply. In turn, the entrepreneur learns over time to assess a consumer's response to his supply, and is able to anticipate the degree of impulse buying, stock up for habitual choices, and forecast the degree of problem solving behavior involved.

Figure 130 represents the structural part of the consumer's participation in the retailing subsystem. The *spatial* aspect of this process is the particular spatial pattern of shopping trips from residence or other location to the store. The *temporal* aspect is the way in which, over time, the consumer allocates his perceived budget between particular commodities—in other words, consumer demand. The entrepreneurial structure is also shown over time; it appears as a functional mix of goods in the store, or of establishments arranged in nucleations or ribbons (over space this structure approximates the central place hierarchy). The consumer's and retailer's structures are related through the feedback of information between the two.

The entrepreneur's response to the pattern of consumer demand will of course play a large part in determining whether he stays in business and so (presumably) makes a profit. Over time the quality and scope of this response will be revealed through management traits, inventory administration, receptiveness to innovations in business techniques, and use of advertising. Over space the same process translates into the dynamics of market area competition, which leads to changes in retail locations and the spatial births and deaths of establishments and centers. Finally, the process from the consumer's standpoint is reflected in learning behavior: the consumer stores and filters information through time as he gains experience of the retailer's ability to supply his needs and wants. Over time this is reflected in the consumer's brand loyalty, repeat buying, or degree of shopping enterprise; in spatial terms, he may develop store loyalty, make repeated trips to particular shopping centers, or exhibit a degree of spatial mobility. In short, figure 130 provides a geographical framework into which we can slot both the ideas about consumer behavior developed in the previous chapter, and the empirical evidence of retailing structure set out below.

Retailing Structure

As was noted in the opening sections of chapter 10, there is a consistent pattern or structure of similar business types and commercial aggregations, despite the multiplicity of factors involved. Retail and related service establishments are grouped spatially according to the special location needs of the type of business concerned. Most shops seek out other shops or groups of shops, and there appear to be regularities in the resulting system or grouping of business types. Knowledge of these regularities has been built up over many years of observation, particularly by B. J. L. Berry and his colleagues in the University of Chicago geography department.

From this work four major empirical constructs emerge, related to the structure of commercial facilities in North American cities:

1. *Retail and related service functions are grouped spatially according to a tripartite schema consisting of:* nucleations, *or* centers, *a hierarchy of planned and unplanned shopping centers from the corner grocery store up to the metropolitan central business district;* ribbons, *highway oriented facilities characterized by their dependency on traffic;* and specialized areas, *the groupings of one or more business types that agglomerate for mutual benefit. As figure 131 shows, these categories are not discrete but overlap and are interrelated.*

2. *The numbers of retail and related service functions are related to the amount and distribution of consumer income. Put simply, the average number of retail facilities is a function of an area's population and that population's income characteristics. Figure 132 shows the close relationship between retail sales and consumer income in Chicago.*

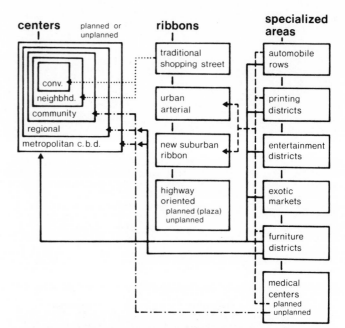

Fig. 131. *The structure of business and commerce in North American cities. (From B.J.L. Berry et al., "Commercial Structure and Commercial Blight," Research Paper No. 85, 1963, p. 20, reprinted by permission of the University of Chicago, Department of Geography.)*

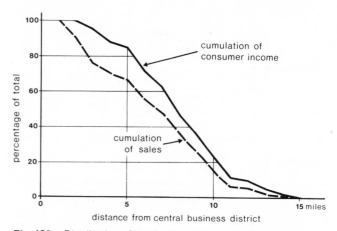

Fig. 132. *Distribution of retail sales and consumer income in Chicago. (From J. Simmons,"The Changing Patterns of Retail Locations," Research Paper No. 92, 1964, p. 14, reprinted by permission of the University of Chicago, Department of Geography.)*

3. *Different retail facilities pay differing amounts of rent.*

4. *There is a variation in the value of commercial land. This is obviously linked with (3). Figure 133 shows long ridges of high land values along major routes, with peaks of high values at important intersections. Although some of these variations are due to the varying size of parcels or their shape and servicing, land value is essentially created by location and accessibility to parts or the whole of an urban area, and hence their proprietors vary in need and willingness to pay the price of good accessibility. Other factors are also important, although geographers to date have dealt only marginally*

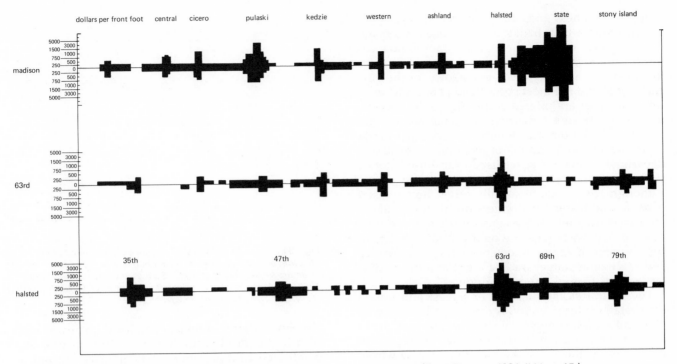

dollars per front foot   central   cicero   pulaski   kedzie   western   ashland   halsted   state   stony island

madison

63rd

halsted

35th   47th   63rd   69th   79th

Fig. 133. *Land value profiles of three selected Chicago arterial streets. (From Simmons 1964, ibid., p. 17.)*

with the so-called theory of the firm, that is, with entrepreneurial location decisions.

The Hierarchy of Retail Nucleations

Table 46 sets out a representative selection of functions at each of the center levels: street corner, neighborhood, community and regional centers.

The *street corner center*, or *isolated cluster*, comprises one to four business types, the most common of which is the grocery-drug store combination. Serving the occasional convenience purchases of consumers who live or work within a few blocks of the store, they are scattered throughout an urban area, and are the most frequent form of tertiary activity.

The *neighborhood center* comprises a whole group of retail and service functions for a local area, and allows ready and frequent purchase of convenience goods. Its functions include those of a small supermarket ("superette") or grocery store, a drugstore, a laundry, dry cleaner, barber, beauty salon, and small café. Sometimes units with other functions, such as hardware stores and real estate offices also occur. These centers serve home-based convenience trips for a local area in which are nested the smaller trading areas of the isolated cluster or isolated store.

The *community center* is more complex, since it contains a group of retail and service facilities serving several neighborhood areas. It serves for the pur-

Table 46. *A Sample of Business Types Found at Certain Levels of the Hierarchy*

isolated cluster or isolated store	community
general store	*variety store*
grocery	*clothing*
drugstore	*dairy*
	lawyer
neighborhood	*branch bank*
	jewelry
supermarket	*florists*
bakery	*furniture*
barber/beauty salon	*post office*
dry cleaners	
hardware	regional
laundry	
real estate agents	*department store*
	millinery
	hosiery
	shoes
	sporting goods
	furriers
	cameras
	professional offices

Source: B.J.L. Berry, "Recent Studies Concerning the Role of Transportation in the Space Economy, "Annals of the A.A.G.," vol. 49, 1959, p. 147.

chase both of necessities (neighborhood level goods) and of the less frequently demanded and more specialized goods at this level. Variety and clothing stores, dairies, jewelry, florists, or a post office may be all marks of this new level. There may also be a group of business and office services—lawyers, insurance agents, trust banks, branch banks, and so on.

The *regional center* is the highest order of noncentral business center. It provides goods and services for several community areas, and allows for the purchase of all but the most specialized goods and services (the latter are offered at the highest level of all, the central business district). Regional centers are distinguished from community centers particularly by the variety and number of functions they offer—department stores, specialized furniture stores, clothing stores, record and hi-fi stores, and so on. Although these centers still serve home-based trips, as the lower level centers do, they also allow for a greater variety of consumer purchases, and thus cater to and encourage the multipurpose shopping trip. As a result, regional centers are fewer in number and serve much larger trading areas in terms of distance, density, and purchasing power.

The *central business district*, or largest and dominant retail center in a city, is the pinnacle of a complex and varied commercial structure, serving areas beyond the city's limits. It is the retail center of the first order, at the top of the hierarchy, below which occur the regional centers and all the others. The central area of a city has many functions. It is not only the major retail center but also the main location for administrative functions, both private and official, as well as wholesaling and certain types of recreational activities. In other words, all the principal tertiary activities are represented there. The retail functions are predominantly in shoppers' goods (clothing, furniture, and department stores) and specialty goods (custom jewelry, winemaking equipment, etc.). It is usually, though not always, the largest retail center in the city. For example, Berry reports that, at the peak of the land values surface, the Chicago central business district sells eight times as many shoppers' goods as the largest outlying regional center, and has ten times the total retail sales. Besides size in these terms, the range of the central business district is also greater, since its trading covers not just part of the city, like all other centers, but the entire urban area and its hinterland.

The existence of the retail nucleation hierarchy is partly explicable in terms of the concepts of **threshold** and **range** and in part in terms of consumer behavior and the propensity to search for various types of goods. The hierarchy for Chicago is expressed in figure 134 as a relationship between functions and numbers of shops in 68 shopping centers. It will be seen that the average neighborhood, community, and regional center provided 24, 37, and 56 functions respectively.

Analyses have also been carried out of the actual floor space in use in the hierarchy of centers. Figure

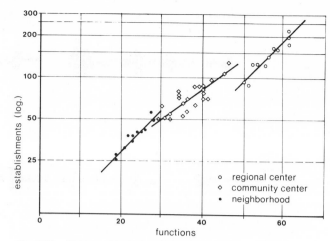

Fig. 134. *Chicago: hierarchy of shopping centers, number of functions and establishments. (From B.J. Garner, "The Internal Structure of Retail Nucleations," Studies in Geography, no. 12, 1966, p. 45, modified and reprinted by permission of Northwestern University, Department of Geography.)*

135 shows that functional complexity increases with each higher level of the hierarchy. This relationship is reflected in the amount of floor space utilized by convenience and shopping goods, as well as by other functions (obviously, in order to overcome the disparity of sizes between centers, floor space is portrayed in proportional terms). The proportion of convenience goods (drugs, groceries, etc.) decreases as the number of business types and establishments increases—a clear reflection of the importance attached to higher level centers for multipurpose shopping goods trips.

However this simple notion of hierarchies is upset by a number of factors. One is the factor of *ribbons* and *specialized areas*, considered below; another is

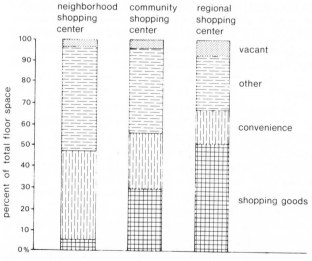

Fig. 135. *The proportion of total floor space devoted to convenience shopping and other goods, by level of retail nucleation. (From Garner 1966, ibid., p. 88; see fig. 134.)*

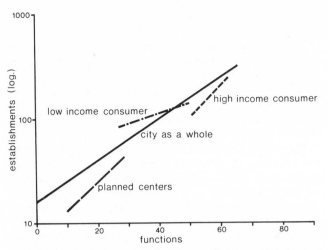

Fig. 136. *Retail functions, income levels, and planned centers in Chicago. (From B.J.L. Berry et al., "Commercial Structure and Commercial Blight," Research Paper No. 85, 1963, p. 134, reprinted by permission of the University of Chicago, Department of Geography.)*

the existence of *discount houses;* third is the factor of consumer motivation; and fourth the quasi-monopoly enjoyed by certain highly specialized forms of retailing, as described by R. Leigh in a 1965 study. Moreover, detailed analysis of the hierarchy of shopping centers in Chicago has suggested the existence of more than one hierarchy within cities.

Figure 136 again shows the relationship between establishments and functions, but this time with allowance made for differences in consumer income. The relationship for the whole city obscures great differences between various parts of the city, and between older and newer centers. The figures for the low income areas of Chicago, especially the lower correlation between functions and shops, suggest greater duplication of functional types in areas where demand is lower and of a different nature. Planned centers appear also more likely to offer fewer functions than unplanned centers, probably because planning involves greater selectivity and a higher initial outlay.

Ribbon Developments

The function of ribbon developments is to serve demands that originate from highway traffic. They include such activities as gas stations, restaurants and drive-ins, motels, and so on. In general, the greater the volume and intensity of traffic, the greater the demand for and density of highway oriented facilities. Since most trips to them are likely to be single purpose, often on impulse, they are seldom functionally linked. Most are unplanned strip developments like the one on U.S. Highway 99 be-

tween Seattle and Everett, Washington, though some planned service plazas do occur. Table 47 summarizes the functions typically found along ribbon developments. As Pred has pointed out, the central place model cannot account for these retailing ribbons since it does not allow for the combination of the shopping trip with other trip purposes; in ribbons thresholds are met because the shops and services lie on heavily trafficked routes where they attract consumers who may well have some other trip purpose in mind. Thus there is little relationship here between the order of goods and services and the distances consumers travel—that is, little relationship between order and range.

Among the types of ribbon development is the *urban arterial* location. It results from the seeking out of accessible routes that need access to an urban market but, because of space requirements or the ways in which they are utilized by consumers, can function independently of the nucleations described above. Among the common functions often served in this way are automobile repair, furniture and appliance stores, discount houses, department stores, funeral homes, plant nurseries, and lumber yards. These are either uses for which the consumer has an infrequent special demand, or that attract a large market by

Table 47. *Selected Functions in Ribbon Developments*

automobile service districts (highway-oriented facilities)	arterials close to CBD
gas station	*printing*
restaurant	*office equipment*
motel	*funeral homes*
fruit and produce stand	urban arterial rows
	missions
space-consuming service districts (highway-oriented facilities)	*second hand stores*
	groceries
building services and supplies	*bars*
lumber yard	
repairs, incl. plumbing	automobile row
radio-television sales and service	*new car sales*
	used car sales
urban-arterial oriented	
car repairs	
bars	
shoe repairs	
furniture	
car accessories	
appliances	
fuel	
gifts and novelties	
food lockers	
florists	

Source: B.J.L. Berry, "Recent Studies Concerning the Role of Transportation in the Space Economy," *Annals of the A.A.G.,* vol. 49, 1959, pp. 147–148.

virtue of advertised low prices. Whole rows of such uses occur because, although they may not be functionally linked, they tend to seek out a common arterial location.

Other arterial or ribbon types of development are the *new suburban ribbons*, which consist of concentrations of drive-in restaurants, discount houses, and so on, and the traditional *shopping street*, so common in Europe, that still occurs in the older parts of American cities. These latter types essentially perform the function of centers at the convenience and neighborhood levels of the center hierarchy, as the links on figure 131 indicate.

Many urban arterial functions are found from the village level up. Automobile repair is one example; bars are another. As the size of the urban area increases additional functions are added, until at the metropolitan level arterials adjacent to the central business district are characterized by such fairly specialized functions as printing or office equipment and supplies. Such large urban areas also commonly have a skid-row, with its cheap saloons and flop houses, and an "automobile row," formed by one or more concentrations of dealers in used and new automobiles.

Specialized Functional Areas

Functions of several types cluster together in what are called specialized functional areas. The clustering of new and used car dealers in "automobile rows" is one example, as is the clustering of doctors, dentists, and medical specialists into "medical districts." Such functional areas remain clustered because of the close linkages between their component establishments. Linkages are provided by comparative shopping opportunities, related services, sharing of specialists, and referrals. Most specialized functional areas require good accessibility to the part of the urban area that is their threshold support. Thus automobile rows occur adjacent to good arterial links, or nodes on those links, and medical centers may locate with reference to public transport or good highway links. Many of these centers remain unplanned, although there is an increasing trend toward planned medical centers.

Land Values

Land values have traditionally played a strong role in the location of retail facilities, since they underlie much of the physical urban structure. Land values are in fact basic to a study of spatial systems in urban areas.

The Concept of Land Value

Most explanations of land value rest on the notion of complementarity between **site costs** and **transportation costs,** which together form "friction of space." The land values "surface" thus varies spatially, so that different locations and thus different retail businesses will vary in the amount of rent, or land return, that they pay.

High and low land values reflect fairly faithfully the land use category and areal status of a given location. Land values are in fact affected by many elements of the urban system. Of particular importance is the spatial location of a piece of land with respect to the overall spatial distribution of land uses. Also important is its location with respect to other sites within one particular land use type. In a 1949 study, Ratcliff observes that:

Each parcel of land occupies a unique physical relationship with every other parcel of land. Because in every community there exists a variety of land uses, each parcel is the focus of a complex but singular set of space relationships with the social and economic activities that are centered on all other parcels. To each particular combination of space relationships, the market attaches a special evaluation which largely determines the amount of the bid for that site which is the focus of the combination. Thus certain locations are more highly valued for residential use than other sites because of greater accessibility to shops, schools, place of work, and so on. Corner locations command a higher price for certain types of retail use because of greater convenience to streams of pedestrian traffic.

Implicit in these statements is the concept of *accessibility*. The returns from particular sites represent savings in movement costs, savings from minimizing distance relationships and so increasingly accessibility. Accessibility increases inversely with distance, so that competition among land use sites will reflect distance and transportation costs. Thus, in theory, savings obtained by minimizing movement costs can be set against the higher returns payable on the most accessible sites: the greater the savings on movement costs the greater the availability of surpluses to pay for land costs. From this viewpoint, the land use activity occupying a particular urban site is not just the activity of the highest bidder but the activity that has the greatest positive movement cost advantages. Thus the greater the accessibility the higher the land value, and the lower the accessibility the lower the land value. This relationship is complicated by the fact that accessibility—and hence the relationship with the whole spatial land use system—varies from land use to land use. For commercial uses, it is accessibility to consumers or purchasing power that matters; for industries (if they are vertically or horizontally integrated) it is accessibility to other industries; for schools, shops, or places of work, it is accessibility to residential uses. In all cases, of course, there are modifying factors. For instance, residential land users, particularly those with high incomes, may be less concerned with minimizing time-cost distance relationships, and more concerned about life style relationships.

Thus a particular parcel of land receives a value through its relationships with the whole urban system. The land economist still looks to classical rent theory for the analysis of supply and demand relationships and the pricing of land in the market. But he also sees the total pattern of land use as a compromise between accessibility, costs, and satisfaction. The total pattern of values as now seen is the cumulative result of these sorting processes and market decisions.

A Simple Model

One view of the urban value mechanism is shown in figure 137. For any activity, the utility to be derived from the land tends to fall with distance from the central urban area as shown in (a). In a way this is similar to the von Thünen formulation, as an orderly pattern of land use would result, with a maximization of rents and utility. In (b), a particular entrepreneur would have to pay a certain value in order to derive a given utility at a certain distance from the central business district. In order to obtain the utility for the distance XY, the entrepreneur incurs costs $XYZA$. But the total returns, BB_1, exceed the costs by the amount $ACBZ$. As a result of competition this excess becomes the amount of "rent" that could be paid to a landowner, lease owner or mortgagor. This is similar, then, to the "land return" noted in the von Thünen model, and following that produces a value gradient that could be erected for each land use activity or type, as with PP_1 in (a). If now a number of value gradients are erected for different land use activities—PP_1, QQ_1, RR_1 in (c)— the spatial effects can be deduced. Thus X to Y would be devoted to land use P, and Y to P_1 to land use Q, and P_1 to R_1 to land use R. Accessibility, as we have seen, means different things to different activities, so the rent gradients—QQ_1, PP_1 and RR_1—will vary too. Using the logic derived from the von Thünen model, if QQ_1 represents wholesaling and industry, PP_1 commercial activities, and RR_1 residences, then XY will be occupied by commercial land uses, YZ by wholesaling and industry, and ZR by residences.

However, the operation of the urban land values system is more complex than this simplistic model, as several authors have pointed out.

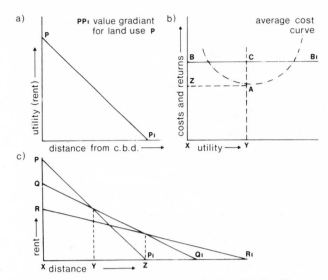

Fig. 137. *Economic rents in an urban situation. (Cf. figs. 46 and 47.)*

The Development of Land Value Theory

The process by which land acquires value has been investigated in great detail. Some of the factors examined are summarized in table 48. It will be seen that analysis of the influence of distance and location, as reviewed in the previous section, is here sharpened by consideration of the relative accessibility of different urban sites. Then $A(1)$, *relation of district to city center*, has been studied with reference to a hypothetical isolated city in which accessibility to the central core is the dominant aim. It is further assumed that individuals and businesses want to minimize site rents and transportation costs. Under these assumptions, it can be shown that central core area has accessibility to all parts of the city, and that therefore all activities find the center the most convenient point for location. Thus rents or land values will be the highest at this point, and competition to use this central area will displace activities that can only afford lower rental values. The owners of the relatively accessible sites will impose a rent equal to the saving in transportation costs afforded by that site. Implicit in these ideas is the theory that congestion and increasing transportation costs from outlying areas will raise site rents and values, and, conversely, that an improvement in transport and a lowering of transportation costs will reduce site rents and values in the central area.

In another study, the factors influencing the value of urban land were classified into three groups: factors affecting income (demand and supply); factors affecting the rate of capitalization; and factors affecting the direct satisfaction from land ownership.

Table 48. *Summary of Factors Influencing Urban Land Values from Current Valuation Literature*

A. physical factors (i.e., tangible)
  1. *relation of district to city center*
  2. *street characteristics, size, type, etc.*
  3. *access to property*
  4. *distance: time-cost effort to reach suitable employment*
  5. *amount of land available for similar use*
  6. *nearby buildings, type and equipment of newer ones*
  7. *attractiveness or otherwise of neighborhood*
  8. *density of adjacent buildings*
  9. *exposure (winds, sunshine, etc.)*
  10. *size, shape, and topography of lot; restrictions or advantages for future land use*
  11. *competition from vacant lands*
  12. *firmness of substratum for foundations*
  13. *elevation in relation to street and adjacent lot*
  14. *location in block*
  15. *surface drainage*
  16. *transition in land use*

B. economic factors
  1. *world trends, booms and slumps*
  2. *national wealth, living standards, cost of living, purchasing power of dollar, bank credit*
  3. *special local conditions affecting cost of living*
  4. *supply and demand — surplus or shortage for homes, etc., of similar class*
  5. *construction costs*
  6. *competition with other districts and comparison with competitive locations*
  7. *real estate market*
  8. *values generally in district and in competitive areas*
  9. *general trend of values in area*
  10. *rate of transition in land use*
  11. *deed or title restrictions or advantages*
  12. *utility of lot — present potential*

C. social and demographic factors
  1. *population trends: increase, decrease, direction, rate of change*
  2. *relation of district to city structure (i.e., ecological place)*
  3. *employment records of accessible industries*
  4. *surplus, or shortage (demand for houses of similar class)*
  5. *attractiveness or otherwise of neighborhood (social prestige, social mobility)*
  6. *social characteristics (racial, etc.) of neighborhood*
  7. *local prejudices*
  8. *effect of directional growth of city*
  9. *special local conditions affecting cost of living*

D. service availability factors
  1. *water, sewer, gas, electricity (buried, exposed)*
  2. *fire and police protection*
  3. *schools, churches, libraries*
  4. *recreation: movies, parks, beaches, lakes, etc.*
  5. *transportation: bus, tram, train, etc.*
  6. *serviceable roads*

E. other factors
  1. *government trends and influences*
  2. *zoning and planning*

The actual supply of urban sites was seen as influenced by such factors as physical quality and layout of an area, speed and cost of transportation services, zoning, taxation, public controls, and the costs of production. Any depressing effect that transportation improvements may have, in this case by increasing the supply of urban landsites, was considered offset by the bolstering influence upon values of sites in areas specifically affected.

Movement of land values can also be treated in relation to the physical expansion of the city. Increases in a city's size and changes in its structure are reflected in changes in land values. Accordingly, these values reflect out-migration from city centers and resettlement at the periphery—phenomena often referred to respectively as urban blight and suburban sprawl. The areas of highest value (the central business district) usually have some stability. But their actual gains in value are small compared to those at the subcenters, as satellite business communities proliferate. Indeed, it is possible that this differential rate of rise from center to periphery may be due to improvements in transport, particularly the flexibility given by the automobile.

It can also be argued, in line with classic rent theory, that the value of urban land services derives mainly from location, and that the value differences among sites reflect location advantages at different points in the urban system. According to this view, value is the capitalized expression of economic rent, and market prices of land tend to reflect forecasts concerning its future "productivity." Thus the highest payment for a particular landsite is justified by the "highest and best use" to which it can be put.

One contemporary economist who thinks that the preceding ideas on land values depend on too many simplifying assumptions is P. F. Wendt. In particular, he claims that transportation costs have been overstressed. Instead, he proposes a model of the general form

$$\text{Land Value} = \frac{f \cdot A - B}{f \cdot C}$$

where f = expectations, A = aggregate gross costs, B = total expected costs, and C = capitalization rate.

In this model Wendt stresses the importance of distinguishing between factors that affect the aggregate of land values, and factors that operate on an individual site. Thus there may be variations in land value stemming from changes in economic conditions, and there may also be variations due to conditions inherent in a particular locality. The revenue component A includes such factors as the urban area's competitive pull, the availability of alternate land sites, and the income spent for various urban services within the market. The expected cost component B is the sum of such variables as property taxes, operating costs, interest on capital, and depreciation allowances. Finally, C represents interest rates, risk, and capital gains.

Other models stress other functions. Thus L. Wingo (1961) has combined an analysis of traffic flows and the theories of land economists into a model of the residential land market. Rents and transportation costs are looked at as complementary, their sum being equal to a constant that equals the transportation costs to the most distance residential location occupied. This is similar to Haig's view, and parallel to that of von Thünen. Wingo further allows the size of the site to enter his model, by using a consumption function of quantity of land with price. In this way, he finds the equilibrium level of the market through the balancing of supply and demand quantities. For example, he uses transportation costs to establish the distribution of residences at one or another *position rent*, defined as "the annual savings in transport costs compared to the highest cost location in use." The rent that a household is willing to pay for a site is based on a classic utility notion: the greater the unit rent, the fewer the units of space utilized.

W. Alonso (1965), whose model parallels to some degree that of Wingo, uses a **bid-price curve** instead of a demand function. He then treats bid-price curves and the price structure of land as bases for allocating agricultural, business, and residential users to their sites. Beginning at the center of the city, land is put up for bid. On the basis of these curves the bid for the most central site is compared to the next preferred alternative, the latter being the marginal combination of price and location for that particular use. On the basis of the steepest bid-price curve, the highest bidder takes the most central site, the next highest the next most central site, and so on.

Empirical Evidence

The factors and processes noted in these various methods of assessing land value can be found in most cities, though of course there are variations in site quality, morphology, and functions. The physical quality of the site, for example, affects the location of economic activities and thus the entire city structure. Figure 138 shows a land values surface for an urban area, with the lofty peak of the central city falling into the deep valleys of blighted areas, only to rise again toward suburban centers, though

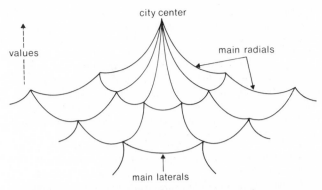

Fig. 138. *A model three-dimensional land values surface.*

at a decreasing rate. The peaks mark the junctions of important lateral routes with the main radials, with the result that the surface looks rather like a three-dimensional spider's web.

At least three of the elements shown in figure 138 appear to be present in most cities:

1. *Land values reach a peak at the center and decline toward the periphery.*
2. *Land values are higher along major traffic arteries than away from them.*
3. *Local peaks of higher value occur at major traffic intersections.*

The pattern detected here is most evident in large metropolitan areas, where there are strongly formalized notions of local commercial centers. In this case the site for such a center is located at a point of maximum consumer accessibility (i.e., the junction of a radial artery with a main one). In other cases, however, secondary nuclei may coincide with preexisting cores of engulfed settlements. But usually the land values surface will reflect accessibility within an urban area.

The existence of the land values surface and the importance of accessibility have been demonstrated in many empirical studies of market-exchange economies. Thus M. H. Yeates was able to show the importance of six or seven variables to the Chicago land values surface between 1910 and 1960. These were: distance from the central business district; distance from the nearest shopping center; distance from a rapid transit line; distance from Lake Michigan; distance from the main radial routes; population density; and the percentage of nonwhites living in a particular block. Distance from radial routes was one of the most significant variables.

Another discussion of land values in Chicago is based on the work of Hoyt:

From a peak at the city center values diminished outwards with increasing distance . . . since commercial values

*exceeded those for residential property, the long
business ribbons stood out as sharp ridges above the general
residential value levels . . . just as the residential values
diminished with distance, so did the backs of the ridges
representing commercial values. At regular intervals on the
ridges, the commercial values took a sudden up turn, to a
maximum at an intersection, followed by an equally
sharp drop to a point where the value pattern of the ridge
was resumed. . . . The basic features of Chicago's land value
skeleton were already in existence in 1935, and they persist
to this day . . . wherever there is a peak there is a business
center; wherever there is a ridge there is a (commercial)
ribbon development . . . the land values map of Chicago
indicates several hundred peaks. Most rise barely $50 or
$100/front foot over the prevailing height of the ridges
(which usually run $200 plus or minus $50/front foot) . . .
the local street corner nucleations . . . the largest peaks on
the other hand, rise to more than $4,000/front foot (the
peak of the CBD exceeds $40,000).*

Figure 139 shows the distribution of peaks with
values over $750 per front foot, which in the study's
terms excluded local neighborhood business centers, but included all higher order business centers.

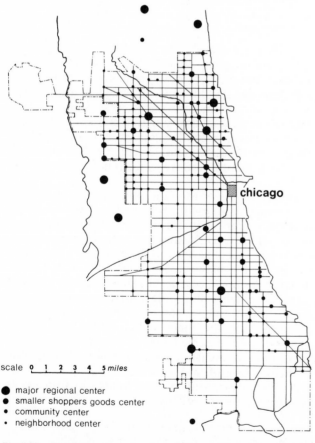

scale 0 1 2 3 4 5 miles

● major regional center
● smaller shoppers goods center
• community center
· neighborhood center

Fig. 139. *Retail structure of uptown Chicago. (From Berry et al.
1963, ibid., p. 32; see fig. 136.)*

From Land Values to Retail Structure

The relationship of land values with the retailing
structure should now be obvious. The long ridges of
high land values along major thoroughfares are
associated with the various types of *ribbon* development, because the level of values and the intensity of
business depend on the intensity of traffic along
these arteries. The peaks of high values at the important intersections are associated with *nucleations* and
with some *specialized areas*, the whole comprising
the *hierarchy of functions*. The variations in land
value are in part due to variations in land parcels,
size, topography, and services. But essentially they
are created by the location of the land site: location
in terms of relative accessibility, nearby land use,
existing traffic patterns, and potential customers.

Thus Berry notes that in Chicago the smaller
neighborhood centers are generally found at points
with values about fifty dollars higher than the surrounding values surface. Regional centers, needing
more accessible locations to serve larger trade areas,
occurred where values rose about $4,000 above the
surrounding surface. However, other factors such as
quality or income level of trade area are also important, and land values are probably most useful
in identifying the arrangement of functions within
a center. Figure 140 shows one such arrangement.
The central business district is depicted as comprising two distinct parts in a "core-frame" pattern:

1. *There is an inner core of intensive use of high value
land, with consequent marked vertical usage (skyscrapers),
and strong functional links between shops and various
offices (clusters of functions forming small land use
zones).*

2. *There is a less intensively developed frame in which,
since it has much lower values, there is more likely to be
horizontal than vertical expansion, and the various
functions are not so strongly interlinked (except of course
by location).*

There is also a relationship between values and
arrangement of functions in centers other than the
central business district. Thus figure 141 shows the
ordered arrangement of land use within three levels
of shopping centers. The competition between business functions with varying threshold values for the
use of the sites leads to the kinds of spatial arrangement shown. The inner core of high values for a
given level of center is occupied by the functions
that distinguish this particular center from those
lower in the hierarchy. This core of high order functions is surrounded by the functions typical of each
lower level of center, and by successively lower
values of land.

Thus in figure 141a the core comprises high thresh-

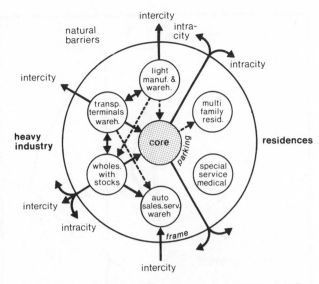

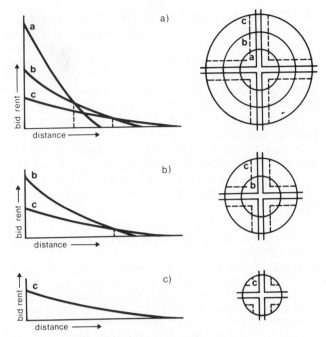

a highest order business type *regional*
b medium order business type *community*
c low order business type *neighborhood*

Fig. 141. *Hypothetical internal structure of regional, community, and neighborhood level retail nucleations. (From B.J. Garner, "The Internal Structure of Retail Nucleations," Studies in Geography, no. 12, 1966, p. 112, reprinted by permission of Northwestern University, Department of Geography.)*

— primary goods flow ---- secondary goods flow

Fig. 140. *The Horwood-Boyce CBD core-frame concept. A schematic diagram with selected functional centers, indicating the principal flow of goods. (From E.M. Horwood and R.R. Boyce, Studies of the Central Business District and Urban Freeway Development, 1959, p. 21, reprinted by permission of the University of Washington Press. Copyright © 1959.)*

old, high rent paying functions of a high order, surrounded by progressively lower threshold, lower rent paying functions. At the next lower level, shown in figure 141b, those highest level functions are excluded because the threshold entry level cannot be upheld, and the core is now occupied by the next lower level functions, surrounded in turn by the lowest level functions. The lowest level—figure 141c—has the simplest structure, since only one level of service is provided. Thus a, b, and c, representing the three orders, can be interpreted as the *regional, community,* and *neighborhood* shopping functions discussed above. This hypothetical structure was empirically tested in Chicago, and was found to represent the structure of centers quite well, especially at the community and neighborhood levels. However, the real-world arrangements were found to be complex. This does not destroy the premise of the model, as has been noted earlier in agricultural and industrial location models. The geographer B. J. Garner states that although "the simplicity of land use patterns is destroyed once and for all . . . this does not mean that the order and system are destroyed. It means that the order imposed by the influence [of other factors] . . . takes on increasingly more complex forms. . . ." The same author notes that his simple model should be modified for the effects of *product differentiation* (the complex of goods, tastes, and needs), and for a modification of the threshold concept, in order to allow for the whole range of goods offered.

The Dynamics of the Retailing System

Thus far we have reported work that has dealt with the retailing subsystem as largely static and unchanging. However, retailing structures at any one time are in various stages of development, particularly when the rate of urban growth is taken into account. Some centers will be at various stages of maturity, others will be in decline. Thus the open-ended system that represents the urban tertiary and retailing subsystems will be undergoing the effects of physical, economic, and social change. The transportation pattern will be modified by these changes, and they in turn will affect the urban-commercial subsystems, and vice versa. All these changes will of course be reflected in changed patterns of accessibility and changed land values surfaces. Mobility to and within urban areas is reflected in changing patterns of consumer taste and demand. Changes in the actual technology of retailing may also have an effect on the commercial system. Thus the urban landscape is dynamic and in a constant state of flux.

The impact of highway changes on the retailing hierarchy has been studied by W. L. Garrison and his coworkers. The study area was at Marysville, on U.S. 99 a few miles north of Everett, Washington.

In 1954, through traffic was diverted to a new freeway west of the city, which led, immediately after diversion, to a 66 percent reduction in the amount of traffic entering Marysville. At this point in time Marysville was a small service center (population 2,500) quite low in the hierarchical order. It supplied the surrounding agricultural areas with goods and services, served highway travelers, and had its own lumber industry.

It was found that diverting the highway had a more complex effect than just reducing the number of travelers. In fact, six broad areas of impact were identified, all of them related to the town's tertiary activities:

1. *There was a marked reduction of travelers, particularly in the summer.*

2. *Traffic congestion was eased, not just in Marysville, but for several miles north and south of the town (figure 142). This made trips easier to make from Marysville to Everett—including shopping trips, of course. It also made Marysville a more pleasant place to live, as it became more accessible and freer from congestion. Home construction rose.*

3. *Decongestion of the Marysville town center also made it more accessible and attractive.*

4. *The improvement of the north-south route made Marysville and Everett more competitive with other small towns to the north.*

5. *These changes in accessibility seem to have had two overall effects. First, they made Marysville more attractive; its first- and second-order tertiary functions increased by 121 percent. Second, since it was now easier to get to Everett from the rural areas around Marysville, the greater range of higher order functions in the former attracted more customers, while Marysville's sales of those higher order functions dropped to 83 percent of previous volume.*

6. *Finally, there was evidence that a number of businessmen had changed their methods of operation, as well as the lines of goods and services they offered, in response to these changed relationships with consumers.**

This study shows very clearly that a "complex set of travel and amenity charges operates concomitantly with highway change." Figure 143 illustrates the effect of such changes on a pattern of hypothetical retail centers. Here, the greater accessibility achieved by the new highway system encourages a centralization of business activities—but centralized with references to the new network and its dispersed residential areas. Thus as highway changes occur in one part of the overall economic system they affect

*Since this study was undertaken in 1955–59, the freeway has been extended northwards and southwards as Interstate 5.

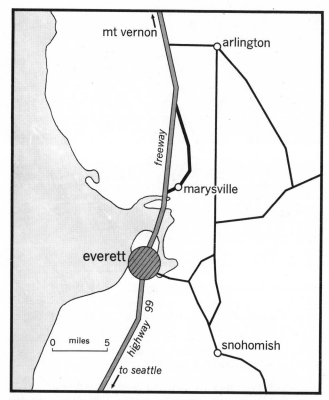

Fig. 142. *The impact of highway change: Marysville, Washington, 1955. The introduction of the new freeway section bypassing the town of Marysville increased the town's access in terms of lower order goods; but it also made Everett more accessible for higher order goods than under the pre-bypass conditions.*

the other components, which change correspondingly and are reoriented.

Change takes many forms. Within an urban area, a business center faced with change may find that the threshold level is falling below the minimum entry level for certain business types. When this happens the most specialized types, which need the highest threshold levels, drop out first, followed by the less and less specialized functions (some of course may wish to hold on, despite liquidation of capital). Vacancy rates in such declining areas are likely to be high. Land values do not react immediately, but in time they too fall. Growth in other areas—say, on the periphery of a metropolitan area suffering from "urban blight" leads to the development of new shopping centers. The central business district may also develop new habits as accessibility to it decreases and competition from large regional centers increase. This is associated with a shrinkage of the core area and the gradual encroachment of the frame land uses, which leads in turn to areas of "blight" and low grade establishments.

Various studies of retailing dynamics have shown that the turnover of stores in cities may vary from 4 to 48 percent over ten years. The research at Chicago

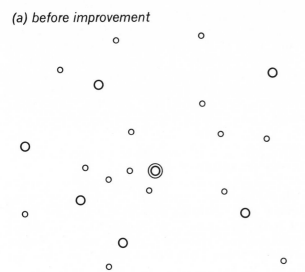

(a) before improvement

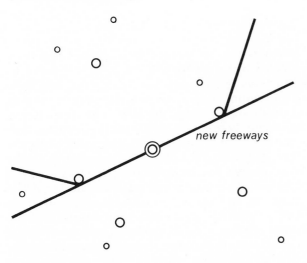

(b) after new freeways

new freeways

◎ regional   ○ community   ○ neighborhood

Fig. 143. *Hypothetical representation of impact of highway change on the tertiary landscape, represented here by three orders of shopping centers. (From W. Garrison et al.,* Studies of Highway Development and Geographic Change, *1959, p. 137, reprinted by permission of the University of Washington Press.)*

has documented some of the factors that lead to the spatial births and deaths of stores. Some have already been mentioned—the growing suburbanization of population, the increasing mobility of the consumer, rising affluence, changing technology in retailing, and social change in the inner city. Such changes in the North American city have caused the decline of the isolated grocery store, the growth of

decentralized regional shopping centers, and increases in the size of the centers and shops themselves. No doubt there are other changes yet to come.

Conclusion

Drawing on the four empirical constructs mentioned at the beginning of this chapter, as well as on the principles set out in land value theory, the central place model, and the various paradigms of consumer behavior, we can make the following kinds of synthesizing statements:

1. *Each retail store has a threshold, or minimum amount of sales below which it cannot operate. Usually that sales level will be based on a balance of profit and loss. But establishments can and do endure loss situations if the entrepreneur perceives a turn of fortune in the future.*

2. *In order to tap a sufficient quantity of purchasing power, the manager of a retail store has to ask himself who might be expected to make purchases at that store. Thus the store may attract consumers directly from their homes, or may depend on a supply of passersby who are attracted impulsively or by chance.*

3. *Each firm consciously or unconsciously erects a market area from which it expects to draw customers. Usually, it chooses to be as accessible to that potential market area as possible. Firms in a monopolistic situation (e.g., because they carry very specialized goods) may not be so concerned. But in both cases the chosen location is usually linked to the firm's conception of its rent paying ability. This conception is based on the firm's conscious or unconscious assessment of probable customers, population and income distributions, traffic flows, and the location of competitors.*

4. *Rent paying ability is linked to the actual surface of land values across a city by the concept of highest and best use. In other words, peak land values are occupied by stores that need maximum accessibility and can afford to pay for it.*

5. *Not all sites are chosen within nodal centers: there are stores with location needs that may be arterial or functional, so that a whole different set of possible locations emerges.*

6. *The retailing structure varies with the limited or full search nature of consumer behavior. Shopping goods that invite full search activities tend to cluster in higher order centers, unless they are in a monopolistic situation. Convenience goods are frequently purchased and fairly standardized. They are thus subject to more limited search activity, and are more dispersed through the urban area. Shopping goods stores may be subdivided into primary categories, which are more frequently purchased and need near-optimal locations, and secondary categories, which are less frequently purchased.*

These six points give a fairly complete summary of the retailing subsystem as seen by geographers. More space has been devoted to this subsystem because it constitutes such a large part of the tertiary subsystem, and because geographers to date have made it their principal concern in this area.

Recreational Activities

In terms of numbers employed, recreation may be one of the smaller components of the tertiary subsystem. Its importance to the consumer, however, increases as the working week grows shorter.

Recreational activities include the operation of theaters, movie houses, dance halls, bowling alleys, sports arenas, and groups of activities that overlap to some degree with such tertiary components as hotels, motels, camps, eating and drinking places, gas stations, or souvenir and gift shops. The economic input of tourist traffic is important to some such groups of recreational activities, since they cluster along major highways leading into and through resorts, ski centers, and scenic areas. For other groups the concern is with the theatrical, literary, artistic, and athletic milieu of an urban area. These differences arise as the result of differing demand patterns. There are *day-to-day* demands of leisure, which can obviously be satisfied in reasonable proximity to the consumer's place of residence or work, and more *infrequent* demands and needs that are met by excursions of longer duration.

Frequent Leisure Demands

The locations of daily or frequently demanded leisure facilities are very similar to those of retailing activities: they must seek a threshold of purchasing power by being located near their customers. Similarly, their size and spacing depends in part on the intensity of use and the threshold entry level of the facility. Major metropolitan areas can normally support activities with a very high threshold level. These include major league sports teams, race tracks, art galleries, museums, planetariums, musical and theatrical events of high caliber, and the more familiar amusement parks, first-run movie theaters, exhibitions, and zoos. Such activities can exist in areas of smaller population or purchasing power, but usually in a more rudimentary form. Even metropolitan areas may find difficulty in supporting the more esoteric activities, and the existence of wealthy patrons and patronage organizations may inject a noneconomic factor into their continued existence at below-threshold levels.

Normally, a whole range of such leisure time ac-

tivities can be expected to develop in relation to the distribution of consumer demand. The most frequently used facilities are likely to be located near the consumer because of time constraints. But other, less frequently demanded activities will usually locate so as to be most accessible to a large number of consumers, yet concomitant with the land values surface.

Infrequent Leisure Needs

Among the more infrequent leisure needs are air displays, rock festivals, parades, and so on. What they have in common is their capacity to attract consumers from relatively long distances. Also in this category are activities that, because they are designed for people with more than several days of leisure at their disposal, can be located at sites far from the consumer, and can therefore be located where conditions are particularly favorable. An obvious example here is skiing.

Recreational and Vacation Resources

Infrequent leisure needs can be divided into those demanded by **recreationists** and those demanded by **vacationists.** It has even been suggested that there is a continuum of vacation needs, with recreationists and vacationists at opposite ends. The recreationist, who is activity oriented, will want to spend less time in traveling and will be less concerned with the nature of the journey from the urban area to the recreation area. Such a figure is the daily or weekend sportsman. The vacationist, at the other end of a continuum, will be concerned with seeing as many places as possible in a fixed time period, and the journey itself may be of greater significance to him than any activity en route. Along this continuum we find other categories, such as the *recreational vacationist,* who may want, for instance, to spend three to four weeks mountain climbing, but at some place more distant from his home than if mountain climbing were his sole concern (see figure 145).

The patterns of movement associated with these different types of vacation needs may also determine the character of the frequented recreational area. Thus the urban recreational hinterland may extend to a periphery some two days driving away; it may extend along major corridors of movement; or it may be nucleated, to serve a variety of products to the specialized recreational vacationist.

The recreational or vacational resources utilized by these consumers are of course very varied. Some are natural, while others are man-made. In both cases, however, the primary consideration seems to be the availability of facilities to provide particular desired experiences that happen not to be normally available to large numbers of patrons. Since the bulk of the population in market-exchange economies is urbanized, so-called ideal vacation sites often incorporate open areas of country, with trees, rugged terrain, and access to streams or lakes for fishing, boating and swimming. Summer vacationists may demand cool temperatures; winter vacationists may look for sunny beaches; winter recreationists may want snow for skiing. Other vacationists are attracted to areas or places that offer unfamiliar types of art, architecture, and other cultural objects.

The analysis of recreation and vacation sites involves consideration of resources, inhibiting factors, and user perception. Among the inhibiting factors the most important seem to be the cost and inconvenience of reaching places with the perceived combinations of desirable characteristics. Many North Americans refuse to devote more than about ten percent of their vacation period (which may be only two to four weeks in length) in reaching the desired site, and they may well prefer one with inferior characteristics that is nearer to them in travel time. The emphasis is on time-distance rather than on physical distance, so that the distance that can be traveled is a function of the consumer's economic resources. For instance, Australia can be reached in 24 hours from Seattle if the consumer has the air fare—the same amount of time it would take him to drive to Los Angeles. However, improvements in transportation tend to reduce these time-distance constraints.

M. Clawson and J. L. Knetsch have sought to apply certain economic principles to the *demand* for recreational facilities. In a 1966 study they identify three categories of recreational resources:

1. *User oriented recreational areas.*
2. *Resource-based recreational activities.*
3. *Intermediate types.*

These categories are based on use as a measure of demand, translated into demand curves relating costs and number of visits. A user oriented resource such as a golf course or riding stable is located close to the consumer. An intermediate area caters to weekend or day activities such as camping, swimming, and skiing. These two categories are basically what we have already called recreational activities, with the emphasis on the activity. A resource-based user is primarily a vacationist traveling a longer distance to some outstanding natural or man-made vacation site. This categorization is of course somewhat misleading, since *all* recreation and vacation

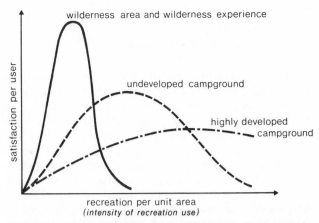

Fig. 144. *Outdoor recreation: user satisfaction and campground use. (From M. Clawson and J. Knetsch,* The Economics of Outdoor Recreation, *1967, p. 168, reprinted by permission of the Johns Hopkins Press © 1967 for Resources for the Future.*

areas are user oriented, that is, recreational facilities do not exist without the perception, demand, and satisfaction of the consumer. However, some account can be taken of user satisfaction, as figure 144 shows. This graph plots user satisfaction (taking camp grounds as an example) in relation to intensity of recreation area use. Various other measures are available in the same study.

Recreation Use

One of the most comprehensive surveys of recreation ever undertaken is that carried out by the Outdoor Recreation Resources Review Commission (O.R.R.R.C.), which reported in a 28-part series to the U.S. Congress in 1962. The Commission's findings were based on elaborate surveys of existing literature, and on a comprehensive national survey. It set up the following six-fold classification of recreational areas, based on both the users' and the Commission's perception of what the areas provide, and on certain public policy and management criteria:

Class I: *High Density Recreation Areas—areas subject to intense development and managed for mass use.*

Class II: *General Outdoor Recreation Areas—areas subject to substantial development for a wide variety of specific uses.*

Class III: *Natural Environment Areas—areas suitable for recreation in a natural environment, and usually found in combination with other area types.*

Class IV: *Unique Natural Areas—areas of outstanding natural beauty or of scientific importance.*

Class V: *Primitive Areas—wilderness areas, virtually un-*

disturbed by man, with minimal road or track access.

Class VI: *Historical and Cultural Sites.*

The Commission studied consumers as well as sites. The consumer's perceptions and conceptions, ethnic status, socioeconomic group, and age were all taken into account; unfulfilled demands were studied as well as actual participation. Thus the report details such factors as the time required to engage in an activity, the money costs of recreation and vacations, the level of physical activity involved, the level of prestige or status achieved through participation, the level of learning, and other social factors that motivated participation in leisure time activities. Thus any leisure activity requires certain *inputs* in the form of time, financial resources, physical strength, and skills. The fewer the number of inputs required, the larger tends to be the number of people participating in an activity. Conversely, the greater the input in terms of time, money, physique, and skills, the fewer the participants. Other demanding factors, mainly of a sociocultural nature, were also noted—religion, cultural group, ethnic status, and sex differences. Thus religious factors restricted hunting as a possibility for some groups, and the more active forms of recreation were dominated by males and by young people of both sexes.

On the basis of this user information, a fourfold typology of consumers was developed, as follows: (a) backwoods types; (b) boat culture; (c) the country club to picnic ground group; (d) passive participants. These are really distinctive *styles* of recreation, though they are not discrete or absolute, as table 49 shows.

The *backwoods* participants are thought to want to escape from the formal interpersonal relationships and rule observance that characterize so-called normal work or leisure situations. The activities they choose include camping, fishing, hunting, hiking, and mountain climbing.

The *boat culture* is linked to the North American "mobility culture," or desire to spend leisure time on the move—in this case by sailing, boating or water skiing.

The *country club* and *picnic* activities take place in fairly public settings with elaborate game rules and traditions. The chosen activities include swimming, sailing (but not too seriously), bicycling, horseback riding, outdoor games and sports, and picnicking.

Finally, *passive participants* engage in driving for pleasure, walking, sightseeing, and attending outdoor sports events. Although classified as "passive," these participants are also related to the mobility or highway culture mentioned above.

Table 49. *Style of Recreation Participation*

water	passive
sailing	driving for pleasure
boating	sightseeing
water skiing	outdoor sports events
	walking
active	**backwoods**
outdoor games	camping
horseback riding	hiking
bicycling	fishing
picnicking	mountain climbing

Source: O.R.R.C. Study Report No. 19, National Recreational Survey, 1962, p. 83.

Finally, the Commission studied the time spent in recreational activities. Here, the main distinctions were between *vacations, trips,* and *outings.* The average *vacation* was found to be 1,200 miles long and of at least 10 days' duration, with an average (1962) expenditure of eight dollars a day per consumer. The number of vacation trips was functionally related to income level, but the number of such trips taken leveled off at the $8,000 per year bracket. The average *trip* was only 225 miles long and 2½ days away from home; it involved an average expenditure of five dollars per consumer per day. It was found that consumers earning $3,000 a year or less made only half as many trips per year as those earning over $10,000. A day trip, or *outing,* was found to average 8 hours with no overnight stay involved. The frequency of outings levelled off at the $4,500 per year bracket.

Many other things could be said about this very elaborate survey. However, its one overwhelming finding was that the greatest need in the future will be for recreational activities in or near urban centers, so that people can readily avail themselves of recreational opportunities.

A Recreational Model

Besides his distinction between recreationists and vacationists, Campbell has proposed a model of recreation based in part on demand and in part on user satisfaction. There are four preconditions:

1. *The city is the generator of recreational demand (this is based on the findings of the O.R.R.C. report).*
2. *The nature of the recreation market should be clearly defined.*
3. *Attention should be focused on the spatial relationship*

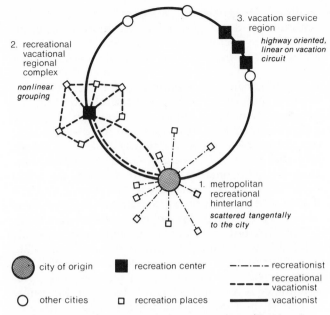

city of origin ●   recreation center ■   –·–·– recreationist

other cities ○   recreation places ◇   – – – recreational vacationist

                                                      ——— vacationist

Fig. 145. *A framework for recreational movement. (Reprinted from C.K. Campbell, "An Approach to Research in Recreational Geography," B.C. Occasional Papers, no. 7, 1966, p. 10, by courtesy of Tantalus Research Ltd.)*

between the city and the recreation areas, and especially on the patterns of movement between them.

4. *Hence, recreation facilities should be regarded as to some degree highway oriented.*

Campbell sees the patterns of movement of the recreationist, on the one hand, and the vacationist, on the other, as determining the characteristics of the frequented recreational area.

Thus in figure 145 the *metropolitan recreational hinterland* is depicted as scattered on the periphery of the urban zone of influence, usually less than two hours' driving time from the city. The *regional recreational complex*, by contrast, is a nucleated group of recreational areas providing a variety of high quality recreational services to the specialized recreational vacationist. Finally, the *vacation service region* consists of linear leisure facilities, mostly of a service nature, that are close to major corridors of movement. Typical examples are gas stations, gift shops, and restaurants.

Conclusion

Recreational activities are an area of increasing interest in North America and Western Europe as working hours decrease while both leisure and affluence increase. Much work remains to be done, but current research has revealed a great many of the

factors involved. These are summarized in table 50. Among them are:

1. *The demographic characteristics of the potential travelers—their age, sex, income, occupation, status, and so on.*
2. *The character of the specific areas from which they come (mainly urban).*
3. *The relationships between the urban areas and their recreational hinterlands.*
4. *The degree of mobility, that is, the availability of transportation.*

Table 50. *Summary: Recreational Activities*

need	location and classification of area	length of trip	traffic orientation	participatory role
weekly, monthly, yearly	high density recreational area: user oriented	outing/ recreation	local recreational	passive boat culture country clubs
	general outdoor recreational area: user oriented	outing/ trip/ recreation	main recreational arterials and routes	passive boat culture
	natural environmental area: resource based	trip/ vacation/ vacationist	resort roads	boat culture active
	unique natural area: resource based	vacation/ recreational- vacationist	resort roads	active backwoods
	primitive area: resource based	vacation/ recreational- vacationist		backwoods
	historical and cultural sites: user oriented	outing/trip/ vacation/ vacationist	resort roads	passive
daily, weekly	internal urban	outing	intra-urban	passive

Medical Services

At first glance it might appear that trips to service facilities such as hospitals or churches could be explained relatively simply in terms of spatial behavior. Actually, the use of these facilities is complicated by "satisficing," public and private policy making, and the ways in which users perceive particular physicians and hospitals. In this subsection these two categories of medical service, physicians and hospitals, will be examined in the context of the United States medical system.

Physicians

Like facilities that distribute goods, service facilities have a threshold level of support. As noted earlier for retailing, most of the market or catchment areas overlap. Thus the patients of some physicians undertake long, uneconomic journeys in response to quite subtle gradations in the attractiveness of the services available. People may continue to visit their family doctor long after they have moved many miles away, or go some distance to a large medical center on the expectation that the quality of medical care will be higher.

Distribution of Demands and Services

For these and related reasons, physicians' services operate in a fairly indeterminate spatial system of market areas. However, they are linked both horizontally, through the transportation network, and vertically, through the professional hierarchy. The latter extends from the general practitioners through varying degrees of specialists—or, in other words, from the *locals*, with a commitment to particular communities or organizations, to the *cosmopolitans*, who have a more general commitment to the profession, and who therefore locate near medical centers. Moreover, each separate hierarchy of specialists operates with a varying range, threshold, and size of market area. Although these factors may vary they are usually in close association; indeed, specialists are encouraged by their common interests to aggregate in medical centers. Hence we often find a group of general practitioners' medical service areas within the service area of a single hospital specialist.

One might naively assume that the demand for medical care in a given area depends on the amount of illness and infirmity in it, and so on the biological characteristics of its population. In reality, however, such factors as income, availability of medical insurance, rural as against urban residence, distance from a doctor, education, and ethnic group membership all influence the demand for medical care—at least in the United States. The demand for services, then, depends on the total socioeconomic picture presented by an area and its population, together with its relative location and accessibility.

It would be equally naive to assume that the demand for care coincides with the distribution of facilities. Hospitals, for instance, tend to be concentrated in the larger, older, and more prosperous cities, while doctors are concentrated in high income areas, where patients are more frequent in their visits.

We have already mentioned the hierarchy that exists in medical care. Here, it is useful to distinguish between two basic types of physician: a *general practitioner*, or family doctor, who handles the large proportion of medical care that is routine in nature; and a *specialist*, such as a gynecologist or ophthalmic surgeon, who handles cases in his own particular field. There is no sharp break between the family doctor and the specialist, and many doctors do to some degree carry out some specialist functions.

The distribution of general practitioners generally coincides with the distribution of population. But since consumers are willing to travel farther for medical care than for most other services, this correspondence is not so close as it is for them. Rimlinger and Steel, in 1963, studied the extent to which economic factors influence the distribution of physicians. Do the economic forces at work within a given institutional arrangement favor a distribution that is consistent with the efficient use of health resources? It appears that doctors tend to gravitate toward middle and high income areas, and that they locate elsewhere only through medical and economic necessity. As might be expected, specialists are heavily concentrated in the larger metropolitan areas, and consumers are usually willing to travel very long distances to reach them. In contrast, the distribution of family doctors is such that many movements for medical care tend to be local, and in some cases are to the nearest physician. For specialists' care, however, there is considerable regional and interregional movement. Within urban areas, most doctors locate in medical centers of larger or smaller size adjacent to other tertiary activities.

The Dynamics of the Subsystem

Changes in medical care have occurred through technological progress, urbanization, rising incomes, and specialization of certain medical practices. But the availability of medical care has not kept pace, despite increasing ease of transportation. Pressing shortages of medical personnel have accompanied population growth. As a result, medical services now tend to be differentiated and concentrated in urban areas, whereas in the past they were more evenly spread.

The history of this phenomenon is worth recapitulating. To begin with, the United States population was predominantly rural and of relatively low density. Medical practice was undifferentiated. The physician went to the patient's home on horseback.

Since the investment of time and money in each visit was high, doctors did not see many patients or serve a large population or area. Since in rural life demands for medical care were fairly uniform, doctors were distributed fairly evenly, being sited in almost every village. This pattern has since changed fundamentally for three principal reasons: the rise of cities and the increased differentiation of incomes; technical and scientific change; and increased automobile ownership. The rapid growth of cities since the late nineteenth century has created large and concentrated demands for medical care, as well as creating new medical problems. As medical science developed it led to the introduction of specialization into medical schools. The new specialists located in the cities, where a sufficient market for their more costly services could be assured.

Urbanization resulted in a great differentiation in the attractive power of rural areas and urban settlements alike. The concentration of purchasing power in cities caused a rapid divergence in the ability of areas to compete for medical care. Put simply, this meant that most doctors were attracted to cities because incomes were higher there, other amenities were greater, and research and hospital facilities were more readily available.

The rapid increase in automobile usage affected both the distribution of physicians and the relation of patients to doctors. Among the first users of the car were the doctors themselves, who could now see more patients in one day. Soon the patients themselves were visiting the doctors' offices by car, which in turn increased the number of patients a doctor could see in a single day, while transferring the burden of travel distance to the patients themselves. Even in rural areas the relationships have changed. Thus F. Dickinson reported that, in rural Illinois, sixteen doctors in 1951 were providing more services to more people than forty-two doctors had done in 1920. In that latter era the roads had been so poor that a doctor could spend one and two hours getting five miles to and from town on a rural call, and it took six hours to travel forty miles to the nearest hospital. Now, however, patients can reach town in ten to twenty minutes, and hospital services are at the most an hour away.

The general effect of the automobile has been to concentrate doctors into fewer settlements and to enlarge the catchment areas for medical services. In some cases, because of the greater attractiveness of cities, rural areas have been left with inadequate local medical care.

Subsystem Structure

Empirical studies of the structure of medical care services tend to emphasize that the utilization of medical services is not just a function of the prevalence of illness. Most major illnesses are treated in the United States. Nevertheless, the overall utilization of a medical service varies according to the characteristics of the population and the availability of that service, both of which are especially subject to variations in the patient's income and in the supply of doctors. Other contributing factors are ethnic origin, education, occupation, and distance.* The distribution of doctors, which leads to the differential availability of services mentioned above, reflects potential income, the ratio of rural to urban characteristics, and the size of a settlement.

In total, the approximate supply of doctors is roughly equivalent to the total medical demand, so that any maldistribution in the system is a function of the distribution of doctors rather than of the number of doctors.

In the United States doctors concentrate in the largest urban nodes. Some 30 percent of the total U.S. population is concentrated in less than 1 percent of all U.S. cities. But these cities—the ones with 100,000 or more inhabitants—have 50 percent of all U.S. doctors. About 50 percent of the population, residing in the 9 percent of towns with over 10,000 population, were served by 76.5 percent of all doctors.

How many people are needed to support a doctor's services? Estimates based on empirical studies range from about 1,000 for an ordinary physician up to 40,000 for specialists (table 51). These threshold populations might be more accurately characterized in terms of their purchasing power, but the data are not available.

Movements or trips for medical care have also been analyzed (table 52). They have usually proven to be among the longest trips made for any purpose, which reflects the importance often attached to a particular doctor or quality of service. This study, conducted in western Pennsylvania, illustrates very clearly how increased urbanization makes medical services relatively more accessible.

Hospital Care

An interesting way to trace the distribution of hospital care is to examine briefly the work done by R. Morrill and R. Earickson in 1969 in conjunction with the Chicago Regional Hospital Study. Their purpose was to ascertain the location factors of hospitals, and to estimate shifts in the location of ca-

*Since people are willing to incur high time-costs for medical care, often transportation time-costs can approach the cost of the care itself. In the case of specialist care at regional medical centers, demand can be so great that time-costs may far exceed the costs of the care itself.

Table 51. *Threshold Population for Physicians' Services*

	threshold population
physician	*900*
general practitioner	*2,500**
pediatrician	*6,000*
internal medical, surgery, eye and ear	*10,000*
obstetrician	*7,500*
opthalmologist, radiologist	*20,000*
urologist, orthopedist, neurologist, etc.	*40,000*

Source: From Garrison et al., *Studies of Highway Development and Geographic Change.* Reprinted by permission of the University of Washington Press.

*In small towns without specialist thresholds, general practice thresholds may range from 800 to 1500.

Table 52. *Distance Traveled to Physicians, Western Pennsylvania*

	av. distance to general practitioner (miles)	av. distance to medical specialist (miles)
allegheny	*2.97*	*3.12*
lesser metropolitan areas	*3.60*	*6.00*
areas adjacent to allegheny	*4.30*	*10.00*
areas adjacent to lesser metropolitan areas	*5.30*	*14.10*
other	*5.00*	*14.40*
average	*3.87*	*6.10*

Source: Garrison et al, *Ibid,*, p. 241.

pacity (number of beds, doctors, etc.) that would raise the level of satisfaction of patients, physicians, and hospital management. They defined satisfaction in terms of:

1. *The patient's desire for easier access, both temporally and spatially, to hospitals and doctors with certain desired characteristics.*
2. *The physician's desire to increase his access to hospitals and to make full use of their capacities.*
3. *The hospital management's desire for a high rate of occupancy without congestion or excessive waiting.*

First, Morrill and Earickson analyzed the actual use of the hospital system. They found that for most patients the trip to hospital is a two-stage affair, although both stages do not usually occur together. The patient first visits a doctor, who in turn assigns the patient to a hospital. While the patient may have preferences and opinions about particular hospitals, it is the doctor, not the patient, who chooses the hospital. In terms of distance, this decision com-

monly benefits the doctor more than the patient. Thus while the trip to the doctor tends to reflect to some degree the patient's own appraisal of the number of physicians and the time it takes to reach them, the hospital trip predominantly reflects the doctor's evaluation of the distance, size, and number of suitable hospitals. This explains why so many patients travel beyond the hospital closest to them.

Second, it was pointed out that the availability of medical care in the United States is maldistributed. That is, some patients cannot afford to go to doctors at all, nor can they afford to pay for hospital care. To the extent that they must have care, their needs are met by only a small proportion of suitable hospitals, such as the few designed only for charity patients, and the few that take some charity patients for medical interest under state or federal subsidy. Such a restriction means that many poorer patients go without treatment, or have to travel much further to a hospital than they would otherwise need to.

Third, Morrill and Earickson point out that patients differ in the severity of their medical problems, and that hospitals differ in their ability to provide specialist care. In large metropolitan areas at least four kinds of hospitals are found: a few very large teaching and research hospitals that can deal with even the most specialized and acute medical needs; a few large hospitals that can treat a variety of intermediate level problems; many smaller hospitals, equipped to handle only routine medical needs; and a few special purpose hospitals that will treat or care for only one specialized medical need. The effect of such a structure is to restrict the choice of hospital, especially for the patient needing more specialized treatment. Other hospital types exist that cater to particular groups of patients, such as children and pregnant women. But not all hospitals have wards for these classes of patients, while some hospitals emphasize them. This complicates choice still further.

Fourthly, ethnic differences, particularly between black white, have a dramatic influence on hospital use. The low income Afro-American population is restricted to the few hospitals taking charity patients. But even the paying Afro-American patient is likely to be treated by Afro-American doctors, who in turn are likely to be restricted to a few wholly Afro-American hospitals. Clearly, the Afro-American patient does not have equal access to hospitals and must travel farther than average in order to obtain medical care. Sometimes limited substitution is possible between a fairly close Afro-American hospital and a very distant hospital that will at least accept Afro-Americans.

Finally, Morrill and Earickson discovered that religion can play a role in choice of hospital. Thus a patient may have to choose between a distant hospital operated by the religion of his choice and a closer one of some different persuasion. In the Chicago area for example, it was found that many patients were willing to travel greater distances in order to reach Protestant, Catholic, or Jewish operated hospitals.

In sum, patients require different levels of care, but only a minority of hospitals are similarly differentiated. Patients also differ in ethnic status and their ability to pay, while hospitals differ in their willingness to care for charity or Afro-American patients. Finally, patients' religious beliefs lead some of them to perceive advantages in hospitals under the control of their denomination.

Wholesaling

As a category of tertiary activities, wholesaling has received considerable attention from the commerce and marketing disciplines, though somewhat less from geographers.

The Wholesaling Subsystem

Between the manufacturer and the retailer there often stands an array of intermediary channels of distribution. In the early years of the Industrial Revolution, manufacturers tended to be small. Thus wholesalers came to dominate distribution systems. This was an important factor in leading manufacturers to adopt brand names and to attempt to build up consumer demand for specific brands. In time, some manufacturers decreased their dependence on the wholesaler in a number of ways. One of these was to establish their own sales forces and distributing their goods directly to the retailer. Some manufacturers went further and established their own retailing outlets; still others compromised by retaining the wholesaler for distribution, but utilizing their own missionary salesmen to supplement their promotional efforts.

The Structure of the Subsystem

Despite efforts to circumvent the wholesaler, or *middleman*, he is still an integral element of the marketing system. One way of defining his role is as that of an independent businessman who buys, resells, or negotiates sales of merchandise to other organizations such as retailers, other wholesalers, manufacturers or institutions. The butter manufacturer in New York State, the manufacturer of electronic components in Colorado, and the vegetable grower in California have one important thing in common: the

need to reach their markets by some *channel of distribution.*

Within the wholesaling subsystem there are several identifiable subcomponents, as shown in tables 53 and 54. These roles have arisen in response to changes in economic conditions. For example, the *rack jobber* is a relatively new type of limited function wholesaler who originated as the sales of nonfood items in supermarkets increased. Although nonfood items account for only about 5 percent of total store sales, wide profit margins and often fairly rapid turnover may make these items earn up to 8 percent of all store gross profits. The rack jobber came into being to supply food stores who would find it relatively inefficient to handle their own nonfood items, especially since a relatively small proportion of total store volume is involved, and warehousing and handling costs can be quite high. As retailing conditions have changed further, the rack jobber has spread into a relatively wide line of retail supplies, and now services variety stores, discount stores, and hardware stores besides supermarkets.

For a particular product or good there may be several alternative distribution channels, as figures 146 and 147 show. These channels can be of varying complexity, efficiency, and cost. Thus the manufacturer of lighting fixtures can sell his good directly to the user via a retail store or mail-order house, or through an agency system, or through various wholesalers and contractors. A manufacturer of records may use several wholesalers before his product reaches the consumer, or he may sell directly, through his own record club.

These patterns are concerned with what have been called the *vertical* aspects of distribution. As shown in table 53 where the wholesaling functions are completely integrated at the producer levels, these channels can be direct from manufacturer to user. This is the system normally used for distributing industrial goods. Where the wholesaling functions

Table 53. *The Wholesaling System: Vertical Aspects of Distribution Channels*

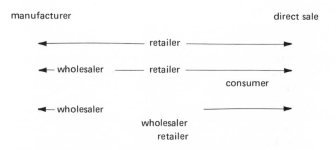

Source: Adapted from G.A. Field, J. Douglas, and L.X. Tarpey, *Marketing Management: A Behavioral Systems Approach* (Columbus, Ohio: C.E. Merrill Books, 1966), p. 422.

Table 54. *Classification of Wholesale Middlemen*

I. merchant middlemen
   A. nonintegrated, full service
     1. full service wholesaler
     2. industrial distributor
     3. importer and exporter
   B. nonintegrated, limited function
     1. cash-and-carry wholesalers
     2. drop shippers
     3. mail order wholesalers
     4. truck jobbers
     5. rack jobbers
   C. integrated, manufacturer controlled
     1. manufacturers' sales branches (with stocks)
     2. manufacturers' sales offices
   D. integrated, wholesale middlemen controlled
     1. converters
     2. wholesaler-sponsored voluntary chain
   E. integrated, retail middlemen controlled
     1. corporate chain buying offices
     2. corporate chain warehouses
     3. retailers' buying pools
II. agent middlemen
   A. nonintegrated, full service
     1. commission agents
     2. export and import agents
   B. nonintegrated, limited function
     1. auction companies
     2. brokers
   C. integrated, manufacturer controlled
     1. selling agents
     2. manufacturers' agents
     3. purchasing agents
III. combination merchant and agent middlemen
   A. petroleum bulk plants, terminals, and gas facilities
     1. independent
     2. chain
     3. commission
     4. refinery controlled
   B. assemblers of farm products
     1. nonintegrated
     2. integrated
   C. multiple-type operations

Source: G.A. Field, J. Douglas, and L.X. Tarpey, *Marketing Management: A Behavioral Systems Approach* (Columbus, Ohio: C.E. Merrill Books, 1966), p. 447.

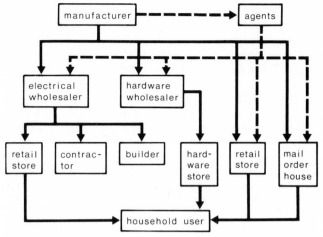

Fig. 146. *Distribution channels for an "industrial" good: residential lighting fixtures. (Adapted from E.H. Lewis, "Distributing Electrical Products in a Dynamic Economy," Electrical Wholesaling, June 1958, p. 119, by courtesy of the editor and the McGraw-Hill Publishing Co.)*

are completely integrated by the producer, the retailer, or both, there is usually a short distribution channel. A third possibility is that an agent or wholesaler can step in between producer and retailer.* Finally, there may be a combination of agents or wholesalers, or of both together. Which kind of dis-

*An *agent* does not own the goods, and may in fact never take actual physical possession of them, as the *wholesaler* does. Before the chain store revolution of the 1920s these were the most usual methods of distributing consumer goods.

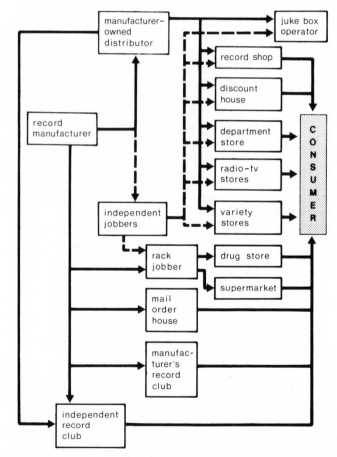

Fig. 147. *Distribution channels for a "consumer" good: phonograph records. (Adapted from K. Hamill, "The Record Business—'Its Murder,'" Fortune, vol. 63, no. 5, pp. 178 and 182, courtesy of Fortune Magazine.)*

tribution channel will be used depends on three basic factors:

1. *What is the nature of the product to be marketed?*
2. *What is the nature and extent of the market for this good?*
3. *What middleman or distribution channel already exists for similar products?*

In other words, is the good to be marketed an industrial, shopping, or convenience good? Is the market seasonal? Is it spatially localized, or is it nationwide? And are there manufacturers, agents, or wholesalers already in existence to market similar products, so that they could cope with this new product too? These questions will usually be posed and answered in the framework of expected cost and sales potentials. But whatever distribution channel is chosen one particular marketing axiom holds true: You can eliminate the middleman but you cannot eliminate his functions. In making a channel selection the marketing manager must decide what sort of cooperation he will get from various middlemen in the way of sales promotion, price guarantees, or other kinds of help. Once the decision is made it is usually periodically reviewed in order to take account of any changes in the wholesaling subsystem, such as the rise of rack jobbers.

Marketing also has its *horizontal* aspects. These relate to the amount and kind of market exposure a manufacturer needs for his product. A producer of convenience goods (breakfast foods, cake mixes, etc.) will want his product on the shelves of virtually every grocery store and supermarket. A producer of certain shopping and specialty goods, on the other hand, may attempt to reach only a limited section of the market, and will therefore select only one or two retailers in a local area to sell his products, which may be appliances or high quality furniture.

Three different types of marketing exposure can be distinguished:

1. Intensive distribution, *or the stocking and selling of a product by virtually every middleman in the market. This is a costly system, but many convenience goods have to be made concurrently available to consumers because the latter are not likely to invest much time in looking for them.*
2. Selective distribution, *or selecting only some of the available middlemen to market a product. This system is adopted when blanket coverage of the market is neither necessary nor desirable.*
3. Exclusive distribution, *or using only one middleman to represent a particular manufacture in a particular market or region. This is often done with specialty goods and less frequently with shopping goods. The usual reason is that the manufacturer wants to control specific*

aspects of the marketing program at the local level. Automobile sales, some household appliances, radios, and television sets may be handled this way.

The rationale behind these three systems of distribution is based first, on the amount of marketing effort expected of each middleman, and second, on the nature of the product. As table 55 shows, these factors are interrelated. The manufacturer of convenience goods might choose policy "A," since he is primarily interested in maximizing shelf exposure and expects little or no in-store promotion other than that already primed by advertising and the distinctive packaging. At the other extreme, a manufacturer of expensive hi-fi components might choose policy "C," and give a reputable local retailer or wholesaler an exclusive franchise. In return he might ask for such in-store promotional efforts as special servicing, local advertising, and maintaining an inventory of spare parts. The nature of the product is therefor a major factor in the manufacturer's choice of distribution channel.

Table 55. *Horizontal Distribution Policies*

	policy A	policy B	policy C
number of middlemen	*many*	*few*	*one*
type of policy	*intensive*	*selective*	*exclusive*
marketing effort by middlemen	*minimum*	*some*	*maximum*

Source: G.A. Field, J. Douglas, and L.X. Tarpey, *Marketing Management: A Behavioral Systems Approach* (Columbus, Ohio: C.E. Merrill Books, 1966), p. 425.

The Location of Distribution Centers

The appropriate location for a warehouse or distribution center depends on the degree of market concentration, the intensity of distribution, the intensity of demand, the location of the production plant or plants, and the adequacy and efficiency of the communications network.

Assuming for simplicity's sake a distribution system, as shown in figure 148, with a single manufacturing source and a two-tier middleman distributive channel, the following comments can be made.

If the market for the product is highly concentrated, the warehouses will tend to be located at or near major points of concentration rather than at minimum cost points. In such cases, warehouses tend to be located at transportation nodes, between the plant and the market areas they serve (figure 149). Thus products moving from the wholesalers can reach local markets in a reasonable length of time, depending on distance, and on the modes

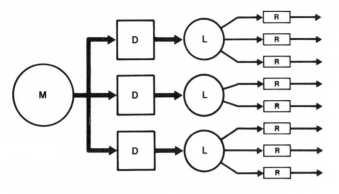

M manufacturing plant   L local distribution
D distribution warehouse R retail store

Fig. 148. *Product flow in a wholesaling system from a single plant. (From J.E. Magee,* Physical Distributions Systems, *1967, p. 116. Copyright © 1967 by McGraw-Hill Inc. Used with permission of McGraw-Hill Book Company.)*

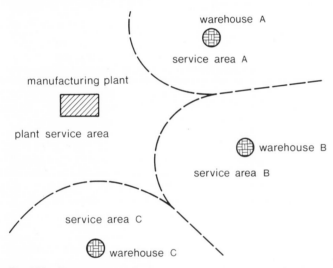

warehouse A

service area A

manufacturing plant

plant service area

warehouse B

service area B

service area C

warehouse C

Fig. 149. *Relationship of manufacturer, wholesaler, and consumer. (From Magee 1967, ibid., p. 117.)*

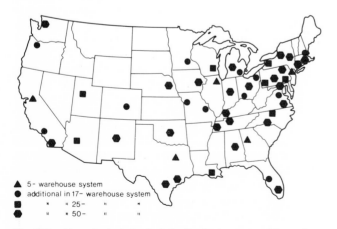

▲ 5- warehouse system
● additional in 17- warehouse system
■   "   "   25-   "   "
⬢   "   "   50-   "   "

Fig. 150. *Hypothetical physical distribution systems, with varying numbers of warehouses. (From Magee 1967, ibid., p. 119.)*

(rail, truck, etc.) and services available. Depending on the time and intensity of coverage one of the four systems illustrated in figure 150 might be used. Thus in the United States distribution from a warehouse could cover an area with a radius of 200–250 miles within one day's journey, 450–500 miles within two days', and 700–750 miles within three days', all depending of course on local highway conditions.

In determining actual warehouse territories, factors such as sales convenience, provincial and state boundaries, or anomalies in service and freight rates may all need to be accounted for, as well as time-distance and transportation costs. A manufacturer setting up his own wholesaling functions will want to relate the present to the projected market, and then identify a number of warehouse locations. These need not be many; for an industrial product with a geographically concentrated market only one to five warehouses may be needed to cover the whole United States. On the other hand, the manufacturer of a convenience good may need fifteen to one hundred locations, and perhaps two or three intermediate systems.

Having selected the warehouse locations, the manufacturer will have to set up provisional boundaries between the warehouse distribution areas. The main criterion here will be the transportation cost function. But this will need adjustment for freight rate boundaries, state or national boundaries, and major physical obstacles such as the Rocky Mountains. The market area that could be served from each warehouse in one, two, or three days will also have to be noted. The sort of pattern that might emerge (in this case based on the calculations of a southern Illinois manufacturer) is shown in table 56. This is a solution for only one manufacturing plant; for more than one plant, the technique is more difficult.

In locating a warehousing system it must also be borne in mind that retailers may find they need to hold their stock or inventory levels fairly low, consistent with consumer demand. Thus the retailer may need to be able to utilize a distribution system that can supply him relatively quickly. In fact the location of warehouses reflects the horizontal policies

Table 56. *Warehousing: Market Area Coverage*

system	number of warehouses	percentage of potential market reachable within		
		1 day	2 days	3 days
A	5	30	78	88
B	17	73	87	90
C	25	81	90	90
D	50	87	90	90

Source: *Physical Distribution Systems* by J. E. Magee, p. 123. Copyright © 1967 by McGraw-Hill Inc. Used with permission of the McGraw-Hill Book Company.

of distribution discussed above. Most numerous and most highly dispersed are warehouse locations for *intensive distribution,* such as wholesale grocery houses or gasoline bulk stations, where customer needs are large and the frequency of purchases is great. Less numerous and more highly centralized are the wholesalers of dry goods, furniture, manufacturer goods, and spare parts, all of which are less frequently purchased items. Even wholesale grocery houses may be confined to cities that are of medium size or larger, since one warehouse can serve a large number of retailers and a much larger number of consumers. Thus furniture, dry goods, and jewelry wholesalers normally exist only in the larger metropolitan centers, the market areas of which include hundreds of retailers. In figure 150 and the "A" row of table 56 a five warehouse system with locations in New York, Chicago, San Francisco, Dallas, and Atlanta could reach 88 percent of the market in 3 days, which would be ample coverage in time and area terms for specialty goods such as wrist watches or jewelry.* In the "B" row, the addition of another 12 centers like Portland, Los Angeles, Boulder, or Tampa could give a 73 percent coverage in 1 day. For grocery wholesaling the best choices would probably be systems "C" or "D."

The advent of the motor truck has brought considerable changes in the wholesaling pattern in recent years. Principally, of course, it increases the radius or market area that can be served quickly by particular warehouses. Overnight deliveries in response to telephone or teletyped orders have reduced even further the inventory holdings of retail stores. At the same time, speedy truck deliveries have greatly increased the number of stores that can be served from one center. The result of these technical changes has been to greatly reduce the number of wholesalers as well as the adoption of systems A, B, or C. Thus wholesalers have become overwhelmingly concentrated in the larger metropolitan centers, especially ones that are major transportation nodes. This trend has been accompanied by an increase in the number of producers with their own distribution channels. In short, the whole process of the elimination of the smaller wholesaler, and the concentration of distributive mechanisms in the hands of a few major wholesalers or manufacturers, is basically a function of improved transportation. This tendency is limited only by the development of specialized wholesaling services, such as rack jobbers, that arise from time to time to deal with special changes in retailing and consumer demands.

*Of course a manufacturing plant in southern Illinois, which is the subject of this example, has a central location that simplifies site selection.

Conclusion

If retailing makes up the bulk of the tertiary subsystem in terms of employees, sales volume, and monetary transactions, it by no means dwarfs the importance of the other components. As table 40 suggests, there is a wide range of other tertiary activities. Some are concerned with our leisure time, an increasingly important part of our total activities. Thus recreational and vacation services range from movie theaters to restaurants, from motels to picnic sites. Some of these activities, together with business and repair services, are governed by all or some of the principles set out in the retailing section. Wholesaling, like retailing, has been the subject of intensive marketing studies, but has not so far been much studied by geographers. Other areas of tertiary activity concern medical, educational and spiritual needs. These "medical and personal service" sectors have their own sets of governing factors, many of which depend more on public policy decisions than on the decisions of the individual entrepreneur. Finally, as we saw in table 40, there is the group that has received least attention of all from geographers; financial institutions, such as banks, trust companies, stock exchanges, insurance, and real estate. Each of these subsystems has its own controlling factors, so that regional banks, for instance, are subject to centralizing factors—and, in the United States, to specific public policies and legislative conditions—while real estate offices, on the other hand, are subject to decentralization.

Despite these disparate factors, this group of activities, with particular and sometimes unique local situations, is bound together by a common goal: service of the consumer, with all his needs and wants.

Summary

1. The retail facilities of a city form a subsystem, a set of interrelated elements that interact to create a recognizable structure. The consumer's demands and responses and the retailer's supplies and responses are linked through a feedback system. Over time these interrelationships lead to the establishment of a fairly consistent spatial pattern of nucleations, ribbons, and specialized areas.

2. In addition, the number of retail functions is related to the amount and distribution of consumer income. Each store has a threshold or minimum amount of sales below which it operates at a loss. Stores are often located so as to best tap the consumer income most likely to patronize them.

3. Each store's location is also related to a land values surface. Peak land values are occupied by stores that need maximum accessibility to consumers and that can afford to pay for it.

4. The retailing structure varies with the limited or full search nature of consumer behavior. Shopping goods that invite full search activities tend to cluster in high order centers (unless in a monopolistic situation) with maximum accessibility to purchasing power and sited at land value peaks. Convenience goods are frequently purchased, searched for in a more limited way, dispersed in low order centers with lower land values and accessibility to more localized purchasing power.

5. With a shortening working week, leisure-time or recreational facilities are of growing importance. The day-to-day demands of leisure can be satisfied in reasonable proximity to the consumer's work place or residence. Movie theatres, night clubs, sports arenas, etc., locate in a similar manner to retail facilities. Other recreational needs can be satisfied by more infrequent weekend or vacation excursions. The location of ski-lodges, motels, hotels, national parks, etc., depends on consumer demand and user perception, economic need, physical amenities and accessibility.

6. Medical facilities in the United States are located by factors like threshold and accessibility, which in turn are influenced by the personal perceptions of the services available. Religious, ethnic, and socioeconomic status can limit a patient's choice to a third-class separate system of medical care. Demands and supplies are warped by the cultural and economic characteristics of an area, and by the medical profession's responses to them. Thus medical services are spatially unevenly distributed, of varying quantity and quality, and particularly oriented to the demands of higher socioeconomic groups in large urban centers.

7. Between the manufacturer, the retailer, motel operator, physician and hospital stands an array of intermediary channels of distribution. The location of this wholesaling subsystem and the degree of specialization of the wholesaler vary with the nature of the goods, consumer demand, and the costs and speed of delivery. The use of trucks, containers, and unit trains has increased accessibility and led to a decline in the total number of wholesalers, as larger and larger areas can be serviced efficiently and quickly from fewer and fewer distribution points.

8. These brief analyses of four components of the tertiary activity subsystem merely introduce us to an ever-expanding area of the work force and national product. Banking, insurance, real estate, charity organizations, education, administration, repairs and services, religious institutions—and many others—

are all part of this same subsystem, and as yet largely await the attention of the economic geographer.

Further Reading

The retailing component of the tertiary subsystem is treated in an extensive number of books and articles, since it has received most attention to date from geographers. A selection includes:

Berry, B. J. L. et al. *Commercial Structure and Commercial Blight,* Department of Geography, University of Chicago, Research Paper no. 85, 1963.

Garner, B. J. *The Internal Structure of Retail Nucleations,* Department of Geography, Northwestern University, Studies in Geography, no. 12, 1966.

Scott, P. *The Geography of Retailing* (Chicago: Aldine, 1970).

Simmons, J. *The Changing Pattern of Retail Location,* Department of Geography, University of Chicago, Research Paper no. 92, 1964.

Simmons, J. *Toronto's Changing Retail Complex: A Study in Growth and Blight,* Department of Geography, University of Chicago, Research Paper no. 104, 1966.

The recreational component is an area of increased interest in recent years, and is covered in

Aldskogims, H. "Vacation House Settlement in the Siljan Region," *Geografiska Annaler,* vol. 49B, 1967, pp. 69–95.

Bultena, G. L. and Klessig, L. L. "Satisfaction in Camping: A Conceptualization and Guide to Social Research," *Journal of Leisure Research,* vol. 1, 1969, pp. 348–354.

Campbell, C. "An Approach to Research in Recreational Geography," *B.C. Geographical Series,* no. 7, 1966, pp. 85–90.

Clawson, M. and Knetsch, J. V. *Economics of Outdoor Recreation* (Baltimore: Johns Hopkins Press, 1966).

Clawson, M. *Methods of Measuring Demand for the Value of Outdoor Recreation* (Washington, D.C.: Resources for the Future Inc., 1966).

Colenutt, R. J. "Modelling Travel Patterns of Day Visitors to the Countryside," *Area,* vol. 2, 1969, pp. 43–47.

Deasy, G. F. and Geiss, P. R. "Impact of a Tourist Facility on its Hinterland," *Annals of the Association of American Geographers,* vol. 56, 1966, pp. 290–306.

Lucas, R. C. "Wilderness Perception and Use: The Example of the Boundary Waters Canoe Area," *Natural Resources Journal,* vol. 3, 1964, pp. 394–411.

Lucas, R. C. *User Evaluation of Campgrounds on Two Michigan National Forests,* USDA Forest Service Research Paper NC44, 1970.

Mercer, D. C. "Urban Recreational Hinterlands: A Review and Example," *The Professional Geographer,* vol. 22, 1970, pp. 74–78.

Mercer, D. C. "The Role of Perception in the Recreation Experience: A Review and Discussion," *Journal of Leisure Research*, vol. 3, 1971, pp. 1–13.

O'Riordan, T. "Environmental Management," *Progress in Geography*, vol. 3, 1971, pp. 173–231.

Outdoor Recreation Resources Review Commission. *Economic Studies of Outdoor Recreation*, Study Report No. 24, Washington, D.C., 1962, as well as some of the other reports (e.g., no. 3 on user-satisfaction).

Tombaugh, L. "Factors Influencing Vacation Home Locations," *Journal of Leisure Research*, vol. 2, 1970, pp. 54–63.

Wolfe, R. I. "The Geography of Recreation: A Dynamic Approach," *B.C. Geographical Series*, no. 8, 1967, pp. 7–12.

Wolfe, R. I. *Parameters of Recreational Travel in Ontario*, Report RBIII, Department of Highways, Ontario.

The medical component, a relatively new area of interest, can be tracked down in

Earickson, R. *The Spatial Behavior of Hospital Patients*, Department of Geography, University of Chicago, Research Paper no. 124, 1970.

Garrison, W. L. et al. *Studies of Highway Development and Geographic Change* (Seattle: University of Washington, 1959), chapters 12, 13 and 14.

Gould, P. and Leinbach, T. R. "An Approach to the Geographic Assignment of Hospital Services," *Tijdschrift Voor Economische en Sociale Geografie*, vol. 57, 1966, pp. 203–206.

Long, M. F. and Feldstein, P. J. "The Economics of Hospital Systems: Peak Loads and Regional Coordination," *American Economic Review*, vol. 57, 1968, pp. 119–29.

Morrill, R. L. Earickson, R. J. and Rees, P. "Factors Influencing Distances Travelled to Hospitals," *Economic Geography*, vol. 46, 1970, pp. 161–171.

Vise, Pierre de. *Slum Medicine: Chicago Style, How the Medical Needs of the City's Negro Poor Are Met*, Chicago Regional Hospital Study Working Paper, no. 4.8, 1968.

The wholesaling component is not so well developed, but see

Field, G. A., Douglas, J. and Tarpey, L. X. *Marketing Management: A Behavioral Systems Approach* (Columbus, Ohio: C. E. Merrill Books Inc., 1966).

Magee, J. F. *Physical-Distribution Systems* (New York: McGraw-Hill, 1967).

Mulvihill, D. *Geography, Marketing and Urban Growth* Princeton: Van Nostrand, 1970).

For a rather different and a very idiosyncratic treatment of the area of wholesaling, see

Vance, J. E. *The Merchant's World: The Geography of Wholesaling* (Englewood Cliffs: Prentice-Hall, 1970).

twelve

The Transportation
System: An Overview

Previous chapters have emphasized the location of *sites*—the places at which economic activities occur. In this chapter and the next we turn to a consideration of *routes*—the links between sites, and the main determinants of their *accessibility*, which is the ease with which communication occurs between sites. We shall also be concerned with *transportation methods*. Many innovations in the field of transportation are concerned with efforts to improve accessibility. Accordingly, insofar as economic activity is extended over space, transportation technology plays a key role in it.

Introduction

Transportation is an essentially geographic concept. The relations and connections between areas are frequently reflected in the character of transportation facilities and in the flow of traffic. But the study of transportation involves more than this. It deals not just with the flow of goods or people but with the flow of such less tangible items as ideas, innovations, money, and credit. Indeed, it deals with all kinds of spatial connections and interactions, which French geographers sum up in one untranslatable term, *circulation*. This term is an apt reminder that "communication," the movement of ideas, and "transportation," the movement of goods and people, are not rigidly separated, but rather grade into each other.

Geographic Relevance of Transportation

The study of *circulation*, in the sense given above, is maintained by some geographers to provide a deeper insight into the meaning of areal differences, and even to provide a key for measuring differences and similarities among places on the earth. Indeed, some geographers have viewed geography as primarily the study of *circulation*. One of these is P. R. Crowe; another is E. L. Ullman. Both saw movement as an indicator of the degree of social connection and as underlying all patterns of interchange. The same idea is implicit in the absolute spatial concepts of W. Bunge, and in the work of J. D. Nystuen.

Traditionally, North American geographers have divided economic geography into four basic components: primary production, manufacturing, marketing, and transportation geography. But this, as should be obvious by now, is a highly artificial division. Thus geographers interested in transport are forced to draw on ideas and concepts from other disciplines like sociology, psychology, planning, engineering, architecture, as well as from other parts of geography. However, in economic geography we are concerned primarily with such questions as: What is the role of transport in the spatial economy? How are economic behavior patterns influenced by the availability and nature of transportation networks? How do improvements in the transportation network affect those patterns? As long ago as 1894 the sociologist C. H. Cooley warned that "there can be no adequate theory of transportation which has regard only to some one aspect of its social function, as the economic aspect. That is not the only aspect nor can one truly say that it is more important than the others. All are coordinate, equally indispensable to social progress." Today this reads like an early plea for systems analysis! Equally pertinent are his following remarks: "The character of transportation as a whole and in detail, at any particular time and

throughout its history, is altogether determined by its interrelations with physical and social forces and conditions. To understand transportation means simply to analyze these interrelations."

Most societal systems are specialized; even the most underdeveloped are showing signs of some specialization. It seems to be a hallmark of economic change that economic activities become increasingly polarized in spatial terms. As economic development occurs there is a marked tendency for the means of production to be concentrated in fewer and larger economic units (what economists call agglomerative tendencies). In the most developed economic systems, as living standards rise economic differences tend to decline. So developing societies are at the same time becoming increasingly differentiated and yet more uniform. This uniformity is also encouraged by other forms of communication — communication of ideas, for instance — and other forces that in some sense or other are making the world more alike. The general effect is to make demands (i.e., the array of goods consumed) more alike and widespread, but supply (i.e., the array of production facilities) more concentrated. Thus economic systems as production units are tied to ever expanding markets. As consumer units, they have needs that must be satisfied from increasingly diverse sources of supply.

In other words, change in the technology of transportation over the last few hundred years has resulted in a great reduction in the costs of movement, and a corresponding general improvement in accessibility. It is this that has made possible the economic specialization of areas. In effect, interdependence has been substituted for self-sufficiency. Transport over land used to be slow and costly — compare, for example, the transportation components of the Christaller and von Thünen models. Bulk movements of raw materials as now undertaken were virtually unknown. Each area of concentrated settlement was therefore virtually a closed system, or household, producing most of its own fuel and food. Most trade was in the form of luxury items that could stand the high cost of shipment. Certainly there were some bulk movements, particularly where the relative cheapness of water transport permitted some crop specialization. Thus fourth-century Athens depended on wheat from what is now the Ukraine, just as first-century Rome depended on corn and other grain crops from North Africa. But both cities relied on transportation by sea. It was the railroad, first as a short feeder route from Northeast England's coalfield to the sea, but later of intercontinental dimensions, that provided cheap overland bulk transport. At last continental agricultural areas could specialize even if they were remote from navigable waterways. For the first time, factors of **comparative advantage** became operative, and locally favorable conditions of land, labor, and capital allowed specialized low cost production of goods for distant markets. Thus instead of local zones around a market city, in the von Thünen model, large and ever more distant regions around a specialized area have become the dominant pattern of economic activity.

This trend toward a single world economic system shows up in local and regional circulation patterns. The complexity of the interrelationships that may arise is illustrated in figure 151. Circulation patterns, however, are also influenced by the particular modal system, as well as the particular network, flows, and so on. The matching of demand, which is becoming increasingly similar and widespread, and supply, which is becoming increasingly specialized and concentrated, is channeled through the communications system. It is the spatial structuring of these patterns of demand and supply that initiates movement, through which any spatial imbalance can be corrected (compare figures 161 and 162, below). The structure of the transportation system affects and moulds the circulation patterns, limiting in some cases the degree and direction of interchange and interaction.

A number of authors have been concerned with the various notions of *distance* implicit in any study of interaction. This concern has been correctly called fundamental to geography. Distance is particularly important in a discussion of *circulation*, since it has an inhibiting effect on movement. There are several concepts of distance, each with its own unit of measurement:

1. *Physical distance (e.g., in miles).*
2. *Temporal distance (e.g., in hours).*

3. *Economic distance (e.g., in dollars).*
4. *Social distance (e.g., in terms of accessibility).*

To these four, a fifth is often added: communications distance in terms of cost, efficiency, and use of telephone calls, newspapers, radio, and television. Physical distance is the mapped, flight, or ground distance; economic distance, measured in terms of transportation cost, is the cost of transporting a commodity from one point to another; social distance refers to distance measured in terms of its meaning to a particular social group, such as Puerto Ricans who migrate to New York (the closest point that means anything very much to them).

To recapitulate: the ultimate aim of an economic geographer concerned with transportation is to both describe and explain *circulation* as a feature of the world economic system. This feature is limited, directed, and channeled by a transportation system that is both composite and conglomerate. The total communications system is a composite of many modes and elements acting either in unison or in competition over a complex of networks. When demands or desires are united with areally separated supplies or fulfillments, the result is *circulation*. The quantity of traffic is a function of those demands and supplies, on the one hand, and of the character of the available transportation systems, on the other. As we shall see, each means or mode of transport has its own technological characteristics, and its own spatial layout or network.

All the basic behavior or activity sectors examined by the economic geographer are implicitly concerned with movement of some kind. Thus agricultural location theory deals with the output shipments from farm to market, and the movement of fertilizers, machinery, and other material inputs from market to surrounding farms. This theoretical sequence of land use is both a reflection and a determinant of agricultural practice. Industrial location theory in both its least cost and profit maximization versions imposes certain patterns on the transportation of fuel, raw materials, and the finished or semi-finished product itself. Central place theory also defines the movement of consumers from place of residence to tertiary good or service outlet.

Each of these theories tends to be *static, deterministic,* and *normative.* That is, it describes conditions as they ought to occur at one point in time if activities were determined in an economically rational way. Real-world deviations from the spatial interaction patterns implicit in such deterministic economic location theories are usually explained in terms of distribution patterns already dictated by that same body of theory. However, these deviations are more likely to represent conditions that are the opposite of economically rational.

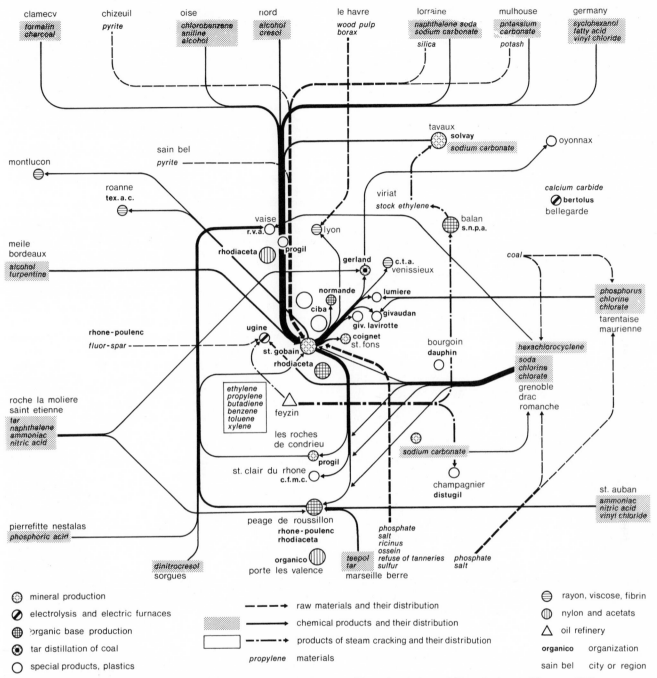

Fig. 151. *Economic goods flows: the Lyons industrial region. (From Jean Labasse,* L'Organisation de l'Espace, *1966, p. 193, reprinted by permission of Hermann, Paris.)*

Legend:
- ⊚ mineral production
- ⊘ electrolysis and electric furnaces
- ⊕ organic base production
- ◉ tar distillation of coal
- ○ special products, plastics
- - - -→ raw materials and their distribution
- ▦ ──→ chemical products and their distribution
- □ -·-·-▸ products of steam cracking and their distribution
- *propylene* materials
- ⊖ rayon, viscose, fibrin
- ⬚ nylon and acetats
- △ oil refinery
- **organico** organization
- sain bel city or region

The Transportation Subsystem

How then are we to approach transportation, if its systemic relationships are so complex? There are a number of alternative ways; here, only two with particular geographic relevance will be examined.

The Six-Question Systems Approach

One approach is to pose a series of questions concerning transportation routes:

1. What is meant by a route?

2. *What are the conditions for interaction, and so for the emergence of a route?*

3. *What is the nature of routes?*

To these three basic questions, three further questions can be added:

4. *What controls actual route location?*

5. *How do routes grow and change?*

6. *What is the relationship of the route structure to other economic activities?*

The Meaning of "Route"

A route is a regularly traveled path of some social and economic significance. A path is a link between two communities or places that is not used on any regular basis, and may not be considered a link at all. Figure 152 shows diagrammatically the kinds of paths and routes that may develop in response to economic and social conditions. What are the factors that result in a limited number of paths becoming routes?

The first factor must be a desire to travel or move a person, good, or piece of information from one place to another—the need or desire to overcome the effects of the physical separation of producer and consumer, buyer and seller. This separation, or spatial imbalance, and the need to get in contact, together give rise to the selection of a path by which a need or desire can be satisfied. Unfortunately, although the underlying motive explained here is simple enough, the mechanism by which these motives are translated into action or movement along a particular path or route is conditioned by other factors. Among these are the principles of *least cost* and *least effort*, which in turn are subject to environmental factors like topography, political boundaries, and **intervening opportunities.** Of course, it is also conditioned by the particular information available to the group or individual in question.

Conditions for Interaction and the Emergence of a Route

Interaction will occur if there is:

1. *Complementarity, or a demand in one area and a supply (surplus) in another. This factor may arise through the differentiation of areas from natural and cultural causes, or through areal differentiation based on the operation of economies of scale. In the latter case, one large plant may be so much more economical than several smaller plants that it can afford to import raw materials and ship finished products great distances.*

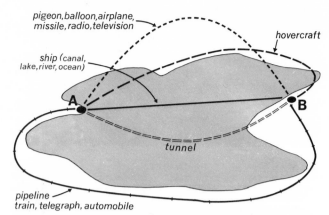

Fig. 152. *The various kinds of paths and routes which can arise in response to spatial differentiation. (From R. McDaniel, "Elements of Economic Geography," 1966, used by courtesy of the author and the Department of Extension and Summer School, University of Western Ohio.)*

2. *Intervening opportunity, or the fact that complementarity generates interchange between two areas only if no intervening source of supply is available.*

3. *Transferability, or the fact that, under certain conditions, alternate goods will be substituted. Among these conditions are if the distance between market or desire and supplier or satisfier is too great and too costly to overcome. Thus we might think of the factor of intervening opportunity as resulting in a substitution of areas, and transferability in a substitution of products.*

Once the complementarity has been identified, the route established, and interchange begins, then the inhibiting effect of distance occurs. Places become established in a time-space framework. A wide variety of data relating to the exchange of information, commodities, and people between paired cities has been examined by George K. Zipf in 1949. For such things as the exchange of telegraph messages, telephone calls, rail, bus, and air passengers, Zipf observed that the number of such occurrences varied directly, according to the equation

$$\frac{P_1 P_2}{d_{12}}$$

where P_1 and P_2 are the populations of the two cities concerned, and d_{12} is the distance between the cities. This measure is called the *gravity model*, being an analogue of the Newtonian concept of gravity. The same relationship is shown graphically in figure 153, which stresses the distance effect, or **distance decay function.**

Two groups of variables influencing movement have now been isolated:

1. *Variables that increase the likelihood of movement, such as complementary or intervening opportunities, trade,*

(a)

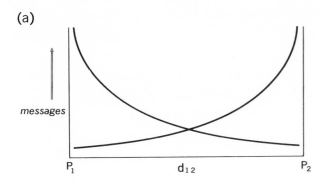

(b)

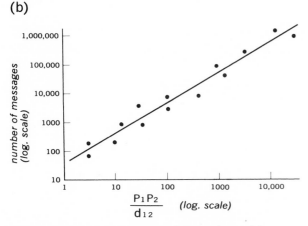

Fig. 153. *Graphical representation of the gravity model.*

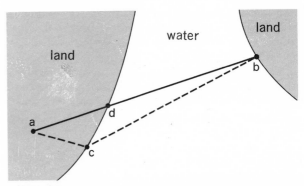

Fig. 154. *Minimum cost route choice. Although route* adb *might be the shortest route, the minimum cost choice might be route* acb, *where the costly portion of the journey (over land) is minimized and, although the water route is increased, the lower costs involved may more than compensate for this longer distance choice.*

tariff preferences, and cultural affinities. To these could be added brand loyalties, political affiliation, or other symbolic attachments, and innovations in transport. This first group of variables could also be represented by the sum of the two populations, P_1 and P_2, in the gravity model.

2. *Variables that* decrease *the likelihood of movement, such as transferability and substitution, movement costs, tariffs, quotas, handicaps of time, and alternative choices.*

Both kinds of variables will be mentioned again later.

The Nature of Routes

The sets of variables mentioned above interact. If the balance is positive, interaction takes place. The problem then becomes one of what kind of route is likely to develop. One approach to this problem is to state it entirely in terms of minimizing costs.

The *minimum cost path* is the route location for which the total cost of a certain arrangement is lowest between two points. In other words, it is the least cost choice amongst alternative paths. Of course, this is just one element in a complex socioeconomic

system. Neither costs nor route can be considered apart from prospective users or environment.

The *minimum cost technique* (or *design*) takes into account the method of transport and type of route construction. Both, of course, must be considered in relation to the environment, service required, traffic volume, and commodity type. For instance, an oil pipeline of large diameter is not a minimum cost design for an oil field where output is not expected to last more than a year or two, nor is a multilane, low gradient, limited access freeway a minimum cost design where the traffic flow consists of only one or two vehicles a day.

The *position of minimum cost transfer points* is obtained by consideration of the whole system of movement involving transhipment points. The movement of a commodity from origin to destination may involve two or more kinds of routes—for example, ocean, followed by railroad and truck. In such a case, *transhipment* would occur, and the problem of path location might make it necessary to consider the whole system of movement, including the location of transhipment points. Thus it might be possible to locate the transhipment points that would minimize travel over some relatively costly transportation link. Figure 154 shows such a situation; rather than choosing ADB which is the shortest overall route, the costliest part of the route, AD, which is over land, could be minimized by choosing route ACB, which though longer is cheaper in cost terms.

The *position of the minimum cost base* refers to the location of operating and repair operations where they can be performed most efficiently. The correct location of a minimum cost base, whether or not it centralizes repair operations and other functions, affords lower total costs. Among the cost factors to be considered are those of managing the movement of certain quantities of traffic, and of maintaining a certain time-cost distribution of traffic.

In the first three of our six questions we have approached the analysis of transportation in terms of a single route or path. But it is obvious that many routes are needed in order to link the various economic activities together smoothly and efficiently. And so a series of supplementary questions arises: What is the *optimal* set of routes? What is the optimal set of techniques, bases, and transfer positions? What is the optimal time schedule of movements? All these questions belong to a fairly new field, **operations research.** The technique involved in solving them is a variant of linear programming known as the "transportation problem." Our three remaining questions, then, will deal with route location, route development, and interaction with other factors such as land values.

Actual Route Location

If a route has to be built between two settlements, *A* and *B*, then the intuitive answer to route location is to join them by a straight line. But few routes follow this straight line form. Four kinds of deviations can be recognized:

1. Positive deviations: *a route may be lengthened in order to collect more traffic. Thus the relationship between the length of the route (the shorter the better) and the amount of traffic (the greater the better) is optimized. In figure 155, case (c) would be the optimal solution.*

2. Negative deviations: *a route may deviate in order to avoid certain barriers or minimize the distance traveled through high cost sections.*

3. Political distortion: *the importance of political factors, particularly boundaries, in distorting route patterns was stressed in a pioneering work by Cooley in 1894. The same theme has been taken up more recently in the 1960s by D. W. Meinig and R. I. Wolfe. Wolfe revealed the striking effect of the United States-Canada border on the railroad pattern (figure 156). The effect of a change in status of a boundary is shown in figure 157, where the establishment of a new political frontier has dramatically curtailed both the number of routes and the flows along them.*

4. Network geometry: *these route deviations are based on certain distance minimization concepts, where route location may be a compromise between user costs and builder costs.*

In figure 158, case (a) is a minimum distance network which, starting at (say) point a, connects the other four towns b-e by the shortest route. Case (b) is the shortest cycle around all five towns—the best route for a mailman or multipurpose shopping trip. Case (c) is the position of one town, d, connected by the shortest routes to all other towns, by itself a rare example. Case (d) is the shortest completely con-

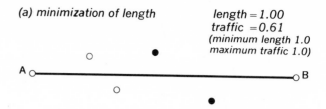

(a) minimization of length

length = 1.00
traffic = 0.61
(minimum length 1.0
maximum traffic 1.0)

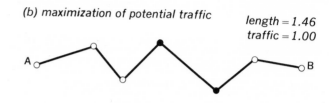

(b) maximization of potential traffic

length = 1.46
traffic = 1.00

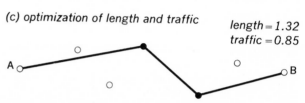

(c) optimization of length and traffic

length = 1.32
traffic = 0.85

Fig. 155. *Route location: optimizational route length and traffic potential. (From P. Haggett,* Locational Analysis in Human Geography, *1965, p. 62, reprinted courtesy of Edward Arnold, London.)*

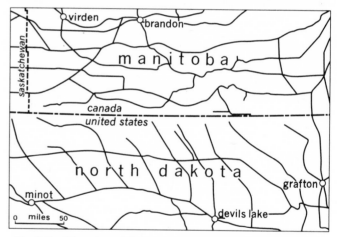

Fig. 156. *Distortion of the railroad network by the U.S.-Canada national boundary. (From an idea by August Lösch in* Economics of Location, *Yale University Press, 1954, p. 447.)*

nected network, containing the lines of all three previous solutions. This is the least cost solution from the user's point of view; it is the shortest and most convenient network to and from any of the 5 cities. Case (e) shows that the shortest set of links joining the five towns does not contain any of the previous elements. This is the least cost solution from the builder's point of view, since it has the shortest route length linking all five towns.

Where large cities are clustered together, the enormous flow of traffic generated between them

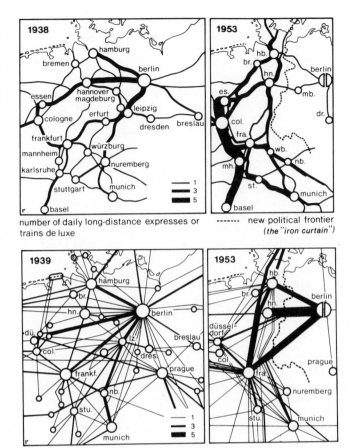

number of daily long-distance expresses or
trains de luxe

------- new political frontier
(the "iron curtain")

air traffic – number of daily flights in both directions

Fig. 157. *The impact of a change in political boundaries on transportation networks: Germany, 1939 and 1943. (Reprinted from E. Ottremba,* Allgemeine Geographie des Welthandels und des Weltverkehrs, *1957, pp. 261–63, by permission of W. Keller and Co., Stuttgart.)*

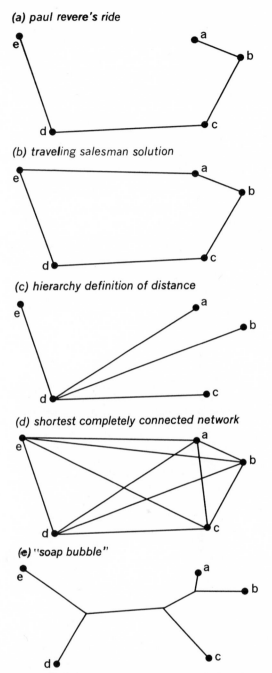

Fig. 158. *Network geometry: minimum distance networks. (From William Bunge,* Theoretical Geography, *1966, pp. 187–9, 193, reprinted by courtesy of the Department of Geography, Royal University of Lund, Sweden.)*

might favor solution (d). This is basically the pattern seen in the railroad network of the northeastern United States. Where cities are more widely spaced and traffic is light, building costs could become of prime importance and solution (e) might be the dominant one, as in much of the western United States.

Route Growth and Change

Routes and communication systems are of course not stable or static; they change and develop in response to changes elsewhere in the socioeconomic system. That is, there is a feedback effect, since the socioeconomic system and the communications system are mutually interdependent.

A number of geographers have tried to sketch the changes in the communications system over time. They have analyzed network and route changes, and have shown that the growth of road, rail, air, or canal networks are interwoven with the whole process of socioeconomic growth and regional development.

Underdeveloped Areas. One simple model of transportation development in underdeveloped countries is based on empirical studies in Ghana, Nigeria, Brazil, Malaysia, and parts of East Africa. It relies on a 4-phase sequence of development representing

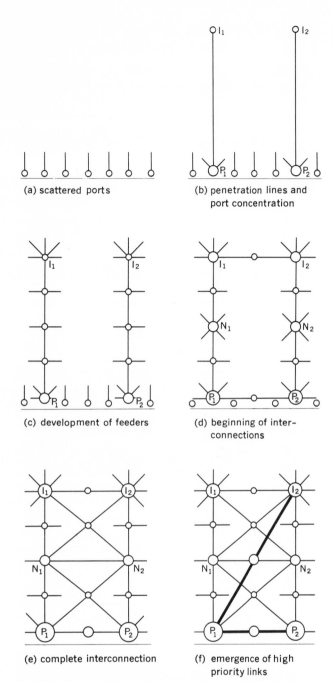

(a) scattered ports

(b) penetration lines and port concentration

(c) development of feeders

(d) beginning of inter-connections

(e) complete interconnection

(f) emergence of high priority links

Fig. 159. *Transportation network evolution model. The ideal-typical sequence of transport development in an underdeveloped area from initial small coastal ports to limited inland penetration (I_1, I_2); the development of feeders; the rise of one or two ports (P_1, P_2); intermediate centers (N_1, N_2); and finally the rise of high priority linkages. (From E.J. Taaffe, R.L. Morrill, and P. R. Gould, "Transport Expansion in Underdeveloped Countries: A Comparative Analysis," The Geographical Review, vol. 53, 1963, p. 504, reprinted by permission of the American Geographical Society.*

1. *At first, there is only a scatter of small ports and trading posts along the coast (figure 159a). Each small port or post has a limited inland trading field but little contact with each other, except through occasional fishing boats and irregular traders.*

2. *Next, a few major lines of penetration develop inland. The coastal ports expand their immediate hinterlands (figure 159b). Diagonal inland trunk routes begin to focus on growing areas of settlement in order to extend political and military control over the interior, to tap exploitable mineral resources, and to develop areas of potential agricultural production.*

3. *Eventually, feeder routes develop, and the beginnings of lateral intercommunication occur (figures 159c and d). The growth of feeder routes is accompanied by continued growth of the main seacoast terminals what is known as a multiplier situation. At this stage some intermediate centers grow up between the central and interior nodes.*

4. *Finally, linkage and concentration occur, as high priority linkages emerge between the most important centers (figures 159e and f). The best paved roads and the heaviest rail traffic and airline connections follow these main links.*

In development terms (a) represents a coastal trading position with very limited hinterlands. In (b), the emergence of major penetration routes reduces transportation costs for some ports, and markets expand. In (c), feeder routes allow the major nodes to develop at the expense of smaller nodes. Thus, as certain centers grow at the expense of others, the result is a set of high priority linkages.

Like all "stage" models this one can be criticized. But as its authors warn, "it is probably most realistic to think of the entire sequence as a process rather than a series of discrete historical stages. Thus at a given point in time a country's total transport pattern may show evidence of all phases."

Developed Areas. Our concern here is with development where an existing route system is already functioning. Thus we have to deal with the ways in which networks are adjusted to technological change in transportation itself, and with the ever-widening circles of interaction as socioeconomic levels rise and society grows more complex. Figure 160 shows diagrammatically how these changes could be fused with the idealized landscape model of Lösch. "A" represents the Löschian landscape in which movement routes link each settlement in a direct way. In "B," a rise in socioeconomic level, with accompanying growth of specialization and polarization of economic activities, leads to some centers attaining greater importance than others; thus high priority linkages occur that bypass many of the smaller centers. In "C" we find an intensification of this pattern.

The increasing exchange that results from a con-

certain regularities. Thus the growth of route systems (depicted in figure 159) proceeds as follows:

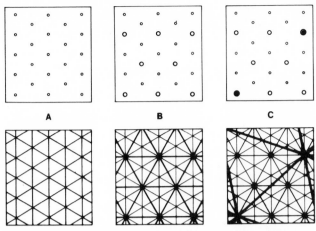

Fig. 160. *Network development by route substitution in developed areas. The latter are represented by a Löschian landscape. (From Peter Haggett,* Locational Analysis in Human Geography, *1965, p. 82, reprinted by courtesy of Edward Arnold, London.)*

centration of human activities may lead to overextension of the transportation facilities. Accessibility may deteriorate through overuse and traffic congestion. This is particularly true of Western Europe, where traffic is usually forced along existing arteries, slightly modified instead of new routes designed to accommodate the increased flow. In the New World, on the other hand, increasing interaction, resulting from the centralization and specialization of activities, has led to demands for increased accessibility. This in turn has led to attempts to improve urban transportation and to the development of an interstate freeway system.

Route Structure and Other Economic Activities

There are paths and routes, interaction occurs, a network is laid out with a particular form and location, the system changes with socioeconomic development. In other words, transportation and economic activities are interdependent. But what *kinds* of relationship exist between them?

Transportation may satisfy human wants directly, as in the case of vacation travel, or it may play a vital role in productive processes, from shipping raw materials to distributing the finished product. That is, transportation adds *place* utility to goods. In particular, it can be related to trade, prices, and land use.

In the area of *trade*, transportation is a prerequisite. Without improved transportation an area is limited to the goods it produces. Transportation also plays a role in regional specialization and the division of labor. It increases productive capacity by increasing

efficiency and allowing economies of scale to take place. Good transportation serves to reduce the costs of production, even though it is itself a cost of production.

In the area of *price*, improved transportation effectively stays the development of local monopolies. It assures that a crop failure in one area will not bring disaster. Improved transportation also increases competition, for when prices for a certain product in one area are raised above the cost of producing it in another area plus the cost of transporting it from that area, that product will be imported (the principle of *comparative advantage*). An important feature of the economic system that relates directly to the adequacy of transportation is the extent of competition between suppliers at the fringes of market areas.

In the area of *land use and values*, the role of transportation should need no stressing (see chapters 6–11, above).

As we saw in earlier chapters, both secondary and tertiary economic activities tend to become increasingly specialized and polarized over time. Primary activities may also become more specialized through such factors as comparative advantage. The greater the specialization and centralization of these economic activities, the greater the need for accessibility and an efficient transportation system. As accessibility is improved, so movement can be speeded up, and larger areas tapped within a given time. Secondary and tertiary activities can serve more people, and perishable primary products can be marketed over greater distances. In turn, this allows even more specialization and further concentration into urban nodes. It seems that transportation and economic activities are perpetuated in a never-ending and accelerating cycle.

Thus activity specialization has separated origin from destination—that is, demand from supply—and the desire to make a trip from the satisfaction of that desire. These origins and destinations are formalized as land use patterns, and the spatial structuring of those patterns helps to initiate movement where a specific complementarity occurs. Movement, in short, has become the means of correcting any kind of spatial imbalance. That is, few journeys or trips are made for the sake of movement itself, but in order to do something that cannot be done at the place of origin. This concept is shown diagrammatically in figure 161. People function at different points in space. In order to do so and to communicate with one another, they must pass through a communications system.

In practice, of course, the relationship is not as simple as this; for example, feedback occurs as the

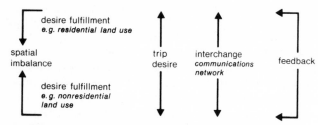

Fig. 161. *Simple land use–travel movement relationships. (Reprinted from M.E. Eliot Hurst, "Land Use–Traffic Generation Relationships,"* Traffic Quarterly, *1969, p. 264, by courtesy of the Eno Foundation.)*

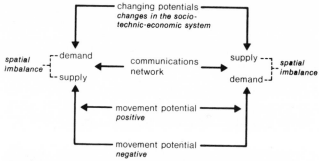

Fig. 162. *Land use–travel movement relationships: a tentative movement system. (From Eliot Hurst 1969, ibid., p. 265; see fig. 161.)*

transportation network influences the development of land use and population distribution, and the network itself is influenced in turn by such developments. So, rather than representing a simple causal relationship, the diagram or model should try to represent a system that veers between balance and imbalance. People in a particular functional relationship have particular travel needs. They therefore pass through a network, or system, that in turn influences and is influenced by those relationships (figure 162). These are the *positive potentials* that we identified earlier. Also implicit in this particular functional relationship are the *negative potentials* that operate to inhibit travel. Finally, there are the *changing potentials* that, with advancing technology, could alter both the positive and the negative potentials.

Conclusion

This 6-question approach is, then, essentially a straightforward systems approach that shows the mutual interdependence of economy, *circulation,* and transportation. The phenomenon of *circulation* results from bringing together spatially separated demands and supplies through trade and interaction. Thus the amount of movement becomes a function of the nature of the demands and supplies and of the character of the available transportation systems. Each means of transportation also has its own technological characteristics and its own spatial layout or network. The total transportation system is a composite of many types of transportation, acting in unison or competition over many networks, that limits, directs, and channels *circulation.* B. J. L. Berry states that: "It is obvious that [these] relationships are extremely complex, whether they be of the economy-circulation-transport type which gives rise to goods movement or the livelihood-settlement-circulation-transport type, which describes the movement of persons. Change in any one part of the system is likely to be precipitated throughout the whole. . . ."

The Functional Approach

In the light of the systems approach to transportation, if one particular area had to be studied, what factors would be examined? Six principal factors could be listed:

1. *General economic development.*
2. *The location of activities.*
3. *Available technology.*
4. *Relative cost structures.*
5. *The interests, perceptions and preferences of the decision makers (including political and military decision making).*
6. *The outlook for the future, as perceived by the decision makers.*

To some extent two further factors would also have to be considered:

7. *The historical pattern of development.*
8. *The natural environment.*

Of course, this is not meant to be an exhaustive list, and there are other influential factors. For instance, the position of nations on international airline routes affects the development of air transportation. The list is, however, essentially a functional one in that it emphasizes development as some *function* of the characteristics of areas. It is also systematic in that it tries to explain transportation in terms of relationships to other elements in a general *system.* A bald statement like this is too general to give much information about the substantive character of transportation. In order to do this, the concept of transportation systems would have to be disaggregated into its component subsystems. But this would be to obscure the fact that by nature they are not independent elements. For example, the transportation network is dependent upon flows, which can be conceptualized in terms of the eight factors listed above or the six questions treated in the previous section.

However, if the transportation concept is disaggregated to some extent, the following elements or components of the system can be identified:

1. *Transportation as an* inventory *(the stock of roads, automobiles, etc.).*
2. *Transportation as a* network *(the structure of the route system).*
3. *Transportation as* flows *(what movement occurs, and how intensively).*
4. *Transportation as* modal systems *(what types of transport occur).*
5. *Transportation as the relationships of transport subsystems to each other.*

Inventory

The stocks, or inventory, of basic transportation equipment can be classified as either *mobile equipment* (cars, buses, trucks, railroad equipment), or as *fixed facilities* (miles of railroad or road). The quantity of these stocks could be explained in varying degrees by functional relationships between them and variables such as income and population. Generally, the distribution of these stocks is most closely related to income, population, and size of area.

Network

The layout, geometry, or pattern of the transportation system consists of the location of routes; the location of intersections, nodes, or terminals; the density and length of routes; the accessibility of individual points on a network to other points, and the distance traveled in order to reach every point on a network. These notions are related to factors conditioning the development of transport.

Flows

The movement of people, commodities, or messages can all be referred to simply as *flows*. Flows are the very activity of transportation, and many of them can be identified. This latter factor gives rise to difficulties of measurement, for if there is to be an attempt to explain the systematic and functional relationships, flows have to be related to some explanatory variables. Flows can be analyzed through a simple temporal sequence, through linear programming, or by certain other means such as the gravity model.

Modes

The various types or modes of transportation can be examined in order to identify their particular spatial and technical characteristics. Each mode plays a different, though often overlapping, role in the total supply of transportation. Thus railroads seem best suited to long haul transportation of heavy commodities, which are often of small value per unit of carload traffic. On the other hand, air transportation specializes in speed, long haul, and high value goods needing rapid delivery. Of course, there is some competition between the modes, and technical change is tending to increase it.

Interrelationships

The concept of interrelationships differs from the previous four factors in that it does not represent an attempted codification of structures or functions, but rather points to relationships among transportation systems and between the latter and the whole socioeconomic system. On the one hand, there are the relationships between, say, highway and railroad networks. Thus in some areas highways are supplementary to the railroad network, while in others they both supplement and complement it, and in still others compete with it. These interrelationships are evidenced by a combination of stock conditions, characteristics of flows, network structures, and other use characteristics. On the other hand, there is the functioning of the socioeconomic system, which requires the use of various transportation mixes. As the system develops, so spatial differentiation increases and relatively more transportation is required.

Conclusion

We have been concerned in this overview with the functional relationships between a transportation system, on the one hand, and the environmental or regional system on the other. However, since both are parts of a greater world system, they are often so intertwined that analysis is extremely difficult.

Any change in a transportation system changes the social and economic environment within which the system operates—and vice versa. The replacement, for example, of a primitive route system in a developing country by a more satisfactory system of railroads may profoundly affect the pattern of development. Places advantageously located on the new railroad system may grow at rates different from those located on the more primitive system; in fact, many nodes of this latter system may actually decline in size. Such an outcome would be comparable to the changes, identified in the Christaller and Lösch models, that took place in Europe and America when rural roads were first paved: the relative positions of hamlets and rural market towns shifted, as did patterns of trade, and many other factors relating to transportation development and use.

There are many other kinds of interrelationships that are of relevance here. For example, the decision rules for development change as the system develops. Thus the development of a network can be looked on as a series of links; one link may be added at one time, and another link at another time. From a formal point of view the second addition is not a replication of the first because the decision or operating rules will also have changed. Systems in which these rules change over time are much more difficult to study than closed systems, for which the operating rules stay constant as the system evolves.

Strictly speaking, then, the relationships stressed here do not involve explanatory variables, because the whole complex environment of the transportation system changes as transportation evolves. The rules implicit in these functional or systematic relationships differ according to the state of development of the transportation system. Further, the transportation system interacts with the so-called determining factors, and these shift during the period of transportation development. All these complications taken together pose an especially difficult situation for analysis.

Summary

1. Previous chapters have emphasized the location of sites. This and the next chapter examine the nature of the links or flows between those sites, as represented by circulation *or* transportation.

2. The spatial structuring of primary, secondary and tertiary activities initiates movement. Movement or transportation becomes the means of correcting the spatial imbalance created by the separation of points of demand and points of supply.

3. Distances separating the varying nodes in the economic landscapes can be measured in purely distance terms, but usually we transpose physical distances into time, cost, or social accessibility measures.

4. The movement generated by spatial specialization, no matter how it is measured in accessibility terms, is channelled and directed by a transportation system, whether it be a system of microwave relays transmitting news or information, or a railroad system circulating people or goods. The amount of

traffic flowing through any transportation media is a function of the demand and supply, as well as some reflection of the characteristics of the particular mode.

5. A systems approach can be used to analyze transportation subsystems. It begins by examining the basic "route," the conditions that exist before interaction can take place and the route emerges; goes on to consider the nature of the route, the controls of the network patterns, the growth and change of routes; and finally looks at the interrelationship of such routes with the rest of the economic activity system.

6. If such an approach is applied to a particular economic landscape, certain further factors must be discerned, such as the general economic development of an area, the availability of various technologies, and the decision makers and their milieux. This allows us to disaggregate the transportation subsystem into its inventory, network, flows, modal systems, and interrelationships, which are to be analyzed in more detail in the next chapter.

Further Reading

For general discussions of transportation geography see

Becht, J. E. *A Geography of Transportation and Business Logistics* (Dubuque, Iowa: Wm. C. Brown, 1970).

Eliot Hurst, M. E. *Transportation Geography: Comments and Readings* (New York: McGraw-Hill, 1973), part 1.

Taaffe, E. J. and Gauthier, H. L. *Geography of Transportation* (Englewood Cliffs: Prentice-Hall, 1972).

One approach to the basic conception of spatial interaction is

Ullman, E. L. "The Role of Transportation and the Bases for Interaction," in W. L. Thomas, ed. *Man's Role in Changing the Face of the Earth* (Chicago: Chicago University Press, 1956), pp. 862–880.

Aspects of the "six-question approach" are also found in

Berry, B. J. L. "Recent Studies Concerning the Role of Transportation in the Space Economy," *Annals of the Association of American Geographers*, vol. 49, 1959, pp. 328–42.

Eliot Hurst, M. E. "Land Use: Travel Movement Relationships," *Traffic Quarterly*, vol. 23, no. 2, 1969, pp. 263–274.

Haggett, P. *Locational Analysis in Human Geography* (London: E. Arnold, 1965), chapters 2 and 3.

Haggett, P. *Geography: A Modern Synthesis* (New York: Harper and Row, 1972), chapters 14 and 15.

Taaffe, E. J., Morrill, and Gould, P. R. "Transport Expansion in Underdeveloped Countries: A Comparative

Analysis," *Geographical Review*, vol. 53, 1963, pp. 503–529.

The "functional" approach developed at Northwestern University's Transportation Center is summarized in

Garrison, W. L. and Marble, D. F. *A Prolegomenon to the Forecasting of Transportation Development*, Research Report, Transportation Center, Northwestern University, 1965.

For further leads to studies of transportation, see

Siddall, W. R., compiler. *Transportation Geography: A Bibliography* (Manhattan: Kansas State University Library), Bibliography no. 1, 1969.

In addition, the Transportation Center at Northwestern publishes a monthly classified bibliography:

Current Literature in Traffic and Transportation.

thirteen

Some Components of the Transportation System

We are now in a position to disaggregate the transportation subsystem still further into four basic elements: *stock aggregates, networks, flows,* and *modal systems.* This approach is of course artificial insofar as it serves to break down an essentially holistic conception. Accordingly, we shall go on to examine some of the ways in which these four elements interact and, by reintroducing the concept of *movement,* propose an integrated view of transportation systems. Finally, we shall examine transportation in two specific contexts: developing areas and human communications.

Inventory

The aggregate measures of the transportation system can be listed as follows:

1. *Number of automobiles.*
2. *Miles of road.*
3. *Miles of railroad.*
4. *Ton miles hauled.*
5. *Number of railroad cars.*
6. *Cost of transportation.*
7. *Number of workers.*
8. *Fuel used in transportation.*
9. *Number of trucks.*
10. *Transportation industry profits.*

This list is less than all-inclusive. The things measured can be classified into two subgroups: *mobile facilities* (such as buses, cars, and trucks), and *fixed facilities* (such as miles of railroad and highway).

Our earlier list of eight factors and this list are postulated to be in some functional relationship with each other.* Thus the notion can be developed that stock aggregates (inventory) are functionally related to such factors as level of economic development, just as the structure of networks is related to the level of technological development. The effect of an area's stage of economic development on its transportation system can be analyzed by comparing such indices as income and population levels with the numbers of different kinds of vehicles in the area, and so forth.

One of the basic difficulties associated with an analysis of this sort is finding suitable indices for comparison. If we wanted to estimate the number of motor vehicles in an area we could perhaps use the number of gas or service stations as a guide. Of course, data on both gas stations and motor vehicles may be equally inaccessible. Moreover, although they both result from a common set of causes, they do not explain the existence of one another.

Surveys have therefore used such data as are available. Often there are no direct measures of such environmental factors as population, gross domestic production, or per capita income. Some factors, such as differences in decision making processes, cannot be measured directly at all. Simple deterministic models have been used to represent processes that include probabilistic or chance occurrences. In short, our measures are imperfect. But they offer some glimpses of the infinitely complicated reality.

*For much of this chapter I am profoundly indebted to the pioneering work of the Transportation Center, Northwestern University.

Stock Factors and Environmental Factors

A study of transportation in Ghana and Nigeria treated highway route mileage as the stock factor to be explained. Among the independent variables — that is, the explanatory factors — were the population and area of these regions. Other such factors were the physical environment, competition from alternative modal systems (rail or waterway), income levels, position within the nation, and level of development.

The results of the regression analysis indicated a close relationship between the distribution of road mileage for a region and the internal distribution of that region's population. It was found that road mileage in a given district or unit was usually proportional to a constant multiplied by the square root of the district's population, multiplied in turn by the square root of the district's area, as follows:

$$S_1 = C \cdot \sqrt{P} \cdot \sqrt{A}$$

where S_1 = stock (route miles), C = a constant, P = population, and A = area. Three-quarters of the internal variation in route mileage was found to be associated with those two factors. In other words, this particular stock factor, highway mileage, can apparently be estimated for a country at a particular time by reference to that country's population distribution. The effects of difficult topography, resource distribution, and competition from other modes are subsumed by that of population distribution.

The total population of an area in the analysis actually accounted for more of the variation in highway mileage than did the area itself. Thus about 50 percent of the internal variation in route length was

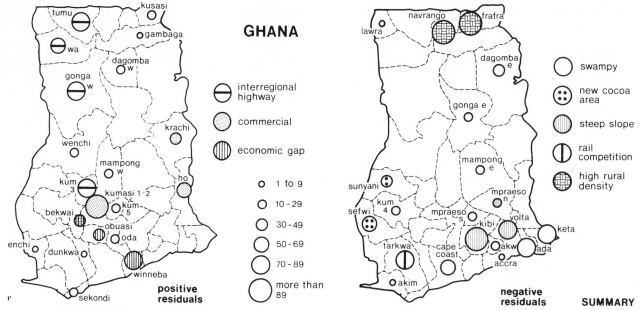

Fig. 163. *Summary maps: positive and negative residuals from highway mileage analysis, Ghana. (From* Geography Research, *pt. 1, 1960, p. 101, reprinted by permission of the director, Transportation Center, Northwestern University.)*

accounted for by population and about 20 percent by area. While the demand for roads in Nigeria and Ghana generally reflects the distribution of population, in fact a large sparsely populated area will require more investment per capita in roads than a small densely populated area. This must be borne in mind when the above relationship is considered.

Further analysis, particularly of the areas where the degree of association between route miles and the population-area relationship fell above or below the 75 percent figure, indicated that five other factors also played a significant role. These were the hostility of the natural environment, the amount of competition from railroads, the number and type of intermediate locations, the level of income and commercial production, and the level of development.

Application to Ghana and Nigeria

Figure 163 summarizes the Ghanaian picture, in an attempt to suggest the relationship between this one stock factor, highway mileage, and the environmental factors. An interregional highway, the Western Trunk Road, accounted for the largest number of positive deviations (that is, for the areas with more than expected highway mileage). High commercial activity associated with agricultural production for export was found at Ho, Krachi, and Kumasi, again accounting for positive deviations. Ho and Krachi also received special consideration as transportation centers because of their former position in British Togoland and their existing links with Togo. Other factors concerned with positive devia-

tions include the government's "economic gap" policy, that is, a policy designed to close a gap in the country's communications system. Under this policy, highway connections between Kumasi, Bekwai, and the coast have been pushed eastwards from a Kumasi-Sekondi line. The high deviations at Kumasi, Bekwai, Obuasi, and Winneba are probably associated with this pattern of highway development.

Negative deviations (areas with less than expected road mileages) occur in southeast Ghana because of swamps and steep slopes. Tarkwa is a case of harmful railroad competition.* Sefwi and Sunyani were areas that lagged behind in the sequence of transportation development, although they had been recently opened to cocoa production. Here, production and population have grown more quickly than the transportation network. In the North, apart from Tumu which deviates positively because it is a major interregional link, transportation development does not seem to have reached the same level as in the South. In technical language this would be called a peripheral lag, related to the historical sequence.

The positive deviations in Ghana from the relationship between population, area, and highway mileage are mostly contained in a zone of maximum activity that includes the early penetration lines, the main routes, and many lateral interconnections, in-

*Competition from another mode can reduce (in this case) road construction by reducing the need for an alternative system. This is not such an obvious point as it sounds: in many cases the opposite effect occurs, and road construction is stimulated as a feeder system to a break-in-bulk point.

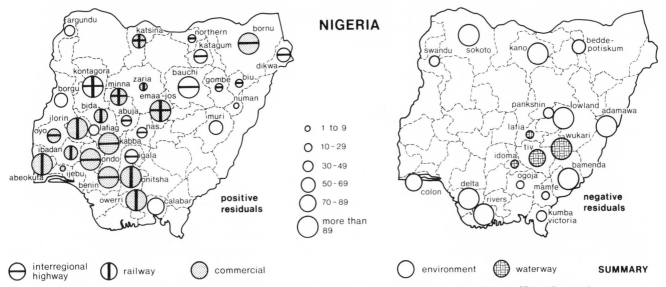

NIGERIA

Fig. 164. *Summary maps: positive and negative residuals from highway mileage analysis, Nigeria. (From* Geography Research *1960, ibid., p. 109; see fig. 163.)*

cluding the railroad triangle (Kumasi-Accra-Tarkwa). Figure 163 summarizes the main features that, in this formulation, explain the number of highway miles, especially as this number deviates from the average calculation based on population and area alone.

Areas with below-average highway mileage for Ghana were swampy and had steep slopes, high rural density, and locally based economies. They were often quite adequately served by railroads. In contrast, areas with above-average highway mileage coincided with the presence of interregional highway links, intensive commercial activity, and regions where it had been deliberate government policy to improve the communications network.

The Nigerian highway stock situation is outlined in figure 164. There is a striking concentration of positive deviations within a zone of maximum transport activity. Most of the areas within this zone rate high in commercial production as well as in either railway mileage or interregional highway mileage. Conversely, the trend for peripheral areas to have less highway mileage than might be expected from the population-area relationship is more marked than in the case of Ghana. The only major exception is in the Northeast, in areas traversed by a major link to the Bornu and Lake Chad districts. The negative deviations occur in the peripheral areas, and in those where a hostile environment and waterway competition tend to reduce highway mileages.

An Extended Analysis

This analysis of transportation in Ghana and Nigeria was part of a larger study, undertaken from 1960 to 1965 by the Transportation Center at North-

western University, that extended to seventy-one nations and to other transportation stock measures. In this extended analysis, area did not seem to have a distinct effect on the quantity of mobile equipment (cars, buses, trucks, etc.), and population alone did not show a distinct relationship with fixed stocks (miles of paved roads, gravel roads, railroad tracks, etc.). For two countries with similar incomes and population, the extended study indicated that the country with the larger area tended to have longer roads and railroad tracks, but it did not necessarily have more cars, and so on. If you compare two countries with identical populations, incomes, and investment abilities, but one has a much larger spatial area and higher road mileages, then, other things being equal, the larger country will have a higher proportion of unpaved roads than the smaller one.

According to the study, income seemed to affect the transportation inventory in two ways:

1. *As more goods were produced, the demand for transportation increased.*
2. *As the wealth of a community increased, its demand for transport as a consumption good increased too.*

Thus two countries with differing incomes per capita are likely to demand different levels of transportation service, both directly (consumption of transportation facilities) and indirectly (production of goods requiring increased transportation). The first of these is indicated by a positive relationship of rising incomes and increasing automobile ownership, as automobiles are substituted for public transit. In this study, calculations showed that each bus was replaced by an average of 15.2 private automobiles. On the whole, levels of stocks seem to be determined by common explanatory relationships. Thus nations with high levels of income and large populations would be expected to consume much transport and so have large stocks. Similarly, one stock can be substituted for another, as when a nation with many trucks needs fewer freight cars.

Obviously, population numbers and income are partial measures. But they do have some independent significance. Two countries that differ only in population size, with per capita income, and so on, identical, may show different transportation stock levels as a result of the direct effect of population size on the total demand for (say) passenger transport. Likewise, two countries with the same income and population may still have a different mix of transportation facilities because they have different needs and cost structures. If the two countries have different areas, their population density will vary—a crucial factor in transportation, as we have seen. The shape of a country's terrain may also have some effect on the cost of transport in general, and on the relative costs of different means of satisfying similar transportation requirements. Thus we can see that the wealth and population of a country do exert a distinct effect on its mix of transportation facilities as measured by stocks or inventories.

All these relationships result from human effort rather than from any constraint imposed from without. The question therefore arises, Do forces external to the system have any effect on transportation stocks? Superficially there do appear to be external influences. Thus higher than average slopes impose greater construction costs because the routes needed are both longer and harder to construct. This is especially the case with railroads, which are more susceptible to gradients: the steeper the terrain, the higher the operating costs. But although effects like these can be seen at the microlevel, the results of the study suggest that at the macrolevel their influence is negligible. The fact that they are negligible is highly suggestive. In fact, it is tempting to conclude that differences in stock levels between countries are a consequence of their economic or social development, and that these influences create such a diversity in the levels of inventories that, compared to them, the influence of such factors as terrain and weather is small.

In this first disaggregation of the transportation system we have relied on economic measures mainly in the sense of "measures of economic goods." Some of them, however, were "economic" in the more limited sense of "measures of economic relationships." In any case, our analyses so far do show that some relationship exists between stocks and area characteristics.

Network Analysis

Given that movement takes place between points of demand and supply, desire and fulfillment, what sort of network system conducts this movement to its goal? What are the characteristics of route location, the locations of intersections and terminals, the density and length of routes, the accessibility or connectivity of the network? The answers to these questions must convey some notion of how transportation networks are arranged over the earth's surface.

Much attention has been given in geographic and economic literature to the indirect implications of network structure, particularly through the concept of "accessibility." The theories of location examined in earlier chapters contain accounts of varying accessibility and relative location. Such concepts as break-of-bulk points or central place all hinge on the concept of accessibility. But strict definitions of accessibility itself have been lacking. However, in the 1960s several papers appeared that went a long way toward remedying this lack. It is these papers that we shall discuss in the following section.

The Structure of Networks

Transportation systems fall within a double dichotomy of function and nature, on the one hand, and tangible or intangible, on the other (table 57). No matter which type of system is studied, however, its network will be composed of the same elements: *origins, routes* and *destinations*,—or, more simply, *nodes* and *routes* (figure 165). A transportation network is then, "a set of geographic locations interconnected in a system by a number of routes." The spatial structure of a transportation network is the locational pattern formed by those elements, the nodes and the routes.

The research on which this section is based has been conducted with three main purposes in mind:

1. *To ascertain what measures will best describe the structure of transportation networks.*
2. *To ascertain the ways in which these measures depend upon the characteristics of the area in which the transportation network lies.*
3. *To determine if, given knowledge of network measures and areal characteristics, a network can be simulated. That is, given some information about the nature of an area, can the structure of the transportation network in that area be predicted and its spatial structure mapped?*

Table 57. *Schematic Representation of Transportation Systems*

NATURE

	imaginary network network has no virtual existence independent of unit of transportation	objective network exists independently of unit of transportation
FUNCTION intangible messages and information transported	*radio* *television*	*telephone* *cable systems*
tangible goods and people transported	*airlines* *steamer routes*	*railways* *highways*

Source: From an idea by B. Turnbull.

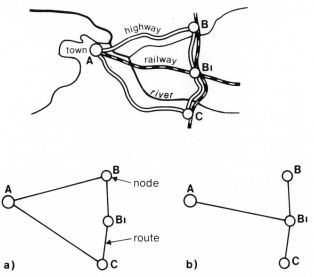

Fig. 165. *A transportation network: conventional map representation and network structure.*

Graph Theory

In order to describe, analyze, compare, and predict network systems, some method of accurate and consistent measurement is needed. Networks have global properties and characteristics; they are composed of sets of relationships between elements and the whole network, on the one hand, and between individual elements, on the other. The measurements chosen should be such that they allow comparison between the networks of different transportation systems.

Networks have been approximated mathematically by the use of **graph theory,** a branch of topology.* More specifically, the methods of graph theory have been used to translate observed network relationships into numerical and symbolic forms. Graph theory is used to measure quantitatively the qualities of transportation networks. The manner in which a number of nodes and routes are interconnected may be measured by several indices developed within graph theory. These indices measure and reflect network attributes, that is, they reveal and translate into uniform and consistent measures the structure of a network. The purpose is not only to describe the network's attributes but to compare it with other networks, and relate it to areal characteristics such as the level of economic development.

Studies of network structure vary in the amount of information they contain. At the very least, they contain information on nodes and routes. More complex network diagrams might include information on the angles, lengths, and capacity of routes.

Analysis of the Venezuelan and Argentine Air Networks

Figures 166 and 167 show the networks of internal air line routes in the Argentine and Venezuela. These are examples of *minimal* network structures, that is, they show only where the routes exist (or do not exist), and where the terminals are located. Route length is implicit on the maps, but means little unless combined with information on flows and costs. In the case of airline route lengths, costs vary

*There is an excellent elementary introduction to graph theory by O. Ore (1964).

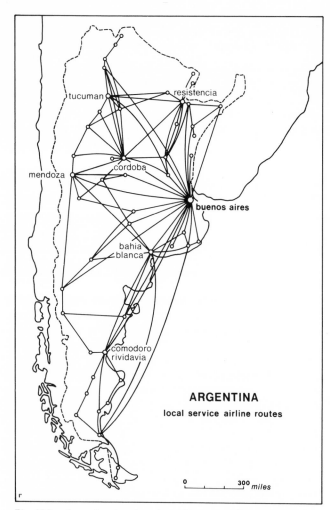

Fig. 166. *Argentina: local service airline routes. (Figs. 166–172 are from* Geography Research *1960, ibid., see fig. 163. This figure is from p. 59.)*

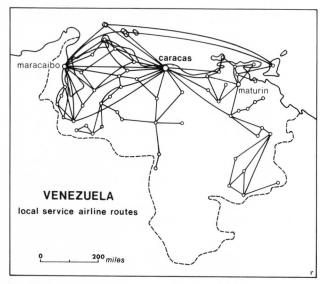

Fig. 167. *Venezuela: local service airline routes. (Ibid., p. 63.)*

from day to day and season to season depending on the exact choice of pilot and other factors.

If we compare the two networks shown, we might ask whether they differ in layout, and if so, how. The Northwestern University group has attempted to answer these and related questions. Most of this research on network structure began with attempts to find meaningful ways to codify these structural differences.

Table 58. *Indices of Local Airline Networks in the Argentine and Venezuela*

	the Argentine	Venezuela
no. of nodes	50	59
no. of routes	91	104
mean no. of links/node	3.8	3.5
*cyclomatic number**	42	46
*gamma index***	7.4	6.1
*alpha index****	3.6	2.8

Source: Northwestern University, *Transportation Geography Study,* 1960–65, part 2, p. 58.

*The cyclomatic number is the count of the occurrence of loops or circuits in a network. It will equal zero where there is no complete loop, one where there is one loop, up to an infinite number. Additional paths provided by loops or circuits are "redundant"; thus the cyclomatic number also gives a measure of redundancy.

**This is the ratio of the actual number of routes in a network to the maximum number of routes if all the nodes were connected directly. As the number of routes decreases the gamma index will approach zero as the lower limit. With the maximum number of routes possible the ratio would be 1.0. In practice the ratio is multiplied by 100, and is thus expressed as a percentage. This can be interpreted as the percentage of connection in the network. Thus a completely unconnected system will have a zero value, and a completely connected system a value of 100%.

***This is the ratio of the actual number of loops or circuits in a network to the maximum number of loops that could be present in a network. The actual number of loops is the cyclomatic number. This index is also multiplied by 100 to give it a range 0 to 100, as an indication of the percentage of redundancy. Thus a network with no loops would have zero redundancy, and a network with the maximum possible number of loops would have 100% redundancy.

Table 58 sets out some actual graph measures used in these kinds of analyses. Combining this table with figures 166 and 167, the graph measures can indicate for us a number of characteristics of the networks— how complete they are, for example. A *complete* network would be one in which each node has a direct route to every other node. One measure of completeness would be to compare the actual number of routes known to occur with the number of routes that would be required to link every node directly with every other node or airport (this is known as the **gamma index**). The networks might also vary in number of *loops* or *circuits;* in number of *end points* (nodes with only one link); in number of links that must be traversed in order to reach every other node on the network from a particular node; and in degree of *redundancy*.* Use of indices like these results in more meaningful comparisons than mere visual inspection.

Civil aviation is actually slightly less well developed in the Argentine than in a number of other South American countries with less well developed surface networks than those of the Argentine. The Argentine air network, with 50 nodes (airports) and 91 connecting routes, was slightly over 7 percent connected and less than 4 percent redundant. In Venezuela the airline routes constitute the major part of the transportation system, serving 59 cities (nodes) via 104 routes. Here, the construction and operation of surface transportation facilities are made difficult by major mountain ranges, swamps, and other hostile environmental factors. As a result, some 80 percent of the total population lives in the Northern Highlands and coastal regions.

Having established such graph measures for the networks, the researchers went one step further and tried to find out if the two networks contained any basic substructure. Four or five basic patterns were abstracted by means of the statistical technique known as **factor analysis**. Some 52 percent of the observed variation in the network structure of the Argentine air route system was found to be accounted for by five factors:

1. *A basic factor that accounted for nearly 22 percent of the observed variation was the total relationship of the nodes in the Argentine network, that is, their total number of direct connections with other nodes. In other words, the larger the city, the larger was the number of flight paths from it.*

2. *Two major regional subsystems within the overall network structure could be identified: (a) a triangular grouping of directly connected cities to the northeast of Buenos Aires, with major nodes at Cordoba, Resistencia, and Tucuman; (b) a second major region to the south of Buenos Aires, centered around the urban nodes of Bahia Blanca, Comodoro Rivadavia, and Buenos Aires itself (figure 168). These major regionalization effects accounted for another 11 percent of the observed variation after the first factor had been identified and removed from the analysis.*

3. *A factor to represent the pull, or field effect, of the primate city, Buenos Aires, "explained" some 9 percent of the remaining variation (figure 169). It is notable*

Fig. 168. *Argentina: local service airlines, the major regionalization effect. (Ibid., p. 64.)*

however, that the major regions had a more dominant influence on the network than the pull of Buenos Aires.

4. *A further 6 percent of the observed variation was accounted for by a minor regional effect centered around Cordoba and Mendoza, with a weak link (the dotted line in figure 170) to Buenos Aires. This minor region appears to be a generally triangular net acting as a feeder for the major northern region identified as part of the second factor listed above.*

5. *Just under 5 percent appeared to define still another minor region centered at Rio Gallegos, south of Comodoro Rivadavia, and weakly linked to both Buenos Aires and the second major region.*

Thus a factor analysis of local Argentine air routes, as shown in table 59, yields five structural influences: the number of connections to a node, apparently related to city size; two major regions; the field effect of the primate city; and two minor disconnected regions, tributary to the major regions and to the central node, Buenos Aires. Two further factors were

*Normally, only one path exists between any pair of nodes, a condition known as *zero redundancy*. Any further paths provided by loops and other connections are thus *redundant*, i.e., provide connections beyond the minimum necessary.

Fig. 169. *Argentina: local service airlines, the field effect. (Ibid., p. 64.)*

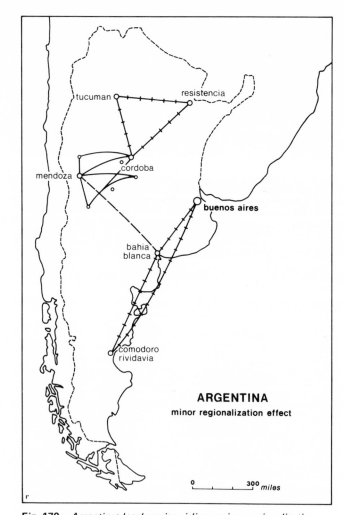

Fig. 170. *Argentina: local service airlines, minor regionalization effect. (Ibid., p. 65.)*

also mentioned: the so-called neighborhood effects (the tendency to establish links to the nearest neighbors), and through-systems connections.

A similar analysis for the local Venezuelan airline network resulted in the isolation of four factors that "explained" about 38 percent of the variation in network structure of the network (figure 167 and table 59). It appears from this that the Venezuelan network is less structured than the Argentine one (figure 166). The four factors were:

1. *Total number of direct connections, scaled directly by city size (19 percent of the variation).*

2. *A major field effect around the city of Caracas (figure 171). This time, the pull effect of the primate city came second, with 7 percent of the remaining variation.*

3. *A major regionalization effect (figure 172) similar to that for the Argentine (about 6 percent of the remaining variation). Again two regions were extracted, though at a somewhat weaker level of internal cohesion than in the Argentine analysis. In the West, the region*

centered on Maracaibo and Santa Barbara; in the east, on Caracas and Maturin. Compared with the Argentine, the positions of importance of the field and major regional effects are reversed.

4. *A weak but detectable minor regional effect. The strongest portion of this pattern is a triangular feeder region centered on Caracas and extending westward toward Maracaibo. Some weaker developments also appear to be associated with the major Maracaibo-Santa Barbara region. However, they were too weak to be classed as further regionalization effects.*

Subsequent analyses of this Venezuelan network, utilizing more sophisticated statistical techniques, have thrown some doubt on these earlier conclusions. However, even these analyses still identify groupings of links and nodes centered on a Caracas-Maracaibo axis (now identified as the major structural influence). They also identify groupings of nodes in the Southeast around Maturin, smaller and more isolated clusters lying south and southeast of Caracas,

Table 59. *Basic Network Structures: Local Argentine and Venezuelan Airline Routes*

Argentine variance "explained" by:	total variance: 192.00	variation %	cumulative %
1. number of flight paths	42.14	21.9	21.9
2. major regions	20.65	10.8	32.7
3. field effect	18.19	9.5	42.2
4. minor region (Cordoba-Mandoza)	10.96	5.7	47.9
5. minor region (Rio Gallegos)	8.61	4.5	52.3
total	100.55 (52.3%)		

Venezuelan variance "explained" by:	total variance: 208.00	variation %	cumulative %
1. number of flight paths	38.88	18.7	18.7
2. field effect	15.50	7.5	26.2
3. major regions	13.70	6.6	32.8
4. minor regions	10.90	5.2	38.0
total	78.98 (38.0%)		

Source: Northwestern University, *Transportation Geography Study*, 1960–65, part 2, pp. 62, 69.

and a subregion in the Northeast between Maturin and Caracas. These analyses are tentative, but it seems that, at least for local airline networks in the Argentine and Venezuela, the following structural patterns can be identified:

1. *A field effect, centered on the major urban center of the area.*

2. *A major regionalization effect, consisting of a series of routes focusing on a set of secondary urban centers.*

3. *A set of nominally triangular subregions or feeder areas that focus upon one or more of the secondary nodes as a gateway to the rest of the system.*

Given these basic structural patterns, the remaining structure of the network could be accounted for by (a) number of direct connections to a node; (b) the "neighborhood effect," or linking of nodes to nearby nodes, as when Maracaibo is linked to five near neighbors; (c) system connections, the existence of loops, circuits, or chains. This kind of analysis could be repeated for various time periods in order to show how the network develops and changes.

Networks and Environment

Having identified the structures of networks by the means described above, it is possible to relate them to various features of the areas within which they are located. Thus a series of regression analyses has been carried out with data from twenty-five countries ranging from Sweden and France to Cuba and Rumania to Angola and Ghana. The data used to represent the characteristics of the areas fell into two broad categories: socioeconomic, representing the level and nature of economic, social, and resource development; and physical, representing the physical makeup of the area. The transportation system was represented by a variety of measures, including number of nodes and links, and average link length for highway and railroad subsystems. The socioeconomic subsystem was represented by measures developed by Berry in 1960 and 1961, who carried out a factor analysis of some forty-three measures

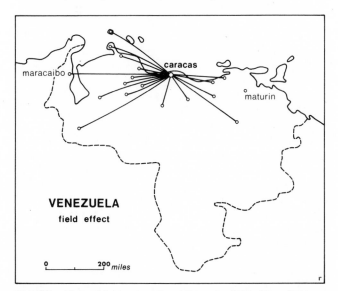

Fig. 171. *Venezuela: local service airlines, the field effect. (Ibid., p. 66.)*

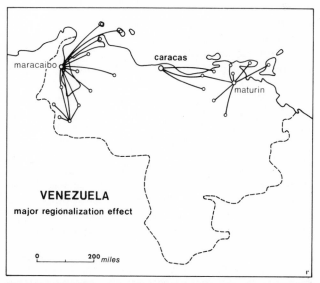

Fig. 172. *Venezuela: local service airlines, the major regionalization effect. (Ibid., p. 66.)*

(value of foreign trade, value of imports, development of energy resources, population density, newspaper circulation, etc.) for ninety-five countries for which relevant data were available. Two of these measures were found to possess the strongest explanatory value: *technological level,* based on degree of urbanization, industrialization, transport, trade, and income; and *demographic level,* reflecting birth and death rates, population density, population per unit of cultivated land, and so on. A low value on the technological scale indicates high trading levels, many international contacts, intensively used transport, high energy consumption, etc. A low value on the demographic scale indicates high birth and death rates, and high population densities. The physical environment was represented by *shape,* a measure of the longest axis across each nation; *size,* a scale representation of square mileage; and *relief,* the ratio of plane distance to relief distance.

In table 60, the results of the regression analysis are summarized in terms of the coefficients of *determination* (100 would equal complete correspondence or explanation, while zero would equal no correspondence at all). These results indicate that technological development is always a major determinant of network structure; other factors are important only in certain cases. Thus the more developed a country's socioeconomic subsystem, the higher the number of nodes, routes, loops, and so on, and the smaller the link length. The demographic measure was of no importance, and size was important only for the last four measures. The greater a nation's size, the greater was the average link length, and so on. This was truer for highways than for railroads. The shape measure was significant only for the degree of connection, and for the *diameter* of the network.* Finally, relief had its greatest effect on the link length of railroads.

The relationship between these network measures and the attributes of the areas through which the networks pass can be summarized as follows.

For *railroads,* the cyclomatic number (a measure of connectivity), indicates that networks change from region to region as an area's economy changes. Thus highly developed regions have railroad networks of high connectivity, and poorly developed regions have networks of low connectivity, that is, their networks are minimal. The degree of connectivity does not appear to be influenced by the size, relief, or shape of a country. Much the same applies to the diameter of the railroad network: highly developed countries have networks of dimensions such that the

*Diameter is a measure of the *span* of the network; it denotes the least number of links that can be used to move between the two points that are the greatest distance apart on the network.

Table 60. *Network-Environment Analysis for 25 Countries.* *
Summary of Results (coefficients of determination).

	technological development	demographic level	size	shape	relief
1. nodes	.73	.73	.76	.77	.77*
2. routes	.73	.73	.75	.76	.77
3. alpha index	.42	.44	.46	.54	.57
4. gamma index	.37	.40	.41	.52	.56
5. cyclomatic no.	.54	.56	.59	.62	.62
6. diameter	.62	.62	.67	.75	.80
7. average link length (highway)	.45	.46	.66	.67	.67
8. average link length (rail)	.43	.51	.63	.65	.77

Source: W.L. Garrison and D.F. Marble, *A Prolegomenon to the Forecasting of Transportation Development* (Evanston: Research Report, Transportation Center, Northwestern University, 1965), p. 62.

*The 25 nations were Algeria, Angola, Bolivia, Bulgaria, Ceylon, Chile, Cuba, Czechoslovakia, Finland, France, Ghana, Hungary, Iran, Iraq, Malaya, Mexico, Nigeria, Poland, Rumania, Sudan, Sweden, Thailand, Tunisia, Turkey, and Yugoslavia.

**It may aid understanding to regard each value as a percentage explanation, and for each column move to the right to be regarded as cumulative percentages.

diameter is a small portion of the total network length. In poorly developed countries the diameter is a large portion, equal or almost equal to the network's total length. Moreover, highly developed countries have railroad networks with a larger number of nodes than the less developed areas. A high level of technological development is also associated with shorter average link lengths (i.e., shorter distances between nodes). Finally, the length of the average route or link is significantly correlated with the size of a country and its relief.

Similar conclusions can be presented for *highways.* Variations in the structural properties of highway networks were found to be equivalent to the variations in the railroad networks, except that the average link length on highway networks was not significantly related to relief.

Logically, the next step would be to build on analyses of this type in order to generate or simulate a network from known area or regional characteristics. Most such attempts to date have produced only crude results, although networks in Sicily and Northern Ireland have been fairly successfully reproduced by means of simple deterministic and stochastic techniques.

In summary, the graph measures described here aid our understanding of network structure and point to its connections with certain regional characteristics, especially technological development.

Flow Analysis

So far we have seen that spatial interaction occurs, that networks exist to channel that interaction, and that the physical stocks of those networks also vary over space. We are now in a position to examine how much moves where—in other words, the *flow*, the very activity of transportation.

Methods of Study

Many studies of flow patterns center largely around the flow of goods or commodities. For example, one line of inquiry deals with the demarcation of port hinterlands. Another, pursued largely by economists, looks at the broader interregional or international patterns of commodity flows. Still others used advanced techniques such as linear programming to forecast or project such flow patterns. At a more general level, efforts have been made to clarify the complexities of individual regional economic structures. The classic description of an intranation commodity flow is an examination of flows in the United States in 1957 by E. L. Ullman, who posed the question: What is the pattern of spatial connections in the American economy? Ullman believed that he had found an obvious link between geographic patterns and their spatial settings, from which he postulated his 3-factor typology of spatial interaction: **complementarity, intervening opportunity,** and **transferability.**

As a result of this work, geographers and allied researchers have postulated that there is a relationship between the network structure examined in the previous section, and the flow of goods or movement of people over that network. This structure-flow relationship is thought to be due in part to the fact that the provision of a communications system modifies relations between a set of locations. Thus in channeling the volume, direction, and intensity of movement, the network is in turn influenced by the volume of the flow it conducts. The relationship between certain graph theoretic measures and the corresponding areal characteristics is based on the intuitive assumption that the structure of a transportation network is a reflection of the network's traffic flow pattern.

By *flow* is meant simply the volume and direction of the movement of goods, people, and messages. Thus flows, and the interaction that they involve, are the chief objects of many geographical investigations, from the diffusion of innovations to the movement of consumers. Although movement is often a continuous phenomenon, it is nearly always treated as static and discrete. Taking the existence of routes

and stocks as given, we are now concerned with accounting for the volume of traffic that flows over different routes or through different nodes.

The models used to explain or represent movement, flow, or exchange, have employed six principal techniques:

In *regional input-output techniques*, flows of various kinds are examined simultaneously for their effects upon the activities of an area.

The technique of *linear programming* is frequently used in regional and other flow models. It is an extension of the *least cost idea*, which allows simultaneous consideration of several alternatives. Flows are looked on as part of a maximization technique applied within the restrictive framework of a particular situation. This technique is examined below.

The more general approach represented by *diffusion models* is concerned with the spread or flow of a variety of phenomena: new ideas and techniques, rumors, disease, cultural traits, and many others.

Another technique is *analysis of transactions;* it is used to examine flows of money, mail, telephone calls, and similar phenomena.

The use of *traffic flow models,* based on empirical studies of road capacities, speeds of vehicles, width of road, existence of junctions, and so on, is virtually confined to traffic engineering.

Finally, mention has already been made of *gravity models,* which are based on an analogy with classical Newtonian physics.

Flow patterns will now be examined in the light of two basic approaches that utilize two geographic conceptions: *temporal variation* and *spatial variation.* These approaches are:

1. *By examining the temporal sequence of flow activities, to show how they relate to the agricultural and industrial mix of an economy.*
2. *To take a more precise approach to the spatial distribution of flows by means of linear programming.*

Temporal Sequences of Flows

As economic growth proceeds, temporal sequences of flow activities reflect changes in the differential demands for goods and ideas. How can these developmental sequences best be measured? One way might be by improving the previous graph theoretic measures. This could be done by using weighted graphs in which each route or link would bear some value corresponding to the flow through the network. The pattern of weighting would then reveal how the functional interdependency between nodes and regions changes with time. The next step would be to see if there is a detectable sequence of change related to the rate and nature of economic growth.

Flow Patterns in India

From the previous analysis of graph-theoretic measures, several structural components are known to exist. It follows that a network can be broken down into field effects at both a regional and a national level. In this way complex regional interdependencies are revealed, with their accompanying nodal connections and neighborhood effects.

The following extended example deals with three important linkage-flow patterns in India (figure 173). Over a period of years, Berry and his coworkers examined more than sixty-three commodity flows between thirty-six nodes (representing major regions and cities). Figures 174 to 185 summarize the patterns for just four of these commodities: cattle, grain and grain products, baled raw jute, and iron and steel. The sample years were 1956, 1959, and 1961. These provided a reasonable coverage both in terms of the spatial organization of the Indian economy and in terms of changes in this organization due to events since the end of the colonial regime, including the Indian program of planned economic development. The map analysis in figures 173 to 185 is drawn from a 36 × 36 matrix of the nodal areas; flows between the nodes are represented either in volumetric terms or as converted values of some sort. A straight line connecting two nodes is known as a *desire line*. In these figures, desire lines link the principal receivers to the principal shippers. Thus the figures show the existence of organizational regions comprising groups of adjacent states that receive commodities from specialized production areas. Taken separately, each figure depicts the spatial flow patterns implicit in each commodity flow matrix, based on common patterns of spatial organization between and among shippers and receivers.

The first map (figure 173) just shows the nodal regions, or areas utilized in the analysis. Figures 174, 175, and 176 illustrate the effects of the field phenomenon: nodal regions of varying scale exist for the various agricultural commodities, so that there is a sort of hierarchy of field effects. Figure 174 illustrates how the areas dominated by major metropolitan centers each have their own specialized source of cattle. Note, however, that grain production is more spatially restricted; the grain production areas serve much broader regions of India (figure 175). In figure 176 Calcutta is shown to be the major source from which all India drew baled jute in 1956.

But this pattern is somewhat illusory, since it obscures the movement of jute from the actual production centers — rural Bihar (3) and West Bengal (10), from which 95 percent of the baled jute originates — to the traditional distribution center, Calcutta. However, as figures 180 and 184 show, India finally came to depend less on this traditional center, and the movement of jute from the production centers became more important.

Whereas in 1956 various types of nodal organization characterized the production and receipt of agricultural goods, a more complex form of regional flow and interdependency characterized the shipment and receipt of iron and steel (figure 177). Each of the major metropolitan areas shipped to the others, particularly Bombay (29), Madras (33), and Calcutta (30). In addition, there were links in 1956 between the Calcutta, West Bengal (10), and Bihar (3) production areas. Finally, Calcutta shipped to its own hinterland and to that of Bombay; Bihar shipped to the Calcutta hinterland; and Madras shipped to its own hinterland in the South. Thus there were complex interconnections between the metropolitan centers and the manufacturing centers, and the metropolitan centers acted as nodes for their nonproducing hinterlands.

Figure 178 repeats the pattern of figure 174, although the hinterland of Bombay, with Bombay State as its specialized source, is more clearly defined. Increasing specialization in the production of grain in the Northwest led to increased focusing of flows on that area, as figure 179 shows. The opposite was true for jute: small alternative sources were being tapped and long-distance commodity flows eliminated (figure 180). By this stage, India no longer relied on Calcutta, and the importance of the Bihar-West Bengal production area was being emphasized. Figure 181 shows the effects of increased domestic production of iron and steel in Calcutta, West Bengal, and Bihar, and the elimination of many of the imports through Madras. The complex intermetropolitan cross flows had been removed: Calcutta and West Bengal were serving the hinterlands of Bombay and Delhi, Bihar was shipping through the Calcutta region, and there were still some complex cross flows between Calcutta, West Bengal, and Bihar.

Fewer changes are shown in figures 182 to 185. Some penetration of the Madras hinterland by Bombay appears in figures 182 and 183; in figure 184 the Bihar-West Bengal-Calcutta triangle stands out more clearly; in figure 185 the effects of new steel production at Madhya Pradesh are in evidence. The Bihar-West Bengal-Calcutta triangle stands out complex cross flows, particularly to the immediate Calcutta region; Calcutta serves the Madras hinter-

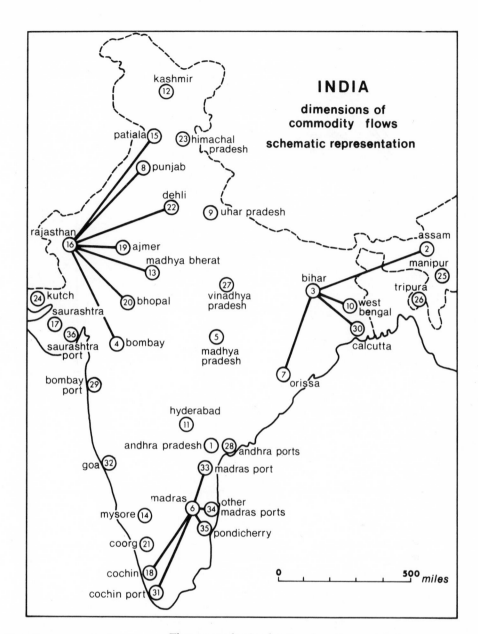

INDIA
dimensions of
commodity flows
schematic representation

Fig. 173. *Schematic representation of commodity flows in India — the basic nodes and regions. (From W.L. Garrison and D.F. Marble, "A Prolegomenon to the Forecasting of Transportation Development," Research Report, 1965, reprinted by permission of the director of the Transportation Center, Northwestern University.)*

land; West Bengal that of Delhi. But the new steel mills of Bihar and Madhya Pradesh also ship to the port-metropolises of Bombay and Madras, and Bombay, in turn, has been reestablished as the node for its own hinterland.

Conclusion

Several conclusions can be drawn from these examples of flow patterns through time:

1. *As production becomes divided among specialized areas, local field effects are replaced by ones broader in scale. Ultimately, these latter may embrace the whole nation.*

Thus as production becomes less dispersed and more specialized, the field effects grow from one city hinterland or region to cover the entire national economic landscape. This point applies to the flow patterns of different commodities at any point in time and to any particular commodity through time.

2. *Later stages of the productive process, such as manufacturing, are more likely to be characterized by complex regional flow interdependencies than are earlier stages, such as primary production. The most prominent interconnections or flows will be those linking manufacturing areas and metropolises by multiple cross-hauling. This point, in fact, specifies some of the conditions under which complex regional organization emerges at high levels of economic development.*

3. *Certain field effects repeat themselves in a variety of com-*

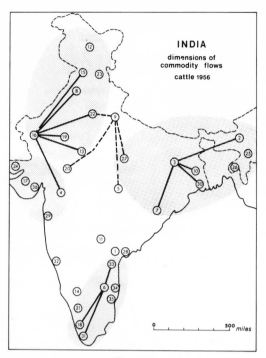

Fig. 174.

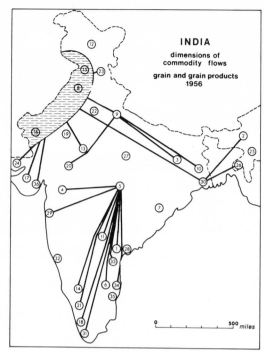

Fig. 175.

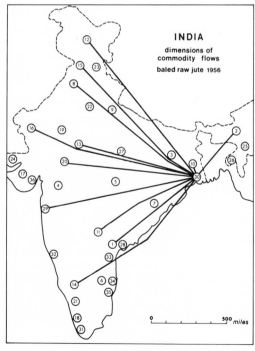

Fig. 176.

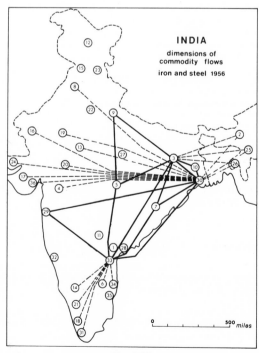

Fig. 177.

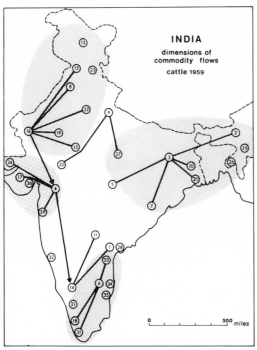

Fig. 178.

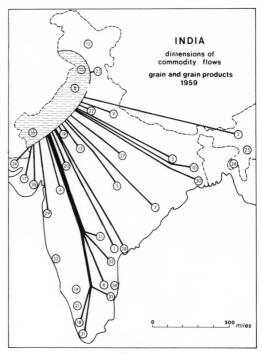

Fig. 179.

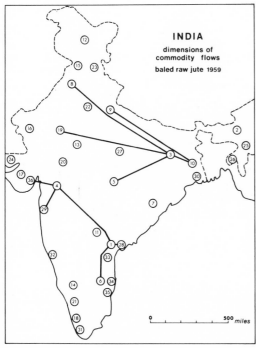

Fig. 180.

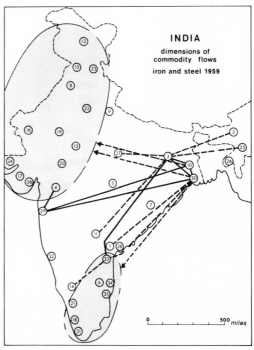

Fig. 181.

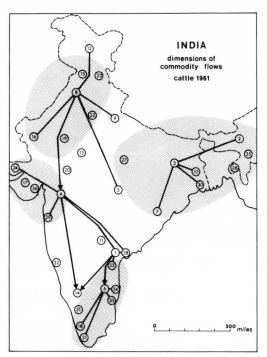

Fig. 182.

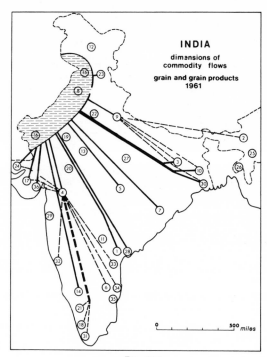

Fig. 183.

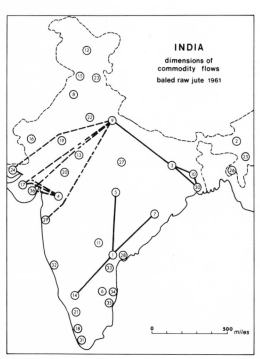

Fig. 184.

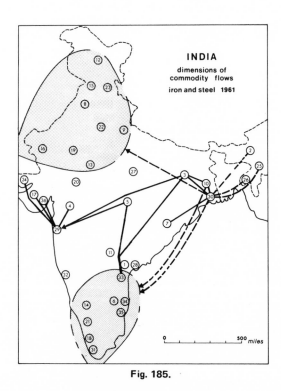

Fig. 185.

modity flows and appear to be stable through time, even though the part of the region serving as the node varies from one commodity to another. The most notable of the stable fields or regions are the hinterlands of the major metropolitan centers.

4. *Whereas there are on the one hand stable elements of structure, there are on the other hand individual commodity flow patterns that display great changes in spatial structure over relatively brief periods of time. Increasing specialization and polarization, the emergence of new production centers, governmental and other political activities—all have immediate and often drastic effects upon flow structures.*

The sum total of these changes and effects is to increase the influence of the nodal regions and to make regional interdependencies, in the form of complex interconnections between metropolitan and manufacturing nodes, more pronounced. Thus we saw that, as economic development increased and the network displayed changes in structure toward greater complexity and density, and as the specialization of areas increased, so too did the flows over the networks. Since, at these higher levels of development, increasing proportions of the flows came from more specialized production areas and involved output from manufacturing industry, the aggregate flow patterns took on a wider and more complex form.

The "Transportation Problem"

If flow patterns are so complex, is there any way they can be analyzed in detail? Of the five or six models suggested earlier, only one will be examined here in detail. This is the technique of *linear programming*, as illustrated by the so-called **transportation problem.**

Linear programming rests on the assumption that there is a linear relationship of the form $A + B = C$. Typically, there is a series of *simultaneous equations*, which represent the basic conditions of the problem, and a *linear function*, which represents the objective. The word "programming" merely means that a set program or series of rules is followed in order to solve the equations. Suffice it to say here that we are concerned with: (a) *supply centers* with known surpluses; (b) *receiving places* with known demands; (c) known *connecting routes* and *transportation costs*. The problem is, How are the flows arranged between the nodes? This is a restatement of a problem mentioned earlier. Given the network, stocks, and relation of demands to supplies, what flow pattern results? However, a rider must be added to condition (c), namely, that the flows should follow *least* cost routes. Thus the linear programming technique, outlined in the following pages, is a step-by-step measure to allocate the flows from and to known points of demand and supply to the optimal least cost routes.

The Technique

Given supply centers with known surpluses, receiving places with a known demand, and known connecting routes and transportation costs, the problem is to arrange the flows between the supply and demand points so that they follow least cost routes. This is essentially a stepwise linear programming algorithm. It is adapted from the 1965 work of K. R. Cox.

Destinations (deficits)

i \ j	1	2	3	......	j	......	m	......	Totals
1	C_{11}	C_{12}	C_{13}	......	C_{1j}	......	C_{1m}		a_1
2	C_{21}	C_{22}	C_{23}	......	C_{2j}	......	C_{2m}		a_2
3	C_{31}	C_{32}	C_{33}	......	C_{3j}	......	C_{3m}		a_3
⋮	....								
i	C_{i1}	C_{i2}	C_{i3}	......	C_{ij} X_{ij}	....			a_i
⋮	....								
n	C_{n1}	C_{n2}	....						a_n
⋮	....								

Origins (surpluses)

Totals b_1 b_2 b_3 ...... b_j ...... b_m $\sum_i ai = \sum_j bj$

The *problem matrix* is a diagrammatic way of representing this. Here, areas of surplus are listed on the left, and areas of deficit or demand along the top. The last column, a_1 to a_i, shows the total amount of a given commodity that is available for export from the particular area of surplus. All the surpluses added together are represented at the bottom by $\sum_i a_i$, which is the total amount of surplus available for export. The total amount of demand by deficit areas 1 to j is represented by b_1 and b_j. The total amount of a good demanded by all areas of deficit is $\sum_j b_j$. The fact that total demand is equal to total supply is signified by the equation $\sum_i a_i = \sum_j b_j$. In the body of the matrix, c_{ij} is a representation of the cost of transporting one unit of the commodity from the surplus area i to the deficit area j. The unknowns, that is, the flow or quantity of the good shipped from *i* to *j*, are represented by x_{ij}. Thus the problem to be solved can be represented symbolically as a linear equation

$$\sum_i \sum_j X_{ij} C_{ij} = minimum\ solution$$

What this means is that the product of transportation costs, C_{ij}, between areas of surplus, *i*, and areas of deficit, *j*, and the flows between them, should be at a minimum.

In a series of further equations, Cox shows symbolically that, in this transportation problem, total surpluses are equal to total deficits.

The solution can be presented in the following ten stages, with the use of hypothetical data. Let us imagine that three companies manufacturing auto bodies supply four auto manufacturing plants. Locations are randomly assigned to the latter. In the matrix shown below, which represents *Stage 1*, A, B, and C are the car body makers (areas of surplus) and W, X, Y, and Z the auto manufacturers (areas of deficit). The row totals represent the supply of auto bodies; the column totals represent the demand for these bodies from the four areas of deficit. The individual cell entries indicate the transportation cost, let us say in dollars, between an area of surplus and an area of deficit. The problem now is that the auto body suppliers wish to organize their transportation costs, that is, set up a pattern of flows that satisfies the criterion of minimizing costs.

Stage 1
Areas of Demand

		W	X	Y	Z	Row Totals (*n*): surpluses
	A	20	40	70	50	400
Areas of Supply	B	100	60	90	80	1,500
	C	10	110	30	200	900

Column Totals (*m*): deficits	700	600	1,000	500

In an algorithm, a basic feasible solution is said to contain not more than $n + m - 1$ variables, all with positive values. Here, then, we can expect $3 + 4 - 1 = 6$ cells occupied by figures. In the matrix illustrating *stage 2*, transportation costs for each cell have been ranked, the cheapest 1, the most expensive 12.

Stage 2

	W	X	Y	Z
A	2	4	7	5
B	10	6	9	8
C	1	11	3	12

Proceeding to *stage 3*, if we take the cell with the lowest unit movement cost, which is C/W, ranked 1, we find that this represents a supply of 900 auto bodies, and an auto manufacturer who needs 700 bodies. Thus 700, the number used, is entered in this cell, and the row and column totals are adjusted accordingly. In other words, we are allocating to W the 700 bodies he needs, leaving 200 to be allocated elsewhere.

Stage 3

	W	X	Y	Z	surpluses
A					400
B					1,500
C	700				200
deficits		600	1,000	500	

We saw in *stage 2* that the second lowest transportation costs were those of auto body manufacturer A to auto fabricator W. We also saw in *stage 1* that A can supply 400 bodies. But there is of course no demand now from W, since he has already been supplied by C at a lower transportation cost. Hence we move on to the cell with the third lowest movement costs, which is that of body supplier C and manufacturer Y. After supplying W, C has only 200 bodies left. Since Y needs 1000 bodies in all, 800 must come from elsewhere. Accordingly, 200 is entered in cell C/Y, and so on, to obtain the matrix shown in *stage 4*.

Stage 4

	W	X	Y	Z
A		400		
B		200	800	500
C	700		200	

The fourth cheapest transportation costs are those for cell A/X, so that X gets all 400 of A's bodies, but still needs another 200. The fifth cheapest are for cell A/Z, but A's supplies are now exhausted. The sixth cheapest are for cell B/X. Here, only 200 are needed, although B could supply 1,500. And so on.

The total transportation cost of this allocation would be $153,000, or the total gained by multiplying the $700 of *stage 4* by the $10 of *stage 1*, and so on through the *stage 4* matrix. What we do not know about this allocation, however, is whether it is the cheapest possible pattern of flows. This is our concern in *stage 5*. We first compute what are termed *fictional unit costs* for every row, n_i, and column, m_j, and then compute the fictional cost for each cell as the sum of the values for the respective row and column, $n_i + m_j$. These fictional unit transportation costs are then compared with actual costs.

The method of calculating fictional costs is as follows. Costs for the first row are first set at zero. Then the known unit costs are inserted in the matrix at the points where we showed flows could occur. Having fixed the A row total at zero, we can make the other row and column figures follow in sequence, as shown in the *stage 5* matrix.

Stage 5

			n_i	
50	40	70	60	
	40			0 m_j
	60	90	80	20
10		30		−40

NOTE: $40 + 0 = 40$, and $60 − 40 = 20$, which then fixes 70 and 60, which in turn fixes the −40 and the 50.

We must now fill in the *fictional* costs of the cells not used in stage 4, given the framework already calculated in *stage 5*—that is, the series $50 + 20 = 70$, $40 − 40 = 0$, and so on. This is done in the matrix for *stage 6*, below.

Stage 6

50	40	70	60	
50		70	60	0
70				20
	0		20	−40

In *stage 6a* (no matrix shown) the fictional costs are compared with the true costs. Three alternatives result:

1. *If the fictional transportation costs for an unoccupied cell of* stage 4 *are* larger *than the true cost, then a final solution has not been reached, and further stages of readjustment are needed.*
2. *If the fictional costs for an unoccupied cell are* equal to *the true cost, readjustment could occur, but without a further reduction in total transportation costs.*
3. *If the fictional costs for an unoccupied cell are* less than *the true costs, then readjustment would lead to an increase in total transportation costs rather a decrease. In other words, the minimum cost solution has been found.*

A comparison of the true costs of *stage 1* and the fictional costs of *stage 6* shows that for the first cell, A/W, the fictional cost is in fact higher than the true cost. Thus the minimum cost solution has *not* been found, and readjustment *is* necessary. Accordingly, in *stage 7* we adopt the following rules, which together constitute a *stepping stone procedure*:

1. *Values are transferred along a circuit that moves from the empty cell of stage 4 by steps that use occupied cells for the rest of the time.*
2. *The steps take alternate horizontal and vertical lines.*
3. *Each step is alternately negative and positive in value, the first step away from the empty cell being negative.*
4. *The value of the transfer (the latter consisting of the number of auto bodies) is determined by the minimum value in any cell that will have a negative value during the course of the procedure. In this particular case it proves to be cell A/X. Taking A/W as the empty cell, we trace a circuit along alternative horizontal and vertical moves, alternatively negative and positive in value, as shown in the matrix for* stage 7. *Thus for C/W we subtract 400, for C/Y we add 400, for B/Y we subtract 400—and so on, until we again reach A/W, an empty cell to which we now add 400.*

If these additions and subtractions to and from the values of *stage 4* are entered into a new matrix, the

Stage 7

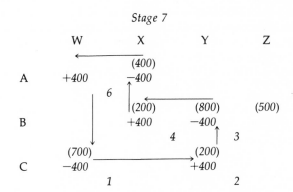

following values are found, as seen in *stage 8*:

Stage 8

	W	X	Y	Z
A	400			
B		600	400	500
C	300		600	

As already remarked, A/W was empty, but we have transferred 400 auto bodies into it (the total produced by plant A). The other values have been adjusted accordingly. Thus instead of plant C supplying manufacturer W with bodies, which on the surface seemed the cheapest solution, rearrangement through linear programming shows that the minimum cost solution calls for plants A and C to supply manufacturer W. Multiplying out the values in *stage 1* by the new figures in *stage 8* gives a total transportation cost of $141,000 instead of $153,000.

For this to be proved the minimum solution it must, as noted in *stage 6a*, be tested by comparison with fictional costs. The latter must be recomputed,

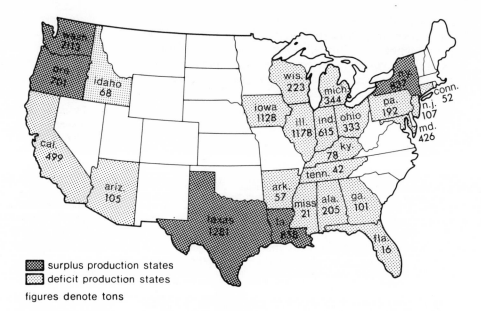

Fig. 186. *The transportation problem: (a) areas of U.S. surplus and deficit production of aluminum bars. (Figs. 186–189 are reprinted by permission from "The Application of Linear Programming to Geographic Problems," Tijdschrift Voor Econ. En. Soc. Geografie, Nov.-Dec. 1965. This figure is from p. 232.)*

▨ surplus production states
☐ deficit production states

figures denote tons

and the calculations compared with the true costs of the unoccupied cells, by means of the tripartite test already described. This is done in *stages 9* and *10*, which resemble *stages 5* and *6*. Thus in *stage 9*, as in *stage 5*, true costs of the *now* occupied cells are entered

Stage 9

			n_i	
20	10	40	30	
20				0
	60	90	80	50
10		30		−10

Stage 10

20	10	40	30	
	10	40	30	0
70				50
	0		20	−10

in the matrix, and the values of n_i and m_j are calculated as before (the first row value, m_{ji}, is set at zero). In *stage 10*, as in *stage 6*, there is a substitution for the unoccupied cells. If *stage 10* is compared to *stage 1*, it will be seen that no cell has a fictional cost that is larger than its true cost. It follows that the adjusted flow of *stage 8* is indeed the final solution, that is, the minimum cost one.

A companion problem, the obverse of the one just considered, is the *maximization problem*. Thus in the above case we could calculate the maximum total excess of delivered value over the value at the factory. In this way the locational advantages of the

three auto body plants could be compared and perhaps readjusted.

An Application

Given such a technique—three conditions and a least cost solution—one could calculate the optimal flow for a given commodity, and compare them with real-world flows. In this way, a better understanding of the latter could be achieved. A specific example can be found in figure 186, which shows the distribution of surplus and deficit areas for a given product, aluminum bars. The existence of such **complementarity** is one prerequisite for the emergence of flow patterns. In this case, the Pacific Northwest, southwestern California, and New York State would be the areas of supply, and the Midwest an area of demand. Figure 187 applies the linear programming results to the distribution of surpluses and deficits by allocating interstate movement of aluminum bars to the minimum total distance flows.* This optimal or normative flow pattern can then be compared with actual flows (figure 188).

Tests were made by Cox to ascertain whether the differences between the two patterns were statistically significant, that is, whether they were due merely to chance or whether they gave indications of some further meaning. The tests indicated that there were indeed significant differences between the two patterns shown in figures 187 and 188. Cox then proceeded to compute regression equations based on the normative flows, but containing data

*Minimum distance was used, because of the paucity of data concerning the costs of moving aluminum bars.

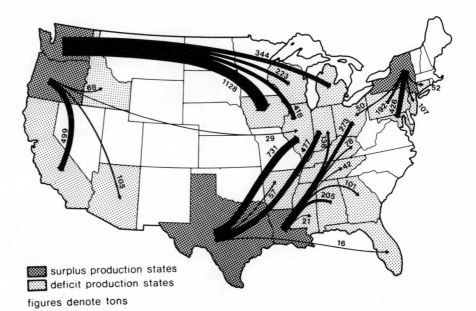

surplus production states
deficit production states

figures denote tons

Fig. 187. *The transportation problem: (b) the optimal movement of aluminum bars. (Ibid., p. 232.)*

drawn from the real world. The *residuals* from this regression (i.e. those parts unaccounted for by the normative conditions of distance minimization) could then be plotted and used to indicate why deviations occur from the postulated least distance conditions.

Figure 189 shows the distribution of those residuals from the regression of actual flows on optimal flows. The mapped residuals indicate that positive deviations from the optimum refer to states separated by long distances (Washington to Illinois, New York to Indiana), and negative deviations to states separated by short distances (Louisiana to Mississippi, Texas to Arkansas). These deviations illustrate that transportation costs are in fact not directly related to distance in a linear manner. In the case of railroads, the cost per ton mile tends to decrease between origin and destination, since most of the costs are terminal costs not actual movement costs, and the longer the journey the longer the total mileage over which those terminal costs can be spread. Thus it may be cheaper per ton mile to transport aluminum bars from Washington to Illinois than from Washington to Idaho. Because of the lack of cost data noted earlier, Cox had to use estimates based on whatever cost data were available.

Conclusion

Flows are *volumetric measures* of spatial interaction. Flow patterns can be analyzed and explained in terms of areal characteristics, the positive or negative factors being supply and demand, on the one hand, and cost and distance (among other factors) on the other. Economic development, regional growth and change, consumer taste preferences, cultural traits, or governmental and military direction can all alter the spatial imbalance that usually has to be present to initiate movement. Flow analysis, by any of the methods mentioned, can act as a link between the concept of interaction and the analysis of spatial distribution and relationships.

Modal Systems

Demand and supply—in noneconomic language, desire and fulfillment—generate movement. If movement occurs, it is through a network with a structure containing certain stocks or units of transport. Intensity of movement from X to Y can be measured by volume, or flow. We are now in a position to note that these relations are also measurable in terms of different modes of transport.

Each mode of transport—air, road, rail, waterway, or pipeline—has its own distinctive characteristics and spatial relationships. Moreover, each plays a different though often overlapping role in the supply of transportation. Thus railroads seem best suited to long haul transportation of heavy commodities that are often of small value per unit load. Trucks excel in door-to-door specialized traffic, with emphasis on the shorter haul. Air transport specializes in speed and in long haul high value goods needing quick delivery. Inland waterways and ocean shipping have an advantage in hauling bulk goods of low value that can slow transportation and are amenable to bulk handling and movement; pipelines can transport liquids, semiliquids, or (more recently) solids, in a one-way flow at reasonable speed and in a continuous stream (table 61). Technical change is tend-

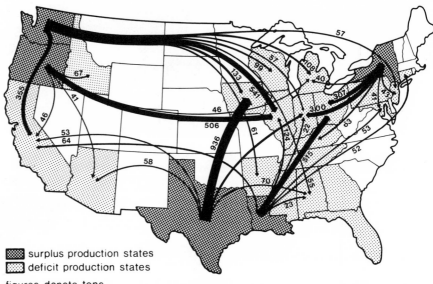

Fig. 188. *The transportation problem: (c) the actual movement of aluminum bars. (Ibid., p. 233.)*

▨ surplus production states
▦ deficit production states

figures denote tons

ing to increase the already considerable overlap or competition between the modes.

Table 61. *U.S. Domestic Transportation, Relative Modal Shares*

	% ton miles	% revenue
railroad	42.0	42.0
truck	25.0	40.0
pipeline	17.0	3.5
inland water	15.9	1.5
air	0.1	13.0

Source: M.T. Farris and P.T. McElhiney, eds., *Modern Transportation: Selected Readings* (Boston: Houghton Mifflin Co., 1967), p. 2.

Table 61 gives two measures of U.S. domestic modal shares: by ton miles hauled (which overemphasizes modes carrying bulk goods long distances), and by revenue generated (which overemphasizes high value goods and high value charges or rates). These relative shares have not been constant over time; railroads were formerly the dominant mode of transport, and even up to 1945 they hauled 60 percent of the total U.S. ton mileage. While at present in the United States all the modes haul more ton miles in total than they did in 1945, their relative shares have changed. Most of the increase in ton mileage has gone to the newer modes of transportation, particularly trucking.

The highly developed market-exchange economy produces an atypical modal pattern. Western Europe on the other hand, shows a smaller relative drop in the percentage of ton miles and passenger miles moved by rail, and a very limited dependence on air travel. These differences arise from different standards of living, population densities, and conceptions of distance. The redistributive economies, such as the U.S.S.R., place a much stronger emphasis on railroads for both passenger and freight traffic; the Soviet railroad system carries over 70 percent of intercity freight. Japan, another market-exchange economy but with different developmental characteristics, also emphasizes railroads, which carry something over 50 percent of its freight ton miles. Since Japan is a group of islands, water transport plays an important role; between 30 to 40 percent of the ton miles of freight are moved by coastal shipping. Only more recently has Japan begun a major road building program, just as the U.S.S.R. has begun to expand its airlines.

Like Japan and the U.S.S.R., countries emerging from peasant-subsistent economies tend to favor railroads. India, Pakistan, and China, for instance, depend on rail movements backed up by inland waterways. But in developing countries with lower population densities the emphasis tends to be on highways, with air routes and pipelines sometimes playing significant roles, as in Venezuela. According to W. Owen, in Columbia 57 percent of freight traffic in 1960 was carried by truck, 16 percent by inland rivers, 17 percent by rail, and 7 percent by coastal shipping and pipelines—a response to very different spatial and developmental conditions.

Railroads

In marketing-exchange economies, the history of railroad development is in large part a history of efforts to raise enough capital. In other words, this mode is capital intensive. And no wonder: it has to provide not only actual rolling stock but the right

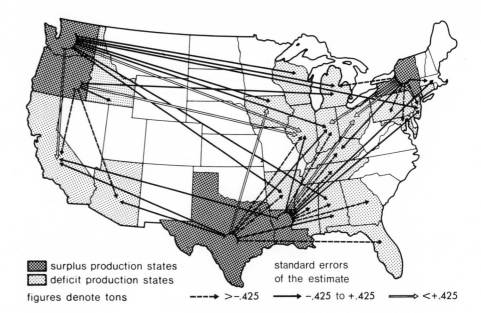

Fig. 189. *The transportation problem: (d) estimation of residuals from regression analysis involving the optimal and actual flows of aluminum bars. (Ibid., p. 233.)*

▨ surplus production states
☐ deficit production states

figures denote tons

standard errors of the estimate

---▶ >-.425   ──▶ -.425 to +.425   ⟹ <+.425

of way, which motor carriers do only indirectly, and airways not at all. The profitability of this investment depends on intensity of use, so to be economic a railroad requires sufficient traffic moving over a given route to permit economy-of-scale operations. In Europe, the figure needed to justify a section of railroad economically is usually 350,000 tons per mile per year. In North America, a figure of about 400,000 tons is used to justify the building of a new rail link. These are economic conditions; usually there are social justifications as well. About 37 percent of U.S. railroad mileage cannot be justified on the economic grounds noted above, since it carries less than 1,000 tons per mile per day. About 50 percent of U.S. rail freight traffic is carried on only 10 percent of the network, which averages 39,000 tons per day per mile. There are two broad bands of movement; west to east across the industrial belt of the United States, and from the east Kentucky coalfields to the East and Northeast. Potential traffic may also justify construction, though if large movements are not expected for some time it may be justifiable to begin with some other mode.

The world railroad map gives the impression of a system in which one movement follows another without impediment. This impression is misleading. There are thirty-nine different track gauges in use today, ranging from 1 foot 3 inches to 5 feet 6 inches; 13 of these gauges are the principal track gauges in one or more countries. India has about 52 break-of-gauge points; Australia has three dominant gauge widths. The geographer W. Siddall reports, "Choice of gauge was sometimes made by a committee . . . and in more than one case the decision of the committee was a compromise . . . in South Africa the first railroad was built to a gauge of 4'8½", and a

later line was built at 2'6". The government took over the railroads in 1873 and opened the question of a proper gauge, whereupon a Parliamentary Committee compromised on 3'6"."

Railroads become increasingly efficient with length of haul, as the high costs of terminal operations are spread over an ever greater number of ton miles. For example, the operating costs for Nigerian railroads, assuming a five ton shipment, are 32 cents a mile for 10 miles, 8 cents a mile for 50 miles, and 3 cents a mile for 500 miles. For a larger shipment the cost is lower, on both long and short hauls. As table 62 shows, railroads meet competition here, particularly for heavy volumes of industrial raw materials, since the unit cost of movement by pipeline and waterway can be one-fifth to one-third of the cost of moving comparable volumes by rail. We have already seen that rail rates are not linearly related to distance, but are curvilinear due to the effects of terminal and handling costs. In the United States there are five additional factors that influence rates.

1. Freight rate territories. *Until recently, rates varied among five regions, with the eastern price set at 100, the southern at 139, the western at 147, the southwestern at 175, and the mountain Pacific at 191. Since this practice was ruled discriminatory, although it reflected varying intensities of traffic and thus produced lower operating costs per ton mile, the territorial differentials were eventually eliminated.*

2. Rate-group principle. *This means that rates are grouped in steps; nodes along each route are divided into groups, and all points in the same group have the same rate over broad zones. The rates rise in steps at the zone boundaries.*

Table 62. *Modal Systems: Comparative Characteristics (North America)*

Mode	Costs	Unit Cost (Mile) (Rail = 1.0)	Distance	Rates	Characteristic Goods	Distinction	Drawbacks
Railroad	*Capital intensive; large initial investment (incl. right of way). Profitability rests on intensity of use: 350,000 to 500,000 tons/mile/ year is operational margin. Terminal costs high.*	*1.0*	*Increasing effectiveness with length of haul. Large shipments cheaper by long or short haul.*	*Subject to class rates, freight rates, territories in-transit rates, etc.*	*Minerals; un- processed agric. products; building mats, chemicals. Pass'rs minor.**	*Large volumes of bulk goods in comparatively short time at low costs.*	*Cost and time of assembling units.*
Waterways	*Investment low, especially where natural waterways utilized. Terminal and hand- ling costs several times line haul costs.*	*0.29*	*Increasing effectiveness with length of haul.*		*Marine: semi- finished and finished prod- ucts. Inland: bulk raw goods— coke, coal, oil, grain, sand, gravel, cement. Pass'rs negligible.*	*Low freight rates; slow speed; spec. of goods carriage.*	*Slow speed.*
Motor Transport	*Fixed costs negli- gible. Operates on small margins — operating costs high; vehicle turnover high.*	*4.5*	*Short hauls, less costly than rail. Wide areal coverage.*	*Rail acts as price leader.*	*Perishable goods; lumber. Pass'rs important.*	*Light loads, short distances, short time. Flexible and convenient. Improved serv- ice. Minimizes distribution costs.*	*Inadequate capacity for moving heavy volumes, bulk materials. High costs of long hauls. High vehicle oper- ating costs.*
Air Transport	*Fixed costs low. Investment in stock very high. Terminal, take-off costs, high.*	*16.3*	*Long hauls, economy with distance.*	*Rates set by national and international regulations.*	*Pass'rs dominant. Perishable, light weight, high value goods.*	*Speed.*	*Very high costs.*
Pipelines	*Fixed costs high. Large economies through diameter of pipe. Costs increase almost directly with distance. Viscosity adds costs.*	*0.21*	*Long haul in bulk.*		*Crude oil and petroleum products in large volume. Natural gas. Some solids.*	*Bulk movement of liquids.*	*Restricted com- modity use. Regular flow and demand needed. Large market.*

*In Europe, passenger revenues usually exceed freight revenues.

3. Class rates. *The Interstate Commerce Commission (I.C.C.) authorizes rates applicable to items moving in small quantities. These rates vary for thirty classes. Thus a commodity in class 400 has four times the base rate (100), while the rate for class 13 would be 13 percent of the base rate.*

4. Commodity rates. *These are specific rates allowed by*

the I.C.C. for goods moving in large quantities between specific origins and destinations. They are the rates commonly used for the great majority of freight.

5. In-transit rates. *These are special privileges granted by the I.C.C. that allow goods to travel at an initial raw freight rate, despite intermediate processing. Thus railroad*

rates are highly complex systems of prices based both on costs and on considerations of demand.

At one time, railroads were the dominant long haulage carriers. More recently, however, railroads have undergone an adjustment to the traffic to which they are most suited, so that they are now carriers of such items as unprocessed agricultural products, building materials, and chemicals. In the United States 55 percent of rail traffic is the haulage of minerals; in eastern Europe, 65 percent consists of fuel, ores, and metals; in the U.S.S.R., 70 percent consists of these same three commodities with the addition of lumber. Conversely, there has been a decline in certain types of traffic that formerly moved by rail. Thus perishable goods are now largely sent by truck and crude petroleum by pipeline, while coal has declined in importance with the development of new energy sources. Passenger service yields only a small portion of total revenue in North America, and its effect on profits may well be negative. Railroads find it difficult to compete with buses and aircraft for the 9 percent in the United States who do not travel between nodes by automobile. An attempt to revitalize and nationalize U.S. rail passenger service has come with the introduction of a quasi state system, Amtrak. This is a federally financed institution to coordinate and run the main rail service in the United States, using existing company rolling stock and track. It is too early to comment on the ultimate success of this scheme; so far, its achievements are not impressive. Efforts to compete in the freight area are being carried out with the unitized train, which is an entire train devoted to carrying a single commodity from one node to another. Other such devices are so-called piggyback services—transfer of containers directly from truck to freight car and back again—and faster schedules. With regard to the latter, it should be noted that average speed in normal rail freight operations can be as low as 15–20 m.p.h., because of delays in terminal operations.

The advantages of railroads lie in their capacity to carry large volumes of heavy items in comparatively short time at low cost. Their drawbacks include assembly and terminal costs, and time costs. The unitized train, and various kinds of large-capacity freight cars, are among the ways of overcoming these difficulties.* In short, railroads seem better for long hauls than for short ones.†

---

*For instance, the *pregnant whale* is a supertanker with 30,000 gallon capacity, compared to the regular 8,000 gallon tanker.

†This brief survey cannot possibly cover all aspects of railroads. In particular the reader is advised to look at the W. H. Wallace (1963) review of geographic railroad structures.

Water Transport

The leading characteristics of water transport are low freight rates, specialization in a few bulk commodities, and low speed (e.g., barges on inland waterways move at an average of 5 miles an hour). In the United States, inland waterways carry about 16 percent of all intercity freight. In 1946 the comparable figure was 3.1 percent, so an increase has taken place, as waterways have become increasingly competitive through technological improvements. If natural waterways are used, the investment is small compared to the railroads. Inland waterways tend to carry such bulk goods as oil, grain, or sand.*

The position is slightly different for marine transport, which is free from much of the competition of fast inland media. Hence marine transport hauls a much larger proportion of semifinished and finished commodities. However, handling costs are high, and the terminal and handling costs together can exceed the costs of the voyage proper (the *line-haul costs*) by as much as three times. Other costs, imposed in part by other media, are packaging and containerization, and the turnaround costs. Even for railroads, which have heavy terminal costs, terminal costs are usually equal to line-haul costs for a movement of 300 miles. By sea, however, terminal costs can still be double or triple line-haul costs on a 3,000 mile journey.

The *general costs* of the marine transportation system are also important. The system suffers from periods of excess capacity alternating with periods of high demand. Capacity responds very slowly to changes in demand, and reductions in force are slow, since the lifespan of a ship is over twenty years. Voyage costs are fixed independently for the most part of the cargo carried, and the marginal costs of carrying extra cargo up to the vessel's capacity are small. As a result, there are often economic pressures in times of excess capacity to accept extra cargo at any price in excess of the handling costs for the marginal cargo. Since in the short run the supply of vessels is inelastic, shortages of shipping are reflected in upward price swings.

Marine rate structures are complex, governed by international rate agreements that are essentially restrictive, that is, they hold down competition and keep up prices. They also reflect national practices in subsidizing ship construction or giving preference to certain types of cargo. Marine vessels are undergoing technical changes, particularly to

---

*This is true in North America and Western Europe. But in Bangladesh (formerly East Pakistan) jute and rice are hauled. In Nigeria, 70 percent of the Niger River traffic downstream was ground nuts and palm kernels; upstream, it was 20 percent salt and 50 percent cement.

increase capacity and usage. There are now tankers (which, since they are partly automatic, lower handling costs) for liquid sulphur, latex, fruit juices, and liquid gases. Container use is also growing, too, and ships specifically designed for containerization have been developed.

It should be clear from the foregoing discussion that we cannot ignore the special terminal point for marine transportation: the seaport. A model to simulate the growth of ports and their seaward and landward connections has been proposed by P. Rimmer in a 1967 study; it is summarized in figure 190.

Inland waterways are in direct competition with overland media. Their advantage is cheapness; their disadvantages are slowness, vulnerability to weather conditions, and so on. We have already seen that water carriers have an advantage over railroads in that they bear only a small proportion of their route costs. The fully distributed costs of river barge transport are about 2 cents per ton mile, or five to ten times lower than the equivalent rail costs. Thus the economy of water transport for bulk movement of commodities that do not require prompt delivery is sufficient to absorb all terminal and transshipment costs, and still remain below rail costs. Cost advantages also revolve around the quantities carried. A single barge can carry up to one million gallons of petroleum. With eight barges in tow, this exceeds a rail train capacity by three or four times. Another illustration of the low costs is the fact that a gallon of crude oil can move 1,700 miles by waterway for less than the cost of moving a gallon of gasoline 10 miles from a refinery by truck. However, the full potential of water transport can be achieved only by shipments in very large quantities.

Average length of haul is 532 miles in the United States, compared with 464 miles for railroad, 267 for trucks, 314 for pipelines carrying crude oil, and 261 miles for pipelines carrying refined oil. Speeds are slow: the journey from Pittsburgh to New Orleans takes 8 days and 18 hours for 1,852 miles downstream (9 miles per hour), and 14 days upstream (5 miles per hour).

In summary, the place of water transport in the total transportation market may be said to be characterized by low cost for large volume movements. Water transport is slow. For commercial purposes, then, it is restricted to longer route mileages than the other methods of transportation.

Motor Transport

Motor transport is now a very important part of the domestic transportation systems of North America and Western Europe. A part of nearly all shipments in those areas now goes by truck, and in some in-

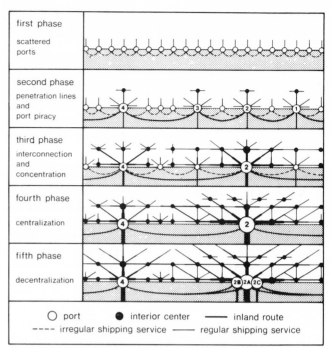

Fig. 190. *A model of port development. (From P. J. Rimmer, "The Search for Spatial Regularities in the Development of Australian Seaports, 1861–1961/2," Geografiske Annales, series B, 1967, vol. 49, p. 43, reprinted by courtesy of the editor.)*

Phase 1. *Dispersed pattern of seaports scattered along coast, limited hinterlands, irregular service.*
Phase 2. *Emergence of main landward penetration routes; certain ports expand at the expense of others (1,2,3,4). These four ports develop as foci for separate route networks.*
Phase 3. *Feeders continue to develop until 1, 2, and 3 link; 2, in its central position, captures the trade of the other two, and 1 and 3 revert to former status. 4, unlinked to the other network, survives.*
Phase 4. *The networks of 2 and 4 link up; but 4 gains sufficient momentum (inertia) to survive, despite the centralization of economic activities at 2, by providing specialized services. Port 2, however, continues to grow at a faster rate.*
Phase 5. *In this final phase, the continuing expansion of the network and of economic activities leads to the provision of specialized functions at ports 2B and 2C, while the initial port (now 2A) concentrates on general cargo services.*

dustries more than a part. This is a relatively recent phenomenon; only with the provision of improved highways in the last thirty to forty years has it been technically able to expand.

Truck transport is particularly well adapted to moving light loads short distances in a short time; on short hauls, trucks can cost less than railroads. In most countries, governments build and maintain roads. For this reason, many shippers find it cheaper to send long distance shipments by trucks. In the United States, the ton mileage of intercity freight has grown from 53 billion ton miles in 1939 to 331.9 billion in 1966—an increase of more than 500 percent. In Canada, growth has been less impressive but still marked: from 1.5 billion ton miles in 1938 to 17 billion ton miles in 1966. There are three principal reasons for this marked trend: the economy and reliability of road transportation has increased rapidly with improved roads and improved vehicle performance; on many routes with light traffic, this may be the only feasible method of mechanized transport; and as the economy develops, there may grow a greater concern for improved service and a correspondingly lesser concern for transportation costs.

The concern of a shipper is not just with the costs of movement, but with total production and distribution costs. Various modes of transport can have significant effects on these total costs. Thus the economy of rail transport may be impaired by slow deliveries. For a wide range of shipments, including both perishable and highly valued manufactures, time is important. To carry large inventories of goods simply for the purpose of overcoming time lags in delivery may be very costly and tie up needed capital. An advantage of road transport is the wide and flexible areal coverage offered by the highway network, which can be upgraded in stages; a gravel road will do for light traffic, but this can be improved as traffic increases. Other media, especially rail, water, and pipeline, are designed for substantial capacity from the beginning. The fact that trucks are able to offer a complete door-to-door service is a distinct asset: it avoids transshipment, and allows flexibility of scheduling. Truck transportation can be more readily integrated into the total production process, especially if an industry operates its own trucking line, thus reducing its inventories and eliminating the need for storage.

Diversions to road transport can occur even when the competing mode is cheaper, in order to minimize the total costs of distribution. However, the benefits are most marked for shorter hauls. In a survey of the movement of fresh fruit and vegetables in the United States, it was found that for all shipments destined for points less than 100 miles away, 88 percent moved by road and only 6 percent by rail. On trips of 1,000 miles and more, railroads carried 66 percent, and at over 2,000 miles, 93 percent went by rail.

A number of cost factors are interesting here. Motor carriers operate on very small margins; some 96 percent of all revenue may be operating expenses. The required investment is small, however; the trucking business is highly competitive, but it is relatively easy to enter. However, there are only very limited economies of scale; large firms do not have decisive cost advantages over small firms. A more unusual characteristic is the rapid wearing out of vehicles, particularly when they are used intensively; four years may mark the average life of a truck. Because of this about one million new trucks enter

Table 63. *Distribution of Shipments by Truck, Selected Industries U.S.*

industry	total mills. of tons shipped	% by truck
beverage-tobacco-confectionery	51	79
clothing	4	73
meat and dairy product	43	72
canned and frozen food	128	40
primary iron and steel products	121	40

Source: U.S. Census 1965 (for 1963); J.B. Lansing, *Transportation and Economic Policy* (New York: The Free Press, 1966), p. 261.

Table 64. *Passenger Transportation: Comparative Costs, U.S. (costs in cents)*

	cost/seat-mile	cost/pass'r mile
railroad	1.90	6.93
bus	1.29	2.73
automobile	2.15	4.50
airline (truck)	3.81	6.20
airline (local)	5.45	12.30

Source: J.B. Lansing, *Transportation and Economic Policy* (New York: The Free Press, 1966).

the U.S. highways each year and about 500,000 are scrapped. In this way, technical innovations are diffused very quickly, and excess capacity is kept to a minimum. Rates charged usually take their lead from railroad prices, and compete by offering better service, door-to-door speed, and overnight delivery.

In summary, truck transport is inadequate for moving heavy volumes of bulk materials, and is costly for long hauls. However, it offers greater flexibility, better service, and low costs for short hauls. The average length of haul for trucks is 267 miles in the United States compared to 464 miles for railroads. In the United States it has been most successful in the confectionery, beverage, tobacco, clothing, and meat and dairy product industries, though as table 63 shows it does move a substantial proportion of iron and steel products, principally in the category of goods that travel less than 400 miles.

Motor transportation, unlike most of the other modes, also has a substantial importance as a passenger carrier, particularly in urban areas: Table 64 compares the costs of the modes: Railroads can provide passenger services on heavily trafficked main routes at 1.9 cents per mile, but the low load factor increases the cost to the passenger to 6.9 cents per mile, higher than the popular trunk airlines. Buses provide the cheapest transport and automobiles the next cheapest, although they carry 91 percent of U.S. intercity passenger traffic. The reasons for the advantages of automobiles are convenience, flexibility, and their ability to supply cultural wants and needs. Quite frequently the owner-driver does not perceive all the costs involved, and in evaluating alternative modes is more concerned with relative levels of service or time than with cost considerations. Surveys have shown that most auto drivers do not estimate their driving costs, a factor that is consistent with the relative inelasticity of response to changes in fares of public transit systems.

Air Transport

One of the newest of the transportation modes is air transport. It has expanded very rapidly since 1945. Airlines are the specialists in transport; principally passenger carriers, by efficient operation they have captured a high proportion of the "for hire" passenger market. A small but important freight market exists for goods with such characteristics as high value, light weight, and perishability or need for speedy delivery.

Air transport can play a different role according to the development characteristics of a region. According to K. S. Sealy, there are three main stages:

A *pioneer phase*, where aircraft are used for various topographical, forest or mineral surveys. In some cases, where potential resource exploitation seems to warrant it, aircraft are used to establish the first camps and to aid in the construction of surface links.

With the establishment of primary land routes, there is a *phase of exploitation* in which aircraft begin to specialize in passengers and freight.

In a *final phase*, growth of industry and settlement may follow, in which case surface modes rise to dominance. Air transport now assumes a more "normal" role, concentrating on passengers, mail, and specialized freight carriage.

The demand side of air transport is complex to evaluate. In short haul conditions, other modes offer services that are close substitutes. But in the long haul passenger market there are distinct advantages. The long haul market is constrained, of course, by the consumer's ability to pay for travel; and only if he has an annual income of $7,500 or more does an American adult have a more than 10 percent likelihood of making an air trip in any one year. There is little variation in the rates charged between airlines; in the United States, for example, interstate airfares are regulated by the FTC, and international flights by the International Air Transport Association agreements. Some promotional fares exist, varying with season, family size, and so forth. Competition usually takes the form of advertising gimmicks and ownership of the most technically advanced aircraft.

Fixed costs in air transport are either small or absent. Operating costs, on the other hand, make up about 27 percent of flying operations, maintenance 20 percent, services 43 percent, and depreciation 10 percent. Economies of scale between airlines are small, but there are economies among aircraft types; for instance, there is a strong tendency for operating costs per seat mile to be lower when the aircraft is large (table 65). The important factor is the percentage of seat miles, flown in a scheduled service, that are *sold*. This is because the cost of operating an aircraft between two points depends only to a limited extent on whether the aircraft is full or empty; the same terminal costs, crew costs, and fuel costs are incurred. The utilization rate of the aircraft is also important, since each represents a substantial capital outlay, and so are such other factors as route density, route structure, and length of stage flown. With regard to the last-mentioned factor, it should be noted that costs per aircraft mile are not constant; they fall as distance increases, since the costs of taxiing, takeoff, climbing, and landing are spread over more miles; cruising costs are much lower. However, there comes a point at which the additional fuel needed to fly longer distances begins to be expensive. Table 66 shows some estimates for the Boeing 727 at the time of its introduction.

Air freight charges are many times higher than freight charges for competitive modes. Average freight revenues per ton mile were about 22.7 cents in 1950, though technical improvements lowered it to between 10 and 16 cents per ton mile in the late

Table 65. *Jet Aircraft: Operating Costs, 1964*

jet type	av. seats /mile	cost/seat mile (cents)
Caravelle	64	3.1
Boeing 720	111	1.5
DC-8	123	1.4
Boeing 707	124	1.4
DC-8	127	1.7

Source: Air Transport Association, *American Aviation*, May, 1965, p. 41; J.B. Lansing, *Transportation and Economic Policy* (New York: The Free Press, 1966), p. 318.

Table 66. *Cost Estimates, Boeing 727*

stage length	direct operating costs ($)	costs/seat mile (cents)
400 miles	1.55	1.40
600 miles	1.40	1.25
over 1,000 miles	below 1.30	1.15

Source: W.S. Reed, "Boeing Reveals Final 727 Design Details," *Aviation Week*, March 6, 1961, p. 41; J.B. Lansing, *Transportation and Economic Policy* (New York: The Free Press, 1966), p. 318.

1960s. The reason that air freight is used at all is that it can serve to minimize *total* costs. Its customers range along a continuum from those who use it only in emergencies to those who use it regularly. A typical example of an emergency use would be flying out replacement parts for a ship rather than letting it be held up for weeks. Commodities regularly sent by air freight include perishables like flowers, fruit, and information (i.e., newspapers). There are also instances where there is no alternative to air freight, as in much of ·Alaska.

Future developments may see the emergence of air transport as a substitute for other modes rather than as a complement. Although it is usual to think of surface transport as the norm, this may change with changing technology. Already there is some evidence of changing attitudes. Thus the World Bank recommended that Libya make use of aircraft to service remote communities rather than build roads (Libya chose to ignore this advice), and in Venezuela meat is flown out of points that are otherwise inaccessible.

Pipelines

The main characteristics of pipelines, apart from their newness, is that they are *specialized, cheap,* and *slow.* Basically, they carry liquids, although they have some potential for moving solids. Their increasing role in commodity movements has been made possible by various technical advances: large-scale production of inexpensive pipe, the use of electric welding, and improved and more economic ways of laying pipes. There are certain disadvantages to pipelines, such as their inflexibility once laid and their relatively fixed capacity, which can be only marginally improved by the installation of extra pumping equipment. The advantages of pipelines lie in their ability to cross most terrain practically unaffected by climate, and to carry petroleum and natural gas in particular at very low unit costs. Where volume and market demand are sufficiently great and steady, pipelines are more economic than other forms of transport. Land costs can often be minimized by burying the pipeline, and 70 to 75 percent of the costs of installing an average pipeline are the costs of the pipe itself. Pumping stations are installed at intervals between 30 and 150 miles, and they can be largely automatic. Annual operating costs run about 3 to 10 percent of original costs. The actual costs vary with size of pipe, efficiency of use, cost of capital, nature of terrain, and the viscosity of the fluid being transmitted (the more viscous, the harder it is to pump). The average costs of a ten-inch pipeline in North America 1,000 miles long, is $37,000 per mile, excluding rights of way. A comparable length of twenty-inch pipeline, carrying three and one-half times as much liquid, is about $66,000 per mile, with operating costs about a third as much. Moderately large volumes of any liquid can be moved by pipeline to waterways at about 15 to 25 percent of rail costs and 15 to 18 percent of truck costs. Something like 70 percent of U.S. energy resources move through a million-mile pipeline network (table 67). The total movement of oil, especially of crude oil, is very large, and pipelines account for about 17 percent of U.S. intercity freight ton mileage. The larger share of the crude petroleum market revealed by table 67 is due to the special suitability of pipelines for very large movements, such as flows from oil fields. Distribution of refined products to individual points of consumption is in much smaller quantities. Natural gas is another major product carried by pipelines; there are twice as many miles of gas pipeline in the United States as there are miles of rail track.

It is clear, then, that the most important determinants of cost in pipeline transportation are economies of scale associated with pipe diameter. Thus for 1,000 miles of pipe, with a throughput of 100,000 barrels a day, an eighteen-inch pipe would average about 16 cents per barrel, but 400,000 barrels in a thirty-two-inch pipe would cost 8 cents per barrel. Obviously in this case it would be wasteful for, say, four competing refineries in a consuming area, taking crude oil from the same area, to use four separate pipelines, since they would double the costs of moving the oil. It follows, then, that the cost of moving oil on a route equipped with a large-diameter pipeline will be lower than on another route not thus equipped.

Western European pipeline systems have not grown at anything like the pace of North American ones. In spite of the growth of Western Europe's oil market there have been few individual markets large or regular enough to warrant pipeline installation. Figure 191 illustrates why the availability of cheap water transport, and the smaller size of European markets, have held back European pipeline growth. In recent years, however, the growth of large inland markets for oil at Cologne, Vienna, and elsewhere, has justified the construction of a considerable mileage of crude oil pipelines. The most

Table 67. *Distribution of Crude and Refined Petroleum by Mode, U.S.*

	% crude	% refined
pipeline	76	20
water	18	38
truck	6	36
rail	–	6

Source: American Petroleum Institute, ''Petroleum Facts and Figures, 1959,'' p. 197; Lansing, 1966, p. 371.

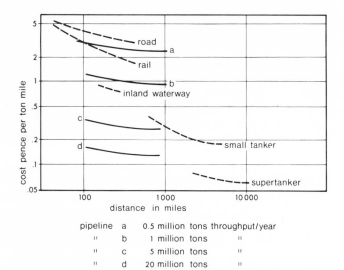

pipeline a 0.5 million tons throughput/year
     "   b 1 million tons   "
     "   c 5 million tons   "
     "   d 20 million tons   "

Fig. 191. *Alternative costs of transporting oil in Europe (c. 1960). (Reprinted by permission from G. Manners, "The Pipeline Revolution," Geography, 1962, p. 157.)*

recent change has been the growth in products pipelines, brought about by increasing demand inland, and demand for lighter, less viscous products. The development of supertankers underlines this change: refining capacity is becoming concentrated at fewer coastal points.

There has been much interest in the use of pipelines for moving solids, an operation that can be accomplished by the use of a carrying fluid, or by breaking down the solids in the form of capsules. The test example was a 108-mile pipeline constructed in Ohio to move coal to a power plant near Cleveland. The ten and one-half inch pipeline, including land, cost $125,000 per mile, with a capacity of 1.2 million tons of coal per year. The coal was ground to a coarse sand size, and mixed with an equal amount of water (the result is known as *slurry*). This mixture was pushed by three pumping stations over the 108-mile route in 30 hours. However, the introduction of unitized trains over the same stretch has caused the closure of the pipeline.

Other Modes

We live in a period when new developments in transportation are in the offing. For example, there are *hovercraft,* operating on cushions of air, that can utilize areas of unstable ground and operate over water or in areas with no fixed routes. They are limited only by the steepness of the terrain (costs of operation have yet to be determined). Vertical takeoff and landing (VTOL) craft, including helicopters, could reduce both terminal costs and the

problem of access to airports, but they are relatively costly to operate. Helicopters can carry freight short distances for about 16 cents per ton mile with a 75 percent load factor. But they are essentially short haul operators, and for hauls over fifty miles some combination of fixed-wing and VTOL aircraft would be necessary for economic operation. Yet another development is the *hydrofoil* for river and coastal services. It is capable of speeds from 45 to 100 knots, and of carrying 5,000 to 20,000 tons of freight. Besides these actual vehicular changes there may be novel technical developments such as fuel cells, gas turbine engines, and nuclear engines. Any of these may again alter the balance between the modes noted above.

Conclusion

The modal systems cannot of course be considered in isolation. Thus the railroad system is influenced both by the absence or presence of other modes of transport, and by these other modes' location and relative efficiency. Table 62 compares the basic characteristics of the modes discussed; table 68 shows the relative shares of the market for the principal modes of transportation in the United States and Canada.

Table 68. *Modal Systems, Relative Shares of Market, U.S. and Canada*

(a) intercity freight traffic (ton miles), United States 1939–1964 (%)

	1939	1949	1959	1964
railroad	62.3	58.3	45.6	42.9
motor carrier	9.7	13.8	21.5	23.8
inland waterway (incl. Gt. Lakes)	17.7	15.2	15.3	15.9
oil pipeline	10.2	12.6	17.6	17.2
airways	0.002	0.026	0.052	0.100
total ton miles (billions)	543	916	1278	1555

(b) intercity passenger-miles (for hire), 1950–1964 (%)

	1950	1960	1964
railroad	46.3	27.6	19.7
bus	37.7	25.5	24.3
inland waterway (incl. Gt. Lakes)	1.7	3.4	3.0
airway	14.3	43.5	53.0
total passenger miles (billions)	70.2	78.1	93.4

Table 68. *(continued)*

(c) intercity freight traffic (ton miles, Canada 1938–1961(in millions of ton miles and in %)

	1938	1941	1951	1956	1961
water	*20,688*	*19,688*	*24,625*	*33,594*	*39,169*
	(42.2%)	*(27.4%)*	*(24.5%)*	*(23.8%)*	*(25.8%)*
railroad	*26,835*	*49,982*	*64,300*	*78,820*	*65,828*
	(54.7%)	*(69.5%)*	*(63.8%)*	*(55.8%)*	*(43.3%)*
road	*1,515*	*2,237*	*8,238*	*10,614*	*16,099*
	(3.1%)	*(3.1%)*	*(8.2%)*	*(7.5%)*	*(10.5%)*
airway	*1*	*2*	*11*	*39*	*45*
oil pipeline	*–*	*–*	*3,551*	*18,141*	*21,483*
			(3.5%)	*(12.9%)*	*(14.2%)*
gas pipeline	*–*	*–*	*–*	*–*	*9,308*
					(6.1%)
total ton miles					
(millions)	*49,039*	*71,909*	*100,725*	*141,208*	*151,932*

Source: For (a) and (b), J.B. Lansing, *Transportation and Economic Policy* (New York: The Free Press, 1966), p. 371; for (c), Camu, Weeks, and Sanetz, *Economic Geography of Canada* (New York: St. Martin's Press, 1964), p. 257.

Relationship Between Elements

We have already seen some of the ways in which the different modes of transport overlap and compete. But they may also complement each other. Thus a ferry system cannot exist in isolation, but must be linked at each end to some other form of transportation. Moreover, each separate mode of transport is part of an overall transportation system, and the transportation system in any one area is a complex of interacting subsystems, each dominant, complementary, or in competition. Thus it can be shown, as in figure 192, that at certain distances from a market differing types of mode are dominant, and that transfer costs are adjusted to reflect this situation. Thus no mode can be considered in isolation: the flows, costs, and network structure of all other forms of transportation acting in unison could influence the flows of any one mode in particular. Similarly, individual determinants of economic behavior such as the policies of bodies like the Interstate Commerce Commission, or technological change, can be treated separately. But each is only a component in the overall transportation system.

We began with a holistic concept of transport as a system related functionally to the characteristics of the area in which it occurs. We then disaggregated the system into component elements consisting of stocks, networks, flows, and modes. But it does not follow from this that any one structural element is

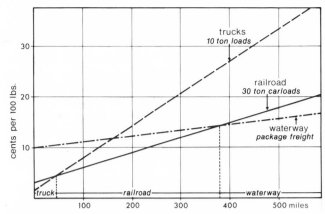

Fig. 192. *Mileage costs for three modes of transport for commodities or equivalent (data for lower Mississippi Valley, 1939–40). (Reprinted from E.M. Hoover,* The Location of Economic Activity. *Copyright © 1947, McGraw-Hill Inc. Used with permission of McGraw-Hill Book Company.)*

more important than any other. Thus the layout of a network depends on flows, intensity of use, the modes and stocks available, and area characteristics. Nor is this a static conceptualization; the element of change is introduced through man's changing technical development, and his ability to use what he perceives and develops. Nevertheless, our concept of a transportation system still lacks a sound theoretical base because we lack a generally applicable concept of movement, or *spatial interaction*. The following sections review some of the attempts that have been made to develop such a concept.

Toward a Theory of Movement

A number of geographers have raised quasi-philosophical questions about interaction. J. R. Whitaker (1932), P. R. Crowe (1938), R. S. Platt (1949), and E. L. Ullman (1956) have all made statements in which movement, or spatial interaction, is treated as the focal point of geography

Mechanical Postulates

Many of the attempts to construct a general theory of movement, or to erect a model to represent movement, are essentially mechanistic. Here, we shall review two of these attempts: Ullman's threefold typology of movement, and the so-called gravity model.

Ullman proposes that all interaction (i.e., movement between two points) has three bases: **complementarity, intervening opportunity,** and **transferability.** By complementarity he means that there is a demand in one area that is matched by a supply in other. If complementarity exists then interaction takes place—provided that there is no intervening opportunity, or intermediate source of supply. However, alternate goods will be sought if the distance between demand and supply is too costly to overcome; this is the principle of transferability. Up to a point, Ullman's model is a satisfactory and even useful tool. But it has certain inherent defects that make it less than the general conceptualization of movement it pretends to be. There are three points at which it is especially vulnerable to criticism:

1. *Ullman contends that movement is always to the nearest market, or human opportunity. This follows from the principle of intervening opportunity, according to which complementarity generates interchange between two areas only if no intervening source of supply is available.*

2. *He also contends that opportunities that occur elsewhere in a system than between an origin and a destination (or within a circle whose diameter stretches from the origin to the destination) can have absolutely no effect on spatial interaction between that origin and destinations within that circle.*

3. *The principle of complementarity implies that decision makers on both the supply and demand side are fully aware of each other; like von Thünen's farmers or Weber's industrialists, everyone in this model has complete information available to him and enjoys perfect rationality of action. As we know from our study of economic behavior, this is far from the truth.*

Ullman's model can be extended to an urban context, with suburban residences viewed as points of demand and the hierarchy of urban commercial centers as points of supply. Thus supply and demand, complementarity, intervening opportunity, and so on, are often translated into terms of urban land use. A. M. Voorhees postulates that all journeys made from the urban dweller's residence are attracted, or "pulled," to various land uses, in apparent accordance with certain empirical relationships that he calculated. He found that trips made from the home to work could be estimated by an "attractor," measured as the number of workers employed modified by a distance factor (the square root of the distance). Similarly, he measured social interaction by the number of residences and distance cubed; trips for convenience goods by the floor area in food and drugs at the "attractor" sites and distance cubed; and trips for shipping goods by floor area in apparel and distance squared.*

Just as Ullman's conceptualization is unsatisfactory as a working theory of transportation, so is the

---

*Figure 163 can be utilized in an urban framework too; instead of supply and demand, we could think in terms of the *desire* to make a trip and the fulfillment of that desire.

interactance hypothesis or gravity model. As we have seen, in this model spatial interaction of any kind between pairs of places or points is a positive function of their population, and inversely proportional to the intervening distance. One formulation of this (more elaborate than the one used earlier) is as follows:

$$I_{1-2} = G \frac{W_1(P_1)^\alpha - W_2(P_2)^\beta}{D_{1-2}^b}$$

where I_{1-2} = the movement or interactance between points 1 and 2, P_1 and P_2 = the respective populations, W_1 and W_2 = weights attached to the population component, G is an empirically derived constant, and α, β, and b are empirically derived exponents.

Other versions weight the weights; in place of population others have used number of automobiles, the population or floor space devoted to a particular activity, and the population characterized by sex, age, income, occupation, education. Distance has been measured by airline distance, actual distance, time distance, cost distance, road tolls, and number of traffic lights. One variant of the gravity model uses an index based on Ullman's notion of complementarity. However, no matter how much the gravity model is manipulated, it is inadequate as a general model of movement because: (a) it does not admit that places are influenced simultaneously by more than one other point in an interacting system; (b) it is essentially an empirical and nonbehavioral notion with little, if any, theoretical grounding. What has occurred is that researchers have taken an analogous situation from Newtonian physics, and then have tried to apply it, with varying degrees of success, to observed patterns. But although it happens to fit observed patterns—with some manipulation—it does not tell us why these patterns occur. Consequently, it can never account for deviations from the pattern. In fact it seems purely coincidental that this physical analogy fits some of the observed data; it is no more than a proxy for certain explanatory variables. The problem is to find out what the explanatory variables are.

Movement Space

Many transportation surveys take the same kind of mechanistic approach that we have just criticized. They rely on only a small number of variables such as car ownership, family size, or travel time and costs. But these macroscopic parameters all involve assumptions about human behavior. A great many other attributes, individual values and goals, seem to be important at the microlevel, varying with group and individual values and goals. What we really want to know in a study of spatial interaction is how

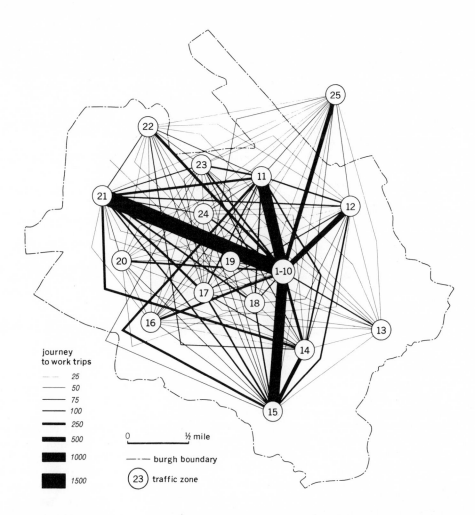

Fig. 193. *Urban travel movements. A desire line map of a journey to work pattern in the Scottish burgh of Perth. (From M. E. Eliot Hurst, "An Employee Work-Journey Survey,"* Traffic Engineering and Control, *vol. 10, no. 4, 1968, p. 166, reprinted by permission of the editor.)*

journey
to work trips

```
- - - - -  25
———————  50
———————  75
———————  100
━━━━━━  250
━━━━━━  500
━━━━━━  1000
━━━━━━  1500
```

0 _____ ½ mile

–·–·– burgh boundary

㉓ traffic zone

individuals themselves view the choice situations in which they make travel decisions (contrast the behavioral matrix of chapter 5). In short, the unique particulars of those situations seem to be at least as important as the more impersonal characteristics normally used in transportation analyses. Instead of the rational tripmaker who instantly perceives and adopts the "best" line of action in any situation, this approach substitutes an *intendedly* rational tripmaker whose rationality is bounded by his values, his experiences, his conceptions of space, and his varying ability to perceive opportunity or fulfillment.

The framework for this approach is based on a number of concepts from the social sciences, especially the concepts of *life space, activity space* and *migration space.* To Lewin all behavior is the result of the organization of the individual's perceptual field. According to the manner in which this field is organized, the individual will act. An individual's behavior therefore depends on his entire life space — that is, the individual *plus* his "psychological environment" — in which all parts are interdependent, so that a change in one part results in a change in another. It is now generally admitted that Lewin's

model does not offer a completely satisfactory explanation of how man conceives his environment; for instance, it needs to be supplemented by S-R theory (see chapter 4). In contrast, the framework adopted here — the inductive framework, as it will be called — requires understanding of the individual's apperception of his environment as related both to his personal goals and to the goals of his socioeconomic group. We have already seen how man's experience is affected by the filtering processes of perception and cognition, and how both in turn are affected by experience, feelings, values, and socioeconomic organization. Thus the apperceived environment is not a place that can be located in physical space, but rather only in the *psychic space* of the individual or group. Man operates within a reality that he does not wholly perceive; what he sees, reacts to, and reacts in is this *psychic space* created by his needs, desires, abilities, and awareness.

To supplement the conventional urban transportation measures of *age, income,* and *household size,* seven additional elements can be used (figure 193).

1. *The* trip itself, *the movement from one point to another*

for a particular purpose by an individual making a trip, by any mode or modes.

2. *The* goals *that influence the initiation of a trip. The objective of movement is to accomplish* goal events *at one or more intended destinations. The goal event is a*

3. *The* value system *of the individual or group affects many of the other elements in the situation.*

4. *The* positional utility, *or net gain derived by the tripmaker from his new intended spatial position. When an individual has a need or needs that cannot be fulfilled where he is, he must seek out a destination where he believes fulfillment is possible. The notion of utility is embedded in that of the "intendedly rational man" who differentiates courses of action in terms of relative utility, even though he has a finite ability to perceive and calculate. The tripmaker has a level of aspiration and expected attainment, adjusted by experience. Thus the positional utility at which he aims is a function of his previous experience, as well as his goals and value system. This positional utility may be either positive or negative, an indication of attraction (net gain) or repulsion (net loss). Thus the tripmaker will move to a destination whose characteristics, as he perceives them, promise a relatively higher utility than those of any other destinations known to him. Some of the processes involved here are very simple — the journey to work, for instance — but others, such as social visits or pleasure trips, are more complex.*

5. *The tripmaker's* style of life, *which has been defined as "a meaningful composite of values, activities, possessions, and motives. . . ."*

6. *Various* socioeconomic determinants *related to the life style, value system, and so forth. Thus M. M. Webber has stated that the propensity to perceive movement and movement opportunities results from a composite of socioeconomic and cultural factors that produces a conflict between the unbounded mobility patterns and the bounded value systems of particular types of socioeconomic organization.*

7. *The tripmaker's* level of satisfaction. *There will be degrees of satisfaction and dissatisfaction with the whole process. Wolpert notes that "the process itself is self adjusting because aspirations tend to adjust to the attainable. Satisfaction leads to slack which may induce a lower level of attainment. Dissatisfaction acts as a stimulus to search behavior."*

The perceived part of the environment within which movement occurs or is seen to occur is known as *movement space*. It is a specifically restricted space within which the tripmaker receives stimuli and makes his responses. It is therefore only a limited portion of the actual environment. Three types of movement space can be identified (figure 194). There is a *core*, which is the most frequently traveled space, and the one within which regular journeys are made; there is a *median area*, which is the occasionally traveled space, such as visits to relatives and vacations; and an *extensive area*, which is the world of

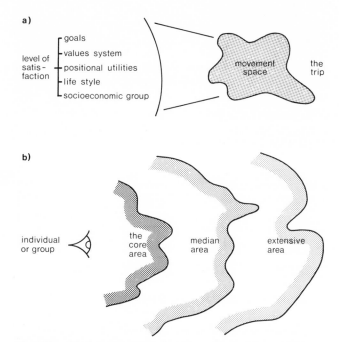

Fig. 194. *(a) The conception of a "movement" space and the determination of making a journey.*
(b) The varying intensities of information about "movement" space.

abstract concepts and of things known only in theory ("cosmological space"). The boundaries to these are shown in figure 194 in a deliberately uneven manner, since there is no way of carving space up into tidy portions. Thus movement space includes the range of choices defined by an individual's evaluatory abilities and presented to him through a combination of search, experience, ability, and communication.

The concept of *individual action space*, which is very close to that of movement space, has been developed by F. E. Horton and D. R. Reynolds. It has been shown that route choice varies with habit, experience, tension, and amenity. For example, it was found that tripmakers tend to choose a route not just as a least time or least cost path, but rather in terms of the "psychological hazard" presented. The head of household's core movement space was in many cases more limited than that of his wife, who had wide spatial limits. The higher up the socioeconomic scale, the broader these limits became, irrespective of whether the wife drove or not.

Conclusion

These criticisms of the gravity model and the Ullman typology, the two most frequently cited representations of interaction, point to the need for an alternative explanation. But at present there is none. Obviously, any adequate explanation should be able to encompass person-to-person or group-to-group variations in both the availability of information about alternative opportunities and the ability to use it. If any general theoretical framework is to be constructed, then we must take such behavioral factors into account. Among these factors we may list:

1. *Evidence from marketing studies that the capacity of consumers to reduce uncertainty varies from person to person according to income, social support received from others, and so forth.*
2. *The individual's subjective perception of the environment and its spatial arrangement.*
3. *The context of varying search abilities.*
4. *Field theory of search behavior.*
5. *Random and probability elements.*
6. *Interactance hypotheses of the Ullman variety.*
7. *Movement space.*

A combination of these and other elements might eventually lead to a reasonable representation of movement, for both human beings and commodities.

Transportation Systems

Lacking any sound theoretical framework in which to arrange the components of the transportation system, one can use only a simple scheme, like the one shown in figure 195. The first stage in the development of any transportation system is the need or desire for interaction to take place. Interaction arises because of the spatial separation of the means of satisfying those needs or desires. Interaction, movement, transportation, are not ends in themselves; they exist for the sake of some broader objective. The term "place utility" expresses this fact.

The basic components of a transportation system are modes, stocks, and networks. Movement is constrained by the channels of the network; the characteristics of particular modes; and the facilities of the fixed and mobile stocks. The mobile stocks, such as vehicles, provide the interface between the items being transported and the fixed stock of the network, such as the road or rail track. With some modes—pipelines, television and radio, the pedestrian—while there are no mobile stocks, there is still some interface between the "goods" and the fixed stocks. The networks consist of nodes and links; each node corresponds to the demand or supply (desire or fulfillment), each link to specific transportation channels. The links may be tangible and well defined, or relatively diffuse and intangible (see table 57). Some nodes may be interchange points

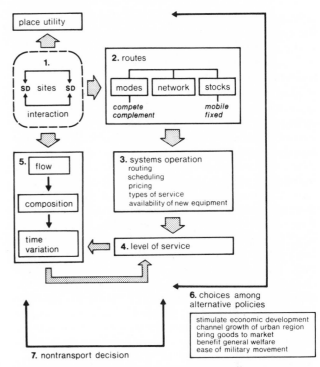

Fig. 195. *The transportation system: a tentative breakdown into the components of circulation.*

between links of the same mode (railyards, highway interchanges), while others may be interchange points between links of different modes (the seaport, ferry, rail or air terminal), where these modes are complementary. Often, however, modes may compete for traffic over similar link paths. Networks exist to channel movement, whether of objects, people, or ideas. Modes and stocks interact over space and time, competing with or mutually complementing each other, but in any case flowing through the channels in a variety of interacting paths. Changes in the movements of one set of factors will normally affect the movements of others.

The decision maker has open to him a wide choice of movement. In contrast, the ordinary individual, whether potential traveler, broadcaster, or shipper, tends to see the transportation system as essentially fixed, since he can only choose a routing and time schedule offered by the system. The operators and policy makers, however, can establish both routes and schedules, pricing and reliability, not to mention other factors that determine level of service. They also determine the types, numbers, and availability of stocks in the system; add new links and abandon old ones; improve operating characteristics by dredging rivers, widening highways, and so forth; and regulate competition, assigning operating rights and rates. Only in redistributive economies does one agency exercise this full set of systems functions. In other types of economic organization many different agencies may be involved. In any economy, however, the types of option will differ from time to time. A specific trip decision can be implemented rapidly, but changes in the entire network or transportation technology may take a considerable time.

The interaction system is a complex of demand factors, transportation facilities, operating characteristics, and level of service. Before movement occurs a decision maker considers the several characteristics that make up the level of service. This in turn is a function of the spatial characteristics of demand and supply, and the characteristics of modes, stocks, networks, and operating abilities. Thus a decision maker may consider not just cost and travel time, but safety, comfort, reliability, indirect costs (e.g., total transfer costs), and frequency of service. Level of service therefore includes such variables as total trip time, schedule times, direct transport charges, loading costs, warehousing costs, probability of accident, number of transfers, and—for passengers—physical comfort, privacy, general amenities, aesthetic experiences along the route, and so forth.

The level of service at which transportation is provided varies both spatially and over time. It responds to demand in a highly complex way because of the many interactions that take place among flows in the course of their movement through the network (e.g., the congestion that very rapidly develops on an urban freeway when an accident occurs at rush hour).

In response to demand, routes, systems operations, and level of service, a flow of persons, objects, and ideas moves through the system. This flow is a volumetric measure of the degree of interaction and the successful interrelationship of the other components. Flows vary in actual composition, as well as over time and space; thus the flow of traffic through a city on a Sunday differs from the flow on any week day. There is a feedback effect to level of service, operating characteristics, routes, and—ultimately—demand itself.

Transportation decisions are not made in isolation. On the contrary they are influenced by a wide variety of factors, both direct and indirect. The direct factors include general investment decisions to achieve the overall socioeconomic development of an area or region. In urban areas, planned changes in the basic structure of the transportation network, such as the San Francisco Bay Area rapid transit scheme, have feedback effects throughout a region. Such general investment decisions are almost bound to affect not only supply and demand but the general welfare of the people in a region. There may also be military decisions based on strategic mobility (e.g., the Interstate and Defense Highway System in the United States). Other such developments include the introduction of basically new transportation technologies. All of these options can affect the workings of the factors previously described.

Besides direct influences, there are a number of other external factors that must be considered. Nontransportation decisions can affect demand for and use of transportation systems. National economic policies can affect the distribution of demand over space and time, and hence the demand for freight services. Other influences are land use controls, the provision of public utilities, industrial logistic systems, differential regional growth policies, and the impact on those who do not use the system.

The threads drawn together here underlie the great variety of interactions present in the socioeconomic landscape. The scheme is not an exhaustive one, but the principles implicit in it are equally applicable to communications in general, urban transportation, intercity movements, regional and national interactions, and world trade flows. At the same time it brings together the transportation system's disaggregated components—modes, networks, stocks, flows, the reasons for interaction—and shows how they interact and operate within a systems framework.

Transportation Analyses

The six-question approach and the Northwestern University approach both deal with vertical cross sections of the transportation subsystem. Table 69, however, suggests that it is also possible to view the subsystem horizontally, by looking at specific amalgams of transportation routes, stocks, modes, networks, and flows. Of these horizontal sections, some represent particular settings, such as the city, or recreational areas, while others represent particular situations, such as the impact of new transportation structures. One section represents a particular situational context—human communication.

It is not possible here to examine all these horizontal cross sections in detail. Accordingly, just two are examined below; developing areas and human communication. The other sections noted in table 69 are just as crucial to the transportation subsystem. Some however, such as the impact of new freeways on the tertiary structure, or that of recreational travel on the general economic landscape, have been partly covered in chapter 11.

Urban transportation, another cross section, is a vast topic with a substantial literature of its own. Suffice it to say here that two distinctive patterns exist today in urban transport: pre-and postmotorized. The time and space flexibility of the truck and automobile, coinciding with a period of urban population growth, smaller family size, change in life style, and greater spatial mobility, have led to an extensive utilization of urban space. The premotorized city, on the other hand, was characterized by patterns of more intensive land use. Urban interaction in both types of city is a function of land use patterns (figures 162 and 163), and differences in the distribu-

Table 69. *Transportation Analyses*

	inventory	network	flow	mode	relationship
human communication	words, sounds, symbols, smells, taste	fields of personal, public and visual contacts; distribution channels, radio-T.V. networks	flows of ideas, facts	face-to-face, telephone, radio, television, printed word	social communication
urban transport	cars, trucks, buses, trains; miles of street, freeway, subway	streets, sidewalks, tracks, freeways	flows of ideas, money, goods, people	pedestrian, automobile, truck, bus, rapid transit	balanced urban transportation system
developing areas	cars, trucks, freight cars, etc. miles of road, track, etc.	road, rail, water air networks	flows of goods, equipment, machinery, people, ideas	railroad, truck, automobile, water trans., airplane, hovercraft	transport as a neutral factor; concomitant with growth; sometimes a catalyst
highway impact	new and projected highway miles; expected traffic units	new freeway, roadway network	volume of diverted, generated, non-diverted traffic	automobile, truck, bus	impact on region—growth and change of tertiary activities, and other economic activities
recreation	cars, buses, planes, ski lifts, etc.; highway, airline miles	road, rail, air networks	flows of people, money	automobile, bus, plane, skidoo, etc.	increased leisure time; regional impact; growth of tertiary activities

tion and dispersion of urban land usages lead to a spatial imbalance of supply and demand. In the postmotorized city increasing use of the car and the resulting spatial dispersion of land uses has almost inevitably led to a decline in the use of public transport. Nevertheless, as long as the downtown core dominates urban travel patterns, public transit remains the most efficient and least costly means of reaching it. Contributing to the decline in public transit facilities have been the flexibility and convenience of the automobile, public ignorance of actual car commuting costs, lack of investment in efficient transit systems, and a powerful "freeway lobby." These and other factors have given rise to the myth that public transit systems are necessarily slow, run-down, and inefficient. Despite this myth, public transport is making a comeback, though so far more as an idea than an actuality. The subject is a fascinating one for economic, cultural, and urban geography; some readings in it are suggested at the end of this chapter.

Transport and Development

H. Hunter has posed the question: Is ample transport capacity a prerequisite for economic development? As he points out, the conventional Western attitude tends to view transport as playing such a role, although the attitude of redistributive economies has tended to make transport a secondary sector of the economy. One of the factors which Hunter stresses in the course of his examination of Soviet and Chinese transportation development is that transport improves in any economy as a concomitant of economic development, not a precondition for it. He draws on evidence from outside those two countries, such as the role of railroad development in the nineteenth-century United States, to show that "massive expansion of transport capacity is not a prior condition for economic progress."

We know that the functioning of an economy requires the use of transport, and that, as economies develop, specialized production increases and relatively more transport is required. It might be possible, therefore, to analyze economies with varying structures and levels of development, see how transport is used, and discover how the variations in its use relate to other determinants of spatial variations. This would be a complex undertaking because of the many ways in which transport is used in an economy. One could list all the outputs of an economy—beef, steel, aluminum, automobiles, and so on—and calculate for each the amount of transport required for each unit of output. Thus a summary of transportation intensity in a country would consist of a list of numbers showing the input of transport per unit of output for every economic activity.

However, the role of transport is not completely unambiguous. Rather than being autonomous, it is always a part of something else. Without the resources that are going to be utilized, access has no meaning. Investment in transport may be contingent upon the fact that it is already being provided but, as Heymann points out, there is no assurance that this fact will necessarily call forth investment. It thus becomes essential to consider transport within a matrix of potential demand. Otherwise, it may become an underutilized facility within its region. Frequently one reads such remarks as: "Lack of adequate transport can be one of the greatest obstacles to economic progress . . . the difficulty comes when the choice has to be made between the various types of transport. . . ." What is rarely mentioned is the choice within the socio-economic context, which may dictate not so much *which* mode of transport is used but how much (or little) investment in transport is needed at all.

Of itself, then transport is a neutral factor; it needs to be related to what it is going to be used for, and to who is going to use it, before any development and investment can take place.

A Possibility Matrix

There are two ways to examine transport's role in development: to erect a theoretical framework or model, and to examine an empirical case study.

The first method, utilized by Storey in 1970, is to erect a matrix (table 70). Essentially, Storey has isolated one factor from a complex system of inter-dependency (the economic system), and has constructed a static, two-dimensional model. The components of his model relate to *causal* and *time* precedence. By causal he means direct stimulation of certain economic activities by the provision of transportation facilities. Three causal possibilities seem to arise:

1. *A positive effect (+), whereby new productive activities are the direct result of providing transportation facilities.*
2. *A neutral effect (0), whereby transport does not affect the growth of economic activity either way.*
3. *A negative effect (−), which we can say intuitively does not usually occur in reality, whereby transportation developments reduce the level of economic growth.**

The temporal component of the model relates to the period of development:

1. *The provision of transportation facilities* predates *economic growth in temporal terms. (PRE).*
2. *Provision of transportation is* concomitant *with economic growth (CON).*
3. *The provision of transportation* postdates *economic growth (POST).*

*Thus a newly developing country's overambitious and prestigious efforts to create a national airline may well divert investment from areas where it could have led to economic growth.

Table 70. *A Possibility Matrix*

		causal factors		
		positive	neutral	negative
		+	0	−
	pre condition	x		
temporal factors	con comitant		y	
	post dates			

Source: K.J. Storey, "The Role of Transport in Economic Development," M.A. thesis, Simon Fraser University, 1970.

These components are set out in table 70. The letter X in the matrix indicates a common view of transport as a precondition or prerequisite of development, implying both causal and temporal precedence. However, as the case study set out below indicates, place Y in the matrix is a more reasonable representation of reality. This is because transport plays a neutral role, developing concomitantly with the expansion of productive activity and economic growth.

Transport's Role in Part of the Canadian North

The part of the Canadian North to be examined here consists of the Yukon and the Northwest Territories. Within these two areas the basic networks have in fact already been formed. We are really concerned with two separate systems, which historically have had few links between them, and which have evolved from different bases, even though in fact both areas were originally penetrated by Europeans as part of the fur trading system (figure 196).

The Transportation Networks. To some extent, especially in the Northwest Territories, the fur trading period was the basis for some of the existing routeways. On the other hand, of particular importance to the Yukon were the gold discoveries of the late nineteenth century, culminating in the Klondike strikes of 1896. The gold rush was on such a scale as to bring substantial investment, which included development of a narrow gauge railroad from Skagway, in Alaska, to Whitehorse. The latter was a break-of-navigation point on the Yukon River system, and led north to Dawson. Since the river was seasonal, the river route was paralleled by an overland trail from quite an early period. This overland trail, with subsequent realignment, became the backbone of the area's road system.

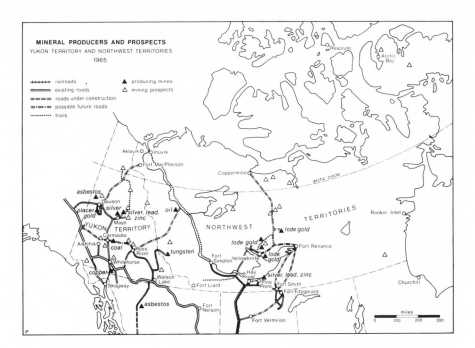

Fig. 196. *Mineral resources and transportation links, Yukon and Northwest Territories, Canada. (From M.E. Eliot Hurst and A.L.P. Horsman, "The Role of Transport in the Developing Canadian North," B.C. Occasional Papers, no. 8, 1967, p. 32, reprinted by courtesy of Tantalus Research Ltd.)*

The realignment in question was predominantly a response associated with the development of lead and silver resources at Mayo, on the Stewart River. The Alaska Highway was constructed in 1942–43, partly traversing areas not previously tapped with its ancillary limbs. It proved to be of greater importance to northern British Columbia than to the Yukon. The potential of this route as an alternative to the rail link has been implicit ever since, although until now it has not been used often enough as a freight route for a comparative cost relationship to become clear. Thus at the end of World War II, two major access corridors existed in the Yukon: the rail and road route, and the Alaska Highway. Air services, developed in the 1930s, had competed with the road route north of Carmacks (just south of Fort Selkirk). Since most of the movement had been in the form of passenger traffic, this northerly extension of the route had deteriorated considerably.

By the 1950s, renewed interest in the base metal resource at Mayo, which was unable to rely on the relatively high cost and seasonal waterway, led to an upgrading of the land route north of Carmacks. Since then other extensions have taken place. These have basically been of two forms: all-year gravel roads of a quality equivalent to the main roads, such as the Dawson branch from the Whitehorse-Mayo road; and winter roads built for temporary access, predominantly in response to oil exploration, as in the Bell River and Peel Plateau areas. The Canal Road, which had been allowed to fall out of use in 1945, was reopened as far as Ross River in the 1950s. Although maintained as a year-round road, it is of lower quality than many others in the Territory. Cur-

rent road building in the Yukon is essentially linking the termini of this basic system.

It will be seen, then, that the Yukon has really had a very stable network morphology. The pattern of the late 1880s is still discernible, although it has been translated into overland freight movements. Since the actual scale of settlement has been too small to call into being its own system, the one that has been developed is almost solely a response to the exploitation of known resources.

In contrast, the fur trading economy of the Northwest Territories, with its larger Indian population, its associated Indian trading posts, collecting points, and so on, has played a greater role in establishing the general outline of the settlement pattern. Mining did not play any major role here until the years following World War I, when the general pattern of settlement and routeways had already been established. The Mackenzie waterway system played a more substantial role in the transportation network, since the pressures of a nonmining economy could be fed more easily into a seasonal flow pattern. Overland routes were few and primarily designed to augment the water system. Not until World War II did the movement of goods by truck threaten the dominance of the river routes.

In the Northwest Territories, the winter roads have played a much larger role than in the Yukon. A winter road system, with roads of varying quality according to the extent of clearing and packing, is much more favored by terrain and water surfaces in the Northwest Territories. Winter road construction has become highly efficient, and the more advanced techniques have cut yearly costs down to about $100 a mile, one-tenth of the Yukon costs. However, there are only about 500 miles of permanent and semipermanent roads in the Northwest Territories, compared to about 2,000 miles in the Yukon. Permanent road construction costs do not vary so much between the territories; the range is from $30,000 to $60,000 per mile. The mining industry, interested in low inventory costs and a fairly regularized supply system, has increasingly turned to these alternatives. As the emphasis on precious metals has declined, there has arisen a corresponding demand for a transportation system capable of handling high freight tonnage. In the Yukon this sector of the mining industry could function within the system already provided. But in the Northwest Territories the larger-scale development of Pine Point made a prerequisite of the rail system. Despite these developments, however, and despite a decrease in importance in relative terms, river traffic remains an important primary supplier for settlements in the Northwest Territories.

Transport and Development. Three broad categories of reasons can be found for investment and development in these northern areas:

1. *The first arises from the presumed existence of resources —the identification of the North as a "storehouse of minerals." Implicit in this identification is the assumption that the North is only waiting for a better developed transportation network.*
2. *There is a feeling that Canadians have an obligation to use resources, both from national self-interest, and as a kind of challenge, made stronger by indirect "moral" pressures. These two points were translated into a Canadian government report,* Vision of the North, *which included a "Road to Resources" program.*
3. *Less emphasized, but often mentioned, is Canadian responsibility for the native population. For example, the Minister of Northern Affairs for Canada said in 1966 that the solution of transportation problems and the education of the Indian and Eskimo populations were the keys to the North's future development.*

Transportation, then, plays a major role in these three viewpoints, the implicit assumption being that access is the prerequisite to development, which is itself inevitable. But the assumption stops there; it does not go on to inquire into the relative costs of the resources that would be made available.

Economic stimulation and development, whether governmental or private, can take two forms: either transportation is oriented to a resource in order to service it; or development can be promoted in order to provide access to potential resource areas. The recent road expansion program of the Canadian federal government appears to have been shaped by some concept of accessibility. In announcing the program, the government noted that its completion would bring all potential areas of resource development within 200 miles of a road.

To date developments within the Yukon and Northwest Territories have consisted of finding and exporting natural resources, on the one hand, and generally increasing accessibility, on the other. In this connection we can recognize two levels of transportation: the servicing of communities, especially mining communities; and the transportation of equipment, personnel, output, and so forth, associated with resource utilization. The second level involves two different concepts. In the first, a resource is not of itself large enough to warrant its own transportation system, and is made viable by the development of a *corridor of access*—in this case, the Alaska Highway. At the other end of the scale are large developments like Ross River or Pine Point, where transportation is an integral part of the investment decision. Here, the scale is sufficient to warrant an entirely new system. In reality, of course, these two concepts tend to be combined, as where a route developed for a major resource site opens up a corridor for small-scale development. Conversely, small-scale operations that by themselves justify only low grade access may nonetheless open an area to more intensive exploration.

The developments associated with the present network have been at precisely three levels of interest. Relatively few brand-new discoveries of minerals have been made, and a great deal of recent development has been the result of a reevaluation of resources, the actual presence of which has been known in some cases for several decades. This is precisely the advantage we do *not* have in projecting routes beyond the existing network. To build extensions almost at random, at a cost for a permanent road of between $30,000 and $60,000 a mile, is rather difficult to justify. For instance, what justification is there for a link between Dawson and Fort McPherson, when hardly anyone can be expected to travel between these two points? It would make more sense, both socially and financially, to improve the short links between existing population concentrations in the District of Mackenzie. Since this evaluation in the mid-1960s, the concern for environmental protection and for the oil fields on the Alaskan North Slope and the Canadian Arctic has caused some reassessment. Confronted by a choice between a tanker route in the Pacific Coast or an overland pipeline in Canadian territory, the Canadian federal government announced plans to provide a road through the Mackenzie area to Inuvik. Such reevaluations, however, have not changed the basic challenge: namely, that many links are unnecessary and harmful to the environment.

Modal Systems. It is interesting to note here the role of particular modes, insofar as they reflect the Canadian government's general concern with economic growth.

As we have seen, *railroads* need a certain threshold tonnage before construction and operation can be justified. Perhaps a production of about one-fourth million tons a year would be sufficient to justify development. However, when anticipated tonnage is close to the threshold, it becomes economically possible under some conditions to use roads.

Transport by *road* is becoming more efficient as a result both of technological improvements and of administrative reforms within the operating companies. Noncommercial operations within the Yukon have reported ton-mile costs as low as 4.06 cents on a one-way haul. Future developments may see a further decline in costs, particularly if in the North use could be made of a virtually closed system, similar to forest roads.

Similarly, *air* transportation has improved its efficiency, and costs are quite often lower than one associates with air freight. A turboprop plane with a 15-ton payload and a 75 percent load factor has been costed as low as 8 cents per ton mile; a helicopter was reported at about double that under similar conditions. Air freight may well play a greater role in the future, particularly if future mining developments take the form of relatively temporary camps rather than permanent settlements. As technological change reduces the work force for any given output tonnage, even a relatively high price for air transport may become acceptable. Commonly, where surface communications are primitive, it actually costs less to establish an air transportation system than to develop other kinds of transportation.

In the case of *waterways,* the prevailing impression of cheapness has to be modified in the North by considerations of the seasonality of navigation (15–20 weeks open), limits on size, and so on. As a result, only occasionally do costs fall below those of trucks. The Mackenzie waterway system has costs only slightly lower than those of the Alaska Highway. The main importance of waterways may in the future be as routes for winter roads or tracks for hovercraft, though costs for the latter have so far been high. However, the potential development of the hovercraft has by no means been exhausted, and it is quite possible that it could change the whole transportation pattern in the North.

Conclusion. Only by avoiding the assumption that transport has a life of its own, by acknowledging the necessity for the presence of other passive resources, and by noting that the presence of such facilities is part of the growth process that needs to be explained (rather than an explanation in itself),

can a satisfactory investment pattern be devised for such areas as the Canadian North. It is clear that the Canadian government, the oil companies, and the mining companies, well informed or not, have committed themselves to certain developments over the next decade. However, these investments and commitments have not been made with clear objectives in view. Empirical evidence from North America, Western Europe, Russia, and China confirms that transportation infrastructure did in fact develop concomitantly with, rather than prior to, economic growth. Admittedly, some limited development of facilities ahead of demand could be useful, and anticipation of future facilities may be of some significance. However, since neither *ensures* subsequent development, investment procedures along these lines may lead to a less efficient allocation of resources than investment that occurs concomitantly with development.

Both Storey's matrix and this empirical study underline the fact that transport may be a catalyst. In other words, the provision of transport facilities may activate development, *assuming all other requisites for growth are present.* In the case of the Canadian North, this is not true. Potential resources remain potential without some means of access to them, but access itself has no meaning unless those potential resources are available. It is difficult, as noted above, to abstract one element from the economic system. But if areas like the Canadian North are to develop to benefit the whole nation state, then recognition must be given to the neutrality, concomitancy, and *occasional* catalytic role of transport.

Communications and Circulation

It is now time to elaborate on the sketch of communication and circulation given in previous chapters. Both concepts refer to the movement of ideas and knowledge in human society. But they do so in different ways. Let us deal with communication first.

Communication

It is possible to define communication as a cooperative attempt on the part of a **sender** and a **receiver** to exchange ideas, impressions, and experiences—a cooperative attempt, because unless the receiver is aware of the **message,** no communication can have taken place. There must also be some **channel** or route for the message. As far as economic geography is concerned the receiver must then take

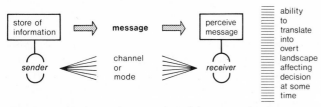

Fig. 197. *A simplistic representation of the communications process from sender to receiver and the landscape.*

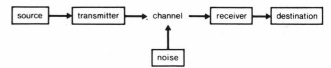

Fig. 198. *Shannon's minimal communication system.*

a course of action that affects landscape patterns in some way (figure 197).

The sender initiates the flow or transmission of information. Quite frequently transmission has become institutionalized and is undertaken by writers, musicians, announcers, salesmen, and other professional communicators. A sender ceases to be such when he stops and listens or observes, when he becomes a receiver. A sender can shift channels (modes) and still remain in the same role, for example by switching from the written word to the spoken word. Expert senders can use several modes in rapid alternation, and thus help a complex message to get across.

The message itself can be chosen from a large storehouse of information available to the sender. In order to be communicable the ideas or information must be translated into symbols that are intelligible to the receiver. The channels or modes of communication include writing, the printed word, the spoken word (whether face to face or via an electronic medium), visual images, and, in certain situations, touch, odor, and taste.

The receiver has the opportunity of completing the communication process by being aware of the message. He may select channels, messages, and senders, according to his perception. His degree of awareness will vary according to his personality, perceptual abilities, and socioeconomic status. Highly perceptive and gregarious individuals will tend to come into contact with more "bits" of information than will individuals of a different temperament. These factors will also affect the *quality* of information in a person's possession; studies have shown that the higher the socioeconomic status of the receiver, the more selective he is in his choice of senders. So how a person perceives either messages or senders depends on his past experience and his learning abilities. These factors predispose his attitude toward messages, determining the level or content of information that he deems relevant. Past experience can be decisive in determining whether a piece of information is found useful or discarded. Thus the flow of messages is constrained not just by the physical channels of message dissemination, but by the sender's receptiveness.

Once the message has been received, we as geog-

raphers are interested in whether the perceived information is used to help arrive at a decision. Whether a decision is reached or not can affect the economic landscape. Of importance here, are such factors as aspiration levels, goal seeking, group norms, and social support.

A Model of the Communication Process

C. E. Osgood and T. A. Sebeok have described the erection of a model of the communication process. They begin with a minimal system (figure 198), which has been applied to such widely different information processes as electricity transmission, biological and psychological systems, and telephone networks. In a telephone network the message produced by a speaker is in the form of variable sound pressures and frequencies that have to be transformed into electrical signals by a transmitter, which in turn are carried through a wire (the channel) to a receiver, which then transforms the signals back into the variable sound pressures and frequencies, so that it can be comprehended by the listener. The transmitter is said to **encode** the message, the receiver to **decode** it. An additional concept of **noise** is introduced to take account of unpredictable variations that can distort the message after it has left the source.

This basic scheme has to be modified to fit the human communication system, in which transmitter and receiver are not separate (figure 16). Each human communication unit is "equipped to both receive and send messages . . . and . . . is regularly a decoder of the messages he himself encodes through various feedback mechanisms." In decoding, some form of physical energy (sound, light, etc.) is first recoded into sensory nerval impulses via the receiving apparatus and interpreted by what we earlier called the black box. In encoding, some motive centered in the black box is passed via the transmitting apparatus in the motor areas and recoded into the physical movements that are the output of the communications unit. Thus the input is the *stimulus*, the receiver is *perception*, destination and source become the *cognitive processes* of the black box, the transmitter is the *motor skill* and organization, and the output becomes the *response* (for these terms, see chapter 4).

The third stage in building up a satisfactory model

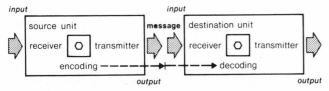

O mediator *destination/black box/source*

Fig. 199. *The essential communication act. (Cf. fig. 16.) (Modified from C.E. Osgood and T.A. Sebeok, eds., "Psycholinguistics: A Survey of Theory and Research Problems,"* Journal of Abnormal and Social Psychology, *vol. 49, supplement, 1954, p. 3. Copyright © by the American Psychological Association and reproduced by permission.)*

of communication must entail putting the communication unit into a social setting. In other words, there must be a source unit (speaker or sender) and a destination unit (listener or receiver). Between the two flows a message. In the words of Osgood and Sebeok:

We will define message as that part of the total output (responses) of a source unit which simultaneously may be a part of the total input (stimuli) to a destination unit. When individual A talks to individual B, for example, his postures, gestures, facial expressions and even manipulations with objects (e.g., laying down a playing card, pushing a bowl of food within reach) may all be part of the message. . . .

As noted earlier, messages may be *immediate* (face to face) or *mediate* (written, recorded, expressed as art). Figure 199 thus represents the human communication process, with the encoding of a message by a *source unit*, and a decoding of that message by a *destination unit*.

An Operational System

We can think of the individual as having to hand informational resources consisting of: *private information*, received by person-to-person and face-to-face contact, or by telephone calls, and written exchanges; *public information*, received from printed and electronic media; and *visual information*, the perceived and experienced information in the surrounding landscape.

Private Information. The quantity and quality of private information is affected by an individual's site and situation. Person-to-person contacts are inclined to be most numerous at very short distances; they decline very rapidly with distance. There is considerable evidence, empirical and theoretical, concerning this distance-decay of human interaction. Theoretically, it should decline in a circular pattern — that is, if the decay in information is equal in all directions. J. L. Moreno, in 1934, thought of this in social-psychological terms: the individual was a "social atom" situated in a "field." Here, we prefer

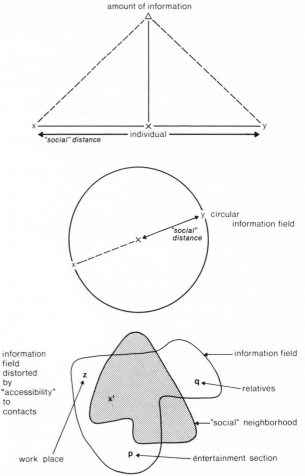

Fig. 200. *The "private" information field.*

the idea of a circular *private information field* (figure 200), with single individuals as the central points. This field (or as we can now think of it, an individual's total array of personal contacts) does not have a circular form in the real world. One reason is that the shape of the field varies with the distribution of the population around the person who is the center of the field. Thus the shape would be different in an urban area, where there are complex and overlapping information fields. Another reason is that variation will occur according to the specific individual's personality, perceptive abilities, socioeconomic status, and **movement space.** Thus highly perceptive individuals will gain relatively large quantities of private information, in contrast to less perceptive individuals who will have relatively small quantities. Irregularities of distance and direction will also arise through differences of sex, age, income, education, occupation, marital status, political affiliation, and religion. Not only the amount and spatial spread of information is affected in this way, but also its quality. Studies like that of H. F. Lionberger (1960) have shown that the higher the socioeconomic status of an information seeker, the more selective he is in the choice of others as sources of information. Thus we could consider that "potential information" is available in a more or less uniform way, given a uniformly distributed and informed population, and that variation occurs in reality because the *achieved* information level varies from person to person.

Public Information. The quantity and quality of public information available to an individual is influenced again by his geographic situation. Major spatial biases exist in the circulation of such information. Evidence has shown that public information percolates downward through the urban hierarchy of a country or region. Thus T. Hagerstrand (1952) has noted the tendency for a funneling of information through cities; he found that many innovations entered Sweden through Skane, the southernmost province, only to jump to Stockholm and then to spread down to progressively lower order centers. J. Wolpert, again from work in Sweden, also noted that agricultural information diffused by steps, from a core zone of "experts" in the Stockholm-Uppsala area to the central offices of agricultural organizations, and "then to the local county offices which are situated typically in the county's leading city." Thus people are in positions of varying access to public information according to the hierarchical position of the city in which they live, or (if in a rural situation) according to the order of the city to which they live near. This is probably explicable in terms of the siting of mass communications media and central offices: the higher the order of the city as a central place, the greater the depth and variety of public information sources upon which its residents can rely.

Personal factors are again important, in two principal ways:

1. *Educational and personality factors govern an individual's direct exposure to printed matter and other media.*
2. *All the differentials of age, sex, and other factors mentioned earlier as influencing the private information field will also come into play, insofar as public information is diffused by the overlapping and interactance of those fields.*

The concept of a "two-step" flow of communication can be applied to this process. According to E. Katz and P. F. Lazarsfeld" ideas often seem to flow *from* radio and print *to* opinion leaders, and *from them* to the less active sections of the population." Thus particular better informed individuals, termed *influentials* or *opinion leaders*, either perform a relay function (relaying public information to the previously unexposed), or a reinforcement function (explaining or clarifying the meaning or effectiveness of some particular piece of information), or both. It seems that the so-called influential engages in more face-to-face communications than the other group members or, alternatively, that he has a denser private information field, which leads to greater accessibility to information and greater accessibility to other group members. However, the influential is working not apart but very much within the confines of his group. Should he come across information that does not accord with his group's norms and values, then he will tend not to transmit it.

Visual Information. The visual impressions accumulated by an individual are primarily related to the space immediately around him, and to his normal channels of movement. Visually acquired information varies from place to place, and assumes particular importance when it is combined with either private or public information, or both. The visual information field of an individual, like his private information field, falls off in intensity quite rapidly with increasing distance, making him highly dependent on the objects visible either in his immediate vicinity or along well traveled routes. Again, personality factors will influence the visual part of an individual's total quantity and quality of information. An individual can in fact attend to only a small part of the information recorded in his memory and presented by his environment (see chapter 4).

Information and the Individual

As we have seen, the way an individual perceives the contents of public, private, or visual information fields depends on past experience and learning abilities. Suffice it to say here that these perceptual and learning processes predispose a person's attitude toward information, determining the level or content of information that he finds relevant. Where information falls outside that latitude, it is rejected or suppressed; where it falls within, it is incorporated, in modified form, into the personal information field. Past experience, by giving the individual an optimistic or pessimistic outlook, can also be decisive in determining whether information is used or discarded. Thus variations in perception, experience, and learning can distort the eventual landscape patterns formed from decision making processes. Other factors of this order are also important: the rate of receipt of information, the timing of receipt, the order in which it is received, and the size of the information bundle. Still further considerations include how the individual looks at an information source, public or private, and whether he feels it is objective or biased. This, too, obviously involves past experience.

Information and the Firm

The receipt and flow of information is important not only to the economic behavior of an individual, but to the economic behavior of a multiperson firm. Here information availability and use can be summarized in terms of the firm's own properties. For example, if a firm happens to be dissatisfied with its present location, wide differences probably exist in the quantity and quality of information to hand at the time of a decision to move or to stay put, because: (a) information is not given, but sought only when a time of dissatisfaction arises or awareness of a problem materializes; (b) firms, like individuals, differ in their ability to assemble, store, recall, and perceive information.

If a firm is viewed as a coalition of individuals, then its exposure to information, for example concerning a specific locational problem, will depend on the overlap and interaction of the public, private, or visual information acquired by the members of the firm who are to make the decisions. The composition of the total private information sources will be related to the distance-decay of contacts around the center of each member's information field, and to the distortions created in those individuals' fields by personal attributes. The common center of this mosaic of information fields will be the place of work. Once more the quantitative and qualitative exposure to information will be associated with the hierarchical position of the city in which the firm or its members are situated. Because of the circulation of public information through private information fields—the two-step flow of communication—the firm's public information possibilities will also frequently depend on the groups that its information gatherers belong to, as well as on their educational background, age, and so forth. In this respect, face-to-face contacts are important for the firm. We know also from research in cultural geography that information is diffused mostly by these contacts between individuals. As before, if visual information exists, exposure will be highly dependent on the firm's location, and will tend to fall off with distance because of the qualities of each individual's visual information field.

How the firm perceives and recalls the information it accumulates will usually depend on: its past experience as a business organization; the past experience of its individual decision makers; the order in which the information is received; the timing of acquisition and the size of different information bundles; and personal attitudes toward sources of information, both public and private. Past experience is important because it is through such experience that the firm learns to pay attention to certain portions of the total information available.

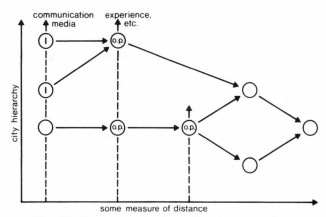

Fig. 201. *Communication of information through a settled landscape.*

The information that the firm actually processes, recalls, and utilizes may also reflect the goals and orientations it has adopted, and the hopes and expectations it holds as a result of previous experience. A firm's size and internal organization may also have some effect, since larger size or better organization may increase the distance from which potential information can be sought or perceived. Once more it is difficult to separate the perception of information and the firm's apparent ability to utilize that information.

Implications

Figure 201 tries to portray some of the sequences of the circulation of information for individuals or firms. Obviously this is an oversimplified picture that does not include all the screens through which information must pass. However, the relevancy of even this brief discussion to locational and economic behavior should be obvious. Finally, it should be noted that we are dealing with a dynamic not a static communications area. It has been suggested by Marshall McLuhan (1964) that changes in media of communication, particularly the shift toward electronic media (table 71), affects the whole socio-economic system and hence the economic landscape —for instance, through the growth of giant industrial corporations. However, other observers find McLuhan's premises empirically questionable. While it is possible to accept McLuhan's argument that the increasing use of an urban based electronic communications system rather than the printed word is *one* causal factor of change in the modern landscape, change does not seem to be occurring in the direction of McLuhan's **global village.** Rather, changes in mass communication are seen as breaking down the socio-economic landscape into groups that can best be described as diverse and tribal in character. But

Table 71. *The McLuhan Schema*

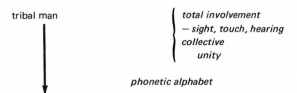

tribal man

total involvement
— *sight, touch, hearing*
collective
                    unity

phonetic alphabet

disintegration of tribal involvement, loss of audio-tactile abilities - - - -
becomes visual

invention of printing press

hot
medium

exclusively visual logic of
print; individualism

electronic revolution

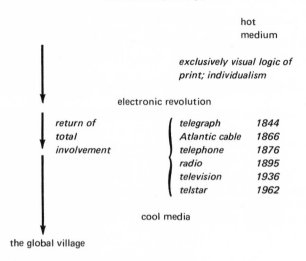

return of	telegraph	*1844*
total	Atlantic cable	*1866*
involvement	telephone	*1876*
	radio	*1895*
	television	*1936*
	telstar	*1962*

cool media

the global village

recreation of tribal society on a global scale

whether the change is toward uniformity or diversity, the communications process undoubtedly plays a fundamental role in shaping the landscape.

Conclusion

A number of the areas examined in this and the previous chapter illustrate that we have a long way to go before we can set up a fullfledged theory of transportation. Many empirical studies have been cited, and a number of models or frames of reference have been used. The gravity model, Ullman's typology, Pred's behavioral matrix, the concept of movement space, and the systems analyst's viewpoint are all attempts at providing a general theory. But so far they have not added up to anything usable. Sufficient evidence has come to hand, however, that we do have reason to reorientate our study of routes that link sites. Rather than just describing those links, economic geographers must now analyze the decisions and causes that lead to their establishment and maintenance.

Summary

1. The first component of the transportation subsystem to be examined is the inventory — the vehicles, containers, and channels. The mobile *facilities (buses, cars, trucks) are the containers which provide the interface between the items being transported and the* fixed *facilities of the system like roads and tracks. There is some relationship between the transport inventory on the one hand and the technical, economic, and cultural "environment" on the other.*

2. Networks consist of origin and destination nodes and the interconnecting links. The links may be tangible, intangible, imaginary, and objective. The paths of vehicles, people, or units of information through a network are through a succession of links and nodes. As a common means of measurement and analysis of many different kinds of network, certain graph theoretic measures can be used.

3. Although some of these measures may seem unfamiliar, they do permit us, at one level of analysis, to understand more clearly the relationships of nodes and links to the characteristics of the region in which they are located.

4. Another level of description is the pattern of flows of persons, ideas, or goods through the subsystem. Flows are the volumetric measure of the amount of interaction and hence are the very activity of transportation. These flows are constrained by the channels of the network, but for many analyses we can ignore the description of the physical facilities and simply show the patterns of flow, as, for example, in the movement of goods across India, and the flows of aluminum bars in the United States.

5. Each mode of transport — railroad, road, air, inland waterway, marine transport, and pipeline — has its own distinctive technological characteristics and its own spatial relationships, which affect its role in the space economy. Each plays a different role in the supply of transportation — sometimes complementary, often overlapping and competitive.

6. None of these four components exists in isolation; they are parts of the transportation subsystem. However, to interrelate the four, with notions concerning movement motivation, decision making, and the operational milieu, is not so easy as it sounds. A number of attempts have been made to understand these interrelationships, but they have largely failed because, as with models of primary, secondary, and tertiary activity systems, they are static, deterministic, and make unreal behavioral assumptions.

7. One avenue of approach seems to be to discern how individuals themselves view the choice situations in which they make travel decisions. Then, having found a sounder behavioral base with which to explain interaction, the mechanical components (stocks, networks, flows, modes) and the management side of transportation can be rerelated, provided they are firmly entrenched in the characteristics of a particular societal framework. The transportation subsystem has little meaning without reference to the other components, including the operational milieu, of the socioeconomic landscape.

8. Having viewed the transportation subsystem until this point as a set of vertical cross sections, it is now possible to take a horizontal viewpoint and examine such areas as urban transportation, transportation's role in economic development, and communications.

9. In examining the development of socioeconomic landscapes, it has not always been possible to demarcate clearly the role of transportation. There has, in fact, been some dispute as to the importance of that role. Few question the basic necessity of transportation as a medium of accessibility, but many do question whether transportation as such is neutral or whether it acts as a stimulant to further growth. Occasionally transportation may act as a catalyst for change in the landscape, but more frequently it seems to be concomitant with human decision making and a stimulus as an agent of change, rather than a precondition.

10. At a number of points through this book, the communication of information—symbolically or directly—has been alluded to. Having now introduced the idea of interaction in a spatial sense, we can return to the notions introduced in chapter 4. The act of communication is a cooperative attempt on the part of a sender and a receiver to exchange information. The process can be broken down into a sender, a message, a channel, and an aware receiver. To this, in economic geography, we can add the decision which ultimately results in some landscape change.

11. It is possible to think of the farmer, industrialist, retailer, consumer, or worker as having available to him three information resources or fields—private, public, and visual. The strength and extent of these fields depend on the geographic site and situation of the individual and a number of personal attributes like his gregariousness, awareness, aptitude, and socioeconomic status. Similarly the corporation is subject to site-to-site variations in information availability and ability to receive, assemble, store, and recall information.

12. The impact on the economic landscape of the mechanistic side of transportation and all the other

economic subsystems is mediated through channels of information flow. That fact alone is enough to begin to get a much clearer understanding of the disparate landscape patterns in the world.

Further Reading

Information on networks of the transportation subsystem will be found in

Haggett, P. and Chorley, R. J. *Network Analysis in Geography* (London: Edward Arnold, 1969).

An earlier and shorter exposition on the same theme is

Haggett, P. "Network Models in Geography," in R. J. Chorley and P. Haggett. *Models in Geography* (London: Methuen, 1967), chapter 15.

on flows in

Berry, B. J. L. *Essays on Commodity-Flows and the Spatial Structure of the Indian Economy*, Department of Geography, University of Chicago, Research Paper no. 111, 1967.

A review of techniques will be found in

Smith, R. H. T. "Concepts and Methods in Commodity Flow Analysis," *Economic Geography*, vol. 46, supplement 1970, pp. 404–416.

Among the modes of transport and their impact, the following are worth study:

Bird, J. *The Major Seaports of the United Kingdom* (London: Hutchinson, 1963). This includes an explication of the Anyport model.

O'Dell, A. C. and Richards, P. S. *Railways and Geography*, 2nd ed. (London: Hutchinson, 1971).

O'Flaherty, C. A. *Highways* (London: Edward Arnold, 1967).

Sealy, K. R. *The Geography of Air Transport*, 3rd ed. (London: Hutchinson, 1966).

Of the many articles on modes of transport the following could be noted:

Brooks, P. W. "The Development of Air Transport," *Journal of Transport Economics and Policy*, vol. 1, 1967, pp. 164–83.

Fleming, D. K. "Independent Transport Carriers in Ocean Transportation," *Economic Geography*, vol. 44, 1968, pp. 21–36.

Manners, G. "The Pipeline Revolution," *Geography*, vol. 47, 1962, pp. 154–163.

Meinig, D. "A Comparative Historical Geography of Two Railnets: Columbia Basin and Southern Australia," *Annals of the Association of American Geographers*, vol. 52, 1962, pp. 394–413.

Pinkney, J. F. "Motor Carriage: The Long and Short of It," *Annals of the Academy of Political and Social Sciences,* vol. 345, 1963, pp. 66–72.

Siddall, W. "Railroad Gauges and Spatial Interaction," *Geographical Review,* vol. 59, 1969, pp. 29–57.

Taaffe, E. J. "Trends in Airline Passenger Traffic: A Geographic Case Study," *Annals of the Association of American Geographers,* vol. 49, 1959, pp. 392–408.

Economic and management aspects of transportation are covered by

Farris, M. T. and McElhiney, P. T., eds. *Modern Transportation: Selected Readings* (Boston: Houghton Mifflin Co., 1967).

Lansing, J. B. *Transportation and Economic Policy* (New York: Free Press, 1966).

Sampson, R. J. and Farris, M. T. *Domestic Transportation: Practice, Theory, and Policy* (Boston: Houghton Mifflin, 1966).

Troxel, E. *Economics of Transport* (New York: Rinehart, 1955).

Aspects of freight rates and cost-distance are explained in

Alexander, J. W. et al. "Freight Rates: Selected Aspects of Uniform and Nodal Regions," *Economic Geography,* vol. 34, 1958, pp. 1–18.

Johnson, J. F. "The Influence of Cost Distance Factors on the Overseas Export of Corn from the U.S. Midwest," *Economic Geography,* vol. 45, 1969, pp. 170–179.

The interrelatedness of transport and space economy on abstract and empirical levels is covered by

Garrison, W. L. "Spatial Structure of the Economy," part 2, *Annals of the Association of American Geographers,* 1959, pp. 471–82.

Hoover, E. M. *The Location of Economic Activity* (New York: McGraw-Hill, 1963).

Isard, W. *Location and Space Economy* (Cambridge, Mass.: M. I. T. Press, 1956), chapter 2.

Transport and economic development is treated by a wide range of literature. The following may prove particularly useful:

Abramovitz, M. "The Economic Characteristics of Railroads and the Problem of Economic Development," *Far Eastern Quarterly,* vol. 14, 1955, pp. 169–78.

Cootner, P. H. "The Role of the Railroad in U.S. Economic Growth," *Journal of Economic History,* vol. 23, 1963, pp. 477–521.

Fogel, R. W. *Railroads and American Economic Growth* (Baltimore: Johns Hopkins Press, 1964).

Fromm, G., ed. *Transport Investment and Economic Development* (Washington, D.C.: Brookings Institution, 1965).

Hunter, H. "Transport in Soviet and Chinese Development," *Economic Development and Cultural Change,* vol. 14, 1965, pp. 71–84.

Martin, B. and Warden, C. "Transportation Planning in Developing Countries," *Traffic Quarterly,* vol. 19, 1965, pp. 59–75.

Stanley, W. R. "Evaluating Construction Priorities of Farm to Market Roads in Developing Countries: A Case Study," *Journal of Developing Areas,* vol. 5, 1971, pp. 371–400.

Communication studies have been infrequent in geography, other than the general aspect of diffusion:

Abler, R. "The Geography of Communications," in Eliot Hurst, M. E. *Transport Geography: Comments and Readings* (New York: McGraw-Hill, 1971), selection 17.

Brown, L. *Diffusion Processes and Location,* Regional Science Research Institute, Bibliography Series no. 4, 1968.

Gould, P. R. *Spatial Diffusion,* Association of American Geographers, College Commission, Resource Papers no. 4, 1969.

McLuhan, M. *Understanding Media: The Extension of Man* (New York: McGraw-Hill, 1964).

Olsson, G. *Distance and Human Interaction,* Regional Science Research Institute, Bibliography Series no. 2, 1965.

Osgood, C. E. and Sebeok, T. A., eds. "Psycholinguistics: A Survey of Theory and Research Problems," *Journal of Abnormal and Social Psychology,* vol. 49, supplement, 1954, pp. 1–3.

Pred, A. *Behavior and Location* (Lund: C. W. K. Gleerup, 1967), part 1, pp. 32–62.

Wagner, P. L. *Environments and People* (Englewood Cliffs: Prentice-Hall, 1972).

In addition the following readings may be useful to those interested in urban transportation:

Breecher, R. and E. "Getting to Work and Back," *Consumer Report,* February, March, and April, 1965.

Creighton, R. L. *Urban Transportation Planning* (Urbana: University of Illinois Press, 1970).

Hoover, E. M. "Motor Metropolis: Some Observations on Urban Transportation in North America," *Journal of Industrial Economics,* vol. 13, June 1965, pp. 177–92.

Horton, F., ed. *Geographic Studies of Urban Transportation and Network Analysis,* Northwestern University, Studies in Geography, no. 16, 1968, especially pp. 1–101.

Oi, W. Y. and Schuldiner, P. *An Analysis of Urban Travel Demands* (Evanston: Northwestern University Press, 1962).

A review of some areas of current interest in transportation geography has been undertaken by

Wheeler, J. O. "An Overview of Research in Transportation Geography," *East Lakes Geographer,* vol. 7, 1971, pp. 3–21.

fourteen

The Total Spatial System

This book began by considering the concept of a general system: it was postulated that the spatial economy of the real world seemed to satisfy the definition of such a system. An overlay of behavioral, operational, and decision making factors was added in such a way as to modify the pattern within the basic system. This world system, or spatial economy, was then disaggregated into the two major subsystems of *sites* (primary, secondary, tertiary) and *routes* (transportation), each of which was examined separately. These component subsystems must now be reaggregated in order for us to see if some total spatial system or economy does exist.

The Spatial Organization of the Economy

Human activities are distributed through space and time in certain patterns. The factors contributing to these patterns include chance, satisficing behavior, imperfect knowledge, the operational milieu, economic circumstances, and the impact of existing patterns or later developments.

Patterns of economic behavior are not static; they change with shifts in societal structure, whether they lead to changes in demand and supply, in level of technology, or in the sociopolitical organization of an area. The behavior patterns that make up the economic and social organization of an area are reflected in its patterns of agriculture, industry, and settlement, and in its flows of money, ideas, people, and goods. If there is a spatial pattern corresponding to each evolving level of socioeconomic development, then there may, at least in theory, be an optional strategy for each level.

In the early period of development marginal returns to the factors of production vary from region to region. But with further development economic and social functions become more and more spatially differentiated, and the scale of many functions increases. At an advanced level of development the socioeconomic structure is nationwide and there is an integrated hierarchy of functional areas, with population and activities heavily concentrated into urban and metropolitan regions.

Table 72 emphasizes the total spatial system; both the factor of space and the factor of interaction over space are utilized, and both are contained within a systems framework. This table draws on the factors explained in previous chapters: the behavioral environment; regions; locations; movement of ideas, peoples, and goods; and patterns of behavior as partially explained by the theories of von Thünen, Weber, and Christaller.

This spatially identifiable economic organization can be represented in a number of ways. One way is to represent economic behavior and activities by the equation

$$(1) \qquad H \pm A(R \cdot S) \rightarrow O$$

where H = human motives and capacities, or *demand*, A = accessibility, R = resources, S = resistances, and O = occurrence of an economic activity or *supply*.

By *human motives* and *capacities* we mean all those behavioral factors that lead to the demand, need, or desire for a good or service. By *accessibility* we mean the location of an activity with respect to other sites and the ease of transportation to it. By *resources* we mean the physical existence of resources in the landscape, modified by the group's perception of them, their accessibility, and the *resistances*, by which we mean such features of the landscape as climatic variations and soil erosion. By *occurrence* we mean the visible evidence of a particular economic behavior system.

Thus, on the one hand, at any particular site we have *demand*—what is wanted or needed from the landscape—modified by other factors, in particular by how the landscape is perceived and operationally organized. On the other hand, this leads to the occurrence—that is, to *supply*. Thus, in the landscape, we find *primary occurrences* (agriculture, animals, etc.), *secondary* and *tertiary occurrences*, and *transportation networks*, coexisting as distinct subsystems.

Now this is both a static and an isolated view of economic activities; each activity is viewed separately, and the interactions between them are not considered. But, as we now know, a particular farmer's decisions are related to other parts of the system. He does not make decisions in isolation, but in relation to what other farmers are doing nearby. His decisions also depend on his perceptual abilities, which are culturally determined, and on what the market demands. So economic behavior must be viewed in a spatial setting.

Fig. 200, an example of an particular form of economic behavior—the West Coast logging industry—can be used to illustrate this point. It is immediately clear that there is a specific areal location. The organization of this particular activity arises from a particular way of appraising forest resources. In addition, it rests on accumulated experience and technology—a very different basis for appraisal from

Table 72. *The Spatial Factor in Interaction*

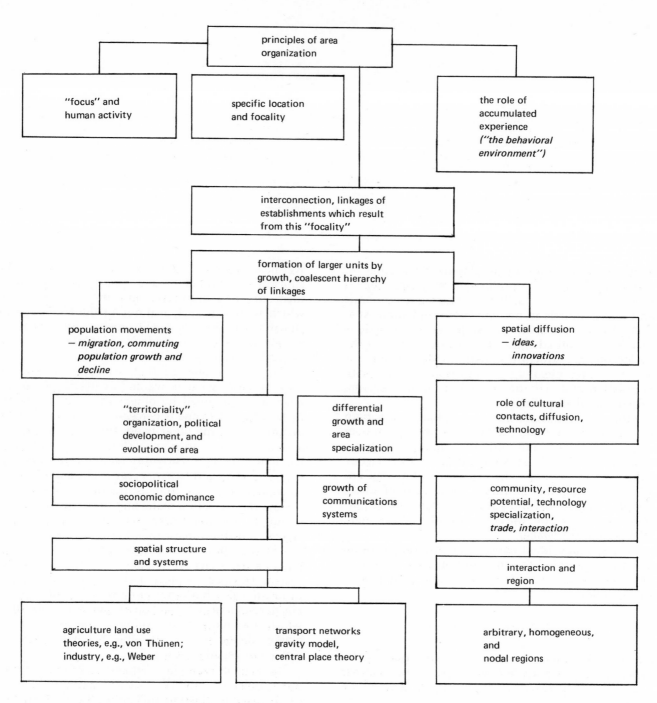

principles of area organization

"focus" and human activity

specific location and focality

the role of accumulated experience ("the behavioral environment")

interconnection, linkages of establishments which result from this "focality"

formation of larger units by growth, coalescent hierarchy of linkages

population movements — *migration, commuting population growth and decline*

spatial diffusion — *ideas, innovations*

"territoriality" organization, political development, and evolution of area

differential growth and area specialization

role of cultural contacts, diffusion, technology

sociopolitical economic dominance

growth of communications systems

community, resource potential, technology specialization, *trade, interaction*

spatial structure and systems

interaction and region

agriculture land use theories, e.g., von Thünen; industry, e.g., Weber

transport networks gravity model, central place theory

arbitrary, homogeneous, and nodal regions

Source: K. W. Rumage and L. P. Cummings, "Introduction to Geography: A Spatial Approach," Commission on College Geography, Publication No. 4, 1967, pp. 111–166.

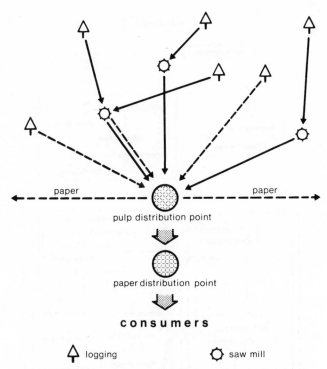

paper ←--------------------→ paper

pulp distribution point

↓

paper distribution point

↓

consumers

⌂ logging   ⬡ saw mill

Fig. 202. *The formation of a total spatial system: the linkage of sites and routes in the West Coast logging industry.*

that possessed by, for instance, the West Coast Indians. The specific *focus* of the present-day activity is the marketing of softwoods. The specific *location* is a West Coast maritime climate, very suitable for softwood growth, and with advantages for logging. These particular *site characteristics*—the existence of softwoods, and the desire by people to exploit them—lead to particular *production points* in the economic landscape. But of course they do not occur in isolation. Certain interconnections arise because of the very nature of the activity—for example, rivers may play a role as a means of transportation.

In time these isolated point activities have grown, as have spatial interconnections between them. Flows or routes have been established between logging sites, sawmill, pulp mill, paper mill, and distribution point (figure 202).

The growth in size and complexity of the units, with the increasing demands that result from rising socioeconomic levels throughout the entire spatially organized system, has led in turn to population movements, some of them seasonal, and the population supported by the activity has grown. Ideas and innovations in forestry have spread among the sites —a clear example of diffusion through space and over time. The growth of this particular activity has had an effect on the economic growth and viability of the region both in which it occurs and to which it is related. This in turn has given rise on occasion to particular political feelings, communication systems,

and landscape patterns—in short, to regional distinctiveness.

Thus the formula is not just $H \pm A(R\ S) = 0$, but

$$H \pm A(R \cdot S) = 0$$
$$H \pm A(R \cdot S) = 0$$
$$H \pm A(R \cdot S) = 0$$

This is meant to express the fact that an economic occurrence, the result of a particular behavior pattern, does not exist in the real world in the static, isolated form implied by equation (1), above. Not the least of its relationships is with other places. As was stressed in chapter 2, the simple notion of location—*where* as the point of reference—is fundamental to geography. To find out where something is requires defining its spatial relationships to known points. *To locate is to relate.* Moreover, the relationship between places or sites in the various subsystems implies interaction, that is, the existence of connecting routes. Interaction implies overcoming distance through movement, or *circulation*. Table 72, above, links interaction and points, or focalities, in an overall spatial system.

Also implicit in this analysis is the factor of time. Pred conceptualizes this as **initial advantage,** which he sees as the fact that:

1. *"Existing locations are usually characterized by tremendous inertia and a temporal compounding of advantages."*

2. *"Existing locations often exert considerable influence on subsequent . . . location decisions."*

3. *"Once concentration is initiated it has a self-perpetuating momentum."*

Economic landscape patterns are thus as much a product of previous decisions as they are of present ones.

A number of other factors also intervene to prevent the occurrence of worldwide patterns. There are cultural variations that influence the way people perceive the landscape, and variations in the operational milieu, including variations in the political environment. This latter factor gives rise to the notion of the **nation-state,** which may lead to the placing of barriers across the total spatial system in the form of customs unions or tariffs. Conversely, it may lead to the setting up of supranational economic communities or institutional regions (see below).

These factors, with the factor of time, mean that not all types of occurrence are found at the same level of development. Thus level of development and economic organization is an important variable in the world economic landscape. Figure 4 shows the locational pattern of five major types of economic area as determined by certain factors or measures of economic progress (see p. 17). It should be stressed that there is no implication that any areas have gone or will have to go through all five levels.

Type 1. The United States, southern Canada, Western Europe, and parts of Australia all have predominantly commercial or market-exchange economies, with relatively high levels of productivity.

Type 2. Market-exchange and redistributive economies, with more moderate levels of productivity, characterize parts of Argentina, Chile, Venezuela, South Africa, Japan, and Spain, as well as much of Eastern Europe and the U.S.S.R. All of these countries contain large sectors that still have a subsistence economy.

Type 3. Central America, parts of Africa, China, India, the Middle East, and the Balkan countries are mostly distinguished by large sectors of subsistence activities, though some points do occur where a market-exchange or redistributive economic organization exists. In general, however, activities are at a low level of productivity.

Type 4. This type consists of areas that are almost entirely subsistent in nature and have a very low productivity level.

Type 5. This type (shown on the map with type 4) represents largely undeveloped, very sparsely populated areas. Much of South America, the Middle East, interior China, and Africa fall into type 4, while type 5 includes the Arctic North, the deserts, Central Australia, and other such areas.

Most of the world's population is located in areas where the level of economic development is very low. On the other hand, the areas where the level of development is high are small in extent. This theme will be pursued in chapter 15.

Figure 203 by way of illustration shows how at three levels, variation occurs in both the isolated relationship, $H \pm A(R \cdot S) = 0$, and in the amount of interaction between the different activity sites. At a subsistence level, with low incomes, demand (H) is localized, consisting mainly of food and shelter for the family unit. Perception is severely constrained by the environment and by such operational factors as culture and religion. Accessibility (A) is low, the areas are inward looking and small in extent, and transportation technology is very limited, as, in consequence, is spatial interaction. The resource base (R) is small, local, and agriculturally based, and the resistances very great. Man at this level is much more subject to the vagaries of the physical environment. Thus the demand and supply sides are virtually coterminous in space.

At a different level of organization and economic development, the economic landscape changes. Demand (H) is now much wider, and the first set of

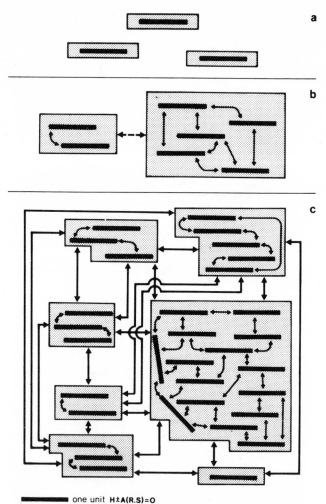

one unit $H \pm A(R.S) = 0$

Fig. 203. *Three levels of spatial systems. H = human demands; A = accessibility; R = resources; S = resistences; O = occurrence (supply).*

demands is for industry. Accessibility (A) is much greater. There is an increasing specialization of areas, as each looks to the other for trade. As the factors of complementarity, intervening opportunity, and transferability become important, there is a spatial separation of demand (H) and supply (O). Thus raw materials become separate from the market and there is increasing spatial interaction, not just as a spread of marketable goods, but of ideas, innovations, information about new machinery and techniques, and new opportunities. The resource base (R) thus seemingly expands, while resistances (S) decline in importance. The occurrence (O), in the form of economic and social satisfactions, is now a more marked feature of the socioeconomic landscape. Most of the models of economic landscapes and systems, in their unrefined state, apply to this level of situation. Activities (O) become concentrated at a few centers, which grow more rapidly and attract toward themselves the more dynamic elements from the more static environment around. As a result, these latter areas may become relegated to an inferior peripheral position. This interplay between center and periphery can be thought of in systems terms as a flow of energy (negentropy) that proceeds from the environment into an open subsystem and arrests, then reverses, the tendency toward disorder (i.e., economic depression). The flow, therefore, may not be one-way; feedback or counterflow may be generated, resulting in increased demands for the periphery's products. A. O. Hirschmann calls the first process *polarization* (the formation of a "growth pole," or center) and feedback **trickling down effects.** These ideas are examined in more detail below.

At the most complex stage of economic organization and development, an era of sustained growth and innovation is reached. Demand *(H)* is at an increasingly specialized level. But specialization and technological development go hand in hand, so that there is an ever-increasing interdependence between areas, and ever-increasing spatial interaction. Finally, there is an elaborate communications network: the resource base becomes worldwide, and resistances are reduced. Economic activities also become specialized in location; there is an increasing tendency to centralize in large urban areas, accompanied by a "growth pole" or multiplier effect.

This conceptualization is very similar to that of J. R. P. Friedmann, who has related certain aspects of location theory and agglomeration economics to the spatial changes associated with economic growth. He notes that, as economic development proceeds, there is an increase in areal specialization, functional differentiation, and spatial interaction between different areas. Thus economic structures develop from systems characterized by small, isolated, and functionally undifferentiated communities into hierarchies of interdependent regions. At the highest level of development these become linear cities and conurbations of very large size. A very high level of specialization and interdependency characterizes these later stages.

These variations in development and related spatial systems occur not just from nation to nation, or from market-exchange to subsistence economies, but from area to area within nations. A great diversity in levels of development occurs within all countries, including the most advanced. The United States, for example, has large areas of abject poverty and almost equally large areas of unprecedented affluence. In many nations, the contrast is not just twofold but threefold. For example, in many underdeveloped nations there are often islands of affluence associated with European or American petroleum interests, mining developments, or plantations; islands consisting of the native urban economies, which often possess more extensive links with the outside world than with the rest of the nation; and peasant-subsistence rural areas.

In other words, the total spatial system described in previous chapters appears in the landscape as a mosaic of **regions.** Each of these regions is characterized by a complex set of relationships of the order $H \pm A(R \cdot S) = 0$ and their interactions, or in other words by a complex set of *sites* and *routes*. In this way the total spatial system becomes a set of interlinked and overlapping economic regions, each with its distinct set of characteristics and occurrences, sites and routes.

Regional Organization

The regional concept is invoked here not in the narrow sense of a set of unique demarcated areas with prescribed boundaries and specified activities — the sense usually used by geographers — but as a useful representation of a particular *subsystem* located on the earth's surface. The term subsystem is emphasized, because all regions have relationships, links, and routes that extend beyond their own boundaries, and no region can be conceived as isolated and unique. Thus the regions shown in figure 203c are clearly interdependent both internally and externally. It is the strength and volume of the internal linkages of a particular regional subsystem that distinguish it from neighboring regions.

Traditionally three approaches have been taken to defining regions: The first approach emphasizes the *homogenous* or *uniform* region, that is, the homogeneity or similarity of one or a combination of physical, economic, social or other characteristics. The second approach emphasizes the *nodal* region, that is, polarization or centralization around some focus or node, which is usually a central place. The third approach emphasizes the *policy oriented area,* a more or less arbitrarily defined unit erected mainly for administrative coherence or convenience.

These three approaches are not mutually exclusive; in fact, they are really variants on the homogeneity criterion. The difference lies in what kind of homogeneity is sought. Thus an administrative region is homogenous in being entirely under one jurisdiction, a nodal region is homogenous in its dependence upon certain trading links, and uniform regions are homogenous with respect to certain physical, economic or social characteristics. But much of this seems doubtful in the light of systems analysis. Perhaps the pragmatic, problem solving approach of J. L. Fisher is the most acceptable one: "The most helpful region in many instances is what might be called the *economic development region. . . .* The emphasis is is on the development of policies, programs, and actions to move the region from where it is economically toward predetermined economic objectives."

Economic Regions

For our purposes, five forms of the spatial system, or total economic landscape, can be recognized.

Small Economic Regions

Areas drawn together by close economic bonds, such as those of commodity flows, labor supplies, or flows of capital, are often known as *small economic regions.* The concept is comparable to that of R. Vining's *economic community.* Vining bases his analysis on flows, structure, and stages of production. "In broad outline, . . . an area can be divided into an irregular patchwork of subareas, each characterized by some form and substance . . . lines of union along with matter and energy flow connect these subareas into some kind of functioning system of entities."

Vining's subject is not an isolated industry, nor even a set of industries in isolation, but rather the structural and operational characteristics of his economic community, which

seems to be organised around its "export" industry, this being the source of the flows which this community injects into the larger interdependent system and which act as a balance for the flows diverted from the larger system and channeled into this community. . . . [Thus] links [exist] between, not nations as such, but population structures or concentrations. The activity of given sets of firms is to be regarded as tied in with the national (and international) economy but being integrated with respect to a group of population structures—in some cases to a single population concentration and in others for all population concentrations within the general interrelated system of population structures. . . . A system of population cluster patterns [or] nets of areas are grouped into higher order nets, each with a population cluster as a nucleus and so on to a prime population concentration which is the central nucleus of a hierarchical system of population clusters. The region, then, is the area including this primary unit, and it corresponds approximately with the familiar primary trade area.

Somewhat similar to Vining's ideas are Lösch's *systems of economic areas,* developed on a homogenous plain on which population is distributed, and over which labor specialization and transportation costs occur in response to population needs. The interrelationships of these market areas or economic regions are very complex, and in reality may be quite difficult to identify. A clear economic region would seem to be a fortunate accident rather than a natural subdivision of the landscape. Still, beneath a veneer of irregular market areas Lösch believed a regional substructure of varying importance existed: "The economic landscape is a system of *different* markets; an organism, not merely an organ." Despite this complexity, Lösch identified three types of economic area: *simple* market areas, *nets* or subsystems of such areas, and *systems* of nets (compare figure 80). The simplest is dependent upon trade within a closed system; the most complex is also based on trade, but with areas external to the basic subsystem.

Thus both the economic areas or communities of Lösch and Vining depend on trade between areas and within the area. Each area has its trading center and its hinterland within which trading is carried on in much greater value than it is with outside areas, though interaction with the latter does occur. Spatial interaction in the form of flows of goods, money, and ideas provides the matrix within which these economic regions are set. If these flows are regarded as bonds which link components of the system to one another, it can be seen that the greater the magnitude of these flows in any area, the more highly related are the components in that area. According to W. Isard and Freutel, the problem of where to locate any kind of boundary is to find the locus of points where flows fall to a minimum, due to the impact of distance. "Our criterion for regional demarcation would then be internal interdependence of income, as revealed through flow phenomena. Furthermore, if there are such natural aggregations, and if the aggregations display a hierarchical tendency, then we might expect to find regions of varying order."

The City-Region

A second type of economic region is the *city-region complex.* Here, trading links are still very important, but there are also many spatial links consisting of flows of passengers, telephone calls, newspapers, and so on. A metropolitan community has been defined by Bogue as

. . . an organization of many communities, distributed in a definite pattern about a dominant city, and bound together in a territorial division of labor through a dependence upon the activities of the dominant city . . . the metropolitan community is not independent of the physical environment, but is, rather, an adaptation to the environment. It utilizes the techniques of production and exchange which are common to populations with industrial commercial cultures in order to exploit environmental resources. . . . The complete structure of the metropolitan community may in-

clude the functions of finance, government, education, religion, and innumerable other aspects of the institutional composition of the individual hinterland community.

As we saw earlier, the metropolitan community has come to be a characteristic feature of the spatial system of advanced market-exchange economies. Such "communities" are really large urban centers of industry, commerce, and administration; together with their hinterlands, they are usually "growth poles," or regions of great potential growth.

J. R. P. Friedmann has identified a hierarchy of such metropolitan or urban city-regions (figure 204). Within each major area there are a number of *regional cities,* smaller in size and performing fewer functions than a *primate city.* Below these are the towns in the lower orders of a hierarchy. Between some of the cities are *regions of interdependency,* or "development axes," the elongated corridors along principal transport routes. The prospects for development are said to be roughly proportional to the size of the centers they link, and inversely proportional to some functions of the distance separating them.

Natural Resource Regions

A third type of economic region is the *natural resource region.* Here the area is identified by the homogeneity of certain features that distinguish it from surrounding areas. For example, it is a common administrative device in water resource management to use a river basin as a regional unit, as is done by the Tennessee Valley Authority. The validity of such all-purpose regions based on a single resource has been questioned, particularly in urban industrial areas where the particular resource may be of little relevance to development.

Institutional Regions

A fourth type of economic region in the total spatial system is the *arbitrary region,* chosen as an aid to decentralized administration by many institutions such as government agencies, businesses, and banks. These institutional regions also arise on an international basis, through nation-states that are willing to participate in such institutional arrangements as preferential trade areas or economic communities.

A number of such supranational regional organizations exist today. One of the oldest of the European economic regions was Benelux. It began in 1921 with an economic union between Belgium and Luxembourg, and was joined by the Netherlands in 1944. Common tariffs were established for many

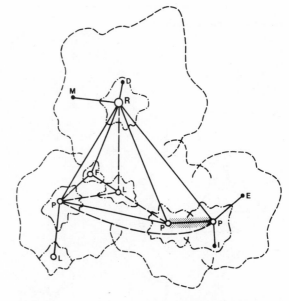

primate city (not shown)
R regional city
P provincial city
L local service city
M mining community
E educational community
F manufacturing city

I industrial satellite community
D dormitory city
▦ potential linear city
⟨_⟩ region of interdependency
⌐.⌐ city region
—— stronger economic relationships
– – weaker economic relationships

Fig. 204. *Simplified model of the spatial structure of locational matrices in a developed economy. (Reprinted by permission from J. R. P. Friedman, "Locational Aspects of Economic Development," Land Economics, vol. 32, 1956, p. 216. Copyright © 1956, by the Regents of the University of Wisconsin.)*

goods, and plans were set in motion to eliminate such factors as import licenses and quotas. Another celebrated regional union was the Organization for European Economic Cooperation (O.E.E.C.), set up in 1948 to administer the Marshall Plan in Europe. In 1961 this was replaced by the Organization for Economic Cooperation and Development (O.E.C.D.), which is now concerned with economic stability, aid to developing regions, and expansion of world trade.

Six members of O.E.E.C. — France, West Germany, Italy, and the Benelux countries — took the first steps towards forming a large integrated economic region in 1951. This European Coal and Steel Community removed the national boundaries impeding the flow of raw materials, finished products, labor, and investment between the six nations. The great combines (Thyssen, Blöckner, ARBED, Schneider Geusat, etc.) were satisfied with the resulting expanded markets and with the degree of control over an enlarged spatial territory enabling them to exploit the new market more profitably.

The success of this and other economic regional unions led to the formation among the six nations of a European Economic Community (E.E.C.) or Common Market. This large protected market was

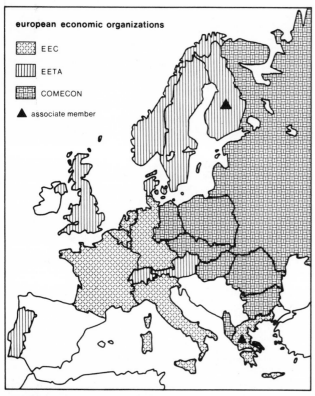

european economic organizations

EEC

EETA

COMECON

▲ associate member

Fig. 205. *European economic organizations in the late 1960s. By 1973 the United Kingdom, Ireland, Norway, and Denmark will have joined the E.E.C., and the future of E.F.T.A. is in doubt.*

established in stages. Tariffs and trade restrictions were removed over a fifteen-year period (except for some agricultural products that are not yet flowing freely), while flows of labor and capital were freed immediately. Today the six nations have free movement of population, capital, and certain services, as well as common rules of economic competition, common social welfare policies and transportation services, and a common external tariff.

In effect, a spatially large and economically powerful economic region has been created within which businesses can operate freely and under uniformly favorable legal and socioeconomic conditions. Some measure of its growth can be seen between 1958 and 1966, when the gross national product of the E.E.C. increased by 51 percent, while those of the United States and the United Kingdom increased by 45 percent and 30 percent respectively. Within this integrated economic region of some 186 million people, the goal was to improve the standard of living by more *efficient* spatial organization—efficiency as always, being defined by a particular perception of what it might stand for.

The effects of such changes in the total economic spatial system of the six nations have been to create increased interaction, as many political and legal

impediments to movement were removed. Increased interaction has fed back to economic activity and behavior patterns, and in particular has encouraged the growth of oligopolistic and monopolistic businesses. Since the welfare of large established firms is now at stake, there has been a marked increase in government resistance to political pressure from localized and working class groups seeking their own benefits. Such shifts in scale have led to the establishment of internation rather than intranation spatial patterns.

Larger scales also affect the market, which means increasing scales of production, more spatial specialization (especially in agriculture), and more efficient production. To some degree this move toward regional grouping of nations reflects changing technologies: automated mass production requires assured mass markets, as in the United States. Relocations or reallocations of factors of production from less to more efficient producers has led to the further economic depression of some peripheral areas (Brittany, Southern Italy) and to the concentration of new growth in already established growth poles (Paris, the Ruhr). The E.E.C., recognizing this danger at the time of its establishment, set up a European Investment Bank to offset socially undesirable capital flows. But such attempts have met with little real success. Relationships and trade flows with the rest of the world economic system have also undergone modification as new trade links have been established or intensified, especially at the expense of those Western European nations outside the community.

The nations not participating in the Common Market when it was founded, particularly the United Kingdom, were concerned over some of these trends. It must be remembered that economic groupings of this type are intended to improve economic growth only within their own boundaries. The new patterns of economic flows that result may actually contribute to a decline in economic prosperity in outside areas —and, indeed, to some harmful dislocation within the community itself. Accordingly, seven states, the United Kingdom, Norway, Denmark, Sweden, Switzerland, Austria, and Portugal, decided in 1957 to form their own preferential trade area, the European Free Trade Association (E.F.T.A.). This area, or region, was poorer and less populated than the E.E.C., but it gained from the presence of the United Kingdom with its trade ties to the Commonwealth.

The objective of E.F.T.A. was to eliminate tariff barriers among the member states. But E.F.T.A. did not erect a common external tariff as the E.E.C. countries had done; instead, each member met foreign trade in its own manner. The lesser economic strength, spatial fragmentation, and lack of common social and legal institutions of the E.E.C. type, together with the great economic success of E.E.C. itself, doomed E.F.T.A. almost from the beginning to a lower rate of economic growth. A number of approaches were made by the United Kingdom and other E.F.T.A. nations seeking entry into E.E.C. Finally, in 1970, four countries—the United Kingdom, Denmark, Norway, and Ireland—began negotiations to establish certain concessions (such as a phasing out of the British Commonwealth trade preference links) and made successful application to enter the Common Market in 1973. This even wider economic grouping will no doubt continue to lead to changes in the spatial economic patterns in Western Europe and the rest of the world.

Such economic regionalism is not confined to market-exchange economies. In 1949 the redistributive economies of Eastern Europe and the U.S.S.R. also organized an economic union, the Council of Economic Mutual Assistance (C.E.M.A.). Its purpose was to centralize and administer trade agreements, and to operate a system of credit and technical assistance. Neither are such economic regions confined to high levels of economic development; a number already exist among developing nations. For example, the Alliance for Progress among South American nations was, in a sense, the O.E.E.C. of the Americas. Established in 1961, the ten-year program provided for the allotment of some $20 billion in financial aid to shore up economies and get reform programs underway. This particular regional grouping, dominated by the United States as metropolis and the South American countries as satellites, failed in almost every respect to change the basic economic patterns. This failure was largely due to the inability to remove the basic malfunctioning of the economic systems concerned (see chapter 15). In Asia, there is the Colombo Plan, or, to give it its full title, the Plan for Cooperative Economic Development in South and Southeast Asia, established in 1950 to combat poverty, illiteracy, and disease. It was led by Britain, United States, Canada, Australia, and New Zealand, with Borneo, Cambodia, Ceylon, India, Laos, Malaya, Pakistan, Singapore, South Vietnam, Burma, Nepal, Indonesia, Japan, and the Philippines as the Asian participants. The aims of the Colombo Plan differ somewhat from that of any comparable European organization because of the difference in levels of development, and most aid has gone to improve the agricultural base through irrigation schemes.

Finally, there are several international economic regions in Africa. The Common Services Organization joins Uganda, Kenya, and Tanzania in a loose economic union; it reflects the former British colonial region in East Africa. Another economic regional union is the Entente in West Africa, founded in 1959 with the Ivory Coast, Upper Volta, Dahomey, and Niger as its original members. Members of the Entente have a common currency, common official language, common overseas representation, common education, and a common airline. The basic purpose is to coordinate economic activities. There is also a central fund into which each country makes an annual contribution proportional to its revenues, and out of which the poorer states draw the largest amount. Associated loosely with the Entente is the Abidjan Group, formed in 1960 for similar purposes. This group includes the ex-French colonial territories of French Equatorial Africa (Chad, Gabon, Central African Republic, and People's Republic of the Congo), Senegal, Cameroun, and Mauritania.

The Economic Development Region

The proliferation of economic problems and opportunities that can be best treated on a regional basis accounts for the popularity of the *economic development region*. It may overlap with some of the previous regional types (e.g., the Colombo Plan, in some respects, is a supranational development region). One of its subtypes is the *depressed region*, or economic problem area—an area with a declining or stagnant economy, which offers only modest development prospects, and provides many of the migrants for areas of new growth. A typical example of a depressed area is Northeast England, examined later in this chapter. Also in this category is the *frontier region*, or area of economic opportunity, which would be greatly aided by investment in resource development and transportation networks (see chapter 13). Examples are Alaska, the Yukon, and northern British Columbia. These frontiers are either adjacent to older developed areas, or are associated with large-scale resource development. Sometimes they form relatively isolated **exclaves,** usually with an urban focus, but at a considerable distance from existing metropolitan regions. As J. L. Fisher notes, "Each economic development region has a particular problem or set of related problems; each has a susceptibility to a particular kind of policy and program which will reduce its problems and help in realising its opportunities." Few regions are content just to fade away; instead, they generally try to do something about their future.

Analytical Methods

Regional economics and regional analysis offer a number of methods for systematizing the relationships within and between economic regions. Much of the early work in these fields concentrated on depressed areas; the eventual purpose was to revitalize the area's rate of economic progress so that it conformed to some national level. In many countries experiencing rapid economic growth, a not unusual occurrence is the existence of a **dual economy.** This generally means that the newly industrialized urban areas are so far ahead of the rest of the country that they constitute a virtually separate economic system. Attempts are often made to overcome this duality by means of special regional development programs such as that in Southern Italy (the so-called Mezzogiorno Project). One of the earliest and most ambitious of these schemes to redistribute economic opportunity geographically was the New Towns policy in the United Kingdom. It was followed by the National Plan, part of which is described below.

The Transportation Study

Other studies have evolved around the metropolitan region, particularly in relation to transportation surveys. Data are collected in so-called **O-D surveys,** in which a sample of households, transit passengers, automobile drivers, and so forth, are questioned as to their origin, destination, mode of transport, and trip purpose. The main objective is to gauge present habit patterns, so as to estimate the current level of demand for transportation facilities within an urban area, and to project that demand to some future date. Quite frequently the **gravity model** is used to estimate traffic flows between pairs of traffic zones.

Many attempts have been made to improve the projective abilities of these models. Thus the development of land use models has made the projection of population distributions and transportation demands somewhat more sophisticated, though still very mechanistic. The Penn-Jersey Transport Study, for example, distributes future population and thus demand for transport by reference to economic rules of residential choice applied by means of a linear programming model. Nor is regional analysis in an urban context limited to planning for transport. Thus both the Pittsburgh Regional Planning Association and the New York Metropolitan Region Study have analyzed the interdependence between transport, land use, population growth patterns, and industrial development. Similarly, not all the transportation problems studied by regional analysis are urban. For example, the regional structuring of railroads, trucking lines, and airlines in the United States has led to studies of rail passenger volume and freight flows, region by region. The North East Corridor Program and the Appalachia Study are two

such examples. Transportation is in fact a favored sector in programs of regional development, and plans to stimulate regional economic growth frequently begin with expenditure on transport.

Regional and Interregional Multiplier Analysis

The notion of a **multiplier effect** was introduced above. In an individual region, fluctuations in the activities of basic industries may lead to fluctuations in retail and service activities. In other words, fluctuations in basic industries may have a multiplier effect. Regions, of course, are not isolated units; a system or mosaic of regions exists, and fluctuations in one region's exporting or importing abilities will be felt in neighboring and linked regions. Hence the concern is not just with a regional multiplier but with an interregional one, that is, with the expansion and contraction of the economic bonds between regions.

The first step in the use of these concepts as analytical tools is to define certain activities as being *exogenous,* or determined outside the economy under analysis. Thus the economic base of a region is that group of industries primarily engaged in exporting from the region under analysis to other regions. An empirical multiplier is determined by observing the historical relationship between this export activity and total economic activity in the region. This multiplier is then applied to estimates of economic base to forecast total economic activity. The problem therefore arises of how to estimate the size of the economic base, and of how relevant this base concept is anyway. Where the concern is to improve economic growth rates in a region, usually some attempt is made to estimate the extent of new export activities that might have a chance of economic survival, and so of creating a base for the general expansion of the economy of the region studied. Usually, new export possibilities are estimated by means of comparative cost analysis. This procedure involves a set of cost comparisons for supplying certain products to specified markets from the region studied, as compared with alternative sources of supply for those same markets. Such comparisons usually center around transportation costs, labor costs, or even energy costs if some heavy consumer of energy is being considered. Other factors, however, are more difficult to include. Among these are economies of scale and agglomeration economies. Isard has used industrial complex analysis, which is an attempt to delineate more meaningful industrial groupings by means of the input-output matrix.

Broadly, then, the multiplier concept concerns the way in which a rise in income, production, or employment in one group of economic activities in a region stimulates the expansion of other groups through an increased demand from the former group and its workers for the goods and services produced by the latter. Usually, these rises are induced by changes within the total economic system, that is, changes external to the region itself. The interindustry stimulus may take the form of an expansion of demand for actual production inputs needed by the original group, or it may operate indirectly through growth in demand for consumer oriented goods and services on the part of the better paid workers employed through increases in that group. Thus Vining divided regional economic activity into two groups, the "carrier" industries and the "passive" industries, corresponding respectively to industries that produce for export and industries that are locally based. He derived a multiplier ratio of about 1.2 for employment growth in those industries in the Pine Bluff trading region of Arkansas.

Linear Programming

Use has also been made in regional studies of linear programming techniques (see chapter 13). The most ambitious of such efforts to date has been the Penn-Jersey Transport Study household location model, mentioned above. It began with the simple notion that different types of households have certain specific amounts that they can budget for the "bundle of services" associated with households of each type. This of course includes land consumed, which obviously in turn gives rise to different land use patterns. Families with varying incomes and occupations, as well as different numbers of children, were assumed to select particular housing types and residential areas. Transport, structure, and amenity costs were subtracted from a household's total available budget to determine how much remained to pay for buying land or renting it. Households were then assumed to bid for land up to the maximum, subject to such constraints as total land availability. However, certain behavioral assumptions were also made (e.g., economic rationality) that cast much doubt on the actual results.

This account is not meant to exhaust all the known methods of regional analysis. A number of other techniques have been utilized. Some of them are grounded in Löschian and post-Löschian location theory. Some have utilized computer systems simulations. Still others have used multi-equation dynamic products that include behavioral, technological, and institutional components. In this latter group also falls the work of the Cowles Commission at the University of Chicago in the 1940s and 1950s. These and the methods reviewed above are all contributing to the analysis of the regional mosaic.

Regional Development

Having examined the general time-space distribution of economic activities, and having seen this expressed as a mosaic of economic regions, we are faced with the question of what can be done to promote development or change in a particular region. It has already been suggested that certain institutional arrangements, like removing political hindrances, may begin to solve this problem; other "malfunctions" are examined in the following chapter.

The resources available to an area depend very much on what that area or region wants to do and what it is able to do. Indeed, as Zimmermann has noted, "the word 'resource' does not refer to a thing or to a substance but to a function which a thing or substance may perform or to an operation in which it may take part." Regional economic development is concerned with investment in resources, and thus with actions that are a function of the group that occupies an area. Resources are a function of human perception and therefore reflect the cultural variation that is distributed over the earth's surface. Resources, in short, only become such as humans see a use for them. Uranium, for example, only became a major resource when man found a use for it in the production of nuclear energy. Many resources, however, must remain *potential* resources because it is technologically or economically unfeasible to exploit them.

It is not unusual for the cumulative environmental factors, the total spatial system of a region, to be considered a resource in itself. In the same way, available transportation systems, buildings, and even whole cities can be considered as *capital* resources to be exploited for the benefit of the human population.

Regional development, then, is concerned with investment in total resources (potential, natural, human, cultural, and capital) and is either a function of the group that occupies an area or a function of external aid from some group outside the area. Given the goal of increased economic activity in a region, or of some change in the spatial system, how can a particular group achieve these changes? Would it, for example, reallocate labor and capital in order to maximize some human welfare goal, or would it take some alternative action?

Cumulative Causation

Economic development varies from region to region. High levels of development are concentrated at particular points, producing the mosaic of regions that we noted earlier. One conceptualization of this differential growth process is that of Gunnar Myrdal

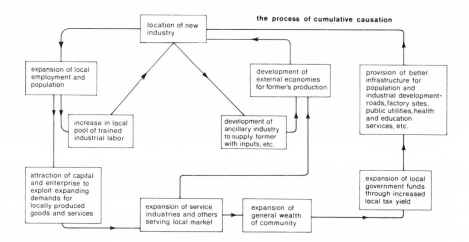

the process of cumulative causation

Fig. 206. *Myrdal's process of cumulative causation: a simple illustration. (Reprinted by courtesy of D.E. Keeble, from R.J. Chorley and P. Haggett, eds.,* Models in Geography, *Methuen and Co., 1967, p. 258.)*

(1957). In particular he invokes the notion of **cumulative causation,** according to which "the play of forces in the market normally tends to increase rather than to decrease, the inequalities between regions." In other words, should some region gain some initial advantage, new growth will tend to concentrate in this already expanding region, because of its derived advantages, rather than in other regions.

Figure 206 illustrates a simple case of the cumulative process. However, Myrdal also explains differential regional growth in terms of the spatial interaction between the expanding regions and the others. Once economic growth has begun in a region, then spatial flows of labor, capital, and goods begin to focus on that region at the expense of the remaining regions. Faced with higher returns in a growth region, most of the factors of production become mobile; lagging regions may lose their skilled workers and locally generated capital. Simultaneously with the in-migration of production factors to the growth region, there is an outflow of goods and services to the other regions that competes to the detriment of locally based secondary and tertiary activities. Multiplier and feedback effects occur in the sphere of health services, education, and many other specialized activities. This leads to even poorer servicing of the lagging regions.

Also of significance are what Myrdal calls "certain centrifugal 'spread effects' of expansionary momentum from the centres of economic expansion to other regions." By stimulating demand for such things as agricultural and mineral products in other nearby regions, expansion in one region may initiate growth in others. If the impact of such demands is strong enough to overcome the disadvantages of lagging, a process of cumulative growth may begin leading to another center of self-sustained economic growth. Such effects are most likely to occur where the lagging regions are already at a fairly high level of economic development, since they will have the

necessary transport, communications, and educational facilities. Myrdal assumes in his model that self-sustaining growth occurs without the necessity for government intervention. He does suggest, however, that stronger spread effects tend to occur where government policies are aimed at fostering growth in backward regions, and that such action can only be interpreted as yet another aspect of cumulative causation. Certainly, there does appear to be greater government concern with regional inequalities in advanced than in developing economies.*

There has been some criticism that Myrdal's "backwash" and "polarization" effects hardly constitute a satisfactory explanation of regional backwardness. Others, however, seem to believe that these concepts represent important explanatory variables for differential development.† Most commentators seem to approve of the idea of cumulative causation, and to agree that regional economic development does tend to occur in areas where there has already been most growth. Among other processes they stress the cumulative advantages or cumulative processes of growth in the regions of concentration.

Backward and Forward Linkages

Using the terminology of Hirschmann, we might suggest that stimulation of economic activities in a region can be achieved through the most significant *backward* and *forward linkage effects.*

A *backward* linkage effect is a situation in which every nonprimary economic activity will induce attempts to supply the inputs needed in that activity

---

*There are many papers on developed areas, but few companion studies for developing areas.
†The criticism seems about equally balanced with the agreement.

through domestic production. It is sometimes called the *input provision,* or *derived demand.*

A *forward* linkage effect, sometimes called *output provision,* is concerned with outputs to a consumer. Here, every activity that does not by its nature cater exclusively to final demands will induce attempts to utilize its outputs as inputs in some new activity or other.

Thus an economic activity should attempt to get its inputs *produced* locally and its outputs *purchased* locally, because in this way the outputs can be utilized in a further manufacturing process. Such attempts would lead to more intensive use of local resources, both human and natural, thus stimulating the formation of social overhead capital in the form of transportation routes, power sources, or schools, and the institution of directly productive activities in the form of factories, mines, or farms. This accumulation of capital resources could lead in turn to significant agglomeration economies and increased population, thus contributing to sustained growth through the establishment of service and consumer oriented industries. The activities that generate the large linkage effects desired could be selected via an input-output matrix. In this way it would be possible to ascertain which industries have the kinds of input-output relationship through which the use of the resources in a particular region might be maximized.

It is the lack of interdependencies and linkage effects that is characteristic of the less developed regions. Agriculture, especially subsistence agriculture, is characterized by a scarcity of such linkage effects. All primary production by definition should exclude any large degree of backward linkage. As was noted, however, in the input-output analysis (chapters 7 and 9), modern technology has introduced the outside purchase of agricultural products like fertilizers and insecticides. Thus the more primitive the agricultural activity, the more truly primary it is. Forward linkage effects are also weak in this sector, as a large proportion of agricultural output is destined directly for consumption or export. Another part of the total production is subjected to some processing but, as in wheat milling, only small costs are added in relation to the total value. Particularly in underdeveloped areas, relatively little produce receives elaborate processing. The importance of this absence of linkage effects to economic growth is obvious, since there will be no direct stimulus to the setting up of new activities without such effects. Thus the primary products from mines, large farms, and so forth, can be shipped out of a region without effecting further growth in the region's economy.

Industrial linkage effects are more complex. Industrialization can start only with industries that deliver to final demand, otherwise there will be no market for intermediate goods. This means that development can begin with only two kinds of industries:

1. *Those that transform domestic or imported primary products into goods to supply final demands.*
2. *Those that transform "imported" semi-manufactures into goods to supply final demands.*

To the pioneer industrial areas only the first course was open. This explains the towering importance of a few industries such as textiles, iron and steel, pottery, and so on, during the early stages of the Industrial Revolution. Today, textiles, food processing, and construction materials industries based on local materials may still be of great importance. But to a significant degree industrialization can now occur through industrial plants that perform a few final stages on an almost-finished industrial product imported from outside the region. This trend has some advantages, particularly in providing an investment outlet for small amounts of capital that might not be available to a pooled resource development, and it removes the first industrial plants from direct reliance on what may be unreliable local sources. In this way many regions of new development may be said to set up "last" industries first, if one thinks in terms of the input-output flows of the more advanced areas. This kind of pattern has often proven to be a powerful stimulus to the development of agriculture.

Hirschmann also sees an implicit geographic imbalance in the growth process, as economic growth is channeled to a few leading areas and the powerful forces of concentration and specialization reinforce the inequality of areal development. He suggests that despite this polarization tendency economic pressures will eventually develop to change that unbalanced situation, particularly through government intervention. Governments, he suggests, need support from all sections of society, and will therefore tend to disperse investment funds over a large number of small projects scattered over the national territory. From the point of view of public investment policy he sees three different stages:

1. *Widespread scattering of public investment.*
2. *A stage of geographic concentration of public investment.*
3. *An attempt to "ignite development in the hitherto stagnant areas through 'autonomous' public investment."*

The key role in Hirschmann's study is played by spatial interaction between growing and lagging regions—factors similar to Myrdal's spread and feedback effects. However, Hirschmann's model depends on more than cumulative causation, since it implies that if a centrally determined imbalance between regions develops during the early stages of economic growth, counterbalancing forces, especially government intervention, will in time operate to restore the situation to an equilibrium position.

Both Myrdal and Hirschmann posit feedback and centralization effects in the form of interregional flows of capital, labor, and goods from lagging to growing regions. Such flows have been shown to occur in Indonesia, Pakistan, Brazil, and Spain. The spread, or down-flow, effects have not been identified so clearly, perhaps in many cases because of the considerable cultural, social, and economic differences between the regions of the developing countries studied. In more advanced economies, however, the geographic spread of development does seem to have occurred.

Export Base Model

According to the *export base model*, growth in a given region is initiated by the response of the industries within it to an increase in demand arising outside it. This results in an expansion of economic activities, particularly of local trade and service activities. The key role in a region's growth belongs to the exportable commodities and services, the idea being that capital investment will tend to flow into a region to develop the export industries. This process includes improvement of production processes and further development of specialized services to the exports. The resulting increase in income will tend to augment demand for secondary products and induce investment in a variety of other industries. The rate at which a region grows will thus depend on the rate at which the export base expands in response to the increase in the demand for the region's exportable commodities and services.

This formulation is based on a 1961 study by Perloff and Wingo of the growth of U.S. spatial economic structure. The authors claim that "regional growth typically has been promoted by the ability of a region to produce goods or services demanded by the national economy and to export them at a competitive advantage with respect to other regions."

D. C. North has put forward a five-stage regional export base model that he suggests could be applied to most market-exchange economies with no population pressure problems:

1. *There is a brief subsistence stage.*
2. *There is rapid development in the exporting of staple commodities to more advanced regions as the basis of the regional economy.*
3. *With the growth of external economies, inflows of capital, and provision of an export-oriented infrastructure, a stage of export intensification and regional development occurs.*
4. *In time, residentiary or locally based industry develops to serve the local market.*
5. *Finally, the expansion of resident industries, together with footloose industries located by chance, may reach a point where they too enter the export market, thus diversifying the region's export base.*

The same author has suggested that capital investment tends to flow into a region to develop its export industries in the manner described above. The resulting increase in income tends to increase demand for secondary products and to spill over investment into a number of other industries. Here, too, the rate at which the region grows ultimately depends on the rate at which the export base expands in response to the increase in demand for the region's exports. The general implication is that growth is dependent on a high overall level of economic development within the nation and a continued demand for the region's export products.

Growth Centers

Finally, a body of ideas has grown up about spatial variations in economic prosperity within regions. These focus around the concept of a *growth center*, which is, roughly speaking, the idea that economic development rarely occurs uniformly over a particular region, but rather tends to be concentrated in certain areas that expand at a higher rate than the surrounding ones. This is comparable to Friedmann's concept of metropolitan centers, which he locates at the core of the spatial system as the principal centers of growth. The growth centers are almost always either urban-industrial concentrations or concentrations of activity of an economic and social nature that seem to lead to rapid and sustained growth. Through the media of communication and money this growth "filters down" to the less developed regions, thus raising their economic status. Such a growth pole is seen as owing its existence to the location within it of one main growth industry that attracts other linked industries as the growth pole expands. Other agglomeration economies come into play to encourage further growth. So, too, do high rates of technological change and the easy and rapid exchange of ideas.

Many economists doubt whether there can be just one main growth industry, and in fact it has been shown to act as an inhibitor of other industries. Most growth areas, however, do seem to be concentrations of industrial development, and several policy making bodies have accepted the idea as a key concept in regional economic planning. This acceptance reflects the belief that concentrated investment and industrial activity will in the long run stimulate a higher level of economic development than investment spread over a wider area. It also reflects "the hope that prosperity will spread outwards from the chosen points in concentric ripples."

This concept of "growth centers" stems from the work of French economists, particularly F. Perroux (1964), who developed the abstract notion of a *growth pole*. Perroux's approach is based on two basic assumptions: first, that there exists a closed system; and second, that the maximum acceleration of regional growth follows an unbalanced pattern. Within these constraints he maintains that the analysis of regional growth should concentrate on the process whereby various activities appear, grow in importance, and in some cases disappear. Perroux's growth poles (firms, industries, or groups of firms or industries) are located in an abstract economic space "from which centrifugal forces emanate and to which centripetal forces are attracted." The firms or industries are envisaged as being "propulsive units" transmitting growth through the economy when: they have high interaction with many other firms; they have a high degree of dominance; they are very large; and they are part of a rapidly expanding sector of the economy. These growth poles are seen to initiate and transmit economic growth through multiplier effects and factors such as Hirschmann's backward and forward linkage effects. Strictly speaking, however, Perroux's model deals with nongeographic economic space, whereas the practical concept of "growth centers" belongs to geographic space. That is, "growth poles" tell us nothing about the location of a firm or industry in real space, nor of the consequences of a pole having a particular location in real space. Some confusion has arisen between the practical and abstract notions, and recent literature has attempted to clear it up.

Although these concepts of "growth centers" and "growth poles" have gained currency in regional development programs, they are open to criticism. Thus N. M. Hansen (1968) questions the ability of a large industry to stimulate growth; for instance, establishment of the Lorraine steel industry was not followed by accelerated development of steel consuming industries. Similarly, in Denmark prosperity has been neither initiated nor sustained by a big propulsive industry, but rather by scattered, relatively small agricultural units. In other words, although growth centers can be identified in some areas, the growth pole concept is only a partial explanation of regional growth.

There are, of course, other possible explanations of regional development. Some of them are explained in chapter 15, where theories of economic development and social change are detailed. A valid alternative to the growth center concept may well be the metropolis-satellite concept of A. G. Frank, who views regional growth as centered in certain favored areas in the capitalist system that exploit the other areas.

Benefit-Cost Analysis

It was noted earlier that regional economic development and growth is concerned with investment in resource development. Yet it has been suggested in subsequent pages that there are a number of ways those resources can be used — indeed, there may be more than one use for a given resource. How then, should one develop a particular resource within this context? The solution of this problem requires a technique known as *benefit-cost analysis*. The calculation of a benefit-cost ratio for each of several competing resources or projects may enable one to decide which one confers the largest net benefit on the region as a whole. The technique has been used for a number of such choice situations: highway locations, water resource development, and so on. In the latter, benefits may take the form of hydroelectric power, navigation, flood control, irrigation, recreation, and pollution abatement.

Benefit-cost is based on the following principles:

1. *The goods and services produced have value only to the extent that there is, or will be, a demand for them.*

2. *The best alternative for development must also be the most "economic" one. The next best alternative, with its cost of procedure, establishes an upper limit to the value of the labor, materials, and so on, that will need to be employed.*

3. *The best or most economic alternative should be the one that exhibits the highest benefit-cost ratio. Selection of this alternative alters the economic circumstances in terms of which the rest are evaluated. Thus more analyses must be undertaken once the initial decision is made.*

4. *To determine the scale on which the project should be built or the resource developed, economic effectiveness must be maximized by comparing it to the next best alternative.*

Economic comparisons can then be made as follows.

(A) *Comparison of net benefits* establish the ratio of excess benefits to costs. Thus two schemes for resource use could be present, both with equal surpluses of benefits over costs and both at face value equally desirable. However, if project A costs $1 million and produces an excess of benefits over costs of another $1 million, while project B also produces $1 million in net benefits but costs ten times as much as project A, then project A will offer the best resource development opportunities (table 73).

(B) *Comparison of rates of return on investment* reveals the relative profitability of different types of

Table 73. *Comparison of Net Benefits*

	project A	project B
total costs	$1,000,000	$10,000,000
total benefits	1,000,000	1,000,000
net benefit	$1,000,000	$ 1,000,000
benefit-cost-ratio	2.0	1.1

Source: W.R.D. Sewell, J. Davis, A.D. Scott, and D.W. Ross, *Guide to Benefit Cost Analysis* (Ottawa: Queen's Printer, 1962). Reproduced with the permission of the Queen's Printer for Canada.

investment. It can be determined by computing the ratio of annual net benefit to capital invested in the project. Naturally, its main use is in capital intensive developments. Finally, *comparison on the basis of benefit-cost ratios* is the principal method used in the early stages (later in the assessment one could look at net benefits). The benefit-cost ratio is, of course, a relative and not an absolute measure.

Thus we could use this form of analysis to determine which of two industries that wish to use the same land, forest, or water resources should be given the preference. This could be an important decision in a region's economic growth. For example, if industry *X* is already in possession of a resource, and industry *Y* also wishes to use it, a benefit-cost analysis can help to determine the advisability of using the resource *with* industry *Y* as against using it *without* industry *Y*. Another example might be a mining company wishing to have for its own use an area of forest land surrounding a mine site. How many acres, if any, should it have? By comparing the *net benefits* of forest production which are sacrifices (that is, the discounted future value of the stand of trees, plus any intangible value of the forest, less future logging and forestry costs) with the *net benefit* of mining (and in this case subtracting from the net benefit of mining either the probable damage from forest fires started in mining areas or the cost of preventing such fires by extra vigilance) it would be possible to discover whether or not, and how extensively, forest land should be transferred to the mining company. Thus the calculation of a benefit-cost ratio for competing uses may enable one to decide which use confers the largest net benefit on the regional economy as a whole.

Regional Studies

It is possible to identify two basic types of approach to analyzing regions. One deals with the economic mosaic of regions from a historical-behavioral point of view. The other is concerned with finding a quantifiable, predictive, and mathematically rigorous framework for the study of regions. Of course, these approaches are not discrete; each draws on the techniques of the other.

The historical-behavioral approach stresses the analysis of trends and evolutionary patterns. The variables of interest are the motivations behind regional structural changes, and the purpose is to forecast future changes in the light of current or apparent trends in behavior. Thus stress is placed on entrepreneurship, market structure, and initial advantages and patterns. None of these is usually incorporated into the formal approach because of difficulties in quantification and manipulation. In contrast, the analytical-quantifier approach emphasizes formal structure and consistency, while behavioral concerns are the exception rather than the rule.

A Regional Model

Isard has attempted a synthesis of these two approaches through a five-stage model. In stage I (figure 207) the basis of the approach is an interregional input-output matrix enlarged to take account of both comparative cost and the industrial complex analysis mentioned earlier. In order to project future regional growth reliance is placed on demographic characteristics, changes in technology, tastes, and so forth. Thus the population, with its labor force and productivity, is projected into the future. Through government expenditures and capital formation, Isard also estimates **social accounts**. Initial regional markets are established on the basis of current data and predicted from growth assumptions involving flows of money, labor, and goods, as well as economic base, multiplier concepts, and the impact of community attitudes on industrial location.

In stage II (figure 208, minus the block "probability, etc.") Isard's model emphasizes the urban-metropolitan regional structure. For the interregional matrix he uses a specific regional input-output matrix backed up by central place theory. As before, a set of assumptions is made for the system, as well as regional market estimates. A predictive factor is then added, and a meaningful hierarchy of regions is set up. This hierarchy consists of a system of major metropolitan regions, a set of subregions, and a set of local areas. Thus comparative costs, outputs, and so on, are allocated to such a system.

In stage III an attempt is made to incorporate the agglomerative forces and economies and their social equivalent, the "behavior of social masses." In order to do this, notions of gravity, potential, and energy notions are incorporated (figure 208). Using gravity models of the probability type, spatial patterns of

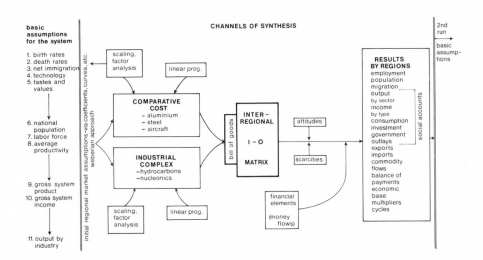

Fig. 207. *Simulation of the total spatial system: Stage I. (Reprinted from Walter Isard, Methods of Regional Analysis, p. 571, by permission of the M.I.T. Press, Cambridge, Mass. Copyright 1960 by the Massachusetts Institute of Technology.)*

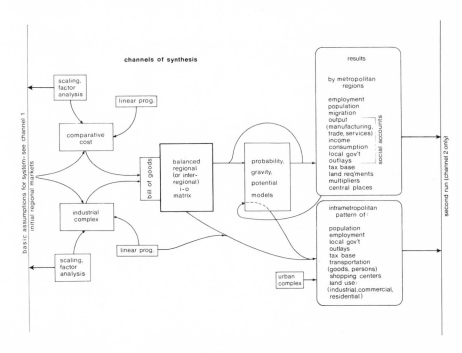

Fig. 208. *Simulation of the total spatial system: Stages II and III. (From Isard 1960, ibid., p. 649; see fig. 207.)*

phenomena within metropolitan regions and their subregions—employment patterns, residential patterns, shopping center patterns—are projected forward. Certain spatial interactions are implicit: journeys to work and shop, certain commodity flows, and so on. Actual and optimal patterns for these flows can be compared, and rearrangement of the spatial systems can be undertaken. In this way, the effect of adjusting one component is accounted for through its effects on all the other components of the spatial system.

In stage IV (figure 209) central emphasis is placed upon cultural values and social goals, so that economic efficiency (the basis of the previous three stages) is just one basic goal among several. From a strictly quantitative point of view this model is non-operational. Isard gives as the reason that "accumulated historical study and political, sociological and other social science theory and empirical investigations offer insufficient understanding of the goal-setting process—that is, how to proceed from values and culture through the decision framework to system and subsystem goals." In Isard's model the specific cultural goals would have to be translated into social accounts worked out by means of a linear programming technique.

In stage V (figure 210) this lack of operationality is overcome by fusing stages I–III and the quantifiable portions of stage IV. Major values and social goals, for example, are inserted into the framework of

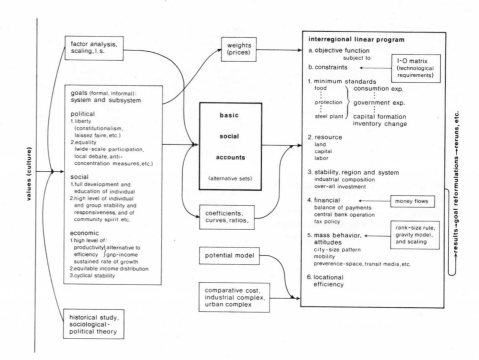

Fig. 209. *Simulation of the total spatial system: Stage IV. (From Isard 1960, ibid., p. 684; see fig. 207.)*

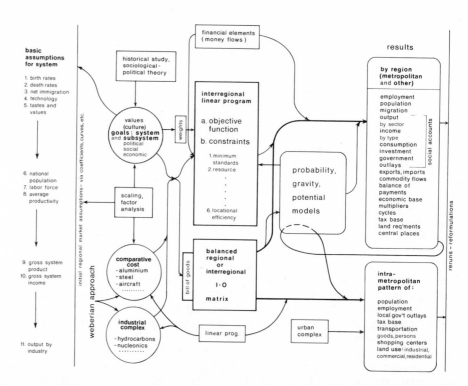

Fig. 210. *Simulation of the total spatial system: Stage V. (From Isard 1960, ibid., p. 720.)*

state I by translating social goals into specific accounts. This is done regardless of whether "the statement of such goals is relatively simple as in an armaments reduction program, or exceedingly complex as in an ideological goal." The accounts are placed in the final demand sectors of the several regions.

Isard summarizes the use of the five stages as representations of the total spatial system in the following words:

Of all stages, stage V is the most advanced, operationally speaking. It achieves the highest level of synthesis of analytical techniques. Thus its fused framework is the most effective in attacking the interrelations which pervade

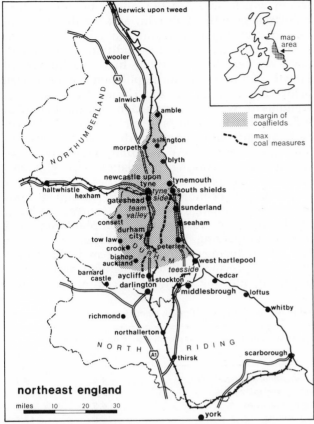

Fig. 211. *Northeast England: a landscape of nineteenth-century development.*

an interregional system and its diverse subsystems. *Of the variants [stage IV] looms as the most promising one, provided the investigator judges that high speed electronic computation capacity and practice will be able to cope with the general interregional linear program involved.*

An Empirical Study

As an example of a regional spatial system that has undergone a phase of expansion and then a phase of declining opportunities, Northeast England will be analyzed in some detail (figure 211). First, however, it is necessary to discuss the nature and origin of depressed areas in general.

All regions of stress tend to share similar characteristics. Among them, almost by definition, is a level of per capita income that falls below some generally accepted standard. A proxy measure, the usual one in the United Kingdom, is the level of unemployment among males.

Typically, depressed regions exhibit resource immobility. For labor this involves the inability or unwillingness of workers to migrate to areas where they may either escape unemployment or earn

higher real wages than they are presently earning. The most promising adjustment for both depressed and underdeveloped regions is for labor to move out. Of course, it also helps if capital moves in. Accordingly, governments attempt to aid depressed areas through increasing their stock of capital. This was the purpose of the Area Development Act of 1961, the Appalachian Regional Development Act, the Public Works and Economic Development Act, and the Public Works and Economic Development Act of 1965.

Other typical characteristics of depressed regions are low rates of labor productivity and a substantial rate of emigration. Frequently, there is also a scarcity of such items of the social infrastructure as housing, roads, and schools. Faced with these problems governments have usually reacted with little regard for the total spatial system or system of regions, or for the reasons underlying regional decline. In many cases, as with the Casa per il Mezzogiorno (Fund for the South) in Southern Italy or British government policies in Scotland and Northeast England, the government has invested heavily in the infrastructure under the assumption that improving it and bringing in new industries will put an end to the backwardness of the region. Events have shown these policies to be unsuccessful. This need not surprise if the situation is viewed in a holistic framework, that is, if one sees the causes rather than the symptoms of regional problems. Solutions lie not just in attracting replacement industries but in correcting the whole national (or international) economic system.

A clue to the existence of depressed areas is to be found in the simultaneous existence of points of rapid regional growth elsewhere within the same country. Thus stagnation in Sicily is matched by the rapid increase of employment and productivity in Milan; the decline of the economy of the Massif Central is equaled by the growth of the Paris metropolitan region; and unemployment in the Highlands and Northeast England coexists with labor scarcity in the London-Birmingham-Manchester complex. These phenomena are closely related; in fact, explicit recognition of regions of growth as well as regions that are depressed is the first step in the understanding of regional problems, whether one uses Myrdal's, Hirschmann's, or Perroux's conceptual frameworks. Such a center-periphery pattern is implied in Gundar Frank's metropolis/satellite hypothesis (see chapter 15) and has been very clear in Caesar's 1964 study of British industrial growth.

It has been pointed out that even if initially there are a number of regions equal in income per capita, chance and temporal processes lead to a situation in which one region is most favorably endowed while the resources of another are used less. The movement of factors of production and goods and services between regions, far from equalizing regional income, tends to increase the relative advantage of some at the expense of others. Thus interregional differences in factor productivity tend to increase over time, unless there are radical changes in the structure of demand or technology.

The British Situation

Britain's growth as a manufacturing nation in the nineteenth century was based on industrial specialization. This involved narrow specialization — roughly speaking, Lancashire for cotton, Yorkshire for wool, Clydeside for ships, and the Northeast for coal and iron. This basic structure served Britain well in the years of expansion. But after 1918, partly because other nations had industrialized and become Britain's rivals, and partly as a result of the so-called economic depression that spread across the world in 1929, the structure weakened. The stagnation and depression of this period affected the older basic industries, particularly the ones that were export oriented, far more severely than the new. Moreover, the newly expanding consumer-durable goods industries were drawn to the new growth areas, where they saw their main markets. Thus a sharp difference grew up between the traditional industrial areas of Central Scotland, South Wales, and Northeast England, all of which suffered major decline and unemployment, and newer areas such as the London-Birmingham axis, where the expansion of modern and technically innovative industries kept unemployment down. Indeed, by 1932 unemployment levels in the older areas were as high as 40 percent, but as low as 10 percent in the London area. The discrepancy would have been greater but for the large and continuous movement of labor from the depressed areas to the growth centers.

It follows that the origin of the depressed areas is in part linked to the existence of growth areas. Therefore any understanding of Northeast England's problem must be based on study of increases in employment and productivity, with the accompanying technological change, in the growth regions and in the world economic system.*

Northeast England

For some fifty years Northeast England has been a depressed region. The area has been described as "the prototype for the coal-mining heavy industrial

*A number of regional economic planning councils exist in Britain under the auspices of the Department of Economic Affairs. Some of their reports are of interest to economic geographers.

region which provided the sinews of 19th century industrial growth in Britain, and for the past half century has been struggling to adapt to fundamentally changed economic conditions." Unemployment has remained relatively high and the rate of growth of the employed population has been well below the average for the United Kingdom. The stimulus of wartime production and the period of inflation that followed only served to mask the underlying difficulties, which did not reappear in force until 1957–58. At that time one-third of the region's total working population was still employed by the older basic industries (table 74). But a period of economic difficulty, coupled with technological change in energy sources, reduced employment in coal mining, shipbuilding, and marine engineering. By 1963 the Northeast Coalfield had 124 producing coalmines, compared with the 174 five years previously. The consequent drop in employment, affecting nearly 11 percent of the region's

Table 74. *N.E. England: Employment Data and Industrial Sectors*

(a) % distribution of insured population in basic industries

	1948	1957
shipbuilding and repairing	4.6	4.4
mining and quarrying	15.5	14.8
metal industries	4.3	4.5
engineering	10.6	11.1
chemical and allied industries	3.0	3.9
total basic industries	38.0	38.7

(b) regional unemployment and U.K. index of industrial production

	unemployment N.E.	unemployment G.B.	excess N.E. over G.B.	U.K. index of industrial production
1946	5.2	2.4	2.8	
1947	4.0	2.2	1.8	
1948	3.1	1.8	1.3	100.0
1949	2.8	1.5	1.3	105.9
1950	3.1	1.4	1.6	111.7
1951	2.4	1.2	1.2	115.6
1952	2.8	2.0	0.8	113.0
1953	2.6	1.6	1.0	119.3
1954	2.5	1.3	1.2	126.6
1955	1.9	1.1	0.8	133.2
1956	1.7	1.2	0.5	133.8
1957	1.8	1.5	0.3	136.0
1958	2.6	2.1	0.5	—
1959	3.6	2.2	1.4	141.2
1960	3.0	1.6	1.4	148.5
1961	2.6	1.5	1.1	149.9
1962	3.7	2.0	1.7	151.0

Source: W.R. Snaith, "The Future Development of the Northeast: The Economic Background," Town and Country Planning Association: Regional Conference, Newcastle, 3 April 1963, pp. 3, 4.

Table 75. *Analysis of Insured Employees in Five Basic Industrial Groups (1959–1961)*

	1959 thousands	1959 %	1961 thousands	1961 %	total change 1959–1961 thousands	total change 1959–1961 %
mining and quarrying	160.0	14.5	143.0	12.9	–17.0	
shipbuilding and marine engineering	64.1	5.8	55.6	5.0	– 8.5	–25.5
metal manufacture	51.1	4.7	57.4	5.1	+ 6.3	
engineering and electrical goods	94.0	8.4	101.0	9.1	+ 7.0	
chemicals	50.5	4.6	52.0	4.7	+ 1.5	+14.8
total	419.7	38.0	409.0	36.8		–10.7

Source: W.R. Snaith, "The Future Development of the Northeast: The Economic Background," Town and Country Planning Association: Regional Conference, Newcastle, 3 April 1963, p. 6.

working force, was from 161,470 to 125,530. This decline particularly hit the western part of the coalfield (figure 211), where thin, broken coal seams, high costs of extraction, and difficulty of mechanization, led to coal being produced at an average loss of about $2 per ton. This decline continued to occur, and by 1970 only some 70,000 employees worked in the coalfield, a decline of over 45 percent from the 1963 figure.

Shipbuilding and the marine engineering industry have also suffered decline (table 75). Both industries were affected by the depression of shipping freight rates after 1958, and by increased foreign competition. Since 1950, the latter has reduced the United Kingdom from first to sixth position among the world's exporters of ships. In employment terms there was a fall from 47,000 workers in shipbuilding and repairing in 1957 to 37,000 in 1963. The concurrent decline in marine engineering was from 18,170 to 11,180 workers. Even as late as 1957 the region produced about 46 percent of total U.K. shipbuilding output. Improvements in technology, and increased efficiency to meet foreign competition, have had the effect of reducing employment in the industry still further.

Between 1948 and 1958 there had been little change in the total workers attached to the five basic industrial groups. The declining importance of shipbuilding and coal mining had been offset by the expansion of chemicals, metal manufacture, engineering, and electrical goods. Until 1957 it was possible to argue that diversification of industry in the region was being brought about by the changing relative importance of the five industries within the basic group. But by 1962 it was no longer possible to accept this optimistic argument. The decline of mining and shipbuilding from 1958 onwards was too large and too rapid for the other basic heavy industries to make good the loss. It seems clear that further development of the service industries and of the expanding lighter manufacturing industries will be required if the Northeast is to provide sufficient job opportunities for its working population.

The importance of the basic industries in the industrial structure of Northeast England makes the region sensitive to the multiplier effects of cyclical downturns in the national economy. It is particularly sensitive to variations in the level of fixed capital investment. In the years up to 1957 the United Kingdom as a whole enjoyed a high degree of prosperity, with rising levels of demand and output. The decline of regional unemployment from the end of the war until 1957 was a reflection of the rising level of industrial production, which stimulated demand for the capital goods in which the Northeast specialized. As is shown in table 74, this sustained rise in industrial production came to an end in 1955. But the backlog of orders, built up in the boom period, was sufficient to maintain full employment in the Northeast until 1957.

Yet another aspect of the postwar period of falling unemployment was the increasing importance of the manufacturing sector of the regional economy. Expansion took place in chemicals, electrical goods, electrical machinery, textiles, clothing, and the food, drink, and tobacco group. This was not, however, at the expense of the older traditional industries. Rather, it coincided with a relative decline in agriculture and the service industries. Insofar as the aim of regional development policy was to provide an alternative to heavy basic industry by building up the light consumer goods industries, this aim was not achieved. Until 1957 heavy industry maintained its importance, while the development of light industry brought about the relative decline of agriculture and the service industries. What was happening was that the Northeast was becoming more dependent upon manufacturing industry, and therefore more exposed to the multiplier effects of cyclical variations in the level of demand.

Early Prosperity

The relative prosperity of the Northeast in the postwar years up to 1957 depended upon certain advantageous circumstances.

1. *The prolonged postwar boom and rising level of industrial production in the United Kingdom as a whole had stimulated demand for the heavy capital goods in which the region specialized.*
2. *The shortage of coal had concentrated the attention of the state-controlled National Coal Board upon production as such rather than upon production of coal in the most economic pits and areas.*
3. *There was a high postwar demand for new ships which was artificially stimulated and prolonged as an aftermath of the Anglo-French Suez escapade.*

These rather artificial conditions of the earlier postwar period successfully disguised the weaknesses of the area and delayed any adjustments in its industrial structure. Thus the reversal of these advantageous circumstances after 1957 was bound to inflict a severe strain upon the economy of the region. An industrial redistribution of the working population was essential if the Northeast was to regain its prosperity. But, as noted earlier, this did not occur.

Employment Ratios

An analysis of the working population in the districts suffering from heavy unemployment shows a close relationship between industrial structure and employment (tables 76 and 77). In nearly all districts of high unemployment a large proportion of this population is attached to the mining and shipbuilding industries, and in most of these areas the service industries are poorly represented. The exceptional area is Tees-side, which still suffers from heavy unemployment in spite of the fact that mining and shipbuilding have played a relatively small part in its industrial structure. More important to Tees-side are the iron, steel, and chemical industries, which in 1959 employed about one-third of the total working population. Throughout the postwar years Tees-side has been the one growth point of the regional economy; for instance, it was the first to recover from the recession of 1959. A large part of the unemployment in Tees-side in the winter of 1962–63 was of a cyclical nature. With the resumption of capital investment and national economic expansion, it disappeared. At the same time, it is as well to point out that both chemicals and iron and steel are capital-intensive industries in which technical innovation is already making it possible to increase output without a proportionate increase in labor.

Table 76. *Unemployment in Certain Districts of N.E. England (November, 1962)*

	male	female	total	
The Hartlepools	12.0	5.0	9.6	
Wearside	9.3	4.1	7.5	high
South Tyne East				unemployment
(Jarrow area)	7.7	5.3	7.0	districts
S.W. Durham	7.6	4.6	6.8	
Tees-side	6.7	4.7	6.1	
North Tyne West				
(Newcastle)	4.5	3.0	3.9	low
Darlington	3.8	2.6	3.4	unemployment
Rural Northumberland	3.6	2.4	3.2	districts
total N.E. region	5.8	3.7	5.2	

Source: W.R. Snaith, "The Future Development of the Northeast: The Economic Background," Town and Country Planning Association: Regional Conference, Newcastle, 3 April 1963, p. 8.

Among the areas of low unemployment Newcastle, the regional center, had a high proportion of its working population attached to the service industries. Coal mining and shipbuilding are more important in the areas to the east of the city, where unemployment is correspondingly high. Darlington is perhaps the least typical area of the region because it has the most diversified industrial structure. It has, however, a significant proportion of its labor force attached to the vehicles group, nearly all of whom were at that time employed in the railway locomotive shops. The planned contraction of the British Railways workshops was fortunately offset by the new location, through American investment, of a large truck assembly plant.

Migration

Detailed information on the migration of workers from the Northeast is not available. However, estimates based upon the exchange of national insurance (i.e., social security) cards between districts suggest that in the decade 1951–61 total net outward migration of insured workers was 59,000 of which 39,000 were men. Outward migration increased toward the end of the decade: from 1959 through 1961 it totaled 40,000, of which 26,000 were men. Migration on this scale reduced the male insured population of the region by about 5,000 per annum, and was particularly concentrated in the areas of mining and heavy industry.

Both migration and the slow growth of the regional economy are direct reflections of the Northeast's industrial and social structure. Of the twenty-four industrial groups in the British standard industrial classification, six groups were responsible for 80 percent of the total increase in employment in Great

Table 77. *Percentage of Insured Workers Attached to Certain Industries and Percentage Male Unemployment (November, 1962)*

	shipbuilding and engineering	coal mining	iron and steel	service industries	male unemployment
The Hartlepools	13.4	—	9.1	53.7	12.0%
S.W. Durham	—	30.4	2.1	34.5	7.6
S.E. Tyneside	15.1	9.8	2.0	42.9	7.7
Wearside	13.7	15.8	1.3	45.2	9.3
Tees-side	3.8	0.9	16.5	41.3	6.7
Newcastle Area	4.7	5.0	1.0	62.7	4.5
Darlington	—	0.4	5.7	52.3	3.4

Source: Snaith, 1963, p. 9.

Table 78. *Percentage of Insured Workers Attached to Growth Industries and Regional Share of Growth Industries*

	N.E. total employees	% N.E.	G.B. total employees	% G.B.	N.E. as % of total in G.B.	
vehicles	13,820	1.2	894,370	4.0	1.5	
engineering and electrical goods	100,992	8.6	2,133,060	9.5	4.7	N.E.
paper printing and publishing	13,065	1.1	615, 620	2.7	2.1	England has 5.6%
professional and scientific services	93,856	8.0	2,059,680	9.2	4.6	of total
banking finance and insurance	15,367	1.3	560,000	2.5	2.7	population of G.B.
distributive trades	146,122	12.5	2,829,340	12.6	5.2	
total %		32.7		40.5	4.2	

Source: W.R. Snaith, "The Future Development of the Northeast: The Economic Background," Town and Country Planning Association: Regional Conference, Newcastle, 3 April 1963, p. 10.

Britain during the last decade. The Northeast is poorly represented in all the industries belonging to this growing sector of the national economy. With the exception of the distributive trades, the Northeast has a smaller proportion of its working population attached to these growth industries than is the average for Great Britain as a whole (table 78). Even within the engineering and electrical goods group the region tends to specialize in sections that have shown less than average growth in the last decade. Three of the growth industries at the national level, particularly banking and finance, are heavily concentrated in the London area. In none of the six groups does the Northeast have a share proportionate to its regional share of the total working population. This does not indicate the unsuitability of the region for growth industries. A comparison of the top industries in terms of employment growth shows that their rate of expansion in the Northeast in the last decade has been slightly greater than the national average. The main reason for the slow growth of the employed population in the region has been its underrepresentation in growth industries and its overrepresentation in declining industries.

The relative lack of choice in employment and the relatively unattractive and unsatisfactory social environment have contributed to the flow of out-migrants. The cultural landscape created in the late nineteenth and early twentieth centuries consists of poorly sited settlements, with (for the most part) low quality row housing overlooked by factories, coal mines and waste tips, and a minimally developed social infrastructure. Little was invested in this infrastructure in the depression years of the 1920s and 1930s, and since 1945 only short-term, piecemeal, and spasmodic investment has occurred. Frequently in the post-1945 period investment was channeled only into spot points of high unemployment. Industries were also pressured by various governmental and institutional means into locating into such areas during these periods. But high unemployment here was usually coincidental with minimal industrial development at the interregional level. The climate of economic uncertainty in Britain, the minimal investment in social capital, and a general lack of confidence in the Northeast really deterred entrepreneurs from relocating or investing in such an area.

Possible Solutions

A successful employment policy for the Northeast would seem to require:

1. *A reduction of present male unemployment to the national level.*
2. *An increase in job opportunities to make good the expected decline in shipbuilding, coal mining, and the railroads.*
3. *A reduction by at least half in the present rate of male migration.*
4. *An increase in job opportunities to allow for the natural increase of men of working age within the region.*

Part of the expansion of employment could come through a partial revival of the traditional products such as iron and steel, and shipbuilding. The main emphasis, however, would have to be on the industries with the greatest growth potential—chemicals, engineering, and electrical goods. Unfortunately, these industries are not of the type that increases its demand for labor in proportion to increasing output. Most future growth, therefore, will probably mean increased production with little or no increase in the labor force. As **capital intensive** industries they are unlikely to expand their labor requirements sufficiently to make good the loss of job opportunities in the highly **labor intensive** mining and shipbuilding industries.

Efforts have been made by the central government to attract a more diversified industrial sector. Since 1938 the light manufacturing industries have doubled the number of their employees, and they now represent about 16 percent of the working force. A significant contribution has been made by the Trading Estates (planned industrial areas) which by 1962 employed about 65,000 people. Under the Distribution of Industry Act of 1945–60, most of the Northeast was scheduled as a development area. Within this area various forms of government assistance could be made available, including the provision of rentable government-financed factories, mostly organized into industrial estates or parks.

As it is, new industry has been guided to the subregions with the highest unemployment rates, irrespective of their potential for long-term growth or decline. At first nearly all districts fell within this category and a wide scattering of industrial estates and sites resulted. However, as growth began and unemployment fell, new industries were guided to

the "most deserving areas" without reference to each area's total economic spatial makeup. Thus the "most deserving areas" did not include the three growth poles—Darlington, Tees-side, and Newcastle. A disproportionately large share of the more vital industries were directed to locate in remote and industrially less attractive areas, where the highest rent subsidies were paid. Thus successive British governments of the time tended to treat the development problem as small-unit social welfare rather than as a problem of total social welfare and spatial organization. Since 1945 more than 200 firms, the largest number belonging to the engineering and electrical goods group, have moved by this method into the Northeast. Other important contributions have come from chemicals, textiles, and the food, drink, and tobacco group. Altogether the new entrants are representative of fourteen different industrial groups. There seems to be ample evidence that a wide range of light manufacturing industry can succeed in the Northeast.

The long-term interest of the region could not be saved by seeking industrial diversification for its own sake. A narrowly based policy of taking work to the pockets of unemployment that arise here and there was discontinued temporarily in 1963 on publication of Lord Hailsham's report on the Northeast. The new policy recognized that West Durham was unsuitable for most types of male-employing manufacturing industry, and that the only solution was an out-migration of excess workers from the subregions to the lower cost areas of the Northeast. The report therefore proposed a growth zone in which the greatest investment would occur. It was hoped that such investment in the coastal mining-industrial-urban tract (figure 211) would trickle over to benefit the western part of the region. Efforts to promote regional development were to be concentrated on the central and eastern parts of the region, with special emphasis on the three growth poles mentioned above. A larger volume of public service investment was to be concentrated into the growth zone between Tyneside, Tees-side, route A-1, and the coast. However, there was still an inbuilt bias in these policies toward the encouragement of labor intensive industries, irrespective of any long-term growth potential, although the most spectacular growth rates among manufacturing industries have come from those with a high ratio of capital to labor.

The other implicit feature of this policy has been to erect a "balanced structure of industry" by introducing a wide range of new industries, the belief being that such diversity bolsters an area against too high unemployment in times of cyclical depression. However, the Hailsham report did indicate some weakening of this assumption, and there seemed to be an effort to build up the region's electrical goods and motor vehicles industries. With the change of political party in 1964, this idea of a growth zone was replaced by a policy of selected growth poles consisting of Tyneside, Wearside, Tees-side, and Darlington, together with a number of selected nodes outside these large urban centers. The general idea was to spread the benefits of development more widely. Regional Economic Councils were founded in order to "assist in the formulation of a regional plan, having regard to the best use of the region's resources; to advise on the steps necessary for implementing the regional plan on the basis of information and assessments provided by [the national government] . . . and to advise on the regional implications of national economic policies." One such regional plan, *Strategy for the North*, was produced by the Northern Economic Planning Committee, outlining the rather meagre future of the area. As House remarks, ". . . not for the first time in its long economic history the industrial North East finds itself poised at a critical stage in its progress."

This is only a brief sketch of a complex problem; for instance, no mention is made of upgrading the infrastructure, or of housing the migrants from the western zone in the growth zone. But it does illustrate some of the attitudes that can be taken toward regional development. In summary, the following general conclusions seem worth drawing:

1. *The origin of depressed regions seems to be linked to the origin of growth regions: the two cannot be satisfactorily explained apart from each other. We cannot properly understand the problems of Northeast England or Scotland without understanding the causes of the increase in employment, productivity, and technological change in the "growth" region of London-Birmingham. Similarly, the problems of the U.S. South or the Appalachians cannot be considered apart from the growth in such areas as California or New York.*

2. *Consequently, no policy to improve conditions in the distressed regions can succeed without simultaneously affecting conditions in the growth regions. Specifically, a policy to increase productivity and employment in the North of England will adversely affect the rate of growth both in London-Birmingham, and in the nation as a whole. In other words, growth must be envisioned as part of a total socioeconomic spatial system. Some British researchers were wrong in suggesting that measures to increase employment would at the same time increase the income of the United Kingdom as a whole. On the contrary, quite often the same amounts of capital and labor would have added more to national income if they had been employed in the South.*

3. *The bonanza days of the mid-nineteenth century, when population growth and economic development rates were prodigious, have left their mark in the twentieth-century landscape. The tremendous rate of physical development then, and the narrow economic base which gave birth to those boom conditions, now pose very substantial problems in terms of the social infrastructure and the economic base. Emphasis today on growth industries, with no reference to their capital and labor intensity, may well achieve the appropriate multiplier effects, but, as the history of the Northeast continues to show, at the expense of substantial out-migration. The one factor of continuing importance has been the role of the central government's trading estate, which has provided a more diversified employment base and has received worldwide acclaim as an outstanding success in industrial planning.*

4. *The magnitude of the effort required, in monetary terms, to arrest the trend of decline in the depressed regions is far greater than is commonly supposed, and certainly exceeds that envisaged in the regional policies, past and present, of the British government or any of the nation's central planning agencies.*

Conclusion

The total spatial system is an extremely complex landscape pattern. As we have seen, it cannot be satisfactorily represented either by simple models or by simple symbolic representations on the order of $H \pm A(R \cdot S) = 0$. The real world is very complex and the patterns that occur in, say, Northeast England, can be only partly represented even by landscape simulations as complex as Isard's stage IV and V models. However, these analyses, and the concept of a system or mosaic of overlapping economic regions, can shed light on the spatial arrangements that shape production, exchange, and consumption —in short, economic behavior. Such concepts and analyses are of help to the geographer or economist in disentangling current events, and to the entrepreneur in deciding where to locate a factory, warehouse, or retailing outlet. They are also of help to city planners and national governments facing decisions of how to best make use of the available resources, both physical and cultural.

A major feature of growth is the increasing division and specialization of labor, a process that leads in turn to spatial specializations—the specialization of areas. The latter kind of specialization is at the root of many of the formal and functional regions that arise with advancing growth and development. Such specialization could not take place without the growing flows of ideas, goods, money, and people between areas. The spatial effects from the regional point of view include:

1. *The formation of interlocking formal and functional regions, which interact ever more broadly as growth takes place.*

2. *The tendency for economic regions to agglomerate, as when farming separates out from urban-based industries*

into farming regions, and for secondary and tertiary industries to come together in an urban hierarchy.

3. *The emergence of regions within the larger urban areas — central areas, regional shopping centers, and so forth.*

All the regions of an economic spatial system are subject to the pervading influence of the national direction of that economy, whether planned or laissez-faire. At the same time the regions are characterized by a great variety in their physical features, accessibility, existing plant and equipment, population density, industrial structure, and economic history. Given their special requirements, industrialists and other decision makers making locational choices will inevitably find certain regions more attractive than others. But these requirements change over time. Shifts of activities are an integral part of a dynamic economy, in which some regions will come to play the growth role while others play a relatively lesser role. This is implicit in the increasing specialization within the economic system.

Economic growth, then, is spatially differentiated, since modern economic development begins at only a few points and then spreads outward. In looking at the spatial structure of economic development, that is, at the total spatial system, we must consider both *physical* and *activity* patterns. Physical patterns are the spatial arrangements of settlement, production points and facilities, transportation networks, land uses, and so forth. Activity patterns, another aspect of the same reality, are the flows of capital, labor, money, and ideas that link those physical points over space. The links and flows between the physical patterns stimulate regional economic development. As we saw in earlier chapters, it is accessibility that allows urban areas to concentrate and expand. But once the criterion of accessibility has been met, and activities disperse, flow patterns also become dispersed, carrying with them the stimulus to economic growth.

The spatial structure of an economy comes into being from the interaction of physical and activity patterns, constrained by the technological levels of the society in question, and revealed in patterns of growth areas, functional urban hierarchies, and metropolitan regions. As the technical skills, cultural attributes, and economic organization of the society all change, so also do the spatial structure and pattern of activities, though historical relics may still remain as pointers to earlier technological levels.

Summary

1. *This chapter deals with the problem of reaggregating all the economic activity subsystems into a total spatial system.*

2. *Such a reaggregation is very complex. One simplistic way is to use a primitive model to represent supply and demand, human motives and attitudes, resources and resistences, and the overt result of this interaction in the landscape (the occurrence). When we relate many occurrences in a spatial setting to varying degrees of specialization and complexity, a rough approximation to economic landscapes at varying levels of "development" is achieved.*

3. *Such variations in degree and type of interrelationships among the landscape-forming variables appear finally as a system or mosaic of regions. The term* region *is not used in the sense of a discrete, isolated unit, but rather as an area in the economic landscape which is interdependent internally and externally, though the force and orientation of internal linkages serve to distinguish it from neighboring regions or subsystems.*

4. *At least five types of economic region are identified — small economic regions, the market area or hinterland of such primary units as a small town or a small group of primary or secondary activities; the* city region, *the hinterland of a city or metropolis with important message flows between the core and surrounding area, as well as links through economic bonds;* natural resource regions, *distinguished by their functional orientation to a single or few resources, like the T.V.A.;* institutional regions, *chosen by many governments and institutions to aid administration, improve economic flows, and/or encourage population movements, like the European Common Market; and the* economic development region, *which arises in part from the previous category and includes the concept of the distressed, marginal, or "underdeveloped" area.*

5. *A number of analytical methods exist to help break down and examine the component elements of a regional system, such as transportation studies, regional and interregional multiplier analysis, and linear programming. These techniques have been introduced in part in earlier chapters, and it is interesting to see how they can be used in studying the total spatial system.*

6. *Regions are not static; they change both positively and negatively. Very few groups, if they perceive the resources and are aware of the social and economic investment in an area, are content to let it simply fade away; others work actively to maintain a region's growth pattern.*

7. *A number of models and concepts exist which try to explain or increase our understanding of regional development. Myrdal, for example, visualizes a process of* cumulative causation *whereby initial advantages accruing to a region are compounded by a multiplier effect; Hirschmann identifies backward and*

forward linkages *that must be present to ensure de-velopment; Perloff identifies a necessary* export base *or group of export oriented, regional industries; finally, a French economist, F. Perroux, has put forward the idea of a* growth pole, *which has subsequently been developed by a number of regional planners. The basic notion in this latter concept is that a group of growth industries can attract to them considerable subsequent development.*

8. For a region to take such advantages, it may be faced with deciding between alternative resources and several courses of action. To help in this choice, benefit-cost analysis may be invoked, which places economic values on alternative criteria. This tool is not infallible, however, since many criteria, par-ticularly cultural ones, are not measurable in eco-nomic terms alone.

9. There are two ways of aggregating the components identified in this chapter—first, to use a model like Isard's five-stage synthesis which attempts to bring together both historical-behavioral and the analytical-quantifier approaches to the regional sub-system; secondly, to examine an empirical study of one region, such as Northeast England, in order to appre-ciate both the intra- and interregional linkages of such a subsystem.

Further Reading

One world view of the spatial distribution of varying regional economic landscapes is

Ginsburg, N., ed. *Atlas of Economic Development* (Chi-cago: University of Chicago Press, 1961).

The economic situations that lead to the development of regional disparities and inequalities in the Western world are summarized in

Balassa, B. *The Theory of Economic Integration* (Homewood: Irwin, 1961).

Beckmann, M. *Location Theory* (New York: Random House, 1968).

Bos, H. C. *Spatial Dispersion of Economic Activity* (Rotter-dam: Rotterdam University Press, 1965).

Friedmann, J. *Regional Development Policy* (Cambridge, Mass.: M.I.T. Press, 1966).

Friedmann, J. and Alonso, W. *Regional Development and Planning: A Reader* (Cambridge, Mass.: M.I.T. Press, 1964). Contains important essays on "space and planning," "location and spatial organization," "theories of regional development," and "national policy for regional development" by Lösch, Berry, Perroux, Friedmann, Hoover, Chinitz, Hirschmann, etc.

Hirschmann, A. O. *The Strategy of Economic Development* (New Haven: Yale University Press, 1958).

Hoover, E. M. *Location of Economic Activity* (New York: McGraw-Hill, 1948), chapters 9–11.

Isard, W. *Methods of Regional Analysis* (New York: M.I.T. Press/Wiley, 1960).

Myrdal, G. *Economic Theory and Underdeveloped regions*, (London: Methuen, 1957).

Needleman, ed. *Regional Analysis* (Baltimore: Penguin Books, 1968).

Nourse, H. O. *Regional Economics* (New York: McGraw-Hill, 1968).

Ontario Department of Economics and Development, International Conference on Regional Development and Economic Change, *Proceedings*, February 15–17, 1965, Toronto.

Oules, F. *Economic Planning and Democracy* (Harmonds-worth: Penguin, 1966).

Perloff, H. S. et al. *Regions, Resources and Economic Growth* (Baltimore: Johns Hopkins Press, 1960).

Some journal articles which look to the abstract notions of economic regions, as well as give some empirical under-pinnings, are

Beckmann, M. and Marschak, T. "An Activity Analysis Approach to Location Theory," *Kyklos*, 8, 1955, pp. 125–143.

Chinitz, B. "Contrasts in Agglomeration: New York and Pittsburgh," *American Economic Review*, 51, 1961, pp. 279–289.

Curry, L. "Landscape as System," *Geographical Review*, vol. 54, 1964, pp. 121–124.

Guthrie, J. A. "Economies of Scale and Regional De-velopment," *Papers and Proceedings*, Regional Science Association, vol. 1, 1954, pp. J–1 to J–10.

Hirsch, W. Z. "Interindustry Relations of a Metropolitan Area," *Review of Economics and Statistics*, vol. 41, 1959, pp. 365–73.

Isard, W. "Regional Science, the Concept of Region, and Regional Structure," *Papers and Proceedings*, Regional Science Association, vol. 2, 1956, pp. 13–26.

Keeble, D. E. "Models of Economic Development," in R. J. Chorley and P. Haggett. *Models in Geography* (Lon-don: Methuen, 1967), pp. 243–302.

Olsen, E. "Regional Economic Differences," *Papers and Proceedings*, Regional Science Association, vol. 20, 1968, pp. 7–18.

Thomas, M. D. "Regional Economic Growth," *Land Eco-nomics*, vol. 45, 1969, pp. 43–51.

Ullman, E. L. "Regional Development and the Geography of Concentration," *Papers and Proceedings*, Regional Science Association, vol. 4, 1958, pp. 179–198.

Von Boventer, E. "Spatial Organization Theory as a Basis for Regional Planning," *Journal of the American Institute*

Regional planning policies and forecasting are noted in —

Bondeville, J. R. *Problems of Regional Economic Planning* (Chicago: Aldine, 1966).

Chisholm, M., Frey, A. E. and Haggett, P., eds. *Regional Forecasting* (London: Butterworths, 1971).

Denton, G., Forsyth, M. and MacLennan, M. *Economic Planning and Policies in Britain, France, and Germany* (London: Allen and Unwin, 1968).

McCrone, G. *Regional Policy in Britain* (London: Allen and Unwin, 1969).

Tunnard, C. and Pushkarev, B. *Man-Made America: Chaos or Control?* (New Haven: Yale University Press, 1963).

Ways and means of measuring economically depressed areas, and some suggested solutions are covered in

Wood, W. S. and Thoman, R. S., eds. *Areas of Economic Stress in Canada* (Kingston, Ontario: Queens University, 1965).

fifteen

Malfunctions of
the System

A glance at the socioeconomic landscape just outside the lecture hall or seminar room reveals that reality does not often coincide with the optimality of some of the earlier chapters. The sensory deprivation tanks we call universities are of course a safe haven for teaching the myths and models of economic geography. Carefully segregated from reality, even when our university is situated right in the community, and wrapping ourselves in the threadbare flag "value neutrality," we can map land use, transportation networks, manufacturing linkages, and even the distribution of incomes, without relating anything we observe to socioeconomic reality.

This chapter is intended to counter these shortcomings. It therefore describes some of the disparities that occur in the geographic landscape. In the terms of our systems approach, such disparities could be labeled "malfunctions," since they are deviations from what ideally many of us would like the world economic system to be like. Among the topics to be considered here are "underdevelopment," population growth, other environmental issues, poverty, and the rise of the corporate state. The list could have been greatly extended.

The "Underdeveloped" World

There has been considerable neglect by economic geographers of the disparities in world spatial structure that have arisen through such factors as enforced colonial economic patterns, imperialism, artificial political boundaries, nationalism, and variations in ideology. In fact, geographers have paid little attention to problems of political or economic development—or, as it is more usually expressed, to the problem of underdevelopment. This neglect has been explained in terms of the scale of problems considered by different social scientists: geographers, it is argued, have been overly concerned with unique landscapes and regions, and have also fallen victim to the imprecision and general misuse of the concepts involved. Such excuses seem surprising when one considers that even by the most conservative definitions over 2 billion people live in areas variously designated as "lesser developed," "developing," or "Third World" (from the French *Tiers Monde*).

Definitions

Geographers so far have been only marginally concerned with the problem of development, despite its urgency. Lack of agreement on a definition of development and inability to decide how best to facilitate change have both compounded this neglect. Among the reasons for this are the multidimensional causes and symptoms of so-called underdevelopment, as a result of which the presence or absence of any one factor is neither a barrier creating lesser development nor a precondition of greater development.

One or two geographers, especially B. J. L. Berry, have tried to objictify the concept of development. Berry submitted forty-three economic and social indices of development from ninety-five countries to factor analysis. In particular, he was able to isolate two important indices from the forty-three originally used. The first one was a **technological index,** a measure of transportation, trade, energy consump-

tion and production, national product, and so forth, that accounted for some 84 percent of the variation in factor analysis. "The highest ranking countries are, of course, those which trade extensively and have many international contacts and well-developed internal systems of communications, including dense and intensively used transport networks. They produce and consume much energy, have high national products, are highly urbanized, and are well provided with such facilities as medical service." The second one was the **demographic index,** which accounted for 26.3 percent of the variance; this represented population density, rates of birth, death, and population growth, infant mortality rates, population densities of cultivated areas, and so on. The highest ranking countries were those with the highest scores on these measures.

From these results, and because the figures were distributed along a continuum (figures 212, 213, and 214), Berry concluded that

"an underdeveloped country apparently is not a member of some discrete group with very special characteristics. It is simply a nation which tends to lie low on various scales relative to other nations. For this reason we should probably think of less developed rather than underdeveloped countries. More specifically, lesser development is represented by low rank on a technological scale and high rank on a demographic scale. These factors, together with a third factor which isolates a group of poor, trading countries located around the Caribbean, comprise the extremely simple fundamental structure underlying an original 43 proposed indices to underdevelopment."

Superficially, this approach might seem to be helpful. But notice that it imposes on all countries Berry's own notion of greater development—consuming more energy, high GNP, high rates of environmental spoilage, and so forth. This would seem to be highly suspect. Berry also omits social conditions and past history (notably, colonial impositions), while saying nothing about how change should be brought about, although he conveys the implicit inference that we should control birth rates, increase industrialization, and jack up GNP. As will be noted below, these are highly questionable suppositions. For example, it is not clear at present whether there are too many people in the world. This will not be clear until the waste of resources and the insane living conditions of the United States and the Soviet Union are altered. It has been estimated that the world in the long term could support only 500 million people living at the North American standard of living. But why should we accept that as a yardstick of development, as Berry apparently does? Exploitative economic systems that lay waste the environment must be curtailed before we can announce that the North American pattern of living is the pinnacle of "development." Thus curtailment of population in the United States would not automatically stop the forests of the Pacific Northwest from being depleted for the remainder of North American society's Kleenex and toilet paper.

Similarly, in a so-called underdeveloped country such as India food shortages are not simply a symptom of overcrowding, but rather a function of ownership factors such as land monopolies and large land owners who utilize the agricultural subsystem in an inefficient way, and in some cases not at all. These same landowners are also frequently the merchants who find it more profitable to deal in imported North American grain than in Indian grain. Add to these factors poor storage conditions, which lead to dampness, rot, and rats, and the result is a set of malfunctions that go much deeper than Berry's simplistic indices. It may be that, when we have corrected those malfunctioning components and substituted an economic system that is oriented toward widespread human needs rather than the accumulation of material goods by a few, that we may then decide population levels are "too high" in India and countries like it. But this economic ethnocentrism has been questioned by a number of social scientists. Thus Katheleen Gough, an anthropologist, notes that whenever she uses the term "underdevelopment" she is referring to "societies which have until recently had particular features of their economic structure produced as a result of several decades of overt or covert domination by Western industrialist capitalist nations." Underdevelopment, she implies, is not "innate"; so far from being the natural state of any nation, it is the result of certain economic conditions imposed from without. In other words, "underdevelopment" de-

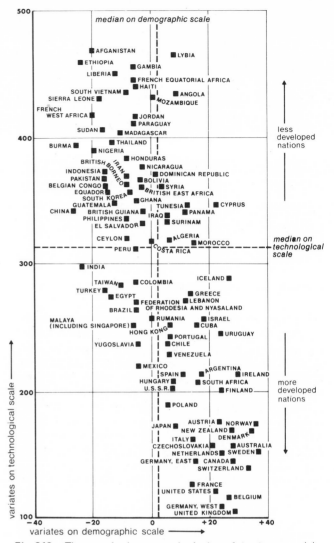

Fig. 212. *The quantitative geographer's view of development: (a) a scale of economic-demographic development. (From N. Ginsburg, ed., "Geography and Economic Development," Research Paper no. 62, 1960, p. 91, reprinted by permission of the University of Chicago, Department of Geography, and B.J.L. Berry.)*

velops—and develops by standards that we in the West impose on those areas. Thus our economic-cultural bias as to what development is warps our view of so-called underdeveloped nations and "commonly produces distortions of both theory and fact."

J. E. Spencer, a geographer, makes the same point when he demands to know whether

all "underdevelopedness" as defined in Occidental terms, [is] bad for the residents of the region in question, or is it so for the residents of the developed region at some far distance? Why is it so for the residents of the developed region at some far distance? Why is it so urgent that the dense jungle of some distant rival region be reduced to a "developed" state of deforestation? . . . For whom is the substitution of factories in the forest essentially good? These and other

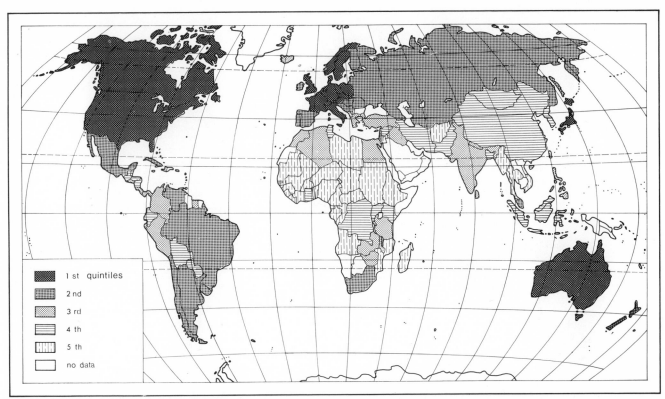

Fig. 213. *The quantitative geographer's view of development: (b) quintile groupings on the technological scale. (From Ginsburg 1960, ibid., p. 86.)*

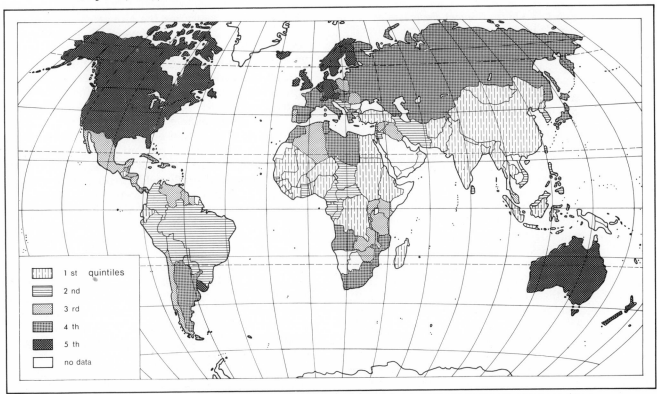

Fig. 214. *The quantitative geographer's view of development: (c) quintile groupings on the demographic scale. (From Ginsburg 1960, ibid., p. 87.)*

The "Underdeveloped" World **349**

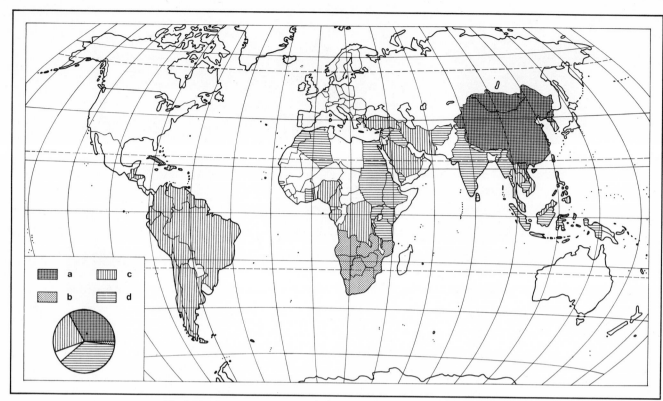

Fig. 215. *An economic-ideologic view of development. (Based on Gough 1968.)*

*questions remain unspoken in the frequent discussions of
"underdevelopedness," which so often stress high Occidental
status and the need for development, by the Occidental
World, of these parts of the world once so far away from our
doors. Too often these discussions [make] . . . the assumption
that everything the Occident has and is is essentially what
other parts of the world must be. . . . There are some who
feel that the current Occidental worry over "underdeveloped"
areas is compounded out of a desire for a new mechanism
for economic exploitation of the old colonial world, and out
of fear that the Occident is in danger so long as
"underdeveloped" areas remain—they may become
Communist.*

In other words, just because an area does not
possess certain economic factors, or does not carry
on certain economic functions that we in the West
see in our own socioeconomic landscapes, it does
not follow that other area is "underdeveloped." "The
populations and cultures of New Guinea and Tibet
are not those of the United States, and a comparison
of the United States and either of the two far regions,
on current American economic criteria of 'devel-
opedness' is initially invalid." Thus the "developed-
ness" of a particular area is a function of the economic organization and culture held by the people
of that area (i.e., is an integral part of that particular
socioeconomic system), and can be measured only
in terms appropriate to that culture.

Figure 215 summarizes the Gough view of development. Some 2,300 million people live in the area
defined by her as "underdeveloped." One-third, or
773 million, live in *category a* areas that have passed
through revolution and out of the sphere of Western
imperialism since 1945; these are China, Mongolia,
North Korea, North Vietnam, and Cuba. The remaining 1,579 million people are in non-Western nations
with capitalist or mixed economies. Of these, some
49 million, or about 2 percent, are in *category b*,
representing colonial nations such as Angola, parts
of South African illegally held territory, and so forth.
Another 511 million, or 22 percent, are in *category c*,
which represents what Gough calls "satellite or
client states." These include Colombia, Argentina,
Chile, the Philippines, South Vietnam, South Korea,
Nigeria, Turkey, and a number of others. Such states
have indigenous governments but are constrained
by Western military or economic aid, or by private
investments that have "strings attached." Most of
these governments allow only limited social reform.
About 14 percent of the people in this category live
in states under the aegis of United States aid either
in South America or in a fringe around China.

Finally, in *category d* we find 873 million, or 37
percent, living in independent nations, most of
which overthrew European colonialism within the
last twenty years. The anthropologist P. M. Worsley

has called this group "populist," since they rely on a multiclass ideology and tend to have "a public sector of the economy and an emphasis on national planning, as well as a large private sector dominated by foreign capital." This category includes India, Burma, Syria, Iraq, the United Arab Republic, Morocco, Algeria, Sudan, and others (figure 215). In the past fifteen years at least 227 million (about 16 percent) have, after a longer or shorter period of relative independence, moved back into a client relationship with the United States. These include Guatemala, the Dominican Republic, Venezuela, and Bolivia. In fact one could now claim that at least 48 percent of the world's population, as either client states or colonies, are heavily dependent on the United States.

The definitions noted here are not necessarily mutually exclusive. If one compares Berry's analysis with that of Gough, it seems that the lower the level of development the greater the likelihood of colonial status and economic dependency. Each definition is acceptable within its own philosophical framework —something that will be stressed below. Thus development can be conceived as: (a) an economic-ideological factor, the result of an economic system imposed from without by colonial and imperialist nations; (b) as a continuum from lesser development to greater, according to measures of technology, trade, energy consumption, or demographic factors; (c) as a value judgment, part of a complex cultural process.

Two Models or Views of Underdevelopment

Another geographer, J. M. Blaut, has pursued this matter of value judgment and ethnocentrism still further by utilizing analyses and accounts written by social scientists, historians, and others who were born and raised in the so-called underdeveloped areas. The contrast between the Western and Third World models of development, he points out, becomes even stronger if we first note certain truisms enshrined in the Western model:

1. *The West has a definite spatio-temporal coherence; although the center of world civilization and empire lay in Europe, it has now shifted to the United States. Thus there is an inner sphere (the "West") and an outer sphere (the "underdeveloped" countries), with a finite boundary between.*
2. *The rise of the West has been generated mainly by inner processes. Thus non-Western peoples played no role of importance in such events as the Reformation or the Industrial Revolution.*
3. *All non-Western cultures are more or less "primitive" at the time of colonization by the West. They are also less*

virtuous, less progressive, less intellectual, and—as a result of all this—less robust than the culture of the "inner sphere."
4. *The outward expansion of the inner sphere is a "striving outward," an "urge to expand"; any part of the outer sphere gains its important attributes from contact with the core.*

Blaut maintains that these four repulsive myths are integral parts of the Western operational milieu. We therefore tend to see **imperialism** as a matter of dispensing civilization, making the world a better place to live in—and taking natural resources as our just reward. In the West, therefore, both **colonialism** and imperialism have acquired the status of natural and inevitable processes.

In contrast, according to Blaut, the Third World commentator sees the same historical events in terms of three stages:

1. *The period of slave-based Industrial Revolution (1450–1750). So far from being an exclusively European phenomenon, this revolution had spatial bonds extending from Atlantic Europe to West African and thence to the West Indies and the Atlantic coast of South America. The period opened with chartered piracy along the Guinea coast, and ended with a crude factory system and the transference of profits to the West. As profit and experience grew, the orbit of Western influence enlarged until the New World was reached, and settlement on the Brazilian coast began. Here warfare, European diseases, and slavery decimated the native Amerindian population. In time, Europe reached the final stage of imperialistic expansion: a massive, commercial, slave-based agricultural system. Thus from the Third World point of view the only respect in which European civilization proved itself "superior" to the civilizations of Africa and America was in the ability of its representatives to seize large quantities of land that had been emptied of its human inhabitants by disease. The so-called European urge to expand is a myth, nor did Europeans have any significant technical advantages except better ships. Europeans merely reached the New World first, and won it by means of genocide.*
2. *The period of classic colonialism. This was a time of large-scale territorial conquest by certain European powers. It began slowly in the mid-eighteenth century, but by the end of the nineteenth century had spread over nearly all of Africa and Asia. In addition, China had become a kind of giant colonial condominium. This stage ended with the formal granting of independence to most of the European colonies in the period immediately after the Second World War. In this second stage two vital ingredients of "development" were drawn into the West: the system of industrial capitalism, which evolved under plantation slavery; and the profits from plunder, slavery, the Asiatic trade, new markets in the New World, and so forth. As the European merchants acquired money they also acquired political power and legitimacy. Thus European governments began to seek colonies as extensions of European marketing and sources of*

European raw materials. Rising industrial and military power provided the technology and capital needed for large-scale conquest. Of course, once investment had been established the newly acquired raw material sources and markets had to be protected, and the new economic motives operationalized and institutionalized.

3. *The period of neocolonialism. In this third and most recent period, some of the outward colonial structures noted in the second period have been dismantled. To Western eyes, these facts are evidence that colonialism is on its deathbed. The Third World, however, sees colonial exploitation continuing, but without overt political control. A state exploited in this way is called neocolonial. It has a number of defining properties:*

   (a) *Its economy is connected to the West, but without full-scale territorial occupation by Westerners. However, this connection implies a transfer of wealth not from the richer to the poorer nation, as Westerners would maintain, but in the reverse direction. For instance, as a result of direct U.S. overseas investments between 1950 and 1965, there was a net inflow of $16 billion to the United States—and this was just part of the negative transfer. This process has been called "growth without development."*

   (b) *Its internal political structure is effectively controlled by an elite of businessmen, civil servants, and military, who are committed by self-interest or ideology to maintaining this subservient neocolonial economy.*

   (c) *This neocolony lies under an implicit or explicit threat of invasion or some other hostile act (such as a trade embargo) if the imperial economic interests are not properly protected; hence its sovereignty is contingent.*

   (d) *Since the exploitation in a neocolony is much like that of classical colonialism, the interests of the colonizing power must be backed up by military assistance pacts and the like. Thus the United States maintains military groups in some sixty-four countries, including nineteen in South America, ten in Southeast Asia, eleven in Africa, and thirteen in Europe.*

We can also distinguish between phase 2 and phase 3 of this model by: (a) the shift from geostrategic maneuvers for the purpose of carving up territory to a policy of protecting the capitalist system from contraction and holding on to as many of its economic and financial benefits as possible; (b) the shift from European to U.S. leadership; (c) the use of a wide range of cultural, economic, and financial inducements, amounting to a state of permanent and total psychological war; (d) the rise of an "international" kind of technology—computers, nuclear energy, communications satellites—which helps to diffuse the ideas of the Western powers, especially those of the United States, and coincidentally provides dominance over the Third World. If the Western notion of development is accepted, then no nation can afford to be without links to the U.S.-

dominated system of technical innovation and development.

It will be seen, then, that the articulation of an opposing view of development is a task of profound importance for social scientists. There is obviously a pervasive scepticism in the Third World about Western pronouncements on development, especially when they seem to entail increased benefits to the West, when there seems to be no real difference between economic aid programs and former colonial technical services, and when population control seems to be imperialism under a new guise.

According to the Western view, imperialism is under control, economic development is just around the corner provided we invest $X in the exploitation of resource Z, and securing world peace is only a matter of right thinking. To the Third World, on the other hand, imperialism is far from dead; in fact, it has changed to neocolonialism, and has shifted its center of gravity from Europe to the United States.

Three Worlds

A number of commentators, among them a geographer, Keith Buchanan, have carried the notion of a Third World even further. As background to this type of analysis, we need a picture of all three worlds (table 79).

The *First World*, dominated by the United States, Western Europe, and their satellites, is characterized by a capitalist system, private ownership, "free" market structure, corporate wealth, middle-class values, and (frequently) a minimum of planning. This is basically the commercial-exchange system discussed above, but with political, societal, and military systems added to it. Thus the First World is characterized by parliamentary democracy, in which strategy rather than ideology differentiates the political parties. It is also highly urbanized, has a high level of mass consumption, and increasing time for leisure activities. Its birth rate is low, as is its death rate. Last, but not least, it has a professional military class.

The *Second World*, which consists mainly of the Soviet Union with its allies and satellites, is characterized by a socialist system, state ownership in a strictly controlled exchange system, proletarian values, and an emphasis on secondary economic activities. This is basically what we have called the redistributive system. The political system of the Second World is dominated by democratic centralism and based on the historical-economic ideology of Communism and Socialism; usually, there is only one political party. Other Second World characteristics include medium to high urbanization,

Table 79. *The Three Worlds of Development*

	first world	second world	third world
constituents	*U.S.A., Canada, Western Europe and satellites*	*Soviet Union, Eastern Europe, parts of Asia, and satellites*	*nonaligned and nonsatellitic states in Africa, Asia, and Latin America*
economic system	capitalist — *private ownership, "free" market, corporate wealth, and monopoly*	socialist — *state ownership, controlled market, investment through public sector*	mixed *economy — public and private sectors, economy in conflict between internal and external orientation*
	planning *minimal, middle class, and based on individual "entrepreneurial" effort*	planning *maximized, proletarian values, based on common human welfare*	planning *various; often moving towards socialism*
	economy — *emphasis on services and consumer goods*	economy — *emphasis on heavy basic industries*	economy — *based on peasant agriculture, with stress on heavy basic industries where possible*
	unions *growing in strength, highly organized*	unions *perceived as part of state*	unions *radical and unstable, with little economic role*
societal system	*highly* urbanized; *rapid growth of middle class; status differentiation through occupation and income*	*medium to highly* urbanized; *still a sizeable peasant sector; bureaucratic elite*	*rapidly* urbanizing; *dominance of primate city; traditional status differentiation diminishing; social mobility low; labor market still unspecialized*
	highly bureaucratized society	*highly bureaucratized society*	
	liberal, mass education	*technical-scientific mass education; education plays an important role in society*	*mass literacy, technical-scientific secondary education*
	leisure *increasing*	leisure *slowly increasing*	leisure *activities low*
	high level of mass consumption	*low level* of mass consumption	*low level* of mass consumption
	low birth and death rates	*low to medium birth rate and low death rate*	*high birth rate, medium to low death rate*
	religion — *Christian*	religion — *socialism*	religion — *Moslem, Hindu, Buddhist, some Christian, and various local categories*
	ethnic *pre-eminence — North West European*	ethnic *pre-eminence — Slav and East European*	ethnic *pre-eminence — Negro and Indian*
	cultural affinities — *Puritanism and secular enlightenment*	cultural affinities — *Byzantine and secular enlightenment*	cultural affinities — *philosophical rationalism; often no clear separation between secular and religious values*
military	professional — *centers of military power dispersed; low level of political involvement*	professional — *works closely with elite at decision making level*	*political, strong role in formulating and executing political decisions; rise of military politics; ideologically committed — in prerevolutionary countries to conservative Caesar models; in post-revolutionary countries to radical-charismatic models*
political	parliamentary democracy — *based on economic law of market*	democratic centralism — *based on historical-economic ideology of communism and socialism interpreted through ruling elite with high doctrinal rigidity*	mass democracy —*based on highly articulated and politically grounded ideology of nationalism and socialism, with a strong charismatic leader*
	ideologically — *conservative and middle-of-the road*		ideology *radical and socialist, but much variation*
	few major parties, differentiated by strategy rather than ideology	party elite large (up to 10% of population); party activity all-encompassing*	*few or one party; highly centralized state; party elite small; military role usually very strong*
	party elite very small and active only during elections		

Source: Based on I.L. Horowitz, *Three Worlds of Development* (New York: Oxford University Press, 1966), pp. 39–46.

Table 80. *Paradigms Representing Economic Growth and Social Change*

	attribute	process	advantage/disadvantage
Hoselitz (1960) functional	*pattern variables*	*generative cities as bearers of change*	*inflexible, incomplete, unreal*
Frank (1966, 67) conflict	*metropolis-satellite structure of the capitalist system*	*stress, alienation, revolution*	*one materialistic dimension*
Lockwood (1964) neofunctional	*core institutional order, material sub-structure, system integration*	*transformaton of the core institutional order*	*dynamic nonactive functional model, with fusion of conflict ideas*
diffusion	*spatial/temporal spread of capital, technology, and institutions*	*migration, colonization, conquest, trade, etc.*	*a definite process, but effectiveness challenged*
MClelland (1961) psychological	*entrepreneurs*	*motivation*	*one factor*
Hagen (1962) psychological	*motivated individuals* *value system*	*change in creativity/problem solving ability and in attitudes towards work*	*multidimensional but not eclectic*
economic theories, etc.	quantified indices	production and maximization of income for utility of an aggregate of individuals	one dimensional

rapid growth of the working class, a high level of mass communication, high social welfare benefits, a medium to low birth rate, a low death rate, and professional military.

The *Third World* is made up of nonaligned and nonsatellite nations. They tend to have mixed economic systems, moving toward socialism in many cases. Typically, they are based on a peasant agricultural sector. Sources of capital are varied; short-term foreign aid is the most usual, and savings are often small. The political system may be a mass democracy with a charismatic leader; in any case, the state is highly centralized, and often controlled by an elite. The rate of urbanization is so rapid that there is often a gulf between the primate city and the others. There is little leisure activity, a low rate of consumption, a high birth rate, and a medium to low death rate. The military are distinguished by their political role. Buchanan attempted to define the Third World in terms of such factors as political attitudes and degree of national integration. He concluded that the Third World is a universe of radical scarcity, with a legacy of warped economies, poverty, degradation, cultural inferiorization, and alienation. The geographer, he argued, is usually unwilling to see the Third World for what it is: not a malfunction to be reduced by population control and economic development, but as a malfunction caused by imperialism. It follows that the continuance of imperialism in any form is to the detriment of the Third World.

Theories of Economic and Social Change

Just as there are varying philosophical and ideological frameworks for understanding development and underdevelopment, so there are many ways of explaining how to overcome the malfunctions attendant upon either process. These explanations include, on the one hand, the *functional* view that change occurs through the harmonious modification of certain pattern variables and, on the other, the *conflict* view according to which change is the result of conflicting values and roles. There is of course a wide range of other viewpoints, some of which are summarized in table 80.

The Functional View

Another name for the functional approach to development is the **index method.** The basic idea has been expressed that "the general features of a developed economy are abstracted as an ideal type and are then contrasted with the equally ideal typical features of a poor economy and society." Alternatively, one can think of this as the "gap" method. That is, if one subtracts the indices of underdevelopment from those of development, then the gap or difference between the two is what the so-called developing area is supposed to achieve. According to this model, then, in order to change from an "underdeveloped" to a "developed" state it is only

Table 81. *The "Functional" View: Indices or Patterns of Development*

pattern variables	
"development"	*universalism* *achievement orientation* *functional specificity*
"underdevelopment"	*particularism* *ascription* *functional diffusiveness*

necessary to change the particular variables, roles, or parts of the social system, not the whole structure of the system itself. Thus change is seen as a function of one or more of the social system's components, as reflected in the indices of development.

Table 81 shows the indices associated with the two extremes of development; they approximate the economic types identified earlier as "subsistence" and "peasant," on the one hand, and "market exchange," on the other. Here, **particularism** denotes exclusive attention or devotion to the interests of the local group. Within this group, social, economic, and political roles are distributed by **ascription**— that is, the attributes of status are ascribed, not earned, so that status is achieved through heredity rather than achievement. Moreover, roles are **functionally diffuse** rather than specific, so that one person may hold or practice many jobs at the same time. This lack of specialization is held to generate "underdevelopment," while the contrary is held of role specificity. Malfunctioning, then, is identified as particularism, ascription, and functional diffuseness.

In contrast, **universalism,** which is seen as an element of a well functioning system, denotes an almost worldwide range of knowledge, interests, or activities. In a universalistic society, achievement is determined by what has been achieved on the scale of values held by that society, that is, through merit rather than by esteem of birth. Moreover, specialization within the society has led to an individual carrying out a specific task, for which he may be best equipped. The gap between particularistic-ascriptive and universalistic-achievement values is what a developing country would have to cover in order to become "developed."

It has been argued by B. F. Hoselitz that the actual mechanism of change has been the growth and expansion of cities, which act as a stimulus to technical change and development, including industrialization. It should be remembered that Berry, in his index method of identifying "development," noted a high positive correlation between economic development and urbanization. Hoselitz makes a

further distinction between *parasitic* and *generative* cities. This division reflects Hoselitz's belief that some cities have a favorable impact upon economic growth, while others have an unfavorable effect. Thus parasitic cities are primate cities of an established order, functioning to restrain growth; far larger than any other cities, they dominate the economic social and political subsystems and have a dampening effect on economic growth and change throughout the system. Thus the economy stagnates, and the city serves to maintain the ascriptive and particularistic value system of the local self-sustaining culture. On the other hand, generative cities are specialized, have become integrated within the economic system, and function as centers of change. Change occurs first in the city and is then diffused throughout the economic spatial system, which in turn leads to a highly integrated spatial complex centered on the city itself. By process of acculturation, these cities develop quite frequently under influences external to the local culture. In this way they come to represent achievement oriented value systems based on specialization and interchange. Specialization increases with greater differentiation of functions, and as specialization increases so do exchange, trade, and interdependence. Such developing economic systems are often bearers of rapid social change, and so in conflict with the older indigenous cultures.

This whole approach is open to a number of criticisms, some of which center around the **functional paradigm.** For instance, it has been claimed that the tripartite pattern variables are unreal, and certainly not mutually exclusive. Thus in our society, which most of us perceive as "developed," achievement is frequently based on ascriptive norms (accidents of birth, etc.) rather than merit. Others have criticized the functional approach itself, taking to task its reliance on an organic analogy and on the assumption of a state of equilibrium. Societies, according to these critics, do not tend to a state of equilibrium; rather, they are full of stresses and strains. This alternative paradigm can be termed **conflict theory.**

Both the conflict and the functional approaches fall within the same major theoretical school of **holism.** According to the holistic paradigm, behavior is a comprehensive, organically unified system. The alternative major approach is the **atomistic** one, where patterns of social life are thought to be secondary, and the actions of persons and individual behavior are thought to be more important.

It is important to bear these differences in mind when considering behavior in the context of something as controversial as economic development, since all the explanations and criticisms are based on particular paradigms and viewpoints. Thus in comparing Hoselitz's functional view of change with Frank's conflict view, these fundamental differences must be borne in mind.

The Metropolis-Satellite Hypothesis

Gunder Frank's metropolis-satellite hypothesis of economic underdevelopment is grounded in conflict theory. Conflict and tension in this case occur between the capitalist metropolis and its exploited satellites. The theory is holistic because it regards underdevelopment as part of a larger capitalist economic system. Frank maintains that underdevelopment is not an original or traditional stage from which every country must begin. For example, "the now developed countries were never *under*developed, though they may have been *un*developed." One does not have to be a conflict theorist to agree with that statement, although it does stand opposed to the views of change expressed by Hoselitz and Rostow. Frank points out that "contemporary underdevelopment (it is said) of a country can be understood as the product or reflection solely of its own economic, political, social, and cultural characteristics of structure. Yet historical research demonstrates that contemporary underdevelopment is in large part the historical product of past and continuing economic and other relations between the satellite underdeveloped and the new developed metropolitan countries."

Frank's theory can be stated as a series of three hypotheses, with a corollary:

1. *The development of the world metropolis, the organizing center of the world capitalist system, because it is no one's satellite, is unlimited. In contrast, the development of subsidiary capitalist metropolises is limited by their satellite status.*

2. *Satellites experience their greatest economic development when their ties to their metropolis are weakest. A corollary to this is that when those investment and trade ties are at their strongest, that is, when the satellites are fully incorporated into the economic system of the metropolis, development and industrialization are choked off.*

3. *Those regions that are the most underdeveloped and feudalistic today are the very ones that had the closest ties to the metropolis in the past. However, they are not to be confused with underdeveloped areas. The source of a region's underdevelopment is neither its isolation nor its precapitalist institutions, but rather its legacy of exploitation from the metropolis.*

These hypotheses were tested and substantiated in Latin America. Examples of the first hypothesis are the metropolitan regions of Buenos Aires and São Paulo whose growth, beginning only in the nineteenth century, was largely unaffected by the colonial system, yet whose overall development resembles that of satellites, first with Britain and then with the United States as a metropolis. Examples of the second hypothesis can be found during periods of world war or depression, when many Latin American countries did in fact face their greatest periods of economic development and were able to initiate autonomous industrialization and growth. Finally, the third hypothesis is supported by evidence of the former development and present underdevelopment of the once sugar-exporting West Indies, Northeast Brazil, and the ex-mining province of Minas Gerais.

Frank's conceptualization, like Hoselitz's, is open to criticism. Frank separates out the essentially economic aspects of a society, and abstracts the individual from the web of social institutions in order to define a specialized aspect of behavior, the maximization of satisfaction. This is a one-sided materialistic interpretation of culture and history. The variation among underdeveloped countries appears to suggest that although economic factors — particularly the institutions of world capitalism — are indeed important, they are not all-important. For example, can the structure of the capitalist system alone explain the differences in development between Japan and Thailand? The answer seems to be no; there are in fact other factors, both cultural and political, besides the ones outlined by Frank. Of course, this does not invalidate Frank's hypotheses in explaining some variations in development, and the role he ascribes to the capitalist-colonialist system is a valid one in many cases. He also makes a valuable contribution by conceiving "underdevelopment" as a changing dynamic factor, and not as static and innate.

A methodological problem has been haunting us all through this discussion of "underdevelopment." If two men can observe the same societal group, yet abstract different relationships, or see change as coming about in diametrically opposed ways, whose perception is the correct one? Can there be a correct perception—or is every answer equally subjective?

The best answer to give at this stage is probably that there is no one Grand Theory. Rather, a plurality of understandings has given rise to a plurality of paradigms and theories. Just as there can be no single definition of "development," so there can be no single causal explanation of it. Each of the theories or paradigms noted in table 80 contains some applicable factors, but their applicability varies from situation to situation and from time to time. The causes of "underdevelopment," as far as can be ascertained, are multidimensional. Certain factors may be of more importance than others, but this importance can be gauged only in the context of the behavioral-operational milieu of a particular society or nation. Purely economic theories of growth, for instance, are obviously inadequate, since both growth and malfunctioning are part of a larger social pattern. Much more work needs to be carried out to find additional and perhaps more realistic representations of economic growth and social change.

World Economic Development

Where does this get us? Stress has been placed on the difficulty of finding an adequate definition of development, and on the role of subjective factors in this. Hopefully, we can now go a little further and identify both the barriers and the aids to "development."

Obviously, the variations of the economic system go farther than the usually quoted factors of population resource ratios or capital formation. The political and ideological goals of a particular nation state may run counter to the optimal functioning of the total economic system as identified by, say, location theorists. Differences in the operational milieu may drastically alter the final perception of an economic system. Frequently, internal or external policy restraints result in departures from the economic norm; for instance, in wartime a capitalist government may take over the country's privately owned shipbuilding industry.

We have already seen that if we begin with the idea of a virtually undifferentiated space, such as the homogenous plain of von Thünen, Christaller, or Weber, and then introduce certain real elements of the economic system—transportation costs, capital availability, agglomeration economies, population, resources, and so forth—then we achieve certain distinctive spatial activity patterns, whether or not they correspond to economic reality. But we also know that to represent reality, economic or otherwise, we must add to the distinctively economic notions of cost, utility, and so on, distinctively *cultural* notions such as values, preferences, and goals, as well as distinctively *political* notions such as nationhood, community, and ideology. Then, and only then, do the spatial patterns come to represent real-world conditions. In fact, it is the interjection of economic, cultural, and political factors into the world economic system that leads to marked deviations from a perceived optimum, and so allows us to identify, each according to his personal standpoint, areas of growth or decline, development or underdevelopment (for examples, see figures 213, 214, and 215)

Three basic variants of an economic system have been identified and used throughout this book.

Table 82 summarizes some of the structural and operational attributes that can be applied to these three organizational types. It is not suggested, of course, that any column is necessarily optimal, though the reader may perceive one as such within the context of his or her own socioeconomic value system. There are of course many variations of each basic type, and the particular characteristics of each nation-state, each culture area, each value system, lead to still further variations. This is why there are an almost infinite number of points along the continuum in figure 212.

Despite the difficulties encountered in identifying and defining economic structures, and in explaining the differences between them, certain general trends in the world economic structure can be enumerated:

1. *The number of Socialist and mixed economies (viz state capitalist subsystems, as identified in chapter 8) is on the increase, and such systems may soon dominate the world economic structure.*
2. *There is a slow but sure extension of advanced interdependent economic structures all over the world. Some of this has resulted from the decline of colonial forms.*
3. *These two developments will probably bring about change and redistribution in present economic structures, so that new centers of economic power may arise.*

Barriers to Development

The barrier to development that is most frequently cited, particularly by geographers, is the population-resource ratio, although it is a concept with little independent meaning. Since it is treated in a separate section below, we need say here only that to cite population growth *in itself* as a barrier to development may well be to overlook the very socioeconomic structures that are causing the imbalance between population and resources. Some of the other barriers, which may be more meaningful from a multidimensional point of view, are summarized in table 83.

The Cultural System

The traditional value systems of developing areas may well be in conflict with the veneer of Western technology and culture that is so often imported with the concept of "development." The traditional values may include an emphasis on nonmaterial, noneconomic values; savings may be channeled into traditional nonproductive investments; and attitudes may be so locally oriented that nothing beyond the village is seen to matter very much. These and other

Table 82. *Variations in Cultural and Economic Criteria, According to Three Types of Economic Organization*

	peasant/subsistent	commercial/market	redistributive
income head	*low; may be declining*	*high; increasing in many cases*	*medium; increasing*
proportion of population directly dependent on *primary* activities	*very high (75% or more)*	*very low (25% or less)*	*medium to low (20 – 50%)*
proportion of population directly dependent on *secondary* activities	*very low*	*high and rising (25 – 30%)*	*high and rising*
proportion of population directly dependent on *tertiary* activities	*low*	*high and rising; sustained increase with urbanization*	*high and rising*
population in cities and large towns	*small, but primate cities do occur*	*very high*	*high*
technology	*static or traditional*	*dynamic with rapid innovations*	
goals of production	*family consumption and survival*	*income and net profit*	*net community profit*
decision making	*arational or traditional*	*satisficing, intendedly rational*	*economic, planned, intendedly rational*
intake of food	*deficient*	*abundant to superabundant*	*sufficient to abundant*
proportion of diet from starches	*high*	*low*	*medium*
death rate, birth rate, infant death rate	*high*	*low*	*low*
level of literacy	*low*	*high*	*high*

Source: N. Ginsburg, ed., "Geography and Economic Development," Chicago: University of Chicago, Department of Geography Research Paper No. 62; J. Rutherford, M.I. Logan, and G.J. Missen, *New Viewpoints in Economic Geography: Case Studies from Australia, New Zealand, Malaysia, North America* (Sydney: Martindale Press, 1966), chap. 1; C.R. Wharton, "Research on Agricultural Development in Southeast Asia," *Journal of Farm Economics,* vol. 45, 1963, pp. 1161–1174.

cultural attributes have been commonly quoted as barriers to development. However, some scholars believe that such attributes do have a role to play in the development process, even if it cannot be clearly identified at present.

Value systems are frequently quoted in the literature as barriers to development. A typical comment is that "this behavioral and attitudinal complex . . . is obviously highly detrimental to the proper functioning of large organizational structures . . . modernization cannot proceed, has no chance of success, unless it is matched by concomitant shifts in attitudes and values. There must be a readiness to take risks, inherent in operating outside the groove of tradition." However, the role of value differences should not be overemphasized. Values and other cultural attributes are not static and immutable. Moreover, as P. M. Hauser (1959) has pointed out, it is easy enough to show that certain values are *associated* with the development of Western technology and economic organization, but quite another thing to prove that they are *prerequisites* for such development.

Quite often these value differences that are sup-

posed to hinder development are put down to the existence of a so-called prescientific attitude system —that is, a system of attitudes and values inconsistent with Western science and technology. It is claimed that behavioral patterns governed by magico-religious beliefs and by the lack of a distinction between man and the rest of nature conflict with and often preclude forms of behavior and attitudes that facilitate technological and economic advancement. Thus Hauser lists, among other elements likely to retard development: an emphasis on spiritual rather than material values and on the life to come rather than the present life; pressure to conform to traditional patterns of value and action; relatively fixed roles and statuses, both in the local community and in the society at large; great importance attached to kinship ties; and the allocation of relatively large resources to traditional customs and rituals. Traditional value systems are also said to recognize and ascribe status to those roles in the social structure that have least to do with economic growth. They provide neither a general orientation to a money economy nor Western ethical conceptions of work. The fact that all these so-called traditional

Table 83. *Summary: Barriers to Development*

	attributes
Population	*Death control increasing; birth rates high; rapid population growth.*
Resources	*High population ratios / perceived or developed resource base. Technological deficiency.*
Colonialism	Initial Advantages — *cumulative advantages of early capitalist development.*
	Colonialism — *"god, gold, and greed." Viable socioeconomic structures wittingly or unwittingly destroyed and replaced with an "alien" European-oriented system. Economic control and exploitation; satellite of mother country.*
	Neocolonialism — *monopoly capitalism, system imposition, metropolis orientation. Warping of indigenous development by external pressures.*
Political	Obstacles to national unity — *artificial boundaries, divided groups.*
	System capability *of certain political structures —the* development syndrome — *failure to maintain law and order, corruption, lack of planning, etc.*
	Ideology — *divert attention from crucial economic factors; justify prestige projects or military adventures.*
Cultural Structure	Value system — *prescientific, traditional, age-deference, religious.*
	Stratification — *caste systems, class systems, elite power groups, peasant groups; lack of mobility between groups.*
	Atomism — *individuation, lack of group consciousness, lack of concern for human welfare.*
Economic Structure	Domination *by external economic forces; foreign "aid" with strings attached.*
	Lack *of "preconditions" — insufficient capital, savings nonexistent, infrastructure undeveloped, markets too small, consumer purchasing power negligible.*
	Lack *of "motives" — few entrepreneurs, risk takers, achievement motivation minimal.*

features can be found in Western culture, both past and present, is generally overlooked.

"Status satisfaction" has been mentioned as yet another barrier to development. Traditional societies generally have highly stratified social orders, and very little social mobility. Age grading is relatively inflexible, and the usual source of economic and political status is social class. Such a system hampers economic growth by limiting opportunities for people who have ability but lack the appropriate status.

If the wealth, power, prestige and status of a society is the exclusive property of two or three groups, then social and economic change are unlikely; new economic opportunities may not be the concern of the dominant group or groups, and may not even be perceived by rest of society.

Institutional changes of various kinds are frequently prescribed for economic growth. For example, lack of savings institutions is often quoted as a reason why capital accumulation does not occur in developing areas. Similarly, technological improvement and scientific research are said to have been institutionalized in Western Europe some time before the most rapid phase of economic growth took place. Entrepreneurship, that very elusive property, is also reported as institutionalized at an early stage in various developed countries. Hoselitz notes that "the rapid structural and organizational changes affecting the productivity of a society . . . are made possible because in a previous phase social institutions were created which allow the successful overcoming of supply bottlenecks, chiefly in the field of capital formation and the availability of a number of highly skilled and specialized services. The creation of these social institutions in turn . . . requires the establishment of a social framework within which these new institutions can exist and expand."

Other institutions, of course, may have the reverse effect and restrict growth. Livestock in much of Asia and Africa are regarded within an institutional framework. For instance, under Hindu law cattle of an inferior quality cannot be slaughtered or sterilized even though the number of animals may be more than the land can efficiently maintain. In addition, the cattle are not efficiently used, either for meat or for milk. By Western standards, this is incomprehensible. In Africa, cattle may be accumulated for their own sake as a measure of status and wealth.

It is difficult to categorize all the variables that may aid or retard economic development. Existing attempts have succeeded in uncovering a great deal of speculation, partial theory, and sociocultural description, but not in drawing up a diagnostic schema. The complexity of the interlinkages in the development process, as well as the way in which the role of certain factors have been overstated, make the task a formidable one. All we can say with certainty is that cultural factors do have a role to play in the development process, but that it cannot at present be clearly identified.

The Economic System

The removal of various economic barriers is also frequently mentioned as a prerequisite of development. Among these barriers are low incomes, which produce few or no savings; markets too small to induce investment; and lack of investment in the infrastructure, especially transportation. The truth is, however, that many factors besides these determine the transition of an economy from one level to another. At particular points along a growth continuum some economic factors become more important than others. But each factor alone is meaningless; it must first be related to the cultural system, the behavioral-operational system, the workings of the world capitalist or socialist system, and the past history of development. No economic system, of lesser or greater development, is a closed system; rather, it is open both to external economic influences and to the influence of cultural factors, both economic and noneconomic, internal to the system itself.

R. L. Heilbroner and other investigators have stressed that underdeveloped areas are "poor societies because they are *traditional* societies—that is, societies which have developed neither the mechanisms of command nor the market by which they might launch into a sustained process of economic growth." He goes on to ask why the agriculture of such countries is so unproductive.

One apparent reason is that the typical unit of agricultural production . . . is far too small to permit efficient farming . . . agriculture suffers from a devastatingly low productivity brought about by grotesque man/land ratios.

These are, however, only the first links in a chain of causes for low agricultural productivity. Another consequence of these tiny plots is an inability to apply sufficient capital to the land . . . even fertilizer is too expensive . . . this paralyzing lack of capital is by no means confined to agriculture. It pervades the entire range of an underdeveloped economy. The whole industrial landscape of a Western economy is missing: no factories, no power lines, no machines, no paved road. . . .

The lack of capital is frequently cited as a malfunction. Capital accumulation, industrialization, and economic growth are, to many writers in this field, virtually identical processes; they argue that although some increase in industrial production is possible without the application of capital, it is very limited in scope. For large advances in industrial production, capital on a large scale is required. Developing areas rarely accumulate such amounts of capital, largely because they find it difficult to break out of what R. Nurske (1953) has called the "vicious cycle of poverty." Low real incomes mean low buying and saving capacity; minimal savings mean a low rate of capital formation; lack of capital means low productivity; and low productivity means low incomes. So poverty reacts in a feedback effect on the size of the market and the capacity to save, which in

turn limits capital accumulation. It should be noted that the actual amount of capital required per worker in modern industry is very high. At present most developing countries with peasant based economies can save only 4 to 5 percent of net national income, whereas industrial development would need 12 to 15 percent savings. One of the reasons is that often up to 40 percent of national income in such areas is in the hands of a few thousand landowners and elitists who squander much of it in ostentatious consumption. Taxation rates, which could absorb such marginal income for national use, usually favor such elites with low rates. It is obvious, then, that domestic saving can contribute only part of the investment capital needed.

Another source of capital is self-capitalization (reinvestment of profit, instead of distributing it as dividends). But this assumes initial investment of some order. A greater role has typically been played by imported capital, especially through the erection of a social and operational base upon which to erect the industrial superstructure. At present, the demand for infrastructure capital cannot be met, since as a form of investment it does not offer a sufficiently attractive rate of return. Capital alone, however does not create development. In the words of Simon Kuznets, "the major capital stock of an industrially advanced country is not in its physical equipment; it is the body of knowledge amassed from tested findings and the capacity and training of the population to use this knowledge effectively." Rather than being a precondition of growth, capital may act as a kind of catalyst.

Another highly relevant aspect of the economic system is the existence of a market. For development to succeed, produce must be sold and distributed either internally or externally. A common feature of developing areas is the small size of the internal market. As was noted above, this smallness is largely a function of the low purchasing power of the consumer in such a society. Average yearly incomes of less than $75 are common, and 60–70 percent of this is spent on food, leaving very little for consumer durables in either absolute or relative terms. Such small markets can usually be adequately supplied by imports; a national supplier would soon go out of business if he had to rely on supplying his own national market alone. The need, of course, is to develop a market that offers wider scope, and so is capable of supporting industrial development.

Whereas capital and markets are restricted in the poorer nations, labor can be both abundant and cheap (though restricted in terms of skill). However, this needs qualification: wages may well *appear* low in comparison with those paid in developed countries, but efficiency and productivity are usually low too. Thus A. Mountjoy reports that in the 1950s the Egyptian textile industry required 16 operators per 1,000 spindles compared with 5 or 6 in the same circumstances in the United States. The training of such a labor force is likely to be both costly and time-consuming, particularly since so many of its members may be illiterate. For this reason, W. A. Lewis has suggested that initial industrial development may be a period of high cost production as these new skills are acquired. In any case, while the population may be an initial drag on capital formation, an abundant labor force is a major resource, provided that it can be trained and effectively used.

One geographer, B. W. Hodder, has identified three divergent views as to which economic sector should be developed if economic growth is to be maximized:

1. *That increased agricultural production is the only sure foundation for successful industrialization at a later stage.*
2. *That industrialization is the panacea, and only its stimulation will lead to economic growth.*
3. *That these two sectors are of equal importance in economic development.*

The first argument revolves around the fact that an agricultural revolution preceded industrial development in Western Europe, and that for more than a century before the Industrial Revolution scientific and technical knowledge had reached a higher level than in most developing countries today. Thus, according to this view, an industrial superstructure cannot be developed without an agricultural base into which investment capital has been poured in order to improve efficiency and productivity.

Given the existing stage of agricultural organization and technology, can the developing economies, without first effecting radical changes in this base sector, sustain a program of industrial development that will include a substantial movement of population from primary production to other forms of employment? The agricultural base is frequently static, largely because any present cash crop production was designed originally to fit into the traditional system of agriculture. Thus agriculture has a great potential for development. The domestic market for agricultural products would be large, and agriculture is not nearly so capital intensive as industry.

In contrast to this, the second view is that increasing the efficiency of agriculture is "unlikely to foster self-sustaining economic growth and may even frustrate it." Agriculture is assigned to a relatively minor role, and prime emphasis is placed on industrialization. A number of arguments are put forward to support this point of view: (a) that industrialization leads to higher living standards, as

the value of output per worker is greater and grows more rapidly than with agriculture; (b) that industrialization results in greater economic diversification and stability, whereas agriculture relies on a few exported primary products that are extremely vulnerable to fluctuations in world demand; (c) that industrial growth is cumulative, and can stimulate growth in other sectors including the social infrastructure; (d) that industrial expansion can absorb the excess of agricultural workers (who may well be underemployed); (e) that the agricultural base does not contain the prerequisites for rapid growth; (f) that the demand for agricultural products is relatively inelastic, as is its response to changes in market conditions; (g) that industrialization is a "magic term" that offers a distinct psychological advantage, since it conjures up in the minds of the people vistas of increased incomes and higher levels of living; and (h) that industrialization, urbanization, and declining birth rates seem to be coterminous.

Thirdly, there is the view that agriculture and industry are interdependent, and that there are feedback effects from one to the other. Thus industrialization alone is seen as neither panacea nor prophylactic. Instead, there is an interdependent cumulative effect: surplus agricultural population is absorbed by industry, as agriculture under the stimulus of greater demand becomes more efficient, and industry in turn expands the market for agricultural products.

Obviously, any economic plan for the developing areas that emphasized investment in one sector rather than another would in many cases not produce the desired economic growth and improvement in living standards. Hodder has suggested that any division between the agricultural and industrial sectors is probably false and arbitrary, and that there is in fact a **development continuum.** According to Hodder, "quite a large part of the industrial sector . . . both depends upon agriculture for its raw materials and is itself aimed at feeding back into agriculture the products and techniques of industry. After a certain critical stage in the development of agricultural systems, the feedback of technology from industry into agriculture is crucial." In other words, we are dealing with a *total economic system.*

Figure 216 illustrates Hodder's notion, relating it to different systems of agriculture and to population density. At the two extremes of the continuum are shifting subsistence agriculture and so-called industrial agriculture. Between lies a shift of population density upwards, which in turn is one of the chief stimulants of change in the agricultural sector. Although this continuum is only a suggestion it does seem to have some relation to reality, and fits well with the earlier notion that "developed" and "developing" are not themselves rigid categories.

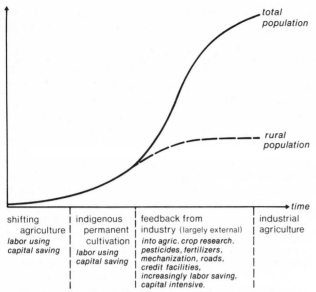

total population

rural population

time

| shifting agriculture | indigenous permanent cultivation | feedback from industry (largely external) | industrial agriculture |
| *labor using capital saving* | *labor using capital saving* | *into agric. crop research. pesticides, fertilizers, mechanization, roads, credit facilities, increasingly labor saving, capital intensive.* | |

Fig. 216. *The development continuum from agriculture to industry. (Reprinted by permission from B.W. Hodder,* Economic Development in the Tropics, *Methuen and Co., 1968, p. 167.)*

Political Structures

Many states are "artificial," that is, they did not exist prior to colonization. Often the very notion of "nationality" is an alien one. A new colonial acquisition was often a conglomerate of tribal or peasant groups, and the colonial boundaries were drawn for convenience rather than to reflect ethnic, linguistic, or cultural differences. Many colonial administrations were short-lived, so that any binding together of these diverse groups usually lasted no longer than a few decades. Even when the idea or value of one national identity could be introduced, short time spans could not erase the differences between such peoples as the Ibo, Hausa, Yoruba, and seven other major tribes, all of whom were expected to regard themselves as "Nigerians." As one Nigerian politician has remarked, "Nigeria is not a nation state. It is a mere political expression." The truth of this remark received tragic expression in the attempt to form a breakaway state of Biafra, and the resulting civil war (1967–70). The formation of a new nation, Bangladesh, out of the artificial creation of another colonial compromise, adds even further strength to this contention. There are still many territories that have little cultural or economic reason for existence. Not only are disparate groups loosely joined together within common boundaries, but the boundaries themselves cut across common groups. The result of this is often the emergence of subgroups that have more in common with subgroups in other such "nations" than with any in their own. Thus many of the Shan people, who live in Burma, China, and

Thailand, have only tenuous national feelings. Similarly in West Africa, where national boundaries were drawn approximately at right angles to the coast, cultural groups aligned parallel to the coast were severely dismembered. The most notorious example is probably that of the Ewe tribe, divided between the two neighboring states of Ghana and Togo. Formerly the Ewe were divided between two areas administered by Great Britain and a third under French mandate.

Another obstacle to national unity has been the policy of certain colonial administrations to prevent the formation of any political or national identity. Belgian and Portuguese colonial policy, in particular, discouraged national political parties and utilized primarily European administrators. The Portuguese have kept to the idea of a single corporate state consisting of motherland and overseas territory, so that the idea of a colony gaining "independence" has no meaning for them. In the Congo, the Belgians decided not to educate Africans for higher positions, thus making the transition to independence even more difficult and perhaps perpetuating the regionalism and localism that have hindered the emergence of a Congolese state. British and Dutch colonial policies may have been different, but their use of "indirect" rule also tended to foster local loyalties by maintaining traditional chiefs.

All these factors have left many countries with groups that have no loyalty or attachment to the "nation-state" to which they are supposed to belong. Obviously, the resultant instability and localism militates against overall economic development.

It was suggested above that the external boundaries to the so-called developing nations, imposed as they were from without, were artificial and often caused as much dissension as unity. Instability or dissension, it was suggested, could be a barrier to economic growth. If this is true of political boundaries, is it also true to any degree of the internal political subsystem? Historically, of course, growth has taken place within a wide variety of political systems and under quite different public policies. From a strictly economic point of view, is any system necessarily "the best"?

One difficulty here is that the population of a developing nation is concerned with a complex of factors, only one of which is material advancement, and it is difficult to disaggregate such a complex. Another problem is that many commentators in pursuing such analyses seem to assume that the process of political development has only one end product, *viz*, the one pursued by "typical" industrial nations. However, it has been stressed throughout this book that we cannot regard our values and practices as universally valid. In fact, there may be no specific end product at all.

The argument, then, becomes reversed in this section. Whereas we might concede that population numbers, resource bases, imposed colonial structures, and so forth, can contribute to "underdevelopment," can we also concede that only if a society is to perform as a modern industrial state, with all the attendant Western institutions and practices, will it be able to develop economically? Do all nations have to share the same Western concepts about law and the nature of public authority? Is the question, "Who is in charge here?" always meaningful? According to *our* logic every territory should fall under some sovereignty, defined as a common loyalty and the same legal obligations. To the Western mind, an orderly legal process is a requisite of political development and economic growth. Indeed, the success of a colonial regime is frequently measured according to the extent to which it left behind a working administrative framework.

It can be argued that various political frameworks are capable of providing an environment for economic growth. Among the political factors that can impede economic development either directly or indirectly are: failure to maintain law and order; corruption in public administration; exploitation of certain social classes or groups; maintenance of a rigid class system; failure to provide critical assistance to certain economic sectors; diversion of capital into unproductive sectors of the economy; unfair taxation; demoralization of population; waste of resources in needless militarism; and indulgence in "political monuments" such as airlines and convention centers that divert capital from growth areas. To these factors Joseph Spengler has added ability or nonability to support education and public health; research and technical development; overhead capital; banking and credit systems; planning and conservation policy; legal structure; and the institutionalization of public and private initiative. Failure to create this last-named group of facilities is seen by Spengler as a major economic barrier. According to Spengler, most "developing" nations, despite strong efforts at national planning and at attracting foreign capital, are failing from a sociopolitical point of view, and thus are contributing to economic stagnation.

A. Eckstein is another who has noted that the failure of the political structure is frequently reflected by deficiencies in capital formation and in the growth of entrepreneurship:

In many traditional societies, accumulations of merchant and other forms of capital tend to be dissipated because of: (1) the absence of adequate and contractual arrangements to protect these holdings from the more or less arbitrary ravages of officialdom, and (2) the failure of the state to institute a social security system. . . . At the same time, condition (1) tends to reinforce the economic risks of various

types of business and industrial investments . . . the same condition further encourages the flow of capital into land investment, which . . . represents one of the safest and most profitable forms of holdings . . . in effect the state . . . through sins of commission and omission . . . tends to undercut actual and potential sources of capital accumulation.

What, then, is the relationship of development to social attitudes and cultural values? Certain political factors, as we have seen, do appear to influence economic development. But such influences seem not to be the specific property of any one political structure. Individualistic democracy, collective democracy, authoritarian, elitist, or totalitarian political systems—all have recorded successes and failures. Obviously the answer lies in a complex of factors, only some of which are political.

An interesting development, noted by F. R. von der Mehden, has been the evolution of personal, party, and national ideologies. These ideologies have been syntheses of capitalist, socialist and indigenous elements, and as such have often been of a unique nature. In particular, they tend to be introverted and xenophobic, merging fact and value to produce the desired version of reality. Ghandi, for example, believed that "Indian civilisation is the best and that the European is a nine days' wonder . . . the tendency of Indian civilisation is to elevate the moral being, that of the Western civilisation is to propagate immorality." The relationship between ideology of this kind and economic growth is not a simple one, but it can be costly for a government to adhere persistently to economic doctrines that run counter to social and other indigenous relationships. Thus in both China and East Germany the barriers to economic improvement seem to be fewer than in India, with its very uneven record of growth.

Some applications of von der Mehden's ideological categories are set out in table 84. No attempt will be made here to tie in one kind of ideology with economic growth and another with underdevelopment; the relationship is not as simple as that. It is worth noting, however, that ideology can:

1. *Divert popular attention away from important internal problems, as when a campaign against the former colonial power is used to obscure real domestic problems.*

2. *Be used as a basis for justifying militaristic adventures, at great cost to the state.*

3. *Lend legitimacy to primarily political or individually motivated acts, which again could be harmful to economic development.*

This brings us once more to the concept of "colonialism." As noted earlier, the vestiges or continuing presence of an imposed colonial system can seriously affect the operation of a developing na-

Table 84. *Summary: Selected Nations, Colonization, Political Structure and Ideology*

country	colony	independence	political structure	ideology
Afghanistan	—	—	one party	elitist
Algeria	France	1962	one party	collective democracy
Argentina	Spain	1816**	multiparty/military	capitalist elite
Bolivia	Spain	1825**	dominance of one party/military	capitalist elite
Brazil	Portugal	1822**	military	military elite
Burma	U.K.	1948	military	socialist-minded military rule
Cambodia	France	1953	monarchy/one party	personality oriented
Cameroon	France	1960	multiparty	collective democracy
Ceylon	U.K.	1948**	multiparty	collective democracy
Chad	France	1960	one party	elitist
Chile	Spain	1818**	multiparty	mixed democracy
China	—	—	proletariat	proletarian democracy
Congo (Leopoldville)	Belgium	1960**	military	elitist
Cuba	Spain	1898	proletariat	proletarian democracy
Dominica	Spain	1821	dictatorship	elitist
Egypt	U.K. control	1952	one party	guided democracy
Ethiopia	—	—**	monarchy/traditional oligarchy	elitist
Gabon	France	1960	one party dominant	collective democracy
Ghana	U.K.	1957**	military	elitist
India	U.K.	1947**	multiparty	mixed democracy
Iran	—	—**	monarchy	elitist
Jordan	U.K.	1946**	monarchy/multiparty	elitist/guided democracy
Liberia	U.S.	1822**	one party	Whig
Malaysia	U.K.	1957–63**	multiparty	mixed democracy
Mexico	Spain	1821	one party	collective democracy
Morocco	France	1956	monarchy/two party	elitist
Nigeria	U.K.	1960**	military	military elite
N. Korea	Japan	1946	proletariat	proletarian democracy
N. Vietnam	France	1954	proletariat	proletarian democracy
Pakistan	U.K.	1947	multiparty	mixed democracy
Panama	Spain	1903*	multiparty/military	mixed democracy
Philippines	Spain/U.S.	1946*	two party	mixed democracy
Saudi Arabia	—	—	monarchy	elitist
Sierra Leone	U.K.	1961**	multiparty	mixed democracy
S. Korea	Japan	1946*	U.S. dominated	elitist
S. Vietnam	France	1954*	U.S. dominated	elitist
Thailand	—	—	military	elitist
Tunisia	France	1955	one party	collective democracy
Uganda	U.K.	1962	multiparty	collective democracy
Uruguay	Spain	1825*	two party	capitalist elite — mixed democracy
Venezuela	Spain	1811**	multiparty/military	mixed democracy

Source: F.R. Von der Mehden, *Politics of the Developing Nations* (Englewood Cliffs, N.J.: Prentice-Hall, 1964); J.S. Coleman, "The Political Systems of the Developing Areas," in G.A. Almond and J.S. Coleman, eds., *The Politics of Developing Areas* (Princeton, N.J.: Princeton University Press, 1960).

*neocolonial metropolis orientation still strong
**neocolonial orientation present in economic system

tion's economic system. The already "developed" nations grew at a time when they had few rivals. Hence their gains were great, and tended to be cumulative. These initial centers of capitalist development then diffused to their colonial territories and satellites only those economic factors that served their own interests. In the words of A. G. Frank, "the metropolis (the centre of the market-exchange system) suppressed the technology in the now underdeveloped countries which conflicted with the interests of the metropolis and its own development, as the Europeans did with the irrigation and other agricultural technology and installations in India, the Middle East, and Latin America, or as the English did with industrial technology in India, Spain, and Portugal." The situation regarding markets is now very different for a nation attempting to develop an industrial or agricultural sector, from the advantages gained and secured by the already developed locations.

Such impositions frequently had disastrous effects. Thus K. E. Gough describes peasant revolts in nineteenth century India as follows:

The biggest revolts were . . . in Malabar . . . such uprisings stemmed from the increasing exactions of the colonial economy. During the first two-thirds of the 19th century the British instituted capitalist agrarian relations throughout most of India. Land became the personal, marketable property of former land-managers and revenue collectors. Landlords acquired the power to raise rents or evict tenants freely. Serfs and slaves became landless laborers. Cash crops were produced for foreign and Indian markets in response to the government's extraction of heavy cash revenues. . . . In Kerala the 19th century saw a great increase in population and a vast expansion of export crops. . . . Landlords forced more and more produce from their too numerous tenants, evicting them if they failed to pay their rents. . . . Tenancy Acts passed after 1887 gave increasing security to rich and middle peasants and non-cultivating middle tenants, but did little for poor peasants and landless laborers.

Among the economic elements introduced by the British were Tamil laborers who, for various reasons, formed a new social group rather than assimilating. Moreover, they encouraged population movements that brought the different ethnic groups into close proximity, thus heightening the dangers of intergroup clashes. Such internal divisions were frequently strengthened by the way the British instituted community boundaries.

The result of these colonial impositions was to create a new network or system of international economic, cultural, and political relations. It was a dynamic relationship that changed shape and emphasis over time as a result of new acquisitions, differential rates of industrial or resource development, the exhaustion of resources, and cyclical business depressions. The net result for the colonized was frequently a barrier to development. Thus in Buenos Aires, after it fell under the financial domination of London, local manufacturing was ruined by foreign competition.

Colonialism has now given way to neocolonialism, so that today only a handful of nation-states remain completely subservient to some foreign political master. But the vestiges of this system are still implanted in virtually all ex-colonial territories, whose very economic functioning has been weakened by decades of colonial tampering with their system. The frequently invisible systems links of neocolonialism can dominate a country's political, economic, and cultural structure without resort to overt colonial rule. Neocolonialism is carried forward not so much on a wave of soldiers as on a barrage of Coca-Cola, *Time, Reader's Digest,* "Sound of Music" type movies, telestar relays, and Al Capp cartoons. This barrage has been termed the very *culture* of neocolonialism.

The roots of neocolonialism are in monopoly capitalism and the military-industrial complex. Its branches are corporate and financial institutions, with their internationalized capital. Its means are the business and political elites of the imperialist nations and their puppets in the underdeveloped world. Its end results are the same as under classic colonialism: the ever-widening gap between metropolis and satellite, and the warping of indigenous development by external pressures.

In one analysis of international U.S. corporate enterprises, net capital outflows of U.S. parent companies to their foreign subsidiaries were estimated at between $2 to $3 billion per year and inflows of royalties and dividends at some $5 billion per year. It is notable that the General Foods Corporation, whose international corporate structure was disaggregated above, has in recent years received its most rapidly growing profit area from its holdings outside North America. Foreign corporations attract and absorb scarce domestic capital and skills, thereby depriving the "host" nation of its own resources. Similarly, the provision of foreign technology and skills is frequently seen as a means of drawing off scarce human resources, as the few available skilled scientists and technicians are siphoned off to other areas. Such foreign investment can also bring with it a milieu of uncertainty and instability, since, according to Vernon, "every [nation] . . . is aware that a multinational corporate group which is able to provide export markets for the product of the host country is also capable of withholding such markets and cutting off the jobs that depend on such exports. If Nigeria should eventually become a lower cost producer of widgets than Italy, the corporate group

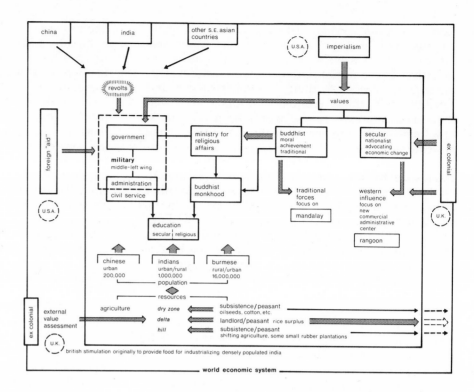

Fig. 217. *Burma: the national system; a generalized profile. (In part from M. Nash, "Some Social and Cultural Aspects of Economic Development," Economic Development and Social Change, vol. 7, 1959, pp. 137–150.)*

may shift the locus of its operation out of Italy into Nigeria."

Neocolonial influences do not seem to be the specific property of any one political structure. Individualistic democracy, collective democracy, authoritarian, elitist, or totalitarian political systems have all recorded successes and failures in this area. One difficulty in identifying neocolonial barriers to development is that the population of a developing nation is concerned with a complex of factors, only one of which may be material advancement or political stability. Many commentators seem to assume that the process of development can have only one end product, and that it follows the course of allegedly typical Western industrial nations. However, we cannot regard *our* values and practices as the universal standard or system. In fact there is no specifically definable end product; we may well be dealing with system capability rather than with fixed institutional forms, economic patterns, or normative policies.

Forces Working Toward Equalization

Despite the negative barriers, there are also forces at work that are leading toward some equalization of development, albeit slowly. Greater mobility, the breakdown of status distinctions, the development of mass communications and resulting contact with the outside world, the increasing availability of educa-

tion and technology, development aid (both sefless and selfish), the slow breakdown of capitalist and colonial dependency, economic planning, a concern for general human welfare, and the sheer will of a society to alter its traditional socioeconomic structure, have all had a role to play. But the process is not an easy one. For example, the following factors have been said to aid development: increased technology, capital, labor, and more efficient resource utilization. All of these factors were provided for over a ten-year period under the Alliance for Progress—which has proved to be a failure. Briefly, the reason appears to be that, although South America is relatively rich in resources, a one-dimensional aid program is not capable of benefiting the mass of its population. Wealth either continues to flow from the resources to the native elite, including the bourgeoisie, or from the indigenous economy to the international corporations. Unless the forces of equalization radically alter the economic and social structure of these countries, they will be trapped in a cycle of **perverse growth.**

Figures 217 and 218 illustrate some of the interlocking forces that must underlie the impetus toward equalization. Development is a process that involves behavioral, spatial-temporal, and operational factors. Not all of these dimensions can be shown here. In both cases, there are elite groups with their own distinctive values and activities, both political and religious. There are also wide differences between the social structures of the rural peasant communi-

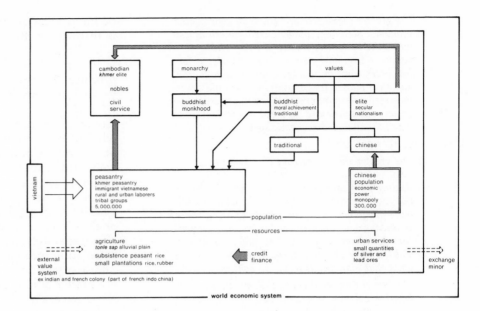

Fig. 218. *Cambodia: the national system; a generalized profile. (Ibid.)*

ties and the urban populations. Of course, the full sociological and historical ramifications of these relationships are hard to present in a diagram of this type. Thus, Manning Nash, in 1959, argued that Burma had greater potential for development than Cambodia because, among other advantages, it had succeeded in incorporating the large and vigorous Chinese merchant class into the general economic system, whereas in Cambodia this same class was more or less forced to keep to itself. But a great many things have happened in both countries since Nash made his study, so that their comparative prospects for development have to be entirely reassessed. Nevertheless, Nash's schema of developmental factors is still highly relevant. The following is an adaptation of that schema, with the addition of a few categories not found in the original.

A. CULTURAL FACTORS

1. Social Stratification

(a) *The more extreme the polarization of wealth, power and prestige between groups in a nation, the less likely that economic opportunities will be perceived and acted upon. The corollary of this statement is that the lower the degree of social stratification, the more the concern for general human welfare and the more likely that economic changes will benefit a nation's growth.*

(b) *The fewer the legitimate opportunities for social mobility, the more likely that the "lower" strata will seek alternative means of mobility, including military or guerrilla revolt. One corollary of this is that the more legitimate opportunities for social mobility, the more the concern with human welfare and the larger the opportunities for seeking development.*

2. The Value System

(a) *The greater the stress on nationalism, the greater the probability of development being made one of the national goals.*

(b) *The greater the exposure to other than national values and ideologies, the easier it is likely to be to win a commitment to development.*

(c) *The more equalized values are between segments of society, and the greater the degree to which those values are other than traditional values, the easier it is to achieve development.*

B. ECONOMIC FACTORS

(a) *Greatest development occurs at times when the links to the world capitalist metropolises are at their weakest. This is not to deny the importance of "aid" or the work of certain United Nations agencies. But it does indicate the inverse causal relationship between imperialism or neocolonialism and "development."*

(b) *The lesser the subsistence element in the economy the less likely that the system will be localized and activities diffuse. Conversely, the higher the proportion of nonsubsistent elements, the more likely that savings will be accumulated and steered into supplying the metropolis, and that economic growth to the benefit of the satellite nation will not take place.*

(c) *The greater the level of savings, the greater the time perspective of investment, and the greater the availability of entrepreneurs and others who can foresee potential growth, the more likely that economic activities of a secondary and tertiary nature will occur. The more developed the institutions available to deal with accumulation and investment, the more significant the amounts of capital that are likely to be channeled into economic activities with growth potential.*

(d) *The greater the degree of nationally coordinated economic planning, and balanced growth investment, the better the chance of successful and balanced economic change. The plea here is for less investment in prestige projects such as iron and steel plants, transportation links, and other imagined preconditions of Western-style economic growth, and for more balanced investment in a carefully analyzed economic system.*

C. POLITICAL FACTORS

(a) *The greater the sovereignty of a government over its territory, the more organized the group holding political power, the more broadly based the government's recruitment practices, and the more allegiance that people have to a centralized political group, then the better the environment for centralized cultural and economic planning, and the more people will try to identify with what that planning is trying to achieve.*

(b) *The less the external political domination, whether colonial or neocolonial, past or present, the greater the hope for developmental equalization.*

(c) *The less the political aggrandizement, the less likely that prestige, military or territorial expansion projects will be undertaken, with consequent effects on economic growth patterns.*

(d) *The less elitist and divorced from the general welfare the attitudes of politicians, the greater the hope for development.*

This is not a complete list; for instance, certain spatial dimensions have been omitted.

Conclusion

Development is a complex historical process. So, too, is underdevelopment; there is nothing innate about it, if the area is reasonably habitable. The relationships between the various sectors of the spatial system are part of the dynamic process by which socioeconomic systems develop. These relationships are both positive and negative, functional and conflicting; at times one element may stimulate and induce development, at others it may act as a barrier. Some, like Spengler, would go so far as to identify specific political preconditions to development; Rostow sets out economic preconditions; both Hoselitz and Smelser are more interested in a variety of cultural prerequisites; Frank has identified a particular world capitalist system that imposes lesser development. None of these explanations is very satisfactory in itself. Any theory specifying a certain precondition for development is vulnerable to the objection that development has occurred elsewhere without that precondition's help. Thus development at any one time in any one nation may

be impossible unless a colonialist or imperialist yoke is thrown off. But this alone will not insure growth and change: the economic, cultural, and political factors must be combined in some unique way to produce an ongoing system of development.

We must also pose the question "Development for whom?" Obviously, we are concerned with the behavior of such people as industrial entrepreneurs, wholesalers, retailers, and regional planners, all of whom no doubt form a part of some well fed, well paid elite, whether a capitalist or a communist economy is in question. But what about the rest of society? What about the Burmese or Vietnamese peasant, the sugar cane worker in Northeast Brazil, or the Uganda coffee farmer? Many of these people are desperately poor; in fact, over half the world's population receives less than the recommended daily calorie intake *every* day of their lives. Their behavior is a matter of bare survival. Development for whom? Need we ask?

There are of course other kinds of malfunction to consider. But the impact on the world economic landscape of this particular malfunction is so considerable that most of this chapter has been devoted to it.

Population and Resources: To Feed the Billions

The most striking demographic event of the past three centuries has been the unprecedented increase in world population. In previous centuries the overall population total grew very slowly. Carr Saunders estimated that in 1650 the world population stood at 545 million. In 1950, on a much firmer basis, world population was estimated at 2.5 billion and in 1960 at 2.99 billion. United Nations demographers estimate that in 1975 it will reach 4 billion. Around 1700, the expectation of life at birth of the population of North America and Western Europe was about 32 years. It had probably been at that point for the previous three or four centuries. Today, the average for western countries is 69.8 years, an increase of over 100 percent. There is no evidence to suggest that any measurable part of this remarkable increase in average length of life has been due to changes in the genetic constitution of the population. Rather, all evidence points to man's increasing control of his environment as the chief cause. This increasing control has been made possible by four developments:

1. *The opening up of new continents, which provided additional sources of food and other resources, and which also acted as an outlet for surplus population.*
2. *The expansion of commerce, which made possible the*

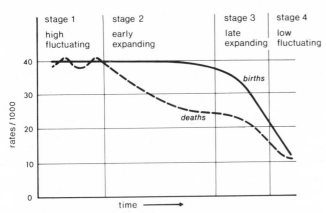

Fig. 219. *A stylized population cycle.*

stage 1 — high fluctuating
stage 2 — early expanding
stage 3 — late expanding
stage 4 — low fluctuating

births
deaths

rates / 1000

time

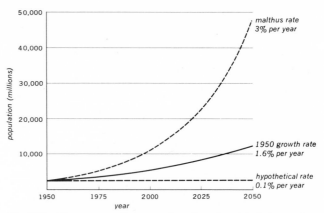

Fig. 220. *Three contrasting rates of projected population growth.*

malthus rate
3% per year

1950 growth rate
1.6% per year

hypothetical rate
0.1% per year

population (millions)

year

transportation of food and capital goods over long distances.

3. *Technological changes in agriculture, together with the development of modern industry.*

4. *Increasing control of disease through improved housing, hygienic food and water supply, the adoption of public sanitary measures, advances in preventive medicine, and, more recently, such chemical discoveries as antibiotics and the new insecticides.*

Rates of population increase vary considerably over the surface of the earth. The area of fastest growth is tropical Latin America, which has a natural increase rate of 30–40 per 1,000 population. In absolute numbers, however, mainland China is growing faster because of its huge population base of 700 million; the natural increase rates are 25–28 per 1,000 population. On the other hand, some Western European countries have natural increase rates as low as 5–10 per 1,000 population.

The population problem can be summed up in terms of a historical model of birth and death rates (figure 219). In stage I, the prescientific stage, both birth and death rates are high, though they tend to fluctuate a great deal. Population increase at this stage is slow, irregular, and frequently static. This stage ended in Western Europe in the early eighteenth century. But it continues to this day in the essentially "undeveloped" areas of Africa and Australasia.

In stage II, death rates decline, but birth rates remain high and fluctuate. This is the stage at which medical and sanitary improvements greatly reduce mortality rates, particularly of infants. It is therefore a stage of rapid population increase. Much of Western Europe remained in this stage until the 1880s; thus England and Wales had a birth rate of 36 per 1,000 in 1870. At this stage, population increases of 2 or 3 percent a year are common. In Western Europe, both stage II and stage III were accompanied by rapid economic growth. But this is not true today

of areas with similar demographic characteristics such as Asia and much of South America.

In stage III, mortality continues to decline, but at a slower rate, since for obvious reasons the adult death rate is more difficult to reduce. Perhaps in response to higher standards of living, better education, the changing status of women, and so forth, families become smaller and a decline in birth rates occurs, though there can still be quite substantial population increases. Britain had these demographic characteristics from about 1875 to 1920.

Finally in stage IV both birth and death rates fluctuate at a low level, with small and slow increases in total population. This phase applies today to much of Western Europe and North America.

This sketch is of course a gross simplification. It does illustrate, however, the possible role of population growth as a barrier to development. If a sharp fall in the death rate occurs without a change in fertility rates, and if the economic structure remains unchanged, then the result may be a severe strain on the socioeconomic structure of a particular area. If absolute numbers increase without a sharp fall in growth rates, and if it is accepted that continuing "development" means increased per capita income, more plentiful consumer goods, and an expanding gross national product, then the "explosion" of population could be seen as producing a definite economic imbalance and a retardation (in net terms) of the overall growth rate. This is the classic Malthusian situation. If we assume constant growth rates we get the kinds of growth curve illustrated in figure 220. Thus a growth rate of .01 percent per year would cause a tenfold increase every 2,300 years. Malthus assumed a rate of 3 percent, which would result in a doubling of population every 25 years! The third curve is a projection of the actual 1950 increase rate which, if continued, would result in a world population of 12 billion by 2035, 25 billion by 2065, and 50 billion by 2100.

Any such portrayal is of course very simplistic, and there are numerous theories to explain how such imbalances between population and resources can be resolved. To the neo-Malthusian the "space ship earth" is filled to capacity and running out of resources. To the computer model maker, who elegantly projects the same trends in terms of natural resources, capital investment, pollution, and so on, we are headed for eco-catastrophe. To both, the solution is ZPG, or zero population growth. Both are wrong. The truth is that the factors governing population growth and differential fertility rates are very variable. Total numbers may be less important than population structure—education, sex, age, values. More importantly, the future is not as exact and predictable as the Malthusian view would have it. In particular, we do not need to base our calculations on the North American standard of life. Nor do we have to adopt the Malthusian concept of "natural resources" as the substance and processes of which the earth is composed here and now. In this sense, "resources" would indeed be finite on a finite globe. However, in Zimmermann's functional conception only substances and processes that are perceived and utilized by man at one point in time become resources. In this sense, resources are almost infinite. For many societies, and for mankind as a whole, the future vis-à-vis population and natural resources is open-ended. Perhaps what we should worry about are not the population growth rates of India, but the production ratios of the United States and the Soviet Union. The Malthusian assumption that population will inevitably outgrow food supplies holds good only under the condition that man and his socioeconomic systems are unchanging and that man is unable to alter his resource system. This is not to preach complacency: increasing the food supply *is* a challenge. But it can be met without resort to extreme measures.

Despite this, the population-resource crunch is probably the barrier to development most frequently cited by geographers, who assume that for the welfare of people in lesser developed areas to improve resources should become available at a rate faster than population growth. It is true that in some areas the increase in population is threatening to outrun *present* efforts to increase productivity per capita. Such efforts commonly take one of three forms:

1. *Increasing productivity by technological means.*
2. *Reducing the rate of natural population increase.*
3. *A combination of the two above.*

The ultimate goal is to produce a surplus of goods over and above those needed for current consumption, and thus to provide the means for capital forma-

tion and the improvement of social and instrumental capital. Of course, the question arises whether there are alternatives to these three solutions. Thus technical means exist to increase agricultural yields and industrial production. But these may not be utilized to the full. For instance, in the United States in 1968 the federal government paid farmers $4 billion to keep 35 million acres of agricultural land out of production. When something like 50 percent of the world's population goes hungry every day, such a policy seems paradoxical. But the argument used is that though there may be demand, there is no "market" for more food—or in other words, that in North America food is grown for profit, not to feed people. When this kind of malfunction occurs, that is, when the problem is one of "surplus" amid starvation, hunger is not just a matter of lack of food; it is also a lack of money. This is a different order of malfunction altogether, and actually easier to adjust.

On the other hand, a substantial body of opinion, rightly or wrongly, perceives population increases as a barrier to further economic growth. These writers see death control as much more widespread than birth control. They point out that present social structures encourage high birth rates, that standards of living are bound to decline, and that the gap between developed and underdeveloped nations will grow as resources are outstripped by population growth. But what are resources? The concept varies by culture, both subjectively and objectively. It might be possible to determine a ratio of population to resources that would be appropriate for each cultural group. For each group we would have to know how much they can and do produce, how much they do and would like to consume, and how much they need to consume. This is not to deny a minimum threshold; below a certain level of food intake (the U.N. figure is 2,200 calories) all men, no matter what their attitudes or beliefs, are going to starve. But anything above that minimum is difficult to measure, and it is only too easy to fall back on Western notions of what constitutes an acceptable standard of living.

E. A. Ackermann has put forward a schema in which the ratio of population to resources is described for five different types of area (figure 221).

Areas of the *first type* are technologically advanced, with a low ratio of population to resources (example: the United States).

Areas of the *second type* are technologically advanced, with a high ratio of population to resources (example: much of Western Europe).

Areas of the *third type* are technologically deficient, with a low ratio of population to resources (example: parts of South America, such as Brazil).

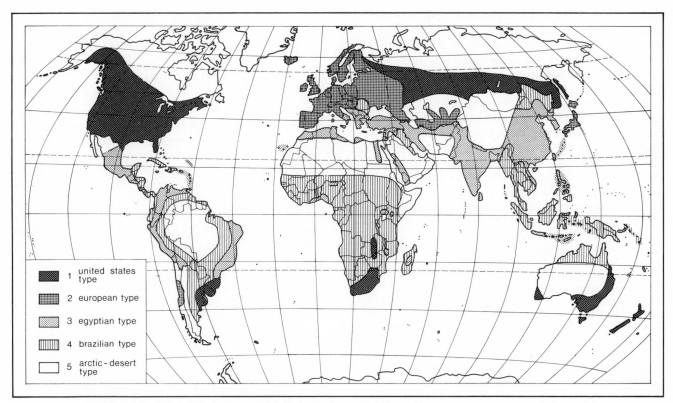

Fig. 221. *Generalized population-resource regions. (From W. Zelinsky,* A Prologue to Population Geography, *1966, pp. 108–9, reprinted by courtesy of Prentice-Hall Inc. and the University of Chicago Press.)*

Areas of the *fourth type* are technologically deficient, with a high ratio of population to resources (example: parts of Southern Europe and Southeast Asia).

Areas of the *fifth type* are technologically deficient, with very few food-producing resources at all (example: the Arctic and Antarctic areas).

It should be clear even from this brief discussion that it is not possible to treat population and resources by themselves; the addition of some operational component — in this case technology — is necessary if we are to understand, say, the differences between the United States and Brazil. W. Zelinsky gives detailed examples from each of these categories. For instance, he points out that type 3 areas, for a variety of reasons, have a resource base that is extensive by Western standards, but only minimally developed. Underdevelopment of resources has occurred through lack of capital, colonial exploitation, and political, ideological, and cultural barriers. Type 4 areas have an imbalance of population and resources by Western standards, are densely populated by these standards with regard to available means of subsistence. Zelinsky warns that "these lands are doubly stricken: their excessive numbers confront deficient material and social capital, and their

chances for escape upwards to the status of European type countries are very slim." However, he does not explain how Japan or Puerto Rico, which some years ago might have fallen into this category, escaped such a fate. On the other hand, an explanation could be constructed in terms of some of the other structural defects noted above and in table 83.

To sum up: one viewpoint sees hunger and overpopulation as being defeated by control *of* people, the other as being overcome through control *by* people.

The New Foundling: Ecology

In the 1930s, in a book called *The Idea of Progress,* the British historian J. B. Bury optimistically predicated that science, technology, and the other paraphernalia of the modern state assured mankind of virtually millennia of continued existence on the earth's surface. Just under four decades later, man's very physical survival seems to be open to question. In fact a group of biologists and other scientists at the University of Toronto give us probably only another four decades *to* survive.

As with underdevelopment and population, we have a paradox. On the one hand, there is a very real environmental crisis: we have devastated natural environments, rivers, the very air we breathe. Ecosystems from Lake Erie to Lake Baykal are in danger. On the other hand, there are means to reverse the consequences of pollution. Yet we seem incapable of utilizing them.

There are a number of reasons for this—reasons that cannot be stated in traditional economic terms. Economists reduce the ecological problem to a narrowly defined technical exercise that ignores the broad range of social and political change needed within our operational milieu. In so doing, they refuse to acknowledge that their traditional analyses are inadequate, and that what needs to be challenged is the very basis of our social and economic system, including the high premium we place on material growth. Heilbroner states:

There is no doubt that the main avenue of traditional capitalist accumulation would have to be considerably constrained; that net investment in mining and manufacturing would likely decline; that the rate and kind of technological change would need to be supervised and probably greatly reduced; and that, as a consequence, the flow of profits would almost certainly fall. Is this imaginable within a capitalist setting. . . . ? It is tantamount to asking a dominant class to acquiesce in the elimination of the very activities that sustain it. . . .

These words of a liberal go to the heart of the problem. What we need is not zero population growth but zero *economic* growth.

What does not seem to be clearly understood in today's environmental crisis is that the emphasis on economic growth is only one feature of a value system that needs to be radically revised. The solution of course, is not simply a matter of stopping the measurement of GNP, introducing pollution taxes, or halting population growth. All these deal with symptoms of malfunctioning rather than root causes. To go to root causes must entail far-reaching changes in society and in man's relation to man. In Mao Tse-tung's words: "If you want knowledge, you must take part in the practice of changing reality. If you want to know the taste of a pear, you must change the pear by eating it yourself."

Technologies by themselves are socially neutral. But the attitudes that go with technologies, are cultural products, the results of particular socioeconomic relationships that human beings establish with one another. To make clear the attitude of the typical Western businessman, we need only quote Milton Friedman, the well-known American economist:

The view has been gaining widespread acceptance that corporate officials . . . have a "social responsibility" that goes beyond serving the interest of their stockholders. . . . This view shows a fundamental misconception of the character and nature of a free economy. In such an economy, there is one and only one social responsibility of business—to use its resources and engage in activities designed to increase its profits so long as it stays within the rules of the game, which is to say, engages in open and free competition, without deception or fraud.

A common twist in the argument over who is to blame for pollution is to blame us, the general public, rather than the corporate structure and business ethics. For instance, a common myth is that the automobile is the primary cause of air pollution, and thus we, the drivers, are at fault. But in many cities more than half the air pollution comes not from automobiles, but from industrial plants. Meanwhile, industry passes the bill for environmental damage on to us. Thus the one-way bottle can actually cost us more than the old returnable type because about 30 cents in taxes are required for its disposal.

The dilemma facing North American society is that the rapid rate of growth necessary to service large corporations, war machines, and wasteful consumer items, ultimately involves an increasing degree of environmental destruction. Even if cleaner processes are created, the complete recycling of wastes will be technologically impossible and, in our economic system, economically unfeasible. The unavoidable conclusion is that without a significant slowdown in the rate of economic growth, the environment will simply be destroyed. Technological breakthroughs may occasionally offer a respite, but they will not provide an ecological panacea. The only way out of the malfunctioning seems to be to adopt institutions, beliefs, and technologies that will allow us to maintain a stationary economy—zero GNP.

The changes demanded may be almost impossible for a society in which organic community relationships, which placed a premium on cooperation, have given way to *market* relationships, which involve reducing everything man and nature, to a resource for exploitation. In our society, life is structured around two axioms: "Production for the sake of production," and, "Consumption for the sake of consumption." Just as men are negated and converted into commodities, so every aspect of nature is converted into a commodity, a resource to be manufactured and merchandized at will. Cities become market places, continental areas are treated as factories. Bookchin has remarked that "the plundering of the human spirit by the market place is paralleled by the plundering of the earth by capital. The tendency of the liberal to identify the marketplace with human needs, and capital with technology, represents a calculated error that neutralises the social thrust of the ecological crisis."

In this crisis, the production rates of Western countries are of more legitimate concern than the non-Western countries' rates of population growth. The United States is the prime example since every year it produces 50 percent of the world's goods and consumes 70 percent of the world's resources, but has only 7 percent of the world's population. If current industrial projections are correct, then unchecked economic growth over the next thirty years will demand a five-fold increase in electric power production, based presumably on nuclear fuels and coal. But at what cost to the environment? The enormously increased burden of radioactive wastes and other effluents is almost beyond imagination. And in the shorter term, the picture is no brighter: it is estimated that over the next five years, the United States will increase its production of lumber by 20 percent, of paper by 5 percent, of folding boxes by 3 percent, of metal cans by 4–5 percent, and of plastics by 7 percent—annually!

It may be that the planet conceived as one huge garbage dump can support these enormous increases in economic production in the short run, although one shudders to project the condition of the economic landscape in, say, twenty-five years time. But the earth conceived as a place for people cannot survive such ecocide. The question then becomes, can the earth survive these ravages long enough for us to replace the present malfunctioning and destructive economic system with something better? Do we have a better model to turn to? Certainly not to the Soviet Union, where the high priority given to economic growth and rapid industrial development has led to serious environmental disruption. Perhaps we have most to learn from the Chinese, whose environmental ethic is one of frugality and cooperation—the direct opposite of the competitive consumption on which Western life is based. Abandonment of "production for the sake of production" would of course involve an entirely new ethics, in which technology and industrial production would be placed at the service of meaningful human needs, and all industrial outputs would be carefully gauged to permit recycling of wastes into the environment. Economic development and progress would be measured not in terms of the rise of GNP but of net human benefit (NHB). Gurley remarks that, as in China, the ideal would be to "raise the level of material welfare of the population, [but] . . . only within the context of the development of human beings and of encouraging them to utilize fully their manifold creative powers. And it [would] be done on an egalitarian basis. . . ." Unhappily, established institutions, values, and beliefs are very difficult to overturn. Bringing man and his economic system into harmony with the phenomenal environment is going to require very concentrated effort.

Apartheid

Racist policies and values can have profound effects on the functioning of an economic system and its consequent landscape patterns. Such effects are most immediate and obvious when "racial" segregation becomes the official policy of the state concerned. A prime example is *apartheid*, the official policy of the Republic of South Africa. The rationale of apartheid is that the so-called racial groups should be allowed to develop separately, insofar as this is possible within the boundaries of one country. To this end, a partial territorial separation is under way, with special areas for Africans, Coloreds, and Asiatics; outside these areas Europeans have priority.* Separation, however, does not imply equality. Africans are restricted to certain fields of employment, largely on a migrant labor basis. Social and residential segregation is everywhere enforced, and contact is reduced to a minimum. Apartheid even has the blessing of the Dutch Reformed Church.

The economic development of South Africa has centered on a number of growth poles, or centers of intensive development, with underdeveloped areas between. A modern industrial society has been developed in a region inhabited by peasants whose labor supports it. The demand for labor has in turn created urban-rural differences in incomes, and has drawn more and more from rural to urban areas. Many of the laborers are semipermanent urban dwellers. This has had profound effects on the peasant economic organization, since it siphons off the young men and women from the land and allows at the same time the support of an unbalanced population in the African rural areas, or reserves, by means of income earned outside. The major industrial complex occurs in the southern Transvaal-northern Orange Free State area, with about 2½ million people. It includes the whole mining-industrial complex of the Witwatersrand, as well as the Pretoria and Witbank areas and the Orange Free State goldfield. It contains about half of all industrial employees—4 out of 10 Europeans and 1 in every 5 Africans. Development of other areas, such as the bush veld of Transvaal, with the northward expansion of the Natal sugar belt, has led to increasing European settlement. Of more importance, however, are the African reserves, where average family income is in the range of $75–$150 per year, with between 33 and 57 percent coming from local production and the balance from wages earned outside. Labor migration thus becomes an economic necessity. A handful of Africans can earn up to $100 or $160 a month in

*These group distinctions are the ones made by "white" South Africans.

urban areas, but earnings in the region of $18–$20 In his study of South Africa, Brookfield notes: "Generally speaking, the African areas are backward, neglected, and run down. Their agriculture still depends on extensive, unscientific pastoralism and on shifting cultivation yielding pitifully low returns." The reserves are carrying their maximum possible number of cattle, which is not the optimum number.

The rural-urban migration has siphoned off all the most able and ambitious Europeans and Africans, so while the traditional economic relationships in rural areas have been only partly disturbed, in the cities those relationships are no longer extant. Thus Asiatics in Durban could have taken control of all commercial activities, so thoroughly had they penetrated the tertiary sector; the fact they did not was due to government restrictions. Africans are subject to greater restrictions: short-term migrants are housed in barracks in or near the employment location, while the more permanent male and female migrants live in assigned city sections. This African migrant force provides the bulk of the labor needed by the secondary industries. However, this increasing urbanization of Africans is controlled quantitatively as well as areally. In Brookfield's 1957 work the author observes that by various administrative techniques the government is placing "a limitation and control of the urban influx, direction of immigrant labor to primary production, and an attempt to direct African cultural development towards the reserves, and around tribal traditions." Other techniques include locating new industries on the *margins* of reserves, but within largely European areas. In this way the industries can easily draw on African labor, but will remain permanently in European hands. A serious proposal at one time was to remove all Africans west of a line in the Cape Province.

Economically, government policies rely on the development of the "reserves," which are expected to contain the whole anticipated natural increase of the African population until the year 2000. Thus within central areas of cities, whites would far outnumber non-whites. On the flanks of these white islands would be densely populated African urban sections, and somewhat less populated Asiatic and Colored sections nearer the towns. Outside the towns would be white rural areas, although Europeans might compose only 15 percent of the population, with Africans dominating east of the line noted above, and Colored dominating west of it. In the eastern half of the country would be African reserves carrying very high rural population densities, and sending migrant laborers to the non-white proletarian urban settlements. As Brookfield points out, many of these policies are going to lead to increasing difficulties; in fact, territorial apartheid will be virtually impossible to carry out. Apartheid policies as outlined here would only diffuse integration without actually strengthening the European strategic position. Without integrated development, cutting the African reserves off from the nation's economic system would lead only to economic stagnation for the reserves, and to increasingly glaring economic differences between "white" and "black" South Africa.

Thus by deliberate government policy, an economic system is being shaped with dual components: a European system, similar to the market-exchange systems described in this book, but relying on African "slave" labor; and an African system, quite separate, peasant oriented, but receiving some income flows from participation in the European system. Apart from Rhodesia, no other intranational economic system is shaped quite in this way as a result of overt government action.

It would be mistaken to think of apartheid as confined to South Africa and Rhodesia; unfortunately, it flourishes elsewhere in the world, though in less obvious forms.

In North America it affects a number of groups, from French-speaking Canadians to Puerto Ricans, native Indian groups, and Mexican-Americans. These groups are doubly handicapped by racial prejudice and poverty. The process of residential segregation in North American cities has resulted in *ghettos*, which can be defined informally as areas from which the inhabitants would like to but cannot escape, because of economic and labor discrimination. The ghetto is a kind of urban reservation that becomes firmly entrenched in the spatial structure of a city when, in addition to the barriers of discrimination, institutional barriers are thrown around the urban enclaves. These can take a variety of forms, but the most common are various restrictive zoning and land-use controls. In suburban areas they can be used to prevent the development of low income housing, thus giving rise to what Robert Wood has called the "garrison suburb." Apartheid policies of this type in the United States are reinforced by government and local tax revenue structures, whereby the poor are seen as both economic and social liabilities.

Most but not all ghettos are centrally located. But the same processes occur regardless of location: restriction of interaction with the remaining urban neighborhoods, restriction of employment opportunities, immobility, and inadequate services, including housing. Such separation appears to be a permanent feature of North American capitalism; it is useless to talk of "restructuring the metropolis," and the like, when the entire socioeconomic system is to blame.

Poverty itself, in or out of the ghetto, is a form of economic apartheid. Approximately one out of every five North Americans lives below the poverty line.

In some individual regions and cities, the proportion is even higher. With poverty, as with the ghetto, go a whole range of symptoms: poor education, poor health, substandard housing, and personal disabilities of one kind or another. Many geographers and other commentators see these latter factors as the *causes* of poverty, rather than as what they are—its symptoms. It is of course profoundly demoralizing to live in a place where the young have as little hope as the old; where many are so poor that they find a can of dog food a good meal; where the unemployed people are so dehumanized that many commit suicide or become alcoholics. But these negative characteristics of the poor did not arise in a social vacuum; rather, they are responses to objective deprivation. Poverty begets poverty; for the most part it is a function—or rather, a malfunction—of the economic system, not the individual.

A common objection is that since even the poorest Canadian or American disposes of more income than an average worker or peasant in India, Bolivia, or one of the South African native reserves, that there really is no poverty in North America. But such a comparison is meaningless. Every society has its own standards for measuring poverty; and every socioeconomic subsystem has its own *subsistence minimum,* or list of basic wants. Poverty, as a systems malfunction, is the condition in a particular society when certain of its members have insufficient incomes to achieve the subsistence minimum. In these terms at least one out of every five North Americans is poor, and the system as it currently functions seems incapable of raising their incomes to any appreciable degree. It is no accident that the system is also incapable of assuring full employment, curbing inflation, distributing resources equitably, and rewarding achievement in a fair way. At the community level, local city governments and welfare agencies all too frequently fall into the hands of those who wish only to ensure that poverty and its consequences will not become a political issue.

Thus apartheid at the subsystem level can affect people in both spatial and behavioral terms: spatially, they may be restricted to some urban or rural area, while behaviorally they suffer racial discrimination and living standards below the subsistence minimum.

The Corporate Society

A crucial question concerning any economic system is that of *who holds power.* Who has the power to make the decisions that determine the shape of the economic landscape? How do those who hold that power exercise it? How will they exercise it in the future? Such questions arise naturally at this point in the book because maldistribution of economic power is a frequent cause of economic malfunction such as poverty. In North America a preponderant share of this power resides in the hands of large corporations and conglomerates, and is used to make profits and in other ways to promote the interests of those corporations and the small class of people who own, direct, and manage them.

This virtually uncontrolled use of power is a major malfunction, being responsible for many of the persistent inequalities in the North American economic landscape: the failure to meet many people's basic needs, the proliferation of waste in the form of military adventures and weaponries, the many useless consumer goods, and the roadblocks placed in the way of serious social reform. In part, such unfettered power feeds back to some of the other malfunctions listed in this chapter.

Except by birth or marriage, it is not easy to enter the class that constitutes the economic elite (for which see chapter 4). At the least, it usually requires a long and expensive apprenticeship at one of the establishment's guardian institutions. Thus there is throughout our socioeconomic system an abstract ideal of equal opportunity, but no equality of individual human beings. On the other hand, most of us live in a world dominated by the decisions of this same elite class. As small retailers, manufacturers, and marginal operators of all kinds are squeezed out of existence, more and more of us are obliged to work in or service one of the giant corporations. In fact, the corporation has become the key unit of what we can now call **neocapitalism.** This is true even of such activities as fishing, mining, lumber, agriculture, energy, manufacturing, transportation, and retailing. The 100 largest U.S. corporations own about one-half of all manufacturing assets, and the 500 largest own over two-thirds. Since the United States accounts for about 50 percent of all manufacturing in the world, the power of such corporations can hardly be underrated. For instance, General Motors Corporation, one of the world's largest in terms of sales, has revenues larger than the annual gross national product of all but 13 of the Western nations. After the governments of the United States and the Soviet Union, it is purported to be the third largest economic organization in the world. In almost any system of ranking—by number of employees, gross national product produced, or total assets—most large corporations are more important economic units than all but the largest of the industrial nations. Thus the U.S. Steel Corporation mines more iron ore and produces more steel than most nations in Western Europe. Multiple corporations, known as conglomerates, have also brought together widely disparate activities under one umbrella. Such activities range from parking lots to record companies and their performers; indeed, the conglomerates recognize no bounds to their activities, either industrial or national.

The decisions that corporations make about prices, wages, and locations strongly influence the economic system. Their investment decisions are crucial in determining the pace and direction of economic growth. Many take the lead in developing and applying new technologies. Their advertising dominates the media, and they strongly affect political and social organization. Despite the system of public ownership through shareholding, their profits reach the pockets of very few of us. To what use, then, do they put the economic surplus that they generate? The answer in many cases is that they use it to pay the costs of marketing, advertising and selling their products, which very often exceed the cost of producing them. Since corporate income is not taxed anywhere near as heavily as personal income, the social benefit to be derived from corporate profit-making is not obvious.

Baran and Sweezy, in their book *Monopoly Capital*, note that apart from the actual costs of transporting commodities from their place of manufacture to their points of retail distribution, most distribution costs are "wasteful." For instance, if annual style changes for automobiles and similar expenditures for what economists refer to as "product differentiation" were eliminated, then a vehicle of comparable performance, and superior safety and durability, could be produced for less than $1,000 (of course, allowance must be made for inflation since the mid-1960s). The difference between that price and the average selling price of $3,000 is what the consumer is presently paying for advertising, unnecessary style changes, and so forth. This is what they term "capitalist waste"; it is due to the way in which capital is used in capitalist society, not to the nature of capital itself. Baran and Sweezy also point to the tremendous expenditure of resources in the military sector of the economy, whose main reason for existence they see as a means to perpetuate tolerance for capitalist social relationships in as much of the world as possible. Adding together all these modes of surplus, they offered the conservative estimate that at least 56 percent of the GNP of the United States in 1963 was expended for purposes of maintaining the social order of capitalism, and that it therefore represented productive forces of which the population at large was deprived.

Even with the Federal Trade Commission and all the other federal regulatory agencies, the U.S. economic system remains dominated by the corporation and its management. This is not to say government has no role, for indeed government is strongly interlinked both with the corporate economy and with the military sector. Indeed, in some areas there is little difference between corporate officials and government officials, since each sector draws its personnel from the other. The truth is that, in the corporate state, the government guarantees the profits of the corporation. In so doing, the government redistributes national income in favor of the economic elite and to the detriment of the 20 million Americans who are malnourished, the 10 million whose jobs pay less than the federal minimum, and so on. The richest 2 percent of the U.S. population gets more income each year than the poorest one-third. This 2 percent controls one-third of the nation's private wealth, which is so considerable that the richest 200 American families have more wealth than the entire GNP of black Africa! The affluent world that we see portrayed in advertisements and television commercials is beyond the grasp of well over 90 percent of Americans. We are not shown the true picture of life in a corporate state where the average factory worker's real wage has not risen since 1967 and which has a higher rate of infant mortality than sixteen other nations. We rarely see how many of the goods purchased by most Americans are in fact shoddy.

To sum up: the corporate structure that makes such an impression on the economic landscape generates a vast output, but it cannot distribute the wealth from that output in an equitable way. Distribution is so badly skewed that the richest one-third of Americans each year receive twice as much income as the bottom two-thirds. Only about 5 percent of Americans have incomes of more than $20,000 a year; while more than two-thirds have incomes of less than $12,500. A malfunction indeed.

The corporate state is a malfunctioning one, then, in that it is not able to supply what its citizens need. If incomes were distributed equally in the United States, the average American family would get something like $15,000 a year. The corporation is indefensible because such a small minority of people benefit from it so excessively. It also has an excessive influence: businessmen exist to serve it; highly trained lawyers and government professionals exist to regulate it; and universities exist to train the technicians and managers who will service it.

What is needed is a dismantling of the corporate state, followed by a redistribution of wealth and power to all the community, at home and abroad.

Conclusion

The relationships between the various sectors of the spatial system and of the behavioral-operational milieu are very complex. This is particularly apparent when we come to examine the efficient and rational functioning of particular socioeconomic systems. Obviously, a number of assumptions have to be made: that indeed we are looking for an economically and socially efficient economic system, whose parts interlock to produce a harmonious way of life; that a harmonious way of life can be achieved by roughly equal distribution of resources; that economic efficiency is not incompatible with social welfare; that if they are compatible, the welfare of human beings must come before the welfare of machines; that our aim is net human benefit rather than ever upward surges in gross national product—and so on. To set out such a group of assumptions says of course a great deal about the writer, his society, and his hopes. Having created our model socioeconomic system, we can then regard deviations from it as "malfunctions." Many of them interlock: the rise of the corporate state, poverty, unemployment, environmental desecration, and the exploitation of the Third World have many characteristics in common.

As an illustration, we can reflect that only a few years ago, the Gulf Oil Company discovered large oil reserves in the African nation of Angola, a part of the African continent that until then had only poor oil resources. In exploiting these new resources, this multinational corporation provided the Portuguese government with sufficient funds to pay for at least 50 percent of the costs of suppressing anticolonial liberation movements in Angola and Mozambique, and also supplied South Africa and Rhodesia with a guaranteed source of oil for their economies, since they have only meager oil resources of their own. In one fell swoop, an American corporation, whose assets are held by a small economic class to the deprivation of others, supplied life to the economies of two racist governments and a colonial power, while contributing to the desecration of the environment and making a profit, too!

Summary

1. *Development is a difficult term to define. Development in relation to what criteria? Development for whom? By some measures all parts of the world are underdeveloped, in that they contain sections not developed to some optimum criteria (as set out in the previous chapter, for example).*

2. *Development can be thought of as an economic-ideologic factor—as the result of an economic system imposed from without by colonial and imperialist nations; as a continuum from lesser development to greater development according to measures of technology, trade, energy consumption, population density and growth rates; as a value-judgement; as a complex cultural process.*

3. *Just as there is a wide variety of definitions of development, there is a wide range of explanations for the differences in economic growth rates. The functional view incorporates notions of pattern variables, and claims that change comes about by changing the particular patterns (localism, ascription, lack of specialization); the conflict view sees change as the result of conflicting values and roles, and claims that much underdevelopment has been imposed by the world capitalist system; other views include stages of growth models, diffusion models, the psychological approach, and economic indices.*

4. *There is no final explanatory system. Each of the explanations contains some applicable factors, but these factors vary from situation to situation and from time to time.*

5. *On a world scale then, we may begin with an undifferentiated spatial system, in the sense of the economic landscape identified in the previous chapter, but the influence of economic activities and cultural and political systems soon produces a highly differentiated and partitioned space. Although there may be questions as to how to measure or explain these differences, this partitioned spatial system shows extreme ranges of economic development and organization.*

6. *The causes of development, as far as they can be ascertained, are multidimensional; there is no single explanatory cause. Population densities and growth rates, ratios of resources to population, the initial advantages of developed locations, the artificiality of many imposed colonial boundaries, the imposition of a metropolis oriented economic system, political ideologies and instabilities, cultural attitudes and value systems, traditional motivations, the lack of capital and restricted markets, all have their role to play. The lack or presence of any one of these factors is neither a precondition of underdevelopment nor one of development.*

7. *Besides these negative aspects, there are forces at work which are leading towards the equalization of development, albeit slowly. Greater mobility, the breakdown of status distinctions, unity of purpose, the development of mass communications and contact with the outside world, the breakdown of colonial and capitalist dependency, economic planning, increased capital application, political stability, and concern for general human welfare can all contribute to such a process.*

8. *In addition to the broad matter of "underdevelopment," another commonly labelled malfunction, the matter of increasing world population, is considered. Despite warnings from neomalthusians, the*

growth of world population seems to be less important than an improved distribution of resources.

9. Of more immediate importance seems to be the continued environmental desecration which the pursuit of ever-increased economic progress seems to bring with it. Nothing short of a change in our individual value system would seem to be enough to overcome this malfunction.

10. Spatial segregation and racial segregation through economic apartheid affects a number of the world's economic landscapes; overtly in the case of Rhodesia and South Africa, covertly in much of the rest of the world.

11. As a final example of malfunctioning, the rise of the corporate state and its channeling of wealth into only a few hands is described.

12. Malfunctioning is obviously a relative term, based on the individual's conception of what makes a harmonious economic system. But no matter what relative conceptions are chosen, the examples cited above are real.

Further Reading

This final chapter has covered a very broad canvas indeed, but, unfortunately, one barely touched by geographers. One account of one part of the earth's landscape —probably the first regional geography to date that accounts for the economic landscape in a felt and experienced way—is

Buchanan, K. *The Transformation of the Chinese Earth* (London: G. Bell, 1970).

An earlier paper by the same author is also worth consulting:

Buchanan, K. "Profiles of the Third World," *Pacific Viewpoint*, vol. 2, 1964, pp. 97–126, especially when it is backed up by an article by another geographer:

Blaut, J. M. "Geographic Models of Imperialism," *Antipode*, vol. 2, 1970, pp. 65–85.

A slightly wider-ranging than usual collection of essays, also gathered by a geographer, is

Mountjoy, A. B., ed. *Developing the Underdeveloped World* (London: Macmillan, 1971).

Appropriate back-up information from the other social sciences will be found in

Baran, P. A. and Sweezy, P. M. *Monopoly Capital* (New York: Monthly Review Press, 1966).

Christoffel, T., Finkelhor, D. and Gilbarg, D., eds. *Up against the American Myth* (New York: Holt, Rinehart & Winston, 1970).

DeGregor, T. R. and Pi-Sunyer, O. *Economic Development: The Cultural Context* (New York: Wiley, 1969).

Fann, K. T. and Hodges, D. C., eds. *Readings in U.S. Imperialism* (Boston: Porter Sargent, 1971).

Frank, G. *Capitalism and Underdevelopment in Latin America* (New York: Monthly Review Press, 1967).

Magdoff, H. *The Age of Imperialism* (New York: Monthly Review Press, 1970).

Rhodes, R. I., ed. *Imperialism and Underdevelopment* (New York: Monthly Review Press, 1970).

Other aspects of a malfunctioning system are also dealt with by

Morrill, R. and Wohlenberg, E. *The Geography of Poverty in the U.S.* (New York: McGraw-Hill, 1971), though unfortunately this book describes only symptoms, not causes.

Ramparts, eds. *Ecocatastrophe* (San Francisco: Canfield Press, 1970).

Weisberg, B. *Beyond Repair: The Ecology of Capitalism* (Boston: Beacon Press, 1971), probably the best book to date on the "ecological crisis."

sixteen

A Conceptual
Framework

We see in the real world around us a complex socioeconomic landscape. This term "landscape" is used to describe the system of interrelatedness between the primary, secondary, and tertiary activities that appear in particular places as the visible results of economic behavior. Some of these arrangements and patterns are matters of extreme complexity. The socioeconomic landscapes in which we live are vast mosaics in which the individual elements display a great variety of characteristics; the recurring patterns in those landscapes can be interpreted in terms of a great variety of forces. These forces vary from the immediate and local to the more distant in time, space, or both. The frame of reference already shown in chapter 5 and repeated here (figure 222) tries to encompass some of these complexities. Among them are: the formalized cognitive structures of *virtual space* and the *operational milieu*; the uncertainty with which information is often presented and selected in the real world; the "satisficing" nature of decision making; the cumulative experience gained by making such decisions over a lifetime; and, finally, the visible effect of all this on the socioeconomic landscape—whereupon the whole cycle begins again.

One attempt to aggregate the many components of the economic system is shown in figure 223, which is based on an idea by R. B. McNee. Here, groups and the individuals within them are placed in decision making situations. The group is at a particular level of socioeconomic progress with an associated technological system. The goals and decisions of the group are constrained by these factors, and filtered through the group's own value system. The value systems, experiences, and learned abilities affect the way in which the goals are perceived, the ways in which the technology is used to implement the goals,

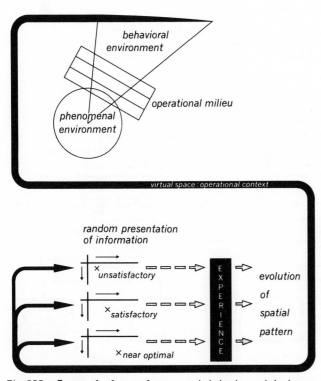

Fig. 222. *Frame of reference for economic behavior and the impact on the environment.*

and the ways in which the landscape symbols are judged and appraised. Essentially, of course, both the diagram and this verbal description are static in conception, whereas in fact the systems will change over time, often at an accelerating rate.

In its desire to organize the phenomenal environment for the sake of its own sustenance or aggrandizement, the group is seen as facing a choice situation: either it can increase economic activities (production) by using the maximum available space and resource; or it can concentrate its efforts at selected points or areas, thus reducing spatial interchange and movement to a minimum. A third alternative is to compromise between these two positions. The decision made is a result of the group's value system and cognitive capacities.

In the *moving point solution*, the group decides to move from place to place in the environment, for example as nomadic hunters and gatherers or as nomadic pastoralists, so that the production system literally moves with the group. Examples in contemporary society include factory ships, some lumber camps, and some recreational activities.

In the *fixed point-area-line solution*, the group sees the production goals as located at specific areas or points of economic activity, linked by interchange and flow.

For each identified type of production—primary, secondary, and tertiary activities—the entrepreneur within the group once more faces a choice situation: the advantages of dispersal versus the advantages of concentration or agglomeration. The solution he chooses will vary with the values held by the group, and from production type to production type. For some primary activities, such as agriculture (see chapters 6 and 7), the production system tends to be dispersed because of the wide availability of certain climatic factors and other environmental attributes. When centralization or agglomeration does occur it is usually because of the costs of transport, perishability of the product, and so on. The patterns are also modified by the nature of the enterprises, economies of scale, and compromises made in other types of production.

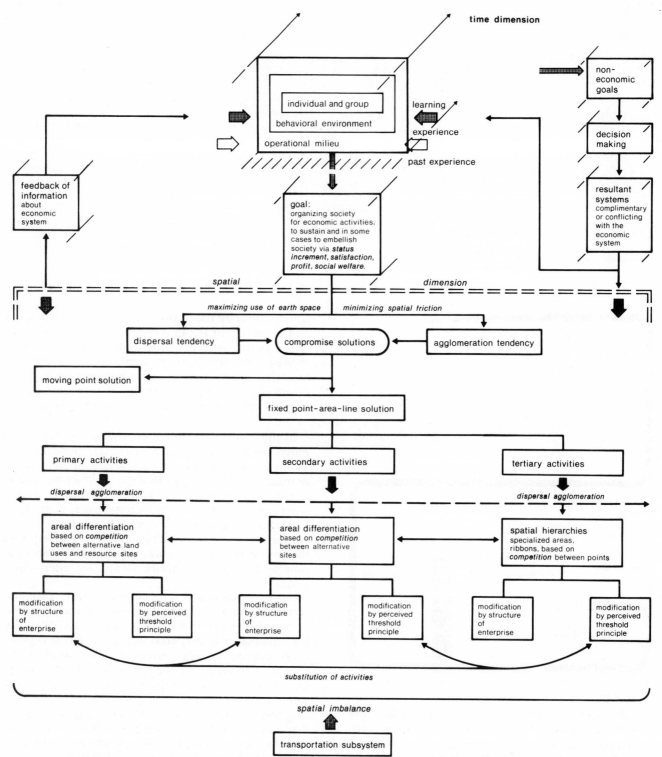

time dimension

non-economic goals

decision making

resultant systems complimentary or conflicting with the economic system

individual and group

behavioral environment

operational milieu

learning

experience

past experience

feedback of information about economic system

goal:
organizing society for economic activities, to sustain and in some cases to embellish society via *status increment, satisfaction, profit, social welfare.*

spatial   *dimension*

maximizing use of earth space   *minimizing spatial friction*

dispersal tendency   compromise solutions   agglomeration tendency

moving point solution

fixed point-area-line solution

primary activities   secondary activities   tertiary activities

dispersal agglomeration   *dispersal agglomeration*

areal differentiation based on *competition* between alternative land uses and resource sites

areal differentiation based on *competition* between alternative sites

spatial hierarchies specialized areas, ribbons, based on *competition* between points

modification by structure of enterprise

modification by perceived threshold principle

modification by structure of enterprise

modification by perceived threshold principle

modification by structure of enterprise

modification by perceived threshold principle

substitution of activities

spatial imbalance

transportation subsystem

Fig. 223. *A conceptual structure for the economic system. (Modified from R.B. McNee, "Toward Stressing Structure in Geographic Instruction," in* Introductory Geography: Viewpoints and Themes, *Commission on College Geography, Publication No. 5, 1967, p. 39, with the permission of the Association of American Geographers.)*

With other primary activities, such as mining, dispersion tends to be the pattern. Mining is the most widely dispersed activity because minerals are widely dispersed over the earth's surface. In volume of production, however, it tends to be very highly agglomerated. The balance between these two solutions varies from mineral to mineral.

Secondary activities such as processing and fabrication (chapters 8 and 9) include handicrafts as well as factory systems. At the handicraft level the units of production tend to be small—often they are households—and so widely dispersed. Concentration occurs with the transference of manufacturing from small units to shops and workshops, and eventually to factories. Major agglomerative forces include economies of scale, market transfer costs, availability of skilled labor, large power sources, cumulative attraction (in the form of mutual positive feedback) and the effects of certain types of transportation network. Patterns of secondary economic activities change with changes in the learning abilities, collective symbolism, and value systems of groups. For example, the location patterns in redistributive economies may be quite different from those in market-exchange economies because they are shaped by a different kind of entrepreneurial decision making.

All service activities tend to concentrate in central places (chapters 10 and 11). The more specialized the service being provided, the greater the population necessary to support it. This is known as the *threshold principle*; it can also be measured as a minimum amount of purchasing power to support such an activity. On the other hand, customers are usually willing to travel further for some services than for others, especially for infrequently used services (the *range principle*). The compromise between these principles is said to produce a hierarchical system of central places, specialized functional areas, and ribbon developments.

All these activities are linked together by a communication or transportation system (chapters 12 and 13). Changes in the flow pattern can alter the balance between dispersion and concentration at each of the production points and areas, and conversely. In this there is a continuing feedback between the *productive* system and the systems of *consumption* and *exchange* that are here represented as the *communications* system. Changes in the latter may take the form of changes in routes, flows, stocks, or the development of new modes and technology. The development and acceptance of a new technology again depends on the value system and abilities of the group.

As noted in chapter 4, the development of the production, consumption, and exchange systems will cause changes in the physical environment. The end result is what we have called the phenomenal environment. Some of these changes may in turn disrupt the economic system, with or without the group being aware of it, while others may stabilize the system or provide stimuli to higher levels of achievement (chapters 14 and 15). In this way, there is a feedback of information about the economic system and its subsystems to the individual or group.

It should be noted that, as with the other model situations, there are constraints. For example, few groups live in isolation or exist as *closed systems*. They are therefore subject to such forces as the diffusion of ideas, conquest, and the resistance of other groups competing for the use of the same environmental space. Similarly the economic system does not exist in isolation from the noneconomic goals of the society and its cultural and political systems (chapters 4 and 15).

Within this behavioral systems framework, firmly placed in time-space dimensionality, we can view the economic system as functioning, malfunctioning, or in conflict. At this level, however, there is a danger of overlooking the individual perceptions and idiosyncrasies that help the group to function or malfunction. Brookfield has remarked:

While we confine our work to the continental, national, or regional levels we can at some risk afford to neglect the minutiae of an alien society, but when an individual human geographer is sitting down in one small corner of a foreign land, and seeks to interpret the geography of that small corner, then it is difficult for him to do so without trying to comprehend the perception of environment among the inhabitants of the area in which he is working. It is still more difficult to do this if, as Wagner and Mikesell would seem to have it, he shuts his eyes to the "inner workings of culture."* There may well be "repetitions of practically standard variation" on the land, but the human geographer is concerned not with the land per se, but with the land as part of the effective environment; with the land as resources. And, as Zimmerman has argued, resources are distinguished from neutral stuff only by the perception and technology of the potential user, and by his ability to organize so as to convert them into wealth.

Although Brookfield was not explicitly referring to economic geographers, we have a lesson to learn from his statement. It should be obvious by now that the complex interrelationships of which economic behavior is only a part are not easily disaggregated.

*Wagner and Mikesell had stated that "the cultural geographer is not concerned with explaining the inner workings of culture or with describing fully, patterns of human behavior, even when they affect the land, but rather with assessing the technical potential for using and modifying their habitats."

Distribution of economic activities, the ways they are organized, systems of conflict and consensus, resultant behavior patterns, and the feedback effects, cannot be analyzed in a static and deterministic way. Economic activities and behavior exist in a dynamic space-time framework, which includes cultural and physical factors. It is a combination of all three types of factor—economic, cultural, and physical—that gives rise not just to an "economic landscape," which is an academic abstraction, but to a *total landscape pattern*. Such landscape patterns are the result of myriad human decisions, as well as of random factors, personal motives, and group values. Above all, as Lowenthal reminds us, we must not forget the individual variations in our separate worlds of illusion and personal symbols:

In each of our personal worlds, far more than in the shared consensus, characters of fable and fiction reside and move about, some in their own lands, others sharing familiar countries with real people and places. . . . Utopians not only make mythic men, they rearrange the forces of nature: in some worlds water flows uphill, reasons vanish, time reverses, or one- and two-dimensional creatures converse and move about. . . . If we could not imagine the impossible, both private and public worlds would be the poorer.

In short, we must not shut our eyes to the "inner workings of culture." As Brookfield rightly says, "geographers have, in the mass, failed to inquire deeply into patterns of social organization and human behavior and attitudes in their search for explanations. . . ." He sees a number of reasons for this failure:

1. *Geographers have been asking the wrong questions. "Where [these questions] concern the cultural landscape*

they lead . . . to a point short of full inquiry into the motives of human action. . . ."

2. *Geographers have confined themselves too narrowly to the descriptive. This has resulted in, among other things, an overreliance on and unimaginative use of quantitative techniques.*

3. *Geographers have studied origins at the expense of ongoing processes. As a result, they have succeeded in reconstructing past societies but have neglected the world we live in.*

4. *Geographers have been reluctant to accept* **microgeography** *as having more than illustrative or anecdotal interest.*

In this book, on the other hand, the study of economic behavior has been presented as the study of *process* in time and space. At the same time, it recognizes the need to inquire into human organization, motivation, perception, symbolic behavior, and learning processes—in short, all the "inner workings of culture." Only by understanding the actions and interactions of the farmer, fisherman, entrepreneur, company vice-president, retailer, wholesaler, consumer, and distribution manager *within their own operational milieu* can we ever hope to explain the landscape patterns that surround us.

Take note of the meaning of the ancient song;
That what there is shall belong to those who are good for it, thus
The children to the maternal, that they thrive;
The carriages to good drivers, that they are driven well;
*And the valley to the waterers, that it shall bear fruit.**

*Bertolt Brecht, *The Caucasian Chalk Circle*, translated by James and Tania Stern, with W. H. Auden.

Appendix:
Some Basic Concepts

	concept	original contributor	successive contributors	basic reading
1.	systems analysis	Von Bertallanffy (1950)	Chorley (1962) McDaniel and Eliot Hurst (1968) Harvey (1969)	Harvey (1969) ch. 23
2.	phenomenal environment	Kirk (1952)		Kirk (1963)

3.	behavioral — perceived
	  milieu
		Lowenthal (since 1961)
		Sprouts (since 1956)
		Kirk (1952)
		Sonnenfeld
		based on: concepts from
		  psychology (Gestalt, S–R,
		  cognitive theory)
			Pred (1967)
			Gibson (1970)
			Yi Fu Tuan (since 1967)
			and many others
				Saarinen (1969)

4.	the operational milieu	Eliot Hurst (1968)
		based on: Vidal de la Blache
		  ("genre de vie")
		McNee
				McDaniel and Eliot Hurst
				  (1968)

5.	the satisficer	Simon (1957)	Pred (1967, 1969) Wolpert (1964)	Pred (1967)

6.	adoption and adaption
	  (of entrepreneurs
	  after nonoptimal
	  location decisions)
		Tiebout (1957)
		based on:
		  Weber (1909)
		  Alchian (1950)
		  Katona (1952)
			Thomas (1961)
			Pred (1967)
			related work:
			  Greenhut (since 1956)
				Pred (1967)

7.	quarternary activities	Gottmann (1961)		

	concept	original contributor	successive contributors	basic reading
8.	stages of growth	Hoffman, W.G. (1931, 1958)	Clark (1939) Fisher (1933, 1939) Gold (1964) Hirsch (1965, 1967)	Thomas (1963, 1969)
9.	agricultural location theory	Von Thünen (1826)	Brinkman (1922) Waibel (1933) Lösch (1941) Dunn (1952) Gould (1963) Hicklare (1963) Alonso (1964) Wolpert (1964) Peucker (1966, 1967) Horvath (1969) Peet (1969)	Hall (1966)
10.	comparative advantage	Ricardo (1817)		McDaniel and Eliot Hurst (1968)
11.	land rent, based on fertility difference	Ricardo (1817)	Marshall (1890)	
12.	application of game theory to land use decision making	Gould (1963) based on: Von Neumann and Morgenstern (1928–1944) Koopmans and Beckmann (1951) Garrison (1959)	Pred (1967)	Gould (1963)
13.	behavioral aspects in spatial decision processes (agriculture)	Wolpert (1964) based on: Simon (since 1952) Walker (1960) Cyert and March (1963)	Pred (1967) related work: Gould (1963)	Wolpert (1964)
14.	manufacturing: least cost locations (assuming continuous and homogenous plane and linear transport functions)	Weber (1909) partially based on Launhardt (1885)	Predohl (1928) Palander (1928) Isard (1956) Moses (1958) Tiebout (1957) Isard (1967) Smith (1966, 1970)	Thoman, Conkling, and Yeates (1968), pp. 183–203
15.	manufacturing: spatial limits model	Smith (1966) based on: Weber (1909) Losch (1939) Greenhut (1956, etc.)		Smith (1966)
16.	manufacturing: competition in space (location as a variable in competition)	Hotelling (1929) based on: Cournot (1838) Sraffa (1926)	Smithies (1941) Lerner/Singer Chamberlin Stevens (1961) Isard et al. (1967) Teitz (1968)	Isard (1956), pp. 158–65

	concept	original contributor	successive contributors	basic reading
17.	"range of tolerance" — margin below optimality within which entrepreneur can still succeed	Morgan (1961) Chisholm (1964)	Krumme (1968)	Krumme (1969)
18.	geography of enterprise (emphasis on organizational and corporate aspects)	McNee (since 1958) refers to: Platt, R. Philbrick (1957) Pounds Kerr (1959) Carlson Thoman Boesch (1947) Kenning (1960)	Fleming (1967, 1968) Steed (1968) Krumme (1968, 1969) Townroe (1969) Stafford (1969)	Krumme (1969a)
19.	concepts and methods for analysis of industrial distributions	Adam Smith (concept of specialization) Ricardo (comparative advantage) Marshall, Weber (economies of scale, agglomeration) Hoover, Florence (various distribution coefficients) Ullman/Dacey ("minimum requirements") Duncan (segregation indices) Rodgers (diversification measure) Isard, et al., (industrial complex analysis		Isard (1960) ch. 7 and 9
20.	input/output analysis	Leontieff (since 1936) based on: computer development (adaptation of neoclassical theory of general equilibrium to the empirical study of interdependence)	Isard (since 1950) Chenery (since 1950) Moses (1955) Tiebout (1957) Karaska (more sophisticated multiplier input studies)	Leontief (1963)
21.	principle of substitution (linking production and location theory)	Predohl (1925) based on: Weber Furlan Engländer, etc. Cassel (1923)	Hoover (1948) Isard (1956) Moses (1958) Alonso (1968)	Krumme (1969b)
22.	industrial location games	Isard and Smith (1967) based on: Weber's agglomeration problem (1909) Hotelling (1929) Isard (1956) Stevens (1961)		Isard (1967) Stevens (1961)

	concept	original contributor	successive contributors	basic reading
23.	division of structural and regional components of regional economic change. "shift and share analysis"	Dunn (1959)	Perloff et al. (1960) Ashby (since 1964) Steed (1967)	Ashby (1968)

24.	central place theory, city hierarchies	Christaller (1933)
		based on:
		  Von Thünen
		  Bobek (1928)
		  Kohl (1850)
		  Gradmann (1916)
			Lösch (1941)
			Ullman (1941)
			Vining (1955)
			Berry-Garrison (1958)
			Beckmann (1958)
			Bunge (1962)
			Woldenberg (1968)
			Curry (1968)
			Marshall (1969)
			and many others
				Berry (1967), p. 59 ff.

25.	urban spheres of influence	Jefferson (1939)
		  ("primate city")
		Chabot (since 1938)
		  (urban zones of influence)
		Bogue (1949)
		  (spatial dominance)
		Vance (1954)
		  (metropolitan dominance)
		Scholler (1959)
		  (umland vs. hinterland)
				Dickinson (1964) pp. 235-8

26.	dynamics of urbanization	Gottman (1957) ("megalopolis, urban fields, axis of urbanization, etc.")		Berry and Horton (1970), ch. 2
27.	rank size rule, city–size relationships	Zipf (1949) Auerbach (1913) Christaller (1933) Lösch (1941)	Vining (1955) Isard (1956) Beckmann (1958) Stewart (1958) Berry (1958)	Berry and Horton (1970), ch. 3

28.	urban land use and land values	Marshall (1890)
		based on:
		  Ricardo,
		  Von Thünen
			Hurd (1903)
			Haig (1926)
			Alonso (1964)
				Knos (1962)

29.	commercial structure	Berry (1962, 1963)	Garner (1966) Simmons (1964, 1966) Berry, Parsons, and Platt (1968)	Simmons (1964)
30.	consumer decision processes	Howard and Sleth (1969) Nicosia (1966) Katona (since 1951) Lazarsfeld (since 1936)	Curry (1968) Andrews (1970) Bowlby (1969) Bucklin	Thompson (1966)

	concept	original contributor	successive contributors	basic reading
31.	transportation: interaction concept; flow analysis	Ullman (1956) based among others on Stouffer (1940)	Ackermann (1958) many functional and inter- actional studies, e.g., the commodity flow study (Berry, 1966)	Ullman (1956)
32.	functional systems viewpoint of transport	Garrison-Marble (Northwestern University)		Eliot Hurst (1971)
33.	geometry of transporta- tion networks, "connectivity of a network"	Garrison (1960) based on: Euler (1736) Konig (1936) Shimbel (1953) Berge (1958)	Nysteun and Dacey (1961) Kansky (1963) Warner (1964) Haggett (1966) Haggett and Chorley (1969)	Chorley and Haggett (1967) ch. 15
34.	gravity model applied to social masses	Stewart (1941) Warntz (since 1957) based on: Newton Carey (1858) Ravenstein (1885) Young (1924) Reilly (1929) Zipf (1940)	Isard Warntz Carrothers Ullman Bunge Lowry (1963) Wilson (since 1967)	Luckerman and Porter (1960)
35.	spatial diffusion processes	Hagerstrand (1952) based on: a) general diffusion models b) migration research	Morrill (since 1962) Brown (since 1963) Pitts (since 1963) Tornquist (since 1963)	Brown (1968a), pp. 10–16 Brown (1968b), pp. 9–38
36.	impact of space on behavioral patterns	Hagerstrand (since 1952) plus many others in related disciplines, including Lewin and Hai	"movement space," "action space," etc., as found in trip behavior, etc., based on notions and concepts from psychology and sociology. Golledge Horton Reynolds Eliot Hurst Rushton Tornquist all since 1966	Eliot Hurst (1969a) Hagerstrand (1970)
37.	synthesis of location concepts	Chisholm (1962, 1966) agricultural and industrial location concepts Von Böventer (1963, 1967) industrial, agricultural, urban, and recreational location concepts Alonso (1964, 1967) rent and location concepts Pred (1967, 1969) behavioral matrix		Pred (1967)

	concept	original contributor	successive contributors	basic reading
38.	spatial development of world economy	Predohl (since 1949) based on: Von Thünen Ritschl (1925)	related *work:* Prebisch (1950) Meier and Baldwin (1957)	Friedmann (1966)
39.	development of spatial structure	Friedmann (1956) based on: Lösch (1939) Isard (1949) Hoselitz (1953) Bogue (1950) Lampard (1955) Vining (1955)	Berry (1961, 1963)	Friedmann (1956)
40.	spread effects of economic development	Myrdal (1957)		Myrdal (1957)
41.	polarization effects, trickling down	Hirschmann (1958) based on: Schumpeter (1912) Perroux (1955), but independent of Myrdal (1957)		Hirschmann (1958), ch. 10
42.	growth poles, growth centers	Perrous (1950, 1955) based on: Schumpeter's innovating pioneer entrepreneur	Hirschmann (1958) Boudeville (1966) Darwent (1968)	Hansen (1967)
43.	geographic multiplier concept	Daly based on: Kahn/Keynes multiplier notions	Isard Tiebout (1955) Pred (1966) Czamanski (1964) Artle (since 1959) (regional econometric models — impact studies)	Pred (1966), pp. 24–32
44.	economic regionalization, using systems, field theory, and factor analysis	Berry (since 1960) based on: Lewin (1951) Zobler (1957) Rummel (1965) and others		Berry (1968)
45.	"regional science"	Isard (since 1950) Weber Lösch Leontief Hoover	Stevens Reiner Tiebout Alonso Wolpert Tietz	Isard and Reiner (1968)

	concept	original contributor	successive contributors	basic reading

46.	*ideologic explanation of underdevelopment*	*Gough (1968)*
		Frank (1966, 1967)
		  and many others
		based on:
		  Marx
			Frank (1967a)
			(metropolis-satellite
			hypothesis)
				Gough (1968)

47.	*lesser development*	*Berry (1961)*		*Berry (1961)*
48.	*cultural factors in development*	*Spencer (1961)*		*Spencer (1961)*
49.	*functional view of development*	*Hoselitz (since 1953)* *based on:* *Talcott Parsons (1949, 1951)*		*Hoselitz (1954–5)*

50.	*geography of economic behavior*	*McNee (1967 a, b)*
		Eliot Hurst (since 1968)
		based on:
		  European tradition of
		  "human geography" and
		  on related disciplines of
		  sociology, anthropology,
		  political science, economics,
		  and psychology		

Source: Based on an original format by Gunter Krümme, designed for use in proseminars at the University of Hawaii and Columbia University.

Glossary

Abidjan group. A supranational organization, founded in 1960 at conferences held in Abidjan and Brazzaville. It includes nations such as Senegal, Cameroun, Mauritania, and the former French Equatorial Africa states. The intent was to pool certain educational, transportation and military practices, and to form a crude joint economic framework.

Accessibility. The ease of getting to a place; a variable quality of location. It can be expressed in frictional terms or as a relative quality which results from the relationship of a place to the transportation system.

Achievement orientation. The orientation of a person who, in deciding how to act, focuses his attention on the *achieved* aspects of the other person (e.g., his professional qualifications.) One of Parson's pattern variables.

Adaption. Economic activities rationally adapt themselves to environmental conditions, based on relative information.

Administrative principle. One of three principles governing the distribution of settlements in Christaller's central place model. This principle is based on the notion of political-social factors that govern settlement from the point of view of production or administrative control.

Adolescence. A term used in a number of cyclic growth models to represent the initial stages of immature development.

Adoption. Economic activities are by chance adopted by the environmental condition.

Agglomeration economies. The utilization of scale

economies to ease the costs of operation by concentrating activities at common locations.

Agricultural Revolution. A period in the development of agriculture (vis-à-vis techniques, plant and animal breeding, etc.), characterized by an apparent upsurge in innovations and change.

Alliance for Progress. A cooperative organization established in 1951 to distribute financial aid throughout Latin America, led by the United States.

Alpha index. A term used in network geometry. It is calculated as the ratio of the observed number of fundamental circuits to the maximum number of fundamental circuits that may exist in a network. The observed number of fundamental circuits is the cyclomatic number.

Analysis of transactions. A technique to measure the cohesiveness among individuals and groups as denoted by the extent of their mutual relationship or interaction. Transactions include the interchange of messages (mail, telephone, radio, television), trade, and people (assessed by the frequency of personal contacts).

Apartheid. A racially discriminatory system in South Africa whereby those of European origin and those of African, Asian, or mixed origin are governed by different laws.

Apperception. The process of perceiving and reacting to a stimulus; the mind is conceived of as an aggregate of sense impressions and images.

Areal association. The similarity within the same study area between two or more **spatial distribu-** tions, determined by information collected for the same unit area. Remembering that spatial distributions are assemblages of geographic facts, we can also define *areal association* as the similarity between two or more sets of geographic facts collected for the same unit area.

Areal organization. The recognition of specific spatial patterns of organization; the regional analysis of economic phenomena to better understand spatial patterns.

Ascription. The given qualities of a person or group, such as sex, age, or social class. One of Parson's pattern variables, used by Hoselitz as an index of "development."

Aspiration level. Aspirations are ends or goals which are strongly desired and which an individual tries to achieve. The level of aspiration gives some idea of how high a person seeks to succeed (the small shopkeeper who aspires to own 4 shops and one who aspires to own a chain of 400 shops illustrate two different aspiration levels). Frequently levels are set which do not guarantee easy success.

Atomistic. An approach holding that discrete, finite, and individual elements are the ultimate constituents of society.

Authority. The form of power that orders or articulates the actions of others through commands which are regarded as legitimate by those who are commanded.

Back haul. The return trip of a vehicle transporting goods or freight.

Backward linkage. Hirschmann's term to denote demands derived from nonprimary economic activities, which induce attempts to supply the inputs needed through production in the local area.

Basic costs. Those costs in manufacturing which must be paid irrespective of location, such as the costs of raw materials at the points where they are mined, or the costs of labor at their cheapest point.

Behavioral milieu or environment. The internalized conception of the milieu of an individual or group, which is the result of perception, learned factors, past experience, and cultural setting. The behavioral environment is the subjective milieu which governs a person's reactions or actions, and may only partly reflect "objective reality."

Behavioral matrix. An heuristic device devised by Pred to provide a framework for locational decisions. The axes of his matrix represent the ability to use information in reaching a decision, and the quality and quantity of the information utilized by and available to the decision maker.

Behavioralism. The utilization of the concept of the behavioral environment and other psychological models of behavior in geography, as an alternative to more mechanistic and simplistic views of behavior.

Benefit-cost analysis. A technique that involves consideration and evaluation of all the relevant costs and benefits among a number of alternatives (e.g., in water management, between the use of a lake for water storage, hydroelectric power, or recreation). The aim is to maximize benefits and minimize costs.

Benelux. A customs union begun on January 1, 1948, between Belgium, the Netherlands, and Luxemburg. Now superseded by the European Common Market.

Bid-price curve. A series of price values to which a firm or individual is indifferent—e.g., if the price of land was X at one point and Y at another point, the firm would be equally satisfied with either point (equal satisfaction is here used in the classic economic sense of equal profits).

Black box. A term used by psychologists and others to refer to a group of functions of the brain which are known in outline, but which are not known component by component. Thus a particular response (a feeling, an emotion) may occur to a given stimulus, but how the brain functions in translating that stimulus to a particular response is not known fully.

The boss nexus. A term utilized by Florence to depict a particular entrepreneurial motive—that of the love of power. Such a motive could lead to the rejection of a merger if the entrepreneur were to be submerged in another organization.

Bounded rationality. A notion that represents man's limited capacity to formulate and solve complex problems. The decision maker is conceived of as constructing a simplified model of the real situation which he can deal with, and as behaving rationally with respect to this model.

Bounties. Premiums or rewards offered by a government, usually in agriculture, to encourage or discourage particular farming practices.

Business cycle. A fluctuation in the economic business of an area, nation, or larger segment of the world; the term usually implies recurrent up-and-down swings in business activity.

Capital intensive. An investment where a high proportion of capital is used in relation to the amount of labor employed. An oil refinery or chemical plant where much capital is sunk into equipment and automatic machinery and where a relatively small labor force is needed would be an example of a capital intensive industry.

Capitalism. An economic system based on private enterprise, in which most of the resources and the power to exploit them are in the hands of relatively few private individuals, and are subject to largely uncontrolled economic competition. Frequently the "profit" motive is assigned to the entrepreneur working in such a system, but that is too simplistic an explanation. The values connotation of the term usually implies profit motive and exploitation of the worker.

The cash nexus. Florence's term in entrepreneurial decision making, representing the idea of profit maximization.

Causal interaction. The reciprocal interplay between events or phenomena which presupposes that a prior condition set in motion a chain or multiplying effect.

C.E.M.A. Council of Economic Mutual Assistance; established in 1949 to centralize and administer trade agreements, credit, and technical assistance between the Soviet Union and Eastern Europe.

Central place theory. A theory put forward by Christaller, which asserts that all cities (other than mining settlements and resorts) function as *central places*, providing goods and services to a surrounding market area.

Channel. The mode and route used in the communications process. It includes the written or printed word, visual image, and the spoken word (direct or indirect).

Circulation. A concept used by French geographers to denote all communications movements—ideas, messages, innovations, money, credit, as well as the transportation of people and goods.

Civilization. A term originally derived from the verb *to civilize*, which means to acquire qualities of enlightment, urbanity, refinement, etc. It now means (a) an advanced culture, with organized material and technical qualities, a body of ideas and values, and so on; (b) that society or nation which has reached such a state.

Class. A group or social stratum of people who possess the same life-changes, display similar styles of life, and have similar material and economic bases.

Closed economy. Describes the economy of a society or group where the exchanges that take place are mainly confined within the group, and exchanges with outsiders are limited.

Closed systems. Systems with clearly defined boundaries across which no movement or exchange of material or energy occurs. Closed systems tend toward a state of maximum entropy, and change only through innate or given differences within the system.

Coefficient of determination. This coefficient (r^2) is the square of the correlation coefficient (r). It is the ratio of the regression sum of squares to the total sum of squares. It represents the proportion of the variation in the dependent variable which is "explained" by covariation with the independent variable.

Cognition. A psychological term denoting all the various aspects of knowing, perceiving, thinking, reasoning, etc. A *cognition process* denotes the complex way in which perceptions and stimuli are translated by the human brain into some recognizable structure.

Colonialism. The policy of a nation seeking to extend or retain its authority over another territory implicitly less developed than itself.

Colony. A territory originally separate from a ruling power, but now subjected to the rule of that power.

Columbo plan. The plan for Cooperative Economic Development in South and Southeast Asia established in 1950. A scheme to provide financial aid to a number of developing nations (such as Ceylon, India, Malaysia) led by the United States, Britain, Canada, New Zealand, and Australia.

COMECON. See **C.E.M.A.**

Common Market. The Treaty of Rome established in 1958 the *European Economic Community* (E.E.C.) consisting of Belgium, France, Italy, Luxemburg, the Netherlands, and West Germany. An economic community or common market was set in motion, by which tariffs and other restrictions were to be removed over a period of at least 15 years.

Common Services Organization. An organization that joins Uganda, Kenya, and Tanzania in a loose economic union; in part a legacy of British colonial rule.

Communal tenure. Land held by and belonging to the community without individual ownership.

Community centers. A specific level of shopping nucleation including variety stores, florists, a post office, and certain business and office services such as lawyers, insurance agents, and branch banks. Community centers supply necessities (neighborhood level) and more specialized goods.

Compage. A "total" region, distinguished by a community of feeling among its inhabitants as well as by climatic, physical, or resource characteristics.

Comparative advantage. The tendency of regions or areas to produce products for which they have a special ability or physical advantage, or the least disadvantage compared with other areas.

Complementarity. One factor in Ullman's tripartite movement typology; the existence of a demand in one area and a specific supply in another.

Complex, the. A regional grouping of integrated economic activities; a functionally organized course of integrated activities used in planning in redistributive economies, such as the U.S.S.R.

Conflict theory. The paradigm stating that the conflict within institutions or other social and economic areas is more important in inducing change than are functional or consensus relationships.

Conservation of matter. A notion utilized by Bunge in his "movement theory" to denote the strict accounting of the quantity of phenomena being considered. Hence a transport network will contain as many vehicles as are put into it.

Conspicuous consumption. A term used by Veblen to describe the wasteful and ostentacious use of articles, demonstrating the wealth and social position of an individual.

Consumer, The. One who uses a commodity or service.

Consumption. The using up of goods and services that have some exchangeable value.

Contract. The process of bargaining for advantages, and the socially prescribed and sanctioned norms to which it is subjected.

Core-frame concept. A refinement of the traditional downtown-area notion. The *core* is the central part of the downtown area distinguished by intensive land use, highrise buildings, and concentrated day-time population; it is the focus of the transit system, and the center of specialized functions. The *frame*, which can encircle the core, is distinguished by semi-intensive land use, subareas of wholesaling, off-street parking, light manufacturing, etc., and has an extended horizontal scale.

Cost advantage. The situation where a buyer or seller, a firm or a consumer has some pricing edge — e.g., access to a low-cost resource, labor pool, or cheap means of transport.

Cottage industry. See **Household industry.**

Critical isodapane. The **isodapane** that represents the point where additional transportation costs balance savings in labor costs.

Cultural configuration. A term used by Ginsburg to denote the system of social organization including values, goals, and objectives. Societies possess these factors in different combinations.

Cultural space. The spatial system of shared symbols by which men relate to their spatial milieu.

Cultural universals. Those elements which are fairly common to most cultures, such as age grading, calendars, systems of counting, language, law, and tool making. Anthropologists are by no means agreed as to the existence of such universals.

Culture. A term defined by Geertz as "... an historically transmitted pattern of meanings embodied in symbols, a system of inherited conceptions expressed in symbolic form by means of which men communicate, perpetuate, and develop their knowledge about and attitudes toward life."

Cumulative causation. Myrdal's term to represent the forces in economic growth that support change and encourage cumulative growth.

Cybernetics. Scientific analysis and control of animate and inanimate systems of organization, based on their methods of communication. It emphasizes the unity of *all* systems, stressing such functional parallels between man and machine as neural networks and electrical circuits.

Cybernetic system. A controlled feedback system (e.g., a missile guidance system).

Cyclomatic number. A term used in network geometry. The cyclomatic number indicates the number of fundamental circuits in a network. A *fundamental circuit* consists of the minimum number of links to create a completely connected circuit.

Decode. A term used by Osgood to denote the process by which physical objects in the environment are *interpreted* by a person.

Deduction. A method of building a theory by reasoning from general principles.

Deficiency payments. Payments made by a government to make up for a farmer's loss or deficiency in a particular harvest year or in a situation of severe competition from dumping or cheaper production elsewhere.

Demand. The ability and willingness to buy a certain good at a certain price, and at a given time, taste, income, etc. The term indicates the functional relationship between the quantity purchased and the price of a particular commodity under specific conditions.

Demands. One of two types of inputs to a political system recognized by D. Easton. Demand inputs include demands for wage laws, work-hour regulations, education, public safety, etc.

Demographic index. A measure representing population density and growth rates, birth and death rates, infant mortality rates, and population density in cultivated areas; used by Berry in his factor analysis of development variables.

Dependent variable. A term used in regression analysis to denote which of several variables is dependent upon one or several other variables, being partly controlled by or related to those others; i.e., it seems to depend somewhat in its functioning on those other variables.

Desire line. Straight-line connection between two nodes; between an origin and a destination; also, *dyad.*

Determinism. The view that all human behavior is determined directly by some law or force which compels a particular reaction.

Development continuum. A term used by Hodder to indicate that no one sector of economic activities should be overemphasized as a panacea for development; rather, development depends on a balanced economic system.

Development syndrome. A term indicating the dilemma of "development" — development for whom? Do we support the *status quo*, or is stability merely stagnation?

Diameter. A measure of the "span" of a *network;* the least number of links that are used to move between the two most separated nodes.

Diffusion. The spread or movement of cultural and economic forms over space, either singly or in a complex. Studies of diffusion include the movement of crops, population, settlement, innovations, and information.

Diffusion models. Models representing the movement of cultural and economic forms over space—for example, in agriculture those models concerned with the diffusion of information and the resulting patterns of land use.

Direct embargoes. A government restriction on the import or export of particular goods to or from specified foreign countries.

Discrimination learning. A model of learning behavior involving habitual discrimination among responses according to the type, force, and frequency of reinforcement.

Distance decay function. The direct decline in interaction between two places as distance increases.

Division of labor. The division of the work process into a number of parts, each part undertaken by a separate person or group.

Dryfield farming. An intensive subsistence agricultural tillage system without paddy rice. (Cf. **Sarvah.**)

Dual economy. The existence of two different economic systems in one area; one group of people may take part in both systems (for instance, as peasant farmers on a small holding and as wage laborers on a plantation).

Economic man. A model of human behavior that assumes the maximization of certain utility functions, such as the maximization of profit. Given complete information and a perfect ability to utilize that information in a rational way, economic man maximizes returns and minimizes costs.

Economic rent. The surplus earned over the minimum costs to retain land in a particular crop or farming system. The return after the costs of seeding, tilling, harvesting, labor, land, and marketing have been deducted is called the *land rent* or *economic rent.*

Economic space. A symbolic space, conceived in **utility** terms, which represents various perceived economic interactions.

Economies of scale. The reduction of costs and maximization of profits by *internal economies,* such as mass production, and/or *external economies,* such as locating similar or linked productive activities in the same areas.

Economy. The system of activities and organizations through which a society patterns the flow of goods and services.

Ecosystem. The complex of animals, plants, and habitat (organic and inorganic) that are in approximate equilibrium. The interactions of these elements maintain the balance in the ecosystem.

E.E.C. See **Common Market.**

E.F.T.A. The European Free Trade Association (an organization of seven states—Austria, Denmark, Norway, Portugal, Sweden, Switzerland, and the United Kingdom) was created in 1959 with fewer far-reaching objectives than the *Common Market.* The main objective was the removal of tariff barriers among the members, but no common external barrier or auxiliary provisions for mobility of labor or investment were proposed.

Ejido. A Mexican communal farm operated by the inhabitants of a village or commune on an individual or cooperative basis.

Enabling conditions. A term used by Katona in his explanation of consumer behavior to denote the conditions that make it economically possible to buy a good or service, such as income, credit rating, etc.

Encode. A term used by Osgood to denote the process by which the *intentions* of a person are expressed in physical terms and hence become environmental events.

Engel's law. "As economic development proceeds and people grow richer, they spend proportionately *less* of their income on food, and proportionately *more* of their income on consumer goods and services."

Entente. An economic union founded in 1959, whose original members were the Ivory Coast, Upper Volta, Dahomey, and Niger.

Entrepreneur. A person who coordinates and controls the factors of production, often instituting major innovations and changes, and who bears the risks involved in an innovative situation with imperfect knowledge and competition.

Entropy. A measure of the degree to which the energy of a system has been unable to perform work; used to denote the degree of disorganization in a system. (Cf. **Negentropy.**)

Environmental determinism. The doctrine that represents the geographic (especially physical) environment as the primary causal or determining factor in cultural and economic activities.

Environmental possibilism. The doctrine that sees the geographic environment as containing a finite *range of possibilities.* From this spectrum, societies select according to cultural needs and norms rather than according to a single determining factor.

Eotechnic. A term used by Mumford to denote the first phase of urban and industrial development, characterized by immobile power sources, primitive technology, and undeveloped transportation means.

Equifinality. A systems analytic term denoting that different initial conditions can lead to similar end structures.

Equilibrium. A system's state of balance, implying that there is a normal state with respect to both internal balance and environmental relationship.

Evaluational aspect of the cultural system. The beliefs that a particular cultural system hold as desirable.

Exchange. The giving and receiving of services, goods, money, or other rights and benefits, usually in return for some other service, etc. Strictly in *economics,* the term means transactions in which money is involved.

Exchange economy. An economic system dominated by transactions in which money is involved. Most of the productive capacity of such a system is directed to production for exchange.

Exclave. A portion of an administrative or other kind of area, which is detached from the main area and completely surrounded by another area.

Experiential space. "Objective" reality, the physical environment containing all objects, perceived and unperceived.

Export base model. A model that stresses the key role of a region's *export base.* This base is the exportable commodities or services produced by a region. North has utilized a five-stage model illustrating the growth and diversification of the industries in a region that "export" their goods and services.

Extended family. A composite family structure, which may consist of several basic family units related by descent, marriage, or adoption. (Cf. **Nuclear family.**)

Extractive agriculture. An attitude and practice of agriculture that stresses the short-term benefits of farming; hence little attention is paid to preserving the resource for future use.

Factor analysis. The statistical technique of identifying and measuring the underlying factors or variables involved in a complex ability or trait in a large variety of measures.

Factory. The manufacturing unit in which the form utility of some "raw" material(s) is changed; a concentration of machines, materials, and labor contributing to such a change.

Feedback. The return to the input of part of an output of a system's component. Various types of feedback can be recognized: for example, *negative* feedback opposes the working of the main driving force; *positive* feedback stimulates the main driving force; *amplification* feedback stimulates an ever-widening source of energy, which itself stimulates yet further energy.

Feedback system. A system distinguished from the **simple action system** by its characteristic of feedback.

Feudal economy. An economic system whose basic relationship was between a vassal and his lord. In return for a grant of land, an office, or certain kinds of revenues from the lord, a vassal accepted certain obligations—to return part of the crop from the land, give certain services to the lord, etc. The vassal was strictly a tenant.

Firm, the. The agency or institution that organizes resources to produce an output of goods or services in response to consumer demands.

Fixed capital. Capital investment, accumulated in the form of fixed items such as high-cost machinery, buildings, etc.

Fixed facilities. Transportation stocks such as rights of way, railroad tracks, and roadways, as opposed to mobile stocks such as cars or trucks.

F.O.B. price. Free on board; without charge for delivery to, and placing on board, a transportation carrier.

Folk society. A term used by Redfield to denote an ideal or abstract type of society commonly studied by anthropologists. Folk societies are small, scattered, and isolated, with personal and kinship relations predominating; magic and religious values outweigh secular values. Each folk society is an integrated whole, static, and quiet, utilizing a simple technology, etc.

Footloose industries. Industries or firms that have

no strong locational preference, due to the greater amount of freedom or flexibility derived from technical advances in using raw materials, the relative unimportance of transportation costs, etc.

Form utility. A change in form of a raw material or good—as, for example, with the transformation of iron ore to pig iron, or the fabrication of a metal into a machine. The addition of this form utility increases the use of the original resource.

Forward Linkage. Hirschmann's term to denote the attempts by economic activities (whose outputs are not used in the local area) to generate demands for their products locally.

Freehold tenure. The outright ownership of land without many legal encumbrances, such as share-cropping, etc.

The free man nexus. Florence's term to denote a motivation to be free from the control or power of others.

Full search shopping. A category of consumer behavior that involves full comparative shopping and lengthy search procedures before the costly and/or highly socially visible product is purchased.

Functional diffuseness. A pattern variable cited by Hoselitz as an index of economic development. A society or system with diffuse obligations and work patterns is contrasted to one that contains specific and limited roles and well-defined obligations (functional specificity).

Functional interdependence. The interlocking of economy and society; the idea that the economy is not so differentiated from the rest of society that each would hold different values. Thus the values, norms, and beliefs present in the economy are similar to (and cannot be in conflict with) those in society.

Functional paradigm. A major sociological paradigm concerned with social systems comprising interdependent parts, dominantly considered to be in some stable equilibrium. Functionalists would view the following statement, for example, as a truism—"The social function of religion is the maintenance of group solidarity"—i.e., religion has a certain functional relationship with the wider system of which it is a part.

Game theory. A statistical procedure dealing with the selection of optimal decisions where imperfect knowledge exists.

Gamma index. A term used in network geometry to measure the number of observed connections between nodes or points on a network, as compared to the maximum number of connections in that network.

G.A.T.T. General Agreement on Tariff and Trade. An agreement ratified in the mid-sixties by over sixty nations to regularized international trade, lower tariffs, control dumping of surplus products, eliminate quotas, etc.

Generative cities. Cities that, according to Hoselitz, act as centers of change and stimulate economic growth.

Genetic agriculture. The attitude and practice in farming of maximizing long-term land use and returns by conserving land resources.

Genre de vie. A concept denoting the set of social facts that intervene between geographic conditions and man's behavior. Each group has its own "genre de vie" made up of habits, techniques, and social, economic, and psychological structures.

Geographic facts. Facts that refer to the character of a place or to the quantity or quality of some phenomenon that occupies a place at a given time. (Note that few facts are exclusively geographic in these terms.)

Geographic inertia. A term used to describe the qualities of a location or located facility where the original locative factors have either disappeared or ceased to be relevant, but the location continues to support a facility or have attractive powers because of some other persistent locative force, such as tradition, etc.

Geographic environment. The unified milieu of man and environment, which Kirk sees as comprised of two interacting components—phenomenal environment and behavioral environment.

Geonomic efficiency. Renner's term to denote the degree to which an industry's location corresponds to the "ideal" location.

Gesalt psychology. A "school" of psychology originating in Germany in the early twentieth century, which emphasizes the organization, patterning, and wholeness of human behavior rather than any atomistic elements.

Global village, the. A term used by Marshall McLuhan to indicate the present or future characteristic of the world united by mass media and visual communication.

Graph theory. A branch of topology, closely related to algebra and matrix theory. Commonly used in the analysis of transportation networks.

Gravity model. An analogue from Newtonian physics, which maintains that spatial interaction of any kind between pairs of places or points is a positive function of their populations and inversely proportionate to intervening distance.

Gross. A condition in the processing of raw materials where the manufacture or addition of form utility leads to a decrease in the weight of the product. (Cf. **Pure.**)

Group. An aggregate or category of persons possessing some common features—common relationship through interaction, similar income, same sex, similar occupation, etc. Usually *primary*, *secondary*, and *reference* groups are distinguished.

Growth pole. A concept that holds that economic development never occurs uniformly over a particular area, but is concentrated at particular points or growth poles which expand much more rapidly than surrounding areas.

Guaranteed prices. A device used by governments in cases of uncertain agricultural markets and conditions to guarantee to a farmer a certain minimum price for his crop or livestock regardless of world or regional price conditions.

Hardware. The tangible elements of a social system, such as tools and artifacts.

Hearth areas. Regions or areas that seem to have been the centers of certain agricultural and technological innovations and inventions, and which then spread the information to surrouding areas.

Heterogenetic cities. Cities that, according to Redfield, are bearers of rapid social change, representing universalist, achievement-oriented value systems—usually under influences external to the local culture. (Cf. **Generative cities.**)

Hierarchy. A term used in central place theory to denote an order, grade, or rank of decreasing numbers of larger settlements. The larger centers provide more goods and services than the smaller cities and towns.

Highest and best use. The notion in urban land value literature that competition for the most accessible land in an urban area and its consequent high valuation leads to its use by the entrepreneur with the highest ability to pay for the land.

Hinterland. The market area, trade area, or informational distribution area of a settlement.

Hobby nexus, the. Florence's term to denote motivation through love of work itself.

Holism. The view, particularly associated with Hegel, that to understand some phenomenon it is necessary to understand it in its entirety. In sociology a holistic approach sees societies as constituting social systems, and by studying the whole, the component parts or interrelationships are better understood.

Household or cottage industry. Manufacturing or transformation of a raw material by the addition of form utility, which is conducted in the home of the consumer or in a small workshop attached to the home. Often used to indicate any very small-scale manufacturing process.

Hydroponics. A technical innovation in agriculture that supports plant growth without soil, via a solution of chemical and organic elements.

Ideal limit. The absolute range of a shop or service, beyond which in economically rational terms no purchaser will use that particular shop or service.

Ideal type. An abstraction from experience, which combines the best characteristics and sets them up as an example or measure against which real things may be compared.

Ideographic approach. The approach in geography that stresses the individuality and uniqueness of different areas and regions, in contrast to the nomothetic approach, which stresses their general similarities.

Ideological space. The symbolic space shaped by the ideology of an individual or group—the spatial context of "community," "nation-state," and "nationalism."

Imperialism. An ideology that justifies the acquisition and control of foreign territory in order to exploit its resources (physical, human, etc.); the monopoly stage of capitalism where, according to Lenin, international financial monopolies divide up the world and exploit the territories to their own advantage.

Independent variable. A term used in regression analysis to denote the variables that vary, or are thought to vary, independently. (Cf. **Dependent variable.**)

Index method. A method by which the general features of a developed economy are abstracted as ideal indices and are then usually contrasted with the typical features of a developing area.

Induction. A method of reasoning from the part to the whole, from the particular to the general.

Industrial Revolution. A period, which had various beginnings traceable to Elizabethan England and

West Indian sugar plantations, that ultimately led to the replacement of hand tools by power-driven machines, and to the concentration of industry in large establishments.

Inelasticity of demand. The responsiveness of a quantity of goods demanded in an economic system to a change in price is called the *elasticity* of demand. Demand is termed inelastic when the percentage change in quantity demanded is less than the percentage change in price.

Inertia. The stability of industrial locations, even after the original locative forces have been eclipsed by technological and other changes.

Influence. A category used to explain consumer behavior; "influences" are factors external to the products or service, such as selling methods or advertising.

Information technology. The application of computers and associated information systems to the handling of data in enormous quantities.

Infrastructure. The fundamental underpinning of a modern economy, such as roads, railroads, ports, other public works, hospitals, schools, public health systems, etc.

Initial advantage. An advantage accruing to a city, region, or nation through its being the first to introduce an innovation, invention, or new technique, to establish a market or tributary area, or to develop an advanced socioeconomic structure.

Input. One of three variables used in a model; the input variables are independent of the model, and are usually allowed to vary; in an economic system, wages would be an example of an input.

Insight learning. A term used in psychology to denote the condition in learning where a relationship is suddenly perceived and a problem may be solved in a flash of insight.

Institution. The complex normative patterns governing behavior in certain fundamental and recurring situations. A particular institution is the organized aggregate to which the norms are applied.

Interaction. The movement or mobility of things, ideas, or people between spatially separated points or places.

Interactance hypothesis. The distance/mass relationship of the **gravity model,** whereby interaction is postulated as a function of the distance from an activity and the "drawing power" of that activity.

Interest group. A group of people whose relations are cemented by some common interest (rather than by familial relationship, income, shared

neighborhood) — it may be a common hobby, value system, recreational pursuit, etc.

Internalize. Through learning and social adaptation, the incorporation of an individual or group into the larger cultural value system.

Intervening opportunity. One factor in Ullman's tripartite movement typology — *complementarity* generates interchange only if no *intervening* source of supply is available.

Isocost line. Isolines joining points of equal cost.

Isodapanes. Isolines connecting points of equal, total transportation costs.

Isolated shopping clusters. Street-corner or isolated clusters of one to four business types, usually a grocery-drugstore combination. Serves consumers within a few blocks of the stores. Most shopping nucleations are usually scattered throughout an urban area.

Isosatisfact lines. Isolines joining points of equal "satisfaction" (in economic behavioral terms of *satisficing*).

Isotims. Isolines of equal delivery costs on either material inputs or finished products.

Isotropic. A surface showing equal growth tendencies and equal values in all directions.

Kibbutz. An Israeli community, usually agricultural, organized under collectivist principles. (Cf. **Ejido, Kolkhoz.**)

Kolkhoz. A Soviet collective farm whose land is leased to the collective as a unit and is farmed under the direction of a committee elected by members of the collective.

Labor aristocracy. The members of the labor force, usually professional workers, who, in a developing area, receive the largest wage increases and rewards due to their privileged positions, while the rest of the labor force's wages remain low.

Labor coefficient. Ratio of labor cost to the combined weights of the material input and the produced output.

Labor extensive. The use of labor in an economic activity, whereby labor is minimized and output is usually maximized.

Labor intensive. The use of large quantities of labor, whereby frequently the return from that labor cannot be maximized.

Latifundia. Large landed estates, originally in Southern Europe but now commonly applied to similar estates in South America; usually held by an absentee landlord employing peasant and/or repressed laborers, utilizing primitive farming techniques.

Learned activity. Relatively permanent changes in behavior that result from past experiences or responses. Two main groups of theories exist concerning "learning": the S-R group see learning as a response to particular stimuli, and the cognitive theorists see learning as expectancies, memories, or purposive behavior. Thus the S-R theorists see "habits" as learned, and the cognitive theorists see "cognitive structures" as learned.

Life style. A group's or individual's way of life as shown overtly by manner of dress, eating, consumption of material objects, decor, etc. A class or group often has enough of these attributes in common for a class life style to be identifiable.

Limited search shopping. (a) **Casual:** limited search and little comparative shopping for goods in everyday use, obtainable at many locations and at low price. (b) **Directed:** limited search and little comparative shopping for goods in frequent use, but which are more costly, less frequently obtainable, and more socially visible; although they do not necessitate the prolonged search of **full search** goods, they are more carefully compared before purchase than are convenience goods.

Linear programming. A statistical technique that implies that there is a linear relationship of the form $A + B = C$; a series of simultaneous equations are used to represent the basic problem, with a linear function representing the objective. The term "programming" merely means that a set program or series of rules is followed to solve the equations.

Linkage. A term used to denote a group of geographically associated, though independent, establishments. Links between them exist because they take part in a similar kind of process or in a sequence of operations which involves a number of establishments.

Localization economies. Economies achieved by choosing an industrial site in an area where many component parts of a particular process are manufactured.

Location. Exact position on a grid reference system; position in relation to other spatially positioned activities or objects.

Locational costs. The costs in manufacturing that are additional to **basic costs,** and are caused by such factors as bringing raw materials from the source to the factory.

Loose structure. A term denoting an **atomistic** or individual behavior pattern; such egocentric behavior shows disregard for others and for the social order.

Macroscopic. A level of investigation or research that concentrates on the large-scale patterns rather than on the minutiae.

Margin of profitability. The limit of profitability, below which the firm operates at an economic loss.

Margin of transference. The boundary between two zones of land use in the von Thünen model: on one side the economic rent from one agricultural practice exceeds that of any other practice, and vice versa.

Marginal analysis. Economic analysis that stresses the borders, margins, or limiting areas of an activity or problem, rather than the entire range of the phenomena, in order to identify conditions of equilibrium, disequilibrium, or processes of change.

Marginal producer. A producer at the margins of profitability; should costs rise, for instance, the producer would probably be forced out of business.

Marginal utility. The increase in total utility that results from a unit increase in consumption. Utility refers to the satisfaction of any want.

Market economy. An economy in which the bulk of the output is produced for exhange. The *market* is the institution by which buyers and sellers come together to exchange goods for money, for present or future delivery and consumption. This type of economic system is commonly identified with private capitalism.

Marketing principle. One variant of Christaller's **central place theory,** where the *k*-value equals 3 and is based on the **range** of central goods.

Material culture. The material objects manufactured by a group to satisfy its wants (tools, weapons, utensils, ornaments and other art objects, machines, buildings, bridges), and such alterations to the landscape as irrigation systems, fortifications, etc.

Material index. Weber's index showing whether the optimal site in least-cost terms would be near the source of raw materials or near the market. It is calculated by dividing the weight of the local material inputs by the weight of the final product.

Maturity. The optimal stage of development in the cycle theory of industrial growth, characterized by a broad and balanced industrial structure, the existence of developed skills, and a substantial infrastructure.

Message. A unit of information.

Microgeography. A study of geographic patterns at the level of small groups, subareas, and small-scale regions. Such a study would usually look at individual and small-group behavior and would detail the social, cultural, and economic workings of the group.

Milieu. The whole range of environmental factors, human and nonhuman, tangible and philosophical.

Mobile facilities. A term used in the analysis of transportation stocks to indicate facilities such as railroad cars, trucks, automobiles, etc.

Model. A mathematical, logical, or mechanical replica of a relationship, a system, or a sequence of events so designed that a study of the model can yield some understanding of the real world.

Money capital. Capital in the form of cash, stocks, or bonds, in contrast to the less transferrable forms of capital like machinery, skills, or buildings.

Monte Carlo method. A simulation technique based on stochastic or probabilistic factors. It involves random sampling from a known probability distribution function.

Movement space. The perceived part of the environment in which movement occurs; to this may be added an extensive cosmological "movement" space.

Multifinality. A systems-analytic term that denotes that similar initial conditions can lead to different end effects.

Multiplier effect. The cumulative process whereby economic growth and change can set in motion a chain reaction of further growth and expansion.

National income. The measure of a nation's production, distribution, consumption, and investment over a period of time (usually one year). National income is measured in several ways—as the "output," the value of all goods and services produced (Gross National Product); as "income received" by all persons in the nation, plus incomes which were undistributed by public authorities, companies, and institutions; or as the value of the total amount spent on consumer goods and services, plus totally new investments.

Nationalism. An emotional allegiance paid by groups or individuals to a nation-state or territory.

Nation-state. A political grouping of people occupying a particular area or region, held together by some common acceptance of particular values. The political organization ensures that those common values can be preserved and further developed. Typically the nation-state occupies a clearly defined territory.

Negentropy. A measure of order or organization in a system. Open systems are negentropic, tending to decrease in entropy and to increase the elaboration of their structure.

Neighborhood centers. A shopping nucleation serving a local area for frequent purchase of convenience goods. Typical functions include a supermarket, drugstore, laundry, barbers, dry cleaner, etc.

Neocapitalism. The form of capitalism dominated by corporations, conglomerates, multinational corporations, and the large-scale intervention of the state.

Neocolonialism. The economic and cultural dominance by a nation(s), which, although not contained within the old concept of nineteenth-century European colonialism, subjugates another group or nation to the master group.

Neotechnic. A term used by Mumford to denote the third phase of urban and industrial development, characterized by many technical innovations in industry, agricultural and power resources, and transportation.

Noise. A term in communication theory used to denote random changes which can occur in the process of transmission.

Nomothetic approach. The approach in geography that looks for repeated patterns and generalities, and develops bodies of theory, principles, or "laws" to represent those common structures.

Normative. A method of approach that looks for what "ought to" occur in a particular circumstance, rather than what actually occurs (optimality vs. reality); thus *normative economics* is a closed systems approach to ideal economic conditions and does not necessarily reflect real-world economic conditions.

Normative integration. The degree to which the behavior of individuals conforms to the major values and norms of a society; also, the degree of consistency among the major values and norms in a society.

Norms. Common standards or ideals that guide members' responses in established groups. *Social norms* are those standards that are accepted by individuals for guiding simple actions or complex judgments in ideal situations.

Nuclear family. A small group composed of husband, wife, and immature children, constituting a unit apart from the rest of the community.

O-D survey. Origin-destination survey; used in traffic analyses, usually by questioning a random sample of travelers and ascertaining the origin of their present journey and its destination. More elaborate methods are available to determine journey purpose, journeys made over a longer period of time, etc.

O.E.E.C. Organization for European Economic Co-operation, established in 1948 to coordinate the distribution and use of the Marshall Plan funds, consisting of 18 European nations. In 1961 it was replaced by *O.E.C.D.* (Organization for Economic Cooperation and Development), the United States and Canada becoming full members. This new organization is concerned with economic stability, aid and support to developing countries, and the expansion of world trade.

Old age. The final and declining stage of development in cycle theories of growth; characterized, for example, in the industrial development cycle by a deterioration in infrastructure, immobility of labor and fixed skills, and a declining industrial mix.

Open economy. An exchange economy where exchanges occur both within the group and with economic systems external to it.

Open system. A system that needs an energy supply for its maintenance and preservation, in contrast to **closed systems** across whose boundaries no such exchange takes place. An open system may attain a *steady state* in which the import and export of energy and material are equated by adjusting the form of the system itself.

Operational milieu. The milieu that is interposed between the decision maker and the objective reality of the environment. The milieu consists of interrelated elements, such as a value system, cultural factors, the economic system, etc. In economic behavior terms this milieu governs the machinery of production, consumption, and exchange.

Operations research. The application of a range of statistical techniques and models to the study of complex logistical problems, such as the assignment of flows in a transportation network.

Operative institutions. In this group of institutions a professed purpose is immediately fulfilled; the institution achieves its task within itself and so renders a specific service.

Opinion leaders. Members of a group who expose themselves to information from the outside world more often than do their fellow group members. They then relay information to the unexposed or reinforce previously exposed members.

Opportunity costs. Costs measured not in terms of money spent directly, but in terms of what the money might have been used for, the alternative that was foregone — e.g., a farmer decides to grow barley rather than oats; the opportunity cost of the barley is the oats which he might have grown instead; the cost of military spending is a somewhat lower standard of living than would otherwise be possible — more guns, less butter.

Opportunity set. A term used by Marble and Bowlby to denote the location of all stores that each consumer could have visited.

Optimizer. Rational economic man — certain, all-knowing, making perfect optimal decisions.

Orthogenetic city. A city that, according to Redfield, resists change or any reorganization of the social order: the economy stagnates, and the city maintains the *ascriptive* and *particularistic* value system of culture. (Cf. **Parasitic city.**)

Output. One of three variables in a model; output is entirely dependent upon the structure of the model, its inputs, and its functioning. An example of output in a model economic system would be the generation of demand.

Paleotechnic. Mumford's term to denote the phase of urban development characterized by coal as a power source, a relatively primitive transportation system, fairly localized markets, and compact urban settlements.

Paradigm. Large-scale models or patterns of thought, which are rarely specifically formulated (in contrast to models).

Parallel. The existence side by side of two economic systems, between which there is only minimal interaction.

Parasitic city. A city that, according to Hoselitz, dominates the economic, social, and political activities of an area to such an extent that it has a dampening effect on economic growth.

Particularism. A pattern variable cited by Hoselitz as an index of economic development. A particularistic society or system chooses among alternatives according to their standing in some relation to itself or the group.

Pattern variables. A term introduced by Parsons and Shils to represent types of choices open to individuals and groups. One side of a pattern variable chosen by an individual determines the meaning of a situation for him. Some dichotomous variables are universalism/particularism, achievement/ascription, and specificity/diffuseness. Pattern variable analysis has been used to identify similarities and differences between cultures and to indicate economic development.

Payoff matrix. The matrix used in game theory to set out the alternative strategies available to the players.

Peasant economy. An economic system in which production is centered on small-scale, technologically simple agriculture, fishing, and crafts, usually by family groups. Usually it is pre-industrial or partly industrialized, rurally oriented, and attached to the soil, local community, and tradition.

Perception. The process by which an organism selects, organizes, and interprets data available through its sensory apparatus.

Perfect competition. The rivalry between firms that takes place in a "perfect" market situation—i.e., in a market where knowledge of all data is available to all competitors, and where all resources are perfectly divisible and mobile.

Perverse growth. Growth that undermines rather than enhances the potentialities of the economy for long-term development.

Phenomenal environment. The physical environment plus modifications and alterations caused by man.

Phenomenology. An approach in psychology that attempts to suspend all presuppositions and to observe and describe the world of conscious phenomena, particularly in connection with such problems of perception as space, time, color, motion, sight, and touch.

Place utility. The utility achieved by transportation, which, by overcoming the barrier of distance, can bring materials or goods to a place or region that does not normally have a sufficient supply of such goods.

Planning models. Models that predict a future course of events, but whose outcomes are evaluated in terms of the planner's goals.

Polarization. A term used by Hirschmann to denote the tendency for economic "energy" to flow toward a growth pole or center.

Political system. A system of particular processes and human actions by which conflicts between the interests of subgroups and individuals and the welfare of the society or group as a whole are governed or settled. Frequently such political processes involve the use of, or struggle for, power.

Potlatch. A complex of activities (feasts, dances, dramatic displays) found among the Indians of the Pacific Northwest, the core and climax of which was the conspicuous reciprocal distribution, and at times destruction, of goods. The amassment and destruction of goods in this manner was to enhance the prestige of an individual in the tribe and simultaneously to degrade the competitor.

Power. The ability of an individual, group, or society to effect a certain occurrence or to influence others in intended ways.

Precipitation circumstances. A term used by Katona in his explanation of consumer behavior to denote factors that can cause a purchase or a reorientation of spending habits—income changes, marriage, childbirth, etc.

Predictive models. Models that are capable of stating, with varying degrees of probability, the course of change.

Predisposition. A category used to explain consumer behavior; predispositions refer to an individual's characteristics at the time of decision, such as beliefs, values, past experiences, etc.

Primary activity. Economic activities concerned with agriculture, forestry, fishing, quarrying and mining, whose output is often a product needing further processing.

Primary group. A group that has intimate, close, usually face-to-face relationships, such as the family or extended family.

Principle of substitution. The process of substituting one economic factor for another, until some margin is reached on which either factor will be "indifferently applied" and where the net efficiency of either factor will be proportionate to the cost of applying it.

Private information. Information that reaches an individual by a "private" system of communication, such as face-to-face contacts, personal letters, and phone calls.

Probabilism. The view that rejects the deterministic cause-and-effect notion, and sees an element of uncertainty in social, physical, and economic events.

Probabilistic clues. A term used by Marble and Bowlby to indicate that by chance the outcomes of particular shopping choices may be successful or unsuccessful.

Product attribute. A category used to explain consumer behavior; product attributes are the chemical and physical realities of the objects or services.

Product differentiation. The complex of goods or products, consumer tastes, needs, and preferences.

Production. The process by which raw materials are converted into goods through the addition of place and form utility.

Production cycle. Kolosovsky's term to denote sets of **linkages** between industries in a **complex.**

Productive leisure. A term denoting those groups motivated not by productive effort for monetary profit, but for some less tangible motive like status, prestige, religion, etc. (Cf. **Status increment motive.**)

Profit economy. A term used by the German economist Werner von Sombart in the early 1900s to denote the polar opposite of "subsistence" economy. Today most people would use the term "market" or "commercial" economy instead.

Protective duties. Import duties levied by a nation-state on goods or raw materials to protect the continued production of such items within the state and to exclude items lower in cost than those produced within the state.

"Psychic" income. The enjoyment that an entrepreneur receives from establishing his firm deliberately at a nonoptimal location; his monetary loss is compensated by his gain in enjoyment or satisfaction from that location.

Public information. Information that reaches an individual through public media like radio, television, and newspapers.

Pure. A condition where weight loss after manufacture is zero. (Cf. **Gross.**)

Quaternary activities. Those service activities for which advanced training and education is required, and which make a large contribution to decision making processes.

Rack jobber. A wholesaler whose activities are limited to supplying supermarkets with certain nonfood items.

Range. The distance a consumer is willing to travel to purchase a good or service at a particular price.

Range of tolerance. The range of locations and sites around the optimal manufacturing location, which can be utilized and still have a considerable chance of being successful.

Ratio of advantage. The ratio or degree of advantage gained in producing one crop or commodity instead of another.

The real-cost nexus. Florence's term that includes

the notion of profit motivation balanced against satisfaction from other sources.

Receiver. The completor of the communications process, who is aware of and accepts a message.

Reciprocal economy. An economic system dominated by reciprocal exchange: goods of economic and/or social value are exchanged through duty or some other reciprocal relationship, such as ceremony or tradition.

Recreationists. Vacation needs that are activity oriented—e.g., weekend sportsmen or hunters.

Redistributive economy. An economic system dominated by a strong central agency governing the exchange of goods—the feudal manor or the governments of people's socialist states are examples of this system.

Redundancy. A term in network analysis: normally only one path exists between any pair of nodes—this would be *zero* redundancy; any further paths to that node are called "redundant," since they provide connections beyond the absolute minimum necessary.

Reference group. A group to which an individual may turn to appraise his own or his own group's standing, values, and norms, but of which he need not be a member.

Region. A unit area with some kind of internal homogeneity, which distinguishes it from areas around it. A number of different kinds of regions have been identified—*uniform* regions, which are homogeneous as to some factor such as economic activity, cultural type, or physical factor; *nodal* regions, distinguished by common orientations; *depressed* regions, characterized by economic underdevelopment; *frontier* regions, located on the margins of settlement; and *institutional* regions, created by banks or government agencies to delimit regions of service.

Regional centers. The highest order of noncentral shopping nucleations, providing for the purchase of all but the most specialized goods and services and offering a wide variety of functions, such as department stores, specialized furniture stores, and record stores.

Regional input-output models. A model that relates certain demographic and economic variables of a region through an input-output matrix which generates the employment population, output, etc. of an area when fed information specifying the final demands for each output.

Regression analysis. A statistical technique used to

establish and quantify a relationship between two or more variables which, by their changes of value, produce changes in the value of the first variable. The first variable, which is the quantity under study, is called the *dependent* variable. When there is more than one independent variable the technique is known as *multiple regression analysis*.

Regulative institutions. A group of institutions concerned with the operation of other institutions; they achieve their purpose by enabling the tasks of other institutions to take place.

Relative location, "Where" an object or activity is located in relation to the locations of other activity sites. A *centrally placed* location implies situations relatively close to the center of activities; *peripherally placed* locations are those far from such a center, inaccessible to it, or at the margins.

Representational mediator. Osgood's term denoting how an individual associates a sign with a particular disposition or internal response.

Residuals from regression. The "unexplained" variation between a dependent variable and one or more independent variables, which reflects in part the effect of other unknown variables, as well as sampling error, etc.

Resource process. A term denoting the set of factors that surround resource use, such as perceived organic and physical elements and their agricultural use.

Resources. Perceived environmental factors, which are evaluated within the observational and behavioral contexts of the group concerned. Three categories of resources are commonly recognized — *natural resources*, a slowly changing stock of physical elements; *human resources*, arising from the abilities of a population, such as manpower; and *cultural resources*, including tools, artifacts, attitudes, and beliefs.

Sanction. A reward (positive sanction) or punishment (negative sanction) used to encourage conformity with the standards of behavior or norms that are regarded as desirable by a social group.

Sarvah. A term denoting an intensive agricultural tillage system, emphasizing the production of rice.

Satisficer. A model of man that discards the rationality assumptions of the optimizer or economic man and assumes that man searches for a course of action that is "good enough" or satisfactory in a given situation.

Scale. A relative or proportionate measure or level of generalization.

Scale economy. See **Economies of scale.**

Search activity. The act of searching an environmental milieu for a desired objective; frequently the order of search is important.

Secondary activity. A convenience term used in economic geography to denote the economic activities that add form utility to a primary resource — i.e., manufacturing.

Secondary group. Large, freely associated groups of people brought together by a complex of common goals and beliefs, but without the intimate interdependency of the **primary group.**

Selective perception. The process by which, in addition to the physical filtering process of the sensory organs and the capacity of the brain, certain perceived stimuli and symbols are selected in preference to others. This selective perception process is the result of learning, experience, values, etc.

Sender. The initiator of a message.

Shift-share technique. A technique for measuring regional shifts in industry and changes on a regional scale of the national share of an industrial group. Usually the rate of growth of employment in a given industry is calculated on a national basis. Then, for each region, the difference is computed between the actual employment in the industry and the employment that would have resulted had the region's rate of growth in the industry been the same as the national rate; a positive difference indicates a shift into the region; a negative difference indicates a shift out.

Sign. A stimulus encouraging a specific response that is the same as or similar to the previous responses to that or a similar stimulus. It is a generic term which includes **symbols** and cues. Osgood uses the term to denote the perceived part of a **significate.**

Significate. Osgood's term to denote any stimulus that, in a given situation, regularly and reliably produces a predictable pattern of behavior.

Simple action system. A simple system with one-way relationships and no feedback.

Simulation model. A method of constructing an analogue of a system to test and draw inferences concerning the system's properties; the analogue is an idealized representation of the real system, but retains its basic properties.

Site. The absolute location of an object or activity.

Site costs. The actual costs of a land parcel in a particular location.

Situation. The location of an activity with reference to the broad spatial system of which it is but one coordinate.

Situational feedback. The feedback that occurs between the external stimulus and the internal state of the perceiver.

Social accounts. The analysis of the economic and financial data of a nation, region, group, or individual by which consolidated accounts are produced—these indicate present wealth, the economic transactions which have taken place over a period of time, the balance of wealth, etc. When applied to a nation-state, such accounts are usually called national income accounts.

Social action. A term denoting the functional structure of action, which includes such morphological features as **pattern variables.**

Social capital. Schools, hospitals, community buildings, and certain government-directed irrigation and utility schemes fall under this investment rubric.

Socialization. The lifelong process of inculcation whereby an individual learns the principal values and symbols of the social system in which he participates and the way those values are expressed.

Social physics. The study of society as a phenomenon that is subjected to "forces" and "processes" analagous to those studied by scientists, particularly Newtonian physicists.

Social space. The symbolic space that people use in assigning social ranking and class.

Social stratification. Social differentiation into hierarchical ranks. These ranks or strata are those into which all members of a society may fall, and within which all are equal, but between which are recognized and sanctioned differences placing one member higher or lower than another in the admitted social order.

Social visibility. Life styles, items of material culture, dialects, language, house types, furnishings, and appliances that are common to a particular social stratum and are its visible symbols.

Software. The intangible elements of a social system, like attitudes, beliefs, and behavior.

Sovkhoz. A Soviet state farm owned and operated by the state; its workers are paid employees as in other state enterprises.

Spatial distribution. A *set* of geographic facts representing the behavior of a particular phenomenon or characteristic distributed in many places on the surface of the earth.

Spatial equilibrium. The contention that the aggregate pattern of space usage by a society is in equilibrium, or is relatively unchanging.

Spatial interaction. The relationship, linkage, or flows among or between unit areas.

S-R theory (Stimulus—Response). A psychological theory linking the stimulus (an object or event which elicits some reply) and the response (the activated reply) in the manner of a reflex arc.

State capitalism. An economic system where the government of a nation-state owns and directs substantial sectors of the economy in competition with private capitalist sectors.

State socialism. An economic system where the government of a nation-state owns and controls virtually all of the economic sector, and where the factors of competition and profit motive are minimized.

Status increment motive. Motivation aimed at improving one's place or prestige within a social system, and/or at attaining access to the distribution of rights, obligations, power, and authority within that system.

Status variable. One of three variables in a model. A status variable specifies that certain conditions of the model are held constant throughout its operation—in the case of a model economic system, the specific form of economic organization would be a status variable.

Stochastic process. A process implying *randomness* as opposed to a fixed rule or relation in passing from one observation to the next.

Stratified society. A society whose members fall into obvious strata, castes, estates, or classes, and where there is a marked difference in attitudes, feelings, beliefs, material well-being, etc., between the different strata.

Subsidies. The means by which a government or one or more sectors of society can support an uneconomic activity or protect it from competition.

Subsistence economy. An economic system that involves relatively simple technology and virtually no interchange of goods outside the family, extended family, or group; the family is both producer and consumer.

Supply. The amount of a good or service available for sale or distribution at a given price and time; the rate of flow of that good or service into the market.

Supports. One of two types of inputs to a political system recognized by D. Easton, including taxes, levies, military service, obedience to laws, participation in voting, etc.

Symbiosis. The coexistence in the same group or society of a number of dissimilar institutions and activities, which functionally complement one another. It is derived from biology where it means living together in close association or functional interdependence.

Symbol. Signs that function as stimuli, by virtue of a significance acquired in previous experience.

System. A set of interrelated components and the relations among them, making a complex whole.

Systems analysis. Utilization of the **systems** concept as an analytical tool; an analysis that begins from the premise that activities are complex interrelated wholes rather than individual parts studied in isolation.

Take-off. The crucial stage in economic development when, according to W. W. Rostow, the economy and society "are transformed in such a way that a steady rate of growth can be thereafter regularly sustained." *Take-off* is characterized by a "rise in the rate of productive investment," the "development of one or more substantial manufacturing sectors, with a high rate of growth," and the emergence of "a political, social, and institutional framework" which encourages growth. The term has gained wide acceptance, even among those who severely criticize Rostow's general formulation.

Technique. A specific sequence of coordinated movements or operations through which a task, like the working of a tool, is accomplished.

Technological index. A measure of transportation, trade, energy consumption and production, and national product used by Berry in his factor analysis of development variables.

Technology. A system of techniques and tools by which man attempts to control or modify his natural or phenomenal environment.

Tenancy. The system of rights and duties associated with land occupancy and use, in return for which the tenant pays cash, shares his crop, or pledges his labor to a landlord.

Terms of trade. The relation between two sets of trade by a region or country: the prices of the goods and services that are exported, and the prices of the goods and services that are imported.

Tertiary activity. That section of economic activities that is involved not with the exploitation or growth of primary products, nor with the change in form of goods associated with secondary activities, but with the exchange and consumption of goods and services. Typical activities include retailing, wholesaling, medical services, recreational services, and various repair services.

Threshold. The minimum level of demand needed to support an economic activity, e.g., shop or service establishment. Demand can be measured in terms of population or income per capita.

Time utility. The addition of a time dimension to a good or service, by storage and/or seasonal marketing, which enhances the utility of the good or service.

Tools. Material objects so designed that they utilize and apply energy in precise and controlled ways.

Traffic principle. One variant of Christaller's **central place model** where the costs of transportation and accessibility considerations cause a concentration of towns along routes and a greater number of higher order centers than the **marketing principle** ($K = 4$).

Transfer costs. The total costs of moving a good from point A to point B; they include transportation costs, insurance costs, handling costs, the cost of inventory, etc.

Transferability. One factor in Ullman's tripartite movement typology—if the distance between demand and supply is too great or too costly to overcome, interaction will not take place; alternate goods will be substituted.

Transformation line. A concept used in production theory to denote all combinations of inputs that give rise to a given output.

Transportation costs. The direct costs of moving a good or individual from point A to point B. (Cf. **Transfer costs.**)

Transport gradient. The slope representing the return to the farmer in the von Thünen model, in terms of market price *minus* transportation cost (directly related to distance from the market).

Transportation problem. A form of **linear programming** where, given the supply centers with known surpluses, receiving places with known demands, and known connecting routes and transportation costs, the least-cost route is calculated.

Trickling down effects. A term denoting the feedback effects from a zone or center of growth toward the periphery.

Uncertainty principle. The principle that maintains there is always a final uncertainty and unpredictability to events and occurrences.

Uncontrolled system. A feedback system in which there are no controls, e.g., in a "free" market situation.

Universalism. One of Parson's **pattern variables** denoting "development." Universalism indicates a worldwide range of interests and knowledge.

Urbanization economies. Economies of scale achieved by the existence of a highly urbanized area with a ready market and supply of labor, and a developed social and transportation structure.

Usufruct. Right to use and profit without ownership.

Utility. The direct satisfaction that goods and services yield to their possessors.

Utility measure. The measurement of satisfaction gained in obtaining one choice over another.

Vacationists. Leisure needs where the journey involved may have as great, or greater, significance than the activity itself.

Validation. A term used by Marble and Bowlby denoting the level of correspondence between a choice and the successful attainment of that choice.

Value system. The system of shared cultural and social standards of a group, against which actions and desires, attitudes and needs, can be judged and compared by members of the group.

Vernalized wheat. Wheat grains that have been subjected to a process (such as exposing partially sprouted wheat to low temperatures for a period) that induces a shortening of the final germinating and ripening period.

Virtual space. The subjective space, containing only those objects perceived.

Visual information. The term used in communication theory to denote the information which an individual perceives through his direct sight.

Wurzburg school. A group of late nineteenth- and early twentieth-century German psychologists who saw unconscious factors as entering into decision making, particularly "imageless" thought.

Youth. A term used in a number of cyclic growth models to represent the first stage of development.

Bibliography

Ackermann, E. A. 1959. "Population and Natural Resource," in P. M. Hauser and O. D. Duncan, eds. *The Study of Population.* Chicago: University of Chicago Press, pp. 621–648.

Alchian, A. A. 1950. "Uncertainty, Evaluation, and Economic History," *Journal of Political Economy,* vol. 58, pp. 211–221.

Alexander, J. W. 1963. *Economic Geography.* Englewood Cliffs, N.J.: Prentice-Hall.

Alonso, W. 1965. *Location and Land Use.* Cambridge: Harvard University Press.

Andrews, H. F. 1970. "Consumer Behavior and the Tertiary Activity System," in *London Papers in Regional Science,* vol. 2, pp. 1–14.

Baran, P. and Sweezy, M. 1966. *Monopoly Capital.* New York: Monthly Review Press.

Beckmann, M. J. and Marschak, T. 1955. "An Activity Analysis Approach to Location Theory," *Kyklos,* vol. 8, pp. 125–143.

Berelson, B. and Steiner, G. A. 1964. *Human Behavior: An Inventory of Scientific Findings.* New York: Harcourt, Brace, and World.

Berry, B. J. L. 1967a. *Geography of Market Centers and Retail Distribution.* Englewood Cliffs, N.J.: Prentice-Hall.

———. 1967b. "Essays on Commodity Flows and the Spatial Structure of the Indian Economy," Chicago: University of Chicago, Department of Geography, Research Paper No. 111.

———. 1961. "Basic Patterns of Economic Development," in N. Ginsburg, ed., *Atlas of Economic Development.* Chicago: University of Chicago Press.

———. 1960. "An Inductive Approach to the Regionalization of Economic Development," in Ginsburg 1960, pp. 78–107.

Berry, B. J. L. and Garrison, W. 1958. "Recent Developments of Central Place Theory," *Papers and Proceedings of the Regional Science Association*, vol. 4, pp. 107–120.

Berry, B. J. L., Garner, B., Simmons, J. W., and Tennant, R. J. 1963. "Commercial Structure and Commercial Blight." Chicago: University of Chicago, Department of Geography, Research Paper No. 85.

Blaut, J. M. 1970. "Geographic Models of Imperialism," *Antipode*, vol. 2, no. 1, pp. 65–85.

————. 1969. "Jingo Geography," *Antipode*, vol. 1, no. 1, pp. 10–12.

————. 1961. "Space and Process," *The Professional Geographer*, vol. 13, no. 4, pp. 1–7.

Bogue, D. J. 1949. *The Structure of the Metropolitan Community*. Ann Arbor: University of Michigan Press.

Bookchin, M. 1971. *Postscarcity Anarchism*. Berkeley: Ramparts Press.

Boskoff, A. 1962. The Sociology of Urban Regions. New York: Appleton Crofts.

Boulding, K. E. 1956. "General Systems Theory—The Skeleton of Science," *Management Science*, vol. 2, pp. 197–208.

Brinkmann, T. 1935. "Theodor Brinkmann's Economics of the Farm Business," M. R. Benedict et al., eds. Berkeley: University of California Press.

Brookfield, H. C. 1964. "Questions on the Human Frontiers of Geography," *Economic Geography*, vol. 40, pp. 42–58.

————. 1957. "Some Geographical Implications of the *Apartheid* and Partnership Policies in Southern Africa,"

Transactions, Institute of British Geographers, vol. 23, pp. 225–247.

Buchanan, K. 1962. "Profiles of the Third World," *Pacific Viewpoint*, vol. 5, pp. 97–126.

Bucklin, L. P. 1967. *Shopping Patterns in Urban Areas*. Berkeley: University of California, Institute of Business and Economic Research.

Bunge, W. 1962, 1966. *Theoretical Geography*. Lund: C. W. K. Glearup, 1st and 2nd editions.

Caesar, A. A. L. 1964. "Planning and the Geography of Great Britain," *Advancement of Science*, vol. 21, no. 91, pp. 230–240.

Campbell, C. K. 1966. "An Approach to Research in Recreational Geography," *B. C. Occasional Papers*, no. 7, pp. 85–90.

Carr Saunders, A. M. 1922. *The Population Problem*. Oxford: Oxford University Press.

Chapin, F. S. 1965. *Urban Land Use Planning*. Urbana: University of Illinois Press.

Christaller, W. 1966. *Central Places in Southern Germany*, translated by C. W. Baskin. Englewood Cliffs, N.J.: Prentice-Hall.

Clark, C. 1951. *The Conditions of Economic Progress*. London: The Macmillan Co.

Clawson, M. and Knetsch, J. L. 1966. *The Economics of Outdoor Recreation*. Baltimore: The Johns Hopkins Press.

Cooley, C. H. 1894. "The Theory of Transportation," Publications of the American Economic Association, vol. 9, no. 3.

Cox, K. R. 1965. "The Application of Linear Programming

to Geographic Problems," *Tijds. Voor Econ. en Soc. Geog.*, Nov.–Dec., vol. 56, pp. 228–236.

Crowe, P. R. 1938. "On Progress in Geography," *Scottish Geographical Magazine*, vol. 54, pp. 1–19.

Curry, L. 1967. "Central Places in the Random Spatial Economy," *Journal of Regional Science*, vol. 7, no. 2, supplement, pp. 217–38.

———. 1962. "The Geography of Service Centers within Towns: An Operational Approach," *Land Studies in Geography*, series B., no. 24, pp. 31–53.

Dale, C. 1966. "What Kind of Transport for Developing Countries?" *International Railway Journal*, April, pp. 35–38, 40, 48.

De Gregori, T. R. and Pi-Sunyer, O. 1969. *Economic Development: The Cultural Context.* New York: Wiley.

Dickinson, F. 1951. "Supply of Physician's Services," *American Medical Association Bulletin No. 81.*

Eckstein, A. 1958. "Individualism and the Role of the State in Economic Growth," *Economic Development and Cultural Change*, vol. 6, pp. 81–87.

Enke, S. 1951. "Equilibrium among Spatially Separated Markets: Solution by Electric Analogue," *Econometrica*, vol. 90, pp. 40–47.

Eversley, D. E. C. 1965. "Social and Psychological Factors in the Determination of Industrial Location," in T. Wilson, ed. *Papers on Regional Development.* Oxford: Basil Blackwell.

Firth, R., ed. 1967. *Themes in Economic Anthropology.* New York: Frederick A. Praeger/Association of Social Anthropologists, Monograph No. 6.

Fisher, A. G. B. 1945. *Economic Progress and Social Science.* London: Macmillan.

———. 1939. "Production: Primary, Secondary, and Tertiary," *Economic Record*, vol. 15, pp. 24–8.

Fisher, J. L. 1955. "Concepts in Regional Economic Development Programs," *Papers and Proceedings of the Regional Science Association*, vol. 1, pp. W1–W.

Florence, P. S. 1962. *Postwar Investment, Location, and Size of Plant.* Cambridge: Cambridge University Press.

Frank, A. G. 1967a. *Capitalism and Underdevelopment in Latin America.* New York: Monthly Review Press.

———. 1967b. "Sociology of Development and Underdevelopment of Sociology," *Catalyst*, pp. 20–73.

———. 1966. "The Development of Underdevelopment," *Monthly Review*, vol. 18, no. 4, pp. 17–31.

Friedman, M. 1962. *Capitalism and Freedom.* Chicago: Chicago University Press.

Friedmann, J. R. P. 1959. "Regional Planning: A Problem in Spatial Integration," *Papers and Proceedings of the Regional Science Association*, vol. 5, pp. 167–179.

———. 1956. "Locational Aspects of Economic Development," *Land Economics*, vol. 32, pp. 213–227.

Garner Barnum, H. 1966. "Market Centers and Hinterlands in Baden-Württenburg." Chicago: University of Chicago, Department of Geography, Research Paper No. 103.

Garrison, W. L., Berry, B. J. L., Marble, D. F., Nystuen, J. D., and Morrill, R. 1959. *Studies of Highway Development and Geographic Change.* Seattle: University of Washington Press.

Garrison, W. L. and Marble, D. F. 1965. *A Prolegomenon to the Forecasting of Transportation Development.* Evanston: Research Report, Transportation Center: Northwestern University.

Geertz, C. 1966. "Religion as a Cultural System," *Association of Social Anthropologists Monograph No. 3*, ed. by M. Banton. New York: Frederick A. Praeger, pp. 1–46.

———. 1965. "The Impact of the Concept, Culture, on the Concept of Man," in J. R. Ratt, ed. *New Views of Man.* Chicago: University of Chicago Press.

Ghandi, M. K. 1946. *Hind Swaraj.* Ahmedabad: Navajivan Publishing House.

Goldman, T. A. 1958. "Efficient Transportation and Industrial Location," *Papers and Proceedings of the Regional Science Association*, vol. 4, pp. 91–106.

Golledge, R. G. 1969. "The Geographical Relevance of Some Learning Theories," in K. R. Cox and R. G. Golledge, eds. *Behavioral Problems in Geography.* Northwestern University, Studies in Geography No. 17.

Gough, K. E. 1969. "The Indian Revolutionary Potential," *Monthly Review*, vol. 20, no. 9, pp. 23–36.

———. 1968. "Anthropology: Child of Imperialism," *Monthly Review*, vol. 19, no. 11, pp. 12–27.

Grigg, D. 1969. "The Agricultural Regions of the World: Review and Reflections," *Economic Geography*, vol. 45, no. 2. pp. 95–132.

Gurley, J. 1970. "Economic Conversion and Beyond," *Industrial Management Review*, vol. 2, no. 3.

Gutman, G. O. 1957. "A Note on Economic Development with Subsistence Agriculture," *Oxford Economic Papers*, pp. 323–329.

Hagerstrand, T. 1962. "The Propagation of Innovation Waves," *Lund Studies in Geography*, series B., no. 4.

Hahn, E. 1882. "Die Wirtschafts Farmen der Erde," *Pettermann's Mitteilungen*, vol. 38, pp. 8–12.

Hall, P., ed. 1966. *Von Thünen's Isolated State (Der Isolierte Staet)*, trans. by C. M. Wartenberg. Oxford: Pergamon Press.

Hansen, N. M. 1968. *French Regional Planning.* Bloomington, Indiana: Indiana University Press.

Harvey, D. W. 1967. "Models of Spatial Patterns in Human

Geography," in Haggett and Chorley, eds. *Models in Geography*. London: Methuen.

Hauser, P. M. 1959. "Cultural and Personal Obstacles to Economic Development in the Less Developed Areas," *Human Organization*, vol. 18, pp. 78–84.

Heilbroner, R. 1970. "Ecological Armageddon," in *Between Capitalism and Socialism*. New York: Vintage.

————. 1962. *The Making of Economic Society*. Englewood Cliffs, N.J.: Prentice-Hall.

Helburn, N. 1957. "The Bases for a Classification of World Agriculture," *Professional Geographer*, vol. 9, pp. 2–7.

Hirsch, W. Z. 1959. "Interindustry Relations of a Metropolitan Region: A Study in Agglomeration Projection," *Review of Economics and Statistics*, vol. 41, pp. 360–369.

Hirschmann, A. O. 1958. *The Strategy of Economic Development*. New Haven: Yale University Press.

Hodder, B. W. 1968. *Economic Development in the Tropics*. London: Methuen.

Hoover, E. M. 1967. "Some Programmed Models of Industrial Location," *Land Economics*, vol. 43, August, pp. 303–311.

————. 1948. "The Location of Economic Activity." New York: McGraw-Hill, Inc.

Horton, F. E. and Reynolds, D. R. 1969. "An Investigation of Individual Action Spaces: A Progress Report," *Proceedings of the A.A.G.*, vol. 1, pp. 70–75.

Hoselitz, B. F., ed. 1960. *Theories of Economic Growth*. New York: Free Press.

————. 1957. "Economic Growth and Development: Noneconomic Factors in Economic Development," *American Economic Review*, vol. 47, pp. 28–41.

————. 1954–55. "Generative and Parasitic Cities," *Economic Development and Cultural Change*, vol. 3, pp. 278–296.

Hotelling, H. 1929. "Stability in Competition," *The Economic Journal*, vol. 39, pp. 41–57.

House, J. W. 1966. "Margins in Regional Geography: An Illustration from N. E. England," in J. W. House, ed. *Northern Geographical Essays*. Newcastle: Oriel Press, pp. 139–158.

Howard, J. A. and Sheth, J. N. 1969. *The Theory of Buyer Behavior*. New York: Wiley.

Huff, D. L. 1962. "Determination of Intra-Urban Retail Trade Areas," Berkeley: University of California, Real Estate Research Program.

————. 1963. "A Probalistic Analysis of Shopping Center Trade Areas," *Land Economics*, vol. 39, pp. 81–90.

Hunker, H. L., ed. 1964. *Erich W. Zimmermann's Introduction to World Resource*. New York: Harper and Row; edited edition.

Hunter, H. 1965. "Transport in Soviet and Chinese Development," *Economic Development and Cultural Change*, vol. 14, pp. 71–84.

Isaac, E. 1961–62. "The Act and the Covenant: The Impact of Religion on the Landscape," *Landscape*, Winter, pp. 12–17.

Isard, W. 1960. *Methods of Regional Analysis*. Cambridge: M.I.T. Press.

————. 1956. *Location and Space Economy*. Cambridge: M.I.T. Press.

Isard, W. and Freutel, G. 1954. "Regional and National Product Projections and their Inter-Relations," in Long Range Economic Projections, *Studies in Income and Wealth*, vol. 16, Princeton: Princeton University Press.

Isard, W. and Kuenne, R. E. 1953. "The Impact of Steel upon the Greater New York–Philadelphia Industrial Region: A Study in Agglomeration Projection," *Review of Economics and Statistics*, vol. 35, pp. 289–301.

Joyce, I. 1969. "Subcultural Variations in Responses to the Urban Environment," M.A. thesis, Simon Fraser University, Department of Geography.

Kansky, K. J. 1963. "Structure of Transport Networks," Chicago: University of Chicago, Department of Geography, Research Paper No. 84.

Katona, G. and Morgan, J. N. 1952. "The Quantitative Study of Factors Determining Business Decisions," *Quarterly Journal of Economics* (published by Harvard University Press), vol. 66, pp. 67–90.

Katz, E. and Lazarsfeld, P. F. 1955. *Personal Influence: The Role Played by People in the Flow of Mass Communications*. New York: Free Press.

Kirk, W. 1963. "Problems of Geography," *Geography*, vol. 48, pt. 4, Nov. 1963, pp. 357–371.

Kolosovsky, N. N. 1961. "The Territorial-Production Combination (Complex) in Soviet Economic Geography," *Journal of Regional Science*, vol. 3, no. 1, pp. 1–26.

Koopmans, T. C. and Beckmann, M. 1957. "Assignment Problems and the Location of Economic Acitivities," *Econometrica*, vol. 25, pp. 53–76.

Langer, S. K. 1953. *Feeling and Form*. New York: Scribner and Sons.

Lasuen, J. R. 1962. "Regional Income in Equalities and the Problems of Growth in Spain," *Papers and Proceedings of the Regional Science Association*, vol. 8, pp. 169–191.

Leigh, R. 1965. "Speciality-Retailing: A Geographical Analysis," *B.C. Geographical Series*, no. 3.

Lewin, K. 1951. *Field Theory in Social Science*. New York: Harper and Row.

Lewis, W. A. 1955. *The Theory of Economic Growth*. Homewood, Ill.: Irwin.

Lindsey, R. 1956. "Regional Advantages in Oil Refining,"

Papers and Proceedings of the Regional Science Association, vol. 2, pp. 304–317.

Lionberger, H. F. 1960. *Adoption of New Techniques and Practices.* Ames, Iowa: Iowa State University Press.

Lösch, A. 1964. "The Nature of Economic Regions," *Southern Economic Journal,* vol. 5, no. 1, 1938, pp. 71–78. Reprinted in Friedmann and Alonso 1964, chapter 5.

———. 1954. *The Economics of Location,* trans. by W. H. Woglom and W. F. Stolper. New Haven: Yale University Press.

Lowenthal, D., ed. 1967. "Environmental Perception and Behavior." Chicago: University of Chicago, Department of Geography, Research Paper No. 109.

McCarty, H. H., Hook, J. C., Knos, D. S. and Davies, G. R. 1956. *The Measurement of Association in Industrial Geography.* Iowa City: Department of Geography, State University of Iowa.

McDaniel, R. 1966. "Elements of Economic Geography," unpublished course outline and notes, Department of Extension and Summer School, University of Western Ontario.

McDaniel, R. and Eliot Hurst, M. E. 1968. "A Systems Analytic Approach to Economic Geography," A. A. G. Commission on College Geography, Pub. No. 8.

McLuhan, M. 1964. *Understanding Media: The Extensions of Man.* New York: McGraw-Hill.

McNee, R. B. 1960. "Toward a More Humanistic Economic Geography: The Geography of Enterprise," *Tijds. Voor Econ. Soc. Geog.,* vol. 51, no. 8, pp. 201–206.

———. 1958. "Functional Geography of the Firms, with an Illustrative Case Study from the Petroleum Industry," *Economic Geography,* vol. 34, pp. 321–337.

Magdoff, H. 1969. *The Age of Imperialism.* New York: Monthly Review Press; also in three parts, *Monthly Review,* 1968, vol. 20, no. 2, pp. 11–53; vol. 20, no. 5, pp. 18–64; vol. 20, no. 6, pp. 18–77.

Marble, D. F. and Bowlby, S. R. 1968. "Shopping Alternatives and Recurrent Travel Patterns" in F. Horton, ed. *Geographic Studies of Urban Transportation and Network Analysis,* Northwestern University, Studies in Geography No. 16, pp. 42–75.

Matore, G. 1966. "Existential Space," *Landscape,* Spring 1966, vol. 15, no. 3, p. 5. An Extract from Matore's *L'Espace Humain,* Paris: La Colombe, 1962.

Meinig, D. W. 1962. "A Comparative Historical Geography of Two Railnets: Columbia Basin and South Australia," *Annals of the A.A.G.,* vol. 52, pp. 394–413.

Mighell, R. L. and Black, J. D. 1951. *Interregional Competition in Agriculture.* Cambridge, Mass.: Harvard University Press.

Moreno, J. L. 1934. *Who Shall Survive? A New Approach to the Problem of Inter-Human Relations.* Rev. ed., 1953, New York: Beacon House.

Morrill, R. and Earickson, R. 1969. "Locational Efficiency of Chicago Hospitals: An Experimental Model," *Health Service Research,* vol. 4, no. 2, pp. 128–141.

———. 1969b. "Problems in Modelling Interactance: The Case of Patient Travel for Hospital Care," in K. R. Cox and R. G. Golledge, eds. *Behavioral Problems in Geography.* Northwestern University, Studies in Geography No. 17.

Mountjoy, A. 1966. *Industrialization and Underdeveloped Countries,* 2nd rev. ed. London: Hutchinson.

Mumford, L. 1934. *Technics and Civilization.* London: Routledge.

Murdock, G. P. 1945. "The Common Denominator of Cultures," in R. Linton, ed. *The Science of Man in the World Crisis.* Columbia University Press.

Myers, J. G. 1968. *Consumer Image and Attitude.* Berkeley: University of California I.B.E.R. Special Publications.

Myrdal, G. 1957. *Rich Lands and Poor: The Road to World Prosperity.* New York: Harper and Row. Published in London by Duckworth as "Economic Theory and Underdeveloped Regions."

Nadel, S. F. 1951. *The Foundations of Social Anthropology.* London: Cohen and West.

Nash, M. 1964. *The Organization of Economic Life,* in Sol Tax 1964, pp. 171–180.

———. 1963. "Introduction, Approaches to the Study of Economic Growth," *Journal of Social Issues,* vol. 29, no. 1.

———. 1959. "Some Social and Cultural Aspects of Economic Development," *Economic Development and Cultural Change,* vol. 7, pp. 137–150.

North, D. C. 1955. "Location Theory and Regional Economic Growth," *Journal of Political Economy,* vol. 63, pp. 243–58.

Northwestern University. 1960–5. *Transportation Geography Study.* Pt. 1., July 1960, "Transportation Geography Research, a preliminary report of fundamental research relating to areal distributional aspects of transportation resources, oriented toward the development of transportation forecast methodology." Pt. 2., 1962 (W. L. Garrison and D. F. Marble), "The Structure of Transportation Networks." Evanston, Illinois: Northwestern University, Transportation Center/U.S. Army Transportation Research Command.

Nurske, R. 1953. *Problems of Capital Formation in Underdeveloped Countries.* Oxford: Oxford University Press.

Nystuen, J. D. 1963. "Identification of Some Fundamental Spatial Concepts," *Papers of the Michigan Academy of Science, Arts and Letters,* vol. 48, pp. 373–84.

O. R. R. C. Report. 1962. 28 volumes. Outdoor Recreation Research Review Commission, Washington D.C.

Ore, O. 1964. *Graphs and Their Uses.* New York: Random House School Library Editions.

Osgood, C. E. 1957. "A Behavioralistic Analysis of Perception and Language as Cognitive Phenomena," in *Contemporary Approaches to Cognition: A Symposium Held at the University of Colorado*. Cambridge, Mass.: Harvard University Press, pp. 75–118.

Osgood, C. E. and Sebeok, T. A., eds. 1954. "Psycholinguists: A Survey of Theory and Research Problems," *Journal of Abnormal and Social Psychology*, vol. 49, supplement pp. 1–3.

Ottremba, E. 1957. *Allgemeine Geographie des Welthandels und des Weltverkehrs*. Stuttgand: Franckh'sche Vertagshand-Lung.

Paauw, D. S. 1961. "Some Frontiers of Empirical Research in Economic Development," *Economic Development and Cultural Change*, vol. 9, pp. 180–199.

Parsons, T., ed. 1968. *American Sociology: Perspectives, Problems, Methods*. New York: Basic Books.

———. 1954. "The Motivation of Economic Activities," in *Essays in Sociological Theory*, 2nd ed. New York: The Free Press. Originally published in *Canadian Journal of Economics and Political Science*, vol. 6, 1940, pp. 187–203.

———. 1951. *The Social System*. New York: The Free Press.

Perroux, F. 1964. "Note sur la Notion de Pole de Croissance," in *L'Economie du xx eme Siecle*, 2nd ed. Paris: Presses Universitaires de France, pp. 142–53.

———. 1950. "Economic Space: Theory and Applications," *Quarterly Journal of Economics*, vol. 64.

Platt, R. S. 1949. "Reconnaissance in Dynamic Regional Geography: Tierra del Fuego," *Revista Geografica*, vols. 5–8, pp. 3–22.

Pred, A. 1969, 1967. "Behavior and Location," part 1, 1967, and part 2, 1969, *Lund Studies in Geography*, series B., nos. 27 and 28.

———. 1966. *The Spatial Dynamics of U.S. Urban-Industrial Growth 1800–1914: Interpretive and Theoretical Essays*. Cambridge, Mass.: MIT Press.

Predöhl, A. 1928. "The Theory of Location in its Relation to General Economics," *Journal of Political Economy*, vol. 36, pp. 371–390.

Ratcliff, R. U. 1949. *Urban Land Economics*. New York: McGraw-Hill.

Redfield, R. 1941. *The Folk Culture of Yucatan*. Chicago: Chicago University Press.

Reilly, W. J. 1931. *The Law of Retail Gravitation*. New York: W. J. Reilly.

Renner, G. T. 1947. "Geography of Industrial Localization," *Economic Geography*, vol. 23, pp. 167–189.

Rimlinger, G. V. and Steel, H. 1963. "An Economic Interpretation of the Spatial Distribution of Physicians in the United States," *Southern Economic Journal*, vol. 30, pp. 1–12.

Rimmer, P. 1967. "The Search for Spatial Regularities in the Development of Australian Seaports, 1861–1961/2," *Geografiske Annales*, vol. 49 B, no. 1, pp. 42–54.

Rostow, W. W. 1960. *The Stages of Economic Growth: A Non-Communist Manifesto*. New York: Cambridge University Press.

Siddall, W. R. 1969. "Railroad Guages and Spatial Interaction," *Geographical Review*, vol. 59, pp. 29–57.

Simon, H. A. 1957. *Models of Man*. New York: John Wiley.

Smelser, N. J. 1964. "Toward a Theory of Modernization," A. Etzioni, ed. *Social Changes: Sources, Patterns and Consequences*. New York: Basic Books, pp. 258–75.

———. 1963. *The Sociology of Economic Life*. Englewood Cliffs, N.J.: Prentice-Hall.

Smith, D. M. 1966. "A Theoretical Framework for Geographical Studies of Industrial Location," *Economic Geography*, vol. 42 pp. 95–113.

Smith, W. 1955. "The Location of Industry," *Transactions*, Institute of British Geographers, vol. 21, pp. 1–18.

Snow, J. T. 1967. "The New Road in the United States," *Landscape*, Fall, pp. 13–16.

Sonnenfeld, J. 1968. "Geography, Perception and the Behavioral Environment." Paper presented at the December 27th, 1968, meeting of the A.A.A.S.

Spencer, J. E. 1960. "The Cultural Factor in 'Underdevelopment': The Case of Malaya," in N. Ginsburg, ed. University of Chicago Department of Geography Research Paper No. 62, pp. 35–48.

Spengler, J. J. 1960. "Economic Development: Political Preconditions and Political Consequences," *Journal of Politics*, vol. 22, pp. 387–416.

Sprout, H. and Sprout, M. 1965. *The Ecological Perspective on Human Affairs*. Princeton: Princeton University Press.

Steed, G. P. F. 1968. "The Changing Milieu of a Firm: A Case Study of a Shipbuilding Concern," *Annals of the A.A.G.*, vol. 58, no. 3, pp. 506–525.

Storey, K. J. 1970. "The Role of Transport in Economic Development," M.A. Thesis, Simon Fraser University.

Sweezy, P. M. 1970. "Toward a Critique of Economics," *Monthly Review*, vol. 21, no. 8, pp. 1–8.

Taaffe, E. J., Morrill, R. I. and Gould, P. R. 1963. "Transport Expansion in Underdeveloped Countries: A Comparative Analysis," *Geographical Review*, vol. 53, pp. 503–529.

Tansley, A. G. 1935. "The Use and Abuse of Vegetational Concepts and Terms," *Ecology*, vol. 16, pp. 284–307.

Tax, Sol, ed. 1964. *Horizons of Anthropology*. Chicago: Aldine Publishing Company.

Thoman, R. S. 1962. *The Geography of Economic Activity*. New York: McGraw-Hill.

Thomas, E. N. 1964. "Some Comments about a Structure of Geography, with Particular Reference to Geographic Facts, Spatial Distribution, and Areal Association," in C. Kohn, ed. *Selected Classroom Experiences*, A.A.G. High School Geography Project, pp. 44–60.

Thompson, D. L. 1966. "Future Directions in Retail Area Research," *Economic Geography*, vol. 42, pp. 1–18.

Tiebout, C. M. 1957. "Location Theory, Empirical Evidence and Economic Evolution," *Papers and Proceedings of the Regional Science Association*, vol. 3, pp. 74–86.

Ullman, E. L. 1957. *American Commodity Flow*. Seattle: University of Washington Press.

——. 1956. "The Role of Transportation and the Bases for Interaction," in W. L. Thomas, ed., *Man's Role in Changing the Face of the Earth*. Chicago: Chicago University Press, pp. 826–877.

United Nations. 1963. *The Economic Development of Latin America in the Post-War Period*. New York: United Nations, Economic Commission for Latin America, ECN 12–659.

Vernon, R. 1967. "Multinational Enterprise and National Sovereignty," *Harvard Business Review*, March/April, pp. 156–172.

Vining, R. 1949. "The Region as an Economic Entity and Certain Variations to be Observed in the Study of Systems of Regions," *Papers and Proceedings*, American Economic Association, vol. 39, pp. 89–104.

Von Bertalanffy, L. 1950. "An Outline of General System Theory," *British Journal of the Philosophy of Science*, vol. 1, pp. 134–165.

Von Der Mehden, F. R. 1964. *Politics of the Developing Nations*. Englewood Cliffs, N.J.: Prentice-Hall (a Spectrum book).

Voorhees, A. M. 1955. "A General Theory of Traffic Movement," *Papers and Proceedings of the Institute of Traffic Engineers*, vol. 26, pp. 46–56.

Wagner, P. L. 1960a. *Human Use of the Earth*. New York: Free Press.

——. 1960b. "On Classifying Economies," in N. Ginsburg, ed. University of Chicago Dept. of Geography Research Paper No. 62, pp. 49–62.

Wagner, P. L. and Mikesell, M. W., eds. 1962. *Readings in Cultural Geography*. Chicago: University of Chicago Press.

Wallace, W. H. 1963. "Freight Traffic Functions of Anglo-American Railroads," *Annals of the A.A.G.*, vol. 53, pp. 312–331.

Watson, J. W. 1969. "The Role of Illusion in North American Geography: A Note on the Geography of North American Settlement," *The Canadian Geographer*, vol. 13, pp. 10–27.

——. 1965. "Canada's Regionalism in Life and Letters," in R. L. Gentilcove, ed. *Canada's Changing Geography*. Englewood Cliffs, N.J.: Prentice-Hall, pp. 213–224.

Webber, M. M. 1964. "Culture, Territoriality, and the Elastic Mile," *Papers and Proceedings of the Regional Science Association*, vol. 13, pp. 59–69.

Weber, A. 1929. *Theory of the Location of Industries*, trans. by C. J. Friedrich, from *Über den Studort der Industrien*, 1909, Chicago: University of Chicago Press.

Wendt, P. F. 1957. "Theory of Urban Land Values," *Land Economics*, vol. 33, pp. 228–240.

Whitaker, J. R. 1932. "Regional Interdependence," *Journal of Geography*, vol. 31, pp. 164–165.

White, L. A. 1959. *The Evolution of Culture*. New York: McGraw-Hill.

Whittlesley, D. 1954. "The Region, Theory and Practice," in P. E. James and D. F. Jones, eds. *American Geography: Inventory and Prospect*. Syracuse: Syracuse University Press/A.A.G., pp. 32–51.

Wilson, T. 1965. *Papers on Regional Development*. Oxford: Basil Blackwell.

Wingo, L. 1961. *Transportation and Urban Land*. Washington, D.C.: Resources for the Future Inc.

Wolfe, R. I. 1963. *Transportation and Politics*. Princeton: D. Van Nostrand Co., Search Light Series, no. 18.

Wolpert, J. 1965. "Behavioral Aspects of the Decision to Migrate," *Papers and Proceedings of the Regional Science Association*, vol. 15, pp. 159–169.

——. 1964. "The Decision Process in Spatial Context," *Annals of the A.A.G.*, vol. 54, no. 4, pp. 537–558.

Wood, R. 1965. "The New Metropolis and the New University," *Educational Record*, vol. 46, pp. 306–311.

Worsley, P. M. 1964. *The Third World*. Chicago: University of Chicago Press.

Wright, M. 1965. "Regional Development: Problems and Lines of Advance in Europe," *Town Planning Review*, vol. 36, pp. 147–164.

Yeates, M. H. 1965. "Some Factors Affecting the Spatial Distribution of Chicago Land Values, 1910–1960," *Economic Geography*, vol. 41, pp. 57–70.

Zelinsky, W. 1966. *A Prologue to Population Geography*. Englewood Cliffs, N.J.: Prentice-Hall.

Zimmermann, E. W. 1964. See Hunker.

——. 1956. *World Resources and Industries*. New York: Harper and Row.

Zipf, G. K. 1949. *Human Behavior and the Principle of Least Effort*. Cambridge: Addison-Wesley Press.

Index

Blaut, J.M., 351
Bookchin, M., 372
Bounded rationality, 8, 20, 119
Bounties, 92
Brazil, 102, 259
Brookfield, H.C., 75–76, 374, 383–84
Buchanan, K., 352
Bucklin, L.P., 213
Business cycle, 19

Campbell, C., 240–41
Canada, 304–7
Capital, 88, 136–37, 360; fixed, 137; intensity, 340; money, 137; social, 136
Capitalist system, 352, 356
Central Business District (CBD), 228, 234, 236
Central places, 194
Central place activities. *See* Tertiary activities
Central place theory, 197–206; assumptions, 198; criticisms, 220; extensions, 203–6; structure, 199–203
Chance, 142
Chemical industry, 338, 340
China, 92, 101, 362, 373
Christaller, W., 197–203
Circulation, 252–54
Civilization, 28
Clark-Fisher thesis, 16
Class, 52–54
Clawson, M., 239
Coal mining, 336–37
Cognitive processes, 44, 46–48
Collective farms, 100
Colonialism, 57, 351, 363–66
Colony, 362
Columbo plan, 325
Common Market, 323–24
Common Services Organization, 325
Communications, 46, 118, 307–9. *See also* Information; Learning; Transportation
Comparative advantage, 28–29, 89–90, 254
Competition, 89
Complementarity, 256, 277, 297
Conflict theory, 355

Consumer, 13–14, 210–11, 240
Consumption, 14
Convergence of disciplines, 7
Cooley, C.H., 253
Cooperatives, 94–95
Core-frame concept, 234
Corporate society, 375–76
Corporations, 145, 365
Cost advantage, 113
Costs: basic, 174; locational, 174; site, 230; transfer, 133; transportation, 108–13, 230, 232–3, 376
Council of Economic Mutual Assistance (C.E.M.A.), 325
Critical isodapane, 167
Cultural universals, 51
Culture, 51–52, 72
Cumulative causation, 328
Cybernetics, 36. *See also* System

Decision making, 20–22, 70–76, 84, 116–22, 130, 145, 380
Decoding, 46, 308
Deficiency payments, 92
Demand, 55, 91, 239, 317
Demographic index, 347
Depressed regions, 335
Determinism, 4, 8
Development continuum, 351, 361
Diffusion, 71; diffusion models, 277
Direct embargoes, 92
Distance, 254–56
Division of labor, 28

Earickson, R., 243–45
Eastern Europe, 92, 101
Ecology, 371–73
Economic development, 253, 320, 357; barriers to, 357–66; forces working toward equalization, 366–68; functional view of, 354–55; metropolis-satellite hypothesis, 356. *See also* Regional development; Underdevelopment
Economic geography, 2–9, 16, 43, 50, 253
Economic man, 3, 190
Economic organization, 12, 14–16
Economic rent, 108–9
Economic space, 91

Vining, R., 322, 327
Von der Mehden, F.R., 363
Von Thunen, J.H., 107–13

Warehousing, 247–49
Water transport, 291–92
Watson, J.W., 47
Weber, A., 165–69
Wendt, P.F., 232

Wholesaling. *See* Tertiary activities
Wingo, L., 233, 330
Wolpert, J., 84, 310
Wright, J.K., 47

Yields, agricultural, 87–88

Zimmermann, E.W., 68–70, 327, 370